The Glannon Guide
to Contracts

The Glannon Guide to Contracts

Learning Contracts Through Multiple-Choice Questions and Analysis

Professor Theodore Silver
Touro College, Jacob D. Fuchsberg Law Center

Professor Stephen Hochberg
Touro College, Jacob D. Fuchsberg Law Center

Wolters Kluwer
Law & Business

Copyright © 2013 CCH Incorporated.

Published by Wolters Kluwer Law & Business in New York.

Wolters Kluwer Law & Business serves customers worldwide with CCH, Aspen Publishers, and Kluwer Law International products. (www.wolterskluwerlb.com)

To contact Customer Service, e-mail customer.service@wolterskluwer.com, call 1-800-234-1660, fax 1-800-901-9075, or mail correspondence to:

> Wolters Kluwer Law & Business
> Attn: Order Department
> PO Box 990
> Frederick, MD 21705

Printed in the United States of America.

1 2 3 4 5 6 7 8 9 0

ISBN 978-0-7355-5796-3

Library of Congress Cataloging-in-Publication Data

Silver, Theodore.
    The Glannon guide to contracts : learning contracts through multiple-choice questions and analysis / Theodore Silver, Stephen Hochberg.
       p. cm.
    Includes index.
    ISBN 978-0-7355-5796-3
    1. Contracts—United States. 2. Contracts—United States—Problems, exercises, etc. I. Hochberg, Stephen. II. Title.

KF801.Z9S49 2012
346.7302'2—dc23   2012029236

About Wolters Kluwer Law & Business

Wolters Kluwer Law & Business is a leading global provider of intelligent information and digital solutions for legal and business professionals in key specialty areas, and respected educational resources for professors and law students. Wolters Kluwer Law & Business connects legal and business professionals as well as those in the education market with timely, specialized authoritative content and information-enabled solutions to support success through productivity, accuracy and mobility.

Serving customers worldwide, Wolters Kluwer Law & Business products include those under the Aspen Publishers, CCH, Kluwer Law International, Loislaw, Best Case, ftwilliam. com and MediRegs family of products.

CCH products have been a trusted resource since 1913, and are highly regarded resources for legal, securities, antitrust and trade regulation, government contracting, banking, pension, payroll, employment and labor, and healthcare reimbursement and compliance professionals.

Aspen Publishers products provide essential information to attorneys, business professionals and law students. Written by preeminent authorities, the product line offers analytical and practical information in a range of specialty practice areas from securities law and intellectual property to mergers and acquisitions and pension/benefits. Aspen's trusted legal education resources provide professors and students with high-quality, up-to-date and effective resources for successful instruction and study in all areas of the law.

Kluwer Law International products provide the global business community with reliable international legal information in English. Legal practitioners, corporate counsel and business executives around the world rely on Kluwer Law journals, looseleafs, books, and electronic products for comprehensive information in many areas of international legal practice.

Loislaw is a comprehensive online legal research product providing legal content to law firm practitioners of various specializations. Loislaw provides attorneys with the ability to quickly and efficiently find the necessary legal information they need, when and where they need it, by facilitating access to primary law as well as state-specific law, records, forms and treatises.

Best Case Solutions is the leading bankruptcy software product to the bankruptcy industry. It provides software and workflow tools to flawlessly streamline petition preparation and the electronic filing process, while timely incorporating ever-changing court requirements.

ftwilliam.com offers employee benefits professionals the highest quality plan documents (retirement, welfare and non-qualified) and government forms (5500/PBGC, 1099 and IRS) software at highly competitive prices.

MediRegs products provide integrated health care compliance content and software solutions for professionals in healthcare, higher education and life sciences, including professionals in accounting, law and consulting.

Wolters Kluwer Law & Business, a division of Wolters Kluwer, is headquartered in New York. Wolters Kluwer is a market-leading global information services company focused on professionals.

To all first year law students everywhere

Contents

Acknowledgments

We would like to thank everyone at Wolters Kluwer Law & Business, especially Rick Mixter, Christine Hannan, Dana Wilson, and Lisa Wehrle.

Professor Silver would also like to acknowledge Diane Bennett.

The Glannon Guide
to Contracts

1

You *Must* Read This Very Short Introduction

For too many students, first-year contracts is a heartache, plaguing them perpetually with this demoralizing thought: "I do my work, I go to class, I listen, I participate, and still — I don't know what it's all about or what my teacher wants me to know."

We're here to spare you that sorrowful plight — to grab hold of contracts, tear away its veil of mystery, and flood the subject with such bright light as lets you see it for what it is: a course, like any other — easily understandable with ordinary work and thought.

And How Do You Do *That*?

We bathe this book in simple illustration after simple illustration after simple illustration. We surround our user-friendly teaching with *stories*, each one simple, easy to read, and at the same time tied to a complex legal concept — as intricate as any contracts case can be.

We "hold off" on stating any legal rule until first we show you why the law created it. Others will burden you with abstract precepts of law in a truncated incomprehensible form, followed by lackluster illustrations of their application. But that's not our way. We *first*, with a simple story, show you a problem in need of a legal solution; *then* describe the legal rule designed to solve it. With further illustration, we show you, too, how contract law (like so much law) makes new problems, even as it solves others. Moreover, we speak forthrightly to the misunderstandings and erroneous thinking that surround so many rules of contract so you'll have a depth of understanding that others don't acquire — a mastery that leads happily to a high and happy grade.

This book stands on its own; it's a comprehensive contracts course in itself. Yet most students will (and should) use it as a companion to their first-year contracts course, as taught by their contracts professor. And while we're on that subject, know this:

Contracts Professors Aren't Cut from a Single Cloth

Contracts teachers vary in the way they organize their syllabi. Some begin with the topic of contract formation, some with consideration, and others with remedies. Hence, this book has *three beginnings.*

1. If your professor starts with contract formation (offer, acceptance, "mutual assent," "mechanics of a bargain"), begin this book at Chapter 2 and read through Chapter 11.
2. If your professor begins with consideration ("exchange," "mutuality of obligation"), begin this book at Chapter 12 and read through Chapter 14.
3. If your professor begins with remedies, start at Chapter 25 and read through Chapter 30.

Furthermore, for any topic in contracts, teachers differ in their thoroughness of coverage. Professor X thoroughly covers "this," toic and gives short shrift to "that" one. Professor Y shortcuts "this" topic and belabors the other. That's a problem; when a teacher sweeps through a topic at high speed, she leaves her students confused.

When That Happens Come to Us

We teach simply and thoroughly, everything that *any* contracts teacher purports to cover. If, for instance, your class leaves you in a fog (as it will) about the relationships among reliance, restitution, unjust enrichment, quasi-contract, benefit conferred, and quantum meruit, we'll quickly guide you out of it. When those topics come up in class, you'll read Chapter 26. You'll read our stories and — *very important* — you'll answer our multiple-choice questions.

About the Multiple-Choice Questions

This is a *Glannon* Guide, so it's studded through and through with multiple-choice questions, each followed by an elaborate analysis and explanation. The questions show you, rule by rule, that you do or don't have full mastery. Answer incorrectly, and the analysis reveals your error. Answer correctly, and it tells you whether your *reasoning* was right (or whether you just "got lucky").

About Our Appendix

Ideally, before starting a single first-year course, every law student should acquire a broad understanding of our legal system and a *history* of the law tied to each of her courses. Some might say we should offer you all of that in the very next chapter, before turning to contract law itself. But we don't do that, and here's why.

We Don't Want to Begin by Boring You

With the next chapter's first page, you'll dive into contract law, head first (as we, your lifeguards, keep you safe from drowning). Quickly, you'll see that contracts—learned *our* way—is fun. Were we to start with the stuff in the appendix, we'd turn you off—fast—and *that* we refuse to do.

When *Do* I Read the Appendix?

We don't ask, ever, that you read it as a whole, all in one "swallow." Instead, we send you now and again to certain of its sections. When you're in the midst of this or that chapter, we'll ask that you stop, turn to the appendix, and read one of its parts. Know, too, that the appendix stands on its own as a great introduction to law, the history of law and, especially, the history of *contract* law. And, since this is a *Glannon* Guide, the appendix, too, is replete with multiple-choice questions, analyses, and explanations.

At some point, you might decide to read the appendix from beginning to end, and thus deepen your mastery of law—*all* law. But that's up to you. Read the sections to which we point you—*when* we point you, and all will be well. You'll learn ever so much more, and you'll keep a smile on our faces.

Finally: Have *Fun*

With this book as your constant companion, you'll love contracts, and that's what we want. For you, we want contracts to be engaging, enlightening fun. So turn the page and let the fun begin!

2

How to Form a Contract: The Basics

A. Contracts Arise by Offer, Acceptance (and Consideration)

Nonlawyers often think "contract" means a *writing*, formally drafted and ceremoniously signed. They're wrong. Many contracts do inhere in signed writings, and we call them "written contracts." Many arise from speech alone. They're "oral contracts." Some arise without words at all. They're born of communicative *behavior*, with nary a word of type or talk. Those are "contracts implied in fact." All such creatures are, to be sure — *contracts*, and all arise by the same legal mechanism: *Two (or more) parties form a contract when they **mutually assent to a bargain** that exacts from each some consideration.* Ordinarily they do so by process of offer and acceptance and so we say, *Two parties form a contract when one makes an **offer** that the other **accepts**, each providing consideration to the other.* Equally fundamental to the law of contracts, therefore, are these two topics: (1) offer and acceptance; and (2) consideration.

For that reason, some professors begin their courses with consideration. If yours does that, then begin this book with Chapters 12-14. Come back here to

5

Chapter 2 when your professor takes up offer and acceptance. If your professor begins with offer and acceptance, keep reading this chapter and continue with Chapters 3-11. Chapters 2-13 tackle offer and acceptance— the "ins," the "outs," and the bottom lines.

1. Offer and Acceptance: The Easy Part and the Hard Part

It's easy to *say* "offer" and "accept." It's easy, too, to memorize their legal definitions, which we'll soon present. But it's not so easy (at first) to apply those words to two "real" parties conducting "real" communications. The challenge is to watch what they do, hear what they say, read what they write, and reach a reasoned legal opinion as to whether (a) one of them made an offer and, if he did, (b) the other accepted. With respect to offer and acceptance, *that's* the "hard part."

2. Sometimes the Hard Part Is Easy; Dan, George, Donna, and Gale

Dan and George are strangers standing in a movie line. Dan says to George, "I hereby make you an offer." George responds, "I accept." These chaps used the *words* "offer" and "accept," but Dan did not *make* an offer, which means George had nothing *to* accept. Between Dan and George, there is no offer, no acceptance, and no contract.

Donna and Gale are strangers, seated next to each other in the movie theater. Donna wants to make a phone call but hasn't brought her cell phone. Meanwhile, Gale, without her glasses, is struggling to see the screen. Donna says to Gale, "I'll lend you a pair of theater binoculars for the duration of the movie, if you'll lend me your cell phone for fifteen minutes, right now." Gale responds, "Sure." These two didn't *say* "offer," "accept," or "contract," but Donna made an offer, Gale accepted it, and the ladies formed a contract.

B.   The Meaning of Offer

When Dan said, "I hereby make an offer," George couldn't know what "deal" Dan meant to propose. On the other hand, when Donna proposed to swap binoculars for phone, Gale should plainly have seen that Donna proposed to swap binoculars for phone. And therein lies the critical difference between the stories. Donna proposed a genuine exchange, a bargain, a swap, a trade, a quid pro quo—an "I'll do this if you'll do that." Dan did no such thing. Donna made an offer; Dan did not. And with that, we're ready to define "offer."

Restatement (Second) of Contracts[1] §24 defines it thus:

> An offer is the manifestation of willingness to enter into a bargain, so made as to justify another person in understanding that his assent to that bargain is invited and will conclude it.

Look at the fifth word, "manifestation." As known to the law it denotes an outward showing, not an inward state of mind. Under some (exceptional) circumstances, we manifest thoughts or feelings we don't really possess. One who cries leads others to believe she's unhappy. She *manifests* sadness. Yet, hearing that her first grandchild was born, she might be crying for happiness. With tears streaming down her cheeks, she *manifests* sadness, but isn't sad. One who is deep in intense, silent contemplation, on the threshold of revelation, might lead reasonable persons to think her apathetic. She *manifests* apathy, but she is in fact thoughtfully engaged.

Resting, as it does, on the word "manifestation," the law's definition of "offer" refers to a person who does, says, or writes that which *would lead a reasonable person to believe* that she stands ready and willing to make a bargain. Whether she manifests such willingness turns not on what she truly wants or intends, but on what, to a reasonable person, she *appears* to want and intend. Occasionally, then, one may unwittingly manifest willingness to enter into a bargain although not truly possessed of any such purpose. Suppose Carlos stands by his lawnmower and says, in a serious tone, "I want to sell my lawnmower for $100." Carlos thus manifests a wish to sell *that* lawnmower, even if in his own mind he's thinking of a lawnmower stored in his garage three miles away.

Mindful, now, of what "manifest" means, let's break the Restatement's definition of offer into three pieces.

Piece 1: *An offer is a manifestation* ...   To make an offer, Party A must make an outward showing or communication to Party B. He may do so with *speech, writing, or behavior.*

Piece 2: *... of a willingness to enter a bargain* ...   A's communication must be such as would lead a reasonable person in B's position to understand (1) that A wishes to form a *bargain*, meaning an arrangement that calls on each party to do something for the other; and (2) *what*, specifically, he expects that each will do.

Piece 3: *... so made as to justify another in believing ... his assent ... is invited ... and will conclude it.*   The communication must be such as would,

---

1. An entity called the American Law Institute has written for a large number of legal topics a so-called "Restatement of the Law." For some topics, including Contracts, it has written a "Restatement" and then revised it. Hence there now exist, as they're commonly known (1) a "Restatement (First) Contracts," issued in 1932, and (2) a "Restatement 2d Contracts," issued in 1979. It's not law, but it is what's called "good authority." Learn more about the Restatements—what they are and what they are not in Appendix, section C.

under the prevailing circumstances, cause a reasonable person in B's position to think, "A asks me to say 'yes,' and, if I do, each of us is firmly committed to the other; we have a deal."

Suppose Alice sits on the hood of a small car and in a serious tone says to Bob, a stranger: "I need my car washed urgently—right now. I'll pay you $200 to do it. Is it a deal?" By law, Alice has offered to pay Bob $200 to wash the small automobile on which she's sitting. That's true even if Alice later proves, indisputably—with incontrovertible evidence—that she was "only joking." It is likewise true if Alice proves that she does not own the little vehicle on which she's sitting and that *her* car, a mammoth limousine, is located 900 miles away.

One makes an offer by doing or stating that which, *under the operative circumstances,* would cause a reasonable person to believe that (1) a definite exchange has been proposed to him, and (2) his assent will "seal the deal." The circumstances under which Alice makes her statement include the physical location from which she makes it. Seeing that she's perched atop the little car, a reasonable listener in Bob's position would understand "my car" to mean "*this* car." Since Bob would reasonably think Alice to mean "this car," then, in the law's eyes, that *is* what she means, whether she knows it or not. Stated otherwise, the law holds Alice not to the meaning she truly harbors in her head, but to the meaning she *manifests.*

QUESTION 1. On April 1, Fay sends to Mort this signed fax message: "Mort—April is upon us. I need your services—this Wednesday, please, at 11 A.M. I'll be ready with cash. Okay?" What additional circumstance, if proven, would most clearly mean that Fay's message constitutes an offer?

A. Mort is a skilled landscaper, mechanic and carpenter, and at various times in the past Fay has hired him to perform services related to those skills.

B. Every April for the previous 12 years Mort has trimmed the trees in Fay's front yard, for which Fay has each time paid him $125.

C. Fay does not know Mort, but has heard that he is a skilled landscaper.

D. By signed writing, Mort responds to Fay: "Yes, I'll be there."

E. By signed writing, Mort responds to Fay: "I'll be glad to help you, but my fee is now $35 per hour."

ANALYSIS.   Go back to Restatement (Second) §24 and read it. (That's easy.) Think of its *meaning* and apply it. (That's *not* so easy.) To determine that a given communication is an offer, examine (a) the communication itself, and (b) the circumstances under which it's made. Then ask yourself: "In my opinion, would a reasonable person receiving this communication understand that a definite bargain is proposed to him and that his assent will 'seal' the deal?"

Fay wrote only this: "April is upon us. I need your services. I'll be ready with cash." Viewed objectively, Fay's message communicates almost nothing. It's like Dan's statement to George made in the movie line. Fay's words, by themselves, could not cause a man in Mort's position sensibly to draw any conclusion as to what she wants him to do or how much "cash" she'll pay him.

Yet under some *circumstances*, Mort might reasonably take Fay's little fax as a definite proposition of specified terms. This question asks that we identify such a circumstance. Among the answer choices we're to find some fact that, if added to the story, would logically cause Mort to understand, specifically, what Fay wants of him, what she'll pay him in exchange, and that he need only express his assent to "close the deal."

D and **E** concern Mort's *response* to Fay's message. They don't concern Fay's statement or the circumstances under which she makes it. In no way do they address *the meaning of offer*. **D** and **E** are wrong.

Consider **A**. If Mort were operating under the circumstance it describes, how would he naturally interpret Fay's message? He might think Fay has for him some work tied to landscaping, mechanics, or carpentry, and that she stands ready to pay some amount of money for his service. But he couldn't know with any specificity what Fay actually wants him to do or how much she's ready to pay.

C tells us that Fay has heard that Mort is a capable landscaper — and, so what? **C** tells us something about Fay's state of mind, but it tells *Mort* nothing of what Fay proposes. **C** is wrong.

And what of **B**? It tells us that every April, for twelve-years, Mort has trimmed Fay's trees for $125. *Mindful of that history* — that *circumstance* — a reasonable person in Mort's position would justifiably conclude that Fay once again wants her trees trimmed, and that she's ready to pay, as before, $125 in cash. **B** is right.

QUESTION 2. Over nine years, from 1997 to 2005, Andrea has visited Frank's diner for breakfast about four times weekly between 6:30 A.M. and 11:45 A.M., each time ordering two soft-boiled eggs with toast, and each time paying the menu price for those items. Also over these nine years, Andrea has come to Frank's diner about three times weekly for lunch between 12:15 P.M. and 3:30 P.M., ordering each time, two hard-boiled eggs with toast, paying the menu price for those items. At noon sharp on January 3, 2011, Andrea steps into Frank's diner and sits at a table. Which of the following additional facts would best justify the legal conclusion that on that day, Andrea has made an offer to Frank in which she proposes to buy soft-boiled eggs for the menu price?

A. Unbeknownst to Frank, Andrea had breakfast today at 7:30 A.M. in another diner, which she also has frequented regularly for nine years.

> **B.** Unbeknownst to Frank or Andrea, Andrea's wristwatch is running one hour fast, and Andrea believes the time to be 11:00 A.M.
> **C.** Andrea knows that Frank does not serve breakfast after 11:50 A.M. and begins serving lunch at noon.
> **D.** A moment after taking her seat, Andrea says, "Eggs and toast, please."
> **E.** A moment after taking her seat, Andrea says, "Another morning; the usual please."

ANALYSIS.   A nine-year history gives Frank every reason to know that Andrea has soft-boiled eggs for breakfast and hard-boiled eggs for lunch. He should know, too, that when Andrea wants breakfast she normally arrives before 11:45 A.M.; for lunch she comes no sooner than 12:15 P.M.

Today, Andrea arrives *at* 12:00 P.M. and takes a seat. By doing so she communicates *something*. Frank might justifiably believe that Andrea is proposing to purchase, for the menu price, toast and two eggs. But, because it's exactly noon, he can't justifiably determine that she wants her eggs hard or soft-boiled. Absent additional circumstances, Andrea has *not* made an offer.

Go back to Restatement (Second) §24 and again, take hold of its meaning. Then read each answer choice, and in your mind, add to the story its stated fact. Determine which one, in your opinion, means that Andrea has offered to buy soft-boiled eggs at the menu price.

Neither **A** nor **B** relates to the substance of Andrea's communication or any circumstance of which Frank should know. If Andrea had breakfast earlier in the day or if her watch is fast, Frank has no reason to know anything about it. Neither fact can affect his reasonable understanding of what Andrea means by "eggs and toast." **A** and **B** are wrong.

According to **D**, Andrea asks for eggs and toast. At noon sharp, Frank has no way reasonably to conclude that she wants the eggs hard or soft boiled. **D** is wrong.

According to **C**, Frank doesn't serve lunch after 11:50 A.M. If Frank has reason to think that Andrea knows that policy, he might be justified in believing that Andrea wants lunch. On the one hand, we're not told that Andrea knows the policy or that Frank has any reason to think she does. Nonetheless, some students might assume that Frank has told Andrea of his policy and that he should conclude that she wants hard-boiled eggs. **C** isn't bad, but maybe **E** is better.

In **E**, Andrea refers to her "morning . . . usual." On hearing the word "morning," Frank *should* understand that Andrea proposes to buy toast and soft-boiled eggs for the menu price. **E** is right.

Remember, even with the facts added by **E**, Frank need not give Andrea what she wants. Andrea has made an offer, but since Frank has yet to accept it, the parties do not (yet) have a contract.

For the meaning of offer, we've looked thus far to Restatement §24. But *The Restatement isn't law.* (See Appendix, section C.) We're not confined to its definition of offer (or of anything else it puts forth). We might properly define the term "offer" in a variety of ways. Consider these:

> *An offer is any communication that leads its recipient reasonably to conclude that he is asked to join in an exchange, explicit in terms, and that his assent will create a binding agreement.*

> *An offer is any act or expression that, under prevailing circumstances, naturally causes its witness or recipient to conclude that a bargain of specified terms is available to her and that her assent will finalize it.*

> *One makes an offer by communicating that which would justifiably lead another to think she is asked to partake of an exchange, specific in its terms, and that her accession will conclude it.*

All of these formulations correctly characterize an offer. They're not "official," but neither is the Restatement. Offer is a common law concept, susceptible to many formulations. Be familiar with the Restatement definition because courts, authorities, and some teachers (poor things) lean heavily on it. But don't think that its words are law. Don't think, either, that memorizing the Restatement's definition of "offer" or *anyone's* definition of "offer" (or any definition of *anything*) means you've learned the law.

Knowing words is important only if you comprehend their meaning. Law is about *meaning*, not words. The lawyer must work well with words as the tools by which she gives and takes meaning. But it's all about *meaning*. Words are the conducting wire, meaning the power.

QUESTION 3. Vortech Inc. supplied industrial chemicals to a large number of customers, including Hartco Inc. After years of doing business with Hartco, Vortech sent Hartco this document:

DEFINITIVE OFFER TO SELL

We have available a variety of alcohol- and ammonia-based cleaning products, many of which you've purchased in the past. We wish to sell some or all of the products in good quantities at favorable prices. Let us know, please, if you wish to purchase any now. Please describe specifically the product(s) you want to purchase and the exact quantities you wish to acquire. This is a definite offer, and we look forward to your acceptance.

Did Vortech make an offer to Hartco?

A. Yes, because Vortech described its message as a "definite offer"
B. Yes, because Vortech did not restrict Hartco Inc. to purchasing any particular product and left it free to choose among many

> **C.** No, because a seller cannot bind a prospective buyer without that buyer's assent
> **D.** No, because Vortech did not refer to cleaning chemicals by name
> **E.** No, because Vortech was nebulous as to the transaction it suggested

ANALYSIS.   These "yes, because" "no, because" questions often appear on the Multistate Bar Examination. Before moving to the options, conceive *your* answer and *your* reasoning. That way, when you examine the answer choices, you'll know what you're looking for and thus arm yourself against the traps that question writers set for you.

Think about the *meaning* of offer. Ask yourself: "Under these circumstances could Hartco reasonably see in Vortech's message a proposal for a definite bargain—an explicit exchange?"

Vortech expresses its wish to sell a "variety" of products, in "good quantities" at "favorable" prices. Vortech doesn't specify *what* it will sell or what price Hartco must pay for whatever it is. Hartco cannot justifiably believe that Vortech has contemplated a true exchange of specified terms. The writing is not an offer; it's too vague.

Since your answer is "no," confine yourself to **C**, **D**, and **E**. Ignore **A** and **B** (for now).

C states that a buyer can't bind a seller unless the seller assents. That's wholly true and wholly irrelevant. You're asked not whether Hartco and Vortech formed a *contract*, but whether Vortech made an *offer*. No prospective buyer or seller acting on her own can create a contract, but either can make an *offer*. **C** is bad; keep looking.

According to **D**, Vortech's message fails as an offer because it does not refer to products "by name." That's tempting. The problem with Vortech's message is indefiniteness—failure to propose a clear, specific exchange. Named products are more specific than unnamed ones. Still, **D** isn't good. Were we to supplement Vortech's message with product names but nothing else, the message would fail, still, to specify quantity or price. It would still fail to propose a bargain of *specified terms*. **D** is wrong. **E** features the words "nebulous," "transaction," and "suggested"—words that don't usually arise in connection with this subject. For that reason, the question writer hopes you'll dismiss it.

Surprise her. Read not for buzzwords but for *meaning*. **E** *means* Vortech's message fails as an offer because it's too indefinite ("nebulous") as to any exchange ("transaction") it proposed ("suggested"). *That* correctly tells us why Vortech's proposal is not an offer; it does not adequately specify its terms. But before settling "for keeps" on **E**, look quickly at **A** and **B**.

According to **A**, Vortech's document *is* an offer because Vortech *calls* it one. You know better. Whether a communication qualifies as an offer doesn't depend on the name it carries. One may use the *word* "offer" without making one (as Dan did when talking to George in the movie line). Reciprocally, one may make an offer without using the word (as Donna did when speaking to Gale in the movie theater). **A** is wrong.

B targets your prejudice. From childhood we learn that freedom is good (which it is) and that it's generally better than restriction (which it is). On that basis, some students imagine that **B** just "must be" right. But it's wrong. The freedom to which **B** refers is the very reason Vortech's message fails as an offer. The freedom inheres in the nonspecificity of the Vortech message, which leaves Hartco "free" to consider what chemical he might want to buy, in what quantity, and at what price — which is why it fails outright to propose a definite bargain. **B** is wrong, and **E** is right.

QUESTION 4. Eunice, age 97, is fond of her younger neighbor Alison, age 26. On Wednesday, May 12, Eunice plans to move from her home in Washington State to New Mexico. On the evening before the move, she leaves Alison this voice-mail message: "You've told me that you need a car. Mine is nearly new, but I've decided to give up driving. In gratitude for our long friendship, I offer you my car. I'll sign the title certificate over to you and mark the box that reads 'transferred as gift.' I'll leave the certificate in your mailbox. I'm leaving for New Mexico tomorrow. Our next contact will probably be by mail." By leaving the voice-mail message, Eunice

A. did make an offer because she described her definite good-faith intention to convey property to Alison.
B. did make an offer because she expressed an explicit, unconditional plan, asking no response from Alison.
C. did not make an offer because she did not require that Alison pay money for the car.
D. did not make an offer because she did not call for a return performance from Alison.
E. did not make an offer because she proposed not a commercial transaction but an informal arrangement between friends.

ANALYSIS. Here's another "yes, because," "no, because" question (with "did" and "did not" replacing "yes" and "no"). Steer clear of the answer choices until you first conceive *your own* answer and reasoning.

One makes an offer by proposing a bargain — an exchange — a swap — an "I'll do this if you'll do that." Eunice didn't do that. As a reasonable person, Alice cannot conclude that Eunice asks anything in return for the car; Eunice proposes no *bargain*. Rather, she promises a gift. She's free to do that, but she hasn't made an offer. Hence, the parties can't form a contract. (As you'll learn from Chapter 12, Eunice need not honor her promise; she's free to break it.)

Now we've conceived of an answer and reason: Eunice made no offer because her message proposed no *bargain*. Reading for meaning and not for words, look first at the answer choices beginning with "did not," ignoring for now those that begin with "did."

E implies that one can make an offer only if she communicates in a commercial setting. You know better. One may make an offer to anyone in any setting — commercial, noncommercial, friendly, or unfriendly. **E** is wrong.

C looks better. It notes that Eunice asked for no money. If Eunice had asked for money she'd be asking, plainly, for a quid pro quo, and her message would be an offer. **C** seems correct, but before writing it in stone (or ink), let's look at **D**. **D** uses the phrase "return performance," which means "something done or given in exchange." According to **D**, Eunice made no offer because she did not ask that Alison do anything in return for the car. That sounds right for the same reason that **C** sounds right. So which is better — **C** or **D**? Look at the difference between them.

According to **C**, the message fails as an offer because it asks Alison for no money. One can make an offer without asking the other for money. One may make an offer in which money plays no role at all. X may propose to wash Y's windows in exchange for Y's sweeping X's floor. In the movie theater, Donna made an offer by proposing to exchange binoculars for a cell phone. **D** recognizes that an offer requires not a request for money, but the solicitation of *some* performance that might or might not involve monetary payment. That makes **D** better than **C**.

Before settling on **D**, look at **A** and **B**. **A** ignores the absence of a proposed bargain and implies that one always makes an offer if she proclaims a plan to transfer property. That's wrong (and the happy words "definite good faith intention" can't make it right. Read for *meaning*, not words).

B accurately describes Eunice's message, but tells us that she *did* make an offer. That Eunice's plan is unconditional means it asks nothing back from Alison. For that reason alone, it can't be an offer. Because it calls for no response, it does not ask for Alison's assent. That too means it can't be an offer. With **A** and **B** out of our way, we know that **D** is right.

C. The General Significance (and Insignificance) of Writings and Signatures

We know that one can make an offer by speech, writing, or behavior. As soon you'll see, the same goes for acceptance. Hence, as stated at the beginning of this chapter: Two parties may form a contract with or without a writing. That raises a simple question: If two parties can form a contract without a writing, why do they so often create one?

Here's the answer: To do something is one thing. To *prove* you did it is another. Suppose you pay April's telephone bill in cash, at the phone company office. You take a receipt, but lose it. One month later, the company bills you for May and asserts also that you owe for April too.

You know you've paid April's bill, and you so inform the company. If the company finds a record of your payment and agrees that you've paid, there's no problem. But suppose it finds no such record and sues you for April's bill. As a plaintiff, the phone company bears the burden of proof; it *must* introduce some evidence that you did not pay, or the court will dismiss its case.

At trial, a phone company employee testifies that (1) the company normally keeps records of all customer payments, and (2) it has no record of your April payment. Your attorney cross-examines the employee: "To your knowledge, has the phone company ever lost a record?" The employee answers, "No, not to my knowledge."

The phone company has introduced evidence tending to show that you did not pay April's bill. As a defendant, you have the opportunity to present evidence showing that you did pay the bill. A receipt signed by phone company personnel would be compelling evidence; with that, you'd surely win. But you don't have one. What evidence can you offer? You can testify that you remember paying April's bill in cash. The jury might believe you, in which case you'll win. But the jury might find the phone company's evidence more compelling than yours, in which case you'll lose. Even though you really did pay April's bill, you'll have to pay it again.

Similarly, two parties, Anastasia and Bob, might form a contract by speech alone. If Bob later denies having done so and there exists no writing that documents their agreement, Anastasia will have trouble proving that the contract ever was made. That is not to say she *can't* prove it; she might have other evidence sufficient to convince a court that the parties formed a contract, notwithstanding Bob's denial. Indeed, plaintiffs often succeed in proving they've formed contracts without a writing. Nonetheless, when two parties form a contract, a writing is compelling evidence that they did so, and it's evidence, also, of the terms on which they agreed.

Hence, when two parties put their contract in writing, they do so in contemplation of a future dispute, for reasons of evidence and proof—proof that they formed a contract and proof of its terms. (Some contracts, however, are enforceable *only* if they are recorded in writing, a matter addressed in Chapter 15.)

D. Meaning of Acceptance, Power to Accept, and Identity of the Offeree

1. Acceptance

One accepts an offer if he writes, says, or does that which would lead a reasonable person in the offeror's position to believe that he has assented, unconditionally, to all terms of the offeror's proposed bargain. Restatement (Second) Contract §50(1) states it this way:

> Acceptance of an offer is the manifestation of assent to the terms thereof made by the offeree[.]

As in the Restatement's definition of "offer," we read the word "manifestation." The legal meanings of offer and acceptance are alike in this way: They turn not on one's genuine intentions but on his *manifest* intentions. If, in response to an offer, an offeree says or does that which the offeror would reasonably interpret as "Yes, I assent," then the offeree accepts. So — whether one *makes* or *accepts* an offer depends not on what he truly intends but on the intentions a reasonable person would ascribe to his words or behavior.

2. Power to Accept

The "power to accept" an offer rests only in an *offeree.* As Restatement (Second) §50(1) provides: "Acceptance of an offer is the manifestation of assent to the terms thereof made *by the offeree*[.]" If A makes an offer to B, and C says, "I accept," there is no contract. C has *attempted* to accept, but he is not, alas, an offeree and has no power to do so.

3. Identity of the Offeree

That an offer allows for acceptance only by an offeree raises this question: How do we identify an offeree? As with the creation of an offer, the answer turns on the offeror's *manifest intent* — on what reasonable persons would believe when interpreting the offeror's acts, statements, or writings. Put another way: *With respect to any offer, an offeree is any person who, under the circumstances, reasonably believes that the offeror's proposal is made to him and that his assent is invited.* Restatement (Second) §29(1) states it thus:

> The manifested intention of the offeror determines the person or persons in whom is created a power of acceptance.

James, Nancy and May

Nancy and May are flutists. James visits them, and there follows this conversation:

> James: "Hey, Nancy, if you'll give me five flute lessons, one on each of the five consecutive Thursdays, beginning this coming Thursday, from 8:00 P.M. to 9:00 P.M., I'll pay $50 per lesson. Is that a deal?
> May: "Yes, I'll do it."
> Nancy: "Yes, I'll do it."

James began with "Hey, Nancy," and so manifested his intent to address *Nancy.* Nancy was the offeree; May was not. Nancy had the "power to accept;" May did not. May's assent is no acceptance. After May speaks, James's offer lives on, and Nancy has power to accept it. When Nancy says, "Yes, I'll do it," she and James form a contract.

As in the case above, an offeror's manifest intention might create only one offeree, thus vesting the power to accept in one person only. The offeror might also create two or more offerees, vesting a power to accept in both (or all) of them, providing also, however, that if one offeree accepts, the others lose their power to do so. Consider again, the conversation among James, Nancy, and May, slightly modified:

James: "Hey, you two—I want five flute lessons, one on each of the five consecutive Thursdays, beginning this coming Thursday, from 8:00 P.M. to 9:00 P.M.; I'll pay $50 per lesson. Is that a deal?"

May: "I'll do it."

Nancy: "I'll do it."

Reasonable persons in May's or Nancy's position should understand James to mean, "I'd like to have five flute lessons, and I don't care who provides them. I do not, however, want ten lessons. So, if one of you agrees, it's too late for the other." When May assents, she exercises her power of acceptance; Nancy loses hers.

An offeror might make an offer to two or more persons as a "team," providing that a contract will arise only if *all* of them assent. In that case, all offerees together "share" the power of acceptance; acceptance arises only if all manifest assent. Suppose, for example, Alan says to Beth, Chad, and Trey: "Hey, you three—if you'll perform at my wedding—Beth at the piano, Chad at the drums, and Trey at the bass—I'll pay $500." The three offerees should understand that Alan wants performance from all three together or none at all. If only one or two of the three offerees assent, there is no acceptance. If all assent, they furnish a single acceptance and a contract arises.

Finally, an offeror might make an offer to two or more persons separately, allowing all to accept. Suppose Libroco makes this written announcement to the public: "We will pay $5 to every person who reads our new book, *Cat Tall* and, by August 18, sends us a written review."[2] Any person who reads the announcement is justified in believing that she is invited to assent. All have a power of acceptance independent of the others. Suppose 5,000 persons read the book and, by August 18, send their reviews. With 5,000 offerees, Libroco forms 5,000 contracts.

Restatement (Second) §29(b) speaks to all such possibilities with this one sentence:

> An offer may create a power of acceptance in a specified person or in one or more of a specified group or class of persons, acting separately or together, or to anyone or everyone who makes a specified promise or renders a specified performance.

Realize that one cannot make an acceptance unless he first receives an offer. Suppose Phillip turns to Mei and says, "I was thinking, maybe, of selling this

---

2. But see Chapter 5 as to whether and when an advertisement constitutes an offer.

diamond ring for a very good price." Mei responds, "I accept." By law, Mei did *not* accept, for the simple reason that Phillip made her no offer. *Without an offer, there can be no acceptance.*

QUESTION 5. In the town of Hampshire there live two women named Harriett Folger. One lives at 14 *Chelton* Lane. The townsfolk know her to be an industrial quality control engineer. She is also a talented seamstress, but, as she is well aware, no one knows that. The other Harriett Folger, of 14 *Chester* Lane, is a seamstress, renowned for the high quality of her work. Farah Fuilan, also of Hampshire, writes and signs this letter:

> Dear Ms. Folger,
>
> I know you are a gifted seamstress. I have a dress in need of repair. I'd like you to examine it and determine whether you can fix it. I'll pay you $100 to do just that much. I'd like to meet next Saturday—any time that works for you. Are you agreeable?
>
> Sincerely yours,
>
> Farah Fuilan

Confused as to which Harriett lives where, Farah addresses her letter to Harriett the engineer at 14 *Chelton* Lane. Harriett receives the letter, opens it, and writes back to Farah: "Yes, absolutely. I am agreeable. Let's meet this coming Saturday at 1 P.M., my home."

Farah then learns of her error. She contacts Harriett the engineer and tells her, "By error, I sent my letter to you. I now know that I should have sent it to Harriett Folger the seamstress, at 14 *Chester* Lane." The engineer responds, "You do not know it, but I too am a capable seamstress. You sent the letter to me, I accepted your offer, and we have a contract." Farah asserts that she and Harriett (the engineer) did not form a contract. Her position is best supported by which fact?

A. Farah honestly wished to contact the other Harriett and, under the circumstances, her error was reasonably understandable.

B. Harriett knew that her abilities as a seamstress were unknown to the community.

C. Harriett's principal professional activity is in the field of engineering.

D. Farah cannot be bound to an agreement she did not intend to make.

ANALYSIS. Think, first, of the relevant law: Two parties A and B form a contract when A makes an offer *to B* and B accepts it. B can't accept an offer if A has not made her one.

Let's ask: Did Farah make an offer to Harriett? Harriett was "well aware" that the community knew her not at all as a seamstress. Seeing that Farah's letter referred to a "gifted seamstress," she should have known that Farah meant to make her offer to the other Harriett Folger; that was Farah's *manifest* intention. Harriett of *Chelton* Lane was not Farah's offeree. Possessed of no offer, *that* Harriett had nothing to accept. Her response, "I am agreeable" was not an acceptance, and the parties formed no contract. Among the answer choices, the right one will reflect *that* reasoning.

A refers to Farah's *honest* intent and the understandability of her error. Neither of these factors states the reason for which these parties failed to form a contract. They failed to form a contract because legally, Farah made no offer to Harriett. **C** reminds us that Harriett is not a professional seamstress. But that doesn't matter. What matters is this: Harriett knows that the community is ignorant of her abilities as a seamstress and so should have known that Farah did not intend to make a proposal to *her*. **C** is wrong. **D** makes the false statement that one cannot be bound to a contract contrary to her actual intention. *We know that's wrong.* Contracts arise not by actual intention, but by manifest intention. **D** is for the dumper.

B refers to Harriett's knowledge that the community did not know her as a seamstress. Extend your reasoning from there. Understanding that she was not known as a seamstress, Harriett *should* have known that Farah did not intend to engage her as one. That's the thought for which we're looking, and so **B** is right.

QUESTION 6. Martha secured a patent for a biomedical device she called "Gutmate." Believing that Deborah was a qualified manufacturer of biomedical devices, Martha sent Deborah the Gutmate plans and designs, together with a note: "I am prepared to hire you as manufacturer of Gutmate. I have little capital and propose, therefore, to convey to you a share of the patent ownership in exchange for your services. I invite your acceptance." Deborah responded, by writing: "Yes, we have a deal."

Does Deborah's response constitute an acceptance?

A. Ayes, because Deborah expressed her assent, clearly and unequivocally

B. Yes, because Martha explicitly invited Deborah to accept

C. No, because Martha's writing omits to describe Deborah as a qualified manufacturer

D. No, because Martha's writing proposes no definite bargain

E. No, because it did not present the word "accept" or "acceptance"

ANALYSIS. You are asked to decide only this: That Deborah's response is or is not an acceptance. Martha's message makes no offer because it specifies no exchange. Most blatantly, it fails to indicate how large a "share" of the patent ownership Martha will convey. Because Martha made no offer, Deborah can give no acceptance.

Look among the choices for one that reaches the right conclusion ("no") for the right reason: Martha made no offer.

Choice **C** raises the reddest of "red herrings." One certainly may make an offer without reciting the offeree's qualifications to perform. The offeree may, likewise, accept. Nothing in **C** explains why Deborah's response fails as an acceptance. **E** implies that one may accept only by using the *word* "accept," and that, of course, is nonsense.

According to **D**, Deborah did not accept because Martha proposed no definite bargain. That's the test writer's way of noting that Martha made no offer, and that *is* the reason that Deborah could not accept. **D** seems certainly to be right, but for safety's sake let's look at **A** and **B**.

A tells us that Deborah plainly and unambiguously expressed her "assent." But that to which she assented was *not an offer*, meaning her assent was not an acceptance. **B** suggests that one gives an acceptance if someone else asks for her assent, and she responds by giving it. Choice **B**, like choice **A**, fails to account for the fact that an *acceptance must follow from an offer* and that Martha, in this case, did not make one. **A**, **B**, and **C** are wrong. **D** is right.

E.   Acceptance by Silence

If circumstances are such that a reasonable offeror should interpret the offeree's silence as assent then — *silence is acceptance.*

Wallace Washes Willa's Windows

In April, for $75, Wallace washed Willa's windows. Willa then told Wallace that she would likely want him to wash her windows again in six months. Six months later, in October, Wallace called Willa and asked if she'd like him to wash her windows again. She said "yes," he did so, and Willa again paid him $75. The same occurred every April and every October for eleven years.

On April 2 of the twelfth year, Wallace telephoned Willa and left this voice-mail message: "I'll be by on Tuesday, April 9 to wash the windows. Let me know, please, if that's a problem." Willa listened to the message and made no response.

Hearing nothing from Willa, Wallace appeared at Willa's home, ready to wash the windows. Willa told him that she no longer wished to have her windows washed.

Has Willa Breached a Contract?

Yes, probably. With his voice-mail message of April 2, Wallace made an offer. In view of his request that Willa report any "problem" she had with his plan, and in light of the eleven-year history, Wallace was justified in believing:

1. that if Willa did not want his services, she would come forth and say so and, therefore,
2. that Willa, with her silence, said, in effect, "yes, come on April 9; I have no problem with that."

This exemplifies the (rather rare) case in which *silence is acceptance.*

So What's the Rule?

You already know the rule because you know the meaning of acceptance. Silence may constitute acceptance because, under some circumstances, an offeror manifests assent by doing and saying — nothing. *An offeree's silence constitutes her acceptance when, under the circumstances, the offeror would naturally expect the offeree to come forth and speak up if she wished not to accept the offer.*
Restatement (Second) §26 (illustration) explains:

> Where an offeree fails to reply to an offer, his silence and inaction operate as an acceptance [if] because of previous dealings or otherwise, it is reasonable that the offeree should notify the offeror if he does not intend to accept.

QUESTION 7. RakeCo is a landscaper and CondoHome a residential condominium community. In each of the years 2003 - 2012, the two parties formed a written contract under which CondoHome paid RakeCo $90,000 and RakeCo attended to a CondoHome's landscaping during the months April - October. On February 1, 2013 CondoHome contacts RakeCo:

(1) February 1, **CondoHome** (by signed writing): We have received no contract for this year. Please assure us that you'll take care of our landscaping this coming spring and summer.

(2) February 4, **RakeCo** (by signed writing): Yes, of course we will. We have raised our fees by 3% to all customers. In your case, our fee will be $93,000, not $90,000. None of our customers has objected to this modest increase, and we assume you will not object either. We'll be making all of our plans firm on April 1.

On February 7, CondoHome read RakeCo's February 4 message and issued no response. On March 31, CondoHome advises RakeCo that for 2013 it has contracted with HoeCo, another landscaper, whose fee was $91,000, and that it will not accept RakeCo's services.

RakeCo brings an action against CondoHome, alleging that the parties had formed a contract requiring that CondoHome retain RakeCo as its landscaper for April - October 2011 and pay its $93,000 fee. CondoHome contends that it never accepted RakeCo's February 1 offer, wherefore the parties formed no such contract.

If judgment is for RakeCo, the reason will most likely be that:

A. RakeCo could sensibly conclude that if CondoHome wanted not to accept RakeCo's offer, it would have said so before April 1.
B. RakeCo did not impose the 3% fee increase on CondoHome alone, but rather imposed it on all of its customers.
C. CondoHome should reasonably have anticipated that RakeCo might, after ten years, increase its fees.
D. Before contracting with HoeCo, CondoHome owed RakeCo the opportunity to match HoeCo's price.

ANALYSIS. On February 1, CondoHome made HoeCo an offer. If these parties formed a contract it must be because RakeCo was justified in taking CondoCo's silence as assent.

Let's assess the answer choices. Choice **D** implies this rule: If a Party X repeatedly buys from Party Y and then finds Party Z offering the same commodity at a lower price, Y may not contract with Z until it first gives X the chance to meet Z's price. There is no such rule. **D** is wrong.

C is wrong too. Maybe CondoHome should have expected an increase in RakeCo's fee. But that doesn't mean CondoHome must pay it. Neither does it turn CondoHome's silence into acceptance. **B** implies that because RakeCo raised its price to *all* its customers, CondoHome's silence constitutes acceptance. That, too, is wrong. Whether RakeCo imposed its increase on all of its customers or on CondoHome only, CondoHome's silence is acceptance only if RakeCo should reasonably understand it as such. **B** is wrong.

According to Choice **A**, CondoHome accepted because RakeCo reasonably believed ("sensibly assumed") that, CondoHome would speak up if it objected to the increased fee. Certainly a court could make that ruling. And, when an offeror reasonably reaches that conclusion, the offeree's silence is acceptance.

That's why **A** is right.

F.   Acceptance by Dominion

Suppose DirtCo, showing no return address, mails to 1,000 private homes a bottle of its laundry detergent, "LaundraLust," together with this message:

Dear Homeowner:

We offer you this bottle of LaundraLust for $1.89, and we'll send you another 11 bottles, one per month, for which you will pay (in advance) that same price of $1.89 per bottle. To accept this offer you need only keep this bottle we've sent you.

That's Cute. The Homeowner Accepts by Keeping the Bottle?

No, he doesn't. *An offeree accepts when she says, writes, or does that which, under the prevailing circumstances would cause a reasonable person in the offeror's position to believe that he has assented, unconditionally, to the offeror's proposed bargain.*

That's law. No offeror can alter it. A reasonable person in DirtCo's position would understand that when one receives a product without asking for it, without notice of a return address, he will likely keep it for the simple reason that he knows not what else to do. An offeror cannot manufacture an acceptance by decreeing that he will treat the offeree's natural behavior as assent. Hence, it cannot reasonably believe that a homeowner who retains the LaundraLust assents to its offer.

So the Homeowner Gets to Keep and Use the LaundraLust for Free?

No, he doesn't. If the offeree keeps the property he makes himself a *bailee*.[3]

By law, he must return it when the owner asks to have it back. If, however, the offeree *exercises dominion* over the property, meaning that he uses it, sells it, gives it away, or otherwise treats it as his own, then he accepts the offeror's offer and must pay the offered price. If he refuses to do so, he commits contractual breach.

> An offer is the manifestation of willingness to enter into a bargain, so made as to justify *another person* in understanding that *his* assent to that bargain is invited and will conclude it. Restatement (Second) of Contracts § 69 (2) provides (in part):
>
> > An offeree who does any act inconsistent with the offeror's ownership of offered property is bound in accordance with the offered terms unless they are manifestly unreasonable.
>
> That means this: *If Party A delivers property to Party B, offering it for sale to Party B, and Party B in some way treats the property as his own, then Party B accepts Party A's offer to purchase the property — unless the terms of the offer are manifestly unreasonable.*

What About That Last Clause Ending with "Manifestly Unreasonable"?

Suppose:

1. Seller sends Homeowner a can of shoe polish together with an offer to sell it for *$12 million,* and
2. Homeowner uses it.

---

3. When you "check" your coat at a restaurant you bail it; you're the bailee, the restaurant is the bailor. The bailor must keep and care for the coat, until you ask to have it back, treating it all the while as *your* property. The same is so when you leave your car in a commercial parking lot. Further, the common law *implies* a bailment when you lose your property and another finds it. You are the bailor and the finder is the bailee. The finder has the obligation to care for the property and, ultimately, to return it to you if and when you claim it. (*Statutes* in most jurisdictions allow the finder to bring the property to the local police and thus be relieved of his responsibility as bailee.) Bailment is itself an expansive legal topic in its own right. The subject has spawned multi-volume works, some of them more than a hundred years old. The topic's tentacles touch a great many fields of law including, as we've just seen, contracts, as discussed in this section.

On learning that Homeowner has used the product, the offeror cannot, as a reasonable person, believe that he manifested assent to pay the $12 million.

The offeree's exercise of dominion does not, in that case, constitute acceptance. (It probably does, however, constitute the tort of conversion.)[4]

Can the Offeree Leave the Property in His Mailbox? And If He Takes It Into His Possession, Can He Ever Discard It?

Yes, and yes. If the offeree leaves the seller's property where he finds it (at his doorstep or in his mailbox, for example) he bears no responsibility for its care or return. If he takes custody of it and thus becomes a bailee he may, after a reasonable time, discard it.[5]

But Know This: Where the Offeror Uses U.S. Mail, a Federal Statute Renders This Common Law Moot

A federal statute now provides, generally, that if, on his own initiative, a Party A *mails* property to a Party B together with an offer to sell it, Party B may take and keep the property as his gift.

39 U.S.C. §3009(b) provides:

> [Any unordered merchandise sent by U.S. mail] may be treated as a gift by the recipient, who shall have the right to retain, use, discard, or dispose of it in any manner he sees fit without any obligation whatsoever to the sender.

The federal statute applies only where the offeror uses the *U.S. mails* to send the unordered merchandise. Where he employs some other mode of delivery, the common law continues to operate.

Can We Summarize, Please?

(1) If (other than by U.S. mail), without any request, one receives property together with the owner's offer to sell it, then the recipient may (a) leave the property where he finds it and be free of any responsibility, or (b) take custody, hold it as a bailee, and, after a reasonable time, discard it, or (c) exercise dominion by using it, selling it, gifting it, or otherwise treating it as his own. In that case he accepts the owner's offer (unless its terms are manifestly unreasonable) and, by contract, must pay the owner's price.

---

4. One commits the tort of conversion and thus becomes a "converter" when, without consent or other justification, he exercises such dominion and control over another's property as properly belongs to a true owner, wherefore the law allows the true owner, in essence, to recover from the defendant the value of the property and thus, in effect, to require that he buy it. See: *Am. Jur. 2d Conversion § 2, Restatement 2d Torts 222A*. If a bailee treats a bailor's property as though it is his own he commits conversion.

5. None of this is quite so simple as we might like it to be. Bailment, once again, is a topic unto itself and it happens to cross paths, here, with contracts. In general, however, when one becomes an "involuntary bailee," as happens in the scenarios we now describe, he may, after a reasonable time, conclude that the bailor has abandoned the property and then discard it.

> **QUESTION 8.** CupCo manufactured disposable cups and sold them to distributors. SupCo was a distributor of disposable cups, and on all the cups it sold, stamped its own name and imprint. On August 1, CupCo sent SupCo two thousand disposable coffee cups, in boxes, together with this message:
>
> > We provide herewith two thousand of our new CoffeeFriend coffee cups. We assume you'll want to sell them to your own customers. If you keep them, we'll assume that you've decided to buy, and we'll bill you—$125. If you do not wish to buy, please return to us within fifteen days, COD; we will pay the shipping charges.
>
> Which of the following would most likely mean that SupCo accepts CupCo's offer?
>
> **A.** SupCo keeps the cups in their unopened boxes for more than fifteen days.
> **B.** SupCo writes to CupCo: "We will keep the cups until you come to get them."
> **C.** SupCo writes to CupCo: "We very much like the cups."
> **D.** SupCo stamps its own name and imprint on the cups.

ANALYSIS. On its own initiative CupCo sent its Cups to SupCo. Notwithstanding CupCo's message, mere silence on SupCo's part will not constitute acceptance. Rather, SupCo will accept if either (a) it contacts CupCo and assents to its offer, or (b) exercises dominion over the cups. According to Choice **A** SupCo keeps possession of the cups but does not even open the boxes in which they came. In doing that, it does not accept the offer but, instead, makes itself a bailee. **A** is wrong. **B** is wrong too. By telling CupCo that the cups are available for pick-up, SupCo once again makes itself a bailee.

What of **C**? It is, perhaps, that "we very much like the cups," manifests assent to CupCo's offer. Were it not for **D**, **C** would be best. But **D** is plainly better. By stamping its name on the cups SupCo treated them as its own; it exercised dominion over them and thus accepted CupCo's offer. **D** is right.

G.   THE CLOSER

> **QUESTION 9.** Paula, President of PowerCo, needs diesel fuel for the coming winter. Olivia sells diesel fuel and Frank, her competitor, sells it as well. On a Monday in August Paul, Olivia, and Frank meet, each with a pad of note paper. They discuss PowerCo's need for diesel fuel during the coming winter. OilCo has 15 million gallons of diesel fuel available for sale.

FuelCo has 20 million gallons. On two separate sheets of paper from her pad, Paula writes "PowerCo is prepared to pay $7 million now for a guarantee that 10 million gallons of grade-two diesel fuel oil will be delivered to its tanking facility on or before October 10 of this year." After she signs both writings, Paula hands one to Franco and the other to Olivia. Franco and Olivia read the writing, and all three part company.

On the next day, Tuesday, Franco personally delivers to Paula this written message, "I accept your offer of yesterday." On the same day, Olivia reaches Paula by telephone and says, "I accept the offer you made yesterday." Which of the following additional facts most likely means that Paula is obliged to purchase diesel fuel from Olivia and not from Franco?

A. Franco did not sign the writing that he delivered to Paula.
B. Olivia reached Paula by telephone before Franco arrived at Paula's office.
C. When Franco wrote the words "I accept your offer of yesterday," he had lost Paula's writing and no longer had it in his possession.
D. On Wednesday, Olivia sent by certified mail a signed writing in which she stated: "I hereby reaffirm acceptance, made by telephone on Tuesday, of Monday's offer."

ANALYSIS. With respect to any offer, the offeree is she who reasonably believes the offeror has invited *her* assent. Paula makes her offer by signed writing, orally addressed to "you two." Hence, both Olivia and Franco are offerees. Yet Paula made plain her wish to buy only 10 million gallons of fuel. Consequently, her offerees should know that she invites acceptance from either of them, but not both. As with James, Nancy, and May (section D above), Paula's offer starts a "race" between two offerees; both have power to accept, but *each loses the power if the other exercises it first*. Olivia accepts the offer if she is first to manifest her assent.

Choice **A** implies that an unsigned writing is legally ineffective. Non-lawyers might believe that, but it's not true. As discussed in section C above, signatures have significance. Nonetheless, one may offer or accept with a writing that's unsigned.

C and **D** cite facts that are legally irrelevant. According to **C**, Franco lost Paula's writing before writing his words of acceptance. The law nowhere requires that an offeree have in his possession some written record of the offer when he decides to accept it. **D** states that Olivia sent by certified mail a signed writing reaffirming the acceptance she made by telephone. To that, we say, "so what?" With the phone call she accepted Paula's offer. A second acceptance means nothing (but, as discussed in section C, it creates good *evidence* of the acceptance).

According to **B**, Olivia was first to contact Paula and express her assent. If Olivia does that, she accepts the offer; she and Paula form a contract. Simultaneously, Franco loses his power to accept. When he handed Paula his writing, he did nothing of legal import; the writing is a "legal nullity." **B** is right.

✦ Silver & Hochberg's Picks

1.	**B**
2.	**E**
3.	**E**
4.	**D**
5.	**B**
6.	**D**
7.	**A**
8.	**D**
9.	**B**

3

Understand the Relationships Among Three Critical Phrases

A.   Manifest Intention (Again)

Think again of the lawnmower case described in Chapter 2, section B: Carlos stands by a lawnmower and says, in a serious tone, "I want to sell my lawnmower for $100." Even if Carlos means to describe another lawnmower miles away, a reasonable person, seeing and hearing him, would think he's talking of the mower standing right there. Regardless of Carlos's true intention, *that's* the intention to which the law holds him; it's his "manifest intention." *A party's manifest intention, then, is the intention that, under all prevailing circumstances, a reasonable person would attribute to her on seeing what she does, hearing what she says, or reading what she writes.* When contract law refers to "intention," it almost always means *manifest* intention.

B.   Objective Theory of Contracts

That brings us to the "objective theory of contracts," a pretentious little phrase that refers to the legal doctrine we've been discussing: *A party's intentions are not those that she subjectively carries in her own mind but rather those that an objective reasonable person would, under all surrounding circumstances, attribute to her words and behavior.* In the lawnmower example, a judge, lawyer, professor, or writer who refers to the "objective theory of contracts" means only that Carlos, by law, is deemed to be offering for sale the very lawnmower standing next to him because a reasonable *objective* person would so conclude.

For at least a century, authorities in contract law have subscribed to the objective theory. Authoritative statements to that effect arise as early as the 1400s when, during the reign of Edward IV, an English court wrote: "It is a trite learning that the thought of man is not triable, for the devil himself knows not the thought of man." Brian, in YB 17 Edw. IV, 2. A wide range of jurists and scholars have agreed,[1] and all modern courts are in accord:

> [T]he law imputes to a person an intention corresponding to the reasonable meaning of his words and acts. *Howell v. Smith*, 128 S.E.2d 144 (N.C. 1962); *Roper v. Clanton*, 258 S.W.2d 283 (Mo. App. 1953); *Marefield Meadows, Inc. v. Lorenz*, 427 S.E.2d 363 (Va. 1993).

Yet many commentators write of a historical debate between those who believed in the objective theory of contracts and those who endorsed a *subjective* theory of contracts. According to proponents of the subjective theory, no two persons could form a contract unless they truly, in their heads, intended to be bound by a single set of terms. A difference of genuine intent or interpretation, if proven, meant the parties formed no contract.

Once again, the truth is that no learned authority—of any century—ever fully expounded a system of contract law based on subjective intent. So even though some literature *refers to* a historical competition between subjective and objective theorists, all modern authorities agree that the objective theory of contracts is law. And yet, opinions still sometimes feature the unfortunate phrase "meeting of the minds."

C.   "Meeting of the Minds"

At its heart, the objective theory of contracts means this: When two persons form an agreement, each is entitled to enjoy his *reasonable expectations and beliefs*; and, in turn, must fulfill those of the other. On that principle we define

---

1. *See, e.g.*, N.Y. Trust Co. v. Island Oil & Transp. Corp., 4 F.2d 655, 655 (2d Cir. 1929) (Hand, Learned, J.) (contracts "depend upon the meaning . . . the law imputes"); Hotchkiss v. Natl. City Bank of N.Y., 200 F. 287, 293 (S.D.N.Y. 1911) (Hand, Learned, J.) ("contract has . . . nothing to do with . . . personal . . . intent . . . [but with] certain acts"); O'Donnell v. Clinton, 14 N.E. 747 (Mass. 1888) (Holmes, J.) (intent "is a matter of overt acts, not of inward . . . motives"); Christopher Langdell, *Cases on Contract* 3marg., 13marg. (William A. Keener ann. 1871) ("law only regards consent manifested, not the abstract state of mind"); John E. Murray, *Convention on Contracts for the International Sale of Goods* (1988) (the law "long ago discarded . . . subjective intent"); 1 Samuel Williston, *Treatise on the Law of Contracts* §22 (1922) ("secret intent [is] immaterial, only overt acts" constitute intent).

"offer" as a *manifestation* of willingness to enter a bargain that *justifies* another person in believing his assent is invited. Because we so define "offer," one who reasonably believes that a bargain is proposed to him does indeed have power to assent to it and thus finalize a contract, even if the offeror truly intends no such thing. And it matters not that offeror and offeree, *in their own heads*, give different meanings to the offeror's words or behavior. By law, words and behaviors have such meaning as *reasonable* persons would give them under the prevailing circumstances.

Similarly, we define acceptance as a *manifestation* of assent, so that when the offeror reasonably believes the offeree has assented, the parties form a contract, even if the offeree truly intended no such thing. It matters not that offeror and offeree, *in their own heads*, give different meanings to the offeree's words. By law, they have such meaning as *reasonable* persons would give them under the prevailing circumstances.

1. But Aren't All Words Susceptible to Many Reasonable Interpretations?

Under most circumstances — no. Under most circumstances communicative words or behaviors have but one reasonable interpretation. *Rarely*, however, quirks of circumstance arise in which one's words and behaviors are susceptible to two very different interpretations, both of them perfectly reasonable. In those uncommon cases, if the misunderstanding be material[2] to the purported agreement, the parties do *not* form a contract. That too squares with the objective theory.

2. Illustration: Ilsa v. Ike

Ike operates a used car lot and has in it a 2000 Chacquar X7 with a blue-book value of $5,000. At noon on September 10, he posts on that vehicle a sign that reads: "ONCE IN A LIFETIME DEAL! This Beautiful 2000 CHACQUAR X7 For Sale Now at the GIVE-AWAY PRICE of $4,999." At 12:05 P.M., Victor sees the sign and decides to make mischief. Carefully and skillfully, he deletes the third "9" so that the price now reads "$499." Victor departs.

At 12:06 P.M., Ilsa arrives at the lot and sees the sign. Believing that $499 is truly a give-away price, she enters Ike's office and asks, "Are you really selling the Chacquar X7 for the price shown on the windshield? *That* price?" "Yes," says Ike. "It's a great price for a great car." Ilsa responds, "For *that* price, I'll take it." Ike replies, "And for that price, you've got it. It's a deal." The parties shake hands and step out to examine the vehicle.

Distraught when he sees that his sign now reads "$499," Ike proclaims, "Someone has altered my sign. Did you think the car was selling for $499?"

---

2. The word "material" pops up throughout the law of contract. It refers to that which is significant. When we say "material misunderstanding," we refer to a misunderstanding that significantly affects the burdens and benefits that the contract visits on one or both its parties.

"Yes I did," says Ilsa. "That's what the sign says, and that's our deal." "Oh, no, it's not," counters Ike. "I posted on the car a price of $4,999." Ilsa and Ike then look very closely at the sign and see that someone has deleted the third "9." Nonetheless, Ilsa insists that she is entitled to buy the car for $499. Ike insists that she is not.

All courts and authorities would conclude that Ilsa and Ike formed no contract. For these two parties, "that price" had two different meanings, *both of which, under these peculiar circumstances, were reasonable.* Yet historically (and still today perhaps), many courts have had trouble articulating the reason for their conclusion. They have resorted instead to the misconceived phrase "meeting of the minds."

For example, a court deciding *Ike vs. Ilsa* might reach the right result but write a misleading opinion like this:

> Each of these parties behaved honestly and in good faith. Plaintiff Ilsa genuinely thought that the advertised price was $499 and in light of the words "give-away price," her belief was understandable. She offered to purchase for "that price," by which she meant $499. Defendant accepted the offer, stating that for "that price" he would sell plaintiff the car. *He* believed "that price" meant $4,999, the price he had posted on the vehicle only minutes earlier.
>
> The law does not impose a contract on two persons, each of whom honestly believes the bargain to be one thing while the other believes it to be another. Notwithstanding their offer and acceptance, and notwithstanding their good faith, we hold that these parties failed to form a contract for the simple reason that they failed to achieve a meeting of the minds, without which no offer and acceptance can make a contract.

Plainly, the court is wrong in its stated reasoning: No true "meeting of the minds" is necessary—*ever*—to the formation of a contract. Any and every (competent) court in the nation would hold, and every (learned) lawyer would agree, that the offeror who stands next to a lawnmower offering to sell "my lawnmower" offers to sell the very lawnmower in front of her regardless of her own true intention. None would care that the offeror's and offeree's minds did not "meet."

Properly understood, the objective theory of contracts explains the result in *Ilsa v. Ike* without reference to any failed "meetings" between "minds." Ike and Ilsa failed to form a contract because they did not achieve an offer and acceptance. When Ilsa offered to purchase the vehicle for "that price," Ike reasonably understood her to mean $4,999, the price he had posted minutes before. Consequently, *by law*, Ilsa *meant* $4,999. She did not, of course, in her own mind, mean to pay that amount, but when she said "that price," her words had such *legal* meaning as would be given them by a reasonable person in Ike's position. Ike, under the circumstances, *wrongly but reasonably* believed that Ilsa proposed to buy for $4,999. Consequently, that was her legal intention; Ilsa offered to buy the car for $4,999, although she herself did not know that.

When Ike told Ilsa she could have the car at "that price," Ilsa *wrongly but reasonably* understood *him* to mean that he would sell her the car for $499, the "give-away price" she saw posted on the vehicle. Because that's the meaning Ilsa *reasonably* gave Ike's words, Ike's *legal* intention was to sell the car for $499, even though he had no such *actual* intention. Consequently, by law, Ilsa offered to buy a car for $4,999 (Ike's reasonable understanding of her intention), and Ike agreed to sell it for $499 (Ike's reasonable understanding of Ilsa's intention). The offer and acceptance don't match. These parties failed to form a contract because they did not achieve offer and acceptance; Ilsa made an offer that Ike did not accept. "Meeting of the minds" has no proper place in the analysis.

3. *The Famous Case of the* Peerless

The English case of *Raffles v. Wichelhaus*, 2 H. & C. 906 (Ct. Exchq. 1864), involved a buyer and seller who attempted to contract for the sale of cotton. The 1864 case report does not indicate which of the parties was offeror and which was offeree, but we can imagine it either way 'round; the issue and result are the same. So let's suppose that Seller was the offeror.

Seller offered to sell cotton to Buyer, the cotton to be delivered to Buyer at Liverpool on a ship called *Peerless*, that ship to sail from Bombay to Liverpool. Buyer accepted the offer, and the parties thus thought they had contracted for the purchase and sale of cotton to be delivered to Buyer at Liverpool aboard the ship *Peerless* sailing from Bombay.

Unbeknownst to either party, two separate ships named *Peerless* were scheduled to sail from Bombay to Liverpool during the relevant period, one arriving in October, the other in December. When Seller made his offer and specified *Peerless*, he knew nothing of the October *Peerless* and had no reason to know of it. He, in his own mind, meant to designate the December ship, the only *Peerless* of which he knew. Yet, when Buyer accepted the offer, he knew nothing of the December ship and had no reason to know of it. He, in his own mind, understood *Peerless* to mean the ship arriving at Liverpool in October. Consequently, the parties thought they had agreed on the ship by which the goods would land in Liverpool (and, therefore, the month in which the goods would arrive). Yet they had not done so. Each had his own understanding of the name *Peerless*, and *both understandings, under the circumstances, were reasonable.*

In October, a ship *Peerless* arrived at Liverpool. Buyer sought to claim his cotton and found it was not on board. In December, the other *Peerless* arrived at Liverpool with the cotton on board. Buyer refused to take it, insisting that Seller should have delivered it on the October ship *Peerless,* the one on which he thought the parties had agreed. Seller brought an action against Buyer, alleging that Buyer was obliged to take and pay for the goods delivered on the December ship, the one on which *he* thought the parties had agreed.

The court ruled that the parties formed no contract at all, adopting the argument (apparently) that they had failed to achieve *consensus ad idem* (meaning agreement of idea; meeting of the minds): "[I]t appears that two ships called the 'Peerless' were about to sail from Bombay [to Liverpool.] . . . That being so, there was no *consensus ad idem*, and therefore no binding contract." *Raffles v. Wichelhaus*, 2 H. & C. 906, 907-908 (Ct. Exchq. 1864).[3]

In *Peerless*, as in *Ilsa v. Ike* above, the two pertinent parties, each thinking *reasonably*, gave different meanings to the same words. In *Ilsa v. Ike*, this rare happening arose from the underlying unlikelihood that within a few minutes after the seller posted one price, a meddler should alter it, and a passer-by should immediately offer to buy for "that price."

In *Peerless*, the rare happening arose because of another unlikelihood — that two cargo ships bearing the same name sailed from Bombay to Liverpool at or about the same time. *Peerless* too is readily susceptible to analysis via the objective theory. When Buyer offered to purchase goods delivered on the *Peerless*, he meant the October ship. But Seller, knowing only of the December ship, reasonably understood Buyer to designate that one. Consequently, Buyer, despite what he thought, offered to buy goods to be delivered on the December ship. Seller, when he purported to accept, agreeing to deliver goods on the *Peerless* meant the December ship, but Buyer reasonably understood him to mean the October ship. Consequently, Seller, in his attempt to accept, did not accept the offer made to him. For that reason — for failure of offer and acceptance — the parties formed no contract.

When a judge rules that two parties form no contract because they fail to achieve a "meeting of the minds," she means (but may not know she means) the two parties give materially[4] different meanings to the same word or phrase and that *both interpretations are reasonable.* Restatement (Second) of Contracts §20(1) provides:

> There is no manifestation of mutual assent to an exchange if the parties attach materially different meanings to their manifestations and . . . neither party knows or has reason to know the meaning attached by the other[.]

That jumble of words is the Restatement's *Peerless* provision. (See Restatement (Second) §20 illus. 2.) It means that two parties fail to form a contract if each gives to the same word or phrase, as used by the other, a materially different interpretation, and *both interpretations are reasonable.*

In such cases the parties fail to form a contract because the meaning of the offeror's offer *as the offeree reasonably construes it* differs from the meaning of the offeree's purported acceptance *as the offeror reasonably construes it.*

---

3. Like many English opinions of old, this one was written by a court reporter; it summarizes counsels' arguments and then reports the court's decision.

4. In the *Peerless* case, for example, the difference between the October and December ships is *material*, or significant. If instead, one ship arrived at 12:00 noon on October 5 and the second at 12:10 P.M. on October 5, the difference would be *immaterial*, or insignificant.

Materiality is ordinarily a question of fact for the jury (or the court in a bench trial).

Hence, even though the parties shake hands or sign their names to the *same set of words*, the offeror proposes one thing and the offeree "accepts" another. The parties achieve no offer and acceptance, and *that's* why they fail to form a contract. A failed "meeting of the minds" has naught to do with it.[5]

4. "Latent Ambiguity"

Some speak of "latent ambiguity" instead of (or together with) a failed "meeting of the minds." The phrase "latent ambiguity" represents the same meaning as does "meeting of the minds": a word or phrase that, as expressed and meant by one party, carries a materially different meaning for the other, *both meanings being reasonable* under the operative circumstances. In *Ilsa v. Ike*, the phrase "that price" represents a latent ambiguity; so does the name *Peerless* in *Raffles v. Wichelhaus*. Hence, where some say that two parties fail to form a contract because they failed to achieve a "meeting of the minds," others say (or add) that the contract fails for latent ambiguity. These identical statements bear identical flaws in concept and we hope they'll someday pass away and be superseded by genuine understanding of a *Peerless* situation.[6]

5. So What Should I Know About "Meeting of the Minds"?

Know that

1. Contract formation never requires—*ever*—any true meeting of the minds.
2. When, regrettably, courts do rule that a contract fails for lack of "meeting of the minds," (or fails for "latent ambiguity") they mean that each party has given to some word or phrase a materially different meaning, *both meanings reasonable under the circumstances.*
3. *But recognize* that if Parties A and B give different interpretations to language on which they purport to agree and Party A *has a reason* to know of Party B's interpretation, then Party A's interpretation is *not* reasonable. The divergent interpretations, in that case, do not constitute a latent ambiguity. The parties do form a contract, and the disputed term carries the meaning given it by Party B.

---

5. *See also* Langdell, *supra* note 1 ("contracting parties . . . must, in *legal contemplation*, concur; and this they do whenever an existing offer is accepted," not through "[*unilateral*] acts or acts of the will. . . .") (italics added); Oliver Wendell Holmes, *The Path of the Law*, 10 Harv. L. Rev. 457, 464 (1897) (courts "infer[] . . . no contract because [parties] have intended different things or [did not know] of [each other's] assent. . . . [A] contract depends . . . not on the parties' having meant the same thing but on their having said the same thing.").

6. *See* Murray, *supra* note 1, at XX ("the unfortunate phrase 'meeting of the minds . . . [arises] only where there is no preponderance of objective evidence favoring [the reasonableness of] one interpretation over another."). To make matters worse, many courts employ the misbegotten phrase "unilateral mistake" (see Chapter 22, section E).

6. *Illustration: Chelsea and Otis*

Chelsea has two bookcases in her den, one on the east wall and one on the west wall. For some 20 years, Chelsea has stored her large unabridged dictionary on the western bookcase. One day, however, she leaves the dictionary on her desk, and her nine-year-old son moves it from the desk to the eastern shelf. And there, gathering dust, it remains.

Six months later, Chelsea asks Otis, a painter, to "paint my white bookcase black." Otis enters the den without Chelsea and, seeing two bookcases, shouts to her: "I see two bookcases, both white. Which do you want me to paint?" "The one with the big unabridged dictionary on it," Chelsea shouts back. Otis sees the large dictionary in the eastern bookcase where Chelsea's son had placed it six months earlier and replies, "Okay, I'll paint the bookcase for $100." Chelsea agrees. Two hours later, when Chelsea sees which bookcase Otis has painted, she proclaims, "Oh, I meant for you to paint the *other* bookcase—that's where I always store the dictionary. I can't pay you for this work; it's not the work I intended you to do."

At the time these parties formed their contract, they honestly attributed different meanings to the words "the one with the big unabridged dictionary on it." Otis took them to mean the bookcase that actually held the dictionary, which was in fact the eastern bookcase. Chelsea meant to specify the western bookcase, the one on which she honestly thought the dictionary sat. And although both parties were honest in their divergent understandings, Chelsea's understanding *was not reasonable* (or not, at any rate, so reasonable as Otis's). Chelsea *should* have known—she had *opportunity* to know—that the dictionary was in the eastern bookcase. It was she who absentmindedly left the book on the desk six months earlier, whereupon her nine-year-old son, with access to the desk, placed it on the eastern bookcase. It was then she who, without herself examining the bookcases, directed Otis, from another room, to the case "with the big unabridged dictionary on it."

With precision, let's examine the parties' statements in terms of their legal significance.

Chelsea: I'd like you to paint a bookcase for me today—now. It's in the den. It's white, and I want it painted black.	Invitation to deal
Otis [*entering the room without Chelsea*]: Both bookcases in here are white. Which one do you want me to paint?	Invitation to deal
Chelsea: The one with the big unabridged dictionary on it.	Invitation to deal
Otis: Okay, I'll paint the bookcase for $100.	*Offer:* Chelsea *should* understand Otis to say "I'll paint the *eastern* bookcase for $100.
Chelsea: Agreed.	*Acceptance:* Otis reasonably understands Chelsea to say "Yes, paint the *eastern* bookcase for $100."

By offer and acceptance, these parties formed a contract respecting the *eastern* bookcase.

Analogy to Negligence/Fault. Chelsea's absentminded failure to replace the dictionary on the western shelf six months earlier, and her failure to verify before answering Otis's question that the book was, in fact, on the eastern shelf, amount to a kind of negligence or fault. Chelsea is like the driver who by absentmindedness passes through a red traffic light and causes a collision. Consequently, when assessing the situation in which two parties give different meanings to some term of their purported agreement, we may ask whether (a) the parties are equally blameless (or blameworthy), as in *Peerless* and *Ilsa v. Ike*; or (b) one of the parties is somehow at fault for the misunderstanding, as in the case of Chelsea and Otis.

If one of the parties is at fault for the misunderstanding, then her understanding of the relevant term is not a reasonable one. Consequently, the parties do form a contract and the disputed term carries the meaning given it by the other party—the party who is not at fault. Restatement (Second) §20(2) articulates this same principle:

> The manifestations of the parties are operative in accordance with the meaning attached to them by one of the parties if . . . (b) that party has no reason to know of any different meaning attached by the other, and the other has reason to know the meaning attached by the first party.

If we apply the Restatement rule to Chelsea and Otis, we find that:

1. Chelsea and Otis attached different meanings to the words "the one with the big unabridged dictionary on it."
2. Otis, understanding the phrase to designate the eastern bookcase, had no reason to know of any other meaning attached by Chelsea.
3. Chelsea, intending the phrase to designate the western bookcase, *did* have reason to know the meaning attached by Otis; it was she who left the dictionary out of place and thus caused the misunderstanding.

Consequently, notwithstanding their divergent interpretations of the term, the parties do form a contract for painting of the *eastern* bookcase.

7. Let's Put It All Together in One Big Rule

If two parties do all that is otherwise necessary to form a contract, but they attribute materially different meanings to a word or phrase on which they think they agree, then

(a) where, under the circumstances, both interpretations are reasonable, the relevant term constitutes a "latent ambiguity" and the parties form no contract;

(b) where, under the circumstances, one of the interpretations is unreasonable and the other reasonable, then the parties do form a contract and the disputed term carries the reasonable interpretation.

The *Peerless* and *Ilsa v. Ike* cases fall within subsentence (a), and cases like those cause some courts, regrettably, to invoke the phrase "meeting of the minds." The Chelsea-Otis case falls within subsentence (b). And once again, the rule just stated and the rule of Restatement §20(2) reflect the *objective* theory of contracts, even when some authorities (and professors) fail to see that truth.

QUESTION 1. Sam keeps two bicycles in his garage, a red one that sits at the back of the garage hidden behind old furniture, and a blue one that sits at the front, in plain view. Although Sam placed both bicycles in his garage, he has forgotten all about the blue one; he remembers only the red one hidden at the back. On Monday Babs visits Sam and sees the blue bike in the front of the garage. On Tuesday, Babs telephones Sam:

> **Babs:** I saw the bicycle in your garage yesterday. I'd like to buy it—today. Will you take $90?

> **Sam:** Ninety dollars sounds good—yes, definitely. Come over, we'll take it out of the garage, you'll pay me, and it's yours.

Babs arrives at Sam's garage. As she moves toward the blue bike in plain view, the parties talk.

> **Sam:** Oh, you meant *that* one? I'd forgotten all about it. I thought you meant the bike at the back of the garage, although I see now that it's hidden.

> **Babs:** Well, I want the bike that's right here in front of me. That's the one for which I offered $90.

Sam refuses to sell the blue bike for $90, insisting that it is worth $105. Babs brings an action alleging that Sam breached their contract by failing to sell her the blue bike for $90. Sam contends that because of their misunderstanding, the parties formed no contract. The court rules that the parties did form a contract for the sale of the blue bike. If the court properly understands the law, it might articulate as its reason that

I.   Both parties, by law, intended to contract for the sale of the blue bike.

II. Sam expressly stated that the $90 price was "good."

III. Babs offered to buy the blue bike, and Sam accepted her offer.

IV. Sam had reason to know that Babs genuinely intended to buy the blue bike, and Babs had no reason to know that Sam genuinely intended to sell the red one.

A. I and II
B. I and III
C. I, II, and IV
D. I, III, and IV

ANALYSIS.   Grab ahold of the rule given above in section C.7. In attempting to form a contract for the purchase and sale of "the bicycle in Sam's 'garage,'" these parties attached different meanings to those critical words. Babs did not know and *had no reason to know* a red bike sat hidden in the back of the garage. Sam, although he had forgotten about the blue bike, *had reason* to know of it; he had put both bikes in the garage. Consequently, Sam should have known that the garage housed two bikes and that Babs had seen only the blue one. For those reasons, the case is not like *Peerless* or *Ilsa v. Ike*. Rather, it resembles Otis v. Chelsea.

Stated otherwise, Babs made an offer, and Sam accepted. When Babs offered to purchase the bicycle in Sam's garage, Sam *should have understood her to mean* the blue bike at the front of the garage. By law, therefore, that's the bicycle Babs offered to buy. When Sam said, "yes, definitely. Come over . . ." Babs *reasonably understood* him to mean he would sell her the blue bicycle. By law, therefore, Sam agreed to sell the blue bike, regardless of what he, in his own head, meant to say. He accepted Babs's offer.

Stated yet another way, these parties had corresponding manifest intentions. A reasonable person in Sam's position would understand that Babs intended to buy the blue bike. Consequently, that was her manifest intention. A reasonable person in Babs's position would understand that Sam meant to sell the blue bike. Consequently, that was Sam's manifest intention. The manifest intentions "match," and the parties form a contract.

Option I states that irrespective of their misunderstanding, the parties *legally intended* to contract for the sale of the blue bike. That is precisely correct and precisely on point. Hence, the right answer must include option I, which eliminates **B** and **C**. Option II reports that Sam expressly acknowledged the reasonableness of Babs's proposed price, a fact that's off point. In response to Babs's offer, Sam did say "that sounds reasonable." Yet, if he'd said no such words, the result would be the same. That eliminates **C** because it includes option II.

We're left with **D**, which includes options I, III, and IV. Option I, we know, is correct. Option III correctly observes that regardless of their misunderstanding, Babs and Sam achieved offer and acceptance, which perhaps *best* explains the result. Option IV correctly observes that Sam had reason to know of Babs's intention and that Babs had no reason to know of Sam's. That reasoning reflects Restatement §20(2) and, in essence, means, once again, that the parties achieved an offer and acceptance. Options I, III, and IV make correct statements, and option II does not. That's why **D** is right.

D.   The Closer

QUESTION 2. On May 1, 2012, Yantzi Yard prepared this document:

CONTRACT

The undersigned seller, Zalia Zorinsky ("Seller"), and the undersigned buyer, Yantzi Yard ("Buyer"), do hereby agree that:

(1) On May 15, 2012, Seller will convey to Buyer all jewelry that she owns, and

(2) In exchange, Buyer will, upon receiving such jewelry, pay Seller the sum of $5.

SELLER: **BUYER:**

Signature: _____   Signature: _____
Zalia Zorinsky   Yantzi Yard

Later that same day, Yantzi approached Zalia. The parties were casually acquainted, neither knowing the other well. On meeting, they spoke.

Zalia: Hi. What paper are you holding?

Yantzi: I'm glad you asked. I'm making a study of signatures; I'm interested to know if there really is an identifiable difference between a male and female signature. You can help me. Would you sign your name at the bottom of this paper—right on the line that says "signature"?

Yantzi showed Zalia the bottom of the paper but so leaned himself over its upper part as to conceal from Zalia all but this:

Signature: _____
                Zalia Zorinsky

Zalia, happy to help, signed her name as Yantzi had asked.

Signature: _*Zalia Zorinsky*_
                Zalia Zorinsky

Yantzi thanked Zalia, bid her farewell, and then signed his own name to the writing that Zalia had just unwittingly signed.

Have Zalia and Yantzi formed a contract according to the terms of the signed writing?

A. Yes, because the writing would be admissible evidence of the fact that they formed a contract according to the terms of the writing

B. Yes, because Zalia's signature signified her acceptance of Yantzi's offer

C. No, because the parties did not achieve what some call a "meeting of the minds"

D. No, because neither party made an offer to the other, wherefore neither could issue an acceptance

ANALYSIS. Evaluate the events according to law. Yantzi hid the paper's contents when he presented it to Zalia, professing to ask for a sample of her signature. As a reasonable person, Zalia had no cause to believe that Yantzi was proposing any bargain of any sort. Hence, Yantzi made no offer to Zalia. Consequently, Zalia's signature was not an acceptance—of anything. When Yantzi then took hold of the document, complete with Zalia's signature, Yantzi knew that Zalia had not seen its text. As a reasonable person, therefore, Yantzi should have known that Zalia did not intend to propose any bargain to *him*. Hence, Zalia made no offer to Yantzi, and Yantzi's signature accepted nothing. Neither party made an offer to the other, meaning that neither was an offeree and neither had anything *to* accept.

Plainly then, the answer is "no," these parties did not form a contract—not at all. Whatever the correct answer, its meaning must reflect the reasoning we've just put forth. A correct answer might be, for example:

- No, because the parties never achieved offer and acceptance.
- No, because neither party accepted an offer from the other.
- No, because neither party manifested an intention to propose or assent to a bargain.
- No, because neither party empowered the other to accept an offer.

A begins with "yes," so it's wrong. It then states that the writing would be admissible evidence *tending to prove* that the parties formed a contract, and that's true. As discussed in Chapter 2, section C, a signed writing that describes a mutual exchange of promises or performances is *evidence* that the two relevant parties formed a contract. But the appearance of what seems to be a contractual writing does not mean, absolutely, that the parties formed a contract. Plaintiff might sue defendant for breach and produce a "signed" "contractual writing." Defendant might prove that she never did sign the document, meaning that some forger did so instead. Other circumstances, too, beyond forgery might well prove that what seems to be a contractual writing does not, in truth, represent a contract.

In this case, a court would admit the writing as evidence of a contract, but when presented with the facts (and they are presented to us as *facts*), it would rule that notwithstanding the writing, these parties failed to form a contract. So **A** is out.

B is wrong too. By telling us that Zalia accepted Yantzi's offer, it states, implicitly, that Yantzi *made* an offer, which he did not. **C**, too, is a loser. It invokes that war-torn phrase "meeting of the minds," which applies, if ever, only when the parties give different meanings to their words, acts, or expressions, *both of them reasonable* (see section C of this chapter). That hasn't happened here. In signing her name, Zalia could have but one reasonable understanding; she was providing Yantzi with a sample of her signature—nothing more. Likewise, that's the only reasonable interpretation Yantzi could have given Zalia's willingness to sign. Because there was but one reasonable way to interpret Zalia's willingness to sign, "meeting of the minds" is out of place.

We come to **D,** which states that the parties did not form a contract because neither made an offer to the other, which means that neither made an acceptance. As Goldilocks opined, it's "just right." When Yantzi presented the paper to Zalia, he made no offer. That means Zalia's signature was no acceptance. Further, Zalia's signature did not create an offer, which means that Yantzi's signature was no acceptance. That's why **D** is right.

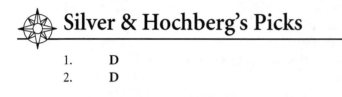 ## Silver & Hochberg's Picks

1.   **D**
2.   **D**

4

More About Offers: Invitations to Deal and Indefiniteness

A. Invitation to Deal
B. Contracts Void for Vagueness, Indefiniteness, or Uncertainty
C. When Material Terms Aren't Explicitly Specified: "Gap Fillers"
D. The Closers
✧ Silver & Hochberg's Picks

A. Invitation to Deal

Let's listen again to Martha from Chapter 2, section D:

> I am prepared to hire you as manufacturer of Gutmate. I have little capital and propose, therefore, to convey to you a share of the patent ownership in exchange for your services. I invite your acceptance.

Martha proposes no bargain and makes no offer. Yet she suggests the *possibility* of a bargain not fully shaped. The law tags such an expression with the labels "preliminary negotiation," "preliminary inquiry," "invitation for an offer," "solicitation of an offer," or, most commonly—"invitation to deal." "Invitation to deal" and these other phrases describe a communication that looks toward *the possibility* of a bargain but lacks the definiteness necessary to an offer, like this one:

> Dear Alex: Your yacht is lovely. I believe it to be worth about $300,000. I'm ready to buy it for that amount. Are you agreeable?—Jaden

That's an offer. But suppose Alex had written this:

> Dear Alex: Your yacht is lovely. I suspect it's worth about $300,000. Have you thought of selling it?—Jaden

This writing alludes to the *possibility* that Jaden and Alex might arrange to buy and sell the yacht. It invites Alex to think along those lines and make a response. Because it suggests that one of the parties *might* ultimately make an offer to the other, *it is not an offer, but an invitation to deal.*

We call a communication "invitation to deal" to tell ourselves not what it is, but what it is *not*—an offer. We say, "X made no offer—only an invitation to deal." Some preface the phrase with "mere:" "X's letter was not an offer, but a mere invitation to deal."

1. *Invitation to Deal as a Circumstance*

An invitation to deal is not an offer, but it is a *circumstance* that might turn some subsequent communication *into* an offer. Suppose Tom says to Jane, "How about Sunday, at my home from 7 to 10, at $15 per hour?" Standing alone, that question means nothing. It proposes no bargain; certainly it's no offer. But consider it as item (5) of this conversation:

(1) **Tom:** Hi, Jane. I must go out this coming Sunday. Might you baby-sit for Jennifer?
(2) **Jane:** Maybe. What hours and what pay?
(3) **Tom:** I'm not sure about the hours. I'm thinking to pay $10 or $12 per hour. What's your usual charge?
(4) **Jane:** I don't have one; I haven't done this in a while.
(5) **Tom:** How about Sunday, at my home from 7 to 10, at $15 per hour?
(6) **Jane:** Okay, great.

Statements 1 through 4 are invitations to deal. They also represent *circumstances* that surround these parties when Tom makes statement 5, and in light of those circumstances, Jane should hear him to mean "I hereby propose that you baby-sit for Jennifer on Saturday night at my home from 7 to 10, in exchange for which I will pay you $15 per hour." Hence, statement 5 is an offer because the prior invitations to deal should tell Jennifer what it means. For, as Justice Holmes taught, "the character of every act depends upon the circumstances in which it is done." Schenck v. United States, 249 U.S. 47, 52 (1919).

QUESTION 1. Jackson, a building contractor, contacts Leister, an electrical contractor.

Jackson: I'm undertaking a construction project for Faith Hospital in Tuttontown. I need an electrical contractor. Interested?
Leister: Yes, definitely, I accept.
Jackson: Great. Can you come by my office tomorrow at 8:00 A.M., to iron out the details?
Leister: Yes, I'll be there.

At 7:00 A.M. the next day, Leister contacts Jackson announcing that she will neither keep the appointment nor serve as his electrical contractor. Is Leister in breach of contract?

A. Yes, because Jackson made an offer and Leister accepted it
B. Yes, because the parties manifested a mutual interest in forming a bargain
C. No, because Jackson's first statement proposed no bargain
D. No, because Leister timely notified Jackson of her altered decision

ANALYSIS.   Leister can't breach a contract on Tuesday unless she formed one on Monday. On Monday Jackson, speaking first, described insufficient detail to pose a bargain. His statement looked toward the *possibility* of a bargain, but was far too vague actually to propose one. Jackson made only an invitation to deal. Receiving no offer, Leister had nothing to accept. *Saying,* "I accept," she expressed only her wish to continue discussion. She too made a mere invitation to deal. Hence, the correct answer must say "no," Leister committed no breach because, with their invitations to deal, these parties never formed a contract.

A and **B** begin with "yes," so they're wrong. According to **A**, Jackson made an offer and Leister accepted it. That didn't happen. Jackson made only an invitation to deal. The statement in **B** is true. Speaking as they did, Jackson and Leister clearly expressed their *interest* in making a deal. But that means only that they began discussion—started negotiation.

We're left with **C** and **D**, both of which properly say "no," Leister is not in breach. For its reason, **D** tells us that Leister "timely" told Jackson that she had changed her mind. And—"So what?" With or without Leister's notice to Jackson, these parties failed to form a contract. **D** is accurate but irrelevant.

We come to **C**, which says that Leister breached no contract because Jackson's first statement proposed no bargain. That's true; it didn't. It was a mere preliminary negotiation (another phrase for "invitation to deal"). Yet if Jackson *had* proposed a bargain—if he had made an offer—then with Leister's response, "I accept,"—these guys would have formed a contract. Precisely because Jackson proposed no bargain they did *not* form one, and that's why Leister committed no breach. **C** is right.

2. Offer or Invitation to Deal? Sometimes It's Arguable

Between offer and invitation to deal there lies no bright line. As with any precept of law, statutory, common law, or constitutional, some cases lie at the extremes and allow for little argument. Others lie nearer the middle and create opposing positions, each of them rational and reasonable.

Read these statements:

1. "Nice bike. I might think of buying it, say, for $900. Have you any interest in selling?"
2. "I like that bike. Would you, do you think, sell it for $900?"
3. "I wish, today, to purchase that bike for $900. Are you prepared to sell?"

All (competent) judges would agree that statement 1 is a mere inquiry, preliminary negotiation, an invitation to deal. All would agree, too, that statement 3 is an offer. Statement 2's status, however, is arguable. One judge might call it an offer. Another might brand it an invitation to deal. It's "in the middle." (If we modified statement 2 by changing "would" to "will" and by deleting the words "do you think, like to" it would read, "Will you sell it for $900?" *That* would likely be an offer.)

QUESTION 2. Dov owned retail store property at 199 Trumbull Avenue. Without naming any price, Portia expressed a tentative interest in buying it. With Dov's permission, Portia hired and paid two professional appraisers to assess the property's value, both of whom reported to her and Dov that it was worth approximately $450,000. Immediately thereafter the parties exchanged these signed writings:

(1) **Portia:** As you know, I'm interested in your 199 Trumbull Avenue property, evaluated by two appraisers at $450,000. Will you sell it to me for that amount?

(2) **Dov:** I won't take less than $500,000. Let me know when you're ready to pay that much.

(3) **Portia:** Very well, $500,000 it is.

Portia then tendered[1] to Dov a $500,000 check and demanded that Dov convey the property. Dov refused, and Portia sued, alleging breach of contract. Dov maintained that he could not have breached a contract because he and Portia never formed one. Which of the following judicial statements constitutes a *plausible* assessment and resolution of the conflict?

I. Writing number 1 was a mere invitation to deal. Writing number 2, likewise, continued as a preliminary negotiation, manifesting Dov's willingness only to *consider* an offer of $500,000. Writing number 3 was Portia's offer to buy for $500,000, which Dov did not accept. The parties formed no contract, and Dov is not in breach.

---

1. One "tenders" a performance when he shows that he is ready, willing, and able to deliver it. If A is to paint B's house, and A arrives at the site, equipment in hand, and says, "I'm ready to begin," he has tendered his performance.

> **II.** Knowing of Portia's interest in the property and allowing her to have it appraised, Dov implicitly offered to sell the property at any price reasonably close to the appraised value. With writing number 1, Portia proclaimed her willingness to purchase for $500,000 and thereby accepted Dov's offer. The parties formed a contract, and Dov is in breach.
>
> **III.** Writing number 1 was a mere inquiry—an invitation to deal. Writing number 2 was Dov's offer to sell for $500,000, and writing number 3 was Portia's acceptance. The parties formed a contract, and Dov is in breach.
>
> **A.** I
> **B.** I and II
> **C.** I and III
> **D.** II and III
> **E.** I, II, and III

ANALYSIS. All legal doctrines and distinctions sit on a spectrum, each having a middle zone that's home to the arguable cases—the cases in which one judge might see it like "this" and the other like "that"—the cases that drive two opposing lawyers to court, each convinced that she should win. Here, we're asked to examine three judicial statements and determine which, in our opinion, are *plausible.* Let's read the parties' statements and determine whether each is (a) clearly one thing or another, or (b) *arguably* one thing or another.

What's writing 1? Maybe it's an offer and maybe just an invitation to deal. It speaks to a particular property and price, and plainly shows Portia's interest in buying. On the other hand, it presents a question, not a statement. Most likely—but not certainly—it's a preliminary inquiry. In *our* legal opinion, it's the latter—an invitation to deal. Yet we recognize, to a possibility of 20 percent perhaps, that some judge might call it an offer.

If writing 1 is an invitation to deal, might we say that writing 2 is an offer? Maybe. Dov expresses his unwillingness to "take" less than $500,000, but then tells Portia to return when she's ready to pay that price. Should someone in Portia's position believe that Dov has *definitively expressed his willingness* to sell the property for $500,000? Let's say, with a confidence of about 60/40, that the answer is "no," meaning that we think there's a 40 percent chance the answer is "yes."

What of writing 3? It's an offer; we're 95 percent confident. Portia pretty plainly manifests her unequivocal willingness to buy for $500,000. Even if writing 3 is Portia's offer, however, Dov never accepted it. Yet, if writing *2* is an offer (which we said is *possible*), then writing 3 seems certainly to be an acceptance, in which case the parties did form a contract.

So maybe these parties formed a contract and maybe they did not. There are at least two plausible ways in which to evaluate their interactions.

Probably: Writing 1 is Portia's invitation to deal, writing 2 is Dov's invitation to deal, and writing 3 is Portia's offer, to which Dov gave no acceptance, meaning the parties formed no contract.

But just maybe: Writing 1 is an invitation to deal, writing 2 an offer, and writing 3 an acceptance, meaning that the parties did form a contract.

Option I describes what we've just called probable. It says writings 1 and 2 are invitations to deal, and writing 3 an offer for which there follows no acceptance.

Option II is nonsense. No sensible judge could think reasonable a person who, in Portia's position, believes that Dov, by allowing the appraisal, had offered to sell the property for a price close to its assessed value. Option II is wrong (and the seductive words "reasonably close" don't make it right).

To option III, we say "just maybe." It calls writing 1 an invitation to deal, writing 2 an offer, and writing 3 an acceptance. Options I and III are plausible, II is not. **C** is right.

B.   Contracts Void for Vagueness, Indefiniteness, or Uncertainty

Suppose Abram says to Beth, "I have an offer for you." She asks, "What's the offer?" When Abram tells her, "Some tickets to this Friday night's Asteroid game," Beth replies, "I accept."

Although Abram used the word "offer," he plainly did not make one. Consequently, Beth accepted nothing, and these parties formed no contract. In assessing this interaction, we need consider nothing more.

Unfortunately, there is more that we must *say.* We know that a contract requires, first, that one party make an offer. That simple truth underlies a host of dubious and superfluous common law statements with which we must reckon, like them or not. Most courts would describe Abram's and Beth's situation like this:

> The supposed terms on which the parties agreed are insufficiently specific, and their contact is *void for vagueness.*

In the same vein, others would say that:

> If not reasonably certain as to their material terms, contracts are unenforceable and, where any kind of property is bought and sold, material terms include quantity and price. These parties specified neither quantity nor price; their contract is *void for uncertainty as to its material terms.*

Consider these two signed writings between EnnerCo and MotoCo.

EnnerCo to MotoCo: Offer to Sell: Large quantity of Grade A Kerosel just received by us at bargain price. We wish to pass savings to you. Will sell some to you at discount price. Please let us know if you accept.

MotoCo to EnnerCo: Purchase Order: Re your offer of yesterday. We accept. What quantities are available and at what prices?

EnnerCo issued a mere invitation to deal. Although MotoCo wrote "we accept," it, too, made only an invitation to deal. Hence, these two companies formed no contract; their negotiations ended before either made an offer to the other. Restatement (Second) of Contracts §33(1) explains it this way

> Even though a manifestation of intention is intended to be understood as an offer, it cannot be accepted so as to form a contract unless the terms of the contract are reasonably certain.

Hence, in the MotoCo-EnnerCo case, the Restatement rightly tells us that the parties formed no contract. All (competent) authorities would reach that same conclusion. Unfortunately, however, some (misguided) courts would *explain* their conclusion by writing that the parties' "contract" is "void for vagueness," "indefiniteness," or "uncertainty as to material terms"—failing to state that the parties formed *no contract at all*.

QUESTION 3. On August 9, BuyCo and SellCo began communicating with these signed writings:

> **August 9, BuyCo:** We understand that you now own the original oil painting *Nightbird*, which is, of course, priceless. Nonetheless, we hereby offer to buy it, and we'd like to hear back from you on any other matters you deem significant, including price. Perhaps an appraiser's report would be helpful. We look forward to your response.

> **August 11, SellCo:** Thanks for your offer regarding our priceless painting *Nightbird*. We accept, and we'll be in touch within 10 days.

Ten days later, on August 21, SellCo tendered delivery of the painting to BuyCo, together with an appraiser's report that valued it at $950,000. SellCo demanded that BuyCo pay $950,000. BuyCo rejected the delivery and refused to pay any price, maintaining that it never formed a final intention to buy. SellCo sues BuyCo for breach. Correctly deciding for Buyco, a court might make which of the following statements (whether we like it or not)?

I. The contract at issue is void for indefiniteness.
II. The contract at issue is void for vagueness.
III. The parties formed no contract because they agreed that the painting was "priceless."
IV. The parties formed no contract because neither made an offer to the other.
V. The parties formed no contract because BuyCo did not fully intend to purchase the painting.

A. I
B. I and II
C. I, II, and III
D. I, II, and IV
E. I, II, IV, and V

ANALYSIS.   BuyCo's "offer" is too vague truly to constitute an offer, meaning that SellCo accepted—nothing. The "contract" on which Sellco sues is no contract at all.

Regrettably, some courts (and teachers) would characterize the case by writing that (1) "The parties' contract is void for indefiniteness, vagueness and uncertainty." Better judicial thinkers (in markedly short supply) would explain that (2) "These two parties formed *no contract at all*, because neither made an offer to the other." The second statement is conceptually correct. The first is not. Yet, from too many courts (and others) the *first* is what we read and hear. For that unhappy reason any option, I - IV, is correct if it resembles statement (1) *or* (2).

Options I and II speak of a contract void for "indefiniteness" and "vagueness." Both resemble statement (1) above and both are correct.

Option III is nonsense. Two parties may describe an item of property as "priceless" or "worthless" and still contract to buy and sell it.

Option IV states that neither party made an offer to the other. *That's* the truth. In a perfect legal world, all judges would decide this by making that observation; IV is correct.

Option V implies that two parties can't form a contract unless both truly intend to be bound. From Chapters 2 and 3, we know that's wrong. By contract law, one's "intentions" are his *manifest* intentions—the intentions another would reasonably attribute to his words and acts. Options I, II, and IV "belong;" III and V do not. **D** is right.

C.   When Material Terms Aren't Explicitly Specified: "Gap Fillers"

Notwithstanding the oft-repeated doctrines of vagueness, indefiniteness, and uncertainty, today's contract law does not require that an offer and acceptance show black and white specificity as to every material term. When two parties omit to mention some important matter and thus leave a "gap" in their agreement, the law often assumes that as to the unmentioned matter, the parties meant to adopt some *reasonable* term. Hence, the law (a court) supplies one. Consider this interaction between RentCo's and BuildCo's presidents:

> **BuildCo:** Do you have a 10-ton forklift available, tomorrow from 9 to 6?
> **RentCo:** Yes, we do. We'll be glad to reserve it for you.
> **BuildCo:** Thank you, please do.

These parties certainly seem to believe they've formed a binding arrangement; but by omitting to discuss price, they've left their agreement with a "gap." A modern court will surely fill it by attributing to these parties an intention to pay and accept a "reasonable price," which, depending on the evidence, might be:

1. the price that RentCo has paid BuildCo in the past for the same or similar machinery, or
2. the price that RentCo normally charges to other customers, if any, to whom it rents the same or similar machinery, or
3. the price that other businesses in RentCo's field normally charge for the same or similar equipment, or
4. the seller's cost plus some ordinary margin of profit, or
5. any other amount that, on the evidence, a court thinks sensibly answers to the phrase "reasonable price."

1. Why the Law Fills Gaps

The truth be known, most contracts create more gap than specificity. Most contracting parties leave most of their agreed terms unstated. In fact, no two contracting parties ever *can* specify in words even a small portion of the terms germane to their agreement. They might agree that work is to be finished by "new year's day" without stating that they mean Euro-American new year, Greek new year, or Chinese new year. They might agree on delivery at 10:00, without specifying "P.M." or "A.M." They might even agree on "10:00 A.M." without specifying eastern standard, eastern daylight, or Greenwich mean time. They might establish a price of "$1,000" without stating that the applicable dollar is American, not Canadian or Mexican.

All human communication takes its meaning not from words, but from the reasonable interpretation *of* words, made in view of the circumstances under which they are used. The point goes deep to the matters of communication and language, and is critical to the law of contract. Let's probe it a little more.

At 6:30 P.M., setting the table, moving a platter from stove to dining room, Henry asks Wanda: "Shall we have dinner?" If Wanda processes only the four words actually spoken, her mind will be awash in a whirl of confusion; "Does he mean we should have dinner now or at some unstated time in the future? Where does he propose to have dinner? Here at home? Elsewhere? When he says 'dinner,' does he mean a European-style afternoon meal or an American-style evening meal? And what does he mean by 'have' dinner? 'Hold' it? 'Own' it? 'Consume' it? I can't answer. I don't know what he's asking."

Henry's statement *is* full of gaps, but if Wanda is a (half-way) reasonable person who lives a (half-way) normal (American) life—who sees both the clock and the action around her, she knows that Henry has invited her to sit down with him for dinner here and now at 6:30 P.M.

When others speak or write to us, we understand them *in light of surrounding circumstance.* With inference and intuition, day in and day out, we all "fill" communicative "gaps." Absent that function, none of us could communicate anything, ever, to anyone—not in any mode, language, or dialect.

It's the "job" of contract law to examine our communications and give them a meaning consistent with the reasonable expectations of those with whom we communicate. We might say, in fact, that *contract law's essential purpose is to fulfill the reasonable expectations that each of us, by communication, has of others.* For that reason, contract law "fills gaps" and in doing so charges all of us with such knowledge, understanding, belief, purpose, inference, and intention as would naturally apply to reasonable persons in like circumstances.

2. Gap Filling Under UCC Article 2

Uniform Commercial Code (UCC) §2-204(3) makes plain that an attempt to contract should not fail for indefiniteness simply because the parties leave some terms unexpressed or incomplete:

> Even if one or more terms are left open, a contract for sale does not fail for indefiniteness if the parties have intended to make a contract and there is a reasonably certain basis for giving an appropriate remedy.

In that regard, UCC §2-305(1) provides specifically for a gap filler as to price:

> The parties if they so intend can conclude a contract for sale even though the price is not settled. In such a case the price is a reasonable price at the time for delivery.

The statute tells us that if two parties outwardly lead each other reasonably to believe that they consider themselves bound in an agreement to buy and sell goods, they form a contract even without mentioning price. The code implies in their contract a "reasonable price." If, when the time for payment arrives, the parties cannot agree on what price is reasonable, seller sues buyer and the court sets a price *it* deems reasonable.

QUESTIONS 4-6. SportCo Inc. operates a chain of sporting goods stores, and BallCo manufactures a variety of articles tied to sports. BallCo publishes a price catalog, which it updates from time to time, ordinarily sending the current edition to all of its regular customers.

In 2005, BallCo published an updated price catalog in which it posted a price of $288 per gross (144) of baseballs. BallCo published no new catalog until January 2011, when it set the price of baseballs at $319 per gross.

During the years 2005-2010, SportCo had ordered a total of 100,000 gross of BallCo's baseballs and paid, always, the catalog price of $288 per gross. In March 2011, the parties began communicating with these signed writings:

(1) **March 1, SportCo writes: Purchase Order:** Please ship immediately to our warehouse at 4400 Raritan Way, Coppertown, PA, 10,000 gross of your baseballs. Will expect invoice with delivery. Thank you.

(2) **March 2, BallCo writes: Sales Confirmation:** Thank you for your order. Will ship promptly, with invoice.

(3) **March 3, SportCo writes:** With apologies we must cancel our recent order for 10,000 gross of baseballs. Please do not ship.

BallCo insists that SportCo is contractually obliged to purchase the baseballs. SportCo maintains that because the parties never discussed price, they never formed a contract.

QUESTION 4. Pursuant to UCC Article 2, is SportCo's position correct?

A. Yes, because when goods are sold, price is a material term

B. Yes, because no two parties form a contract unless one puts to the other a bargain of reasonably specific terms

C. No, because the parties implicitly agreed on a "reasonable price"

D. No, because BallCo changed its published price only once in six years

---

ANALYSIS. UCC Article 2 provides that two parties can contract for the sale of goods without mentioning price, so long as they evidence their intention to be bound. These parties have done that; SportCo made an offer and BallCo accepted; they contracted to buy and sell 10,000 baseballs at a reasonable price

You're not told, specifically, that BallCo has or has not sent SportCo the 2005 or 2011 catalogs, but that matter affects the *numerical value* of the reasonable price, not formation of a contract. If BallCo has not sent SportCo either catalog, a court surely will find enough evidence to name *a* reasonable price—probably $288. Hence, under UCC §2-305, these parties formed a contract.

A and **B** are wrong for declaring that these companies formed no contract. That leaves **C** and **D**. **D** tells us that a contract arose because the seller changed its published price only once between 2005 and 2011. That does not explain how or why these parties formed a contract. If BallCo had revised its pricing every year, then still, this latest transaction would create a contract.

C correctly refers to the rule of UCC §2-305. These parties formed a contract because, notwithstanding their failure to discuss price, they manifested an intention to be bound. The price is a "reasonable price." That's why **C** is right.

QUESTION 5. For this question only, assume that BallCo sent SportCo its 2005 catalog but not the one it published in 2011. When BallCo insists that SportCo is contractually obliged to purchase the baseballs, SportCo agrees and stands ready to pay $288 per gross. BallCo demands $319, the price set forth in its 2011 catalog. All other facts are as originally set forth. BallCo is entitled to be paid:

A. $288, because that is the price it has repeatedly charged SportCo, and SportCo had no notice that the price had been changed.

B. $288, because it is unreasonable suddenly to publish a higher price to a longtime buyer who has customarily and in good faith paid a lower one.

C. $319, because a buyer should reasonably expect to pay according to a seller's published price list.

D. Nothing, because a buyer need not pay a price to which he has not agreed.

ANALYSIS. These parties have a contract. You're to determine the amount the court would likely name as a "reasonable price." BallCo did not provide SportCo with its latest catalog. Together with the relevant history, that fact probably puts the reasonable price at $288.

Quickly eliminate **D**. It does not recognize a contract. Discard **B**, too; it's not founded in law. Certainly a seller may raise prices to any or all of its buyers no matter how long the business relationships, notwithstanding that all have acted in "good faith."

We're left with **A** and **C**. Which one better represents a likely judicial ruling? **C** ignores a relevant fact—that BallCo failed to apprise SportCo of the increased price. If a seller revises its price catalog and fails to so notify one of its regular buyers, is it really *reasonable* that the buyer pay the increased price of which it had no reason to know? Under these circumstances, each party should reasonably have understood that the $288 price continues. **A** is right.

QUESTION 6. For this question only, assume that BallCo sent SportCo a copy of its 2011 catalog, but BallCo never examined it. When BallCo insists that SportCo is contractually obliged to purchase the baseballs, SportCo agrees and stands ready to pay $288 per gross. BallCo demands $319, the price set forth in its 2011 catalog. All other facts are as originally set forth. BallCo is entitled to be paid:

A. $288, because that is the price it has repeatedly charged SportCo, and SportCo had no notice that the price had been changed.

B. $288, because it is unreasonable suddenly to publish a higher price to a longtime buyer who has customarily and in good faith paid a lower one.

> **C.** $319, because a buyer should reasonably expect to pay according to a seller's published price list.
> **D.** Nothing, because a buyer need not pay a price to which he has not agreed.

ANALYSIS. These choices are the same as those of question 5, but the facts differ. Here, BallCo did provide SportCo with a new price catalog, but SportCo didn't read it. That changes everything. Reading SportCo's offer under these circumstances, BallCo was justified in believing that SportCo expected to pay the current catalog price of $319. And if SportCo had read the catalog (as would a reasonable party), SportCo would have taken BallCo's acceptance to *mean* "Will ship promptly, with invoice showing current catalog price of $319."

B and **D** are bad just as they were for question 5. We're left again with **A** and **C**. **A** is wrong for stating that "SportCo had no notice that the price had been changed." SportCo did have notice; it had the new price catalog but failed to read it. **C** correctly states that $319 is a reasonable price because SportCo had access to the new price list. **C** is right.

3. The "Agreement to Agree"

Consider this interaction between two strangers, Victor and Michael:

Victor: I need software that will keep track of my various accounting records. Can you create that for me? If so, how long will it take and what will be your fee?

Michael: Well, that depends on the program's complexity. I don't know what you need.

Victor: I understand. For how long will you warranty your work?

Michael: That too depends on what ultimately I do. Why don't we agree now that I'll write a program for you. Later on, we'll agree on its specifications, the price, and a warranty period.

Victor: It's a deal.

Michael's second response to Victor consigns almost all terms of the contemplated exchange to some future agreement. For that reason, it proposes no definite bargain. The interactions between these two were so utterly nonspecific as to constitute only a series of invitations to deal, meaning that neither made an offer to the other, and, therefore, the parties could not and did not form a contract.

Yet, most courts don't characterize this kind of interaction in quite that way. Instead they invoke what passes for a doctrine regarding the "agreement to agree": *Where two parties purport to reach a final binding arrangement, but leave material terms for later negotiation or agreement, they form only an "agreement to agree," which is not a contract. See* Mays v. Trump Indiana, Inc., 255 F.3d 351 (7th Cir. 2001); Rule v. Brine, Inc., 85 F.3d 1002 (2d Cir. 1996).

Like rules that speak to "vagueness", this one repeated over the centuries, passes for a correct statement of law. Know when to invoke it. Know, too, that it's but another incarnation of the more fundamental rules that (1) no contract arises without offer and acceptance, and (2) one makes an offer only if he is reasonably specific as to the bargain he proposes.

The "agreement to agree" is but one species of a vague, indefinite agreement. It is subject, therefore, to gap filling. If, in the relevant communications and surrounding circumstance, a modern court (a) concludes that two parties intended to form a binding agreement and (b) finds a rational means by which to fill the gap, it might do so. Such is an emerging trend under the common law. For the sale of goods it is statutory doctrine. Look more fully at UCC §2-305(1):

> (1) The parties if they so intend may conclude a contract for sale even if the price is not settled. In such a case the price is a reasonable price at the time for delivery, if:
>> (a) nothing is said as to price; or
>> (b) the price is left to be agreed by the parties and they fail to agree; or
>> (c) the price is to be fixed in terms of some agreed market or other standard as set or recorded by a third person or agency and it is not so set or recorded.

QUESTION 7. BanaCo and StatCo deal in electrical equipment. In its catalog BanaCo lists the prices for some of its products, but not for #4 conducting wire. On July 11, BanaCo sends StatCo this signed written message: "We wish immediately to have 4,000 feet of your #4 conducting wire. We do not see the item listed in your catalog, so we propose that price will be agreed on later. Please ship." On July 12, StatCo responds with this signed writing: "Thank you. We will ship." Have BanaCo and StatCo formed a contract?

A. Yes, because where goods are bought and sold between merchants, price is not a material term

B. Yes, because notwithstanding the open price term, their interaction reflects finality of agreement

C. No, because two parties do not form a contract if they agree that a material term will be subject to future agreement

D. No, because a seller who declines to publish its price shows an intention not to sell

---

ANALYSIS. The transaction concerns the sale of goods, meaning the UCC governs. The communications are unequivocal, meaning that each party manifested its intent to "conclude a contract." Even without specificity of price the writings create a contract under UCC §2-305. The parties must buy and sell at a "reasonable price." If, ultimately, they cannot agree on a price that is reasonable and one sues the other, a court will decide the question. Put otherwise, the court will fill the gap.

C and **D** reach the wrong conclusion. These parties did form a contract. Furthermore, **C** and **D** make legal misstatements. Two parties may, at times, form a contract even when they leave a material term for future agreement. Under UCC §2-305, that's true surely for price, and it represents the modern common law trend as well. As for **D**: that for some product or other, a seller omits to publish his price does not mean, necessarily, that he lacks the intent to sell it.

A is tempting, but it's not quite right. It's true that two parties who buy and sell goods may form a contract without specifying price, but price *is*, nonetheless, a material term.

B is best. It tells us that the parties' interaction reflects "finality of agreement," meaning they show their intent to shore up a contract. When buyer and seller do that, they form a contract without mentioning price. By law, they agree to a "reasonable price." **B** is right.

4. *Gap Filling Goes Only So Far*

Gap filling has its limits. The law goes only so far in supplying terms that the parties fail to specify. For example, where a real estate lease gives the tenant an option to renew at a rent to be agreed on in the future, most courts decline to imply a "reasonable rent." Martin Delicatessen v. Schumacher, 417 N.E.2d 541 (N.Y. 1981). Furthermore, although UCC Article 2 allows for the implication of "reasonable price," it nowhere states that the law should identify "reasonable quantity." It remains law, therefore, that when two parties describe their agreement with such indefiniteness as prevents a court from identifying their bargain, they form no contract or, as some say, "the contract fails for indefiniteness."

D. The Closers

Beginning on October 1, FuelCo Inc. and HeatCo Inc. exchange signed writings:

(1) **October 1, FuelCo to HeatCo: Offer to Sell:** Shipment of Bortex Coal Kindler just received at reduced price. Prepared within next ten days to sell to you any quantity. Please accept promptly.

(2) **October 2, HeatCo to FuelCo: Purchase Order:** Re your offer of yesterday. We accept. What quantities are available, and at what prices?

(3) **October 3, FuelCo to HeatCo: Offer to Sell:** Available: 13 tons. Price depends on amount ordered. What quantity shall we ship? Others are making orders. Supply is shrinking. Please respond soon.

(4) **October 4, HeatCo to FuelCo, Purchase Order:** Re Bortex—will want all 13 tons delivered to our warehouse. Need price.

(5) **October 5, FuelCo to HeatCo, Offer to Sell:** Can deliver. Price: $800 per ton = $10,400. Please advise.

(6) **October 6, HeatCo to FuelCo, Purchase Order:** Thank you. We expect delivery.

(7) **October 7, FuelCo to HeatCo: Sales Confirmation:** Okay:—A.M. or P.M. delivery?

QUESTION 8. Which of the writings 1-7 are best characterized as invitations to deal?

A. 2, 3, and 4
B. 1, 2, 3, and 4
C. 1, 3, 5, and 7
D. 1, 2, 3, 4, and 7
E. All of the writings 1-7

QUESTION 9. Which of the writings 1-7 most likely constitutes an offer?

A. 5
B. 5 and 6
C. 4, 5, and 6
D. 4, 5, 6, and 7
E. None of the writings 1-7.

QUESTION 10. Which of the following italicized modifications would most likely convert the indicated writing to an offer?

A. Writing 1 is modified to read: "Shipment of Bortex Coal Kindler just received at reduced price. Prepared within next ten days to sell to you any quantity. Please accept promptly *and advise us of the price you are willing to pay.*"

B. Writing 2 is modified to read: "Re your offer of yesterday. We accept. *We need 18 tons, $300 per ton. Please ship immediately.*"

C. Writing 3 is modified to read: "*We have 13 tons now available and will hold all until we hear from you.* Price depends on amount ordered. Please respond soon."

D. Writing 4 is modified to read: Re Bortex—will *certainly* want all 13 tons delivered to our warehouse. Need price. *Subject to price we have definite deal.*"

ANALYSIS.   Whether a communication constitutes an offer *does not depend on what the author calls it.* A communication called "acceptance" might be an offer. A communication called "offer" might be an invitation to deal or, for that matter, an acceptance. Names don't matter (much). Mindful of what makes an offer, look at each of the writings and ask: "Is this an offer, and, if not, what is it?"

No reasonable person could read writing 1 to propose a definite bargain. It looks to the possible sale of a particular good, but mentions neither price nor quantity. If HeatCo were to respond by writing "We accept," neither party could know *what* HeatCo had accepted. Writing 1 is an invitation to deal.

Writing 2 purports to "accept." But in writing 1, FuelCo made no offer, so in writing 2, HeatCo can't accept one. Neither does this "purchase order" propose any bargain of its own. It's not an acceptance, and it's not an offer. It's another invitation to deal.

Writings 3 and 4 advance the negotiations, but neither proposes an explicit bargain. Writing 3 tells HeatCo that 13 tons are available, and writing 4 tells FuelCo that HeatCo wants all of it, delivered on October 8, depending on price. Neither party has yet proposed to the other a definite bargain.

Heatco receives writing 5 and should interpret it thus:

> "We're ready to sell you all 13 tons, to be delivered on October 8.
> Price: $800 per ton. Say yes and we have a deal.

That's an offer.

With writing 6, HeatCo plainly manifests its assent, and the parties form a contract. So what's writing 7? It contemplates no exchange. It's not even an invitation to deal. There's no special name for it. It's a communication by which FuelCo courteously asks HeatCo to state a preferred delivery time. If HeatCo states its preference, FuelCo might or might not honor it. The parties formed their contract with communications 5 (offer) and 6 (acceptance). Legally, Writing 7 is nothing.

Let's look, now, at all three closer questions. Closer 1 asks us to identify invitations to deal. We've already found them in writings 1-4, and nowhere else. The answer is **B**.

Closer 2 asks that we find an offer. We've done that too. It's in writing 5. The answer is **A**.

Closer 3 asks that we reconsider the writings with modifications and determine which would most likely amount to an offer. **A**'s modification of writing 1 mentions price but does not specify it. Neither does it specify quantity. It remains an invitation to deal. **C** modifies writing 3 in that FuelCo promises to keep all 13 tons available until HeatCo responds. That's a nice gesture, but HeatCo can't be held to it. It's made no offer, and the parties have no contract.

D alters writing 4 so that it presents the constructions "certainly" and "definite deal." Still, this certain and definite deal is "subject to price." The statement remains an invitation to deal.

B revises writing 2 so that HeatCo proclaims readiness to buy 18 tons of product at $300 per ton for immediate shipment. It does not name the product, but in light of writing 1, FuelCo should clearly understand that "18 tons" means 18 tons of Bortex Coal Kindler. As modified, writing 2 *is* an offer. That's why **B** is right.

✦ Silver & Hochberg's Picks

1.	**C**
2.	**C**
3.	**D**
4.	**C**
5.	**A**
6.	**C**
7.	**B**
8.	**B**
9.	**A**
10.	**B**

5

More About Offers: Advertisements, Solicitations, and Signatures

A. Advertisements, Rewards, and Price Tags
B. Bid Solicitations and Auctions
C. Written Proposals and the Significance of Signatures
D. The Closer
 Silver & Hochberg's Picks

A. Advertisements, Rewards, and Price Tags

An offer needs an offeree, as Restatement (Second) of Contracts §24 make clear:

> An offer is the manifestation of willingness to enter into a bargain, so made as to justify *another person* in understanding that *his* assent to that bargain is invited and will conclude it.

From Chapter 2, section D, we know that an offeree is one who reasonably believes that the offeror means to communicate with *him*. If Party A proposes a bargain but there is no Party B who reasonably believes the proposal is made to him, then Party A makes no offer.

1. *For That Reason the Ordinary Advertisement Is Not an Offer*

Suppose in a newspaper with circulation of 500,000, one sees: "*Lasser's Appliances now offers Tanyo Television Sets, 32," $199.*" In the law's eyes, she should not conclude that Lasser has a number of units sufficient to supply *all* readers of the ad. Hence she should not conclude that her assent to the proposal will definitely finalize a "deal." As to the exchange it contemplates,

Lasser's message is specific, but in the law's eyes it does not lead a reasonable reader to conclude that *her* assent will finalize a bargain. Rather the reader should understand that the retailer invites *her* offer to buy the TV for $199.00. Right or wrong, that's the general common law rule: *The ordinary advertisement is not an offer, but an invitation to deal.* The rule applies to any ordinary advertisement—print, broadcast, billboard, mail, or "pop-up" on the Web.

Yet, if a publicly announced ad embodies such particularity as to lead its reader (or listener) to understand that only a limited number of persons can effectively assent, by doing some specified thing— then it's an offer. Suppose Store publishes this: "1 Black Lapin Stole, Beautiful, Worth $139.50, This Saturday, $1.00. FIRST COME, FIRST SERVED."

Customer is a "reasonable person." He reads the ad and thinks, "The store has made its offer to everyone, but only *one* person can accept—he who, on Saturday, first arrives at the store and proclaims his wish to purchase. If I'm that person, then I accept the offer."

At 1:00 A.M. on Saturday, Customer stands himself outside Store's door. When Store opens at 9:00 A.M., he is first to enter and announce his wish to buy the stole. Store and Customer form a contract because *this* advertisement is an offer. That was the ruling in Lefkowitz v. Great Minneapolis Surplus Store, 86 N.W.2d 689, 691 (Minn. 1957).

Referring obliquely to that case, Restatement (Second) §26, (illustration) explains:

> A, a clothing merchant, advertises overcoats of a certain kind for sale at $50. This is not an offer, but an invitation to the public to come and purchase. The addition of the words "Out they go Saturday; First Come, First Served" might make the advertisement an offer.

So What's the Rule?   *An ordinary advertisement is a mere invitation to deal, but an advertisement is an offer if, (as is not ordinary), it leads a reasonable person to understand that acceptance is limited to (a) a discrete group of persons, or (b) persons who perform some specified act.* Rarely does an advertisement name individual persons as offerees. In the law's eyes, however, it may specify them by describing an identifiable attribute or behavior. Suppose an advertiser publishes this: "Blue-colored contact lenses. $50/pair to all brown-eyed adults who live in Orange County. Dial 1-800-909-9090." The ad designates a group of persons with meaningful specificity—brown-eyed persons living in Orange County. A court might well call it an offer. If the ad proposes to sell lenses to "the *first* 50 brown-eyed adults from Orange County who dial 1-800-909-9090," then more likely still, will a court call it an offer.

Read This Ad; It's Probably an Invitation to Deal.   "Now paying $5 for copies of Charles Godfrey Leland's book *Gypsy Sorcery and Fortune Telling.* Contact: 455 Wayland Street, Hanlin, Mass." The ad offers no specificity as to how many books the advertiser will buy. Hence it does not limit, numerically, the number of persons who may actually accept. Neither does it identify offerees by any distinguishable status. By law, it causes a reasonable reader to believe only that the advertiser wants to buy *some* copies of the book—that he'll entertain offers to sell. It's an *ordinary* ad—a mere invitation to deal.

Read This Ad; It's an Offer.   "Collector wants every extant copy of Leland's *Gypsy Sorcery and Fortune Telling*. Will pay $25 for every copy sent to 455 Wayland Street, Hanlin, Mass." The writer addresses "every person" and asks for "every copy." In the law's eyes, he leads all who read his ad reasonably to believe that he makes his proposal to *them*, and that each will finalize a bargain by sending the book to the address he provides.

2. *Offers of Reward*

One makes an ordinary reward offer when she promises money to the person or persons who do something—apprehend the suspect; find the lost dog. A reward offer is an advertisement, but *not* an "ordinary" one. Every person who knows of it is reasonable in believing that *he* is an offeree, and that he and all others are asked to answer the offeror's request. Suppose Ariela loses her wallet. Hoping to recover it, she publishes this message: "$200 reward for the return of my wallet: black leather, lost near 103rd Street train station. Return to Ariela Martinez, 14 Wayne Way, Scottsdale, AZ. 760-444-7301." All who know of Ariela's offer are offerees. In order to accept, of course, one must be *the* person who returns her wallet. Hence, although all persons are offerees, each knows that only one of them can actually accept.

QUESTION 1. In a national newspaper, Genelco publishes:

> Genelco will pay $45 per share of Westelco common stock to any and every person who agrees to sell us one or more such shares, stating his readiness to do so by signed, notarized written letter mailed no later than May 9, 2012, to Genelco Corporate Headquarters 110-94 Corporate Plaza, Hartstown, Colorado 41567. After we receive your writing, we will arrange, within 30 days, to make payment and collect your share certificates.

Well before May 9, Jacqueline sends Genelco this signed, notarized letter: "I have three shares to sell and I accept your offer." With the letter she includes photocopies of her three share certificates. Has Jacqueline formed a contract with Genelco?

A. Yes, because she specifically wrote the words "accept your offer"
B. Yes, because she manifested assent to Genelco's proposal
C. No, because Genelco's message was an advertisement made to the public
D. No, because Genelco asked for an indication of commitment, not photocopied certificates

ANALYSIS. Expressly addressing *all persons* who own Westelco shares, Genelco (a) plainly states that it stands ready to buy from any and every person, any and every share that he or she may own, and (b) instructs each offeree as to what she must do in order to accept. Its ad is not an "ordinary" one. It's an offer. Jacqueline accepted and the parties formed a contract.

Both **C** and **D** state that the parties have no contract, so both are wrong. According to **C**, Genelco's message is an advertisement to the public and for that reason doesn't constitute an offer. The relevant rule provides that *ordinary* advertisements are not offers. This is no ordinary one, and **C** is wrong.

D implies that an offeree fails to accept if she supplies the offeree with unsolicited matter. There is no such rule. **D** is wrong.

A states that the parties formed a contract because Jacqueline used the *words* "offer" and "accept." Nonsense. One may write the word "offer" one-thousand times and fail to make an offer. And she may *make* an offer using that word not once. One may accept an offer without using the word "accept," and she may use that word without accepting.

What of **B?** With precision, Genelco identifies its offerees (all who own Westelco shares) and what each must do in order to accept. The ad is an offer, Jacqueline accepted it, the parties formed a contract, and **B** is right.

3. Retail Store Price Tags

Traditional common law provides that when a product sits on a retailer's shelf, its price tag represents not an offer but an invitation to deal, inviting the buyer to take the item from the shelf, present it to the cashier, and thus manifest his willingness to pay the stated price. By placing the item on the seller's counter, the buyer makes his offer to buy at the tagged price. The seller is free to accept or not.

Lately, however, that old rule is giving way to a new one. Some courts now hold, under UCC Article 2, that a retailer offers his good for sale when he puts it on his shelf and tags it with a price. *See* Annot., 78 A.L.R.3d 696 (1977). In construing and developing the common law, the nation's courts may well begin to rule that even in the absence of statute, a retailer makes an offer when he places an article on his shelf together with a price tag. The law on that point is, perhaps, in flux.

B.   Bid Solicitations and Auctions

Think of an auction. The auctioneer puts on the block an item of jewelry and asks for bids. Under the law, he makes an invitation to deal—a request for offers. When Bidder 1 says "$50," he offers to buy for $50. When Bidder 2 bids $60, she offers to buy for $60. When Bidder 3 bids $70, she offers to buy for $70. If the auctioneer then says "sold for $70," he accepts the third offer, and the parties form a contract.

The same logic applies when a business puts out a request for bids. Suppose TypeCo publicizes this message: "Now seeking bids for the construction of Shalemart Plaza, specifications detailed on the next 100 pages." TypeCo has asked for bids, which means it has asked for offers, which means it has made an invitation to deal. Each bid that follows is an offer, which TypeCo is free to accept or reject.

QUESTION 2. Acting as Martha's legal representative, Blairehouse Auctioneers announces by newspaper advertisement that it will sell at auction the Remington painting *Color on Canvas* at 3:00 P.M. on September 19. At the appointed time, with hundreds in attendance, the auctioneer begins: "Do I hear $40?" Jack bids $40, Jane bids $50, Jack bids $60, and Jane bids $80. The auctioneer cries out for $90. No one responds, and he says, "Going once, twice—sold for $80!" One second later, Jane declares, "I take back my bid; I don't want the painting. Sell it to the man who just bid $60." Is Jane contractually obliged to buy the painting?

A. Yes, because the seller's representative acceded unequivocally to Jane's express preparedness to purchase for a stated price.

B. Yes, but only if Jane was aware that one who bids at an auction occupies the legal status of an offeror.

C. No, because the auctioneer offered to sell for $90, and Jane failed to raise her bid to that amount.

D. No, because an auctioneer's request for bids represents only an invitation to deal.

ANALYSIS. *A contract arises by offer and acceptance.* An auctioneer makes invitations to deal, and bidders make offers. This auctioneer heard three bids and accepted none of them. When Jane made a fourth bid, offering to buy for $80, the auctioneer, not *immediately* accepting her offer, asked *for an offer* of $90, but none came forth. He then accepted Jane's $80 offer, and the parties formed a contract. The answer, therefore, should be "yes"—Jane has an obligation to buy. The reason? Jane made an offer and the auctioneer accepted.

C states that the parties did not form a contract. For that reason, it's wrong. Further, it incorrectly implies that the auctioneer offered to sell the painting for $90. Let's be clear: The auctioneer never offered to sell the painting, at any price. He *asked* for offers from prospective buyers (the bidders). With his barkings, he made repeated invitations to deal.

D correctly states that a request for bids is only an invitation to deal. Yet it reaches the wrong conclusion. Yes—the auctioneer made only invitations to deal, but all were followed by offers, one of which he accepted (Jane's).

B tells us that Jane must buy the painting. That much is right, but the rest is nonsense. One may make an offer without knowing, legally, that she has done so. In contract law, as in (almost) every other legal arena, the legal status of one's behavior does not turn on her knowledge of law. One who intentionally kills another (without justification) commits murder whether he knows it or not. Offer securities for public sale without first registering with the Securities and Exchange Commission, and you violate federal law, know it or not. **B** is wrong.

A presents not one of the relevant "buzz" words — neither "auction," "bid," "offer," nor "acceptance." Read for *meaning*, not for words. "Seller's representative" means — the auctioneer. "Unequivocally acceded to" means — "accepted." "Jane's express preparedness to purchase for a stated price" means — "Jane's offer." In short, **A** *means* "yes, because the auctioneer accepted Jane's offer." **A** is right.

C.   Written Proposals and the Significance of Signatures

Let's think now about written proposals and the significance of signatures. Look at four versions of a letter from Kirk to Beverly, all written on Kirk's personal letterhead. The letters differ one from another as to a small portion of text and as to whether or not Kirk signs them.

Version 1

Dear Beverly,

I'd like to have you tutor my son Manny in his pre-calculus course — 15 weekly one-hour sessions, beginning this coming Thursday, $75 per hour. If you're agreeable, please sign and return the document to me. Thanks.

Agreed: Agreed:

_____   _____

Kirk Grandel   Beverly Charlotte

Version 2

Dear Beverly,

I'd like to have you tutor my son Manny in his pre-calculus course — 15 weekly one-hour sessions, beginning this coming Thursday at $75 per hour. If you're agreeable, please sign and return the document to me. Thanks.

Agreed: Agreed:

Kirk Grandel

_____   _____

Kirk Grandel   Beverly Charlotte

Version 3

Dear Beverly,

I'd like to have you tutor my son Manny in his pre-calculus course—15 weekly one-hour sessions, beginning this coming Thursday at $75 per hour. If you're agreeable, please sign and return the document to me. Do that and we have a deal; we'll expect to see you this coming Thursday at 7:30 PM.

Thanks.

Agreed: Agreed:

_____   _____
Kirk Grandel   Beverly Charlotte

1. *Offer or Invitation to Deal?*

Let's analyze. With Version 1 Kirk seems certainly to show that he is ready and willing to enter a bargain. Yet he leaves blank the space provided for his own signature. So let's ask: With Kirk's signature line left blank, should Beverly believe that *her* signature will not "seal the deal?" Does Kirk's missing signature mean that the letter is a mere invitation to deal, asking that *Beverly* make an offer to Kirk on Kirk's stated terms?

The answer is "yes, probably," and to explain, we resort to that simple, pliable, ubiquitous word "ordinarily." In the law's eyes, a written proposal with signature lines should, *ordinarily*, cause the reasonable person to realize that the proposor intends signatures to serve as the final showing of assent. With the proposor's own signature missing, the proposee should know that *her* signature will not conclude the bargain. She should realize that the proposor reserves the right to have the "final say," which means that he does not make an offer but, instead, that he *asks* for one. If, as in version 2, the proposor signs his name on the signature line then, *ordinarily*, his writing constitutes an offer, and the proposee, if she signs, accepts it.

To summarize, a proposal or "draft contract" that bears a marked space for the proposor's signature is, ordinarily, an offer if the proposor signs. It's an invitation to deal if he does not.

2. *But "Ordinarily" Doesn't Mean "Always"*

To say that a "draft" bearing the proposor's blank signature line is ordinarily an invitation to deal is to say that in *some* cases (the extraordinary ones), it's *not* an invitation to deal but an offer.

Look at version 3 and ask if it's an offer. Ordinarily the answer would be "no" because it shows a blank space for Kirk's signature. But the proposal isn't "ordinary." It makes clear that Beverly's signature will finalize the arrangement:

"If you're agreeable, please sign . . . Do that and we have a deal; we'll expect to see you this coming Thursday at 7:30 P.M." In light of that language, Kirk's missing signature loses significance. Signed or not, his writing describes a bargain and asks for Beverly's assent. As a reasonable person, Beverly should believe that to "seal the deal," she need only sign and return the document. Hence, Version 3 is an offer.

D.   The Closer

QUESTION 3. By telephone, Stephen Quadra of ConCo contacts Amanda Johnson of WebCo to say that Conco wants to purchase all of WebCo's stock in WebCo's subsidiary corporation, FenCo. The parties talk. At the end of their chat Amanda tells Stephen, "I'll send you a draft contract." Stephen responds, "I'll be expecting it." Amanda then sends Stephen this proposed contract, *un*signed:

CONTRACT FOR STOCK PURCHASE

The undersigned parties, ConCo and WebCo hereby agree that:

(1) ConCo ("Buyer") will purchase from WebCo ("Seller") all shares in the FenCo corporation, the transaction to occur on this next November 15.

ConCo Inc.	WebCo Inc.
By: _____	By: _____
Stephen Quadra	Amanda Jameson
President	*President*

Stephen signs the document and returns it to Amanda. The written exchange probably creates:

I.   a contract between ConCo and WebCo.
II. an invitation to deal from ConCo to WebCo.
III. an invitation to deal from WebCo to ConCo.
IV. an offer from ConCo to WebCo.
V.   an offer from WebCo to ConCo.
A. I
B. II and III
C. II and IV
D. III and IV
E. IV and V

ANALYSIS.   We see two written communications: (1) Webco's unsigned writing to Conco, and (2) the same writing, returned to WebCo *signed* by ConCo.

The first shows WebCo's definite interest in entering a bargain, quite specific in its terms. But let's ask: Should a reasonable party in ConCo's position believe (a) that its own assent will conclude the bargain, or instead (b) that WebCo has reserved for itself the "final say?" Asked another way: As read by a reasonable person in Conco's position, does WebCo's writing (a) make an offer to Conco, meaning that Conco's signature will create a contract, or (b) ask that Conco make an offer to Webco, meaning that Webco's writing is an invitation to deal — that Conco's signature will create an offer *to* Webco?

Webco designated space for two signatures, but sent the writing to Conco, unsigned. Ordinarily, then, Conco should conclude that Webco, reserving the right to sign last, has the "final say" — that ConCo's own signature will not finalize an agreement. Since there appears no extraordinary language or circumstance, this *is* the "ordinary" situation. WebCo's letter to ConCo is an invitation to deal.

By signing the letter and sending it back Conco takes the terms of Webco's invitation, and turns them into its own offer; *ConCo* makes an offer to *Webco*. Hence, Options III and IV are correct, but I, II, and V are not. These parties have not yet formed a contract because WebCo has not yet accepted ConCo's offer. In this written exchange, ConCo made no invitation to deal, and WebCo made no offer. Rather WebCo made the invitation to deal and ConCo the offer. (During the preliminary telephone conversation, ConCo did make an invitation to deal, to which WebCo responded, in writing, with its own invitation to deal.) **D** is right.

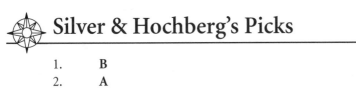

Silver & Hochberg's Picks

1.	**B**
2.	**A**
3.	**D**

6

How Offers Die

A.   Termination by the Offeror's Revocation

Jeff wants Ellen to frame a painting.

(1) **Jeff:** Ellen, I'll pay $90 plus the cost of supplies if you'll frame this painting. I'd like it done by next Friday. Deal?

(2) **Ellen:** I'm not sure. I'll let you know tomorrow morning.

(3) **Jeff:** Never mind. I'll get someone else.

(4) **Ellen:** No, please don't. I'll do it. I'll do it by Friday; I accept.

Jeff and Ellen have *not* formed a contract. With statement 1, Jeff made an offer. With statement 2, Ellen said she'd consider the matter, but did not accept. In statement 3, Jeff *revoked the offer*; he "took it back." That put the offer to its end, and Ellen lost her power to accept. With statement 4, Ellen tried to accept, but she spoke too late. The offer was gone—with the wind. Ellen had nothing *to* accept, and the parties formed no contract.

An Offeror Can Take His Offer Back?

Yes, absolutely. At any time *before an offeree accepts* an offeror is free to revoke. He can do so even if he promises he won't. Imagine, for instance, that the foregoing dialogue had occurred thus:

(1) **Jeff:** "Ellen, I will pay you $90 plus the cost of supplies if you will frame this painting. I'd like it done by next Friday. My offer stands until tomorrow at noon; I won't take it back. I promise

(2) **Ellen:** "Well, thank you. I'll let you know tomorrow morning."
(3) **Jeff:** "On second thought — never mind, I'll get someone else."
(4) **Ellen:** "No, please don't. I'll do it. I'll do it by Friday; I accept."

Even with *that* dialogue, these parties form no contract because Jeff revoked before Ellen attempted to accept. That was his right, even though he had *promised* to hold his offer open. With the offer withdrawn, Ellen lost her power to accept. At statement 4, her *attempt* to accept was, again, ineffective and the parties formed no contract.

The relevant rule is this that: *With respect to any offer, an offeror revokes when he expresses a decision to withdraw, and so long as the offeree has not yet accepted. the offeror is free to revoke, even if he has represented that he will not.* Restatement (Second) of Contracts §42 and cmt. a state it thus:

> An offeree's power of acceptance is terminated when the offeree receives from the offeror a manifestation of an intention not to enter into the proposed contract. . . . [An] offer is revocable even though it expressly states the contrary. . . .

Underlying that rule is another one, fundamental to the whole of contract law: *One party cannot be bound to an agreement unless the other is bound as well.* As to any proposed agreement between two parties, *one party is bound only if both are bound.* If one remains free to enter or not, then the other must be equally free.

That fundamental tenet stands aback of the offeror's right to revoke (and also underlies rules regarding consideration discussed in Chapters 12-14). If the law prevented Jeff from withdrawing his offer while Ellen made her decision to accept or not, then it would bind Jeff without binding Ellen. Picture Ellen, freely pondering her decision—free to bind herself or not. Meanwhile, Jack is at Ellen's mercy. If she snaps her fingers with an "I accept," Jack is bound. His hands are tied, while Ellen's are free. *That*, contract law will not abide. When two parties contemplate a contract, both are bound or neither is bound.

QUESTION 1. WesCo and JenCo exchange these signed writings:

(1) **WesCo:** We need 25,000 units of Bantex 44. Please quote us a price.
(2) **Jenco** (by signed writing): We have no Bantex 44 in stock. We probably can acquire the 25,000 units you request, and deliver within 20 days, but before we research that possibility, you should know that our current price is $8/unit. Interested?
(3) **WesCo:** Your delivery terms are fine, but we are prepared to pay only $6/unit. Please procure product and ship for $6/unit.
(4) **JenCo:** Would you consider paying $7/unit?
(5) **WesCo:** No, thank you. We've changed our mind about the purchase; we'll do without the Bantex.

> **(6) JenCo:** We are able, after all, to order the 25,000 units, and we accept your price of $6/unit. Will deliver.
>
> Thereafter JenCo contacts WesCo announcing that delivery is imminent. WesCo again advises JenCo that it no longer wants the goods and won't accept them. JenCo sues WesCo for breach. WesCo claims it formed no contract. Which of the following judicial conclusions properly supports a decision for WesCo?
>
> **A.** Neither party made an offer to the other.
> **B.** JenCo made an offer, but WesCo did not accept it.
> **C.** WesCo made an offer, but JenCo did not accept it.
> **D.** Each party made an offer, but neither made an acceptance.

ANALYSIS. In order to decide in WesCo's favor a judge must conclude that the parties exchanged no offer and acceptance. Examine the parties' communications. In statement 1, WesCo showed its interest in buying goods. It asked about price, but made no definite proposal. Wesco put forth only an invitation to deal. Then, uncertain of access to the product, Jenco gave its price, but committed to nothing. It, too, made a mere invitation to deal. In statement 3, WesCo responded with an *offer* to buy at $6/unit. It remained for JenCo to accept while the offer remained operative. At statement 4, JenCo responded but did not accept. And, with statement 5, Wesco revoked: "We've changed our mind . . . we'll do without the Bantex." In Restatement terms, JenCo received "from the offeror a manifestation of an intention not to enter into the proposed contract." At statement 6, Jenco tried to accept—too late, for the offer was gone.

According to **A**, neither party made an offer, but that's false. With statement 3, WesCo made an offer. According to **B**, JenCo made an offer. That's wrong too. JenCo made two invitations to deal (statements 1 and 4) and a failed attempt to accept (statement 6). It never made an offer. Choice **D** states that both parties made offers, which is wrong because JenCo did not.

According to **C**, WesCo made an offer but JenCo failed to accept it. That's true: WesCo made an offer in statement 3, but withdrew it in statement 5. JenCo *tried* to accept in statement 6, but had nothing *to* accept. Just as **C** states, "WesCo made an offer, but JenCo did not accept it." **C** is right.

B.   The Option Contract

Although an offeror may revoke his offer at any time before the offeree accepts, the offeree may nonetheless *purchase* an irrevocable offer by forming with the offeror an "option contract."

Victoria and Pamela

Wanting to sell her building, Victoria contacts Pamela and the parties exchange these signed writings:

> (1) **Victoria:** I own a building described in the Frontier County land records at volume 202, page 348. Its address is 4040 Thirteenth Avenue. I will sell it to you for $8 million.
> (2) **Pamela:** I'd like to think about it. Will you allow me 120 days to make up my mind?
> (3) **Victoria:** Yes. I'll hold the offer open for 120 days.

Victoria is free to revoke the offer notwithstanding her promise to hold it open. Pamela has no legal assurance that the building will be available to her for 120 days or even 120 seconds.

Now consider *this* exchange:

> (1) **Vanessa:** I own a building described in the Frontier County land records at volume 195, page 420. Its address is 4040 Twelfth Avenue. I will sell it to you for $8 million.
> (2) **Peter:** I need time to think it over. I'll pay you $10,000 tomorrow morning if you'll agree to hold the offer open for 120 days.
> (3) **Vanessa:** Agreed.

Wanting time to consider Vanessa's offer without risking its revocation, Peter responds, in statement 2, with an offer of his own (a "counteroffer"; see Chapter 7, section A). He proposes to *pay money* in exchange for Vanessa's promise not to revoke her offer. Vanessa accepts and the parties form a contract.

What That Contract Requires

The contract does not require that these parties buy and sell the building. Rather, it requires that Peter pay Vanessa $10,000 and that Vanessa hold open for 120 days her offer to sell Peter the building for $8 million. In essence, for $10,000, Peter has *bought* from Vanessa an irrevocable offer. Reciprocally, for $10,000, Vanessa has sold Peter that same irrevocable offer. For 120 days, *by contract*, Peter has the option to accept it or not. If he decides to accept — to "exercise his option" — then he must pay Vanessa $8 million and Vanessa must convey the building. If he decides not to accept, he loses his $10,000, having received exactly what he paid for — a form of "insurance" — an offer, irrevocable for 120 days called, also, a "120-day option on Vanessa's building."

But I Thought an Offeror Can *Always* Revoke Her Offer at Any Time Before the Offeree Accepts

That's right; an offer is revocable at any time before the offeree accepts. But a *contract* in which an offeror agrees not to revoke her offer is, like any other contract—fully enforceable. Between Vanessa and Peter there stands not a simple offer from one to the other, but a *contract* by which both are bound. Like any other contract, it arose by offer and acceptance (statements 2 and 3 above). And to this sort of contract, we give the special name, "option contract": *An option contract is a contract in which (a) a Party 1 ("optionee") gives value to a Party 2 ("optionor") and, in exchange, with respect to some other prospective contract (b)Party 2 (optionor) promises, for some agreed period, to hold irrevocable an offer so that Party 1 (optionee) for that period has the option to accept it or not.*

Let's apply that definition to Vanessa and Peter.

"*An option contract is a contract . . .* "

An option contract is, first of all — *a contract.* It must arise through its own offer and acceptance. This one arose through Peter's offer, at statement 2, accepted by Vanessa at statement 3.

"*. . . in which . . .*"

An option contract is a particular *kind* of contract about to be described.

"*. . . a first person ("optionee") gives value to a second ("optionor") . . .*"

Peter, the optionee, gives value to Vanessa, the optionor, by way of his promise to pay $10,000.

" **with respect to some other prospective contract**"

Vanessa and Peter contemplate the possibility of another contract not yet formed—a contract for the sale to Peter of Vanessa's land for $8 million.

"**the second (optionor) agrees, for some specified period, to hold open and irrevocable some offer so that the optionee for that period has the option to accept it or not, as he wishes.**"

Vanessa promises that for 120 days she will hold her offer open so that Peter may, any time during that period, accept it, if and as he chooses.[1]

Option contracts come with their own lexicon of words and phrases:

OPTION CONTRACT VOCABULARY LIST

Option: one's contractual right to accept an offer held irrevocable for some specified period.

Optionor: party who sells an option to another.

Optionee: party who buys an option from another.

Option price: price the optionee pays for his option.

Strike price: price the optionee will pay if she exercises her option (Beware: some people use "option price" to mean "strike price.")

Option period: time period during which the optionor must hold her offer irrevocable.

Exercise: optionee's decision to accept the irrevocable offer.

Exercise price: strike price.

---

1. *See* Restatement (Second) of Contracts §25 illus. 1, 2, for additional examples of an option contract.

> **QUESTION 2.** Party G creates this signed writing: "My 300-acre farm is for sale immediately. The land is described at volume 2084, page 782, of the Harrison County Land Records. Price: $10 million, all cash, payable immediately." Party H reads the offer and responds, whereupon G and H exchange writings. Among the exchanges shown below, which creates an option contract?
>
> **A.** (1) **Party H:** I'll pay you $1 million one month from today if you give me five years to decide that I do or do not wish to buy the farm for an additional $9 million.
> (2) **Party G:** Agreed.
>
> **B.** (1) **Party H:** I'm interested. I'll pay you $1 million one month from today. In five years, I'll pay you the remaining $9 million and at that time you'll transfer the farm to me. Agreed?
> (2) **Party G:** Agreed.
>
> **C.** (1) **Party H:** I'm interested, but I'd like to buy an option to purchase the farm. Agreed?
> (2) **Party G:** Agreed. The option period will be five years, the option price $1 million, and the strike price $9 million.
>
> **D.** (1) **Party H:** I'm interested, but I need five years to make a decision. Agreed?
> (2) **Party G:** Agreed.

ANALYSIS.   An option contract is, first, a contract. If an interaction fails to form *a contract* it cannot form an option contract. Consider **D**. Party G offers to sell her farm, but Party H does not accept. Rather, he asks that G wait five years for his answer. With statement 2 in exchange for nothing, G agrees, meaning she purports to make her offer irrevocable for five years. Legally, we know, she can't do that; notwithstanding her promise, she retains the right to revoke. G has made, still, only an offer, and H has not accepted it. The parties have no contract, meaning they have no option contract. **D** is wrong.

Now for **C**. Again with statement 2, H fails to accept. He expresses *interest* in forming an "option contract" but makes no offer to do so. He provides no terms—no option price, no option period, no strike price. Hence, in responding to G's offer, H makes a mere invitation to deal. With statement 2, Party G truly *offers* H an option to buy the farm. She identifies the option period (five years), the option price ($1 million), and the strike price ($9 million). Party H does not respond, and so we're left with G's unaccepted offer to sell H an option on the farm. The parties form no contract, so **C** is wrong.

In **B**, the parties do form a contract. Party H responds to Party G's offer to sell her farm not with an acceptance but with a counteroffer. He proposes definitely to purchase the farm *not* immediately and *not* for "all cash, payable immediately." Rather, he offers to pay $1 million in one month and $9 million five years later, at which time Party G is to convey title to the farm. That's an offer, and with statement 3 Party H accepts it. The parties form a contract, but it leaves neither one with any options at all. These parties *must* buy and sell. Hence, they form a contract, but not an option contract. **B** is wrong.

We're left with **A**. Again Party H receives G's offer and responds with an offer of his own. He proposes to pay $1 million in exchange for the right to buy the farm at any time within the next five years, by paying — if he chooses to buy — for another $9 million. Hence H offers to buy, for $1 million, G's five-year irrevocable offer to sell the farm for (an additional) $9 million. Party G accepts the offer, and the parties thus form a contract — and, more specifically, an option contract. Some would say, "G sold H an option on her farm," or "H bought an option on G's farm."

C.   Termination by the Offeree's Rejection

If in response to an offer, the offeree says "no," she rejects the offer and thus terminates it. Consider this interaction, occurring at 11 A.M.:

> **Party A:** I'll pay you $50 if you'll wash all of my windows by noon today.
> **Party B:** No, thank you.
> **Party B (again):** I've changed my mind. I accept your offer.

B rejected A's offer by saying "no" and thus "killed" it. B changed her mind and tried to accept the offer, but she spoke too late. By saying "no" and rejecting the offer, she lost her power to accept. The parties have no contract.

Now consider this interaction, also occurring at 11 A.M.:

> **Party C:** I'll pay you $50 if you'll wash all of my windows by noon today.
> **Party D:** I wish I could, but I can't wash all of the windows in one hour.
> **Party D (again):** I've changed my mind. I can do it. I accept.

At 11 A.M. Party C made an offer. Party D expressed her wish to finalize the bargain, but stated also that she could not give the requested performance within the specified time. To say that "I wish I could, but I can't" is to say "no" (nicely). Party D rejected C's offer. Her subsequent attempt to accept was ineffective.

The rule, then, is this: *An offeree rejects an offer and thereby terminates it when she leads the offeror reasonably to believe that she has decided not to accept.* Restatement (Second) §38(2) states it this way: "A manifestation of intention not to accept an offer is a rejection. . . ." Section 39(2) adds: "An offeree's power of acceptance is terminated by his rejection of the offer. . . ."

If an offeree responds to an offer not with "yes" or "no" but with "maybe," she neither accepts nor rejects. The offer continues in effect, and the offeree retains her power to accept. Consider this dialogue:

Party A: I'll pay you $50 if you'll wash all of my windows by noon today.
Party B: Well, I'll think about it.
Party B (again): I've thought about it. I can do it. I accept.

In her first statement, B manifests neither acceptance nor rejection. She indicates that she'll *consider* A's proposal. The offer continues in force, just as though B had said nothing. Then, with her second statement, she accepts, and the parties form a contract. Accordingly, Restatement (Second) §38(2) provides:

> A manifestation of intention not to accept an offer is a rejection unless the offeree manifests an intention to take it under further advisement.

QUESTION 3. On March 1, Dennis Storme telephones Mariah Wilson and leaves her a voice-mail message.

(1) **March 1, Dennis (voice-mail message):** Hello, I'm Dennis Storme. You come highly recommended as a math tutor, and I'd like you to tutor my daughter Susan in trigonometry. Would you get back to me so that we can discuss the possibilities?

(2) **March 2, Mariah (voice-mail message):** Hello, Mr. Storme, this is Mariah Wilson. I would be happy to tutor Susan. I have only one opening at present—Saturday mornings from 10:30 A.M. to noon. My fee is $90 for the 90 minutes. I am prepared to commit to the next ten Saturdays. After that we can consider whether Susan needs any additional tutoring.

(3) **March 3, Dennis (fax):** Thank you for your return call. I cannot work with the hours you mention. Would you be able to tutor on Saturday evenings?

(4) **March 4, Mariah (voice-mail message):** No, Mr. Storme, I'm sorry that I cannot tutor Susan on Saturday evenings. Exactly as stated in my last message, I am available for the next ten Saturdays from 10:30 A.M. to noon and would be pleased to tutor Susan on those days at those hours.

(5) **March 5, Dennis (fax):** Very well—we're agreed. Saturday mornings from 10:30 A.M. to noon; I'll find some way to see that we can do it.

Is Mariah free *not* to tutor Susan without breaching a contract?

A. Yes, because Dennis's March 5 message was too indefinite to create a contract

B. Yes, because on March 3, Dennis lost his power to accept Mariah's March 2 offer.

C. No, because on March 3, Dennis plainly continued in his willingness to have Mariah's services

D. No, because on March 5, Dennis assented to the terms that Mariah had set forth on March 4

ANALYSIS. The question is whether these parties formed a contract—whether one of them made an offer that the other accepted—while the offer still lived. On March 1, Dennis spoke to the possibility of purchasing Mariah's tutoring services. He mentioned neither fee nor hours. He made an invitation to deal. On March 2, Mariah responded with an offer. On March 3, Dennis stated that he "could not work" with the hours she had specified. Put otherwise, he expressed an intention not to accept the offer and thus rejected it. At that point, he lost his power to accept it. But on March 4, Mariah restated her proposal and thus made the offer anew. When Dennis assented, he accepted the offer, and the parties formed a contract.

A and B are wrong; they tell us that Mariah *is* free to withhold her services, meaning that the parties formed no contract. It is true, as A states, that Dennis's first message was an invitation to deal. It's also true, as B indicates, that when Dennis rejected Mariah's first offer, he lost his power to accept it. Still, there later arose a new offer and acceptance.

C and D correctly imply that these parties did form a contract. Yet choice C erroneously suggests that Dennis's plain willingness to secure Mariah's services somehow creates a contract. Nonsense. On March 3, Dennis rejected Mariah's first offer and lost his power to accept it; the offer "died," notwithstanding that Dennis continued in his willingness to secure Mariah's services. D has it right: These parties formed a contract because on March 4 Mariah made her offer anew. On March 5, Dennis accepted, and the parties were bound in contract.

D. Passage of Time

Offers are mortal things; they die. We know already that an offeror may kill his own offer by revocation and that the offeree may kill it by rejection. Know now that without death by revocation or rejection, every unaccepted offer dies of "old age." The offeror may expressly provide for that by tagging his offer with a "shelf life." Suppose Barnette Inc. sends to Chadwell Inc. this signed writing: "We are prepared to replace all of the windows in your building at 444 Weston Street, with our new double-insulated windows, #820. Our price: $90,000, payable in advance. Offer good for ten days."

Barnette may revoke its offer, of course, any time before Chadwell accepts. *The offer's last sentence does not and cannot alter that truth.* The last sentence means this: if neither party acts for ten days, the offer expires "for passage of a time stated in the offer." The offer "dies," and the offeree loses his power to accept.

When the offeror does not tie his offer to a timer, the law limits its life to a "reasonable time." Had Barnette not set a ten-day timer on his offer but instead stayed silent on that subject then, by law, his offer would, on its own, die after a "reasonable time."

> **QUESTION 4.** Vlad telephones Esther and tells her, "I stand ready to clean your carpet for $125 on any Friday morning you choose." Esther repeats, "Any Friday morning?" Vlad answers, "Yes, my Fridays are clear." Esther responds, "I'll get back to you." "Very well," says Vlad, "I look forward to hearing from you." For two years neither party communicates with the other. Esther then telephones Vlad: "I accept your offer. Please come this Friday morning." Have these parties formed a contract?
>
> **A.** Yes, because Vlad made an offer and Esther accepted
> **B.** Yes, because Vlad expressly stated that "any Friday morning" would be appropriate
> **C.** No, because Esther failed to accept while Vlad's offer was operative
> **D.** No, because Esther rejected the offer by saying "I'll get back to you"

ANALYSIS.   Vlad made an offer, tying it to no time limit. By law it expired after a reasonable time. As in all other contexts, reasonableness, ordinarily a question of fact, depends on what reasonable persons would do and expect under the prevailing circumstances. For an offer such as this one, two years far exceeds a reasonable time. No reasonable person in Esther's position could believe that Vlad intended his offer to live that long. When Esther attempted to accept, the offer had long been dead. We don't know exactly when it expired, but we know for this offer, that a reasonable time passed, probably after a week, and certainly after a month.

A and **B** state that the parties did form a contract, so they're wrong, as is their reasoning. As for choice **A**, Esther did not issue an acceptance. She *attempted* to accept. But in that effort she failed; one cannot accept an offer that no longer lives. Regarding **B**, Vlad's reference to "any Friday morning" could not justify Esther in believing that his offer was eternally open. She ought to have understood Vlad to mean "the next few Friday mornings." **D** correctly states that the parties formed a contract, but its reasoning is wrong. Esther did not reject Vlad's offer. She said she'd be in touch again. "No" rejects, "maybe" does not. As a reasonable person, Vlad should hear Esther saying "maybe." **C** tells us that Esther attempted to accept Vlad's offer when the offer was no longer "operative," meaning that Esther had lost her power to accept. That's exactly right. When Esther tried to accept the offer, it was long gone. Therefore, Esther attempted to accept after the offer had terminated and so failed to form a contract. For that reason, **C** is right.

E.   Death or Incapacity of Offeror or Offeree

If one dies, his "estate" lives on in his place. Hence, when two parties form a contract and one of them then dies, the contract lives on and, in effect, the surviving party has a contract with the decedent's "estate." Through its executor, the estate asserts the decedent's contractual rights, and must fulfill his contractual duties. (You'll learn all about that when you study wills, trusts, and estates.) That does *not* mean that the decedent's survivors must fulfill his contracts. Rather, the estate must fulfill them, resorting to assets the decedent leaves behind.

Suppose Tom borrows $800,000 from Lender and dies before making any repayment. In addition to the $800,000 borrowed from Lender, Tom has, at his death, $200,000, so that his estate's assets are, in total, $1 million. Tom's will leaves "Everything I own to my son and daughter, Jack and Jill." The estate owes Lender $800,000, but Jack and Jill owe nothing. From its $1 million, the estate first pays its debt. Jack and Jill take the $200,000 that remains.

On January 1, Bess and Lloyd have this interaction:

Bess: I'd like to borrow $100. I'll repay it in six months with an annual 6 percent interest rate, meaning that in six months I'll pay you $103.

Lloyd: I'll make the loan, but I can't do so until February 1, one month from now. Further, I want the interest paid at the outset. That means that you'll pay me $3 on February 1, I'll then lend you $100 on that same day, and you will repay me the full $100 six months later—on August 1. Agreed?

Bess: Agreed.

The parties have a contract. If Lloyd dies two weeks later, on January 15, the contract with Bess lives on. From Bess, on February 1, Lloyd's estate is entitled to $3 and, on that same day must lend her $100, with Bess to repay on August 1.

But an Offer Does *Not* Survive the Offeror Let's modify the original interaction:

Bess: I'd like to borrow $100. I'll repay it in six months with an annual 6 percent interest rate, meaning that in six months I'll pay you $103.

Lloyd: I'll make the loan, but I can't do so until February 1, one month from now. You'll repay me six months from then—on August 1, with, as you say, $3 in interest.

Bess: Let me think about that. I'll let you know by January 25. Okay?

Lloyd: Yes, that's fine.

Plainly, these folks have no contract. Bess made an offer and Lloyd responded with an offer of his own, leaving Bess with power to accept it or not. If Lloyd dies on January 15, his offer dies too; it does not pass to his estate. If Bess then contacts Lloyd's executor, announcing her acceptance, no contract occurs. The same is so if Bess should die with Lloyd alive, his offer still outstanding. Bess's power to accept does not survive her. It terminates.

Analogous rules apply to mental incompetence. If two parties form a *contract* and one then suffers mental incompetence, the contract continues. An "administrator" or "conservator" acts for the incompetent party. On his behalf, she asserts contractual rights and, using the incompetent party's assets, fulfills his contractual duties (perhaps by commissioning another to perform as his substitute). Yet if one makes an *offer* and he or his offeree suffers that fate, the offer terminates — as it does when either party dies. Restatement (Second) §48 addresses both unhappy events:

> An offeree's power of acceptance is terminated when the offeree or offeror dies or is deprived of legal capacity to enter into the proposed contract.

QUESTIONS 5-7. On July 1, Wharton and Xavier create a contract under which Xavier will pay Wharton $9,000 and Wharton will repair Xavier's large yacht, the *Largesse*. Wharton is to begin work on August 1 and on that day Xavier is to pay him $4,500. Wharton is to finish work on August 31, and Xavier is then to pay the remaining $4,500. Also on July 1, just after they have formed their contract, the parties converse:

Xavier: I have another, smaller yacht, the *Peakaboo*, that needs exactly the same repair. For an additional $5,000 will you perform the repair just after you finish this one?
Wharton: I'll think it over and let you know within two weeks.
Xavier: That's fine. Let me know by phone, fax, or e-mail.

QUESTION 5. Xavier dies one week later, on July 8. As a result, Wharton loses:

I. his rights regarding the larger yacht.
II. his rights regarding the smaller yacht.
A. I only
B. II only
C. Both I and II
D. Neither I nor II

ANALYSIS.   If two parties form a contract, and one or both then die, the contract continues. Yet if one makes an offer, not yet accepted, his death terminates it.

As to the larger yacht, these parties formed a contract. When Xavier died, the contract continued. Wharton retained his rights and duties. Xavier's estate must pay Wharton $4,500 on August 1, and Wharton must repair the yacht. The estate must then pay Wharton $4,500 more when he finishes the work on August 31.

Option I makes a false statement, which means that **A** and **C** are wrong. Regarding the smaller yacht, Xavier made an offer, but on Xavier's death it expired; the parties formed no contract. Option II makes an accurate statement, so **D** is wrong. Wharton retains his rights under the existing contract, but loses his power to accept the outstanding offer. Hence, **B** is right.

QUESTION 6. Assume, now, that neither party dies. Instead, on July 8, Xavier becomes mentally incompetent. As a result, Wharton loses:

I. his rights regarding the larger yacht.
II. his rights regarding the smaller yacht.
A. I only
B. II only
C. Both I and II
D. Neither I nor II

ANALYSIS. On mental incompetence and death the law has like effects. Contracts survive. Offers do not. Again, **B** is right.

QUESTION 7. Assume, now, that both parties remain alive and well. On July 8, Xavier contacts Wharton and says, "I've changed my mind about both yachts. Repair neither one." As a result, Wharton loses:

I. his rights regarding the larger yacht.
II. his rights regarding the smaller yacht.
A. I
B. II
C. Both I and II
D. Neither I nor II

ANALYSIS. Xavier is free to revoke his offer, but he cannot destroy the contract. Consequently, Wharton loses his right to accept the offer, but retains his rights under the contract. Again, **B** is right.

F. The Closers

Eyon owns all of the stock in Eyon Inc. He has heard that Orlin, who owns all of the stock in Orlin Inc. might wish to sell it. In April, the two exchange these signed writings:

April 1, 2011, Eyon: I may wish, within the next year, to purchase all of your stock in Orlin. I'll pay $15 million, but I need one year to make my decision. I am prepared to pay $100,000 tomorrow, April 2, for this commitment from you if, during this next year, I wish to make the purchase, you'll sell for that price.

April 1, Orlin: Agreed. Please send the payment.

Eyon sends Orlin $100,000. On April 2, Orlin receives it. Then, on September 1, Orlin contacts Eyon:

September 1, Orlin: Not hearing from you in five months, I have decided not to sell you the stock. I revoke my offer and will return your $100,000.

September 1, Eyon: That is not acceptable. As we agreed, I may still wish to purchase the stock and I will make my decision on or before March 31.

QUESTION 8. Does Eyon retain the right, through March 31, to purchase the stock?

A. Yes, because on April 1 he acquired a one-year option to do so
B. Yes, because he proposed to pay the $100,000 within one day
C. No, because corporate stock is not a good
D. No, because Orlin stood ready to return Eyon's $100,000

ANALYSIS.   With his first statement, Eyon offered Orlin $100,000 for Orlin's promise to sell Eyon the Orlin stock for $15 million should Eyon choose to buy it during the next year. Stated in ordinary plain legalese, Eyon offered to buy a one-year option on Orlin's stock, with an option price of $100,000, and strike price of $15 million. Orlin accepted, and the parties formed an option contract.

We're asked whether Eyon retained the right to purchase the stock until March 31. Plainly, the answer is "yes." **C** and **D** say "no," so they're wrong. **C** reasons that corporate stock is not a good, and that's true. But option contracts do not arise from UCC Article 2 and are not confined to the sale of goods. Option contracts are but one species of contract under the common law. They might concern goods, services, or anything else. **D** says "no" because Orlin offered to return Eyon's $100,000 payment. When two parties form a contract, neither can escape it by returning what the other has given him under its terms. By law, "a deal is a deal." Hence, **D** is wrong.

B says "yes," but its reasoning is askew. When Eyon made his offer, he proposed to pay $100,000 the next day, April 2. One's promise, whenever due, is a *quid pro quo*. Had Eyon proposed to pay Orlin in one week, one month, one year, or five years, then still these parties would form an option contract requiring that (a) Orlin stand ready to sell his stock and (b) Eyon pay Orlin $100,000 — whenever. **B** is wrong.

A tells us that Eyon retains his right to buy the stock because he bought an option to do so. That's true, and **A** is right.

QUESTION 9. Which of the following most accurately characterizes the transaction?

A. Eyon offered to buy stock from Orlin.
B. Orlin sold Eyon an option to purchase stock.

C. Eyon was optionor and Orlin optionee.

D. Eyon presented Orlin with an invitation to deal.

ANALYSIS.   Orlin, as optionor, sold Eyon, as optionee, a one-year option to buy stock. Stated the other way 'round, Eyon purchased *from* Orlin an option to buy the stock. **A**, **C**, and **D** mischaracterize the transaction. As for **A**, Eyon never offered to buy stock. He offered to buy *the right* to do so at his option. What of **C**? Orlin sold the option, so he is the optionor. Eyon *bought* it, so he is the optionee. And **D**? Never did either party make invitation to deal. From the first, Eyon offered to buy an option. Orlin accepted, and Eyon paid him the option price. Hence, Orlin sold Eyon an option to purchase his stock. That's why **B** is right.

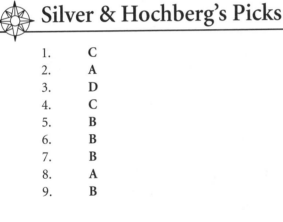 **Silver & Hochberg's Picks**

1.	C
2.	A
3.	D
4.	C
5.	B
6.	B
7.	B
8.	A
9.	B

7

Counteroffer and the Mirror-Image Rule

A. Counteroffer as Rejection
B. The Mirror-Image Rule
C. A "Mere Inquiry" Doesn't Reject
D. The Closer
✛ Silver & Hochberg's Picks

A. Counteroffer as Rejection

One might receive an offer and respond by suggesting a change in its terms, thereby making an offer of his own, commonly called a "counteroffer."

The photocopier, case 1

> **Party A:** I can repair the photocopier by Saturday morning for $320. Okay?
>
> **Party B:** Do it by Friday morning and we have a deal. Agreed?

Party A made an offer and B responded with a "counteroffer"; *With respect to any original offer, a counteroffer is an offer made by the original offeree to the original offeror, similar in subject matter but different in terms.* Restatement (Second) of Contracts §39(1) puts it thus:

> A counteroffer is an offer made by an offeree to his offeror relating to the same matter as the original offer and proposing a substituted bargain differing from that proposed by the original offer.

Common law provides, ordinarily, that when Party A makes an offer to Party B, who then responds with a counteroffer, A justifiably believes that B has rejected the offer initially made to him. In effect, the law writes "no, I reject," at the front of (almost) every counteroffer.

The photocopier, case 2

Party A: I can repair the photocopier by Saturday morning for $320. Okay?

Party B: [No, I reject.] Do it by Friday morning and we have a deal. Agreed?

With the words "no, I reject" implied by law, B's counteroffer has these two effects: (1) it rejects A's original offer, so that B can no longer accept it; and (2) it turns A into an offeree affording him the power to accept B's counteroffer. Let's continue the dialogue and see what that means.

The photocopier, case 3

(1) **Party A:** I can repair the photocopier by Saturday morning for $320. Okay?

(2) **Party B:** [No, I reject.] Do it by Friday morning and we have a deal. Agreed?

(3) **Party A:** I can't do that.

(4) **Party B:** Okay. I accept your initial offer—Saturday it is.

(5) **Party A:** No. I've changed my mind about the price; it will be $380.

Neither party made an offer that the other accepted. With statement 1, A made an offer to which B, in statement 2, made a counteroffer meaning that he (1) put his own offer "on the table" and rejected A's offer, thus shoving it from the table into the dumper. With statement 3, A rejected B's counteroffer, leaving the table empty. With statement 4, B tried to accept A's original offer, but he spoke too late. That offer died when, with his counteroffer at statement 2, B rejected it. With statement 5, A then made a new one, which B is free to accept or not.

About a counteroffer we now know this: it rejects the offer to which it responds. Beyond that, it's an offer like any other. The party who makes it is an offeror (although he was first an offeree). The party who receives it (originally an offeror) is an offeree, free to accept it or not, for so long as it lives—for so long as it does not expire by revocation, rejection, or any other means.

Sometimes a Counteroffer Does Not Reject

By implication of law, as just discussed, a counteroffer "ordinarily" acts as a rejection, meaning that an *ordinary* counter-offer rejects the offer that it answers. But one might overcome the law's implication by making a counteroffer that is not "ordinary."

The photocopier, case 4

(1) **Party A:** I can repair the photocopier by Saturday morning for $320. Okay?

(2) **Party B:** I'll think about that; I might want to accept. Meanwhile, know this: If you'll do the work by Friday morning, we have a deal. Agreed?

(3) **Party A:** I can't do that.

(4) **Party B:** Okay. I accept your initial offer—Saturday it is.

(5) **Party A:** I've changed my mind about the price; it will be $380.

With statement 1, A makes an offer and B, with statement 2, answers with a counteroffer, *making clear his wish to preserve A's original offer.* B's counteroffer is not the "ordinary" one. It overcomes the law's implication that it should act as a rejection. Hence, *this* counteroffer does *not* work a rejection. Party A's offer remains effective, and with statement 4, B accepts it. When, at statement 5, A attempted to revoke his offer and make a new one (at a higher price), he spoke too late. With statement 4, the parties formed a contract.

Neither does a counteroffer operate as a rejection if the original offer*or* makes plain that he will not so interpret it.

The photocopier, case 5

(1) **Party A:** I can repair the photocopier by Saturday morning for $320. Propose a change in terms, if you like. I won't take that as a 'no.'"

(2) **Party B:** I can't wait until Saturday. If you can do it by Friday morning, we have a deal. Agreed?

(3) **Party A:** I can't do that.

(4) **Party B:** Okay. I accept your initial offer—Saturday it is.

With statement 1, A made an offer and plainly told B that he would not take a counteroffer as a rejection. B made a counteroffer and, with statement 3, A rejected it. Meanwhile, A's original offer remained operative. With statement 4 B accepted it.

The rule is that: *One who makes a counteroffer rejects the offer to which he responds, unless (a) he affirmatively manifests his wish to keep the offer under consideration, or (b) the original offeror manifests his intention not to treat it as a rejection.* Restatement (Second) §39 (2) states it a little vaguely:

> An offeree's power of acceptance is terminated by his making of a counter-offer unless the offeror has manifested a contrary intention or unless the counteroffer manifests a contrary intention of the offeree.

In the fourth photocopier case, the counteroffer manifested "a contrary intention of the [original] offeree" because it included the words "I might want to accept." In the fifth photocopier case, Party A, the offeror, "manifested a contrary intention" by saying: "Propose a change in terms, if you like. I won't take that as a 'no.'"

B.   The Mirror-Image Rule

The common law features this long-standing rule: *To accept an offer, the offeree must manifest an assent that mirrors the offeror's proposal in any and every respect. She must show agreement to each and every one of the offeror's proposed terms without alteration.* This, the "mirror-image rule," reflects the simple logical notion that a party can accept only such offer as is actually made to her.

Suppose A and B conduct this conversation:

Party A: I'll wash your car, right now, for $30.
Party B: I accept, but don't wash the car, paint the house instead, and I'll pay you $3,000.

You need no special rule named "mirror image" to conclude that these parties formed no contract. Party B spoke the *words* "I accept," but plainly did not assent to the offer before her. She stated her willingness to enter a bargain *not* offered. She accepted — nothing. To say that acceptance requires a mirror image of the offer is to say only that there can be no acceptance to an offer not made. That's all there is to the mirror-image rule. Don't let anyone tell you otherwise.

This so-called rule applies, of course, whether the difference between offer and acceptance is dramatic or trivial. If Party X offers apples, Party Y cannot accept bananas. If Party X offers red apples, Party Y cannot accept green ones. If Party X offers a quart of skim milk for $1.00, Party Y cannot accept a quart of whole milk for $0.99. Again, *one cannot accept an offer not made.*

Now consider this little conversation:

Party A: I'll wash your car for $30. I'll begin work on Tuesday morning at 9:00.
Party B: I accept, but please begin on Tuesday morning at 9:01.

Party B assented to an offer not made; 9:00 is not 9:01. Consequently, he failed to accept, and the parties formed no contract.

When faced with a problem in which one party makes an offer and the second party purports to accept, but alters the offeror's terms, *say* this: "Because of the mirror-image rule the parties form no contract." But *understand* this: the mirror-image rule means only that a contract requires an offer and an acceptance — *of that offer.*

Now let's ask: when A makes an offer and B issues a non-mirror-image response, what then sits on the "table?" Return to A's and B's exchange over the Tuesday morning car wash. On the table sits (1) A's offer to B, *dead*, because B rejected it, and (2) B's counteroffer to A, which A is free to accept or not. As one court reasoned, "The acceptance may not impose additional conditions on the offer, nor may it add limitations. 'An acceptance which is equivocal or upon condition or with a limitation is a counteroffer. . . .'" Ardente v. Horan, 366 A.2d 162, 165 (R.I. 1976) (quoting John Hancock Mut. Life Ins. Co. v. Dietlin, 199 A.2d 311, 313 (R.I. 1964)). Restatement (Second) §59 states it thus:

> A reply to an offer which purports to accept it but is conditional on the offeror's assent to terms additional to or different from those offered is not an acceptance, but is a counteroffer.

> **QUESTIONS 1 & 2.** Sidney says to Rena: "I'd like to use your recording studio this coming Tuesday from 9 A.M. to noon. Will you rent it to me, and if so, what will you charge?" Rena responds: "Yes, definitely, I accept. The charge is $100 per hour, but on that day the studio is available only from noon to 3 P.M."
>
> **QUESTION 1.** Which of the following responses from Sidney would most likely create a contract?
>
> A. "Fine, noon to 3 P.M. it is, but I can pay only $250."
> B. "Fine, noon to 3 P.M. it is, but I can't afford $300."
> C. "Fine, noon to 3 P.M. it is, but let's make it $95 per hour."
> D. "Fine."

ANALYSIS. An offeree's statement of assent constitutes acceptance only if it mirrors the offer. Sidney first issued a preliminary inquiry—an invitation to deal—expressing interest in renting Rena's studio on Tuesday morning. Rena responded with an offer to rent the studio on Tuesday afternoon for a specific period at a specific price.

Sidney's responses cited at **A**, **B**, and **C** show no assent *to Rena's offer*. In each, Sidney is unwilling to pay the proposed price. But at **D**, he assents to all of Rena's terms without alteration. **D** is right.

> **QUESTION 2.** Assume that Sidney responds to Rena: "Well, that's a high price, and I'd feel better with a price of $95. But that's *my* problem—you've got a deal." Have the parties formed a contract?
>
> A. Yes, because Sidney assented fully to the terms Rena proposed.
> B. Yes, because Sidney's proposed price of $95 differs only slightly from Rena's proposed price of $100.
> C. No, because Sidney did not manifest complete satisfaction with Rena's proposed price term.
> D. No, because as to time, Rena's offer did not conform to Sidney's original proposal.

ANALYSIS. On learning of an offeror's proposed terms, an offeree may gripe, groan, wail, or whine. But if he answers "yes" to *all* of them, he accepts. Here, Sidney expresses dismay over the $300 price, but does, ultimately, accede to it and to all else that Rena proposes. The parties form a contract.

C and **D** are wrong because they tell us that the parties fail to form a contract. According to **C**, an offeree accepts only if he shows "complete satisfaction" with the offeror's terms. There is no such rule. Grumpy or glad, sour or sad, the offeree who assents, fully, to the offeror's terms accepts her offer. **D**

suggests that the difference between Sidney's invitation to deal and Rena's offer somehow defeats the contract. We know better. Parties may exchange multiple invitations to deal, offers, and counteroffers, each differing from every other. If one party ultimately makes an offer that the other accepts, they hatch a contract.

B implies that an offeree may accept with a response that alters the offeror's terms, so long as the change is minor. There's no such rule. One who assents to an offer but varies its terms—ever so slightly—fails to accept. Again, one cannot accept an offer not made.

A correctly states the result and reason. Sidney's response, in the end, does express assent to all that Rena proposes. Notwithstanding his disgruntlement as to price, he responded, "But that's *my* problem—you've got a deal." The parties achieve offer and acceptance, and so form a contract. **A** is right.

C.   A "Mere Inquiry" Doesn't Reject

We know now that the common law ordinarily sees a counteroffer as a rejection of the offer it answers. Yet it sees no rejection in the offeree's simple inquiry about a possible change in terms. Regarding the photocopier repair, let's modify the dialogue between A and B.

The photocopier, case 6

(1) **Party A:** I can repair the photocopier by Saturday morning for $320. Okay?

(2) **Party B:** Can you do it by Friday?

(3) **Party A:** No.

(4) **Party B:** I accept your initial offer—Saturday it is.

(5) **Party A:** I've changed my mind about the price; it will be $380.

With statement 2, B said neither yes nor no. Neither did he make a counteroffer to which the law would impute a rejection. Rather, *he asked a question about a possible change in terms.* When an offeree does that, the law places the words "maybe, but" at the front of his statement: "[Maybe, but] Can you do it by Friday?"

Can We State a Rule?

Yes: *A counter-offer ordinarily operates as a rejection of the offer to which it responds, but a counter-offer differs from a "mere inquiry," as to a change in terms, and such an inquiry is neither a counter-offer nor a rejection.*

Restatement (Second) §39 cmt. b puts it this way:

> [A] mere inquiry regarding the possibility of different terms, a request for a better offer, or a comment upon the terms of the offer, is ordinarily not a counteroffer [i.e., does not terminate the offeree's power to accept]. . . .

Remember too (from section B above) that even a true counteroffer does not act as a rejection if the offeror or offeree expressly makes plain that such should not be so. Combining the two precepts, we arrive at this more comprehensive rule:*(1) A counteroffer ordinarily operates as a rejection, unless the offeror or offeree makes plain that such is not the case, but (2) a mere inquiry as to a change in the offeror's proposal is neither a counteroffer nor a rejection.*[1]

QUESTION 3. On October 30, Tien brings a box full of silverware to Alex's store, "Shine, Sheen, and Polish."

(1) **Tien:** I'd like you to polish all of my silverware by November 1.
(2) **Alex:** I can do the job by November 5, for $75.
(3) **Tien:** What do you think about November 3?
(4) **Alex:** No, I can't do that either. In fact, I've just realized that I can't do it, even, by November 5. How about November 7? Deal?
After Alex makes statement 4,

A. the parties have no contract, but Tien is empowered to accept Alex's offer to complete the job by November 5.
B. the parties have no contract, but Tien is empowered to accept Alex's offer to complete the job by November 7.
C. the parties have a contract requiring that Alex complete the job by November 5.
D. the parties have a contract requiring that Alex complete the job by November 7.

ANALYSIS. Characterize each communication as an invitation to deal, offer, counteroffer, rejection, revocation, inquiry, acceptance — or whatever. Then, for each conversation, assess the legal consequence.

Tien talks first: "I'd like you to polish all of my silverware by November 1." Arguably, that's an invitation to deal, and arguably it's an offer. Tien says nothing about price, but no communication is wholly complete as to all details. Recall the matter of gap fillers (Chapter 4, section C). The law (a court) might impute to Tien's statement an implied willingness to pay a *reasonable* price, or the "going price." On the other hand, it might not. We don't know. Whether Tien's first statement be an offer or invitation to deal is a question you must answer with your best, most thoughtful, educated guess (known also as your legal opinion).

---

1. [A] valid "acceptance must be absolute and unqualified." . . . A qualified acceptance constitutes a rejection terminating the offer; it is a new proposal or counter-offer which must be accepted by the former offeror now turned offeree before a binding contract results . . . "A mere inquiry regarding the possibility of different terms, a request for a better offer, or a comment upon the terms of the offer, is ordinarily not a counter-offer." Comdisco Inc. v. Xerox Corp., 930 F.2d 26 (9th Cir. 1991) (citations omitted).

Yet the answer doesn't matter. If Tien does make an offer, Alex doesn't accept it. Rather, with statement 2, Alex makes an offer of his own, complete with price. With statement 3, Tien poses a mere inquiry; Alex's offer remains effective, leaving Tien with power to accept it for so long as it lives. But with statement 4, it dies; Alex revokes and, simultaneously, makes a new offer proposing to finish the work by November 7.

After all is said, there stands: Alex's offer to complete the job by November 7 for $75. Tien has not accepted it, meaning the parties have formed no contract.

C and **D**, therefore, are wrong. **A** states that the parties have not formed a contract, but describes Tien's right to accept Alex's offer to complete the work by November 5. That offer died when Alex revoked it. **A** is wrong.

And **B?** It describes Alex's offer, open for Tien's acceptance, to finish the work by November 7. **B** is right.

D.   The Closer

QUESTION 4. Which altered conversation from Question 3 above would most likely mean that A and B form a contract?

A. (1) **Tien:** I'd like you to polish all of my silverware by November 1.
   (2) **Alex:** Why sure, let me check my calendar.

B. (1) **Tien:** I'd like you to polish all of my silverware by November 1.
   (2) **Alex:** Why sure, give me the silver.

C. (1) **Tien:** I'd like you to polish all of my silverware by November 1.
   (2) **Alex:** I can do the job by November 5, for $75.
   (3) **Tien:** I accept, but you must finish by November 3.

D. (1) **Tien:** I'd like you to polish all of my silverware by November 1.
   (2) **Alex:** I can do the job by November 5, for $75.
   (3) **Tien:** What do you think about November 3?
   (4) **Alex:** No, I'm afraid not. In fact, I've just realized that I can't do it, even by November 5. I can do it by November 7. Okay?
   (5) **Tien:** No. I accept your initial offer—November 5.

ANALYSIS.   **A, C,** and **D** report conversations that plainly terminate without offer and acceptance. **B** is questionable. As earlier discussed, Tien's proposal, missing a price term, might be an offer and might be only an invitation to deal. If it's an offer, then—in that case—Alex—clearly accepts it with his response, "why sure, give me the silver." We can't confidently conclude that **B** creates a contract, for there remains an arguable question (an "issue") as to how we should characterize Tien's first statement. *Arguably*, it's an offer, meaning, *arguably*, that the parties formed a contract. **B** isn't perfect, but it's better than **A**, **C**, or **D**. **B** is right.

Silver & Hochberg's Picks

1.	**D**
2.	**A**
3.	**B**
4.	**B**
5.	**B**

8

When Acceptance, Revocation, and Rejection Take Effect

A. Acceptance Is Effective on Dispatch; Revocation and Rejection on Receipt

On Monday, A telephones B and makes her an offer. On Tuesday, B writes and mails a letter to A, expressing her assent. On Wednesday, not yet knowing of the letter, A telephones B and says, "I revoke." B protests: "I've already accepted—by letter mailed yesterday." A responds, "I haven't received it. Again, I revoke."

Now let's ask: Did A effectively revoke, or did he speak too late? Now let's answer: *Acceptance is effective when dispatched by the offeree, whereas revocation and rejection are not effective until received by the offeror or offeree, as the case may be.* Regarding acceptance, Restatement (Second) of Contracts §63(a) provides:

> [A]n acceptance . . . [is effective] as soon as put out of the offeree's possession, without regard to whether it ever reaches the offeror.

Regarding revocation, Restatement (Second) §42 provides:

> An offeree's power of acceptance is terminated when the offeree receives from the offeror a manifestation of an intention not to enter into the proposed contract.

Regarding rejection, Restatement (second) Contracts § 40 tells us:

> Rejection or counteroffer [sent] by mail . . . does not terminate the power of acceptance until received by the offeror[.]

Now let's ask: When is a rejection or revocation "received"? Now let's answer: *One receives a rejection or revocation orally made when the relevant sound reaches her ear. One receives a written revocation or rejection when it reaches a destination at which she, in ordinary course, receives communications.* When ordinary mail arrives in one's mailbox, she "receives" it. When an email arrives in one's "inbox," she receives it. When a message churns through one's fax machine, she "receives" it. And, by the same logic, when a message is left on one's voicemail, she "receives" it. Furthermore, one "receives" each such communication regardless of when or whether ever she reads or hears it. Restatement (Second) §68 provides:

> A written revocation [or] rejection . . . is received when the writing comes into the possession of the person addressed, or of some person authorized by him to receive it for him, or when it is deposited in some place which he has authorized as the place for this or similar communications to be deposited for him.

Back to Parties A and B

When B dropped her letter in a mailbox, she accepted A's offer and the parties formed a contract. Notwithstanding that on Wednesday A knew nothing of the letter, he had no power to revoke; B had accepted his offer. Concomitantly, when B mailed her letter and thus accepted the offer, she lost her power to reject. If, before her letter reached A, she had changed her mind, telephoned A, and announced her rejection, she would accomplish nothing.

QUESTIONS 1 & 2. On May 1, Hal tells Gretta, "I'd like you to install my new Betaline video system. When might you do it, and what would you charge?" Gretta responds, "I can do the work on May 9 for $250." Hal replies, "Let me think it over," to which Gretta says, "Fine." On May 2, Gretta writes, dates, and drops in the mail a letter addressed to Hal: "Sorry, I can't install your Betaline system." On May 3, Hal writes, dates, and drops in the mail a letter addressed to Gretta: "I accept your offer." On May 4, Hal receives Gretta's May 2 letter of revocation. On May 5, Gretta receives Hal's May 3 letter of acceptance.

QUESTION 1. On May 2, just after Gretta deposits in the mail a letter of revocation, her offer to Hal

A. remains effective because the letter has not yet reached Hal.
B. remains effective because Hal has had no reasonable opportunity to read the letter.

> **C.** is no longer effective because the letter constitutes a revocation.
> **D.** is no longer effective because she no longer intends to honor it.

ANALYSIS.   Gretta's May 2 letter announces a revocation; it operates when *received* by Hal. On May 2, therefore, the offer remains effective, which eliminates **C** and **D**. According to **C**, Gretta's offer terminates because her letter revokes it. That's wrong; the letter is ineffective until Hal receives it. **D** states that the offer terminates because Gretta no longer *intends* to honor it. That's contrary to law. An offeror's *intent* to terminate her offer means nothing. Revocation requires a *communication*, received by the offeree.

   A and **B** correctly conclude that the offer remains effective, but as to reasoning, one is right and the other wrong. According to **B**, the offer lives on because Hal has had no reasonable opportunity to read Gretta's letter. That's not the law. Revocation is effective as soon as the offeree *receives* it, whether or not he has had the opportunity to give it his attention, and whether or not he ever does so. **B** is wrong. **A** tells us that the offer survives because, as of May 2, Gretta's letter has not reached Hal, meaning he has not *received* it. That's the law. **A** is right.

QUESTION 2. These parties form a contract

A. on May 3.
B. on May 4.
C. on May 5.
D. not at all.

ANALYSIS.   On May 3, Hal dispatches his acceptance wherefore, on that day, the parties form a contract. That's so, even though Hal receives Gretta's revocation before Gretta receives his acceptance. Acceptance is effective on *dispatch* — in this case, on May 3. Revocation is effective on *receipt* — in this case, on May 4. Hal's acceptance precedes Gretta's revocation, and the parties form a contract.

   Now, it's simple. Since these parties did create a contract, **D** is wrong. Because they did so not on May 4 or 5, but on May 3, **C** and **D** are wrong. That means **A** is right.

B.   Exception: Acceptance That Follows Rejection Is *Not* Effective on Dispatch

Suppose (1) on Monday A makes an offer to B, (2) on Tuesday, B dispatches to A this first message: "I reject your offer," (3) on Wednesday, B dispatches to A this second message: "I've changed my mind. I accept." When an offeree sends out those two messages in *that* order, the acceptance is *not* effective on dispatch. Rather, the message that first reaches the offeror dictates the outcome. If B receives the acceptance on Thursday and the rejection on Friday, the acceptance governs, the parties form a contract, and the purported rejection is a nullity. If, however, B receives the rejection on Thursday and the acceptance on Friday, the rejection governs. The offer terminates and the parties form no contract. When, on Friday, the acceptance arrives, it acts as a new offer from A to B (akin to a counteroffer). Regarding acceptance, then, the whole of the rule is this: *Acceptance is effective on dispatch, unless the offeree first dispatches a rejection and then an acceptance, in which case, the message first received by the offeror dictates the outcome.* Restatement (Second) §40 states it (clumsily) thus:

> [A written] . . . acceptance started after the sending of an otherwise effective rejection . . . is only a counter-offer unless the acceptance is received by the offeror before he receives the rejection or counter-offer.

These Restatement folk — this coterie of dreadful draftsmen, mean to tell us that — *if*, in response to an offer, the offeree first dispatches, as message 1, a rejection (or counteroffer) and subsequently dispatches as message 2, an acceptance, *then* — (1) the parties form a contract if the offeror first receives the acceptance, but (2) the offer dies if he first receives the rejection. The would-be acceptance becomes a new offer from (original) offeree to (original) offeror.

QUESTION 3. Eve builds furniture. Ray wants her to make him a desk, the work to be done in his home, with wood that he supplies. Throughout September, the parties discuss the desk in great detail and Ray tells Eve that he wants to have it by November 1. On September 30, the parties fully, finally, and precisely identify the dimensions, design, and specifications suitable to Ray's needs. On October 1, Eve mails to Ray this six-word message: "I will build it for $1,000." On October 5, the message reaches Ray's mailbox and Ray reads it. On October 6, he mails a three-word response: "That's too much." On October 7, Ray writes again and mails to Eve this four-word message: "On reconsideration, I accept." Eve receives the October 6 mailing on October 9, and the October 7 mailing on October 10. She telephones Ray and says, " I have changed my mind. I won't build the desk." Have Eve and Ray formed a contract?

A. No; Eve's October 1 mailing lacks the specificity necessary to an offer.
B. No; although each made an offer, neither made an acceptance.
C. Yes; their September discussions implicitly add all necessary specificity to their October communications.
D. Yes; all of their communications, taken together, manifest mutual assent to a bargain.

ANALYSIS. Acceptance, 'tis said, is effective on dispatch. In truth, that is so when the offeree's attempt to accept "races against" the offeror's attempt to revoke (as in questions 1 and 2 above). But it's not so when an offeree's rejection races with his own subsequent attempt to accept. In that case, the law gives effect to the message that first reaches the offeror.

After receiving Eve's offer, Ray dispatched a rejection and then an acceptance. Eve first received the rejection and the offer met its end. On Friday, Eve received the (would-be) acceptance, but it served only as an offer which, by telephone, she rejected. The parties formed no contract.

Examine choices **A** and **C**. It is true, as **C** implies, that the October communications were, on their face, devoid of specificity. Standing on their own, they would amount only to chatter (like Fay's and Mort's interaction in Chapter 2, section C, Question 1). It's true too, as **C** suggests, that the parties should certainly have understood their October communications to incorporate the details they identified on September 30. Hence, Eve's October 1 message was an offer, and **A** is wrong. But the offer never spawned a contract because Ray rejected it on October 6. **C** is wrong too.

D states that the October communications, all together, manifest "mutual assent" to a bargain. They don't. They embody two offers but no effective acceptance.

And **B?** It correctly states that the parties form no contract because their communications embody (1) Eve's offer, rejected by Ray and (2) Ray's offer rejected by Eve. Each party made an offer, but neither accepted. **B** is right.

C.   Revocation by Indirect Message

Effective revocation requires no *direct* communication from offeror to offeree. If an offeree learns not from the offeror but from some other source that the offeror will not honor her offer, then the offer is effectively revoked.

Colin and Dorothy

On November 1, Dorothy learns that she'll need a chauffeur on the evening of November 17. On November 2, she contacts Colin, who offers to provide the service for $300, stating that for five days his offer will stand firm and irrevocable. By law therefore, Colin's offer will expire on November 7 unless, before that day, Colin revokes it or Dorothy rejects. (Remember that until an offeree accepts, an offeror may freely revoke his offer even if he promises that he won't. Chapter 6, section A.)

While Dorothy ponders the offer, she meets Arnesto, a trustworthy friend. Arnesto tells her that he and Colin have formed a contract under which Colin will serve as Arnesto's chauffeur for all of November 17, day and night. Dorothy then knows (or, more precisely, *should know*) that Colin is no longer available to serve as her chauffeur on that day. Colin's offer is thus revoked, even though Colin himself did not communicate that fact to Dorothy.

Restatement (Second) §43 provides:

> An offeree's power of acceptance is terminated when the offeror takes definite action inconsistent with an intention to enter into the proposed contract and the offeree acquires reliable information to that effect.

After Colin made his offer to Dorothy, he took the "definite action" of forming a contract with Arnesto. That action is inconsistent with a plan to enter a contract with Dorothy. Furthermore, from Arnesto, Dorothy acquired reliable information of what Colin had done.

QUESTIONS 4 & 5. On July 1, by telephone, Dick offers to sell Domina 100,000 paper clips for $200, the clips to be delivered to Domina's address on August 1. Dick says, "my offer expires on July 10."

QUESTION 4. Suppose that on July 2 Domina learns from a reliable source that Dick has sold all his paper clips to another party. On July 2, Domina

A. loses her power to accept because Dick no longer has possession of the paper clips.

B. loses her power to accept because she ought to know that Dick is no longer willing to sell her the paper clips.

C. retains her power to accept because Dick has not himself communicated to her his intention to withdraw.

D. retains her power to accept because Dick's offer does not expire until July 10.

QUESTION 5. For this question assume that the event of July 2 (described in question 4) does not occur. Instead, on:

July 3: There sits in Domina's e-mail inbox a message from Dick advising her that he withdraws his offer.

July 5: Domina deposits in the U.S. mail, a signed letter, addressed to Dick: "I accept."

July 6: Domina reads Dick's July 3 e-mail.

July 8: Dick receives Domina's July 5 mailing.

Have Dick and Domina formed a contract?

A. Yes, as of July 5

B. Yes, as of July 8

C. No, because by July 5 Domina had lost her power to accept

D. No, because on July 6 Domina lost her power to accept

ANALYSIS.   On July 1, Dick made an offer which, he proclaimed, would expire on July 10. By law, Dick's statement meant only that his offer would expire on July 10, unless rejected or revoked before that date. Dick remained free to revoke at *any* time before Domina accepted (Chapter 2, section A). His promise to hold it irrevocable meant nothing. An offer is revoked when the offeree so informs the offeree or, when from some other source, the offeree learns that the offeror intends not to stand by his offer.

As for Question 4, on July 2, Domina acquired reliable information that Dick had sold his paper clips to another buyer. She should then have understood that he intends no longer to sell them to her. Dick's offer underwent revocation and Domina lost her power to accept.

Both choices **C** and **D** state that Dorothy retained her power of acceptance, which she did not. As for a reason, **C** tells us that Dick did not personally advise Domina that he had withdraw his offer. Such reasoning is erroneous since, as we now know, an offer may be revoked without any communication from offeror to offeree, so long as the offeree somewhere acquires reliable information that the offeror will not honor his offer. **C** is wrong. **D** cites as a reason that Dick's offer, by its terms, would not expire until July 10. Wrong. *Unless and until it is accepted, an offer is revocable even if the offeror states otherwise.* Dick's offer is revocable for so long as Domina does not accept it.

Both **A** and **B** correctly tell us that Domina loses her power to accept. As its reason, **A** states that "Dick is no longer in possession" of the paper clips. That Dick *parts* with possession of the paper clips does not by itself revoke his offer. Rather, the offer undergoes revocation when and because Domina acquires reliable information to that effect. Choice **B** correctly explains that the offer is revoked because Domina *learns* that Dick has disposed of the paper clips. Hence, **A** is wrong and **B** is right.

As for Question 5, Dick made an offer on July 1. On July 3, he dispatched a revocation, not by U.S. mail, but by *email*, meaning that Domina received it immediately—a moment (or two) after its dispatch. Hence, on July 3, Dick's offer died. Domina's (purported) acceptance, mailed on July 5, had no effect. For on that day Domina had no offer on her "table."

A and **B** tell us that the parties did form a contract. That's wrong. Both **C** and **D** correctly state that the parties failed to form a contract because Domina lost her power of acceptance. According to D, Domina lost it *on* July 6—the date on which she read Dick's message. That's wrong too. Dick's revocation took effect on July 3, when Donna received it. According to C, Domina "had" lost her power to accept "by" July 5. That's why the parties formed no contract, and that's why **C** is right.

D.   The Closers

On October 1, Bella spoke with Sally:

> **October 1, Bella:** I have a large document that I want you to photo-copy. It's 50,000 pages, and I need 10 copies. Can you do it?
> **Sally:** Oh, I think so, certainly. Let me get back to you with a price and timetable.
> **October 4, Sally (by fax):** Regarding the job: I can complete it by October 10 for $15,000.

On that same day at 1 P.M., Bella composed this signed writing: "Thanks. I'll bring you the document tomorrow morning, October 5." Bella attempted to transmit her writing by fax, but her fax machine did not function.

QUESTION 6. Assume that Bella took the document to a hand courier. At 1:20 P.M. she paid the courier his $15 fee, and he promised to deliver the writing to Sally's office before 3:00. Bella returned to her own office. At 2:00 the courier set out for Sally's office. At 2:30 before he arrived, Sally telephoned Bella:

> **Sally:** I can't do the copy job.
> **Bella:** I've already accepted your offer with a message that you'll receive by hand delivery.
> **Sally:** I don't have it. As I said, I withdraw the offer.

Bella sues Sally alleging breach of contract. Sally responds by asserting that the parties never formed a contract because she effectively revoked her offer. Among the following, which represents a judicial decision most consistent with law?

A. When Sally sent Bella her fax of October 4, she accepted Bella's offer. Consequently, the parties formed a contract.

B. When Bella left her document with the courier, she accepted Sally's offer. Consequently, the parties formed a contract.

C. When Sally announced her revocation, she had no notice of Bella's writing. Consequently, the parties did not form a contract.

D. Bella took no action in reliance on the agreement, and Sally's withdrawal caused her no harm. Consequently, the parties did not form a contract.

ANALYSIS.   Begin here: (1) When an offeree accepts an offer the parties form a contract and the offeror can no longer revoke; (2) Acceptance is effective on dispatch or—as the Restatement tells us—when "put out of the offeree's possession." On October 1, the parties exchanged invitations to deal. At noon on October 4, Sally made an offer, and by 2:00 the courier was bound for her office, Bella's writing in hand. Bella, therefore, had dispatched her acceptance; she had put it out of her possession. By 2:00, the parties had formed a contract, and Sally lost her power to revoke.

A states that Sally accepted Bella's "offer" by faxing her on October 4. That's wrong because Bella never made an offer. On October 1, Bella asked whether Sally might provide the service she needed. Bella did not put forth detail sufficient to create an offer. She made only an invitation to deal. It was *Sally* who, on October 4, made an offer.

C observes that Sally had no notice of Bella's acceptance, an irrelevant fact (in this case). Whether known to Sally or not, Bella's letter worked an acceptance *when dispatched.*

D raises another irrelevancy: that Sally attempted to revoke her offer when Bella had not relied on the "agreement." If two parties undergo offer and acceptance, *they form a contract* whether either relies on it or not.

When Bella deposited her letter with the courier, she put it out of her possession and thus accepted Sally's offer. The parties formed a contract, and Sally lost her power to revoke. Hence, **B** is right.

QUESTION 7. Assume now that when Bella discovered she could not fax her message, she took it at 1:20 P.M. to Binko's Fax Service. There she found a long line of customers waiting to use Binko's only working fax machine. Rather than join the line, Bella left her document with Rob, a Binko employee. She paid Rob Binko's $2 fee and supplied him with Sally's fax number. Bob promised to dispatch the document as soon as the machine was available. Bella returned to her office, and at 2:00 telephoned Binko's. Rob answered, and Bella asked, "Have you faxed the document?" "No, not yet," Bob answered. "Do you still want me to do so?" "Yes, definitely," said Bella, to which Rob replied, "We'll send it by 2:30." At 2:15 Sally telephoned Bella:

> **Sally:** I can't do your copy job.
> **Bella:** I've already accepted your offer with a signed writing that I left with Binko's. You'll have it by fax within fifteen minutes.
> **Sally:** I don't have it now and, again, I withdraw my offer.

Bella sues Sally alleging breach of contract. Sally responds by asserting that the parties never formed a contract because she effectively revoked her offer. Among the following, which represents a judicial decision most consistent with law?

> **I.** Bella accepted Sally's offer when she paid Binko's fee and left her writing to be faxed. Consequently, by 2:15 P.M. she had accepted Sally's offer. Sally's revocation was ineffective.
>
> **II.** For so long as Binko's had not yet sent Bella's message by fax, Bella retained the right to countermand her instruction and to have the document returned to her. Consequently, at 2:15 P.M., she had *not* accepted Sally's offer, and Sally effectively revoked it.
>
> **A.** I
> **B.** II
> **C.** Both I and II
> **D.** Neither I nor II

ANALYSIS.   The issue is whether Bella had accepted Sally's offer by 2:15 on October 4. The relevant *rule* is clear, but the result is not. Acceptance is effective when "put out of the offeree's possession." As to the meaning of that phrase, this case raises an issue: When Bella left her letter with Binko's, did she "put it "out of her possession"? Bella's lawyer might argue: "My client did certainly part with physical possession of her letter. She moved it from her own hands into Binko's. Moreover, she left Binko's premises and returned to her office. At 2:15 Binko's had the letter. Bella did not. It was out of her possession, and her acceptance was complete."

Sally's lawyer might argue: "For so long as Binko's had not sent the message to Sally, Bella had the right to abort its dispatch. She had the right to telephone Rob and direct him not to send it. The writing thus remained in Bella's control and hence in her "possession." For that reason, Bella had not, by 2:15, accepted Sally's offer. Sally's revocation was effective."

Both positions are credible; neither is "right" until a judge chooses between them. Knowing not which argument a judge will endorse and knowing that both have merit, we see that **C** is correct.

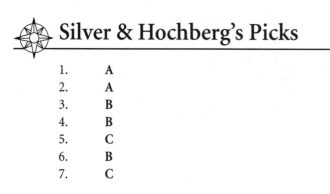 ## Silver & Hochberg's Picks

1.	**A**
2.	**A**
3.	**B**
4.	**B**
5.	**C**
6.	**B**
7.	**C**

9

Mode or Manner of Acceptance; Unilateral and Bilateral Contracts

A.   Master or Mistress of the Offer

As taught in Chapter 2, section D, acceptance is the offeree's unconditional assent to the offeror's proposed bargain. One might attempt to communicate her assent in varied mode or manner including mail, fax, smoke signal, drumbeat, talk, wink, or nod. All of that raises this question: Does the law place limits on the mode or manner in which the offeree may effectively express her assent?

The answer is "yes." Traditional common law provides that in making his offer, the offeror may impose on the offeree any requirements he chooses as to mode or manner of acceptance. If the offeror requires that the offeree accept by writing, sent in ordinary postal mail, then no other expression of assent will suffice. If the offeror requires a certified letter, then such is required for the offeree's acceptance. If the offeror requires acceptance by telephone, e-mail, fax, blast of horn, or bark of dog,—the offeree who expresses assent by any other means fails to accept. That common law rule—that the offeror is empowered to decree the mode or manner by which the offeree may accept—often goes by this unfortunate shorthand: "The offeror is master of his offer" (or, as modernized (by *us*), "The offeror is master or mistress of the offer.") That ill-born expression means that the offeror is master or mistress *of the manner by which the offeree may accept.*

Viewed in full, Restatement (Second) of Contracts §50(1) states that rule in its last nine words:

> Acceptance of an offer is a manifestation of assent to the terms thereof made by the offeree *in a manner invited or required by the offer.*

Further, Restatement (Second) §60 provides:

> If an offer prescribes the place, time or manner of acceptance, its terms in this respect must be complied with in order to create a contract.

That provision, too, reflects the common law rule that the "offeror is master or mistress of the offer."

B.   When the Offeror Does Not Designate a Mode of Acceptance

Most offerors do not exercise their power as "master" or "mistress." Most are silent as to how the offeree should accept. Suppose that in a signed writing, sent by ordinary mail, Andrew offers to redesign Zelda's patio deck for $10,000, the work to be finished by September 10. Andrew writes not a word about how Zelda should accept, and so raises this question: If Zelda does wish to accept, how does she do so?

The common law provides that: *When the offeror imposes no requirements as to the mode or manner in which the offeree must accept, then the offeree may do so in any way that is reasonable under the prevailing circumstances.* Restatement (Second) §30(2) states:

> Unless otherwise indicated by the language or the circumstances, an offer invites acceptance in any manner and by any medium reasonable in the circumstances.

The law presumes it reasonable that an offeree accept in the same mode or manner as that in which the offeror made his offer. Restatement (Second) §60 states it this way:

> Unless circumstances known to the offeree indicate otherwise, a medium of acceptance is reasonable if it is the one used by the offeror[.]

Otherwise, the question of what is reasonable normally belongs to the jury.

Andrew made his offer by signed writing and expressed no requirement as to how Zelda might accept. That means Zelda may accept in any manner reasonable under the circumstances. Probably, therefore, she may accept by telephone call, e-mail, fax message, or face-to-face statement. Certainly and absolutely she may accept by signed letter sent via ordinary mail, for that is the means by which Andrew made his offer.

> **QUESTION 1.** By signed writing sent and delivered by ordinary U.S. mail, TonCo offers to purchase from DumpCo 500 refuse collection trucks, each one for $290,000. In its last sentence TonCo writes, "Please let us know if you wish to accept." DumpCo wants to accept and asks its attorney by what mode or manner it should do so. Wanting to give Tonco the best possible advice, the attorney should suggest that acceptance be made with a:
>
> **A.** hand-delivered message to TonCo's receptionist.
> **B.** signed writing sent by fax.
> **C.** signed writing sent by ordinary U.S. mail.
> **D.** telephone voice-mail message, followed by a signed writing sent via fax.

ANALYSIS. If an offer expressly prescribes the manner in which the offeree may accept, the offeree may accept only that way. If, as is usual, the offer makes no such prescription, the offeree may accept in any manner "reasonable" under the circumstances.

Every choice, **A** through **D** likely describes a reasonable mode of acceptance. Yet we're asked to name the one that's best. If an offeror states nothing as to how his offeree should accept, then it's reasonable, always, that the offeree do so in the manner used by the offeror in making the offer. **C** names the mode of communication that the offeror used in making its offer. Hence, among the options, **C** is best. And if it's best, then it's right.

C. Bilateral and Unilateral Contracts: What They Are and How They Differ

Suppose Anthony offers to pay Barbara $500 to install software. Barbara accepts, and the parties form a contract. At the moment they do so, each party has an unfulfilled duty to the other. Anthony has yet to pay the $500. Barbara has yet to install the software. In legalese, an unfulfilled contractual obligation is an "executory duty." Both these parties, therefore, have executory duties. Stated another way, "the contract is executory on both sides."

When Barbara installs the software, the contract ceases to be executory on her side. It is executory on Andrew's side only. When Andrew pays Barbara, the contract is no longer executory at all. Both parties have fulfilled their duties.[1]

Think back now to the moment at which these two formed their contract—the moment at which Barbara accepted Andrew's offer. The contract was, then, executory on both sides. That means it was a "bilateral contract": *A bilateral contract is a contract which, at the moment of formation, is executory on both sides.* When Barbara installs the software, the parties have a "bilateral contract executory on Andrew's side only." We name the contract, still, "bilateral" because at the moment of formation it *was* executory on both sides.

Aren't *All* Contracts Executory on Both Sides At the Moment They're Formed?

Surprisingly—no. Suppose Maria says to Charles, "I'll pay you $50 to remove all snow from my driveway. You may accept only by *doing the job*—all of it—by removing all snow from my driveway. Do that and you will accept my offer. Fail to do that and you won't." Charles, of course, is free to begin the work or not. Even if he does begin, he's free to finish or walk away. If he finishes, then and only then—at that very moment—does he accept Maria's offer. Only *then*—at *that* moment—do the parties form a contract.

Suppose Charles begins shoveling at 4:00 and removes the driveway's last little snow crystal two hours later, at 6:00. At that moment, he accepts Maria's offer and the parties form a contract. Curiously, *that contract requires nothing of Charles.*

Why Not? *How* Not?

In allowing Charles to accept her offer only by *doing* all that she asks of him, Maria leaves Charles free to begin or not the shoveling of snow. Even if he does begin, he's free to finish or walk away because, Maria, the "mistress of her offer" allowed Charles to accept only by removing all snow from her driveway. The way that Maria has "set it up," the parties form a contract if and when Charles completes work, not a moment before. At 6:00 Charles does complete the work and there occur, simultaneously, these two events: (1) the parties form a contract, and (2) Charles completes his part of it. Consequently and curiously, the contract, from the instant it's born, leaves Charles without any duty at all. And *that* means the parties form a "unilateral contract": *A unilateral contract arises when an offeror allows an offeree to accept only by full performance; from the moment of formation the contract is executory only on the offeror's part.*

---

1. It is, perhaps, oxymoronic to speak of a "contract no longer executory on anyone's part." For if both contracting parties fulfill all of their duties the contract, in a sense, ceases to exist. As to that lego-philosophical question, we can offer only this: If and only if a "dead person" is a *person*, then a "contract executory on nobody's part"—*is* a contract.

QUESTION 2. By fax, MoveCo makes SpaceCo this offer: "We'll handle all of your shipping needs for one full year if you'll allow us to store in your warehouse all of our excess inventory. Agreed?" By fax, SpaceCo responds, "Agreed." The parties have formed a:

A. unilateral contract, because the decision to accept the offer was left unilaterally in SpaceCo's hands.

B. unilateral contract, because MoveCo did not limit the means by which SpaceCo might accept.

C. bilateral contract, because when SpaceCo sent its fax, each party acquired a duty to the other.

D. bilateral contract, because when MoveCo received SpaceCo's fax, each party acquired a duty to the other.

ANALYSIS. To determine that two parties create a bilateral or unilateral contract, identify the moment of formation—the moment of acceptance—and ask yourself: "*At* that moment, is the contract (a) executory on both sides, or (b) executory on the offeror's side only? If the answer is (a), the parties form a bilateral contract. If it's (b) they form a unilateral contract.

Because acceptance is (generally) effective on dispatch, this contract arose when MoveCo *sent* SpaceCo its fax, "Agreed." At that moment, neither party had completed (or begun) performance. MoveCo owed service to SpaceCo, and SpaceCo owed service to MoveCo. From its formation, the contract was executory on both sides, wherefore the parties formed a bilateral contract.

A, **B**, and **C** are wrong because they tells us the parties have formed a unilateral contract. **A** gives this reason: the decision to accept the offer was left "unilaterally" with SpaceCo. *Every* offer leaves the offeree with the power to accept or not. For so long as an offer lives, the offeree is free to accept it or not, a fact that's irrelevant to the difference between bilateral and unilateral contracts. The question writer hopes that in some befuddled way you'll fix on the word "unilaterally" and select this very wrong answer. Don't do it. Bear in mind the *meaning* for which you're searching: that the contract is bilateral because, at the instant of formation, it leaves each party with a duty owed to the other.

B correctly indicates that MoveCo placed no limit on how SpaceCo might accept its offer. That fact suggests the creation of a *bi*lateral contract. After all, if an offeree is free to accept by any reasonable mode, he need not accept by full performance, and acceptance by full performance is the *sine qua non* of unilateral contract.

C correctly describes the contract as bilateral, but gives as its reason that the offeror and offeree sent their communications by identical modes. *That* doesn't make for a bilateral contract. A bilateral contract is one in which both parties, at the outset, have unfulfilled duties.

D correctly states that the parties formed a bilateral contract, but its reason is wrong. Acceptance is effective on dispatch. The contract arose not when MoveCo received SpaceCo's fax, but when SpaceCo *sent* it. That distinction represents the only difference between choices **D** and **C**. Because of that difference, **D** is wrong and **C** is right.

QUESTION 3. Isaac makes an offer to Joan: "If you'll type my manuscript, I'll pay you $6,000." Joan responds: "If I want to accept, how shall I do so?" To that, Isaac says: "You may accept by doing the work—all of it; that's the only way." Thereafter Joan does type Isaac's manuscript, fully and properly. The parties thus form a

A. unilateral contract, since on making her acceptance Joan is free of further obligation.
B. unilateral contract, since only Joan is called on to deliver an actual service.
C. unilateral contract, since only Isaac is required to make a payment of money.
D. bilateral contract, since the two parties are mutually bound only upon Joan's completion of performance.

ANALYSIS.   Identify the point at which the parties form their contract and ask: "At that moment, (a) does each party owe a duty to the other, or (b) does only the offeror owe a duty to the offeree?" If the answer is (a), the parties create a bilateral contract. If it's (b), they create a unilateral contract.

Isaac allows Joan to accept only by fully performing the work he wants of her. When Joan does that, the parties form their contract. At that moment, offeror Isaac owes Joan her payment, but offeree Joan owes Isaac nothing. From its inception, the contract is executory on the offeror's side only; it's a unilateral contract. The right answer will reach that conclusion for that reason.

D tells us that the parties formed a bilateral contract, so it's wrong. Further, **D** gives as its reason that the parties are mutually bound (which means "form a contract") only when Jane completes her performance. That's the very reason that these parties form a *unilateral* contract. **B** reaches the right conclusion for the wrong reason. The parties form a unilateral contract, it states, because only one party is required to deliver "service." It's true that only Joan delivers service (and that Isaac must pay money). That, however, means nothing to the difference between unilateral and bilateral contracts. **C** makes the reciprocal error, suggesting that a contract is a unilateral one if only one party is required to pay money. That, too, is false.

A—happy day—is right. The contract is a unilateral one for this reason: When offeree Jane made her acceptance, and thus formed the contract, she owed to Isaac, the offeror, no duty. Her acceptance *was* her performance. **A** is right.

D.   Unilateral and Bilateral Contracts: Vocabulary and Warning

Know the meaning of "offer for a unilateral contract." It refers to an offer which, if accepted, creates a unilateral contract. Hence: *An offer for a unilateral contract is an offer in which the offeror allows the offeree to accept only by delivering all (not part) of the performance asked of her.* If the offeree does complete that performance, then in the same instant there occur three events: (1) the offeree fulfills her side of the exchange, (2) the contract arises, and (3) an executory duty is created on the offeror's side only.

If an offeror allows his offeree to accept by doing anything *other* than fully performing her side of the bargain, he makes an offer for a bilateral contract. If he allows the offeror to accept by word, writing, smoke signal, e-mail, he makes an offer for a bilateral contract, because the resulting contract subjects each party to a duty owed to the other. If the offeror permits the offeree to accept by completing *half* her performance, he makes an offer for a bilateral contract. If and when the offeree completes half her performance, the contract arises. It leaves the offeree with an obligation, still, to furnish the second half of her performance, and it leaves the offeror with the duty, still, to furnish all of his performance. From the moment it arises, it is executory on both sides.

Watch Out for These Misleading Phrases: "Promise in Exchange for an Act" and "Promise in Exchange for a Promise"

Many authorities (and teachers) carelessly describe an offer for a unilateral contract as one in which the offeror puts forth his "promise in exchange for an act." They describe an offer for a bilateral contract as one in which the offeror puts forth his "promise in exchange for a promise." Those statements are misleading and misconceived, so we'll correct them.

Suppose Beth says to David, "I'll pay you $200 to install my stereo components and my computer system. You may accept by fully installing both the stereo and computer systems." In response, David installs both systems. Beth required that David accept by completing *all* that her offer asked — by installing both the computer and stereo systems. When he completed both jobs, David accepted the offer, and the parties formed a contract. At the moment of formation, the contract was executory only on Beth's part; she was obliged to pay him. David owed Beth nothing because, at the moment he accepted and formed the contract, he completed all that it required of him. The parties formed a unilateral contract — a contract that from the moment of formation was executory only on the offeror's side.

Now suppose Beth says to David, "I'll pay you $200 to install my stereo components and my computer system. You may accept by fully installing *just* the stereo components." Beth requires that David accept her offer by performing *an* act, but not by performing, fully, his part of the proposed bargain. Suppose David installs the stereo equipment. By doing so, he accepts the offer and the parties form their contract. At that moment, each party owes a duty to the other. David must, still, install the computer system, and Beth must, still, pay him. Hence, the parties form a bilateral contract, *even though the offer required the offeree to accept by performing an act.*

QUESTION 4. Frank was a puppeteer. Evelyn telephoned him and the parties spoke:

(1) **Evelyn:** My little boy is turning two. Will you present a puppet show at the party I'm holding that day?

(2) **Frank:** *What* day?

(3) **Evelyn:** Saturday, September 28, my home: 459 Urbana Way, Munsey.

(4) **Frank:** Yes, I'm available at any time that day. My show is 20 minutes long and my fee is $350. If you wish to contract with me, send a check for one-half that amount. The remainder will be due after I conclude the show on September 28.

(5) **Evelyn:** I accept right now; it's a deal.

Frank and Evelyn have formed:

A. a unilateral contract, because there remains only on Frank's part the duty to deliver a performance; Evelyn is obliged only to pay money.

B. a bilateral contract, because Frank's proposal calls on each party to provide some performance to the other.

C. no contract, because the offeree has not accepted the offer.

D. no contract, because neither party has made an offer to the other.

ANALYSIS.   With statements 1 through 3, the parties conduct a negotiation. All of their statements are invitations to deal. None is an offer.

With statement 4, Frank makes an offer. In light of all circumstances (including, notably, statements 1 through 3), Evelyn should understand that Frank has made a reasonably definite proposal, awaiting her assent. He proposes to deliver a puppet show in a specified place, for a specified fee, on a specified day, at any hour Evelyn might name.

Separately (and unlike most offerors), Frank exercised his privilege as master of the offer. He allowed Evelyn to accept only by sending him a check for a specified amount. With statement 5, Evelyn purported to accept, but not in the manner that Frank prescribed. Consequently, she failed to accept, and these parties formed no contract.

A and **B** tell us that the parties formed a contract, and they're wrong for that reason alone. Further, **A** states that the parties formed a unilateral contract because Frank had a duty to deliver a performance and Evelyn had only a duty to pay money. The truth is that neither party had any duty whatever because Evelyn failed to accept Frank's offer. **A** is misconceived for yet another reason. Suppose Frank had not prescribed any mode of acceptance. Evelyn's statement that she accepts "right now" would create a contract. It would leave Frank with the duty to deliver a puppet show and Evelyn with an obligation to pay. The contract, from its inception, would be executory on both sides — a bilateral contract.

B incorrectly implies that an offer ("proposal") calls for a bilateral contract if it proposes that each party take part in an exchange. That's an essential feature of *every* offer whether it contemplates a bilateral or unilateral contract. By definition, an offer proposes a *bargain*. Hence, *all* true offers call for an exchange — a quid pro quo — an "I'll do this if you'll do that." **B** is wrong.

D correctly concludes that the parties have formed no contract, but it falsely states that neither made an offer. Frank did make an offer, so **D** is wrong. With statement 5, Evelyn attempted to accept, but failed to answer the requirement that she do so by sending a check. Choice **C** tells us that the parties formed no contract and correctly states the reason: the offeree (Evelyn) did not accept Frank's offer. **C** is right.

E.   Offers for Unilateral vs. Bilateral Contracts: Why Do We Care?

The difference between an offer for a unilateral and bilateral contract relates only to this question: What must the offeree do to accept? That, in turn, calls for *construction of the offer*, and that's what the whole topic is (or should be) about.

The typical controversy in which the distinction is significant involves (1) an offer, (2) the offeree's *attempt* to accept, followed by either (3) the offeror's attempt to revoke or the offeree's attempt to reject. There then arises this question: Was the attempted revocation or rejection effective or did it come too late? That, in turn, raises this question: Was the attempted acceptance effective? And *that* question requires that we determine what the offer allows as to mode or manner of acceptance.

Suppose Marjorie says to David, "If you'll publish my advertisement, I'll pay $1,500." David replies, "I accept." Marjorie then says, "I've changed my mind, I withdraw my offer." Whether these parties formed a contract depends on the meaning, legally, of Marjorie's phrase, "If you'll publish my advertisement . . ." Does it (1) describe the performance Marjorie wants *and* the manner by which David may accept, or does it (2) identify only the performance sought without addressing the mode of acceptance?

Under older common law (before 1920 or so) an offer looked to a unilateral contract unless the language plainly and expressly allowed for an acceptance by some mode other than full performance. Older courts would have construed Marjorie's offer thus: "If you'll publish my advertisement, I'll pay $1,500. *To accept, you must publish the advertisement.*"

Modern common law takes the opposite view: Unless otherwise clearly and plainly stated, an offer permits acceptance by any mode reasonable under the circumstances (as already described above in section B). If the offeror demands acceptance by full performance, his offer must make that plain, clear, and explicit. He'll have to write or say something like: "You may accept only by complete performance," or "Our agreement takes effect only after you finish the performance described in this offer," or "I will not allow for acceptance by promise. Rather, I require performance." Marjorie made no such statement. Modern courts would construe her offer thus: "If you'll publish my advertisement, I'll pay $1,500. *You may accept this offer in any ordinary way including, of course, the way in which I've made the offer—by simple speech.*"

QUESTION 5. On September 15, Jonathan and Mandy start to exchange signed writings:

(1) **September 15, Jonathan:** I wish to have you repave the parking lot located at my business facility on 100 Grande Street, work to be done, please, this Saturday, September 19. There will be no one on the premises that day, so you'll be able to work without interference. I will pay $25,000 on completion. I am interested in real performance, not empty promises. Please respond.

(2) **September 16, Mandy:** I understand your needs and concerns. You have my solemn promise that I'll complete the work you have requested on September 19; it's a deal.

(3) **September 17, Jonathan:** Thank you for your response, but I've decided not to repave the lots this year. I hope to be in touch with you in the future; my offer is withdrawn.

(4) **September 18, Mandy:** We formed a contract on the sixteenth; I intend to perform and expect you to pay.

On September 19, Mandy does fully and properly repave the parking lot. Have Mandy and Jonathan formed a contract?

A. Yes, because Jonathan's offer contemplated a unilateral contract, and on September 16 Mandy agreed to deliver full performance.

B. Yes, because on September 15 Jonathan plainly demanded acceptance by promise, and one day later, Mandy made the necessary promise.

C. No, because Jonathan's offer was for a unilateral contract, and by September 17 Mandy had not paved the lots to which Jonathan's offer referred.

D. No, because Jonathan's September 15 communication was silent as to mode of acceptance and therefore constituted not an offer but an invitation to deal.

ANALYSIS. The problem typifies those that concern the difference between the offer for a unilateral and bilateral contract. On September 15 Jonathan makes an offer, and on the 16th, Mandy assents to its terms. If the assent qualifies as an acceptance, the parties form a contract, and Jonathan's subsequent attempt to revoke is ineffective. If, on the other hand, Mandy's assent is not an acceptance, the parties form no contract. Jonathan effectively revokes on the 17th, and Mandy loses her power to accept. (The work she performs on the 19th is without consequence in *contract* law per se, but it might leave Mandy with an action for "unjust enrichment"/"quasi-contract" (Chapter 28, section B)).

Whether Mandy effectively accepted Jonathan's offer depends on whether Jonathan (a) allowed her to accept by promise, as she attempted to do, or (b) required that she accept by full performance, as, by September 17, she did not do. In legalese, the question is whether Jonathan made "an offer for a unilateral contract," or "an offer for a bilateral contract." If the offer was for a unilateral contract, Jonathan effectively revoked before Mandy accepted. If it was for a bilateral contract, Mandy accepted before Jonathan tried to revoke.

Examine Jonathan's offer. It features no words like "if you wish to accept" or "you are required to accept in this way" or "you may accept by." *Arguably,* however, Jonathan required an acceptance by full performance when he wrote: "I am interested in real performance, not empty promises. Please respond." *Arguably,* Mandy should understand that to mean: "If you want to accept, you must deliver full performance; a promise will not suffice." *Arguably,* on the other hand, Mandy, as a reasonable person, would note that (1) the sentences do not in "black and white" demand acceptance by performance; (2) Jonathan expresses no contempt for promises in general, but only for "empty" ones; and (3) the words "please respond" suggest that he invites a verbal assent.

Whether these parties formed a contract is, therefore, open to argument. The answer might be "yes" and it might be "no," but neither is correct unless *accompanied by an appropriate rationale.* The correct answer will be akin to (a) "Yes, because Jonathan made an offer for a bilateral contract, and Mandy effectively accepted before he tried to revoke," or (b) "No, because Jonathan made an offer for a unilateral contract, and he revoked before Mandy fully performed." Knowing what we're looking for, let's examine the answer choices.

A and **B** say "yes." As its reason, **A** states that Jonathan's offer was for a unilateral contract and Mandy promised to perform. The reasoning is backwards. An offer for a unilateral contract does not create a contract when the offeree *promises* performance. Acceptance requires that she *actually* perform—fully. **B** reasons that Jonathan "plainly" demanded acceptance by promise and that Mandy gave the necessary promise. Maybe Jonathan *allowed* Mandy to accept by promise, but he did not "plainly" demand that she do so. **B** is weak—*very* weak.

Let's assess the "no" options. **D** tells us that Jonathan's first writing was silent as to mode of acceptance. Arguably, that's true. True or false, however, such silence would not negate the creation of an offer. To constitute an offer, a communication need *not* explicitly provide for a manner of acceptance. Failure to address mode of acceptance means, simply, that any reasonable mode will suffice. **D** rests on an erroneous premise; it's wrong.

We're left with **C**. "No," it states, the parties formed no contract. Why not?—because Jonathan's offer looked toward a unilateral contract and by September 17, the day on which Jonathan tried to revoke, Mandy had not accepted; she had not "paved the lots to which Jonathan's offer referred." **C** posits an offer for a unilateral contract and supplies the appropriate reasoning. **C** is right.

F.   Notice to the Offeror

Julia lives in New York but owns a rental home in New Mexico where a tenant resides. On December 31, her tenant vacates. Lei is Julia's longtime friend, living in New Mexico about 200 miles from the rental home. Julia wants Lei to inspect the rental property, arrange for any necessary repairs, clean the premises, and thus ready it for a new tenant. To that end, on January 1 she contacts Lei by telephone and says, "My tenant has moved out, so I'll pay you $1,000 if you'll travel to the rental home, inspect it, arrange for any necessary repairs, clean all of the rooms, and thus ready the house for a new tenant by January 10. You may accept only by doing all that I ask. Naturally, you may stay in the home as you complete all of this work." Lei responds, "Very well." She travels to the home and, by January 5, completes the work. She does not, however, contact Julia to notify her of that fact. Rather, Lei leaves New Mexico for a vacation overseas.

On January 10, Julia wants to know if Lei has or has not accepted her offer. For that purpose, she tries to reach Lei by telephone, fax, and e-mail. Receiving no response she finds herself "in a bind". If Lei *has* done the work, she and Julia have a contract, requiring that Julia pay her $1,000. If Lei has not done the work, Julia is free to hire another person to do it.

To spare an offeror that dilemma, modern common law provides: *Where an offeree who accepts by performance should understand that the offeror has no meaningful way to know that she has done so, she must notify the offeree that she has, in fact, performed. If, within reasonable time, she fails to give such notice, the offeror is discharged from his contractual obligation.*

Restatement (Second) §62(2) provides:

> If an offeree who accepts by rendering a performance has reason to know that the offeror has no adequate means of learning of the performance with reasonable promptness and certainty, the contractual duty of the offeror is discharged unless
>
>   (a) the offeree exercises reasonable diligence to notify the offeror of acceptance, or
>
>   (b) the offeror learns of the performance within a reasonable time, or

(c) the offer indicates that notification of acceptance is not required.

Lei gave her performance some 3,000 miles from Julia's location. She then departed the country. She ought to have recognized that Julia was without adequate means of learning that she had, in fact, readied the house for a new tenant. After some reasonable time passes and Lei fails, still, to notify Julia that she has done the work asked of her, Julia is discharged from her duty; she need not pay Lei.

QUESTION 6. Harry operates a horse farm in Colorado. Tom, his brother, lives in Connecticut. Dick is Tom's friend, living near Harry in Colorado. Both Tom and Dick know Harry as rather an irresponsible chap. In 2007, Harry urgently needs money and telephones Tom to ask for a loan. Tom then sends to Dick, this signed letter: "My brother Harry needs $100,000. If you make him a loan in that amount, I'll guarantee it; I'll repay you if he does not." Accept my offer by making the loan.

Dick does then immediately lend Harry $100,000, on the understanding that Harry will repay it in five years. Five years later in 2012, Harry fails to pay. Dick contacts Tom and demands that Tom pay him the $100,000 Harry owed. Tom refuses. Dick brings an action against Tom, alleging that Tom has breached a contractual duty to repay Harry's debt. Tom contends that he has no such duty. What additional fact, if proven, would best support Tom's position?

A. Dick made the loan to Harry, expecting that Harry would not be able to repay it.

B. At no time before 2012 did Dick inform Tom that he had made the loan to Harry.

C. In the past, Tom had guaranteed some of Harry's debts, and Harry had always repaid them.

D. When the five years expired, Harry, unable to repay the loan, promised that he would repay it after one additional year.

ANALYSIS. Tom required that Dick accept his offer by actually lending Harry $100,000; he made an offer for a unilateral contract. When Dick did that he accepted the offer and Tom acquired a contractual duty to pay Harry's debt if Harry himself failed to do so. Because Dick knew Harry to be an irresponsible fellow, he had reason to believe that Harry would not advise Tom of the loan. Tom was in a "bind" similar to Julia's. He lacked adequate means by which to learn that Dick had made the loan — no good way to know that Dick had accepted his offer. Consequently, Dick himself had an obligation to tell Tom that he had made the loan. With that, examine the options and find the facts that would most likely free Tom of his contractual duty.

A, **C**, and **D** cite matters of irrelevance. They describe no facts that would affect Tom's duty to pay Harry's debt. **B**, however, offers this: Dick did not advise Tom that he had made the loan. As just discussed, that fact discharges Harry's obligation. **B** is right.

G.   Reward Offers Look to Unilateral Contracts

From Chapter 3, section D, we know that the "power to accept" an offer rests only in an *offeree* and that one is an offeree only if, under the circumstances, he reasonably believes the offeror's proposal is made to *him*. The simplest of logic tells us that if one does not know, even, that some offer has been made, he cannot possibly think it was made to *him* and, therefore, cannot be an offeree. Keep that in mind.

From Chapter 5, section A, we know that an offer of reward *is* an offer. Further, all legal authorities agree that a reward offer is an offer for a unilateral contract. Even if the offeror does not so specify, one may accept only by doing, in full, what the offeror requests.

Suppose Offeror publishes this notice: "REWARD—$1,000 for safe return of LOST DOG. White poodle, answers to the name 'George,' lost near corner of Main and High Streets." The posting proposes a bargain in which Offeree is to return the lost dog and, in exchange, Offeror will pay $1,000. By law, one cannot accept the offer by *promising* to find and return the dog. Rather, in order to accept one must *actually find and return the dog*. By law, therefore, a reward offer is an offer for a unilateral contract. If and when some person does return the dog then, simultaneously, he (1) accepts the offer, (2) performs his part of the bargain, and (3) leaves the contract just formed executory only on the offeror's part; it remains only for the offeror to pay the reward.

Suppose Ernest loses his laptop computer and publishes a notice offering a $1,000 reward for its return. Not knowing of Ernest's offer, Jorge finds a laptop computer, turns it on, and learns that it belongs to Ernest. He returns it to Ernest as would any honest person. Subsequently, he learns of Ernest's offer and asks that Ernest pay him the reward.

Ernest need *not* pay him. Not knowing of the reward offer, Jorge was not an offeree. In returning the computer, therefore, he did not accept the offer. That chain of logic creates this rule: *In order to accept an offer of reward, one must (a) know of the offer, and (b) complete the performance for which the offeror asks.* Restatement (Second) §51 cmt. a provides:

> [I]n cases of offers of reward, it is ordinarily essential to the acceptance of the offer that the offeree know of the proposal made. In general, performance completed before the offer comes to the offeree's knowledge does not have reference to the offer, and the terms of the offer are not satisfied by such action.

H.   The Closers

Sadie is the author of a short story called "Cookie Jar" and owns its copyright. By handwritten fax, on May 8, Baldwin sends Sadie this message: "I am prepared immediately to purchase from you the copyright to your story 'Cookie Jar' for the price of $300,000, half ($150,000) to be paid on June 1 and half ($150,000) to be paid on July 1, on which latter date (July 1) you will actually transfer copyright ownership to me. Please get back to me before May 16, with your written response."

Sadie considers Baldwin's offer. On May 14, she has not made a decision and on that day, by fax, sends Baldwin this handwritten message: "I continue to consider your offer. Might you extend the May 15 deadline by one week—to May 22." By 11:00 P.M. on May 15, Sadie receives no response.

QUESTION 7. For this question assume that at 11:30 P.M. on May 15, with no response from Baldwin, Sadie telephones Baldwin and leaves this voice-mail message: "I accept your offer of May 8." Baldwin retrieves the voice-mail message the following morning, May 16. Then, on the afternoon of May 16, Sadie sends Baldwin this handwritten fax: "In accordance with my voice-mail message left with you last night, May 15, I accept your May 8 offer." In all probability these parties:

A. have formed a contract because, within a reasonable time of leaving her voice-mail message, Sadie sent Baldwin a handwritten fax message confirming her assent.

B. have formed a contract because voice mail represents a reasonable mode of communication in modern-day transactions.

C. have not formed a contract because Sadie failed timely to express her assent in the manner prescribed by Baldwin.

D. have not formed a contract because Sadie could not reasonably expect that Baldwin would hear her voice-mail message before May 16.

QUESTION 8. For this question, make this assumption: at 11:00 P.M. on May 15, Sadie sends Baldwin this e-mail message: "I accept your May 8 offer." The message posts to Baldwin's account at 11:01 but Baldwin does not read it until the following morning, May 16. In all probability these parties:

A. have formed a contract because Sadie accepted Baldwin's offer according to the time and manner prescribed in the May 8 communication.

B. have formed a contract because by May 15, Sadie formed a definite intent to assent to all terms of Baldwin's proposal.

> **C.** have not formed a contract because Sadie did not express her assent in handwriting.
>
> **D.** have not formed a contract because Sadie rejected the offer on May 14.

ANALYSIS. Baldwin is "master of his offer"; Sadie accepts it only if she manifests her assent in such manner as Baldwin prescribes. Further, she must do so before the offer expires by rejection, revocation, or passage of time (Chapter 6). By requiring that Sadie respond "before May 16," Baldwin has limited his offer's life to midnight, May 15. In order to accept, Sadie must manifest her assent *in writing,* no later than that hour on that day.

As for Question 7. Sadie's May 14 fax message certainly did not accept because it did not express assent to Baldwin's proposal. Neither, however, did it reject. Sadie advised Baldwin that she was not ready to make a decision and asked whether she might have more time. (Recall from Chapter 7, section C, that an offeree does not reject an offer by inquiring about a possible change in terms. That applies to an inquiry about terms of the bargain itself or about terms as to time and manner of acceptance.) Baldwin's offer remains open through May 15.

Then, late on May 15, Sadie expresses her assent. She dispatches it—puts it out of her possession—but does *not* do so in writing as Baldwin prescribes. Consequently, by midnight on May 15, Sadie fails to accept, and the offer expires. That Sadie follows the voice mail with a writing on May 16 does not save her; the writing comes too late.

A tells us that the parties did form a contract. For that reason alone, it's wrong, and the happy phrase "reasonable time" can't make it right. That Sadie issued a writing one day after leaving her voice mail means not a thing. She failed to comply with the "master's" decree and so failed to accept.

And **B**? Voice mail is a reasonable mode of communication. If Baldwin had prescribed no special mode of acceptance, Sadie's voice-mail message would have done the job. But **B** overlooks this critical fact: exercising his rights as "master," Baldwin required a written acceptance. Sadie could accept in no other way. **B** is wrong.

D correctly concludes that the parties failed to form a contract, but its reasoning is askew. Acceptance is effective on *dispatch*—when the offeree puts it out of her possession (Chapter 8, section A). That Baldwin would not likely *hear* the telephone message until May 16 does not negate the acceptance. Sadie did dispatch her message on time, but not *in the right way.*

That leaves **C**, which tells us that the parties failed to form a contract because Sadie did not, while the offer still lived, assent to its terms in the manner prescribed by the offeror. **C** is right.

As for Question 8.   Here, Sadie dispatched a *written* message of acceptance *on* May 15. She sent it timely, in the appropriate mode. No rejection or revocation preceded the message, and for all of these reasons, the parties formed a contract.

B and **C** tell us that the parties formed no contract, so they're wrong. Their reasoning is wrong as well. **B** implies that Sadie accepted by forming in her own mind the intention to do so. That's nonsense, of course. **C** implies that an offeree may accept only via the same mode used by the offeror in making the offer. That's false too. First, an offeror may (as did not happen here) specify some mode of acceptance very different from the one by which he makes his offer. Second, when the offeror makes no requirements as to the mode or manner of acceptance, the offeree may effectively accept in any reasonable mode, one of which is, certainly, that by which the offeror made the offer. **D** states that Sadie rejected on May 14. She did no such thing.

That leaves **A**, which correctly states that these parties formed a contract and properly describes the reasons. Acceptance in this case required that Sadie manifest her assent by May 15 in writing. That's what Sadie did, and that's how these parties formed their contract. It matters not that Baldwin first read the message on the following day because, as we know, acceptance is effective on dispatch (Chapter 8, section A). **A** is right.

Silver & Hochberg's Picks

1.	C
2.	C
3.	A
4.	C
5.	C
6.	B
7.	C
8.	A

10

More About the Offeree Who Accepts by Performing an Act

A. When the Offeror Requires Acceptance by *Act*
B. When the Offeror Allows the Offeree to Accept by Promise *or* Performance
C. The Closers
⊕ Silver & Hochberg's Picks

Chapter 9, section A, taught you that the offeror is mistress of her offer. Depending on what she requires, her offeree might accept by (1) making a promise or (2) completing some act.

A. When the Offeror Requires Acceptance by *Act*

If the offeror makes an offer for a unilateral contract, then by definition she allows her offeree to accept only by completing the act(s) that represents his full performance. If the offeror allows the offeree to accept by performing some act(s) other than that which completes his performance, she makes an offer for a bilateral contract. In both cases, she requires that the offeree accept by completing an *act* (Chapter 9, Part D). If the offeree begins to perform the act, he does not accept until he completes it.

1. That Creates a Problem: Sam, Sally, and a Flagpole

We know generally that an offeror may revoke at any time before the offeree accepts. Strictly applied, that rule leads to an unsettling result when an offeree is allowed to accept only by completing some act and *begins* to perform. In the classic illustration, Sam says to Sally, "I'll pay you $100 if you climb to the top of this 100-foot flagpole. You may accept only by fully performing—by reaching the top of the flagpole." Sally begins to climb. After twenty minutes, when she is but an inch from the top, Sam shouts up to her, "I revoke my offer." Sally hangs one inch from the top of the flagpole with nothing to show for it—no contract, no action for breach (and, of course, a long climb downward).

2. Is That Fair? Older Authorities Said "Yes"

If before beginning her climb Sally had consulted her attorney, she would have known that the offeror had the right to revoke at any time before she reached the flagpole's tippy-top. She would have known the rules of the "game" and could have chosen to "play" or not. She might have responded with a counteroffer, *promising* to climb the pole in exchange for Sam's promise of $100. Sam would then be free to accept or not. Because Sally, the offeree, has that option, the older authorities deemed it perfectly fair that the offeror retain his right to revoke at any time before the offeree *completes* the climb. In abstract terms, the older rule was that *an offeror who allowed his offeree to accept only by completing some act retained the power to revoke at any time before the offeree completed the act, even if the offeree had begun and, indeed, nearly completed it.*

3. Modern Law Doesn't Buy Into That

Modern thought finds injustice in the offeror's right to revoke his offer after an offeree begins to perform the act necessary to his acceptance. The common law now provides, generally, *when an offeror allows an offeree to accept only by performing some act and the offeree **begins** to perform, the offeror loses his right to revoke.*

It remains so, under modern law, that to accept Sam's offer, Sally must complete the climb; she must reach the top of the pole. Beginning the climb does not constitute acceptance but, when Sally starts up the pole, Sam loses his right to revoke. As she makes her ascent, Sally knows that Sam cannot take back his offer.

Yet Sam's offer may still expire by events discussed in Chapter 6, sections C, D, and E. The rule, then is this: *If an offeror requires that his offeree accept by performing some act(s) and the offeree begins to perform, then (1) the offer becomes permanently irrevocable, **but** (2) the offer may expire by any of the other usual means: rejection, passage of a stated time, passage of a reasonable time, and death or incapacity of the offeror, **and** (3) the relevant contract does not arise unless and until the offeree completes performance before the offer expires through any such event.*

QUESTIONS 1 & 2. SurveCo surveys and inspects homes for prospective buyers. Peter contemplates buying a home. On June 1, the two parties exchange e-mails:

(1) **Peter:** I'm contemplating the purchase of a home located at 587 Greenery Way in Heightland. I'd like you to survey it, inspect it, and send me a written report on or before June 18 at 5 P.M. Are you able to do that, and what is your fee?

(2) **SurveCo:** Certainly we can accommodate you. We'll begin the survey on June 12 and, if we fail to finish it that same day, we'll certainly finish by June 18 at 5 P.M. Our fee is $1,200 for the survey and report.

(3) **Peter:** Thank you. I am prepared to proceed on your terms, with a deadline of June 18 at 5 P.M. and with this additional understanding: You may accept my offer only by completing all of the work for which I ask.

(4) **SurveCo:** We accept your terms.

QUESTION 1. Assume this: at 10 A.M. on June 12, SurveCo begins the survey and inspection. By 3 P.M., it has completed 75 percent of the work. At 4 P.M., Peter contacts SurveCo and declares his offer revoked. At 4:30 P.M. on June 12, do the parties have a contract that (a) requires SurveCo to complete the inspection and survey, with written report; and (b) requires Peter to pay SurveCo $1,200?

A. Yes, because at statement 4 SurveCo accepted Peter's offer

B. Yes, because on June 12 SurveCo began performance

C. No, because SurveCo has not, at that time, accepted Peter's offer

D. Yes, because Peter's power to revoke would first arise on June 18 at 5 P.M.

QUESTION 2. Now assume that SurveCo begins its survey and inspection on June 12 at 10 A.M. and completes it that same day. On June 13, SurveCo e-mails Peter to announce that its on-site work is complete, adding, "We wish to complete the written report by June 18, but we cannot do so. We'll finish it on or before June 25." Peter e-mails back, "That is not acceptable. I wish not to do further business with you." Later that same day, SurveCo e-mails Peter again to say that it can complete the report by June 18. Peter is firm: "As I wrote earlier, I no longer wish to do business with you." On June 18, SurveCo submitted the written report. Does Peter owe SurveCo $1,200?

A. Yes, because Peter's offer was permanently irrevocable.

B. Yes, because the parties formed a contract on June 12.

> **C.** No, because on June 13, Peter decided to have no further dealings with SurveCo.
>
> **D.** No, because on June 13, SurveCo lost its power to accept.

ANALYSIS.   Examine the first e-mail exchange and ask: Did one of the parties make an offer to the other, and, if so, did the other accept? At statement 1, Peter expressed his interest in purchasing SurveCo's services. Failing to propose a fee, he made a mere invitation to deal. At statement 2, SurveCo named a fee and stated its readiness to do the work by June 18. Probably, SurveCo made an offer. Yet, if it did, Peter didn't accept. Peter took hold of SurveCo's terms, added a new one, and presented it back to SurveCo. He made a counteroffer.

Peter's counteroffer provided that SurveCo could accept only by completing all of its work (thus looking toward a unilateral contract). These parties could form no contract unless SurveCo completed the survey/inspection and report by June 18, Peter's prescribed deadline. When SurveCo began performance, Peter lost his power to revoke. Nonetheless, the offer remained subject to expiration by rejection, by passage of time stated in the offer, or by Peter's death or incompetence.

As for Question 1. Question 1 states that SurveCo began performance on June 12. At that moment, Peter permanently lost his power to revoke, but the parties did not then form a contract. Peter allowed that SurveCo could accept only with a full performance, complete by June 18.

A, B, and **C** tell us that the parties have formed the contemplated contract. On that basis alone, all are wrong. Their reasoning is erroneous too. As to **A,** we know that with statement 4, SurveCo did *not* accept the offer because Peter allowed it to accept only by complete performance. As to **B,** SurveCo's beginning of performance is not an acceptance. It does render Peter's offer irrevocable, but it doesn't form a contract.

D incorrectly states that Peter would acquire a power to revoke at 5 P.M. That's wrong. When SurveCo began its performance, Peter *permanently* lost his power to revoke. After the June 18, 5 P.M. deadline passes, Peter's offer will expire—by passage of a time stated in the offer. Peter can't *revoke* his offer, however, under any circumstance.

C speaketh truth. The parties had no contract because on June 12 at 4:30 P.M. SurveCo had not completed its performance, meaning it had not accepted Peter's offer. That's why **C** is right. (Peter has the right, still, to continue his work and accept the offer by completing it before 5 P.M. on June 18. But as of June *12* at 4:30 P.M. these parties have no contract.)

As for Question 2. According to question 2, SurveCo finished the inspection and survey on June 12. Yet to accept Peter's offer, it had still to submit the written report by June 18. On June 13, it announced to Peter that it *wished* to finish the report by that date but could not do so. From Chapter 6, section C, remember this: "I wish I could but I can't" means "no; I reject your offer." Hence, with its June 13 announcement, SurveCo rejected Peter's offer. Even though SurveCo moved a long way toward completion, it ultimately said "no." Notwithstanding that Peter's offer was irrevocable, ServeCo's *rejection* put it to death. SurveCo's subsequent attempt to accept was ineffective.

A states that Peter must pay the $1,200 because his offer turned irrevocable on June 12. It's true that the offer turned irrevocable on that day, but it died nonetheless on June 13 when SurveCo rejected it. Hence, **A** is wrong. **B** states that the parties formed a contract on June 12. Wrong again; a contract requires offer and acceptance, and the "master" of this offer decreed that SurveCo would accept only if it *completely* performed on or before June 18 at 5 P.M. On June 12 it had not written its report and, therefore, had not accepted the offer. **C** correctly states that Peter owes nothing to SurveCo, but it's reasoning is wrong. That Peter wanted no further dealings with SurveCo is irrelevant. Peter's offer expired because *SurveCo rejected it.*

D, alas, tells us that Peter owes nothing to SurveCo and correctly states the reason: "on June 13, SurveCo lost its power to accept." On that day, Peter's offer, although irrevocable, expired by rejection, and so SurveCo did lose its power to accept. **D** is right.

4. How the Restatement Words the Modern Rule

The Restatement expresses this same modern view by rather a gratuitous, pretentious use of the phrase "option contract" (see Chapter 6, section B). Rather than state simply that an offer becomes irrevocable when it demands acceptance by act and the offeree begins to perform that act, Restatement (Second) of Contracts §45(1) provides:

> Where an offer invites an offeree to accept by rendering a performance and does not invite a promissory acceptance, an option contract is created when the offeree . . . begins the invited performance. . . .

According to the Restatement, the offeree's payment for the "option" inheres in the very fact that he begins to perform the requested act: "[T]he beginning of performance furnishes [payment] for an option contract." Restatement (Second) §45 cmt. d.

In substance and effect, the Restatement rule is exactly the same as the one stated in section A.3 above. The offeree who begins to perform buys an "option" to complete the act, which is tantamount to providing that the offeror's offer becomes irrevocable. In wording and legal "theory," however, the Restatement rule is different. The Restatement reaches its result by creating these fictions:

When This Happens in Fact	The Restatement Draws This Legal Conclusion:
I will pay you $1,000 to register a copyright with the U.S. copyright office. You may accept only by doing what I ask.	Offeror makes two offers: (1) to pay $1,000 in exchange for registering the copyright, and (2) to make that offer irrevocable if offeree will begin the process.
Offeree begins the process of registering the copyright.	Offeree accepts offer #2 and the parties thus form an option contract. That option contract represents this bargain: • offeree has begun the registration process, in exchange for which • offeror must hold offer #1 permanently irrevocable.

As noted earlier, the offer remains subject to termination by the offeree's rejection (Restatement (Second) §45 cmt. e), passage of time, or death or incapacity.

So, what should you know exactly? First, know the rule stated in section A.3 above. Second, know that the Restatement (Second) §45 means to state that very same rule in its own (ridiculous) way.

QUESTION 3. Naomi, a former governor, hopes to publish her memoirs. She submits a manuscript to Publisher, who telephones her after reading it: "Your manuscript is excellent. If you will rewrite the last chapter to include your future plans and submit it within 30 days, we will publish the manuscript and pay you a royalty of 10 percent on gross sales. Our agreement takes effect when you submit the revised chapter." On September 2, Naomi begins to revise the last chapter. Later that day, Publisher calls to say, "I'm sorry, but we've decided against publishing the book." Under modern common law, Publisher's attempt to revoke is ineffective because:

I. Publisher did not communicate its revocation by signed writing.
II. Publisher's offer became irrevocable when Naomi began to revise the final chapter.
III. The parties formed an option contract when Naomi began to revise the final chapter.

A. I
B. I and II
C. II and III
D. I, II, and III

ANALYSIS. Publisher made an offer and allowed Naomi to accept only by completing an act, to wit, the revision of her final chapter. Naomi began the revision, meaning that Publisher's offer became irrevocable. Or, in Restatement terms, the parties formed an "option contract" under which Naomi acquired the "option" to complete the revision and thus to accept Publisher's offer. For these reasons, Publisher's subsequent attempt to revoke was ineffective.

Item I proclaims that the Publisher failed to revoke because it did not communicate its revocation by signed writing. There is no such rule. Publisher's offer became irrevocable when Naomi began the revision. If Publisher had attempted to revoke by sworn statement, smoke signal, or signed writing, he would fail because his offer was irrevocable. Item I is false, which eliminates **A**, **B**, and **D**.

Items II and III correctly explain why Publisher's revocation is ineffective. In plain English, option II tells us that Publisher lost his right to revoke when Naomi began to revise her last chapter. Option III makes the same statement in Restatement jargonese: When Naomi began the revision, the parties formed an "option contract," affording her the "option" to *complete* the revision and thus accept the offer. Because options II and III make true statements, **C** is right.

QUESTION 4. Ivis owns a patent on a machine technology called Manutrix. Anton wishes to purchase from her an exclusive license to build and sell Manutrix machinery. For that purpose, he contacts Ivis by signed writing.

(1) **Anton:** I wish to buy an exclusive license to use your Manutrix technology for five years. In exchange, I'll pay you $300,000 in each such year.

(2) **Ivis:** I'm agreeable to the fee and to the five-year term, but I need some assurance that you will be able to make the payments each year. Bring to me a letter from your bank showing that your bank balance is, as of now, at least $1 million. Do that and we have a deal.

Anton asks his bank to issue the letter. The bank agrees to do so and tells Anton it will be written and ready in five days. Before the bank issues the letter, Ivis contacts Anton: "I've changed my mind. I'm not willing to sell you the license." Which of the following accurately characterizes the parties' legal rights and duties?

I.   Ivis and Anton have a contract requiring that Ivis sell Anton a license to use the Manutrix technology.

II. Ivis and Anton have an option contract under which Anton has the option to purchase the Manutrix technology from Ivis.

III. Ivis and Anton have an option contract under which Ivis has the option to sell the Manutrix technology to Anton.

IV. Ivis made an offer and Anton has the power to accept it or not.

A. I

B. I and II

C. II and IV

D. III and IV

ANALYSIS.   In statement 1, Anton made an offer to Ivis, and in statement 2, Ivis responded with a counteroffer, allowing Anton to accept it only by performing an act—by presenting Ivis with a bank letter attesting to his balance. When Anton *began* his effort to obtain the bank letter, he rendered Ivis's offer irrevocable. In Restatement terms, the parties formed an "option contract" affording Anton the option, if he chose, to complete his acceptance and purchase the license. When Ivis told Anton that she had changed her mind, she made an ineffective attempt to revoke. At that point, the parties had no contract *for the sale of the patent*, but they had the "option contract" that empowered Anton, still, to accept Ivis's offer by securing the bank's letter and presenting it to her.

Option I states that the parties do have a contract for the sale of the license; for that reason it's wrong. Option IV properly reports that Anton is Ivis's offeree with power still to accept Ivis's offer. That's correct: Ivis's offer is irrevocable and thus leaves Anton with power to accept it notwithstanding the attempted revocation. The right answer must include option IV but exclude option I, meaning that **C** or **D** is right, depending on the correctness of options II and III. Both II and III describe an option contract. Option III reports that *Ivis* has an option to *sell* the license. Option II reports that *Anton* has an option to *purchase* the license.

Anton is possessed of an irrevocable offer to purchase the license. If he wishes to purchase, he need only wait for his bank to issue the letter and then deliver it to Ivis. If he does not wish to purchase, he need only abort his efforts. It is for *Anton to decide*, as he wishes, that he will or will not accept Ivis's offer. In Restatement terms, Anton has an "option" to purchase the license. Ivis, meanwhile, has no option but to await Anton's decision. Option II correctly states that Anton has an option to purchase the license. Option III incorrectly states that Ivis has an option to sell it. Options II and IV make true statements, and that's why **C** is right.

In Chapter 9, section F, you learned this: when an offeree accepts by completing performance, the offeror has a right to learn of it; he has a right to know that the offeree has accepted. If the offeree should understand that the offeror has no reasonable means by which to do so then, within a reasonable time of completing performance (and hence accepting the offer), the offeree himself must tell the offeror that he has done so, or the offeror's contractual duty is discharged—the law undoes it; it ceases to exist.

Similarly, an offeror has a right to know if his offer has become irrevocable. Suppose A makes an offer to B, requiring that B accept by furnishing some or all of his performance. B begins to perform, which means that A's offer becomes irrevocable. Suppose that A has no meaningful way to *learn* that B has begun performance and B knows that. B must, within a reasonable time, notify A that he has begun performance, or the offeror may assume that the offeree has not accepted, whereupon his offer expires. Restatement (Second) §54 cmt. b states it all like this:

> [W]here acceptance is invited by a performance which will not come promptly to the offeror's attention, then [the situation] usually requires notification of acceptance.

B.   When the Offeror Allows the Offeree to Accept by Promise *or* Performance

We know now that if an offeror *requires* her offeree to accept by completing an act, her offer becomes irrevocable when the offeree begins to perform. Let's deal, now, with the offeror who permits an offeree to accept by promise *or* performance.

Suppose Bill wants to purchase Leah's computer and makes her this offer: "I'll buy your computer for $300. You may accept my offer by delivering the computer or by promising, right now, that you'll deliver it. The promise or the performance will constitute acceptance." Bill has *allowed* Leah to accept by delivering the computer, but he has not *required* that she do so. He has allowed, also, that she accept by promise. In such a case, the offeree's beginning of performance is, by law, *her promise to complete it.* Hence, by *beginning performance,* the offeree accepts the offer and forms a contract. Restatement (Second) §62 provides:

> (1) Where an offer invites an offeree to choose between acceptance by promise and acceptance by performance, the . . . beginning of the invited performance . . . is an acceptance. . . .
> (2) Such an acceptance operates as a promise to render complete performance.

Further, as we already know, if the offeror is silent as to the mode or manner of acceptance, the offeree may accept in any manner that is reasonable (Restatement (Second) §30(2); Chapter 9, section B). If performance of an act is a reasonable mode of acceptance, then the offeror has implicitly permitted the offeree to accept in that way. In that case, too, when the offeree *begins* to perform, he accepts the offer and the parties form a contract.

QUESTION 5. On April 1, Sylvia mails her accountant Jared statements of income and deductions for the preceding tax year, together with this letter: "I enclose records relevant to my income for this past tax year. If you'll prepare my state and federal tax returns, I will, of course, pay you the usual fee." On April 4, Jared receives and reads the letter. On April 5, he begins work on Sylvia's tax return. The two parties have:

> **I.** a contract in which Jared must prepare Sylvia's tax return and Sylvia must pay Jared's usual fee.
> **II.** an option contract in which Jared has the option to complete Sylvia's tax return.
> **A.** I
> **B.** II
> **C.** I and II
> **D.** Neither I nor II

ANALYSIS.   Sylvia made Jared an offer in which she was silent as to how Jared should accept. Consequently Jared was permitted to accept in any reasonable way meaning, in this case, he was free to accept (a) by promise communicated in any reasonable way or (b) by preparing the tax return. That, in turn, means that Sylvia allowed Jared to accept by performance but did not *require* that he do so. When Jared began to perform he accepted Sylvia's offer; the beginning of his performance operated as his promise to complete it.

As option I states, these parties formed a contract requiring that Jared complete the tax return and that Sylvia pay his fee. Option II incorrectly states that the parties formed an option contract. If Sylvia had *required* that Jared accept by performance, his beginning of the performance would have rendered the offer irrevocable, thus affording him the option to complete it. That, however, is not this case. Option I makes a true statement and option II a false one. **A** is right.

The offeror's "right to know" applies here as it does to acceptance by full performance (Chapter 9, section F) and the beginning of performance that renders an offer irrevocable (above). Suppose A makes an offer to B, *allowing* (not requiring) that B accept by furnishing some or all of his performance. B begins to perform which means that he accepts A's offer and the parties form a contract. Suppose that A has no meaningful way to *learn* that B has begun to perform and B knows that. B must, within a reasonable time, notify A that he has begun performance, or the contract is discharged—the law undoes it; it ceases to exist.

QUESTION 6. On Monday at 10 A.M., Luella brings her computer to Norman's computer repair business. Told to leave it on the front desk with a note describing its dysfunction, Luella does so, writing: "Computer won't boot. Please repair. I'll pay your normal fee, of course. I'll come in tomorrow, Tuesday, to check on the status." Later that same Monday at 3 P.M., Norman begins work on the computer. At 5 P.M., Luella telephones Norman and tells him not to repair the computer. He responds,

"Too late. I've already begun to work on it." "Well, you didn't tell me that you were beginning the work," Luella says, "and I'm directing you now not to repair the computer." Do the parties fail to form a contract because Norman failed to notify Luella that he had begun to work on the computer?

A. Yes; the beginning of performance does not operate as an acceptance unless and until the offeror obtains such notice.

B. Yes; Norman's failure to give such notice shows bad faith on his part.

C. No; by leaving her computer at Norman's facility, Luella waived her right to such notice.

D. No; Luella's stated plan to return to the facility on Tuesday gave Norman reason to believe Luella would acquire the notice.

ANALYSIS. When Luella left her computer at the front desk together with her note, she made an offer. She did not expressly require that Norman accept by giving full performance, but plainly she *permitted* him to do so. Consequently, when Norman began to repair the computer he accepted Luella's offer, and the parties formed a contract requiring that Norman repair the computer and that Luella pay his usual fee.

If Norman had reason to believe that Luella would not learn within a reasonable time that he had begun performance, he himself would be obliged, also within a reasonable time, to notify her that he had, in fact, begun the work. His failure to do so would bring the contract to an end. But Luella's note gave Norman every reason to believe that on Tuesday Luella would learn that he had begun performance. Hence, he had no obligation to provide that notice to her.

We're looking for the answer "no." **A** and **B** say "yes," which makes them wrong. Predictably, they also misstate law and fact. According to **A**, Norman's beginning of performance did not, itself, operate as an acceptance. That's wrong; when an offeror permits—but does not require—that an offeree accept by performing an act, the offeree's beginning of performance *is* acceptance. **B** invokes the time-honored phrase "bad faith." There is not a whit of dishonesty ("bad faith") in Norman's failure to notify Luella that he has begun performance. According to **C**, Luella gave up ("waived") her right to notice by leaving the computer at Norman's facility. There is no such rule. **D** hits the bull's eye. It tells us that these parties formed a contract notwithstanding Norman's failure to notify Luella that he had begun performance. The reason, it reports, is that Luella's stated intention to visit the store on Tuesday gave Norman reason to believe that she would learn, within a reasonable time, that he had begun performance. **D** is right.

C.   The Closers

In the same week, Judge World issued decisions in two bench trials.[1] In the first, she concluded that the litigating parties had formed a contract. In the second, she concluded that they had not. Please read both her opinions.

Case 1: *PoolCo v. Silver Oaks Country Club*
Upon the evidence, I find these facts:

(1)   On August 1, Defendant Silver Oaks Country Club contacted Plaintiff PoolCo and wrote, in pertinent part: "At summer's end, beginning on September 22, we wish to have you winterize all four of our swimming pools, just as you have done in the past. As in the past, we will pay your full fee of $90,000 only when you complete the work, with no payment to be made in advance or on the basis of a contractual promise. Will you be doing the work for us?"

(2)   On August 2, by signed writing, Plaintiff responded: "Certainly."

(3)   On August 3, Defendant again contacted Plaintiff: "We have changed our minds and do not wish to have you winterize our pools this year."

Defendant's August 1 communication was, undoubtedly, an offer. The question before me is whether the offer (a) required that Plaintiff accept by complete performance, thus constituting an offer for a unilateral contract; or (b) allowed Plaintiff to accept by promise, thus constituting an offer for a bilateral contract. If the offer was for a unilateral contract, then Plaintiff's August 2 response did not accept the offer, and since Plaintiff did not begin performance, Defendant effectively revoked on August 3, wherefore the parties formed no contract. If, on the other hand, Defendant's offer was for a bilateral contract, then Plaintiff's August 2 response accepted it, the parties formed a contract, and Defendant's attempt to revoke on August 3 was ineffective.

Defendant cites its language of August 3: "As in the past, we will pay your full fee of $90,000 only when you complete the work, with no payment to be made in advance or on the basis of a contractual promise." Such language, Defendant argues, creates an offer for a unilateral contract. I disagree. There is a difference between an offer

---

1. *Bench Trial* means a trial without a jury, which, depending on the circumstances, may be perfectly proper. In a bench trial, the judge has the obligations of finding fact and applying the law (as she construes it).

that provides, on the one hand, for payment to the offeree only after the offeree fully performs and, on the other, that the offeree may accept only by completing performance. Unless otherwise indicated by the language or the circumstances, an offer invites acceptance in any manner and by any medium reasonable in the circumstances. Restatement (Second) of Contracts §30(2). In its communication of August 1, Defendant nowhere stated or implied that it would allow Plaintiff to accept only by performance. Indeed, with the last sentence of its August 1 communication, it asked for a promissory acceptance. It wrote: "Will you be doing the work for us?" Such a question would justify a reasonable offeree in understanding that the offeror has asked for a promissory acceptance.

Defendant made an offer for a bilateral contract, and on August 2 Plaintiff accepted. Defendant's subsequent attempt to revoke was ineffective.

Case 2: *PoolCo v. High Oaks Country Club*
I find these facts:

(1) On August 1, Defendant High Oaks Country Club contacted Plaintiff PoolCo, writing, in pertinent part: "At the end of summer, beginning on or about September 22, we ask that you winterize our three swimming pools according to the methods and procedures you have used when serving us previously. We do not seek a promissory commitment, but will take as your acceptance the completion of the work, at which point we, as usual, will pay your full fee of $90,000, no money to be paid until the work is complete. We ask that you let us know if and when you intended to begin the work."

(2) On August 2, by signed writing, Plaintiff responded: "We wish to do the work and expect to begin on September 23."

(3) On August 3, Defendant again contacted Plaintiff: "We have had a change of plans. We revoke our offer of August 1 and do not wish to have you winterize our pools this year."

Defendant's August 1 communication was, undoubtedly, an offer. The question before me is whether it (a) required that Plaintiff accept by complete performance, thus constituting an offer for a unilateral contract; or (b) allowed Plaintiff to accept by promise, thus constituting an offer for a bilateral contract. If the offer was for a unilateral contract, then Plaintiff's August 2 response did not accept it; and since Plaintiff did not begin performance, Defendant effectively revoked on August 3, wherefore the parties formed no contract. If, on the other hand, Defendant's offer was for a bilateral contract, then Plaintiff's August 2 response accepted it. The parties formed a contract, and Defendant's attempt to revoke on August 3 was ineffective.

Citing this Court's very recent decision, *PoolCo v. Silver Oaks*, Plaintiff argues that in this case as in that one, Defendant's offer allowed Plaintiff to accept by promise. The reference to completed work, Plaintiff contends, has to do only with time of payment.

It is true that in this case, as in *Silver Oaks*, the offer provided for payment only upon the Plaintiff's completion of the work. Yet Plaintiff overlooks that in this case, Defendant's offer stated, in part, "We do not seek a promissory commitment, but will take as your acceptance the completion of the work. . . . " In *Silver Oaks*, Defendant's offer included no language of like meaning. This Defendant made an offer for a unilateral contract. Hence Plaintiff's response of August 2 was no acceptance, and Defendant effectively revoked on August 3.

QUESTION 7. The Judge found that the parties formed a contract in Case 1, but not in Case 2. Which of the following best describes the reason for which she arrived at the different results?

A. In one case, the offeror was willing to make payment before the offeror completed its work; in the other it was not.

B. In one case, the offeree responded with words of definitive assent; in the other it did not.

C. In one case, the offeree manifested a willingness to enter a bargain; in the other it did not.

D. In one case, the offeror specified the allowable mode of acceptance; in the other it did not.

ANALYSIS. Evidently, before deciding these two cases, the Judge read this book (particularly, Chapter 9, section D). She knows that if the offeror wishes to allow acceptance only by full performance, he must make that plain, clear, and explicit. In each case, therefore, she tests the offer for the high level of specificity that such a restriction requires. In Case 1, she does not find it. She observes that Defendant proposed to make payment only after performance was complete, but she found no indication that complete performance was necessary to *acceptance*. In Case 2, she found what she believed to be the necessary specificity: "We do not seek a promissory commitment, but will take as your acceptance the completion of the work. . . . " In one case she found the necessary specificity and in the other she did not. That's exactly what **D** tells us; **D** is right.

A makes a false statement. In *both* cases, the offeror proposed to pay only after the offeree completed the work. (In Case 1, however (according to the Judge), the offeror did not require that the offeree complete the work in order to accept the offer.) **A** is wrong. As for **B**, it's true that in Case 1, PoolCo responds with "Certainly," whereas in Case 2, it responds, "We wish to do the work and expect to begin on September 23." The first response is more definitive than the second, but the Judge does not seem to think that matters. In her mind, both are sufficiently definite to constitute an acceptance so long as the relevant offer allows for acceptance by promise. For in *both* cases, she writes, "If . . . Defendant's offer was for a bilateral contract, then Plaintiff's August 2 response accepted it." She does not think that in Case 2, PoolCo's response is too tenuous to be an acceptance. So **B** is wrong.

C states that one of the defendants made an offer and the other did not. That's plainly false. In both cases, the Judge writes, "Defendant's August 1 communication was, undoubtedly, an offer." For that reason, **C** is wrong.

QUESTION 8. For both decisions, in the second sentence of the second paragraph, the Judge writes, "and since Plaintiff did not begin performance, Defendant effectively revoked on August 3." She did so because in either case, if Defendant's offer had looked toward a unilateral contract, then Plaintiff's beginning of performance

I.   would have rendered the offer irrevocable.
II. would have formed an option contract.
A. I but not II
B. II but not I
C. Both I and II
D. Neither I nor II

ANALYSIS. Modern common law provides that when an offeror requires acceptance by complete performance only, the offeree's beginning of performance renders the offer irrevocable. In describing that rule, Restatement (Second) §45(1) invokes the phrase "option contract." Statements I and II have the same meaning, and both are true. **C** is right.

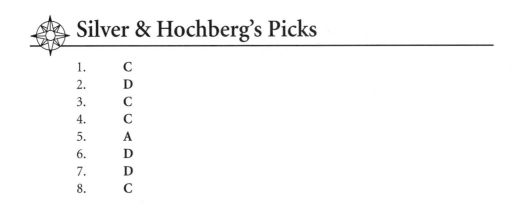

✤ Silver & Hochberg's Picks

1.	C
2.	D
3.	C
4.	C
5.	A
6.	D
7.	D
8.	C

11

Uniform Commercial Code: Offer and Acceptance

A. The "Firm Offer"
B. The Mirror-Image Rule, UCC §2-207(1), and "Battle of the Forms"
C. Modification of Existing Contract: UCC §2-207(2)
D. Offeror's *Silence* as Acceptance of Offeree's Additional Terms
E. UCC §2-207 as Model of Poor Draftsmanship: "Different" and "Additional" Terms
F. More About UCC §2-207(1): The "Written Confirmation"
G. The Closer
✧ Silver & Hochberg's Picks

A. The "Firm Offer"

Please read, now, *Appendix, sections A and D.* Chapter 6, section A, taught you that (a) an offeror may revoke her offer at any time before the offeree accepts, and (b) she may do so even if she proclaims her offer irrevocable, or "firm." That represents long-standing *common law.* Statutes, however, supersede the common law. When a federal or state legislature enacts a statute that conflicts with the common law, the statute governs. That's a precept of the common law itself. The common law renders itself subordinate to statutes. *Statutes supersede the common law.*

1. UCC §2-205

The Uniform Commercial Code ("UCC") is a statute in every state. Its Article 2 governs contracts for the sale of goods, meaning, generally, "movable things." *Some*—not all—but *some* of the provisions within UCC Article 2 apply only to "merchants," so let's define that word as Article 2 uses it: *With respect to the sale of some kind of good, a merchant is one who (a) deals professionally in that kind of good or (b) holds himself out as having special knowledge related to that kind of good.* As to the sale of a piano, a piano dealer is a merchant. So is a piano teacher and a piano tuner. As to the sale of a power saw a hardware retailer is a merchant, as is a power tool manufacturer, a power tool mechanic, and a carpenter. (See, if you wish, UCC § 2-104(1); it's wholly incomprehensible.) UCC §2-205 provides that if a merchant makes an offer in a signed writing and proclaims it irrevocable for some particular period of time, then it *is* irrevocable for that period of time:

> An offer by a merchant to buy or sell goods in a signed writing which by its terms gives assurances that it will be held open is not revocable . . . during the time stated. . . .

Let's take that apart. UCC §2-205 provides that an offer proclaiming itself irrevocable for two days or two weeks or two months is irrevocable for the stated time if and only if it is (a) made by a merchant (b) offering to buy or sell goods, (c) in a signed writing. Suppose Bill, a clothespin manufacturer, by signed writing offers to buy miniature springs from Sam. In his last sentence he writes, "Our offer is irrevocable for ten days." The common law would leave Bill free to revoke any time before Sam accepts. However, because Bill is (a) a merchant who (b) made an offer to buy goods (c) by signed writing, UCC §2-205 applies. Bill proclaimed his offer to be irrevocable for ten days and it *is* irrevocable for ten days.

QUESTION 1. Sally manufactures valves. Betty manufactures tires. On June 1 Sally sends Betty this signed writing: "I am prepared to sell you our standard tire valve #19 at 40 cents per unit, quantity, 100 units, delivered to your facility. You have six weeks to consider this offer; during that period we will not withdraw it." When Sally hears nothing from Betty, she writes again on June 14: "I now withdraw our offer of June 1." On June 19, Betty writes back: "I accept your offer of June 1." As of June 20, Betty and Sally:

A. are parties to a contract because Sally made an offer and Betty accepted it.

B. are parties to a contract because the common law provides that Sally, as merchant, is bound by her promise to hold her offer open.

C. are parties to a contract because Betty is a merchant.

D. are parties to a contract because Betty responded to Sally on June 19 by signed writing.

E. are not parties to a contract because Sally revoked her offer before Betty attempted to accept it.

ANALYSIS. Because tire valves are goods ("movable things"), UCC Article 2 governs the transaction. On June 1 Sally makes an offer, representing that for six weeks she would not revoke it. She (a) is a merchant (b) who made an offer to sell goods, (c) in a signed writing. UCC §2-205 binds her to her word; for six weeks her offer is irrevocable. Two weeks later, her attempt to revoke is ineffective. On June 14 her offer is, still, alive and well. On June 19, Betty accepts, and the parties form a contract.

E states that Sally and Betty formed no contract because "Sally revoked her offer before Betty attempted to accept it." That's exactly what did *not* happen. Sally *attempted* to revoke, but UCC §2-205 denied her that privilege. The offer survived, and when Betty accepted, the parties formed a contract. **E** is wrong.

We're left with **A**, **B**, **C**, and **D**, all of which correctly conclude that these parties formed a contract. Only one of them, however, states the relevant reason. Many students jump at **D**, because (1) they see the phrase "signed writing" as a familiar face and grab onto it, or (2) they hurriedly misread it to state: "are parties to a contract because Sally set forth her offer in a signed writing." If **D** truly read that way, it would be correct. **D** refers not to Sally's offer but to *Betty's response*. Where UCC §2-205 mentions "signed writing" it refers to not the offeree's acceptance, but to the *merchant's offer*. If Betty had tried to accept orally or by unsigned writing, or in any other (reasonable) way, then still the parties would form a contract. So it's not true that these parties formed a contract *because* Betty responded to Sally by signed writing. **D** is wrong.

And **C**? It proclaims that the parties formed a contract "because Betty is a merchant." Again, that's wrong. UCC §2-205 operates when the offer*or* is a merchant and puts forth her offer in a signed writing. The offeree need not be a merchant and need not respond by signed writing. If **C** were to tell us that Betty and Sally "are parties to a contract because *Sally* is a merchant," then it would be correct. But it tells us no such thing. **C** is wrong.

B is wrong because it speaks not of the UCC but of the common law. It states that Sally and Betty "are parties to a contract because the *common law* provides that Sally, as merchant, is bound by her promise to hold her offer open." The common law provides no such thing. Under the common law, an offeror, merchant or not, is free to revoke her offer even if she promises she won't. **B** would be correct if it replaced "common law" with "Uniform Commercial Code," but as truly written, it's wrong.

B, **C**, and **D** teach this lesson: Read the answer choices for what they truly state. Read *every* word. If consciously or unconsciously you overlook or misread a single one, your error will turn 'round and bite you.

A tells the simple truth. Sally made an offer, and on June 19 it remained effective notwithstanding her failed attempt, on June 14, to revoke. Betty accepted and so arose the contract. **A** is right.

2. The Three-Month Limitation

UCC §2-205 allows a merchant to make her offer irrevocable, but it puts a ceiling on the period for which she may do so:

An offer by a merchant to buy or sell goods in a signed writing which by its terms gives assurances that it will be held open is not revocable . . . during the time stated . . . but in no event may such period of irrevocability exceed three months. . . .

Stated otherwise, UCC §2-205 subjects itself to a three-month ceiling. The merchant/offeror may sign in blood that her offer is irrevocable for three months and one day, but it's irrevocable for three months—not a second more. *If a merchant's signed, written offer to buy or sell goods proclaims itself irrevocable, then it is irrevocable for the shorter of (a) the period identified in the offer or (b) three months.* If the offeror states that her offer is irrevocable for one week, then it's irrevocable for one week. If she states that it's irrevocable for two months, then it's irrevocable for two months. If she states that it's irrevocable for three months, then it's irrevocable for three months. But, if she states that it's irrevocable for three months and one day, or four months, or six months or one year then, in each such case, it's irrevocable for *three months* and no more.

QUESTION 2. Wallace manufactures light bulbs, and Shep makes electric sockets. They exchange these signed writings:

June 1, Shep: I offer you type 47 electric sockets for $1 each, quantity 20,000, to be shipped by us to your facility at your convenience. The offer is firm, open, and irrevocable until midnight on September 15.
September 5, Shep (again): I have heard nothing from you regarding my June 1 offer. I now withdraw it.
September 6, Wallace: You made your offer firm until September15. By that date we'll let you know if we wish to accept.

On September 15 Wallace decides to accept Shep's offer. Does he have the power to do so?

A. Yes, because he reasonably expected that Shep would honor his written statement
B. Yes, because Shep is a merchant who made his offer by signed writing
C. No, because Shep effectively revoked on September 5
D. No, because when Wallace contacted Shep on September 6, he did not attempt to accept

---

ANALYSIS. If the case did not concern goods, the common law would govern and the answer would be clear: Shep's offer would expire by revocation on September 5. Because the problem does concern goods, the common law does not govern; the case turns on UCC §2-205.

Shep made an offer on June 1, proclaiming it irrevocable through September 15. The period June 1 to September 15 exceeds three months. Notwithstanding

Shep's promise, he was free to revoke after August 31. On September 5, he did so, and the offer terminated. The answer, therefore, is "no"; on September 15, Wallace had no power to accept.

A and **B** say "yes," so they're wrong. Each also supplies its own erroneous reasoning. According to **A** the offer is extant on September 15 because Shep, a merchant, made it by signed writing. But those facts render the offer irrevocable for no longer than three months. At midnight on August 31, it became revocable and on September 5, Shep revoked. **B** invokes the phrase "reasonable expectation," and too many students believe that all things "reasonable' are happy and right. Realize, please, that a statement might refer to reasonableness and still be wrong. Evidently, Wallace did expect that Shep would hold his offer open until September 15 and, quite arguably, his expectation was reasonable; after all, it's not unreasonable to expect a promisor to keep his promise. Reasonable or not, however, Wallace's expectation conflicted with law. Shep was entitled to revoke his offer on September 1, regardless of Wallace's expectations and regardless of how "reasonable" they might be.

D says "no," but its reasoning is wrong. It's true that Wallace did not try to accept the offer on September 6—but so what? The offer expired on September 5. If, on September 6, Wallace had tried to accept he would have been "too late," just as he is on September 15. The answer would be, still, "no." **D** is wrong.

C correctly says "no," that Wallace has no power, on September 15, to accept Shep's offer. The reason? On August 31, the offer turned revocable. On September 5, just as **C** reports, Shep effectively revoked it. **C** is right.

3. Don't Misunderstand the Three-Month Provision

Let's think again about Shep and ask: why did Shep's offer not expire at midnight on August 31, the date specified *in* the offer? Now let's answer: the passage of three months from June 1 does not by itself *revoke* Shep's offer. Rather, it makes Shep's offer revo*cable*. As of September 1, Shep acquired the *right* to revoke. But if he chose not to exercise that right, the offer, like any offer, would continue until it expired for some other reason such as rejection, passage of time, death or incapacity of the offeror.

Imagine, for example, that Wallace rejected the offer on July 15 by telling Shep, "I have thought about your June 1 offer and have decided not to accept it." The offer dies. If on August 1, Shep changes his mind and tries to accept, he won't succeed. The offer, although it was irrevocable through August 31, died by rejection on August 1.

QUESTION 3. Bonnie is a professional dancer and Sarah sells Dancer's garb. On October 1 Sarah sends Bonnie this signed writing: "I'm offering you the Xavier tights model 9 in your size for $350. The offer is guaranteed for two weeks." On October 2, Bonnie calls Sarah and rejects the offer.

Three days later, on October 5, Bonnie changes her mind, calls Sarah, and says, "I'd like to have the tights after all." Sarah says that she's no longer willing to sell the tights for $350. Bonnie sues Sarah alleging breach of contract. In defending herself, Sarah should direct the court's attention to:

A. the common law mirror-image rule.
B. the three-month limitation embodied in UCC §2-205.
C. Bonnie's communication of October 2.
D. the fact that Bonnie's October 5 statement was not made by signed writing.

ANALYSIS. Think first about the story and then about the question. Regarding the story, consider the legal significance of every fact, communication, and event. On that basis, assess the rights and liabilities, if any, of the relevant parties.

Sarah deals professionally in dancers' garb. In this transaction, therefore, she was a merchant. On October 1, by signed writing, she offered to sell goods, promising not to revoke for two weeks. With that we conclude: Under UCC §2-205, Sarah cannot revoke for two weeks — *period* (even though the common law, if it governed, would allow her to do so).

On October 2, by telephone, Bonnie told Sarah she'd "pass." She rejected the offer and thus "killed" it. There then stood between these ladies no offer at all. The two-week period to which Sarah referred lost its significance.

So much for the story. Let's consider the question. We're to find, among the answer choices, that fact, communication, or precept of law that best helps Sarah demonstrate, legally, that she and Bonnie formed no contract.

A refers to the common law mirror-image rule. That rule has no more to do with this case than the price paid for tea by the woman on the moon. This is not a situation in which Sarah proposed one exchange and Bonnie attempted to accept another. **A** is wrong. **B** suggests that the UCC §2-205 three-month limitation is somehow meaningful to this case. But it isn't. Sarah's offer was irrevocable for two weeks; it doesn't "hit" the three-month ceiling. The three-month limitation has naught to do with the controversy.

D joins **A** and **B** in the dumper. It attempts to "make hay" from the fact that Bonnie attempted, on October 5, to accept not by writing, but by spoken word. UCC §2-205 makes a writing relevant in only one respect: If an offeror is to make her offer irrevocable for a prescribed period (in no case to exceed three months, however), she must do so by signed writing. So long as the offer endures, the offeree may accept in any manner that the offeror prescribes and, if she prescribes none, then in any that is reasonable, including, certainly, spoken word. That Bonnie attempted to accept, on October 5, by speech, not writing, is irrelevant. If the offer had been extant on that date Bonnie, with spoken words, would have accepted it.

Now comes **C**, telling us that Sarah should defend herself by pointing to Bonnie's telephone communication of October 2, in which Bonnie rejected the offer. That's the key to Sarah's defense. By rejection, the offer died on October 2. On October 5, Bonnie's attempt to accept was ineffective. **C** is right.

4. *What If the Merchant Doesn't Prescribe a Time Period for Irrevocability?*

In UCC §2-205, we have thus far left some blanks. Let's complete them.

> An offer by a merchant to buy or sell goods in a signed writing which by its terms gives assurances that it will be held open is not revocable . . . during the time stated *or if no time is stated for a reasonable time*, but in no event may such period of irrevocability exceed three months. . . .

With the italicized words now added, UCC §2-205 comes to mean this: (1) *If by signed writing a merchant offers to buy or sell goods, declaring the offer irrevocable for a specific period, then it is irrevocable for that period, with a ceiling, however, of three months. (2) If by signed writing a merchant offers to buy or sell goods, declaring the offer irrevocable, without specifying a time period for which it will remain so, then, by law, he has declared his offer irrevocable for a reasonable time, with that same ceiling, however, of three months.*

Time Out! Who Decides What Is and Is Not "Reasonable?"

In all fields of law, "reasonable" refers to "that which ordinary reasonable persons would do or perceive under all circumstances surrounding their situation." That is so whether we speak of reasonable belief, reasonable behavior, reasonable perception, or reasonable time. Ordinarily, "reasonableness" creates a question of fact, and questions of fact go to the jury. After hearing evidence of the circumstances surrounding the parties, the jury ordinarily decides the matter of "reasonableness" whether it relates to time, behavior, belief or anything else.[1]

Back to Contracts and UCC §2-205.

Suppose a merchant, by signed writing, makes an offer to buy or sell goods and concludes it with this sentence: "By the way, I won't revoke this offer." Because the merchant did not specify a time for which she would not revoke her offer, her last sentence, by law, means: "By the way, *for a reasonable time*, I won't revoke this offer." In most cases, a jury accounting for all relevant circumstances decides on the meaning of "reasonable."

---

1. Any question of fact, however, can become a question of law. If, in some case, a judge believes that no sensible juror could find the defendant's behavior to be unreasonable then, on appropriate motion, she will take the question from the jury and decide "as a matter of law" that the defendant's behavior was reasonable.

QUESTION 4. Biff is a professional juggler. Shelley sells circus and carnival equipment. The parties exchange these signed writings:

> **April 10, Shelley:** I have twelve surplus juggling pins: height—9 inches; color—blue/yellow striped; bottom circumference—3 inches. I'm ready to sell them to you at $3 each. Think it over; take your time. Don't worry; I won't withdraw the offer.
>
> **April 11, Biff:** Yes, I'll think it over.
>
> **May 15, Shelley:** Regarding our communications of April, I no longer have the pins in stock. The offer is withdrawn.
>
> **Biff:** But just before you contacted me—just now—I had decided to accept. I do accept.
>
> **Shelley:** Sorry; we no longer have the pins.
>
> **Biff:** I've just told you that we accept your original offer. You are obliged to perform.
>
> **Shelley:** Forget it. I'm sorry. We can't.

Which of the following *additional* facts, if proven, would most strengthen Shelley's position that she is not in breach of contract?

A. Shelley's statement 5 on May 15 set forth these additional words: "but for the same price, we have other juggling pins of the same size, different in color."

B. Biff's first statement of May 15 set forth these additional words: "but only on the condition that you reduce the price to $2 per unit; otherwise, we don't want them."

C. On May 15 Biff was truthful in stating that he had decided to accept just before Shelley contacted him.

D. On April 12 Shelley, by signed writing, sent Biff this message: "That's fine, but please realize that the offer expires in one week."

ANALYSIS. Shelley made an offer, declaring it irrevocable. She lost the power to revoke for the shorter of (a) a reasonable time or (b) three months. Yet the offer might terminate sooner by rejection or passage of time. Each answer choice presents a fact, and we're to find the one which, if added to the story, would best support Shelley's position that she did not breach a contract.

By making the statement shown in **A**, Shelley would create a new offer on May 15. But that would not free her of the one she made on April 10. There would be "on the table," two offers from Shelley to Biff: the one of April 10 and the new one of May 15. **A** is wrong. Assessing **C**, let's add to the story this fact: On May 15 Biff was truthful in stating that he had decided to accept just before Shelley contacted him. That fact matters not at all. Biff said "I do accept it."

Unless the offer had expired before he made that statement, his words formed a contract.

D is tempting but wrong. Once an offeror sets a time period for which his offer will be irrevocable, he cannot later shorten it. If we add to the story the fact that on April 12, Shelly told Biff that "the offer expires in one week," we'll be adding an irrelevancy. Such a statement would be insignificant; Shelley's offer would be, still, irrevocable for (a) a reasonable time (whatever exactly that is under these circumstances), and (b) three months—whichever is shorter. **B**'s amendment to Biff's statement 4 creates not an acceptance but a counteroffer and rejection. If in statement 4, Biff had said all of *that*, he'd have rejected Shelley's offer and thus put it to an end. Biff's later statement purporting to accept would come "too late." Consequently, the added fact described at **B** would support Shelley's position that she committed no breach of contract. **B** is right.

B.   The Mirror-Image Rule, UCC §2-207(1), and "Battle of the Forms"

In commerce, buyers often make offers on their own pre-printed forms entitled "purchase order." Sellers often accept (or attempt to accept) on their own pre-printed forms entitled "sales acknowledgment." Imagine that BuyCo constructs large lawns and buys seed from various suppliers. BuyCo makes offers to buy seed on its own preprinted "purchase order" form. The form's front side recites BuyCo's address and contact information, providing blank spaces on which BuyCo personnel write their orders. The reverse side embodies lots of text in teensy type.

SeedCo sells lawn seed. It generally *accepts* (or attempts to accept) offers to buy on its own preprinted "sales acknowledgment" form. The form's front side recites SeedCo's address and contact information. It provides blank spaces on which SeedCo personnel "acknowledge" sales (accept offers) and sign their names. The reverse side, too, embodies lots of text in teensy type.

On one occasion, SeedCo and BuyCo conduct this little interaction:

BuyCo to SeedCo (on the front side of its "Purchase Order" form, signed):

PURCHASE ORDER

Please send to our facility: 18 tons of your grass seed #20. Will pay $200/ton.

NOTICE: THIS PURCHASE ORDER IS SUBJECT TO ALL TERMS ON THE REVERSE SIDE OF THIS FORM.

SeedCo to BuyCo (on the front side of its "Sales Acknowledgment" form, signed):

SALES ACKNOWLEDGMENT

Confirmed: Will send to BuyCo at its facility 18 tons of our grass seed #20 @ $200/ton.
NOTICE: THIS SALES ACKNOWLEDGMENT IS SUBJECT TO ALL TERMS ON THE REVERSE SIDE OF THIS FORM.

Were it not for the "NOTICE" provisions on each form, BuyCo's form would be an offer and SeedCo's an acceptance. Now look at the reverse sides of each form to see how they destroy the transaction.

Buyco's Purchase Order, Reverse Side

This Purchase Order is made under these terms: (1) After BuyCo takes possession of the goods it will have 90 days to pay the agreed price. If BuyCo fails to pay within that period Seller may demand interest at the rate of 4% per annum, but will not be entitled to any interest or damages beyond that amount, notwithstanding that the law might otherwise entitle Seller to additional damages.

Seedco's Sales Acknowledgment, Reverse Side

Acknowledgment and acceptance are made under these terms: (1) After Buyer takes possession of the goods, it will have 15 days to pay the agreed purchase price. If Buyer shall fail to pay within that period SeedCo may demand interest at the rate of 12% per annum, and will be entitled, further, to all additional damages for which the law otherwise provides. Further, SeedCo expressly disclaims all warranties that the law might otherwise imply concerning the goods to be sold, including but not limited to any and all warranties of merchantability, warranties of fitness for a particular purpose, wherefore the goods are sold as is and with all faults.[2]

What Would the Common Law Make of BuyCo's "Purchase Order" and SeedCo's "Sales Acknowledgment?"

SeedCo's purported acceptance (the "acknowledgment" form) fails to mirror BuyCo's offer (the "purchase order") as to three matters:

1. BuyCo's form gives BuyCo 90 days to pay, but SeedCo's form gives BuyCo 15 days to pay.
2. BuyCo's form provides that in the case of breach BuyCo should pay 4% interest and be liable for no additional damages, but SeedCo's form requires that BuyCo pay 12% interest in addition to all other damages provided by law.
3. SeedCo's form excludes warranties, BuyCo's form does not.

---

2. Warranties are discussed in Chapter 23.

Under the common law mirror-image rule,[3] BuyCo made an offer and SeedCo responded with a counter offer which acts, also, as a rejection.[4] The parties fail to form a contract.

Yet businesses operate this way on a daily basis—attempting to make contracts using pre-printed forms whose terms conflict. This shoddy practice creates a problem colloquially called "battle of the forms." By rejecting, in part, the mirror image rule, UCC §2-207 purports to solve it (and in doing so makes shoddy law). UCC §2-207 (comment) states:

> This section is intended to deal with . . . the exchange of printed purchase order and acceptance (sometimes called "acknowledgment") forms. Because the forms are oriented to the thinking of the respective drafting parties, the terms contained in them often do not correspond. Often the seller's form contains terms different from or additional to those set forth in the buyer's form.

1. UCC §2-207(1) as Presently Operative in All States

UCC §2-207, Subsection (1), Lesson 1: The "*Expression* of Acceptance." UCC §2-207(1) invents a legal communication it calls "expression of acceptance" (to which it gives not a word of definition). That phrase refers to a communication that *on its face*—superficially— "looks like," "sounds like," or "smells like" assent. SeedCo's response to BuyCo's offer *seems,* on its face, to say, "Yes—we'll send you the seeds you've requested at the price you've named." Because of its reverse side, the form is not a true, common law acceptance. Yet it is, under UCC §2-207 "an *expression* of acceptance."

UCC §2-207(1), Lesson 2: An expression of acceptance *is* an acceptance even if it fails to mirror the offer.   UCC §2-207(1) provides:

> A[n] expression of acceptance . . . operates as an acceptance even though it states terms additional to or different from those offered. . . .

Those statutory words mean that when Party 1 offers to buy or sell goods and Party 2 responds with a message that, on its face, *seems* to say "yes," Party 2 accepts Party 1's offer, regardless of any different or additional terms that Party 2 might add somewhere in the same message.

In the seed case, BuyCo made an offer to buy, and SeedCo—on the face of things—expressed its acceptance. SeedCo may not know it, but it accepted BuyCo's offer, complete with all terms on the front and back sides of BuyCo's form. Under UCC §2-207, BuyCo and SeedCo form a contract on *BuyCo's* terms. The terms that SeedCo wrote on the reverse side of its form are *not* part of the contract. Hence, the contract requires SeedCo to supply BuyCo with

---

3. Chapter 7, section B.
4. Chapter 7, section A.

18 tons of grass seed at $200/ton. BuyCo has 90 days in which to pay, and late payments will incur interest at 4%. All warranties apply; none is excluded.

SeedCo Is Bound by Terms to Which It Never Really Agreed?

By law, SeedCo *did* agree to all of BuyCo's terms. Under UCC §2-207 it issued an "expression of acceptance." By law, it accepted BuyCo's offer—*as BuyCo made it*. With UCC §207 in place all persons who accept offers to buy or sell goods ought to know: if, on the surface of things, they say "yes," then they accept the offer—all of it—including the offeror's "fine print." Whatever they add to their apparent assent doesn't count; it's not part of the contract.

2. What UCC §2-207(1) Does *Not* Provide

Note that UCC §2-207(1) does not include the word "merchant." The provision operates when both parties are merchants, when neither is a merchant, or when one is a merchant and the other not.[5] Notice, too, that UCC §2-207(1) features no form of the word "write" or "sign." It applies when both offer and acceptance are written and signed, when both are written and unsigned, when neither is written or signed, and when one is written (signed or unsigned) and the other not. Put otherwise, UCC §2-207(1) "doesn't care" whether an offer or an expression of acceptance is unwritten, written, signed, or unsigned.[6]

QUESTION 5. Jared operates a retail hardware store. By telephone, Sarah, a plumber, contacts him:

(1) **Sarah:** Do you have in stock a full set of metric combination wrenches?

(2) **Jared:** Yes, we do. The set is priced at $70, and we'll be glad to hold it for you if you agree to pick it up and pay for it this week. Shall we do that?

(3) **Sarah:** Yes, I'll take it. I don't want to pick it up, however; I'd prefer to have you send it to my office. Of course, I'll pay the transit cost.

(4) **Jared:** No, we won't be able to send it to you.

(5) **Sarah:** Then I don't want it.

Contending that she and Jared have no contract, Sarah refuses to purchase the wrenches. Jared maintains that the parties do have a contract and that Sarah is in breach. Which of the following facts best supports Jared's position?

---

5. Section C below discusses an exception in which the parties' status as merchants does bear relevance, as provided in UCC §2-207(2).

6. Section E below discusses one situation, involving a "confirmatory memorandum," in which the matter of writing *is* significant.

A. Sarah initiated the contact with Jared; Jared did not initiate contact with Sarah.
B. In statement 5, Sarah said she did not want "it," never explaining that "it" meant the wrenches.
C. Sarah is not, in this circumstance, a merchant.
D. Wrenches are goods.

ANALYSIS. Examine the parties' conversation and characterize their statements.

Statement 1: Sarah asked to know whether Jared had a certain item in stock; she made an invitation to deal.

Statement 2: Jared told Sarah that he had the item she sought. He assigned it a price and promised to hold it for Sarah's pickup and payment. He made an offer and left Sarah with power to accept.

Statement 3: Sarah said, "Yes, I'll take it," and then remarked that the wrenches should be sent to her. Under UCC §2-207(1) she issued an "expression of acceptance" thus accepting Jared's offer—all of it—even though she failed to "mirror" its terms.

Statement 4: Jared said "no" to Sarah's new/different terms.

Statement 5: Sarah expressed her wish not to purchase the wrenches, but she did so "too late." At statement 3 these parties formed a contract, and Sarah is bound by it.

Jared is right because (1) the transaction concerns the sale of goods, (2) Jared made an offer, and (3) Sarah, who issued no mirror-image assent, did issue an "expression of acceptance" as that phrase operates in UCC §2-207. Those three facts support Jared's position; they cause the parties to form a contract. Read each answer choice and determine which reflects one or more of those same three relevant facts.

A is wrong. Whether two parties form a contract does not depend, ever, on which of them first contacted the other. **B** is just as bad. These parties formed their contract at statement 3. Nothing Sarah might say at statement 5 could alter that truth.

The statement in **C** is false and irrelevant. Sarah *is* a merchant in this circumstance; by her occupation she holds herself out as having knowledge or skill peculiar to wrenches (See UCC §2-201, section a). But that has not a whit to do with the fact that these parties formed a contract. UCC §2-207(1) applies to any buyer and any seller whether they be merchants or not.

D correctly reports that wrenches are goods. *That's* why UCC Article 2 applies. And *that's* why Sarah's response operates as an acceptance even though it fails to mirror the offer. *That's* why the parties form a contract, and that's why **D** is right.

3. *An Offeree Can Save Herself from UCC §2-207*

UCC §2-207 puts an offeree at risk whether she's a buyer or seller. If she issues an expression of acceptance, she's "stuck" with the offeror's terms. An offeree can avoid that consequence, however, if she expressly states that her acceptance is conditional on the offeror's assent to her new and different terms. Look again at UCC §2-207(1), to which we now add and italicize some text that we earlier removed:

> A[n] expression of acceptance . . . operates as an acceptance even though it states terms additional to or different from those offered . . . *unless acceptance is expressly made conditional on assent to the additional or different terms.*

"Unless" means "but not if." Let's redraft UCC §2-207(1) so you'll better understand it. The provision really means:

> *When one party offers to buy or sell goods, and the offeree responds with an expression of acceptance, that expression of acceptance operates as an acceptance even though it does not mirror the offer, but that rule doesn't apply if the offeree expressly states that his expression of acceptance is conditional on the offeror's assent to the new or different terms that he, in his expression of acceptance sets forth.*

Suppose Simcha makes Bretain this offer: "I offer to sell you 200 widgets for $200, delivered to you next Monday morning." Bretain responds, "I accept, but please deliver on Tuesday, not Monday." He then adds a footnote: "My acceptance is conditioned on your agreement to all of the terms I have here set forth." On its face, the response reads "yes," meaning that Bretain issued an expression of acceptance. The first clause of UCC §2-207 (1) would make it an acceptance were it not for the *second*—the one that begins with "unless." Bretain's footnote puts his expression of acceptance within the second clause. Consequently, *this* expression of acceptance does not operate *as* an acceptance.

UCC §2-207(1) tells us that Bretain's response is not an acceptance, but it doesn't tell us what it *is*. That means we must remember: Where statutes are silent, the common law governs. In order to characterize Bretain's response, therefore, we look to the common law. The common law generally provides that a non-mirror-image acceptance is a counteroffer and rejection. Bretain's response is just that—a counteroffer and rejection.

QUESTION 6. SellCo installs and repairs computer systems. BellCo creates computer software. On July 18, the parties begin an exchange of signed writings:

July 18, BellCo:

PURCHASE ORDER

We understand that you wish to sell an IXM system, with all current software. We wish to purchase it and will pay $40,000, including installation. Our offer stands firm; it will not be withdrawn for 30 days.

THIS PURCHASE ORDER IS SUBJECT TO ALL TERMS ON THE REVERSE SIDE HEREOF.

The reverse side reads: "This Purchase Order and any offer it embodies must be accepted as to each and every term, and BellCo hereby rejects, in advance, any additional or different terms."

July 19, SellCo: Thank you. Please expect our response within three days.

July 20, BellCo: We have decided not to purchase the system.

July 21, SellCo:

SALES CONFIRMATION

Agreed: We will deliver one IXM system to your offices. Installation requires an additional $5,000 charge.

THIS CONFIRMATION IS WHOLLY AND FULLY CONDITIONED ON BUYER'S ASSENT TO EACH AND EVERY ONE OF ITS TERMS.

July 22, BellCo (by telephone): Thank you for your "sales acknowledgment," but as we advised you on July 20, we no longer wish to buy the system.

July 23, SellCo (by signed fax): We accept your original proposal exactly as made.

July 24, BellCo (by signed fax): As we have twice advised you, we no longer wish to purchase the system.

If SellCo brings an action against BellCo for breach of contract, SellCo will:

A. prevail, because on July 23 it manifested assent to all of BellCo's proposed terms.

B. prevail, because BellCo's initial offer was irrevocable for 30 days.

C. not prevail, because on July 20, BellCo effectively revoked its offer.

D. not prevail, because on July 21 SellCo rejected BellCo's offer.

ANALYSIS.   If a merchant, by signed writing, offers to buy or sell goods and declares his offer firm/irrevocable for some particular time period, then the offer is irrevocable for the time stated (but for no longer than three months). Further, if any person (merchant or not) responds to an offer to buy or sell goods with an expression of acceptance, then he accepts the offer as made *unless he expressly provides that his assent is conditional on the offeror's assent to each and every term set forth in the expression of acceptance.*

BellCo is a merchant. By signed writing, it offered to buy SellCo's computer system, stating that its offer was firm for 30 days. For that period, therefore, the offer was irrevocable and BellCo had no power to revoke it. Its July 20 attempt to do so was ineffective, and the offer remained open. On July 21, however, SellCo responded with a non-mirror-image expression of acceptance. That response *would* operate as an acceptance of BellCo's offer were it not for the fact that SellCo expressly provided that *its* assent was conditional on *BellCo's* assent to all of its terms. Consequently, SellCo's response did not operate as an acceptance. It was a counteroffer and rejection, meaning that on July 21, SellCo rendered BellCo's offer inoperative and thus terminated its own power to accept it. When, on July 23, SellCo attempted to accept the offer unconditionally, it accomplished nothing.

According to **A** and **B**, SellCo prevails. Both are wrong. As for a reason, **A** reports that SellCo assented fully to BellCo's offer on July 23. It's true that SellCo did that, but it had rejected the offer two days earlier on July 21. Its mirror-image assent on July 23 came too late. **B** correctly tells us that BellCo's offer was irrevocable for 30 days. Nonetheless, it was susceptible to *rejection*, and on July 21, SellCo did reject it. **C** correctly states that SellCo will not prevail, but its reasoning is wrong. BellCo's offer was irrevocable for 30 days from July 18. On July 20, its attempt to revoke was without effect.

D, alas, speaketh truth. SellCo will not prevail, it says, because, on July 21, Sellco rejected Bellco's offer. By doing so, Sellco rendered the offer defunct. On July 23, its attempt to accept was ineffective. **D** is right.

Question 7. WellCo raises funds on behalf of charitable organizations. In its offices, it uses computers, and it owns an old IXM computer system that it wishes to sell. BestCo wishes to buy it, and the parties communicate:

July 18, BestCo:

PURCHASE ORDER

We understand that you wish to sell an IXM system, with all current software. We wish to purchase it and will pay $40,000, including installation. Our offer stands firm; it will not be withdrawn for 30 days.
THIS PURCHASE ORDER IS SUBJECT TO ALL TERMS ON THE REVERSE SIDE HEREOF.

The reverse side reads: "This Purchase Order and any offer it embodies must be accepted as to each and every term, and BellCo hereby rejects, in advance, any additional or different terms."

July 19, WellCo: Thank you. Please expect our response within three days.
July 20, BestCo: We have decided not to purchase the system.
July 21, WellCo:

SALES CONFIRMATION

Agreed: We will deliver one IXM system to your offices. Installation requires an additional $5,000 charge.

> **July 22, BestCo (by telephone):** Thank you for your "sales acknowledgment," but as we advised you on July 20, we no longer wish to buy the system.
>
> **July 23, SellCo (by signed fax):** We accept your original proposal exactly as made.
>
> **July 24, BestCo (by signed fax):** As we have twice advised you, we no longer wish to purchase the system.

If WellCo brings an action against BestCo for breach of contract, WellCo will

A. prevail, because it responded to BestCo's offer with an expression of acceptance.
B. prevail, because WellCo assented to BestCo's terms within three days of July 18, as it stated it would.
C. not prevail, because WellCo's July 21 response did not mirror BestCo's offer.
D. not prevail, because on July 20 BestCo caused the offer to terminate.

ANALYSIS. WellCo is not a merchant, but that's irrelevant. In response to BestCo's offer, it issued an expression of acceptance under UCC 2-207(1) and did not condition it on BestCo's assent to all of its terms. WellCo's expression of acceptance operates *as* an acceptance—of BestCo's offer—all of it, exactly as made by Bestco. The parties formed a contract on BestCo's terms.

C and **D** are wrong because they state that SellCo will not prevail. As for **C**, it's true that SellCo's July 21 response did not mirror BellCo's offer, but under UCC §2-207, that's irrelevant. WellCo issued an expression of acceptance, and so accepted BellCo's offer *as BellCo made it.* **D** is wrong too. BellCo's offer was irrevocable for 30 days from July 18. **D** is wrong. **B** correctly states that WellCo will prevail. That it assented within three days of July 18, however, is irrelevant. If WellCo had issued its expression of acceptance on July 19, 20, or, at any time before BestCo's offer expired, the parties would form a contract and WellCo would prevail.

A correctly reports that WellCo will prevail, and its reasoning is right: WellCo responded to the offer with an expression of acceptance. The response operated *as* an acceptance, and the parties formed a contract. That's why **A** is right.

C. Modification of Existing Contract: UCC §2-207(2)

If two parties form a (bilateral) contract, then, by a new offer and acceptance, they may agree to modify it. Suppose, for example, that Gary and Jacqueline form a contract in which Gary promises to pay Jacqueline $30 for proofreading his manuscript by August 1. On July 20, Jacqueline makes an offer to alter their contract: "I'll proofread the text *and* retype it at no charge if you'll extend my deadline to October 1." If Gary accepts, the contract is modified; Jacqueline must proofread *and type*. Her deadline is *October 1*.

UCC §2-207(2), Lesson 1: The Offeree's Additional Terms Are an Offer to Modify the Contract

As we now know, when, having received an offer for the purchase or sale of goods, an offeree responds with an "expression of acceptance," he accepts the offer, as made. If his response includes terms that do not conform to the offer, they are not part of the contract. That raises this question: *What is the significance of those terms?* UCC §2-207 subsection 2 (clumsily and ineptly drafted) provides that they are "proposals for addition to the contract." Taken together, subsections 1 and 2 mean this: *If an offeree receives an offer for the purchase or sale of goods, and she responds with a non-mirror acceptance, there occur, simultaneously, these two events: (1) the offeree accepts the offer as made, so that offeror and offeree form a contract on the offeror's terms, and (2) the offeree offers to modify that contract—the one just formed—according to such of her terms as do not mirror the offer.*

Consider these signed writings:

(1) **Ethel:** I am prepared to sell you 20,000 widgets for $20,000, delivered to your warehouse, packed in cardboard boxes and stapled shut. Do you wish to purchase?

(2) **Rohan:** Yes, definitely, and after you apply the staples, you will, please, seal the boxes with one-quarter-inch tape.

Ethel made an offer to sell goods, and Rohan issued a non-mirror-image expression of acceptance. When he did that, there occurred, simultaneously, these two events: (1) Rohan accepts Ethel's offer, so that the parties form a contract on Ethel's terms; and (2) Rohan makes an offer to modify that very same contract — the one just formed. He proposes that Ethel, after stapling the boxes, should seal them with one-quarter-inch tape.

It is for Ethel to accept or not Rohan's offer to modify the contract in that way. If she accepts, then the terms of the contract undergo change: after stapling the boxes, Ethel must seal them with one-quarter-inch tape. If she does not accept, the contract remains as initially formed: Ethel is to shut the boxes with staples; the one-quarter-inch tape has no place in the contract.

Ethel may accept the proposal by announcing her assent to Rohan in any reasonable way (Chapter 9, section B). (Under some circumstances, she accepts by silence, as discussed in section D below.)

QUESTIONS 8 & 9. On May 1, Powex contacts Genex by signed writing: "After much research, we are prepared to purchase your Genex Model T-12 generator for $2 million. Please deliver all component pieces and parts to our main office for assembly. On delivery, we will make payment, by certified check." In response, Genex sends Powex a signed Sales Confirmation form: "Sold—Genex Model T-12 generator, for $2 million, components to be delivered to buyer's facility. Sale is subject to terms printed on the reverse side." On the reverse side, in small print, there appears this text: "For all sales of its equipment, the parties agree that (1) Genex is obliged to assemble the equipment and, for that service, (2) the buyer will pay an additional 10% of the purchase price noted on the front side hererof."

QUESTION 8. If Powex makes no response to Genex's Sales Confirmation, the parties:

A. have no contract, because Genex's sales confirmation amounts to a counteroffer and rejection.
B. have no contract, because Powex's offer does not include any term that concerns assembly of the generator.
C. have a contract for purchase of the generator, but no contract for its assembly.
D. have a contract for purchase of the generator, and for its assembly.

QUESTION 9. Assume now that Powex responds to Genex's Sales Confirmation with a signed writing that carries these five words: "Very well; we are agreed." The parties:

A. have no contract, because Genex's sales confirmation form amounts to a counteroffer and rejection.
B. have no contract, because Powex did not assent to Genex's proposal as to assembly of the generator.
C. have a contract for sale of the generator, but no contract for its assembly.
D. have a contract for sale of the generator and for its assembly.

ANALYSIS. Powex offers to buy a generator in component pieces with no provision as to how or by whom the components will be assembled. Genex issues an "expression of acceptance," that adds a term of its own: Genex is to assemble the components, and, in exchange, Powex is to pay an additional $200,000 (10% of the $2 million purchase price). Simultaneously, therefore Genex (1) accepts Powex's offer as made, thus forming a contract on Powex's terms, and (2) offers to modify that very same contract by adding the assembly term. It is then for Powex to accept or not Genex's offer.

As for Question 8, we are to assume that Powex makes no response to Genex's sales confirmation form. Consequently, the parties form a contract according to Powex's offer and the assembly term does not become a part of it.

A and **B** state that the parties formed no contract, which means both choices are wrong. **A** characterizes Genex's sales confirmation as a counteroffer and rejection. If the common law governed, that would be correct. Under UCC §2-207(1), however, the sales confirmation acts as an acceptance (and simultaneous proposal to modify the contract thus formed). **B** implies that the parties would form a contract only if Powex were to accept Genex's proposal to modify the contract. That's false. With Genex's "expression of acceptance" the parties form a contract on Powex's terms.

D states that the parties' contract includes Genex's additional term. That's false because Powex did not accept it. **C** correctly reports that the parties formed a contract for the sale of the generator, but not for its assembly. **C** is right.

As for Question 9, we are to assume that Powex responded to Genex's sales confirmation form by writing, "Very well, we are agreed." With that response, Powex accepted Genex's offer to modify the contract, and the assembly term became a part of it. Consequently **D** is right.

D. Offeror's *Silence* as Acceptance of Offeree's Additional Terms

Suppose Offeror and Offeree are in the widget business. Offeror makes Offeree this offer: "Will sell to you 400 widgets for $400, delivered to you on May 1 between noon and 1 P.M." Offeree responds: "Yes, we'll buy. When you deliver the widgets you will also supply an invoice." To that proposal Offeree remains silent; he does not, within a reasonable time, "stand up" and object to it.

Let's assess the facts for their legal significance. Facts: Offeror makes an offer to sell goods. Offeree responds with an expression of acceptance ("Yes, we'll buy"). Legal consequence: The parties form a contract on Offeror's terms. Fact: Offeree's response includes a term not set forth in the offer. Legal consequence: Offeree proposes to modify the parties' contract by adding that term to it. Fact: To that proposed modification, Offeror responds with silence.

1. The Legal Consequence of Offeror's Silence

UCC §2-207(2) provides, in substance, *If an offeree responds to an offer with an expression of acceptance that fails to mirror the offer and thus proposes to modify the contract thus formed, the offeror's silence constitutes an acceptance of that proposal if the answers are (1) "yes," (2) "no," and (3) "no," respectively, to these three questions:*

(1) Are both parties merchants?
(2) Did Offeror announce in his offer that he would reject any additional terms put forth by the Offeree?
(3) Is Offeree's additional term material to the bargain—does it alter, in a significant way, either party's contractual burden or benefit?

Again, if (and only if) the answers are (1) "yes," (2) "no," and (3) "no," the offeror's silence amounts to his acceptance of the offeree's proposal to modify the contract.

In our case, the answers *are* (1) "yes;" both Offeror and Offeree are merchants, (2) "no:" Offeror did not, in his offer, state that he would reject any new terms proposed by the Offeree, and (3) "no," the proposed modification does not significantly alter either party's burden or benefit. By remaining silent Offeror accepts Offeree's proposal to modify the contract; when he delivers the widgets he must, also, supply an invoice. If Offeror wants not to accept the proposal, he must not remain silent; within a reasonable time he must "speak up" and object to it.

UCC §2-207 nowhere invokes the *word* "silence" or the phrase "silence as acceptance." Neither does it, in so many words, refer to the three questions and answers we've described. Rather, it provides:

> The [offeree's] additional terms are to be construed as proposals for addition to the contract. Between merchants such terms become part of the contract unless:[7]
>
> (a) the offer expressly limits acceptance to the terms of the offer;
> (b) they materially alter it; or
> (c) notification of objection . . . is given within a reasonable time[.]

The words "between merchants" create our question 1: "Are both parties merchants?" Provision (a) creates our question 2: "Did Offeror announce in his offer that he would reject any additional terms put forth by the offeree?" Provision (b) creates our question 3: "*Is Offeree's additional term material to the bargain—does it alter, in a significant way, either party's contractual burden or benefit?*" If the answers are (1) "yes," (2) "no," and (3) "no," the words

---

7. Because the word "unless" appears just before the colon, the burden of proving that none of the three conditions (a), (b), or (c) applies rests with the party (ordinarily the offeror) who asserts that the offeree's additional terms are not part of the contract. The other party bears the burden of proving that both parties are merchants. As to the relationship between the word "unless" and burden of proof, see Chapter 21, section A.

"such terms become part of the contract," together with provision (c) create the result—that the offeree's silence constitutes his acceptance.

QUESTIONS 10-13. WaxCo is in the business of selling wax to candle manufacturers. CandleCo manufactures candles. On August 10, with a signed, pre-printed "Available for Purchase" form, completing various of its blank spaces in handwriting, WaxCo makes CandleCo this offer: "Will ship to you @$200 per ton, 15 tons of *WaxCo Z-25* Candle Wax, color *White*. Total price: *$3,000*. Delivery within *10* days of your acceptance. Will unload and stack boxes on your receiving platform." On August 11, by signed, pre-printed "Purchase Order" form, completing various of its blank spaces in handwriting, CandleCo responds by signed writing.

QUESTION 10. For this question, assume that on August 11, CandleCo responds thus: "As per your offer of *August 10*, please ship. Additional Comment(s): *You will stack boxes in piles of three*." Making no response to CandleCo, WaxCo delivers the wax and stacks the boxes in piles of four (not three). CandleCo sues WaxCo alleging that WaxCo was contractually obliged to stack the boxes in piles of *three*. WaxCo maintains that the parties' contract included no such requirement. Which of the following facts, if proven, best supports WaxCo?

A. In the wax industry, sellers ordinarily deliver boxes and stack them in piles of four.
B. Many times in the past, WaxCo has delivered wax to CandleCo, stacking the boxes in piles of four.
C. The difference between piles of three and piles of four materially alters WaxCo's obligation.
D. WaxCo and CandleCo have never before done business with each other.

ANALYSIS.   Under UCC §2-207(1) and (2), CandleCo's expression of acceptance produces, simultaneously, these two legal consequences: (1) the parties form a contract on WaxCo's terms, and (2) CandleCo proposes to modify the contract so that boxes will be stacked in piles of three. WaxCo's *silence* accepts CandleCo's proposal if (and only if) to the three questions earlier described the answers are, respectively, (1) "yes," (2) "no," and (3) "no." A given fact will support WaxCo if, for any of the three questions, it fails to provide the answer just mentioned.

Choice **A** fails to address any of the three questions. Whether WaxCo's silence amounts to its acceptance is unrelated to the way in which wax sellers customarily stack boxes. **B** and **D** are wrong because they, too, state irrelevancies.

C is correct. If stacking piles of three would materially alter WaxCo's contractual burden, then the answer to question 3 is "yes," meaning that WaxCo's silence does not constitute its acceptance. That's why **C** is right.

QUESTION 11. For this question, assume that on August 11, CandleCo responds thus: "As per your offer of *August 10,* please ship. Additional Comment(s): *Personnel will not be in vicinity of receiving platform. Please knock twice on front office door to notify us that you have delivered the goods.*" Making no response, WaxCo delivers the wax and leaves *without* knocking on CandleCo's front door. By failing to do that, does WaxCo breach a contract?

A. Yes, because its silence accepted CandleCo's proposed modification to the contract

B. Yes, because the parties formed their contract with signed writings

C. Yes, because under the relevant circumstances CandleCo's proposed modification was reasonable

D. No, because WaxCo gave no assent to CandleCo's proposal that it should knock on the door

ANALYSIS. When CandleCo issues its "expression of acceptance," it forms a contract with WaxCo on WaxCo's terms. Simultaneously, CandleCo proposes to modify the contract so to require that WaxCo, when completing delivery, knock on its front door. To that proposal WaxCo makes no response, meaning that WaxCo accepts only if its silence operates as acceptance. That in turn requires (1) that both parties be merchants, (2) that the proposed addition not materially alter the contract, and (3) that WaxCo's initial offer not limit acceptance to the terms of the offer.

Both parties are merchants, and CandleCo's proposed modification, certainly, does not materially alter the contract. Further, WaxCo's offer did not limit CandleCo's acceptance to the terms of the offer. Consequently, WaxCo, by silence, did accept CandleCo's proposal. The contract includes the door-knocking term. WaxCo is in breach.

Choice **D** tells us that WaxCo is not in breach, so it's wrong. **A**, **B**, and **C** all state, correctly, that WaxCo *is* in breach. **B** implies, however, that WaxCo would not be in breach if the parties had communicated without signed writings. That's false. Nothing in UCC §2-207(1) *or* (2) refers to writings, signed or unsigned. With **C**, the question-writer hopes you'll grab at the word "reasonable" because it seems so very right. But nothing in UCC §2-207(2) makes relevant the *reasonableness* of an offeree's proposed modification. **C** is wrong.

A correctly tells us that WaxCo accepted CandleCo's proposed modification, which it did—by silence. In failing to knock on CandelCo's door, WaxCo breached. **A** is right.

Question 12. For this question, assume that on August 11, CandleCo responds thus: "As per your offer of *August 10,* please ship. Additional Comment(s): *Please include 15 tons of same product, in color*

blue @ same price—$200/ton, for total price of 30 x $200 =
$6,000." On August 12, WaxCo replies, "Sale confirmed as per your
August 11 Purchase Order." WaxCo delivers the white wax but not the
blue wax. By failing to deliver the blue wax, does WaxCo breach the parties' contract?

A. Yes, because both parties are merchants
B. Yes, because CandleCo proposed an addition to the contract, and
   WaxCo accepted it
C. No, because CandleCo's proposed addition materially alters the
   contract
D. No, because CandleCo's request was a proposal to modify the
   contract, and WaxCo did not accept it

ANALYSIS. The parties first form a contract on WaxCo's terms.
Simultaneously, CandleCo proposes to add a term requiring that WaxCo sell
CandleCo a substantial amount of additional product. That proposal would
make a material alteration to the contract. WaxCo's silence, therefore, would
not act as its acceptance.

But WaxCo is *not* silent. After receiving CandleCo's purchase order—its
"expression of acceptance"—WaxCo responds: "Sale confirmed as per your
August 11 purchase order." With that response, WaxCo expressly accepts
CandleCo's proposal. As thus modified, the contract requires that WaxCo
deliver both white wax and blue wax. By failing to do so, it breaches.

C and **D** state that WaxCo did not breach, so they're wrong. **D** incorrectly
reports that WaxCo failed to accept CandleCo's proposal. With the August
12 sales confirmation, WaxCo *did* accept it. As for **C**, it's true that the blue-
wax term materially alters the contract, but that's irrelevant because WaxCo
expressly accepted it. **A** correctly tells us that both parties are merchants, but
that, too, is irrelevant. If the parties had not been merchants, still, the blue-
wax term would belong to the contract because, once again, WaxCo expressly
accepted it. **B** accurately tells us that WaxCo is in breach and correctly states
the reason—WaxCo accepted CandleCo's proposal. It did so not with silence,
but with its August 12 response. **B** is right.

QUESTION 13. For this question please assume that WaxCo's "Available
for Purchase" form, sent on August 10, includes, on its front side, this
language: "SEE ADDITIONAL TERMS ON REVERSE SIDE." The reverse side
features this text: "The buyer's acceptance is limited to the terms shown
on the front side. WaxCo will not accept any additional terms that the
buyer might propose."

On August 11, CandleCo responds thus: "As per your offer of August 10,
please ship. Additional Comment(s): Personnel will not be in vicinity of

receiving platform. Please knock twice on front office door to notify us that you have delivered the goods." Making no response to CandleCo, WaxCo delivers the wax and leaves *without* knocking on the front door. By failing to do that, does WaxCo breach the parties' contract?

A. Yes, because both parties are merchants
B. Yes, because knocking on the door would not materially increase WaxCo's contractual burden
C. Yes, because under the relevant circumstances CandleCo's request was reasonable
D. No, because WaxCo limited CandleCo's acceptance to the terms of its offer

ANALYSIS. Again, CandleCo accepts WaxCo's offer and simultaneously proposes to modify the contract so to require that WaxCo knock on its front door. This time, however, on the reverse side of its "Available for Purchase" form, WaxCo expressly states that it will not accept any terms the buyer might propose. For that reason, WaxCo does not accept CandleCo's proposal. The contract includes no door-knocking term, and WaxCo commits no breach.

According to **A**, **B**, and **C**, WaxCo *is* in breach, and for that reason, they're wrong. As for **A**, it's true that the parties are merchants, but that represents only the first of three necessary conditions through which silence makes for acceptance. **B** correctly states that CandleCo's proposal makes no material alteration to the contract, but that represents only the second of the three necessary conditions. **C**, once again, presents the word "reasonable," to which the writers hope you'll mindlessly attach yourselves. **C** is wrong. We're left with **D**, which states that WaxCo is *not* in breach because it limited CandleCo's acceptance to the terms of its offer. That's exactly right. The reverse side of WaxCo's form prevented WaxCo's silence from acting as its acceptance to CandleCo's proposed door-knocking term. **D** is right.

E. UCC §2-207 as Model of Poor Draftsmanship: "Different" and "Additional" Terms

Although UCC §2-207(1) tells us that an "expression of acceptance . . . operates as an acceptance even though it states terms additional to or different from those offered," UCC §2-207(2) goes on to describe the fate only of "additional" terms; it says nothing of the "different" ones. That peculiarity raises these questions:

- Did the drafters really mean to distinguish "different" terms from "additional" ones, or did they by sheer (characteristic) carelessness, use both words in subsection (1) but only the one word in subsection (2)?
- If the drafters did intend to distinguish "different" terms from "additional" ones, (a) what exactly is the distinction, and (b) what is the fate of the "different" terms?

In answering these questions, the jurisdictions differ and create (roughly) three schools of interpretation, which we'll name School 1, School 2, and School 3.

1. School 1 Jurisdictions

These jurisdictions (understandably) assume sloppiness on the drafters' parts and read the word "additional" in subsection (2) to mean "additional or different." Consequently, these jurisdictions make no distinction between "different" and "additional" terms. They apply subsection (2) to any term that the offeree introduces in his expression of acceptance. Such term is a proposal to modify the contract, and, if the offeror greets the proposal with silence, it becomes part of the contract under the conditions described at subsection (2).

Illustration: White Widgets   Sandy and Barney are merchants. They conduct this exchange:

> **Sandy:** We will sell you 10 white widgets for $10, delivered on Monday before noon.
> **Barney:** Agreed, but deliver *after* noon, and leave an invoice in our mailbox.

Barney expresses acceptance to Sandy's offer, but introduces two terms of his own: One calls for delivery after noon, whereas Sandy proposes to deliver *before* noon. The other calls for Sandy to leave his invoice in Barney's mailbox, a matter that Sandy's offer does not address. School 1 courts do not ask to know whether either of these terms "differ" from or "add" to the offer. Both are newly introduced by the offeree, and to a School 1 court, both represent the offeree's proposal to modify the contract. If the offeror responds with silence, both become part of the contract under the conditions described at subsection (2).

2. Schools 2 and 3 Jurisdictions: Generally

These jurisdictions do recognize a difference between "additional" and "different" terms because the code drafters (seem, perhaps, to) create one. In these jurisdictions, if an offeree's term conflicts with any of the offeror's stated terms, then it "differs" from the offer. Otherwise it "adds" to it.

Illustration: "Different" vs. "Additional."   Reread the exchange between Sandy and Barney. Barney expresses acceptance to the offer, and introduces two terms not included in it. One calls for delivery after noon, and it contradicts the offer, which provided for delivery *before* noon. That term, therefore, "differs" from the offer. The other calls for Sandy to leave an invoice in Barney's mailbox. Sandy's offer states not a thing about the invoice wherefore the buyer's proposed term "adds" to the offer.

3. School 2 Jurisdictions: Discarding the "Different" Terms

These jurisdictions regard the offeree's "additional" terms as proposals for addition to the contract so that UCC §2-207(2) applies to them. If the offeror assents, expressly or by silence (when circumstances satisfy the three necessary conditions) they become part of the contract. If the offeree's terms "differ" from (conflict with) the offeror's terms, they amount to nothing. They are not, even, proposals to modify the contract.

School 2 Illustrated: Reread the exchange between Sandy and Barney. School 2 courts would wholly discard the buyer's statement as to delivery. They would regard it not even as a proposal to modify the contract. These same courts would treat the invoice term under subsection (2) as a proposal for addition to the contract, which the offeror might accept, expressly or by silence (if circumstances satisfy the three necessary conditions).

4. School 3 Jurisdictions: The "Knockout Rule"

Likely representing a majority, School 3 jurisdictions treat the offeree's "additional" terms under subsection (2) as does School 2; such terms are proposals to modify the contract. As to any of the offeree's terms that "differ" from the offer, School 3 applies a court-made "knockout rule" and discards both the offeror's *and* offeree's term. If the term is somehow essential to the contract, then by "gap filling," they replace it with a "reasonable" one under UCC §2-204(3) (Chapter 4, section C).

School 3 Illustrated: Reread the exchange between Sandy and Barney. A School 3 court would apply subsection (2) to the offeree's invoice/mailbox term, as would a court of School 2. It would also "knock out" (remove) from the contract both the offeror's and offeree's terms as to delivery and replace them with a "reasonable" delivery term under UCC §2-204(3):

5. Be Forewarned

With the inexplicable chaos it wreaks on this point (and others), UCC §2-207(2) makes a mockery of the drafters' professed wish to clarify the law and render it "uniform" throughout the states. UCC §2-207(2) is a disgrace to legal draftsmanship and to its drafters. Professor Brian Blum calls it "ugly and misshapen."[8] According to Professor Grant Gilmore, it is "the greatest statutory

---

8. Brian Blum, *Contracts: Examples and Explanations* 115 (5th ed. 2010).

mess of all time."[9] (Both those authorities are too kind.) All that we have said about §2-207 might or might not be the law. All of it should be taken together with a "maybe" and a "who knows?"[10]

QUESTIONS 14-16. SahlCo manufactures planting pots, and BahlCo pots plants for sale to retail customers. On March 1, BahlCo contacts SahlCo by signed writing: "We need 2,000 red clay pots, Model 14-D; priced as per last time—$1/unit = $2,000. Please deliver to our warehouse. Will pay with our business check handed to your driver on delivery." SahlCo responds with a signed sales confirmation form: "Sold to: BahlCo. Red clay pots, Model 14-D; #2,000. Price: $1/unit. Total: $2,000. This Sales Confirmation Includes All Terms Set Forth on Reverse Side." The reverse side of SahlCo's form includes this text:

(1) Full payment to be made by check sent to SahlCo by U.S. Mail.
(2) For contracts that call for delivery by SahlCo, delivery driver will telephone the buyer within 10 minutes of delivery time, and the buyer will post a receiving agent at its receiving platform/facility.

BahlCo receives the sales confirmation form but makes no response to it.

QUESTION 14. With respect to the two terms set forth on the reverse side of SahlCo's sales confirmation form, a School 1 jurisdiction would likely hold that:

A. both terms become part of the contract.
B. term (1) becomes part of the contract, but term (2) does not.
C. term (2) becomes part of the contract, but term (1) does not.
D. neither term becomes part of the contract.

QUESTION 15. A School 2 jurisdiction would likely hold that:

A. both terms become part of the contract.
B. term (1) becomes part of the contract, but term (2) does not.
C. term (2) becomes part of the contract, but term (1) does not.
D. term (2) becomes part of the contract, but term (1) does not, and is replaced by a "reasonable" term of the court's choosing.

QUESTION 16. A School 3 jurisdiction would likely hold that:

A. both terms become part of the contract.
B. term (1) becomes part of the contract, but term (2) does not.

---

9. Mark E. Roszkowski, *Symposium on Revised Article 2 of the Uniform Commercial Code—Section-by-Section Analysis*, 54 SMU L. Rev. 927, 932 (2001) (quoting letter from Grant Gilmore, Professor, to Robert Summers, Professor, Cornell U. School of Law (Sept. 10, 1980) *reprinted in* Richard E. Speidel et al., *Teaching Materials on Commercial and Consumer Law* 54-55 (3d ed. 1981).

10. In their 2003 proposed amendments, not yet adopted by any state, the drafters (without apologizing for what was written 40 years earlier) eliminate from §2-207 both subsections (1) and (2) and offer, instead, a useless provision (born of the original subsection (3), not yet discussed).

C. term (2) becomes part of the contract, but term (1) does not.

D. term (2) becomes part of the contract, but term (1) does not, and it is replaced by a "reasonable" term of the court's choosing.

ANALYSIS. BahlCo offered to buy goods and SahlCo responded, via sales confirmation, with an expression of acceptance which, on its reverse side, presented two terms not included in BahlCo's offer. Term (1) provides that BahlCo should make payment by mail, and thus contradicts BahlCo's offer, in which BahlCo proposed to pay on delivery. Term (1), therefore, "differs" from the offer. Term (2) requires that BahlCo, on receiving a phone call from delivery personnel, post personnel at its receiving platform to accept delivery. BahlCo's offer did not touch on that topic, so Term (2) "adds" to the offer.

Both of SahlCo's terms alter the contract only in trivial ways; they are not material. Both parties are merchants, and BahlCo, in its offer, did not limit acceptance to the offer's terms.

As for Question 14. In applying UCC §2-207(2), a School 1 jurisdiction makes no distinction between "different" and "additional" terms. In view of BahlCo's silence—its failure to object to SahlCo's new terms—both terms likely become part of the contract, and **A** is right.

As for Question 15. A School 2 court treats the offeree's "additional" terms under UCC §2-207(2). Consequently, term (2) is SahlCo's proposal to modify the contract. Because BahlCo responds to it with silence (and because circumstances satisfy the three necessary conditions), it becomes a part of the contract. Term (1), however, "differs" from BahlCo's terms. School 2 jurisdictions disregard it entirely. For these reasons, **C** is right.

As for Question 16. A School 3 court applies the "knockout" rule. Like the School 2 courts, it treats the offeree's "additional" terms under UCC §2-207(2). Consequently, term (2) is SahlCo's proposal to modify the contract. Because BahlCo responds with silence, it becomes a part of the contract. Term (1), however, "differs" from BahlCo's terms. Under the "knockout rule," both the offeror's and offeree's payment terms drop out. Then, under UCC §2-204(3), the court replaces them with a term it considers reasonable. For these reasons, **D** is right.

F. More About UCC §2-207(1): The "Written Confirmation"

With regret, we must show you now that UCC §2-207(1) refers not only to an offer and expression of acceptance, but also to something it calls a "written confirmation." In full, UCC §2-207(1) provides:

> A definite and seasonable expression of acceptance or a written confirmation which is sent within a reasonable time operates as an acceptance even though it states terms additional to or different from those offered or agreed upon,

unless acceptance is expressly made conditional on assent to the additional or different terms.

With this jumble of words, lacking in proper punctuation, the code drafters disgorge some ill-digested meal of half-cooked thought, leaving for others the task of cleaning up.

Tearing the sentence into what are two separate thoughts, we find (a) a provision concerning offer and acceptance, already studied; and (b) a provision that attempts to deal with two parties who form a contract orally or "informally," whereafter one of them confirms the contract in a writing sent to the other. To understand the meanings of these two separate components, we must further dissect this ill-born sentence.

Although the drafters do not define the term "written confirmation," their so-called Official Comment 1 indicates that "written confirmation" means a writing sent by either party to the other, *after* both parties have already formed a contract orally or "informally." The drafters explain that the reference to "written confirmation"

> is intended to deal with [the situation in which] an agreement has been reached either orally or by informal correspondence between the parties and is followed by one or both of the parties sending formal memoranda embodying the terms so far as agreed upon and adding terms not discussed.

The reference to written confirmation would seem, then, to address these parties:

Jack (by spoken word): I'd like to buy from you 200 widgets for $200.
Jill (by spoken word): Sure; I'll send them to your warehouse.
Jill (*signed writing*): This confirms our agreement under which you will buy and I will sell 200 widgets for $200; delivery to be made by me this Friday, March 10.

The statutory provision then *seems* to tell us that Jill's confirmatory memorandum "operates as an acceptance even though it states terms additional to or different from those . . . agreed upon." But the memorandum *can't* "operate as an acceptance." The parties have already formed their contract, meaning they have *already achieved offer and acceptance.* If the reference to written confirmation means anything—*anything at all*—it means only that

1. the additional (and different?) terms set forth in the memorandum are proposals for addition to the contract, which the recipient may accept or not; and
2. if the memorandum's recipient responds with silence, then the additional (and different?) terms become part of the contract under the conditions described in UCC §2-207(2).

Beyond that, the reference to "confirmatory memorandum" means nothing, and no learned lawyer can disagree.

Let's Do the Drafters' Job *for* Them and Render §2-207 Comprehensible. Read UCC §2-207(1) as though it had two separate parts (a) and (b), followed then by UCC §2-207(2):

> (1)(a) *When one party offers to buy or sell goods and the offeree responds with an expression of acceptance, that expression of acceptance operates as an acceptance even though it does not mirror the offer. However, if the offeree expressly states that his expression of acceptance is conditional on the offeror's assent to the new or different terms, then the expression of acceptance is not an acceptance but, instead, a counteroffer and rejection.*
>
> (b) *If two parties form a contract orally or by an exchange of informal writings, and one (or each party) sends a confirmatory memorandum to the other that includes terms different from or additional to those of the contract, then—*
>
> (2) *The additional terms are to be construed as proposals for addition to the contract. Between merchants such terms become part of the contract unless:*
>
> *(a) the offer expressly limits acceptance to the terms of the offer,*
>
> *(b) they materially alter it, or*
>
> *(c) notification of objection to them has already been given or is given within a reasonable time after notice of them is received.*

QUESTION 17. BenCo and SenCo deal professionally in pianos and piano parts. On May 10, BenCo telephones SenCo: "Can you ship to us two full sets of plastic key tops at your catalog price?" SenCo replies, "Yes, we'll ship them on Tuesday." That same afternoon, by fax, SenCo sends BenCo this writing, signed and dated: "Sold to BenCo. Two full sets of plastic piano key tops at catalog price. Payment to be made by check deposited directly to SkyBank using our direct deposit number: 5090319079." BenCo receives the document but makes no response to it. Seven days later, Benco receives the key tops with a bill showing the catalog price of $200. Is BenCo contractually obliged to make payment by depositing a check directly into SkyBank?

A. Yes, because the request is reasonable under the circumstances
B. Yes, because it is for a seller to decide how he shall be paid
C. Yes, if that requirement does not materially affect the contract
D. No, because SenCo sent the confirmation after the parties had formed their contract

---

ANALYSIS. If two parties form a contract orally or by an exchange of informal writings, and one sends a confirmatory memorandum to the other that includes terms different from or additional to those of the contract, then the additional terms represent proposals for addition to the contract (UCC §2-207(1)). If both parties are merchants, and the offeror responds to the proposal with silence, he accepts it unless (a) the additional term materially alters the contract, or (b) in his initial offer, he limited acceptance to his own terms (UCC §2-207(2)).

Here BenCo and SenCo form an oral contract for the sale of key-tops. Thereafter SenCo dispatches a written confirmation in which it sets forth a term not included in the contract, to wit, the payment provision. That term does not *conflict* with the offer, so it's an "additional" one. When SenCo issues the memorandum, therefore, the new term represents a proposal to modify the contract. Both parties are merchants. BenCo in its offer does not limit acceptance to the terms of the offer. There is, perhaps, some question as to whether the direct deposit term materially alters the contract. Hence we can conclude that if the new term materially alters the contract, it does not become a part of it. If the new term does not materially alter the contract, then it does become a part of it.

According to **A**, BenCo must make the direct deposit because such represents a reasonable request under the circumstances. Friendly words do not a right answer make. UCC §2-207(2) nowhere makes relevant the reasonableness or unreasonableness of an offeree's additional term. **B** makes a false statement of law. Decisions on payment (or anything else) belong no more to the seller than the buyer. All contractual terms require *mutual* assent (even if, at times, one manifests his assent by silence). **D** correctly reports that the confirmation came forth after the parties formed their contract. That means, of course, that it can't be an acceptance, as explained above. Nonetheless, an offeree's additional terms, set forth in a written confirmation, do become part of the contract if all conditions of UCC §2-207(2) apply. **C** correctly reports that the parties adopt the offeree's direct deposit term so long as it does not materially affect their contract. **C** is right.

G.   The Closer

QUESTION 18. While surfing the Internet, Beth sees an advertisement for an electric toothbrush called SensaDent. Among other boasts, the advertisement states that the product is "long-lasting." The advertisement invites readers to click on a link, and Beth does so. Her screen then displays a "SensaDent Purchase Request." She completes its required fields, supplying her name, telephone number, mailing address, e-mail address, and credit card number.

The form provides one additional field entitled "Additional Requests or Comments (Optional)." In that field Beth writes:

> I shall have the right to return the item and receive a full refund of the purchase price by certified check (not by credit to my credit card account), within ten years of purchase, if during that period the item should fail to function perfectly.

Having thus completed the purchase request, Beth clicks on the words "I authorize SensaDent to charge $75 to my credit card. SUBMIT." One minute later, Beth receives from SensaDent this e-mail:

> Congratulations! Your Purchase Request is accepted, and the sale is complete. The sum of $75 will be charged to your credit card, and your SensaDent toothbrush will ship within three weeks.
>
> SensaDent Limited Warranty
>   SensaDent Warrants that its product will be free from defects in operation for three years after delivery to the buyer. If the product should fail within that period, then, upon returning the defective product to SensaDent, the buyer will RECEIVE a refund of the purchase price IN WHATEVER FORM OF PAYMENT WAS USED TO PURCHASE THE PRODUCT. The product carries no warranties beyond the face of this document.

Five days after Beth receives SensaDent's congratulatory e-mail, she hears by telephone from a SensaDent representative.

> **SensaDent:** We have just read the additional comment you submitted with your online purchase request form. We warrant the product for three years, not ten, as you were advised in our congratulatory e-mail. Further, refunds are returned in the same form of payment as that used to purchase our product—in your case, by a credit to your credit card account. If those terms are not acceptable to you, then we'll cancel your order if you wish.
>
> **Beth:** Those terms are not acceptable to me, and neither is it acceptable that you cancel my order. I want the product and I want it on the terms put forth in what you folks call my "SensaDent Purchase Request."
>
> **SensaDent:** I'm sorry; we can't agree to that.

Making no charge to her credit card, SensaDent, by certified mail, advises Beth that it has cancelled her order, whereupon Beth visits her lawyer to ask whether SensaDent is in breach of contract. The lawyer answers, "No, certainly not, because you and SensaDent never *formed* a contract." Beth's lawyer is most likely

A. right, because SensaDent cannot be bound by terms to which it never knowingly agreed.
B. right, because SensaDent took no payment from Beth and canceled her order.
C. right, because in this transaction SensaDent is a merchant.
D. wrong, because Beth made an offer and SensaDent accepted it.

ANALYSIS.   The saga starts with SensaDent's advertisement. UCC Article 2 is silent on the subject of advertisements, so common law governs. SensaDent's ad was not an offer but a mere invitation to deal. (See Chapter 4, section A.) When Beth completed the purchase request, *she* made an offer whose terms included the optional comment she wrote about her ten-year right to a refund.

SensaDent (lacking a good lawyer) responded by advising Beth that it had accepted her "order." It thus issued an expression of acceptance under UCC §2-207(1). Its terms differed from those of Beth's offer, but UCC §2-207(1) makes that irrelevant. Consequently, when SensaDent dispatched its congratulatory e-mail, it accepted Beth's offer, and the parties formed a contract. Beth's lawyer is wrong.

Telling us that the lawyer is right, **A** and **B** put forth incorrect statements of law. Under UCC §2-207(1) SensaDent *can* be bound by terms to which it never knowingly agreed. Further, if one forms a contract to sell goods, he cannot extricate himself by returning the buyer's purchase price. **A** and **B** are for the dumpster. **C** states that Beth's lawyer was wrong and offers as a reason that SensaDent is a merchant. SensaDent *is* a merchant, but that's irrelevant. Nothing in UCC §2-207(1) turns on the notion of "merchant." **C** is wrong.

According to **D**, Beth's lawyer is wrong because Beth made an offer and SensaDent accepted it. That's exactly right. Beth made an offer. SensaDent responded with an expression of acceptance, which operates *as* an acceptance notwithstanding that it carries terms different from those of the offer. **D** is right.

 # Silver & Hochberg's Picks

1.	**A**
2.	**C**
3.	**C**
4.	**B**
5.	**D**
6.	**D**
7.	**A**
8.	**C**
9.	**D**
10.	**C**
11.	**A**
12.	**B**
13.	**D**
14.	**A**
15.	**C**
16.	**D**
17.	**C**
18.	**D**

12

Consideration, Part I

A. What's a Contract?

Nonlawyers often think "contract" means a *writing*, formally drafted and ceremoniously signed. They're wrong. Many contracts are embodied in signed writings. We call them "written contracts." Many arise from speech alone. They're "oral contracts." Some arise without words at all. They're born of communicative *behavior*, with nary a word of type or talk. Those are "contracts implied in fact." All such creatures are contracts, and all arise by the same legal mechanism: *Two (or more) parties form a contract when they manifest **mutual assent to a bargain** that exacts from each some **consideration**.*

1. How Two Parties Manifest Mutual Assent

*Two parties form a contract when the first makes an offer that the second accepts, with each providing the other **consideration**.*

We'll understand the meaning of "consideration" only after we know the difference between a "naked promise" and a "contractual promise."

B.   Naked Promise vs. Contractual Promise

You know the meaning of "promise." One makes a promise when she pledges to another that she will or will not do some particular thing. When two parties form a (bilateral)[1] contract, each makes a promise to the other. Consider, for example, this offer and acceptance:

Corporation A: If you will service all of our payroll accounts for the coming year, we will pay your usual fee of $300 per hour.

Corporation B: We accept.

Corporation A proposes an exchange of promises. Specifically, she proposes that (1) B promise to service all of A's payroll accounts, in exchange for which (2) A will promise to pay B $300 per hour. Corporation A thereby makes an offer.

When B accepts the offeror's proposal the two proposed promises come to life so that each party makes to the other its promise as proposed in the offer. At the moment B says (or writes) "We accept." (1) A makes a contractual promise to pay B's usual hourly fees and (2) B makes a contractual promise to service A's payroll accounts. Together the two contractual promises make — a *contract.*

1.   The Law Enforces Contracts

The law enforces the promises each contracting party makes to the other, meaning it enforces promises embodied *within a contract.* But if one makes a promise *outside* of a contract, the law does not ordinarily enforce it. Suppose Robert Waith creates and signs this writing: "I, ROBERT WAITH, do hereby declare this solemn promise: To my nephew, WALLACE WAITH BANNINGTON, on his twenty-first birthday, August 9, 2018, I will give my Symington Swiss gold watch, which watch will then be his wholly, fully, and forever." Because Robert's promise does not follow from an offer and acceptance by which he and his nephew exchanged promises, it does not belong to a contract. It's not a "contractual promise" (our own term, meaning a promise that belongs to a contract). It's an ordinary everyday promise from one person to another motivated, perhaps, by generosity, affection, filial tradition, or who knows what. In the law's words, an ordinary everyday promise that does not belong to a contract is a mere "gratuitous promise" or "donative promise" or, most commonly, a "naked promise." When in the mood to "sound like a lawyer," we use the Latin, *nudum pactum.*

Whether it comes from parent to child, wife to husband, friend to friend, or multinational corporation to the whole of the American public — whether

---

1.   "Bilateral contract" refers to the ordinary contract with which you are familiar in ordinary life — the contract in which two parties, A and B agree that A will do something for B and, in exchange, B will pay A (or do something else for A). The law recognizes, also, what it calls a "unilateral contract" discussed in Chapter 9, section C.

it be made by spoken word or formal writing, signed, witnessed, and notarized, in pencil, pen, or blood, a promise that does not belong to a contract—a gratuitous promise—a naked promise—*nudum pactum*—is unenforceable.

2. The Law Doesn't Hold Us to Our Word?

No; generally speaking, it doesn't. It holds us to our *contracts*, but not (generally) to the ordinary promises we make to one another day in and day out. Let's write a rule: *When, by forming a contract, one party makes a promise to another, the law requires that he keep it. If he fails to do so the other has an action against him for breach. If, however, one party makes to the other a mere gratuitous promise—a naked promise—nudum pactum, the law does not enforce it. The promisor may break his promise for any reason or no reason, and the promisee has no legal remedy.*

We know that two parties form a contract only if one makes an offer that the other accepts. Further, one makes an offer only if he proposes a *bargain*—an arrangement in which two parties make an *exchange*. "Bargain" refers to a "trade," a "swap," a "this" for a "that," or, in Latin—a *quid pro quo*. A contract always reflects a *bargain*. That's why the Restatement definition of offer centers on that word. Restatement (Second) of Contracts §24 provides:

> An offer is the manifestation of willingness to enter into a *BARGAIN* so made as to justify another person in understanding that his assent to that *BARGAIN* is invited and will conclude it.

One accepts an offer and thereby forms a contract, if he manifests assent to the bargain it proposes (Restatement (Second) of Contracts §50(1)).

A contract, therefore, reflects a *bargain* to which two parties commit themselves. Since the law enforces only contractual promises—promises that inhere within a *bargain*, Party Y's promise to Party X is enforceable only if, in exchange, Party Y gets something back from Party X.

3. That Brings Us to the Word "Consideration"

Because two parties form a contract only when they mutually commit to a bargain, simple logic produces this inescapable conclusion: *In every contract, each party (a) must provide something to the other, and that "something" is the consideration he gives; and (b) must receive something from the other, and that "something" is the consideration he gets.* Consequently, the law features statements like these:

- "To form a contract, each party must provide consideration to the other."
- "No promise is enforceable unless it is supported by consideration from the promisee" (meaning that no promise is enforceable unless the promisee gives for it ("supports it with") some promise or performance of his own).
- "Any promise not supported by consideration from the promisee is a naked promise, unenforceable."

Look again at the contract between Corporations A and B. It arose when B accepted A's offer. whereupon each party became bound by a promise to the other.

> **Simple Question:** What consideration does Corporation A receive for its promise to pay $300 per hour?
>
> **Simple Answer:** As consideration for its promise to pay $300 per hour, Corporation A receives Corporation B's promise to service A's payroll accounts.
>
> **Simple Question:** What consideration does Corporation B receive for its promise to service A's payroll accounts?
>
> **Simple Answer:** As consideration for its promise to service A's payroll accounts, Corporation B receives Corporation A's promise to pay $300 per hour.

Hence, it's important that you understand this statement: "A promise supported by consideration is enforceable, and a promise not supported by consideration is not enforceable." You must also understand that it's equivalent to this one: "Contracts are enforceable, but gratuitous promises are not."

4. Come Again? How Are These Two Statements Equivalent

Look at the first clause of each one. Statement 1: "A promise supported by consideration is enforceable." Statement 2: "Contracts are enforceable." We know that a promise supported by consideration is a promise given by one person in exchange for a promise or performance given by another. If two parties exchange promises then, by definition, they mutually commit to a bargain, which means they form a contract. Consequently, a promise supported by consideration *means* a promise that belongs to a contract. To state that "a promise not supported by consideration is not enforceable" is to state that "contracts are enforceable."

Let's now examine the second clause of each statement. Statement 1: "A promise not supported by consideration is not enforceable." Statement 2: "Gratuitous promises are not [enforceable]." A promise not supported by consideration is a promise for which nothing is given in exchange; it's a promise not tied to a contract. "Gratuitous promise" carries the same meaning: a gratuitous promise (naked promise, *nudum pactum,* donative promise) is a promise given in exchange for nothing—a promise not tied to a contract. Hence, "a promise not supported by consideration is not enforceable" *means* "gratuitous promises are not enforceable."

QUESTION 1. MedCo employee Hazel (a Gemini) is approached by her supervisor Nancy: "I have two tickets for this Friday night's game at the Garden. I'm going to give them to you tomorrow as an early birthday present." Hazel, an enthusiastic basketball fan, replies "Thank you!" Is Nancy legally obliged to honor her promise?

A. Yes, because she manifested a serious intention to honor it
B. Yes, because she made it in consideration of Hazel's birthday
C. No, because she received no consideration for it
D. No, because she did not make it in writing

ANALYSIS.   Neither of these parties proposed a bargain to the other. Asking for nothing in exchange, Nancy promised Hazel a gift, meaning she made a naked promise, unenforceable.

A implies that one is bound by her naked promise if she manifests a serious intention to honor it. There's no such rule. One may make a naked promise with the utmost solemnity and still it's unenforceable. **A** is wrong.

B invokes the word "consideration" not in the legal sense, but in the sense of motive. And it's true that Hazel's birthday was Nancy's motive for giving the tickets. Legally, however, consideration does not refer to motive per se. It refers to that which each party gives the other in connection with a bargain—a quid pro quo. **B** is wrong.

D correctly states that Nancy need not keep her promise, but it incorrectly implies that one who makes a naked promise in writing must honor it. That, of course, is false, and **D** is wrong.

And so we come to **C**. It tells us that Nancy need not keep her word, and it correctly states the reason (which, of course, we might express in a number of ways): "[Nancy] received no consideration for the promise." That's why **C** is right.

QUESTION 2. LifeTime Inc. publishes a monthly magazine that derives revenues from advertising. As a promotional strategy, the company offers various businesses the opportunity to advertise free of charge in three consecutive issues of its magazine. On April 1, a LifeTime representative telephones SportsWear Inc.:

> **LifeTime:** We're calling to tell you that in the next three issues of our magazine, free of charge, we'll publish your standard full-page advertisement.
>
> **SportsWear:** We thank you. Please put your promise in a signed writing; we'd like to see it in black and white.

LifeTime then sends SportsWear this signed writing:

> **Confirmation of Binding Contractual Promise**
> This confirms that LifeTime will publish, free of charge, SportsWear's standard full-page advertisement in three consecutive issues of its monthly magazine.

> Thereafter, LifeTime's management decides against its program of free advertising. There follows another conversation with SportsWear.
>
> > **LifeTime:** Please know that we have changed our mind about the free advertising. We will not be publishing your advertisement.
> > **SportsWear:** You made a signed, written promise, and we intend to hold you to it.
>
> Alleging breach of contract, SportsWear sues LifeTime. LifeTime contends that it had no obligation to honor its promise. If the court decides against SportsWear, its reason will most likely be that:
>
> I. SportsWear itself did not sign the writing entitled "Confirmation of Binding Contractual Promise."
> II. LifeTime's promise was not embodied within a contract.
> III. SportsWear revoked its offer before LifeTime accepted it.
> IV. LifeTime's promise was mere *nudum pactum*.
> A. I
> B. III
> C. I and II
> D. II and IV

ANALYSIS.   A contract is enforceable; a naked promise is not. When LifeTime first contacted SportsWear, it proposed no trade, no bargain. Instead, asking nothing in exchange, it promised to publish SportsWear's advertisement free of charge. Consequently, LifeTime proposed no bargain; it made no offer. Neither did SportsWear respond with any offer of its own. Rather, SportsWear requested that LifeTime restate its promise in writing. LifeTime did so. It matters not a whit that LifeTime titled its document with the words "binding" and "contractual." LifeTime proposed no bargain and so made no offer. It made only its own promise in exchange for — nothing.

These events lead to a single conclusion that we might state in a variety of ways:

1. Neither of these parties proposed a bargain to the other, meaning neither made an offer to the other, meaning these parties never formed a contract. Consequently LifeTime's promise is not a contractual promise, and the law will not enforce it.
2. LifeTime's promise does not belong to a contract, meaning it is a mere gratuitous promise, and for that reason it's unenforceable.
3. SportsWear gave no consideration for LifeTime's promise, and for that reason the promise is unenforceable.
4. LifeTime's promise was unsupported by consideration from the promisee (SportsWear), wherefore it is unenforceable.

Those four statements, each in its own way, reflect the single reason for which LifeTime need not keep its word: LifeTime made SportsWear a mere gratuitous promise; the parties formed no contract. Examine options I through IV and determine which, in its way, make(s) that same statement.

Option I tells us that SportsWear did not sign the writing that LifeTime sent it. So what? If SportsWear had signed the writing, in ink and in blood, before 1,000 witnesses and 10,000 notaries then, still, the writing would reflect only a naked promise. The writing and signature are irrelevant.

According to option III, LifeTime revoked its "offer" before SportsWear accepted. That statement is false for the simple reason that LifeTime did not make an offer. It made a promise, but proposed no bargain. Option II states that LifeTime's promise did not belong to a contract. That's true, and furthermore it's the reason LifeTime is free to dishonor its word.

Option IV makes the same statement we see at option II. Because LifeTime's promise does not belong to a contract, it is a naked promise or, in Latin, *nudum pactum*. **D** identifies options II and IV, so **D** is right.

C. Consideration and Value

Two parties, for their own reasons, might agree to a bargain in which they exchange values that are unequal by any normal measure.

1. Adequacy of Consideration: A Tale of Two Cities

Party A owns a $100 million building in Manhattan. Party B owns a tiny little spot of waterfront land in Pago Pago. It's worth $10,000. Party A wants the Pago Pago property. Party B is willing to part with it only in exchange for the Manhattan building. The parties form an agreement in which A promises to convey the Manhattan building to B, and B, in return, promises to convey the Pago Pago property to A.

Notwithstanding that the properties differ in market value, each party promises *something* to the other, meaning each gives and receives consideration. The agreement constitutes a contract and both promises are fully enforceable. *So long as two parties reciprocally manifest genuine intention to form a bargain, the law does not inquire into the value that each conveys to the other.* When asking whether Party A gives consideration to support Party B's promise, we do not ask whether the two promises are equal in market value. With respect to consideration, *value is irrelevant.* As Restatement (Second) Contracts §79 cmt. c explains:

> Valuation is left to private action in part because the parties are thought to be better able than others to evaluate the circumstances of particular transactions. . . . Ordinarily, therefore, courts do not inquire into the adequacy of consideration.[2]

---

2. Hardesty v. Smith, 3 Ind. 39, 41 (1851).

And, as the Indiana Supreme Court ruled, in 1851,

> [Contracting parties] have a right to make their own bargains. The owner of a thing has the right to fix the price at which he will part with it, and a buyer's own judgment ought to be his best guide as to what he should give to obtain it. The consideration agreed upon may indefinitely exceed the value of the thing for which it is promised and still the bargain stand. The doing of an act by one at the request of another, which may be a detriment or inconvenience, however slight, to the party doing it, or may be a benefit, however slight, to the party at whose request it is performed, is a legal consideration for a promise by such requesting party.[3]

2. "Sham Consideration": Ava and Bonnie

Ava, who owns a horse named Ever After, visits her lawyer.

> **Ava:** In seven years my niece Bonnie will turn 21. At that time, I want her to have my horse. Can I promise her such a gift and know that it will be legally enforceable?
>
> **Lawyer:** If, in exchange for your promise, Bonnie pays you $1, the two of you will form a contract and your promise will be enforceable.

Ava prepares this document:

> Bonnie Betts ("Bonnie") and Ava Anson ("Ava") hereby agree that: (1) Bonnie will, immediately after executing this agreement, pay to Ava the sum of $1 in exchange for which (2) Ava will, on Bonnie's twenty-first birthday, convey to Bonnie her horse, Ever After.

Bonnie asks, "Do you really want my dollar?" "No," Ava responds, "but you must pay it to me in order that my promise be legally binding." Both parties sign, and Bonnie pays Ava $1. Seven years later, on Bonnie's twenty-first birthday, Ava disavows her promise and refuses to give Bonnie the horse. Let's ask: Does Bonnie have an action against Ava for breach of contract?

Recall that "offer" means: "the manifestation of willingness to enter into a *bargain*, so made as to *justify another person in understanding* that his assent to that bargain is invited and will conclude it" (Restatement (Second) Contracts §24). Ava made plain to Bonnie that she wished to *give* her the horse and that she did not truly want her dollar in exchange. On listening to Ava, Bonnie should have believed (and did believe) that Ava had presented her not with a bargain, but with the *pretense* of one. Ava proposed that she would promise her horse to Bonnie, and, in exchange Bonnie should do—nothing. Bonnie was to "promise" payment of $1 *not in exchange for the horse* but in an effort to make the arrangement binding.

Hence, Ava's promise does not belong to a contract and that, truly, is the reason for which it is unenforceable. Most authorities, however, state the

---

3. Schnell v. Nell, 17 Ind. 29, 31-32 (1861)

reason thus: Bonnie's promise to pay the dollar was a sham, and *sham consideration is no consideration.* As Restatement (Second) § 71 cmt. states:

> [A] mere pretense of bargain does not suffice, as where there is a false recital of consideration or where the purported consideration is merely nominal.

Because Bonnie gave no consideration for Ava's promise, these parties formed no contract. Ava's promise was mere *nudum pactum,* unenforceable.[4]

When one wishes to render her naked promise enforceable, she and her promisee ordinarily name as "consideration" a petty sum such as $1 or $10 or $25, but no amount of money, however large, constitutes consideration if its purpose is to create the pretense of consideration; *sham consideration is no consideration.*

3. But We Just Learned That One's Promise Constitutes Consideration Regardless of Value

Yes, we did and that's true. If, in exchange for some promise, Promisor asks Promisee for $1, the dollar might constitute true consideration or, on the other hand, a sham. If circumstances are such as cause Promisee reasonably to believe that Promisor truly, genuinely, wants the dollar in exchange for her promise, then the dollar constitutes consideration. If, on the other hand, Promisee reasonably believes (or *should* believe) that Promisor intends her promise as a gift, and asks for the dollar only to create the *appearance* of a bargain, then the dollar is sham consideration; Promisor's promise is not enforceable.

Illustration: The Garage Sale.   At Franco's garage sale, Gary spots a lamp tagged "25¢".

(1) **Gary:** Are you truly selling this lamp for 25¢? I know all about lamps, and this one is worth, perhaps, $100.
(2) **Franco:** Well, I appreciate your honesty but we just want to be rid of the thing. We tagged it at 25¢, and we'll stand by that. Will you pay the quarter?
(3) **Gary:** May I come tomorrow to pick it up?
(4) **Franco:** Yes, and you can pay the quarter then too. Deal?
(5) **Gary:** Deal.

At statement 4 Franco puts forth a proposal. In light of the circumstances, including the conversation that preceded it, a reasonable person in Gary's position would understand that Frank's promise to convey the lamp was truly conditioned on Gary's promise to pay 25¢. A reasonable person in Gary's position would believe that Franco was serious about the 25¢ price, even though the lamp's market value was much higher. Consequently, Franco truly proposes a

---

4. The parol evidence rule, however (Chapter 20), might prevent both parties from offering evidence as to the conversation they held before executing the document, in which case, evidence of the sham would not reach the fact finder.

bargain; he tenders his own promise to convey the lamp asking, in exchange, for Gary's promise to pay 25¢. Hence, Gary makes an offer. When, at statement 5, Franco accepts, the parties form a contract. Their promises spring to life, each one a contractual promise, fully enforceable.

4. *"Liquidated Value": When Disparate Value Does Matter*

The word "liquidate" has several meanings. In one sense, it means "transform to monetary value." If we say that a business owner "liquidates her inventory," we mean that she sells it all in exchange for money; she reduces it to its monetary value. If we say that a monetary investment is not "liquid," we mean that it is not subject to easy divestment and conversion back to money. When we say "the value of item X is fully liquidated," we mean that all reasonable persons would agree on its value in monetary terms—that its monetary value is not a matter on which reasonable persons can differ.

The simplest case of an item fully liquidated is ordinary currency itself. An ordinary quarter is worth 25 cents, and an ordinary dollar is worth a dollar. In the law's estimation, that's indisputable; no sane person can think otherwise. If Party A promises to convey an ordinary dime to Party B and Party B, "in exchange," promises simultaneously to convey one ordinary nickel to Party A, the parties do not form a contract. In net effect, A has promised to give B five cents in exchange for — nothing.

Suppose Stock X is listed on the Chicago exchange. Party A owns two shares and Party A owns one. They cannot know, at every instant, what their shares are worth in monetary terms, but they do know and we all know that each share, at any such instant, has the same value as every other. Imagine that (for whatever reason) A promises to convey his two shares to B who, in exchange, promises simultaneously to convey his single share to A. The law will not enforce their agreement, because it's not a *contract*. In net effect, A promises to give B one share of stock, in exchange for nothing, meaning that B gives no consideration for A's promise, meaning that A makes a mere gratuitous (naked) promise, unenforceable. The rule is this: *If two parties purport to contract for an exchange of items which, as a matter of indisputable reality, are of different liquidated values, then one of the parties fails to give consideration, and the two fail to form a contract.*

It is the lawyer's first lesson that two verbal constructions with identical pronunciations and spelling might, in law, represent different *words*. Consider the phrases, (1) "governmental aid to the *speech* impaired" and, (2) "the constitutional right to free *speech*." In phrase 1 we see a word "speech." In phrase 2 we see another word "speech." As spoken and spelled, the two words are exactly alike, but they are, in fact, different words with different meanings. One who is physically unable to pin on his shirt a political button, is not "speech" impaired. But one whom the government prevents from pinning on his shirt that same political button is denied freedom of "speech."

The same phenomenon applies to such a words as "penny," "nickel," "dime," or "dollar." When we speak, first, of the nickel in your own pocket and then of the "nickel" found in Abraham Lincoln's pocket on the night he was murdered, we refer to entirely different things, even though both are called "nickel." The first is worth, indisputably, five cents. The other acquires its value, not from the words "five cents" embossed on its surface, but from its historical significance. That "nickel" is no longer a nickel as we know the word in everyday life. It is worth, perhaps, $50,000 as is Lincoln's handkerchief, coat, or undershirt. If Party A, as owner of Lincoln's last nickel, promises to convey it to Party B who, in exchange, promises to pay $50,000, the two parties do, certainly, form a contract. Lincoln's "nickel" is not a five cent coin; it's a collector's item. In 1861, in Indiana, (for reasons related to a will contest), D promised to pay P $600 in exchange for P's promise to pay D one cent. The Court held D's promise unenforceable:

> It is true, that as a general proposition, inadequacy of consideration will not vitiate an agreement. . . . But this doctrine does not apply to a mere exchange of sums of money, of coin, whose value is exactly fixed, but to the exchange of something of, in itself, indeterminate value, for money, or, perhaps, for some other thing of indeterminate value. In this case, had the one cent mentioned, been some particular one cent, a family piece, or ancient, remarkable coin, possessing an indeterminate value, extrinsic from its simple money value, a different view might be taken. As it is, the mere promise to pay six hundred dollars for one cent . . . was simply one to make a gift.[5]

> **QUESTION 3.** The law will LEAST likely regard as a contract, which of the following exchanges?
>
> A. X will, *today,* convey to Y $100,000; Y will, *today,* convey to X, the first U.S. postage stamp, issued in 1847, bearing a stated value of 5¢
> B. X will, *today,* convey to Y, 100 single dollar bills; Y will, *today,* convey to X, four $20 dollar bills.
> C. X will, *today,* convey to Y, one 8 ounce bottle of Coca-Cola for which X paid $1; Y will, *today,* convey to X one bottle of Pepsi-Cola for which Y paid 90¢.
> D. X will, *today,* lend Y $100,000; Y will, *one year from today,* repay the $100,000 together with an additional $5,000.

ANALYSIS. If two parties agree to exchange items or services that differ in their fair market values, each nonetheless provides the other with consideration. It is only when the values of the items exchanged are, by law, indisputably unequal—wholly liquidated—that one fails to give the other consideration.

---

5. Schnell v. Nell, 17 Ind. 29, 31-32 (1861).

A refers to the first U.S. postage stamp for which the stated value is 5¢. Such a stamp is no longer an ordinary "five cent stamp," but a collector's item. Its value today is unrelated to the words "five cents," printed on its surface. Hence, its value is not liquidated; it's worth any price on which a buyer and seller agree. **A** is wrong. As for **C,** Coca-Cola and Pepsi-Cola are two different things. We cannot say as a matter of absolute undeniable reality, that for all reasonable persons, one is worth more than the other, notwithstanding that their retail prices differ. **C** is wrong. **D** represents an ordinary loan at 5 percent annual interest. It's true that $105,000 indisputably exceeds the value of $100,000. But $105,000 one year hence does not necessarily exceed the value of $100,000 today. For reasons related to the "time value of money," Money "now" is normally worth more than money "later." **D** is wrong.

B describes the exchange of $100 for $80. A one-hundred dollar bill has a value, indisputably, of $100. Four twenty-dollar bills have a value, indisputably, of $80. Party X promises Y $100 and Y, at the same time, promises to pay X $80. Under ordinary circumstances, the arrangement reflects not a contract, but a naked promise by X to give Y $20. **B** is right.[6]

D. Make Friends with This Phrase: "Bargained for"

In cases concerning consideration, you'll read the phrase "bargained for" in statements like these:

- Consideration must be *bargained for.*
- One's promise (or performance) constitutes consideration only if it is *bargained for.*
- In order that Party B's promise serve as consideration for Party A's promise, Party B's promise must be *bargained for.*[7]

Be familiar with the phrase "bargained for." Know, too, that it reflects, precisely, the fundamental rule you already know: A promise is enforceable only if it belongs to a contract.

1. Let's Explain: Mary and Alice

Mary and Alice are roommates. On Saturday morning they talk:

Mary: I think we've let the yard go for too long. I'll mow the lawn today if you'll trim the shrubs today.
Alice: Okay—agreed.

---

6. *Maybe.* Suppose Party X desperately needs four quarters in "exact" change for use in a washing machine. So desperate is he, that he agrees to pay Y $5 for four quarters. In that circumstance, the quarters are not "ordinary" ones.

7. See also, Restatement (second) Contracts §71.

In its essence, Mary's offer proposes that each party "sell" her promise to the other and, reciprocally, that each "buy" the other's promise. Mary proposes to sell Alice her lawn mowing promise, charging as a "price," *Alice's* promise to trim the shrubs. Because Mary does that—because she demands Alice's promise as payment for her own, she "bargains for" it. Concomitantly, Mary proposes that Alice "sell" Mary her promise to trim the shrubs, with Mary to pay Alice, "as a price," *her* promise to mow the lawn. When Mary assents to the proposal, she "bargains for" Alice's promise and, simultaneously, the parties form a contract.

All of that means, really, that: *A promise is "bargained for" if and only if it belongs to a contract—if and only if, it belongs to an offer that undergoes acceptance.*

Compare Mary and Alice to roommates Marvin and Alex:

Marvin: I think we've let the yard go for too long. I will mow the lawn today.

Alex: That's great. In exchange, I will trim the shrubs today.

Alex says he will trim "in exchange" for Marvin's promise to mow. Nonetheless, Alex makes his promise in *appreciation* of Marvin's, but *not in exchange* for it. Neither of these parties ever proposed a *bargain* to the other. Marvin did not say, ever, "I'll mow the lawn if you will trim the trees." Alex did not say, ever, "I'll trim the trees if you will mow the lawn." Rather, Marvin promised to mow the lawn, asking nothing back from Alex. With Marvin's promise already in place, and in the spirit of cooperative gratitude, Alex promised to trim the shrubs, asking nothing back from Alex. Stated otherwise, neither party made an offer to the other, which means that neither accepted an offer *from* the other, which means that the parties did not form a contract, which means neither of their promises belongs to a contract, which means that neither has been "bargained for." Once again, we reveal this simple truth: *A promise is "bargained for" if and only if it belongs to a contract—if and only if, it arises by the process of offer and acceptance.*[8]

QUESTION 4. For five years Nancy has lived with and cared for her elderly uncle Moses. At the beginning of year six, Moses' sister takes up the task, and Nancy departs to begin the long awaited schooling she has thus far deferred. Grateful for Nancy's services, Moses creates a document entitled "Promissory Writing," which he signs and gives to Nancy. The

---

8. The Restatement writers put it thus: "(1) To constitute consideration . . . a return promise must be bargained for. (2) A . . . return promise is bargained for if it is sought by the promisor in exchange for the promise and is given by the promisee in exchange for that promise." (Restatement (second) Contracts §71) These draftspersons are a lubberly lot. They seem not to know that by their very own precepts and definitions they have stated only this: A promise is bargained for if it belongs to a contract.

document shows a space for Nancy's signature. Nancy does not sign, but she reads it:

> In consideration of and in exchange for her care, devotion, and affection during the past five years, I, Moses Shev, on this 26th day of February, 2012, do promise that should I live to the age of 90 years I will, on my 90th birthday, give to my niece, Nancy Shev, $1 million.

Two years later, Moses turns 90 but refuses to pay Nancy the $1 million he promised. Nancy brings an action against him for breach. Moses' attorney contends that Nancy gave no consideration for the promise, which fact renders it unenforceable. Nancy's attorney maintains that the years of service to which Moses expressly referred was Nancy's consideration for his promise. If the court rules for Moses, which of the following might it likely state as its reason?

I.   Nancy cannot demonstrate that her service to Moses had a monetary value of $1 million, wherefore Moses received no consideration for his promise.

II. Nancy did not sign the promissory writing, wherefore Moses' promise does not belong to a contract and is, therefore, unenforceable.

III. Moses did not bargain for Nancy's service, wherefore he gave his promise without consideration.

IV. The promissory writing does not represent a bargain, wherefore Moses' promise is unenforceable.

A. I and II
B. II and III
C. III and IV
D. I, II, III, and IV

ANALYSIS. After Nancy completes her five years of voluntary service, Moses makes his promise in *appreciation* of her service, but not in exchange for it. Nowhere in these parties' dealings did either propose to the other an "I'll promise X if you'll promise Y." That means neither made an offer, which means neither made an acceptance, which means the parties formed no contract, which means that Moses made not a contractual promise, but a naked promise, unenforceable. Many will say that Nancy's devoted service fails as consideration for Moses' promise because it was not "bargained for." Yet, (whether they know it or not), such persons mean, only, that Moses' promise did not belong to a contract.

Option I implies that Moses' promise is unenforceable because Nancy's service might be worth less than $1 million. We know better. One promise (or performance) may constitute consideration for another regardless of relative values (section C above). Option II reports that Nancy did not sign the promissory writing and that, too, is irrelevant. Signed or unsigned, by Moses, Nancy, John Hancock, or Solon the Sage, the document sets forth only a naked promise. If Nancy had signed it then, still, she would be beneficiary of a $1 million promise—naked and unenforceable.

Having eliminated options I and II, we eliminate also **A**, **B**, and **D**. That leaves us with **C**, which cites only options III and IV.

According to option III, Moses did not "bargain for" Nancy's service. That's true. His promise did not come forth through offer and acceptance; it did not belong to a contract and for that reason was not enforceable. Option IV makes a correct and equivalent statement—that the writing did not amount to a contract. **C** is right.

E.   Past Consideration

1. *Past Consideration Is No Consideration*

Loitering about the law of consideration is this "rule:" *past consideration is no consideration.* That rule represents yet another form of the one just studied: In order that a promise (or performance) serve as consideration, it must be "bargained for" which means, really, that a promise is enforceable if and only if it belongs to a contract.

We know, now, that if B does some service for A *after which* A purports to make a promise in "consideration" thereof, A's promise is a mere *nudum pactum*, unenforceable. Some courts will write that A did not "bargain for" B's service, wherefore B's service is not consideration. Others, regrettably, write: "Past consideration is no consideration." Accordingly, some 180 years ago in Vermont, defendant promised to pay money to plaintiff, "in consideration that" plaintiff had in the recent past done some service for defendant. The court ruled defendant's promise unenforceable, explaining that a "promise made on a past consideration is not binding . . . it is nudum pactum."[9] One hundred seventy six years later, having employed him for four months, plaintiff, a Montana employer, presented defendant, his employee, with a written "agreement." Defendant signed it. The "agreement" recited defendant-employee's promise not to compete with plaintiff, his employer. According to the writing, defendant made his promise "in consideration" of the salary plaintiff had paid him during the previous four months. The court held defendant's promise unenforceable: "The basic precepts of black-letter contract law teach us that 'past consideration is not sufficient to support a promise.'"[10]

Think again of Moses and Nancy. First, Nancy cared for Moses. Then, in appreciation for what she had already done, Moses promised her $1 million,

---

9. Barlow v. Smith, 4 Vt. 139, 143 (1832).
10. Access Organic, Inc. v. Hernandez, 175 P.3d 899, 903 (Mont. 2008).

asking nothing new in exchange. As already noted, some authorities will state that Nancy's services fail as consideration because they were not "bargained for." Others will say "past consideration is no consideration," and some will see that the two statements mean one and the same thing: *a promise that does not belong to a contract is mere nudum pactum,* unenforceable.

QUESTION 5. Jill has a large leak in her roof, but lacks the funds necessary to repair it. Her friend Jack voluntarily makes the repair. Three months later, Jill learns that Jack, short of funds, cannot pay his rent. She contacts him and says, "I'll pay the $2,000 you owe for rent." When Jack protests that he cannot accept such a large sum, Jill responds, "You repaired my leaking roof when I couldn't afford to pay for it. I now promise you something in exchange. In consideration of the roof repairs you made for me, I will pay your August rent." Does Jack's roof repair serve as consideration for Jill's promise?

I. Yes, because Jill made her promise expressly citing the roof repair as consideration

II. Yes, because Jill manifested her serious wish to pay Jack's rent in exchange for the roof repair

III. No, because the roof repair constitutes only past consideration

IV. No, because Jill did not bargain for the roof repair

V. No, because Jill did not record her promise in writing

A. I and II

B. I, II, and III

C. III and IV

D. IV and V

ANALYSIS. In principle, we've seen this case before. Party X does a favor for Party Y. Gratefully, Party Y promises something to Party X "in consideration" of what Party X has done. By law, Party X's service is *not* consideration, for Y's promise, wherefore Y's promise is *nudum pactum,* unenforceable. In this case, Jack is X and Jill is Y. Jack's prior service is not consideration for Jill's promise, and we may state the reason in multiple ways, including these:

- In making her promise, Jill did not "bargain for" Jack's service.
- Jack's service was mere "past consideration," which is "no consideration."
- Jill's promise did not belong to a contract.

Options III and IV make two of the statements just mentioned, so they're correct. Options I and II incorrectly state that Jill's promise is enforceable and each makes (or implies) its own false statement of law. As for I: A promisor does not receive "consideration" by writing or speaking that *word.* As for II: One does not create consideration by earnestly thinking her promise to be given "in exchange" for a service previously received. Jill made her promise because she *appreciated* Jack's prior service, but not *in exchange* for it. Option V correctly states that Jill's promise is unenforceable, but its reasoning is wrong. If Jill had put her promise in a signed writing, it would be unenforceable just the same. **C** endorses only statements III and IV, and so, **C** is right.

2. *Yet Another Redundant Statement: "Love and Affection Are Not Consideration"*

Suppose Daughter cares for Father in his old age. In gratitude Father, by signed writing, makes this promise: "In consideration of the love and affection shown me by my daughter for many years, I hereby promise to convey to her, one year from today, my farm, to wit, the real estate described in Volume 113 Page 422 of the Ashton County Land Records." The "love and affection" to which Father refers came to him before he made his promise. Hence, he did not make his promise *in exchange* for his daughter's love. He did not make it as party of any bargain that either party ever proposed to the other. His promise is unenforceable because it does not belong to a contract.

Nonetheless, legal history is replete with promisors who cite love and affection as the "consideration" for their promises. For that reason, there arose in the courts the statement that "love and affection are not consideration." The statement means, really, that past consideration is no consideration. That statement means really, that consideration must be "bargained for." And *that* statement means no more and no less than this. A promise is enforceable if and only if it belongs to a contract.

F. An Exception to the Consideration Doctrine: Moral Obligation

Notwithstanding all that we've taught, most jurisdictions do enforce one form of naked promise on a theory some call "moral obligation" or "moral consideration." Suppose that on January 1, Lamar and Damon form a contract under which Lamar lends Damon $1,000, Damon promising to repay it with 5 percent interest on or before December 31 of the same year. Damon's promise is, of course, enforceable. It belongs to a contract. As consideration, Damon receives Lamar's $10,000 loan.

On December 31, Damon fails to repay, but Lamar takes no action against him. Six years then elapse, and still Lamar takes no action. In the relevant jurisdiction, the statute of limitations pertaining to contracts and debts provides: "As to any breach of contract or unpaid debt, a plaintiff who fails to bring his action within six years from the time of default shall have no right of recovery." With six years passed since the time Damon defaulted, Lamar loses his right to sue for the debt. Legally, then, *Damon no longer owes Lamar the money*; his "slate" is "clean."

Imagine that Damon then contacts Lamar and says (or writes), "My debt has been discharged by the statute of limitations, but rest assured that I will pay you the $1,000 anyway—within six months from now." From all that we now know, Damon's new promise ought to be unenforceable. Although Lamar furnished consideration for Damon's *original* promise to repay, six years earlier, Damon gives this subsequent promise in exchange for nothing. The statute of limitations has discharged the original debt wherefore, by law, Damon owes Lamar nothing. Yet for his own reasons, Damon promises to pay the 1,000 that he does not (any longer) owe. Damon's newly made promise to pay Lamar $1,000 is *nudum pactum.*

Nonetheless, in some jurisdictions one's promise to pay an old debt, discharged by operation of law, is enforceable because, it is said, the promisor has received "moral consideration," or his consideration inheres in his "moral obligation" to make the payment. With these words, the law means to say that the original loan, although discharged, serves as consideration for the subsequent promise in a way that squares with "good morality" (if not good logic). Hence, one's new promise to pay a debt discharged by operation of law (usually by a statute of limitations) *is* enforceable. The promisee has received no consideration as we otherwise know that word. Nonetheless, for this purpose the law long ago invented the phrase "moral consideration" and, with it, renders such promises enforceable as an exception to the general precepts we've studied thus far.

The relevant rule, then, is this: *If, for a contract under which one owes a debt to the other, the relevant statute of limitations expires but the debtor thereafter promises to pay the debt (fully or in part), his promise is enforceable on the theory of "moral obligation" or "moral consideration" notwithstanding the absence of any new consideration from the creditor.*

Restatement (second) Contracts §82(1) takes that view, but (happily) avoids the phrases "moral consideration" and "moral obligation."

> A promise to pay . . . an antecedent . . . indebtedness is binding if the indebtedness . . . would be [enforceable] except for the effect of a statute of limitations.

Most jurisdictions have modified the common law by statute, providing that any such promise is enforceable only if set forth in a signed writing. In North Dakota, for example, one's promise to pay an old ("antecedent") debt discharged by the statute of limitations is enforceable, but "no [such] . . . promise is sufficient . . . unless the same is contained in some writing signed by the party to be charged thereby. . . . " N.D. Cent. Code §28-01-36.

QUESTION 6. Solomon's business supplies fabric to wholesalers. Bennett is a fabric wholesaler. On November 1, Year 1, the parties form a contract under which Solomon is to sell and deliver to Bennett on December 1, a quantity of cotton cloth for which Bennett will pay Solomon $50,000 on or before December 31. Solomon delivers the cloth on December 1, but by the 31st, Bennett fails to pay. On the next day, January 1, Year 2, and on the first day of every month for *six years* through and including December 31, Year 7, Solomon's automated office procedures send billing statements to Bennett's office, each one requesting payment of $50,000 "within 30 days."

Meanwhile, for all billing statements it receives, from all vendors, every month, Bennett's automated office procedures print a "Billing Acknowledgment" form that reads: "This office acknowledges a debt in the amount shown on your most recent billing statement and will pay the debt by the last day of the current month." On or about the fifth day of each month, Bennett's clerical assistant presents all such acknowledgment forms to Bennett, who hurriedly and routinely signs each one, whereafter the assistant mails one to each vendor who has provided Solomon a billing statement that month. Consequently, for each of the 72 monthly billing statements Solomon sends Bennett over the six-year period January 1, Year 2, through December 31, Year 7, Bennett sends Solomon an acknowledgment form. In response to Solomon's December 31, Year 7, billing statement, Bennett's office mails its acknowledgment form on January 2, Year 8. Solomon's office receives it on January 5.

As to claims for breach of contract and failure to pay debts, the state's period of statutory limitation is six years. Consequently, as to the $50,000 Bennett owes Solomon, the statutory period expires on December 31, Year 7, six years after Bennett was obliged to pay it.

On February 1, Year 8, Solomon engages a financial consultant who studies Solomon's business, including its accounts receivable (meaning moneys owed to it). On discovering the $50,000 unpaid by Bennett since December 31, Year 1, the consultant advises Solomon to bring suit, which he does on March 1, Year 8. Is Solomon entitled to recover the $50,000 from Bennett?

A. Yes, because one's debt to another continues legally, even after the statutory period of limitation expires

B. Yes, because Bennett sent Solomon an acknowledgment form after the statutory period of limitation expired

C. No, because after the statutory period of limitation expired, Bennett made Solomon no express promise to pay the $50,000

D. No, because Bennett ceased to owe Solomon the $50,000 as of December 31, Year 7.

ANALYSIS. On December 31, Year 7, the six-year period of limitation passes; as of that date, Bennett owes Solomon nothing. Yet two days later, on January 2, Year 8, by his "acknowledgment form," hurriedly signed, Bennett (unwittingly) promises to pay the debt. And although the promise would otherwise amount to *nudum pactum* it is, in this case, Bennett's promise to pay a pre-existing debt discharged by a statute of limitations. Consequently (in most jurisdictions), it's enforceable.

C and **D** tell us that Bennett's promise is *not* enforceable. Both are wrong. According to **C**, Bennett made no "express promise" to pay the debt. That's false. Each of Bennett's signed acknowledgment forms referred to Solomon's most recent billing statement and thus constituted an express promise to pay the $50,000 debt. **D** correctly states that Bennett's debt expired with the passage of six years, but ignores the fact that his new promise, made six days later, revives it. **A** accurately states that Solomon will recover from Bennett, but it's reasoning is flatly contrary to law. When the relevant statutory period of limitation expires, one's debt ceases to exist; he need not pay it — ever.

B tells us that Bennett's promise is enforceable because, with the acknowledgment sent to Solomon on January 2, Bennett promised to pay a debt that the statute of limitations had discharged. And, although Bennett got nothing back for this new gratuitous promise, the cotton cloth he originally received constitutes "moral consideration." Or, the consideration Bennett receives inheres in his "moral obligation" to pay (what once was) his debt. **B** is right.

G.   The Closer

QUESTION 7. On September 15, 2012, Benito, a graduate student, asks his friend Lannette for a $10,000 loan.

Lannette: Why do you need the loan?
Benito: The new semester has begun, and I'm $10,000 short on the tuition I owe. Classes have started and I've been attending, but the Bursar is demanding that I pay.
Lannette: That's a lot of money, but I will never forget how you traveled across the country to visit me last year, when I needed emotional support. Certainly I'll make the loan; you'll pay it back if and when you're able. It will take me a week or two to get a hold of the money, but I'll put my commitment in a writing that you can show to the Bursar. Maybe she'll leave you alone until the money comes through.

Lannette then creates and signs this writing:

September 15, 2012
To Whom It May Concern;

In consideration of (i) my long-standing friendship with Benito Bourne, and (ii) the help he has given me and the sacrifice he has made for me in several specific instances, and (iii) his need to pay school tuition, I, the undersigned Lannette Lindstom, as Lender, do hereby promise and commit myself to lend to the said Benito Bourne the sum of $10,000 at 1% annual interest, the loan to be made on or before October 1 of this year, 2012.

> **REPAYMENT TERMS:** The said Benito Bourne is to repay the loan and/or interest when and only when, if and only if, at any time in the future feels himself ready, willing, and able to do so, and otherwise not at all, neither loan nor interest.

On October 1, Lannette tells Benito, "I'm sorry, but I've changed my mind about the loan. I don't think I can afford to part with the $10,000." Benito visits his lawyer, who correctly advises him that Lannette's promise is unenforceable for lack of consideration from Benito. The lawyer is correct because

I.   Notwithstanding her signed writing, Lannette made no promise to lend Benito $10,000.
II. Benito neither did nor promised anything in return for the Lannette's commitment.
III. Among the matters that Lannette cites as consideration for her promise, none was bargained for.
IV. Neither the repayment terms nor any of the matters recited in Lannette's signed writing at (i), (ii), (iii), or (iv) actually describes consideration from Benito to Lannette.
V.   Benito did not sign the writing.
A. I
B. II and III
C. I, II, III, and V
D. II, III, and IV

ANALYSIS.   According to statement I, Lannette made no promise. That's false. She did make a promise; she promised to lend Benito $10,000. Her promise is not *enforceable*, but she did make it. Since statement I is false, **A** and **C** must be wrong. That leaves **B** and **D**, both of which cite statements II and III, meaning that II and III must be true. The two choices differ in that **D** cites, also, statement IV. If statement IV is false, **D** is wrong and **B** is right. If statement IV is true, **B** is wrong and **D** is right.

In statement IV, clause (i) Lannette describes, as consideration, her long-standing friendship with Benito. What goes for love and affection goes, too, for long-standing friendship. Lannette makes her promise *because* of friendship, not *in exchange for it*.

Clause (ii) cites help given and sacrifice made—in the past. Some will read it and say "past consideration is no consideration." Better it is to recognize that Lannette makes her promise *because* of Benito's help and sacrifice, not in exchange for it. In clause (iii), Lannette states yet another reason for which she promises the loan. But Benito's need for tuition is a fact. Lanette cannot and does not receive it *in exchange* for her promise. And what of the "repayment terms"? Their 48 words come to this: Benito need never repay the loan — ever; the "loan" is, really, a gift.

All references that appear in statement IV are bases on which a lawyer should conclude that Lannette has made only a naked promise, unenforceable. Since statement IV is true, **D** is right. We know that without examining III or V, but let's look at them anyway.

Statement III is true. Among all things that Lannette cites as "consideration" for her promise, none has come to her in exchange for her promise; none was bargained for. As for statement V, it's true that Benito did not sign the writing. That, however, is irrelevant to the question. Had Benito signed the writing in ink, wine, or blood, still, he would be giving nothing back to Lannette in exchange for her promise and, still, her promise would be mere *nudum pactum*, unenforceable. Statements II, III, and IV are true; I and V are false. **D** is right.

 # Silver & Hochberg's Picks

1.	C
2.	D
3.	B
4.	C
5.	C
6.	B
7.	D

13

Consideration, Part II

A. "Legal Detriment" or "Loss of Freedom"

We're almost ready now to define "consideration," but we'll first befriend two synonymous phrases, this one first: "legal detriment." *One suffers a legal detriment when she gives a promise or performance to which the law on its own does not otherwise oblige her.* Or, as the U.S. appeals court wrote: Legal detriment is one's "giving up . . . of a legal right[,] the refraining from doing what he has the legal right to do, or the doing of what he has the legal right not to do." Petroleum Refractionating Corp. v. Kendrick Oil Co., 65 F.2d 997, 999 (10th Cir. 1933).

Illustrations. Let's see what does and does not constitute legal detriment. Don't ask why we care or what this all has to do with consideration or contracts. Just learn to recognize what promise or performance reflects a legal detriment.

Al promises that he will drive Betty to the bank on Monday afternoon. No law requires that Al drive Betty to the bank. By promising to do so, Al suffers a legal detriment.

Bob washes Charlie's car. No law requires that Bob wash Charlie's car. By washing it, Bob suffers a legal detriment.

BuyCo promises SellCo: "We might need to buy widgets in 2012. If we do buy widgets during that year, we'll buy them from you. And if we do buy any widgets, we'll pay $1 per widget." By law, BuyCo is free to buy widgets anywhere it likes. By promising SellCo that *if* it buys widgets it will refrain from buying anywhere else, it agrees not to do what the law allows it to do. SellCo suffers a legal detriment.

Frances, a pharmacist, promises her employer PharmCo that if she voluntarily leaves PharmCo's employ, she will not work as a pharmacist for two years within 50 miles of PharmCo. The law allows Frances to work as a pharmacist anywhere she likes. By promising to refrain from doing so for a certain time in certain locations, Frances has agreed *not* to do what the law allows her to do. She suffers a legal detriment.

Wesley promises Quenton: "I will buy your building only if I can secure a license to use it as a medical laboratory." Wesley has not promised to buy Quenton's building. He has promised that *if* he obtains the license, *then* he'll buy it. By law, Wesley may obtain the license and not buy Quenton's building. He has promised to do that which the law allows him not to do. He has suffered a legal detriment.

Janelle promises her mother: "When driving my car, I will obey the speed limit." The law on its own *requires* that Janelle obey the speed limit. Promise or no promise, Janelle must obey the speed limit. By promising to do so, she promises to do that which the law already requires of her. In making that promise, Janelle does *not* suffer a legal detriment.

On March 1, Beth and Hernan form a contract in which Beth must type 100 pages of text by March 15, and Hernan must pay her $700. *Then on March 8, Beth promises Hernan: "I will honor our March 1 contract and type the 100 pages by March 15."* The law (of contracts) already requires that Beth honor the March 1 contract. On March 8, by promising to honor it, Beth promises to do only what the law already requires of her. In making the March 8 promise, she suffers *no* legal detriment.

Kathe, a patrolling police officer in Ward's neighborhood, promises Ward: "I'll always keep a watchful eye for any wrongdoing in the neighborhood." Because of her position as police officer, the law on its own requires that Kathe watch for wrongdoing in the neighborhood. In promising to do so, Kathe promises to do only what the law already requires of her. She suffers *no* legal detriment.

George promises Harriet: *I will either (a) drive you to the fair, or, if I don't, I'll (b) provide you with cab fare for the trip.* No law requires that George do either (a) or (b). By promising that he'll do one or the other, George promises to do what the law does not require. He suffers a legal detriment.

Here, as everywhere in the common law, words run free and loose. Instead of the phrase "legal detriment" (silly in itself), some courts use "loss of legal freedom" to mean the very same thing. For every situation above in which we said that one's promise subjected him to legal detriment, we might just as well say instead, that it subjected him to loss of freedom or loss of legal freedom. (In this book, however, we'll stick with "legal detriment.")

QUESTION 1. Ethel operates a business. To every employee she hires she makes what she calls her "four golden promises," shown in (A)-(D) below. Which of the golden promises subjects Ethel to a legal detriment?

A. Ethel promises never to discharge an employee because he arrives ten minutes late to work.

B. Ethel promises never to discharge an employee because of his religion.

C. Ethel promises never to discharge an employee because she has joined a union.

D. Ethel promises never to discharge an employee because he was born outside of the United States.

ANALYSIS.   By law, Ethel may not discharge an employee for any of the reasons mentioned in choices **B-D**. All four of those choices are wrong. With **A**, Ethel promises to refrain from doing that which the law allows her to do. In promising not to discharge an employee for petty lateness, she suffers a legal detriment. It's as simple as that; **A** is right.

B.   "Legal Benefit"

"Legal benefit" is, simply, the flipside of legal detriment. When one party to an agreement suffers a legal detriment, the other, by definition, enjoys a legal benefit. *One party to an agreement enjoys a legal benefit if and only if the other suffers a legal detriment.*

Suppose Alice and Barry, both adults, form an agreement under which Alice promises to stop smoking and, in exchange, Barry promises to stop drinking.

Because Alice is, by law, allowed to smoke, her promise subjects her to a legal detriment (having nothing to do, of course, with the fact that it subjects her *health* to a benefit). By simple (and silly) reciprocal definition, Alice's legal detriment *is* Barry's legal benefit. Because the law allows Alice to smoke, and she has promised not to smoke, Barry enjoys a legal benefit.

Concomitantly, *Barry's* legal detriment is Alice's legal *benefit.* Barry's promise not to drink subjects him, of course to a legal detriment (even though it benefits his health). Alice's legal benefit inheres in Barry's promise not to do that which the law allows him to do. Barry's promise not to drink is Alice's legal benefit.

QUESTION 2. Alex invites Joan aboard his sailboat, whereupon Joan expresses concern for her safety. With which of these four promises from Alex would Joan *not* enjoy a legal benefit?

> **A.** Don't worry; I'll have on board all safety equipment required by federal and state regulation.
> **B.** Don't worry; I'll have on board more safety equipment than the law requires.
> **C.** Don't worry; I'll be more careful than any sailor ever has been.
> **D.** Don't worry; I'll see that you're perfectly happy, safe, and comfortable.

ANALYSIS.   The rule is simple (and silly): With respect to any agreement, one party's legal detriment is the other's legal benefit. With choices **B-D**, Alex promises to do what the law does not require of him. The corresponding promises confer on Joan, a legal benefit. With **A**, Alex promises to do what the law on its own requires of him. That means it subjects him to no legal detriment, and *that* means it confers on Joan no legal benefit. **A** is right.

C.   "Consideration," At Long Last, Defined

We know that to form a contract two parties must, by offer and acceptance assent to a *bargain*—an exchange, a quid pro quo—an "I'll do this if you'll do that." Defining "consideration" means defining the kind of promise or performance that constitutes a "this" or a "that."

Very simply, now, here's the rule that defines consideration: *A party gives consideration when he suffers a legal detriment, meaning that a party gives consideration when he gives a promise or performance to which the law on its own does not otherwise oblige him.*[1]

Distinguishing the neutral word "agreement" from the legally charged term "contract," let's now use illustrations earlier made to create *agreements* that *do* constitute contracts because each party furnishes consideration to the other, as well as those that *do not* constitute contracts because one of the parties fails to furnish consideration to the other.

1. Bob and Charlie

Charlie (by spoken word): I'll pay you $50 if you'll wash my car. To accept, you must wash the car completely.
Bob then washes Charlie's car completely.

---

1. If we wish to turn the statement 'round and characterize the *receipt* of consideration, we say: *A party receives consideration when he derives a legal benefit, meaning that from some other party he receives a promise or performance that represents, to that other party, a legal detriment.*

Resulting agreement:

> Bob has washed Charlie's car. Obviously, no law on its own required that he do so. By washing the car, Bob suffered a legal detriment and thus provided Charlie with consideration.
>
> Charlie promises to pay Bob $50. Plainly no law on its own requires that he do that. Charlie's promise thus represents a legal detriment, meaning he furnished consideration to Bob.

Consequently, Bob provided consideration to Charlie and Charlie provided consideration to Bob. Their agreement *is* a (unilateral) contract. Charlie's promise is enforceable. (Bob has already performed.)

2. *BuyCo and SellCo*

> **BuyCo (by signed writing):** We might need to buy widgets in 2012. If we do buy widgets during that year, we'll buy them from you. And if we do buy any widgets, we'll pay $1 per widget. We want you to sell us all widgets we request during that year. Agreed?
>
> **BuyCo (by signed writing):** Agreed.

Resulting agreement:

> SellCo promises that for $1 each, it will sell BuyCo all widgets that BuyCo requests during the year 2012. Certainly no law requires that SellCo sell any widgets to BuyCo at any price at all. In making its promise, SellCo suffers a legal detriment, meaning it provides consideration to BuyCo.
>
> BuyCo promises that if it buys any widgets at all, it will buy all of them from SellCo for $1 each. BuyCo has not promised to buy a single widget or to pay a single dollar. Yet it has promised *something*. If it buys any widgets, it will buy all of them from SellCo. By law, BuyCo is free to buy widgets or not, and, if it does, it is free to buy them wherever it chooses. Hence, BuyCo has promised something that the law does not otherwise require. It suffers a legal detriment, meaning it provides consideration to SellCo.

Consequently, BuyCo provides SellCo with consideration, and SellCo provides BuyCo with consideration. This agreement *is* a contract. Both promises are enforceable. If BuyCo buys widgets in 2012, it must buy them from SellCo. If BuyCo demands widgets from SellCo, SellCo must provide them, at $1 each.

3. *Wesley and Quenton*

> **Wesley (by signed writing):** You own a building located at 2576 High Street—the property described at volume 776, page 209, of the Norfolk County Land Records. I may wish to buy it. If I can secure a license to use it as a medical laboratory, then I will buy it for $8 million. Otherwise, I won't. That's my offer. Are we agreed?
>
> **Quenton (by signed writing):** We're agreed.

Resulting agreement:

Wesley promises that *if* he secures the license, then he will buy Quenton's building for $8 million. He does not promise to buy the building. Rather, he makes a *conditional* promise to buy it. His conditional promise subjects him to a legal detriment. By law, Wesley is free to secure the license and not buy Quenton's building (or any building at all). In making this conditional promise to buy the building *if* he secures the license, Wesley agrees to that which the law does not otherwise require of him. He thus suffers a legal detriment, meaning he provides Quenton with consideration.

Quenton promises that if Wesley secures the license, then he will sell Wesley the building for $8 million. Plainly, no law requires that Quenton sell his building to Wesley. In making this conditional promise to sell, Quenton suffers a legal detriment and thus provides Wesley with consideration.

Consequently, Wesley provides consideration to Quenton, and Quenton provides consideration to Wesley. Their agreement *is* a contract, and both promises are enforceable. If Wesley secures the license, he must buy the building and Quenton must sell it.

4. *Janelle and Her Mother*

Mother: If you agree not to exceed the speed limit when operating your car, I'll pay for your prom dress. Agreed?
Janelle: Agreed.

Resulting agreement:

Mother promises to buy the prom dress. No law requires that she do so. By promising to buy the dress, Mother suffers a legal detriment, meaning she provides consideration to Janelle.

Janelle promises to obey the speed limit. The law on its own *requires* that she do that. By promising to obey the speed limit, Janelle suffers no legal detriment, meaning she provides no consideration to Mother.

Consequently, Mother provides consideration to Janelle, but Janelle provides *no* consideration to Mother. The agreement is *not* a contract. Neither party can enforce the other's promise. (If Janelle exceeds the speed limit, the state will subject her to a penalty, but she will not be in breach of contract, because these parties failed to form one.)

(Note here, as always, that the parties failed to form a contract because, really, they failed to achieve an offer and acceptance. Mother's proposal describes no bargain. She says she'll pay for the prom dress, and in exchange she asks Janelle to do — *nothing*. To give a promise or performance to which one is already legally obliged to is, in the law's eyes — *nothing*. A promise or performance that does not exact a legal detriment is—*nothing*. Having proposed her own promise in exchange for *nothing*, Mother proposed no bargain, which means she made no offer. That means Janelle had no offer to accept, wherefore the parties formed no contract.)

5. *Beth and Hernan*

> **March 1, Hernan:** I would like you to type my 10-page manuscript by
> March 15. I'll pay you $700 for the job. Will you do it?
> **March 1, Beth:** Yes, it's a deal.

Resulting agreement:

> Hernan promises to pay $700, and plainly no law, on its own, obliges him
> to do that.
>
> Beth promises to type the manuscript. No law obliges her to do *that*. Both
> parties provide consideration, they form a contract, and both their
> promises are enforceable. Now, as of March 1, because of that contract,
> Hernan *is* legally obliged to pay Beth $700 and Beth *is* legally obliged to
> type the manuscript.

On March 8, the parties speak again:

> **Beth:** I'm working on your manuscript, and I don't think $700 will adequately compensate me. I don't want to finish. However, I make you
> this offer: If you'll pay me an additional $300, I will finish—I'll honor
> our agreement of March 1.
> **Hernan:** Well, okay, it's a deal.

New resulting agreement (of March 8):

> Hernan promises to pay Beth an additional $300. By the March 1 contract,
> Hernan is obliged to pay Beth $700. He now promises to pay her an
> additional $300. No law requires that he do that. On March 8, he suffers
> a (new, second) legal detriment, meaning he provides Beth with (new)
> consideration.
>
> Beth promises to honor the contractual promise she made on March 1. By
> law, Beth must honor her March 1 promise because it belongs to her
> contract with Hernan. In promising now that she will honor a promise
> to which she is already legally bound, Beth promises only to do that
> which the law (of contract) already requires of her. She suffers no legal
> detriment, meaning she provides Hernan with no consideration.

Consequently, Hernan provides Beth with consideration, but Beth provides Hernan with none. The March 8 agreement is *not* a contract, and neither party is bound by promises made on March 8. The March 1 contract continues in effect. Beth must type the manuscript (as promised on March 1) and Hernan must pay $700 (as promised on March 1). Hernan's promise to pay the additional $300 belongs to no contract. It is *nudum pactum*, unenforceable.

(Note that here, as always, the parties failed to form a contract on March 8 because they failed to achieve an offer and acceptance. Beth purported to make an "offer," but she proposed no bargain. She proposed that Hernan should pay her $300 and that she should do what she was already obliged to do. She proposed a "quid" for Hernan, but no "quo" for herself. Because she made no offer, Hernan had no offer to accept and that's why—*really*—the parties formed no contract.)

6. Ward and Kathe (a Police officer)

> **Ward:** I'm worried about crime in this area. I'll pay you $1,000 if, on your patrol, you'll keep a watchful eye for any wrongdoing in the neighborhood.
>
> **Kathe:** I accept.

Resulting agreement:

> Ward promises to pay Kathe $1,000. Plainly no law on its own requires that he do that. His promise subjects him to a legal detriment, meaning he furnishes consideration.
>
> Kathe promises to keep a watchful eye for wrongdoing. Because she is a police officer, the law on its own requires that she keep a watchful eye for wrongdoing. Kathe's promise subjects her to no legal detriment, meaning she does not furnish consideration.

Consequently, Ward provides consideration to Kathe, but Kathe provides *no* consideration to Ward. The agreement is *not* a contract. Neither party can enforce the other's promise. (If Kathe fails to watch for wrongdoing, of course, she might face sanctions from the police department.)

7. George and Harriett

> **George:** If you will baby-sit for my daughter overnight tonight, I will (a) drive you to work tomorrow; if I don't do that, I will (b) provide you with cab fare for the trip.
>
> **Harriett:** I accept.

Resulting agreement:

> Harriett promises to baby-sit for George's daughter. No law requires Harriett to baby-sit for George's daughter, meaning she promises to do what the law does not require. She suffers a legal detriment; she provides consideration to George.
>
> George promises that he will either (a) drive Harriett to work, or (b) pay cab fare for that purpose. No law requires that George do either (a) or (b). By promising that he'll do one or the other, George promises to do

that which the law does not require of him. He suffers a legal detriment, meaning he provides consideration to Harriett.

Consequently, George provides consideration to Harriett, and Harriett provides consideration to George. The agreement *is* a contract. Both promises belong to that contract, and both are enforceable.

8. *In Summary*

For two parties to form a contract, one must make an *offer* that the other *accepts*. One makes an offer only if he proposes a *bargain*. Party A proposes a bargain only if he proposes to give forth consideration in exchange for consideration from Party B. One gives consideration when he suffers a *legal detriment*, meaning that he gives a promise or performance to which the law on its own does not oblige him.

We may now make short work of several phrases and "rules" that follow from the principles just described.

D.   "Preexisting Legal Duty"

The common law purports to feature this rule: *A party fails to give consideration when he promises to perform a preexisting legal duty.* The principle presents itself in section A above in the cases of Ward and Kathe, and Beth and Hernan (reread them now, please). In promising Ward that she would watch for wrongdoing, Kathe promised to fulfill what was her "preexisting legal duty." Before making her promise to Ward, she had a duty as a police officer to watch for wrongdoing. Kathe's promise to perform her preexisting duty does not constitute consideration.

On March, 1 Beth formed a contract with Hernan under which she was to type Hernan's manuscript. On March 1, therefore, the law of contract rendered it her *legal duty* to type the manuscript. Then, on March 8, Beth again promised to type the manuscript. In doing so, she promised only to do what was already her duty. Her promise does not constitute consideration.

Restatement (Second) of Contracts §73 provides: "Performance of a legal duty owed to a promisor which is neither doubtful nor the subject of honest dispute is not consideration." The preexisting "legal duty" might arise from statutory law or common law.

Consider, now, this little two-part story.

Part 1.   Chet and Dana agree that Dana will rebuild the transmission in Chet's truck, and, in exchange, Chet will pay Dana $10,000. Each party makes a promise, and each promise serves as consideration for the other. The parties' agreement *is* a contract.

Part 2.   Ethan is Chet's uncle and knows that Chet's truck has a malfunctioning transmission. Not knowing of the contract between Chet and Dana, Ethan communicates with Dana. "I'll promise to pay you $10,000 if you'll promise to rebuild the transmission in Chet's truck." Dana replies, "It's a deal." That agreement is *not* a contract. Under her preexisting contract with Chet, Dana was already obliged by contract law to rebuild the transmission. In making her agreement with Ethan, Dana promised to do only that which the law—contract law, in this case—already required of her.

Dana's preexisting legal duty arises by common law. In other scenarios, the legal duty might result from criminal law or elsewhere in the common law. Whether the duty arises from statutory or common law, the principle remains the same. When a party promises to perform a preexisting legal duty, she suffers no legal detriment and confers no legal benefit—all of which means she gives no consideration.

QUESTION 3. Lance, a landlord, owns two neighboring residential homes in Roseville. Simeon lives in one and Thad in the other, each as Lance's tenant. By their lease agreements with Lance, both tenants are obliged to "notify the landlord if, at any time, the premises should suffer damage that calls for immediate attention."

Every year, Simeon spends the three winter months in Florida, while Thad remains in Roseville. Thad spends the three summer months in Maine while Simeon remains in Roseville. Thad and Simeon form a contract under which

- Thad will monitor Simeon's home for the three winter months and contact Lance if it should suffer damage that calls for immediate attention;
- Simeon will monitor Thad's home for the three summer months and contact Lance if it should suffer damage that calls for immediate attention.

After the parties form their contract, Lance, knowing nothing of it, approaches Thad.

Lance: Your neighbor, Simeon, will be away for the three winter months. If you will promise to monitor his home and contact me immediately if it should be damaged in some way that calls for immediate attention, I'll pay you $500 when Simeon returns home. Are we agreed?

Thad: Yes, it's a deal.

When winter begins, Simeon leaves for Florida. For three months Thad does dutifully monitor Simeon's home, watching for any damage it might suffer, fully prepared to contact Lance if the damage should seem to call for immediate attention. The three months pass, the home suffers no damage, and Simeon returns home. Thereafter, Lance learns of the contract between Simeon and Thad. He refuses to pay Thad the $500 he promised. Is Lance in breach of contract?

A. Yes, because in their agreement, both Lance and Thad suffered a legal detriment.

B. Yes, because when Thad and Lance reached their agreement, Lance knew nothing of the contract between Thad and Simeon.

C. No, because the agreement between Lance and Thad is not a contract.

D. No, because before Lance and Thad formed their agreement, Simeon had a preexisting duty to inform Lance as to damage that called for immediate repair or attention.

ANALYSIS. Set your mind on the law. A promise is (generally) enforceable only if it belongs to a contract. For two persons to form a contract, each must provide the other with consideration. To provide consideration, a party must do or promise to do that to which he is not by law otherwise obliged. Hence, a party does not give consideration by promising to do that which, by law, he must do *anyway*.

Among all of the promises this story describes, we're asked about *one*—Lance's promise to Thad. If it belongs to a contract, it's enforceable. If it doesn't, it isn't. Hence we must determine that Thad did or did not give consideration for Lance's promise. If he did, the parties formed a contract, and Lance must honor his promise. If he didn't, they didn't, and Lance may freely break his promise.

Before forming his agreement with Lance, Thad formed his contract with Simeon and thus acquired a legal (contractual) duty to monitor Simeon's home for the three winter months. Then, in his agreement with Lance, Thad promised to do exactly that same thing. He promised to do only what he was already bound to do; he promised to perform a preexisting legal duty. That means he suffered no legal detriment, conferred on Lance no legal benefit, and provided no consideration for Lance's promise. The parties formed no contract, and Lance's promise was mere *nudum pactum*—a gratuitous promise—unenforceable.

C and **D** begin with "No," so one of them must be right. Carelessly examined, **D** looks good. It refers to "preexisting duty" and makes a true statement: It's *true* that before this whole saga unfolded, Simeon, by lease agreement, was obliged to inform Lance of damage that called for immediate repair or attention. But *that* preexisting duty is irrelevant to this question. If the lease agreement contained no such provision, then still Thad and Lance would fail to form a contract because of *Thad's preexisting duty to Simeon.* **D** is wrong.

According to **C**, Lance commits no breach of contract because he and Thad never formed one. That might not be the answer for which you were looking, but it's right. In purported exchange for Lance's promise to pay $500, Thad promised to do that which he was already obliged to do under his contract with Simeon. Hence he gave no consideration for Lance's promise, and the parties failed to form a contract. That means that Lance's promise does not *belong* to a contract, wherefore it's unenforceable.

The question writer might have drafted the correct answer differently—using words for which you were looking. She might have written, for example, "No, because Thad's promise to perform what was his preexisting duty to Simeon provided no consideration for Lance's promise." That or similar answers would be right, but the question writer did not offer them. Rather, she tested your *concentration on meaning* by featuring the phrase "preexisting duty" prominently in a *wrong* answer and omitting it from the right one.

E. The Closer

QUESTION 4. On May 1, BuildCo and HotelCo form a contract by which BuildCo is to build a hotel and HotelCo is to pay BuildCo $30 million. GasCo owns thousands of gasoline stations. Knowing of HotelCo's plan to open a hotel, GasCo opens a gasoline station near the building site. GasCo speculates that the hotel will bring increased business to its gas station.

In July, GasCo learns that BuildCo is in financial difficulty and might fail to complete the hotel for HotelCo. Because GasCo wants the hotel completed for its own reasons, on July 15 GasCo exchanges the following signed writings with BuildCo: "We will pay you $2 million if you promise to complete the hotel you are building for HotelCo." BuildCo writes back: "Agreed. We promise to complete the hotel." BuildCo completes the hotel, and HotelCo pays BuildCo $30 million. BuildCo wishes to collect also the $2 million from GasCo according to the promise GasCo made on July 15. Must GasCo pay BuildCo the $2 million?

A. Yes, because on July 15 GasCo and BuildCo exchanged signed, written promises.
B. Yes, because on July 15 GasCo and BuildCo formed an agreement that called for consideration from each.
C. No, because GasCo's promise was *nudum pactum*.
D. No, because GasCo did not ask HotelCo's permission to contact BuildCo.

ANALYSIS.   As always, take hold of the law: Two parties form a contract only if each provides the other with consideration. A party gives consideration when he suffers a legal detriment, meaning that he gives a promise or performance to which he is not already legally obliged. Consequently, a party gives no consideration when he promises to perform a duty that the law already imposes on him.

Here, the May 1 contract with HotelCo imposed on Buildco a legal duty to build the hotel. On July 15, that duty was still in place. When BuildCo promised GasCo that it would build the hotel, it promised only to perform a preexisting legal duty. Hence, it suffered no legal detriment, meaning it gave GasCo no consideration, meaning that GasCo made its promise to pay $2 million in exchange for nothing. The parties formed no contract, and GasCo's promise was *nudum pactum*, a naked promise, unenforceable.

A tells us that GasCo's promise *is* enforceable, so it's wrong. It then makes a statement that's true but, in this case, irrelevant. These parties did exchange promises. But, as just discussed, BuildCo's promise represented only its preexisting legal duty. It did not constitute consideration. **A** is wrong. **B** too begins with "yes," so it's wrong. Further, it makes a *false* statement. BuildCo and GasCo did *not* exchange consideration; BuildCo gave none.

That leaves **C** and **D**, both correctly stating that GasCo's promise is unenforceable. **D**, however, recites an irrelevancy: that GasCo did not acquire HotelCo's permission to contact BuildCo. If GasCo had acquired such permission, the result would be the same; GasCo's promise would be unenforceable for lack of consideration from BuildCo.

And what of **C**? It correctly states that GasCo's promise is unenforceable because it's a naked promise. That's exactly right. Because BuildCo gave GasCo no consideration, GasCo's promise is mere nudum pactum, unenforceable. **C** is right.

✦ Silver & Hochberg's Picks

1. **A**
2. **A**
3. **C**
4. **C**

Consideration, Part III: The Subtleties

A. Conditional Promise as Consideration

Suppose that by signed writing, Quinn offers his building for sale at a price of $8 million. Wesley makes a counteroffer.

> **Wesley (by signed writing):** I will buy the building for that price but only if, within 180 days, I secure a license to use it for pharmaceutical manufacturing.
> **Quinn (by signed writing):** Agreed.

Wesley does not promise, definitely, to buy Quenton's building. Rather, he promises that *if* he can secure the license, then—subject to that condition—he will buy it. Before making his promise, Wesley is free to obtain the license and *not* buy Quenton's building—or any building at all. With his promise in place, he obliges himself to that which the law does not require of him; if he obtains the license, he must buy the building. Hence, Wesley's promise subjects him to a legal detriment. And so it is said that a conditional promise, also called an "aleatory promise," constitutes consideration. For "[i]t is a widely accepted rule of contract law that consideration is not insufficient merely because it is conditional, even though the controlling event may never occur." Charles Hester Enters. v. Ill. Founders Ins. Co., 499 N.E.2d 1319, 1323 (Ill. 1986).

Restatement (Second) of Contracts §76 cmt. c states:

> A party may make an aleatory promise, under which his duty to perform is conditional on the occurrence of a fortuitous event. Such a promise may be consideration for a return promise.

> Illustration: . . . A promises to sell and B to buy goods if A's employees do not strike before the time for delivery. The promises are consideration for each other.

Suppose that Wesley, immediately after making his promise, changes his mind; he decides that he doesn't want the building under any circumstance, license or not. For that reason, he "sits on his hands"; he does not apply for the license. He allows 180 days to pass, and then, having no license to operate Quinn's building as a pharmaceutical factory, he tells Quinn, "I did not obtain the license, so I won't be buying your building."

1. If Wesley Does That, He Will Be in Breach

When, in an agreement with another, one makes a conditional promise and has some control over the condition's occurrence, the law implies his promise, also, to use such reasonable efforts as will tend to make the condition occur. When Wesley promises to buy Quenton's building *if* he can secure the license, he promises, by law, (1) that he will attempt to secure the license, and (2) if successful, that he will buy the building.

Suppose that by signed writing, Buyer and Seller agree on the purchase and sale of realty for $3 million. The contract provides, "Buyer's obligation to buy is conditional on his ability to obtain a 30-year mortgage loan of $2.5 million, at an interest rate of 6 percent or less." *By law* Buyer has promised that he will use reasonable efforts to secure such a loan. Endres v. Warriner, 307 N.W.2d 146 (S.D. 1981). If Buyer then "sits on his hands" and fails to search for the loan, he breaches the contract.

The rule of conditional promises, then, is this: *A party who makes a conditional promise gives consideration, and he implicitly promises as well that if the condition is partially within his control, he will attempt to bring it about through such efforts as are reasonably available to him under the circumstances.*

QUESTION 1. Sandra Salin and Saul Simmons own adjacent farms. Bill Benson wants to buy both of them. On July 1, by a signed writing that is proper in form and content, Bill ("Buyer") and Sandra ("Seller) agree on the purchase and sale of Sandra's farm ("the premises") for $1.5 million. The writing recites Sandra's promise to sell and Buyer's promise to buy. It also provides that:

- Buyer will purchase the premises only if, within 90 days, he succeeds in forming a contract with Saul Simmons, for the purchase of his farm, adjacent to Seller's, at a price of $1.5 million or less.

The parties sign two copies of the writing, and, as a down payment, Bill gives Sandra his check for $100,000. The parties then separate, each keeping a copy of the writing. Seconds later, Sandra changes her mind. She immediately visits her attorney, shows him the signed writing, tells him she no longer wishes to sell the farm, and asks, "Must I sell my farm to Bill?" With which of the following would the attorney respond correctly?

A. "If you revoke your offer before Bill begins to negotiate with Saul, then no, you are not obliged to sell your farm to Bill."

B. "If Bill succeeds in forming a contract for the purchase of Saul's farm, then yes, you will be obliged to sell your farm to Bill."

C. "No; Bill made no promise that he would attempt to purchase Saul's farm, and that renders your promise unenforceable."

D. "No; Bill has given you no consideration which means your agreement is not a contract."

ANALYSIS. These parties have formed an agreement under which Sandra promised to convey her farm to Bill, and Bill promised to pay Sandra $1.5 million — *if* he should be able, first, to form an agreement for the purchase of the adjacent farm. No law, on its own, requires that Sandra convey her farm to Bill. Hence, Sandra's promise to sell subjects her to a legal detriment. By law, Bill's promise requires that he make a reasonable effort to form a contract with Saul for the purchase of Saul's farm. Obviously, however, no law otherwise requires that Bill attempt to buy Saul's farm, and no law otherwise provides that if able to do so, he must, also, buy Sandra's. By promising that he will (a) attempt to purchase Saul's farm and (b) if successful, purchase Sandra's farm, Bill suffers a legal detriment.

Both parties suffer a legal detriment, meaning that each provides consideration to the other; the parties' agreement is a contract. Their promises belong *to* the contract and are, therefore, enforceable. Bill must try to reach agreement with Saul for the purchase of his farm. If successful, he must pay Sandra $1.5 million, and Sandra must convey the farm. If he is not successful, neither party owes anything to the other.

A refers to Sandra's "offer," but between these parties there stands no offer. They have a contract. **A** is very wrong. **C** is wrong too. By law, Bill did promise that he would attempt to reach agreement with Saul. **D** reports that Bill gave no consideration, which is, of course, false.

With **B**, Sandra's lawyer gives good counsel. Sandra has formed a contract under which she must convey her farm to Bill (for which he must pay $1.5 million) if Bill succeeds in reaching agreement with Saul. **B** is right.

B.   Consideration, Contractual Modifications and UCC §2-209(1)

As you learned in Chapter 11, section C, Two parties might first form a contract and later, modify it. As Chapter 11 explained, modification of an existing contract requires that one party make an offer to modify and the other accept. As is so of any offer, an offer to modify an existing contract must introduce a new *bargain*, meaning it must propose that each party to the original contract suffer some new legal detriment. As is more commonly stated: *Two parties modify an existing contract only if, in that regard, each provides consideration to the other.* Borrowing from Chapter 11, section A, suppose that on July 1, Gary and Jacqueline form a contract in which Gary is to pay Jacqueline $30 per hour and Jacqueline is to proofread his manuscript by August 1. On July 20, Jacqueline approaches Gary with this proposal: "I'll proofread the text *and* retype it at no additional charge if you'll extend my deadline to October 1." Gary responds, "I accept." Jacqueline proposed this *bargain*; that she would add to her responsibilities by retyping the text and, in exchange, Gary should extend her deadline. When Gary accepted, each party made a new promise to the other, as proposed in Jacqueline's offer. Jacqueline would *type* the manuscript, which she was not previously obliged to do, and Gary would allow her until October 1 to complete her work which, previously, he had no obligation to do. Hence each party provided consideration to the other and the parties effectively modified their contract.

Imagine that on July 20, Jacqueline approaches Gary with a different proposal: "I'd like you to extend my deadline, so I propose that (1) I will definitely proofread the manuscript as originally agreed, if you will (2) extend my deadline from August 1 to October 1." Gary responds, "Agreed." Jacqueline's proposal does not qualify as an offer. It presents no *bargain*. Gary is to extend the deadline and Jacqueline is to do—*nothing*, except what the existing contract already requires. Hence, when Gary "accepts," he accepts—*nothing*. The parties form no contract, and Gary's promise to extend the deadline is *nudum pactum*, unenforceable. Once again, the applicable common law rule, as usually stated, is that: *Two parties effectively modify an existing contract only if, in attempting to do so, each provides consideration to the other.*[1]

---

1.   The rule (a) that modification of an existing contract requires consideration from both parties is but one application of the broader rule (b) that one gives no consideration when she promises only to perform a preexisting legal duty. On the one hand we said that Jacqueline fails to modify her contract because, in her effort to do so, she gave no consideration. We might just as well say that in exchange for Gary's promise to extend her deadline, Jacqueline promised to perform a preexisting legal duty—to proofread the manuscript which the existing contract already required of her.

1. *The UCC Abandons That Rule*

UCC Section 2-209(1) provides: "An agreement modifying a contract within this article needs no consideration to be binding." The Code rule thus departs significantly from the common law.

Consider this. On May 1, Sabrina contracts to sell Brent 10,000 widgets for $10,000. She is to make delivery on July 1. On June 1, Sabrina approaches Brent: "I know we agreed on a price of $10,000, but I think that's too little. I'll deliver the widgets on July 1, the purchase price to be $11,000. Agreed?" Brent replies, "Yes." Brent now promises to pay $1,000 more than the May 1 contract requires, and Sabrina promises nothing; she will do only what the original contract already requires of her. By common law, the modification would fail. But the contract concerns the sale of goods, and UCC Article 2 governs. Under UCC §2-209(1), the modification is effective. Sabrina is obliged to deliver 10,000 widgets on July 1. Brent must pay $11,000.

QUESTIONS 2-4. On September 1, Roofer and Owner form a contract under which Roofer will repair Owner's roof on or before October 1, for which Owner will pay him $1,500.

QUESTION 2. For this question, assume that on September 12, Owner says to Roofer, "I'd like you also to replace my gutters by, let's say, October 3. Will you do that without any increase in price?" Roofer responds, "Certainly. I'll finish the roof repair by October 1, as agreed, and I'll replace the gutters by October 3." After the September 12 conversation, Roofer is obliged to:

A. repair the roof by October 1 and replace the gutters by October 3.
B. repair the roof and replace the gutters, all by October 3.
C. repair the roof by October 1, and nothing more.
D. repair the roof by October 3, and nothing more.

ANALYSIS. On September 1 each of these parties made a contractual promise, fully enforceable. Roofer was to complete a roof repair by October 1, and Owner was obliged to pay $1,500. On September 12, they attempted to modify their contract. In doing so, Roofer promised to replace gutters by October 3, which the original contract did not require. Owner promised *nothing*. He was to pay only $1,500 as already required by the September 1 contract. Under the new agreement, Roofer enjoys no time extension for the roof repair. He is allowed until October 3 to replace the gutters, but under the original contract he had no duty to replace the gutters at all. Roofer's promise to replace the gutters belongs to no contract; neither does the date October 3. Both parties are bound by their original contract and nothing more. Owner must pay $1,500, and Roofer must make the roof repair by October 1. **C** is right.

QUESTION 3. For this question, assume that on September 12 Owner speaks to Roofer thus: "I'd like you also to replace my gutters. If you agree, I'll give you until October 3 to finish the whole job—roof and gutters. Will you do that without any increase in price?" Roofer replies, "Certainly. I'll finish the roof repair and the gutter replacement by October 3." After the September 12 conversation, Roofer is obliged by contract to

A. repair the roof by October 1 and replace the gutters by October 3.
B. repair the roof and replace the gutters, all by October 3.
C. repair the roof by October 1, and nothing more.
D. nothing.

ANALYSIS. Under the original contract, Owner was entitled to demand that Roofer complete the roof repair by October 1. With this new/modified agreement, he promises not to make that demand. He moves the deadline to October 3. In exchange, Roofer promises to replace the gutters by October 3, which the original contract did not require. Both parties suffer legal detriment, meaning each provides consideration to the other. Roofer gives his promise to replace the gutters, and, for the roof work, he receives a two-day extension. Owner gives the two-day extension for the roof repair, and receives Roofer's promise to replace the gutters. The parties effectively modify their contract and their promises, as revised, belong *to* their modified contract. All are enforceable. Owner must pay $1,500 and, by October 3, Roofer must repair the roof and replace the gutters. **B** is right.

QUESTION 4. Shane sells books wholesale to retailers. Brenda is a retailer. On February 1, Brenda and Shane form a contract under which Shane will sell Brenda 500 copies of the novel *Snowmaker*, to be delivered on March 1, Shane to pay a total purchase price of $750. On February 3, Brenda contacts Shane by signed writing: "Our contract calls for you to deliver 500 copies of *Snowmaker* on March 1. We'd like to have an additional 25 copies, 525 in all for the same $750 total, all to be delivered by February 15. Agreed?" Shane writes back, "Agreed." As of February 3, Shane's contractual obligation is to deliver:

A. 500 copies of the book by March 1.
B. 500 copies of the book by February 15.
C. 525 copies of the book by March 1.
D. 525 copies of the book by February 15.

ANALYSIS. The parties formed a contract for the sale of goods. UCC §2-209(1) permits them to modify it without regard to consideration. On February 3, they attempted a modification under which Shane, in exchange for nothing from Brenda, promised to deliver 25 additional books, 16 days early.

By common law, the parties would fail to modify their contract. They would be bound by their original contract and nothing more. Shane's promise to deliver the additional 25 books would be *nudum pactum*, as would his promise to make delivery 16 days earlier than first agreed. Under UCC §2-209(1), however, the modification is effective. The parties are bound by their contract *as modified* on February 3. Brenda need pay only $750 and Shane must deliver 525 books on February 15. **D** is right.

C. More on Contractual Modifications: Settlement of Claims, Substituted Contract, Executory Accord, Accord and Satisfaction

1. The Rule of Foakes v. Beer

Borrower is a professional roofer in need of a loan. On January 1, Lender lends him $10,000 in exchange for his promise to repay that amount 12 months later, on December 31, together with $500 in interest. On December 1, Borrower contacts Lender.

> **Borrower**: I won't be able to repay all that I owe, and I know that will put me in breach. If you'll forgive the breach, I will pay you $6,000, on the due-date, December 31. Is that acceptable?
>
> **Lender**: Yes, it is; I accept.

On December 31, Borrower tenders[2] $6,000 to Lender as agreed. Lender refuses it and demands the full $10,500 originally owed him. Under the common law, Lender is within his rights; he need not honor the "settlement" to which he agreed, because Borrower gave no consideration for Lender's willingness to take less than he was owed. Lender is entitled, still, to collect from Borrower the full $10,500 originally owed him.

That's often called the "rule of Foakes v. Beer."[3] *When a creditor, in settlement of a fully liquidated*[4] *debt, agrees to take less than he is owed, his debtor giving him no new consideration in exchange, he need not abide by his agreement;*

---

2. One "tenders" a payment or performance when he shows that he is ready, willing, and able to deliver it.

3. L.R. 9 A.C.605 (H.L. 1884).

4. "Liquidated," as used here, means an amount of money that is, under prevailing circumstances, clear, plain, and not plausibly subject to any good faith dispute.

he is entitled to the full amount of the debt originally owed him. This "rule of Foakes v. Beer" is but a corollary to a more fundamental one: Two parties can effectively modify an existing contract only if each, in that effort, gives consideration to the other.

2. When a Debt or Other Obligation Is Not Fully Liquidated; Substituted Agreement and Executory Accord

Lender and Borrower, Episode II

Suppose, now, that the December 1 conversation runs like this:

> **Borrower**: I can't repay what I owe, and I know that will put me in breach. I see, however, that your roof needs repair. If you'll forgive my breach, I will, beginning April 1, repair your roof, the work to be finished by April 30. Is that acceptable?
>
> **Lender**: Yes, it is; I accept.

These parties have achieved an effective settlement, by altering their contract. Lender has given consideration by foregoing his right to be paid $10,500. Borrower has given consideration by promising to do something different from what the original agreement required of him.

Suppose now that April passes, and Borrower does not repair the roof; he breaches the *new* agreement. That raises this question: In view of Borrower's breach of the new agreement, does Lender have an action for the $10,500 originally owed him, or does he have only an action for the damages (if any) that arise from Borrower's failure to repair the roof? Here's the answer: *If* the new contract is what the law calls a "substituted agreement," the original contract terminates. Lender's rights inhere in the new agreement only. He has no action for the $10,500. If, on the other hand, the new contract is what the law calls an "executory accord," then Borrower's failure to honor the new obligation—his failure to "satisfy" it—allows Lender to sue either for (a) $10,500 owed him under the original contract or, if he prefers, (b) damages for Borrower's failure to repair the roof.

When two parties A and B form a contract, and A thereafter alleges that B has breached (which allegation B might or might not admit), and, in settlement of that claim, the parties reach some altered agreement, the law presumptively attributes to them not a substituted agreement, but an executory accord. They form a substituted agreement only if they have plainly manifested an intention to do so. It is relatively rare, therefore that a court attributes to two such parties a substituted agreement. Usually, it rules that they have formed an executory accord. In Borrower and Lender, Episode II, the parties said nothing as to what would be Lender's rights if Borrower should breach the new agreement. Consequently, by presumption of law, they formed an executory accord. Because Borrower fails to satisfy his obligations under the accord, Lender may sustain an action against him for (a) the $10,500 owed under the original agreement, or (b) the damages caused him by Borrower's failure to repair the roof.

3. "Accord and Satisfaction" as a Defense to Breach of Contract

The Accord; Gary and Frances, Episode I

On September 1 Frances and Gary form a contract under which:

(1) Frances, on October 1, is to play 10 violin pieces at Gary's cocktail party, and

(2) Gary is thereafter, on that same night, to pay Frances $3,000.

On October 1, the party starts. Frances plays the 10 pieces, whereafter Gary complains, *sincerely and genuinely*, that as to many notes, Frances had played "flat." Six guests, all musicians, agree with Gary. Frances maintains, sincerely and honestly that she did not play flat. Another six guests, all of them musicians, agree with Frances.

Without knowing whether Frances did or did not play flat, we do know that (1) the parties are in *honest, good faith dispute* regarding that question, and (2) each of their positions is "colorable" (meaning "plausible" under the circumstances). Gary genuinely believes that Frances played flat, and six musicians agree. Frances genuinely believes she did not play flat, and, again, six musicians agree. Each party's position is honestly held and there is, apparently, *some* basis for each. Whatever the truth, each party's position is colorably (plausibly) correct, and honestly held. Frances and Gary converse:

Gary: So, we disagree.
Frances: Yes, we do.
Gary: I think you played flat.
Frances: I think I did not.
Gary: I propose that we settle our dispute on these terms: You play one *more* piece tonight, and I'll pay you, tonight, $2,500 instead of $3,000.
Frances OK, it's a deal.

These parties just formed an executory accord. As is so of any contract or contractual modification, an executory accord requires offer, acceptance, and consideration from both its parties. In this case, Gary makes the offer and Frances accepts. As for consideration, Frances makes two promises (either one of which alone, would suffice as consideration). She promises (1) to play an extra piece, not required under the original contract, and (2) to accept a payment of less than the $3,000 to which the original contract entitled her.

Let's ask: what consideration does Gary provide? Let's answer: Gary, we said, plausibly and in good faith alleges that Frances breached her contract. Consequently, he would be justified in bringing an action against her.[5] He might, of course, fail to prove the breach and, therefore, lose the suit. But, so long as he believes plausibly and honestly that Frances has breached, he has the right to *bring* a suit. *By foregoing that right he gives consideration.* Hence, these parties formed

---

5. One who falsely, or without any plausible basis alleges a breach has *no* right to bring an action. Rather, he commits the tort of malicious prosecution and/or abuse of process.

an executory accord in which (a) Frances promised to do that which the original contract did not require of her, and (2) Gary promised to forego his right to bring suit for the breach that he (plausibly and honestly) attributes to Frances.

The *Satisfaction*

Suppose that after these parties form their accord (their "executory accord"), Frances plays the additional piece. She thus *satisfies* the accord—she does what it requires of her. If Gary right away pays the promised $2,500, he too satisfies the accord. The parties thus achieve "accord and satisfaction," and each loses her/his rights under the original contract.

But suppose now, that Frances, having played the additional piece and taken Gary's $2,500, regrets having made the settlement. She stands ready to prove, she thinks, that she originally gave a note-perfect performance, and she wants the additional $500 that, under the accord, she gave up. She brings an action against Gary under the original contract, seeking a $500 recovery. At trial, as his defense, Gary proves accord and satisfaction. For that reason, Frances recovers nothing. And, once again, that is so even if to the court's satisfaction, she proves that her performance was, in fact, flawless. The accord and satisfaction terminates her rights under the original contract.

Let's state a rule: *If (1) Parties A and B form a contract, and (2) Party A colorably and in good faith asserts that Party B has breached, and (3) in settlement of A's claim, the parties form an executory accord, which means that each must provide consideration to the other, and (4) each party satisfies the accord, then neither party may thereafter assert her rights under the original contract. If either one, as plaintiff, attempts to do so, the other may properly plead the defense of "accord and satisfaction," which, when proven, defeats the plaintiff's claim.*

Remember and understand, please that two parties cannot (under the common law) modify their contract unless each provides consideration to the other. That is so whether they purport to undertake an ordinary, outright modification as discussed in section B of this chapter, or an attempt to settle a dispute by executory accord. Suppose Gary honestly believes that Frances has played her violin to perfection note perfectly, with nary a note flat or sharp. Suppose, further, that (a) Gary nonetheless, insists, contrary to what he truly believes, that Frances has played flat, and (b) Frances, who badly needs money, agrees to Gary's proposed agreement to "settle" his claim. The agreement will not, in that case, constitute an executory accord, because the parties are not in *honest* dispute as to the quality of Frances's performance. Rather, it will constitute an attempt to modify a preexisting contract with Gary providing no consideration to Frances. In essence, the arrangement is one in which Party A makes a promise to Party B, "in exchange" only for Party B's promise to perform a pre-existing legal duty, as discussed in Chapter 13, section C.

With respect to a contract between two parties, A and B, *if Party A, without a plausible, good faith foundation, asserts that Party B is in breach, the two parties are ineligible to form an executory accord; their attempt to do so is ineffective. Party A retains the right to recover under the original contract, and Party B cannot effectively assert the defense of accord and satisfaction.*

When One of the Parties Fails to Give Satisfaction; Gary and Frances, Episode II

Let's return, now, to the facts of Episode I; Gary asserts a plausible good faith claim that Frances has played flat, and the parties form their executory accord, as earlier described. Suppose that Frances plays the additional violin piece pursuant to the accord, but Gary doesn't pay the $2,500 that same night, as required. Rather, he decides to "think it over", and ultimately tenders payment on the next day. Frances refuses the money and decides instead to sue for the full $3000, standing ready to prove she did not play "flat".

Gary can *not* effectively assert the defense of accord and satisfaction because although the parties reached an executory accord as settlement of their dispute, Gary did not *satisfy* it; he did not timely tender his $2,500 payment. Having failed to satisfy the accord, he leaves Frances free to enforce the original contract. If she proves that she properly performed—that she played every note correctly—she is entitled to the full $3,000 originally promised her.

Let's expand our rule: *If two parties, A and B, form a contract, and Party A later sues B for breach, B may effectively assert the defense of accord and satisfaction if he proves that (a) in an effort to settle their dispute, the parties formed an executory accord, and (b) that he satisfied it. If he proves that the parties formed an executory accord but does not prove that he satisfied it, he has no such defense. Party A is, in that case, entitled to pursue her action under the original contract. If she can, after all, prove that she did not breach it, she recovers the damages to which the original contract entitles her.*

QUESTIONS 5 & 6. On May 1, Lender lends Borrower $25,000, to be repaid on April 31 of the next year by ordinary personal check, together with interest of 5 percent, for a total of $26,250. On April 29, Borrower contacts Lender and explains that she cannot pay the full amount.

QUESTION 5. Borrower asks whether Lender will accept $22,000 as a "settlement of the debt." Lender agrees. Borrower sends Lender a check for $22,000, together with a signed note indicating that the check is tendered "in full settlement of what was otherwise my total debt to you of $26,250." Lender deposits the check; three days later, Lender sends Borrower a signed writing: "Your check has cleared; you owe me nothing."

Lender then decides that he wishes to recover the additional $4,250 originally owed him, and he brings an action against Borrower. The court issues judgment for Lender in the amount of $4,250. The Court's reason for not enforcing the parties' settlement is most likely that:

I. the parties reached an accord, but the fact that Borrower owed Lender a liquidated debt of more than $22,000 means they failed to achieve satisfaction.

II. in order that two parties effectively modify a contract between them, each must provide consideration to the other.

III. by first informing Lender, on April 29, of her inability to pay, Borrower gave Lender no fair and reasonable notice of her wish to settle the debt.

IV. the parties were not eligible to achieve accord and satisfaction.

A. I and IV
B. II and IV
C. III and IV
D. I, II, II, and IV

ANALYSIS.   Between these parties, there is no plausible dispute as to the amount that Borrower owes. Her debt is fully liquidated. Nonetheless, she asks Lender to accept less than she owes him, and Lender, receiving no consideration, agrees to do so. The absence of a colorable good faith dispute as to the amount Borrower owes means the parties cannot effectively form an accord, meaning that they cannot achieve accord and satisfaction. Hence, option IV is true. When two parties purport to settle a dispute where, as here, they are not in dispute, they attempt only to modify their contract without exchange of consideration. Hence, options II and IV are true.

Option I offers a sort of double-talk, presenting, meanwhile, a "friendly face." It correctly states that Borrower's debt is liquidated. Incorrectly, however, it reports that these parties formed an accord, but because of the liquidated debt could not achieve satisfaction. That's wrong. Because Borrower's debt was fully liquidated, meaning they were not and could not be in dispute as to its amount, they could not and did not form an executory accord. Option III invokes the happy phrase "fair and reasonable," and on all faces, puts a smile. It sounds so right, but it's very wrong. Call Borrower's notice monumentally fair, wretchedly unfair, outstandingly reasonable, or abjectly unreasonable; it doesn't matter. In this context, no notice of any kind makes a difference to the legal outcome. Lender is entitled to the additional $4,250 for the reasons cited in options II and IV only (which are, in essence, the same). Hence, **B** is right.

QUESTION 6. Assume now that on April 29, after advising Lender that she does not have the funds to pay her full debt of $26,250, Borrower says, "If you will accept $22,000 instead of $26,450, I'll pay you today, two days early. Furthermore, I'll pay you not by ordinary check but by certified check."[6] Lender agrees. On that same day, Borrower engages a courier service that delivers to Lender a certified check in the amount of $22,000. Lender deposits the check, which clears three days later.

Lender then decides that he wants to recover the additional $4,250 originally owed him, and he brings an action against Borrower. The Court issues a judgment for Borrower. Its reason for enforcing the parties' settlement is most likely that

I. Borrower paid two days before she was obliged to and did so in a manner that went beyond her contractual obligation.

II. Lender received consideration in return for his willingness to accept less than the amount originally owed him.

III. Borrower gave Lender consideration in exchange for Lender's willingness to accept less than the amount originally owed him.

IV. in connection with the altered agreement, each party provided the other with consideration.

A. I and IV
B. II and IV
C. III and IV
D. I, II, II, and IV

ANALYSIS. These parties are not in dispute as to the amount Borrower owes Lender or the date on which payment is due. As in Question 7, they are not eligible to achieve accord and satisfaction. However, like any two contracting parties, they can modify their contract so long as, in the process, each provides the other with consideration. (Recall from Chapter 12, section C, that the law does not question the relative value of each party's consideration.)

The parties in this case effectively modified their contract. Lender agreed to accept $22,000 in lieu of the full $26,250. Borrower agreed to pay two days early (itself, adequate consideration), and to pay by certified check instead of ordinary check (also adequate consideration in and of itself) Every one of the options, in its own way, states that the parties achieved an effective modification of their contract, because each provided the other with consideration. Hence, **D** is right.

---

6. As you'll learn in a course called "Negotiable Instruments" or "Payment Systems," Party A issues to Party B a certified check by first writing his own ordinary personal check to B, then taking the check to his own bank and asking the bank to certify it. The bank places various writings on the surface of the check indicating that it is "certified." Once a check is certified payment is positively guaranteed by the bank; the bank is liable on the check (as otherwise it is not). Before the bank certifies a check it examines the customer's account, assures itself that the relevant amount is available, and then sets that amount aside, in order to pay on the certified check when Party B presents it for payment. It is sometimes said that "a certified check is like cash." The reason is that the bank must, by law, pay it. The funds are guaranteed to be present and available, and the issuer of the check (Borrower in this case) has no power to "stop" payment on it (as he otherwise would have). Such, among many other matters, is the subject matter of U.C.C. Articles 3 and 4.

4. *Tender of Check as Offer of Accord; Deposit as Acceptance*

Suppose Jocelyn and Dante agree that Jocelyn will repair Dante's bicycle, with Dante thereafter to pay her $100. When Jocelyn announces completion, Dante proclaims in good faith, on some plausible basis, that performance was defective. He declines to pay the $100. Instead, Dante sends Jocelyn a check for $75 together with a letter stating that, "because I believe you did not properly repair the bicycle, I offer this check for $75 as full and final payment, with the understanding that each of us is fully discharged of all contractual duties."

The letter is Dante's offer of an executory accord. The check is his simultaneous *tender* of satisfaction. Jocelyn may accept the offer or not. If she returns the check to Dante, she does *not* accept. If she simply deposits the check, she *does* accept, and at that moment the parties form an executory accord. If Dante's bank pays Jocelyn's bank (meaning the check "clears"), Dante satisfies the accord, and Jocelyn loses her right to the $100.

It does not matter that Dante and Jocelyn never communicate with each other about the dispute. It matters only that Dante, colorably and in good faith, alleges a breach. If he then tenders his check for $75, he makes an offer of accord. When Jocelyn deposits it, she accepts the offer. And in many jurisdictions, that is so even if Jocelyn writes above her endorsement "without waiver of rights," or "under protest." *One who receives a check in an amount less than she thinks she is owed, together with an offer of an accord, must not deposit it, unless she is willing to forgo what she thinks are her contractual rights.*

Now, let's ask: Who decides that Dante's allegation of breach was made colorably and in good faith? As always, the ultimate answer is *a court*, which makes this decision as it makes all others—upon an evaluation of evidence. Suppose that after Dante's check clears, Jocelyn insists on collecting the additional $25 that Dante withheld. She sues Dante in small claims court for $25, alleging his contractual obligation to pay her that amount. As a defense, Dante asserts accord and satisfaction. Jocelyn insists that the parties formed no true accord because, she says, Dante had no plausible basis on which to believe, in good faith, that her services were deficient. It falls on Dante to show that he believed colorably and in good faith that Jocelyn had failed in her obligations. He tries to do that, perhaps, by (1) testifying himself as to why and on what basis he found the repairs defective; and/or (2) calling in a bicycle repair expert who, after examining the bicycle, offers his opinion on the quality of the repair and whether it was plausible (even if inaccurate) that Dante believed the repair to be defective; and/or (3) presenting the bicycle itself as an exhibit and showing the Court on what basis he believed the repair to be defective.

If, ultimately, the Court finds that Dante did colorably and in good faith believe that Jocelyn's work was defective, then Dante succeeds in his defense of accord and satisfaction. If it finds otherwise, he does not, and it will issue judgment for Jocelyn in the amount of $25.

D. The Illusory Promise and Alternative Promises

1. The Illusory Promise

Let's examine four versions of an offer from Alvin, each of which Betty accepts:

> **Alvin (Version 1):** I'd like you to promise to tutor me in calculus for eight hours on Sunday, without charging me.
> **Betty:** I accept.

Alvin purports to make an offer but does not propose that he himself will suffer any legal detriment. Consequently, he proposes no bargain, wherefore he makes no offer, meaning the parties form no contract. Stated otherwise: The parties' agreement is not a contract because it exacts no consideration from Alvin. Betty's promise belongs to no contract. It's *nudum pactum*, unenforceable. She need not tutor Alvin at all.

> **Alvin (Version 2):** If you'll promise to tutor me in calculus for eight hours on Sunday, I'll do nothing for you in exchange.
> **Betty:** I accept.

This time, Alvin expressly states that he promises nothing. Again, the agreement exacts no consideration from Alvin, and the parties form no contract. Betty's promise is *nudum pactum*, unenforceable.

> **Alvin (Version 3):** If you'll promise to tutor me in calculus for eight hours on Sunday, I'll promise to pay you $400, but I don't promise to *keep* my promise; I might not pay you at all.
> **Betty:** I accept.

Once again, Alvin promises nothing. With one clause he proposes his "promise" to pay and with the next he withdraws it. The parties form no contract.

> **Alvin (Version 4):** If you'll promise to tutor me in calculus for eight hours on Sunday, I'll promise to pay you $400, but please understand that I reserve the right, privilege, entitlement, prerogative, and option unconditionally to dishonor that promise and, therefore, to withhold and refrain from making such payment wholly or in part, permanently or temporarily, with or without notice, if for any reason or no reason, at my own whim and discretion, I should so choose or decide.
> **Betty:** I accept.

This time Alvin promises a great big *mouthful* of nothing. He "promises" to pay $400 but then reserves the right not to pay it for any reason or no reason. Again, Betty promises to tutor Alvin, and Alvin promises *nothing*. In all four offers, Alvin gives no consideration, the parties form no contract, and Betty's promise is unenforceable.

In the fourth version, with all of those fancy words, Alvin creates the superficial appearance — *the illusion* — of a promise but, in fact, makes none. If, as Alvin does in version 4, one purports to make a promise, but then by some attached term reserves the right to dishonor it unconditionally, at his sole whim, for any reason or no reason, then he makes an "illusory promise." An illusory promise is that which, on its surface, might seem to create a commitment but when fully studied comes to nothing because the "promisor" leaves himself wholly free, unconditionally, to honor or dishonor it, as he pleases. An illusory promise is no promise at all. In version 4, Alvin's proposal is exactly the same as proposals 1, 2, and 3. In effect, he says to Betty, "I would like you to tutor me on Sunday for eight hours and in exchange I promise *nothing*."

Here's the relevant rule: *If a party purports to make a promise, but by some attached term or provision provides that he may dishonor the promise, unconditionally, for any reason or no reason, at his sole whim, then he makes not a promise but an* illusory *promise, which is no promise at all and does not constitute consideration.*

2. Illusory Promise vs. True Conditional Promise

In section A of this chapter, we learned that one's conditional promise constitutes consideration. "If it rains, I will drive you to the fair" is a conditional promise, but a true promise just the same. The promisor obliges himself to perform if there occurs some true condition — a matter not governed by his own arbitrary whim. He promises *something* (which the law, on its own, does not require of him) and so suffers a legal detriment. Consider this: "If I can obtain a $2 million, 30-year loan at 6 percent interest or less, I promise to buy your real estate." By law, this promisor obliges herself to pursue the loan and, if she obtains it, to purchase the land. She thus promises *something* that the law, on its own, does not require of her.

Compare those promises to this one: "If I want to, I will drive you to the fair." Here the promisor commits to a performance "conditioned" on his own unbridled desire. By law, one's own unbridled desire is not a condition. Rather, it negates the "promise" to which it is tied. This promisor has made an illusory promise. In the law's eyes he has said, "I promise *nothing*."

It's useful that we supplement the rule of conditional promises so that it expressly distinguishes between a conditional promise and an illusory one:

> *(1) One who makes a conditional promise gives consideration, and he implicitly promises as well that if the condition is partially or wholly within his control, he will attempt to bring it about through such efforts as are reasonably available to him under the circumstances.*
>
> *(2) If one so describes or conditions his promise as to leave himself free to honor or dishonor it at his sole unbridled whim, then he makes not a conditional promise but an illusory promise, which is no promise at all.*

3. Avoid Confusion: Naked Promise vs. Illusory Promise

Remember that a naked promise is a genuine promise for which the promisee gives no consideration. It's a real promise, but the law won't enforce it because it is unsupported by consideration (meaning it belongs to no contract). An illusory promise is no promise at all. If Party A makes a true promise and Party B, in exchange, makes an illusory one, then (1) B makes no promise at all, and (2) A makes a naked promise—a real promise, but because she receives no consideration, she need not honor it. It's unenforceable.

QUESTION 7. DevCo is a real estate developer, and ConCo a builder. By signed writing, DevCo and ConCo form an agreement under which DevCo purports to hire ConCo to build a housing development. The writing embodies 50 pages and 550 paragraphs. Paragraphs 1-20 identify the parties and define various terms. Paragraphs 21 and 22 provide:

> 21. ConCo will build the housing development described herein, according to the timetables, schedules, specifications, and standards also provided herein.

> 22. DevCo will pay ConCo $25 million on each of the dates herein defined and described.

Paragraphs 22-549 describe the timetables, schedules, specifications, and standards by which ConCo is to perform. They also describe the dates on which DevCo is to make its four $25 million payments. Paragraph 550 provides:

> 550. The parties agree that any promise or commitment made by ConCo hereunder is conditioned on ConCo's determination that it wishes to honor it, which determination ConCo alone shall make if and as it wishes.

In this agreement:

I. ConCo makes no promise.
II. ConCo makes only an illusory promise.
III. DevCo makes no promise.
IV. DevCo makes a naked promise.

A. I
B. I and II
C. I, II, and III
D. I, II, and IV

ANALYSIS. The parties signed a lengthy document filled, primarily, with definitions, schedules, timetables, specifications, and standards. At paragraphs 21 and 22, each party purports to make its promise: DevCo is to pay, and

ConCo is to build. The last paragraph provides that ConCo need honor its promise only if and as it wishes and thus renders ConCo's promise illusory. An illusory promise is no promise, and in this agreement ConCo promises nothing. DevCo *has* made a promise—a real one. It promises to pay. Because ConCo has provided no consideration in exchange, DevCo's promise is unenforceable; it's a promise given in exchange for nothing—*nudum pactum.*

Options I and II are true; ConCo made an illusory promise and that's no promise at all. Option III is false. DevCo promised to pay. Option IV is true. DevCo made its promise in exchange for nothing, wherefore its promise was *nudum pactum,* unenforceable. **D** is right.

E. Implied Consideration

In various circumstances, contract law *implies* that a contracting party has agreed to one term or another. Chapter 4, section C, taught of implied "gap fillers." From section A of this chapter, we know that for one who makes a conditional promise, the law implies a promise also to use reasonable efforts to attempt to bring the condition about. Learn, now, of another circumstance in which the law implies a promise.

Jake and Enid
Jake manufactures tires, and Enid operates several retail tire stores. On June 1, 2011, Enid and Jake form an agreement in which Jake allows Enid, for one year, the exclusive right to sell his tires. The substantive portion of the agreement provides:

> Jake hereby promises that Enid will, for one year from this date, have the exclusive right to carry, market, and sell tires manufactured by Jake, and that Jake will not, therefore, during that period, allow any other retailer to carry, market, or sell such tires.

Six months later, on December 1, 2011, Jake wants to dishonor his commitment, and allow another retailer to carry and sell his tires. Jake consults his lawyer, who examines the written agreement and concludes that it does not amount to a contract. "This agreement," the lawyer says, "recites your promise to give Enid an exclusive right to sell your tires, but it exacts no consideration from Enid. Enid promises nothing. You have received no consideration for your promise; it's unenforceable. You may break it."

The lawyer is wrong; he doesn't know this common law rule: *When Party A conveys to Party B an exclusive right to sell, market, or distribute his property or service, Party B implicitly promises that she will, through reasonable commercial efforts, attempt to promote Party A's objectives.*

Here, Jake is Party A and Enid Party B. Jake conveys to Enid the exclusive right to carry and sell his tires. *By law,* Enid promises that through reasonable commercial effort she will attempt to sell the tires. She is obliged, therefore, to sponsor such advertising and marketing as would be usual and customary for a retailer in her circumstance attempting to sell a particular brand of tires. In effect, the law reads the agreement like this:

> Jake hereby promises that Enid will, for one year from this date, have the exclusive right to carry, market, and sell tires manufactured by Jake, and Jake will not, therefore, during that period, allow any other retailer to carry, market, or sell such tires. *In exchange, Enid promises that it will resort to such means and measures as are usual in its industry in an effort to market and sell such tires.*

Consequently, even though the writing shows no express promise from Enid, Enid does, by law, make a promise, and that promise provides consideration to Jake. The parties form a contract, and Jake's promise is enforceable. If Jake allows another retailer to sell his tires, he commits a breach. The rule applies not only under the common law, but under UCC Article 2 as well. UCC §2-209(2) provides:

> A lawful agreement by either the seller or the buyer for exclusive dealing in the kind of goods concerned imposes . . . an obligation by the seller to use best efforts to supply the goods and by the buyer to use best efforts to promote their sale.[7]

QUESTION 8. Shirley is a real estate broker, and Tamara wishes to sell her home. Tamara ("Seller") engages Shirley ("Broker") to represent her in the sale, and the parties form an agreement by signed writing with this substantive provision:

> Seller promises and agrees that Broker will have, for six months, the exclusive right to list and show the home, and to offer it for sale on Seller's behalf. During that six-month period, therefore, Seller will not herself show the home to any prospective buyer and neither will she allow any other person to do so.

The remainder of the writing carries various incidental terms, but recites no promises or commitments from Shirley. Tamara wishes to break her promise and allow another broker to show her home. Is she free to do so?

A. Yes, because she made only a naked promise

B. Yes, because her agreement with Shirley does not amount to a contract

C. No, because she received consideration from Shirley

D. No, because she made her promise in a signed writing

---

7. For a celebrated case citing an analogous rule, see Wood v. Lucy Lady Duff-Gordon, 222 N.Y. 88, 90 (1917) (plaintiff did not "promise in so many words [to] use reasonable efforts to . . . market [defendant's] designs," but "such a promise is fairly to be implied.").

ANALYSIS.   By agreement, Tamara gave Shirley the exclusive right to show her home and offer it for sale. Although Shirley did not expressly make any promise in exchange, the law attributes to her an implied promise to direct reasonable commercial efforts to show the home and offer it for sale. In effect, the law adds this to the end of the parties' signed agreement: "During that same six-month period, Broker will employ such means and measures as are usual, customary, and reasonable in her industry in an effort to show Seller's home and to offer it for sale." With this agreement, therefore, Tamara promised Shirley a six-month period of exclusivity, and Shirley promised Tamara that, during those six months, she would attempt to sell the home. Each party promised to do that which the law, on its own, did not require of her. Each provided the other with consideration. The parties formed a contract, and if either breaks her promise she will be in breach.

According to **A**, Tamara made only a naked promise. If the law did not imply Shirley's reciprocal promise, that would be true. But the law does imply a promise from Shirley, meaning that the parties formed a contract. Tamara's promise belongs to that contract and is not, therefore, a naked promise. **B** states that the parties did not form a contract and, as just explained, that's false. **D** correctly reports that Tamara may not break her promise, but its reasoning is wrong. The rule at issue does not require a writing. If these parties had made their agreement without a writing, then, still, they would form a contract.

C is correct. It accurately states that Tamara may not break her promise and correctly states the reason: Tamara received consideration for her promise. **C** is right.

F.   Enforcing a Promise to Avoid Injustice

1. Promissory Estoppel

Suppose Olivia's uncle says to her, "As a graduation present, I'll give you a car. Count on it." Delighted with the prospect of the car, Olivia plans a weekend car trip. She makes reservations for a two-night stay at a motel, thereby incurring a nonrefundable obligation of $200. Thereafter, Noah tells Olivia that he has changed his mind about the car: "I'm sorry; I won't be getting it for you." Olivia is out $200, and the law of contract affords her no remedy. Uncle Noah has made a naked promise, and the parties have not formed a contract. Stated otherwise, Olivia has given Noah no consideration for his promise, wherefore Noah's promise is *nudum pactum*.

Appended today to the law of contract, however, is the doctrine of "promissory estoppel," rooted not in law but in equity.[8] It renders Noah's promise

---

8.   Appendix, section E.

enforceable — not fully, but to the extent necessary to make Olivia whole. The rule of "promissory estoppel" provides: *If one makes a promise receiving no consideration in exchange, and the promisee reasonably and foreseeably relies on it to her detriment, then the promise is enforceable to the extent necessary to rectify any resulting unfairness.* Restatement (Second) §90 states it thus:

> A promise which the promisor should reasonably expect to induce action or forbearance on the part of the promisee or a third person and which does induce such action or forbearance is binding if injustice can be avoided only by enforcement of the promise. The remedy granted for breach may be limited as justice requires.

Noah, receiving no consideration, made Olivia a promise and, indeed, told her to "count on it." As a reasonable person, he should have foreseen that Olivia might do just that and commit herself to some cost, expense, or detriment[9] as a result. Relying on the promise, Olivia did suffer a detriment by committing herself to a $200 expenditure. Very likely, then, a court will enforce Noah's promise, not in full, but to such degree as is necessary to avoid "the injustice." The car Noah promised has a value, say, of $20,000. If the promise had belonged to a contract, Noah would have to pay that full amount in order to fulfill Olivia's "expectation interest."[10] But the promissory estoppel doctrine won't require that he pay that much. Rather it will likely require that he pay Olivia $200 — the loss she sustains through her reasonable "detrimental reliance" on the promise. That's ordinarily the amount necessary to avoid "the injustice."

Doesn't This Rule Reverse Everything We've Learned About the Need for Bargain and Consideration?   No, it doesn't. To begin, it operates only if the Court finds that the promisee has (1) *relied* on the promise (2) *reasonably*, (3) to her *detriment*, (4) in a way that was *foreseeable* to the promisor, (5) so to cause a resulting *injustice*. Further, when the rule operates, it does not render the naked promise enforceable in full. Rather, it enforces the naked promise only to the extent necessary to correct the resulting injustice. In the case of Noah and Olivia, that's a difference between $200 and $20,000.

QUESTION 9. Becky, age 92, has only $25,000 to her name and is fearful that she will outlive her financial resources. On August 10, 2012, Becky explains her concern to her wealthy great-nephew Logan. On that same day, by signed writing, Logan makes her this promise: "When you exhaust the $25,000 that you now have, I will provide you, as a gift, any amount of money you request, up to a maximum of $50,000 per year for the remainder of your life."

---

9. The word "detriment" in this context does not refer to legal detriment as used earlier. It means only some cost or burden.
10. Chapter 25, section E.

In September 2012, Becky's grandson Thane asks Becky for $25,000. Unable to resist, and believing that she can turn to Logan for any money she may need, Becky gives Thane the $25,000 in her bank account—all that she has in the world. Becky then contacts Logan. Explaining what she has done, she asks him for $25,000. Logan responds, "I did not make my promise to you so that you could give your money away to Thane. I'm not going to keep the promise." To what extent does the doctrine of promissory estoppel require that Logan keep his promise of August 10, 2012?

A. Not at all, because Becky did not reasonably rely on it
B. To the extent of $25,000, because that is the extent to which Becky relied on it
C. To the extent of $25,000, because that is the amount he promised to pay per year
D. Fully, because Becky was reasonable in believing that Logan would honor his promise

ANALYSIS.   Logan can dishonor his promise without committing a breach of *contract*, since these parties formed no contract. The promise was *nudum pactum*. Under the doctrine of promissory estoppel, the promise is enforceable only to the extent that Becky relied on it, reasonably, and in a way that was reasonably foreseeable to Logan. Logan made his promise in response to Becky's concern for her financial future. He had no reason to imagine that Becky would rely on it as a basis from which to give all of her own money to Thane. Becky's reliance was neither reasonable nor foreseeable to Logan. For that reason, Logan need not keep his promise—at all. Consequently, **A** is right.

2. *The Offeree Who Relies on an Unaccepted Offer*

For an offeree who relies on an offer he has not yet accepted, the law sponsors a doctrine similar to that of promissory estoppel. Restatement (Second) §87(2) provides:

> An offer which the offeror should reasonably expect to induce action or forbearance of a substantial character on the part of the offeree before acceptance and which does induce such action or forbearance is binding as an option contract to the extent necessary to avoid injustice.

Illustration: BigCo and ConCo.   BigCo intends to build a school building and invites contractors to submit bids on the project. ConCo wishes to submit a bid. Before doing so, it needs to know how much it will spend on commissioning an electrical contractor to take charge of the relevant electrical work. ConCo contacts both ElectriCo and LightCo, providing them with specifications pertaining to the school building, asking to know how much each will charge for the relevant electrical work. ElectriCo advises ConCo: "Regarding the BigCo school building, we are prepared to do the electrical work for $1.5 million, payment to be made in five equal installments, as we complete 20%, 40%, 60%, 80%, and 100% of the work." LightCo makes an offer on similar payment terms, but the total amount for which it asks is $1.7 million. Relying on ElectriCo's offer, ConCo contacts BigCo and offers to build the building for $30 million. BigCo accepts ConCo's offer, whereupon ConCo decides to accept ElectriCo's $1.5 million offer. Before it does so, however, ElectriCo revokes, whereupon ConCo accepts LightCo's $1.7 million offer.

ConCo brings an action against ElectriCo, seeking to recover $200,000, the difference between the amount it would have had to spend under ElectriCo's offer and the amount it must spend on accepting LightCo's offer. At trial, ConCo proves that (1) in setting its own bid to BigCo at $30 million, it relied on Electrico's $1.5 million offer, (2) if it had had only LightCo's bid and not Electrico's bid, it would have set its bid to BigCo at $30.2 million, and (3) that BigCo would have accepted that bid, wherefore ConCo lost $200,000 in profit as a result of ElectriCo's revocation.

What result? ConCo and ElectriCo did not form a contract, so ConCo has no cause of action against ElectriCo for breach of contract. Nonetheless, ElectriCo made an offer, knowing that ConCo would rely on that offer in making its bid to BigCo. ConCo did just that and offered to build the building for $30 million, instead of the $30.2 million it would have demanded in the absence of ElectriCo's offer. ConCo's likely satisfies the conditions attached to Restatement (Second) §87(2). ConCo reasonably relied on ElectriCo's offer in a manner that was foreseeable to ElectriCo. As a result, it suffered a $200,000 detriment. Probably, ElectriCo will be held to pay ConCo $200,000. *See* Dreenan v. Star Paving Co., 333 P.2d 757 (Cal. 1956).

G.   The Closers

By signed writing, Nancy and Don contract for the manufacture by Don of three new sails for Nancy's sailboat. The contract price is $12,000, and the contract specifies that the three sails will be suitable to function on Nancy's sailboat, with Nancy to have a reasonable opportunity to test their function before making payment to Don. Pursuant to the contract, Don inspects Nancy's boat and then begins to manufacture the sails: one a mainsail, one a jib sail, and one a mizzen sail. When Don announces completion of his work, he delivers the sails to Nancy. Before paying the agreed contract price, Nancy immediately tests their function on her sailboat.

QUESTION 10. After conducting the test, Nancy concludes that the mizzen sail is, to some noticeable degree, not suitable for use on her vessel. She contacts Don by writing: "The mizzen sail is not quite right. It doesn't hang properly and doesn't trim quite right. I will send a check for $8,000 as payment in full under our contract." Nancy does then send an $8,000 check to Don, together with a letter: "I submit this check in accordance with my last writing, in which I described problems with the mizzen sail."

Don deposits the check, it clears, and the $8,000 moves to Don's bank account.

Thereafter, Don asks Nancy when she intends to pay the remaining $4,000 of the contract price. Nancy responds that she does not intend to pay it. She refers Don to the two writings she sent him after testing the sails, and to the $8,000 check she sent with the second one. Don responds that he never agreed to accept $8,000 as full payment and that he has taken the $8,000 only as a partial payment of the $12,000 owed to him. Nancy refuses to pay any additional amount. If Don brings an action against Nancy for the remaining $4,000 of the contract price, and Nancy proves at trial that she honestly and plausibly believed the mizzen sail unsuitable to her vessel, judgment should be for

A. Don, because he received no consideration for the reduction in the contract price from $12,000 to $8,000

B. Don, because he never agreed to accept $8,000 as satisfaction of the $12,000 that Nancy owed under the contract

C. Nancy, because Don's failure to perform one-third of the contract justifies her in withholding one-third of the price

D. Nancy, because Don's receipt of the $8,000 discharged her duty to pay the full $12,000 contract price

ANALYSIS.   Colorably and in good faith, Nancy believes that Don has breached the contract. She tenders a check that, in light of her earlier message, amounts to her offer of an executory accord. By depositing it, Don accepts her offer and the parties form an executory accord. When the check clears, Nancy satisfies her obligation under the accord, and thus achieves accord and satisfaction. **A** is utterly wrong. By forgoing her right to withhold payment and/or to sue on her colorable good faith belief that Don had breached, Nancy does provide consideration. **B**, too, is for the birds. By depositing Nancy's check, Don accepts her offer of an executory accord. To many, both **C** and **D** might seem right. But we don't know, for a fact, that Don did or did not fail to perform one-third of his contract, (or any part of it). We know only that Nancy, in good faith, *believed* he had done so. **C** implies, as a fact, that Don did materially breach his contract, but, once again, we don't know that he did or did not. **D** properly identifies Nancy as the prevailing party and, in its way, correctly states the reason. When Don receives the $8,000, Nancy satisfies the accord. Hence Don loses his rights under the original contract. That's why **D** is right.

QUESTION 11. Now assume that when Nancy tests the sails, she finds them satisfactory. She sends Don this signed writing: "All of the sails function well, and I thank you for your work. However, five other sail makers tell me that $12,000 is out of line — that they would have done the same work for $8,000. For that reason, I will send a check for $8,000 as payment in full under our contract." Nancy does send an $8,000 check to Don, together with a letter that states, "I submit this check in accordance with my last writing, in which I noted that your $12,000 price was excessive." All other facts are as previously set forth in Closer 1. Is Don entitled to receive the remaining $4,000 of the $12,000 contract price?

A. Yes, because Nancy's debt to Don was fully liquidated
B. Yes, because Don never expressly agreed to reduce his price by $4,000 after Nancy complained of it
C. Yes, but only if Nancy failed to believe, colorably and in good faith, that $12,000 exceeded the prevailing market price
D. No, because the parties achieved an accord and satisfaction

---

ANALYSIS. Many students choose **D**, but it's wrong. It is not Nancy's right that Don charge her, for his service, the "going" rate. Don may charge her anything he wishes (so long has he does not, in any way, deceive her). Even if it's true that Don's price is "out of line," Nancy has no right to sue him. In proposing to pay Don less than the contract requires, therefore, she gives up no right to bring an action against him. In exchange for her proposal that Don accept $8,000 instead of $12,000 she proposes, really, that Don sacrifice a contractual right in exchange for — nothing.

B is wrong. Even if Don had expressly agreed to reduce his price when Nancy complained of it, then still, under the "rule of Foakes v. Beer," Don would be entitled to collect the additional $4,000. **C** is just as bad. Even if Nancy's belief as to the excessive price is wholly honest, wholly colorable, and indeed correct, she has no right to have it reduced and hence, with her proposal, offers Don no consideration.

That leaves **A**, which correctly states that Nancy's debt to Don is liquidated; it is indisputable no matter that Nancy thinks it too high. Because it's indisputable, Nancy was obliged to pay it — absolutely wherefore, once again, her proposal called for no consideration from *her*, meaning that when Don deposited the check and received the $8,000, he got $4,000 less than he was owed, and received nothing back for foregoing that money. The parties failed to form an accord and so could not achieve accord and satisfaction. **A** is right.

Silver & Hochberg's Picks

1.	**B**
2.	**C**
3.	**B**
4.	**D**
5.	**B**
6.	**D**
7.	**D**
8.	**C**
9.	**A**
10.	**D**
11.	**A**

15

The Statute of Frauds: A "Defense" in a Suit for Breach

A. The Statute of Frauds: What It Is and What It Means

You now know well that two parties may form a contract without a writing. Yet, as explained in Chapter 2, section C, it's one thing to form a contract and another to *prove* you've done so. When we record contracts on paper, we usually do so to create evidence of what we've done, lest there later be a dispute as to whether and on what terms we contracted. In some cases, however, we put our contracts in writing for another reason. For as we've not yet learned, some contracts are enforceable *only if* set forth in writing.

In 1677 the British Parliament identified six kinds of contracts which, it believed, created too many plaintiffs bringing too many fraudulent actions—claiming to have formed contracts with their defendants when, in fact, they had not. Fraudulent claims, Parliament believed, frequently arose in connection with

1. contracts for the sale of an interest in land;
2. contracts for which it was impossible for both parties to complete their performances within one year;

3. contracts in which one agreed to be surety/guarantor for another's obligations;
4. contracts for the sale of goods at a price equal to or greater than ten pounds sterling;
5. contracts made in consideration of marriage;
6. contracts in which the executor or administrator of an estate promised to answer for damages out of his own funds.

For that reason, Parliament passed "An Act for the Prevention of Frauds and Perjuries." Regarding those six kinds of contract, the statute provided that no plaintiff could sustain an action for breach unless he could show that the contract had been recorded in a writing that the *defendant had signed*.

In America, all states have enacted statutes derived from the old British "Statute of Frauds" (now repealed in England, as it happens). By custom, lawyers and courts refer to all such statutes collectively as *the* "Statute of Frauds," treating them as a single rule of law that operates throughout the nation. When, without specifying a state, we say "the Statute of Frauds," we do not refer to a single statute. Rather we refer generally, to a rule embodied in 50 separate statutes enacted by 50 separate states, all of them founded originally on the old English law. Now know this: In many if not most states there appears in the Statute of Frauds the phrase, "party to be charged." It means (almost always), "the defendant."[1] With that, let's look at a prototypical Statute of Frauds:

> Unless set forth in a written memorandum, signed by the party to be charged, no action may be sustained for the breach of any contract (1) for the sale of an interest in realty, (2) not to be fully performed within one year of its making, (3) in which one person promises to answer for the debt or default of another, or (4) made in consideration of marriage.

Further, UCC §2-201(1), drawn from the British Statute of Frauds and enacted now in every state, replaces "ten pounds sterling" with "$500." And, instead of "party to be charged," it employs the phrase, "party against whom enforcement is sought" meaning, once again, "the defendant":

> [A] contract for the sale of goods for the price of $500 or more is not enforceable . . unless there is some writing sufficient to indicate that a contract for sale has been made between the parties and signed by the party against whom enforcement is sought. . . .[2]

---

1. As just noted, the "party to be charged" is, ordinarily, the defendant. That is, when plaintiff sues defendant attempting to enforce a contract, the defendant is the "party to be charged"; she is the party against whom the plaintiff seeks to enforce the contract. It might happen, however, that a plaintiff brings an action against a defendant on some other basis and the defendant in that action asserts a contract as a defense or counterclaim, in which case the plaintiff becomes the party to be charged. The party to be charged is the party in the substantive position of a defendant, whether she is the defendant in fact (as is the usual case) or a plaintiff against whom the defendant asserts a counterclaim.

2. The most recent amendments to the UCC, not yet adopted by any state, raise the relevant amount from $500 to $5,000. UCC §2-201 (as amended, 2005).

In most U.S. states, the Statute of Frauds applies to five kinds of contracts (for which we'll provide illustrations just a little further on):

1. *Contracts for the sale of an interest in land.* If two parties form a contract for the purchase and sale *of an interest in land,*[3] neither party as plaintiff may enforce it against the other as defendant unless the contract is set forth in a writing ("memorandum") signed by the defendant.
2. *Contracts for which the parties cannot complete performance within one year.* If two parties form a contract for which they cannot possibly complete performance within one year of the date on which they form it, then neither party as plaintiff may enforce it against the other as defendant unless the contract is set forth in a writing ("memorandum") signed by the defendant.
3. *Suretyship contracts.* If two parties form a contract under which one agrees to be surety or guarantor for the contractual obligation of some third person, neither party as plaintiff may enforce it against the other as defendant unless the contract is set forth in a writing signed by the defendant.
4. UCC §2-201(1) provides that if two parties form a contract for the sale of goods at a price of $500 or more, neither party as plaintiff may enforce it against the other as defendant unless the contract is set forth in a writing signed by the defendant.
5. *Contracts formed in consideration of marriage.* If two parties form a contract in which one party's obligation is to marry some third person, neither party as plaintiff may enforce it against the other as defendant unless the contract is set forth in a writing signed by the defendant.

These five contracts, it is said, "fall within the Statute of Frauds," meaning that the Statute of Frauds applies to them, meaning that they are enforceable only if set forth in a writing signed by the defendant.

1. Illustration: Contracts for the Sale of Interest in Land

Shayna and Belle I.   Shayna owns Blackacre, and Belle wants to buy it. In the presence of ten reliable witnesses, Shayna says to Belle, "I'll sell you Blackacre for $1 million. We'll meet in my lawyer's office one week from this Monday at noon. At that time, you'll hand me a $1 million certified check, and I'll hand you the deed to Blackacre. Agreed?" Belle answers, "Yes, agreed." Shayna subsequently decides not to proceed with the land sale, and Belle brings an action against her.

Shayna and Belle formed a contract that falls within the Statute of Frauds. They created no writing, and for that reason neither can enforce the contract against the other; the contract is unenforceable. Belle stands ready with ten witnesses to prove that she and Shayna did, certainly, form a contract. Nonetheless, the Statute of Frauds forbids the court to enforce it, because Belle

---

3. As you'll learn when studying real property, "interests in land or realty" include a fee simple, a life estate, a remainder, and many other so-called estates. All illustrations in this text will concern sales of a fee simple, which means a transfer of full and complete ownership. When, in ordinary speech, we speak of buying land or buying a house, we mean buying a fee simple.

cannot present a writing signed by Shayna, her defendant — "the party to be charged."

Shayna and Belle II.   Suppose after the parties agree orally on the purchase and sale of Shayna's land, they decide to "put" their agreement "in writing." Seated in Shayna's office, they create two copies of a document that fully describes Blackacre, and all other details tied to their agreement. Belle signs both copies whereupon Shayna says, "I'd like to read the document, carefully, once more before I sign. Leave a copy with me, please. After I sign, I'll send it to you. You can then send me the copy with your signature." Belle leaves the documents with Shayna, and she departs.

Shayna studies the document and decides not to sign it. Furthermore, she decides not to proceed with the sale of her land. Hence, Belle brings an action against her for breach. Again, ten witnesses stand ready to testify to the conversation in which the parties made their agreement. Nonetheless the Statute of Frauds forbids the court to enforce it against Shayna. Even though Belle presents a writing that *she* has signed, she does not present one *signed by Shayna* — her defendant — "the party to be charged."

Shayna and Belle III.   Imagine now that Shayna continues in her wish to sell the land, but that Belle decides not to buy it. Let's ask: Can Shayna sustain an action against Belle? Let's answer: Yes, because Shayna will come to court with a writing signed *by Belle* — her defendant — "the party to be charged."

One Party Can Enforce the Contract but the Other Can't?   That's right. Consider two parties, A and B, who form a contract that falls within the Statute of Frauds, and then record it in writing. Suppose first that A signs the writing but B does not. In that case B can enforce the contract against A, but A can't enforce it against B. Suppose, now, that B signs the writing but A does not. In that case, A can enforce the contract against B, but B can't enforce it against A. Suppose, finally, that both A and B sign the writing. In that case, each party can enforce the contract against the other.

2. Illustration: Contracts for Which the Parties Cannot Complete Performance in One Year

Laura and Garath.   On December 1, 2011, Laura and Garath, by spoken word, form a contract under which Garath will serve as Laura's secretary from January 1, 2012 through December 31, 2012 at a weekly salary of $900. Nineteen days later, on December 20, 2011, Laura tells Garath that she won't honor the agreement; she won't employ him.

The parties made their contract on December 1, 2011. It's a logical impossibility that December 31, 2012 should fall within a year of that date. Consequently, the contract is within the Statute of Frauds. Absent a writing signed by Laura, Garath can't enforce it. As with any contract within the

Statute of Frauds, that's so even if Garath can prove unequivocally that he and Laura did, truly, form a contract.

Jason and FinaCo.   Jason is 79 years old, healthy and hearty. FinaCo sells lifetime annuities, and Finn is FinaCo's president. On March 1, 2011, Jason and Finn orally agree that: (1) on June 1, Jason will pay FinaCo $500,000, the bulk of his life's savings, and (2) beginning July 1 and on the first day of every month thereafter, for the rest of Jason's life, FinaCo will pay Jason $8,000.

Jason, we said, is in good health. Probably, he will live for more than one year, but it's *possible* that he won't. It's *possible* that FinaCo will make its last $8,000 payment on July 1, August 1, September 1, or at any time within one year of March 1. That means the parties *might conceivably* complete performance within one year of the date on which they form their contract. Hence, the contract does *not* fall within the Statute of Frauds; it requires no writing or signatures. If either party breaches, the other may enforce it as any two parties may ordinarily enforce any oral contract (provided, of course, that they can prove its existence).

3. Illustration: Contracts in Consideration of Marriage

A "contract in consideration of marriage" means a contract for which one party's consideration is his promise to marry another. It does not include, however, the marriage contract between two persons who commit to marry each other.

Ryan and Frank.   Frank is Abigail's father. He and Ryan form a contract in which Ryan promises to marry Abigail, and Frank, in exchange, promises to pay Ryan $100,000 on the wedding day. The parties record their contract in writing. Ryan signs it; Frank doesn't. One week before the wedding, Frank concludes that Ryan is "a bum." He tells Ryan that he won't honor the agreement; he won't pay the $100,000.

Let's ask: Can Ryan enforce the contract against Frank? Let's answer: No. For his part of the bargain, Ryan promises to marry Abigail. That means the contract is made "in consideration of marriage"; it falls within the Statute of Frauds. The writing is signed by Ryan, but not by Frank—the party whom Ryan wants to sue—"the party to be charged." Ryan can't enforce the contract; he has no action for breach. As with any contract within the Statute of Frauds, that's so even if Ryan can prove, unequivocally, that he and Frank did, truly, form a contract.

4. Illustration: Suretyship Contracts

One becomes a "surety" when he agrees to guarantee another's contractual performance. When one "cosigns" another's obligation to pay a debt, she is a surety, as is one who "bonds" another's contractual performance.

AlCo, BondCo, and Client. Al is a builder[*] and Ben is a bondsman.[4] On March 1, Al forms with Client a contract requiring that he construct an office building, for which Client is to pay $20 million. Client worries that Al might suffer insolvency ("go broke"), and be unable to finish his work. For that reason, on April 1, Client forms a contract with Ben. It provides that, (1) Client will pay Ben $50,000 on May 1, and (2) if Al should become insolvent, and fail to complete the building, Ben will pay Client a sum of money sufficient to have some other builder finish the job. Client and Ben record their contract in a writing. Client signs it, but Ben does not.

The contract requires that Ben act as a surety in respect of Al's performance. That means it falls within the Statute of Frauds. Suppose that on May 1, Ben announces his decision not to bond Al's performance, and refuses to accept Client's $500,000. Let's ask: Can Client enforce the contract against Ben? Let's answer: No; he can show no writing signed by Ben, his defendant—"the party to be charged." As with any contract within the Statute of Frauds, that's so even if Client can prove, unequivocally, that he and Ben did, truly, form a contract.

5. Illustration: Sale of Goods for $500 or More

TileCo and ClayCo. ClayCo manufactures tiles, and TileCo installs tiled bathrooms. On June 1, ClayCo and TileCo form an oral contract whereunder ClayCo is to supply TileCo with 2 tons of tile, delivered on July 1. On delivery, TileCo is to pay ClayCo $7,000. The parties do not record their contract in writing. On June 12, TileCo contacts ClayCo and states that it no longer wishes to purchase the tiles, and will not do so.

The contract calls for the sale of goods at a price greater than $500, and so falls within the Statute of Frauds, meaning, in this case, UCC §2-201(1). ClayCo can show no writing signed by TileCo, its defendant—"the party against whom enforcement is sought." Hence, ClayCo cannot enforce the contract against TileCo; it can't sustain an action for breach. As with any contract within the Statute of Frauds, that's so even if ClayCo can prove, unequivocally, that it did, truly, form a contract with TileCo.

QUESTION 1. To say that a contract "falls within the Statute of Frauds" is to say that

A. it is recorded in a writing signed by both its parties.
B. it is not recorded in a writing signed by either party.
C. it is recorded in a writing signed by one of its parties.
D. it is unenforceable unless recorded in a writing signed by the party against whom enforcement is sought.

---

4. A bonding company or "bondsman" is roughly analogous to an insurance company in that it sells a guaranty—an assurance—that if some specified risk should arise, it will pay compensation.

ANALYSIS. The question tests only your understanding of the phrase, "within the Statute of Frauds." That phrase applies to contracts that are enforceable only if set forth in a writing signed by the defendant—"the party to be charged." That a contract is "within the Statute of Frauds" does not tell us that its parties have or have not recorded it in writing, or that either or both have signed one. That a contract is "within the Statute of Frauds" means only this: it's one of the contracts that the Statute of Frauds "talks about;" it's unenforceable unless recorded in a writing, signed by the defendant. **A**, **B**, and **C** are wrong. **D** is right.

QUESTION 2. Which of the following contracts falls within the Statute of Frauds?

I. A contract, written and signed by both parties, under which one party agrees to sell land to another

II. A contract, unwritten, under which one party agrees to sell land to another

III. A contract, written and signed by one party, in which one party agrees to employ another for a period of two years

IV. A contract, unwritten, in which one party agrees to tend a 40-year-old patient for so long as the patient lives

A. II only

B. IV only

C. I, II, and III

D. I, II, III, and IV

ANALYSIS. Again, the question tests only your understanding of the phrase "within the Statute of Frauds." All of the contracts mentioned at options I, II, and III are unenforceable unless set forth in a writing, signed by the defendant. All of them are "within the Statute of Frauds." (And because they are within the Statute of Frauds, contracts I and II are unenforceable. Contract III is enforceable only by the party who did not sign, against the party who did.) Contract IV does not fall within the Statute of Frauds because the forty-year-old patient might not live for a year. **B** is right.

QUESTION 3. Which of the following contracts, if breached by A, is enforceable by B?

I. An oral contract, whereunder A agrees to sell land to B

II. A written contract signed only by B, whereunder A agrees to employ B for a period of two years.

III. A written contract signed only by A, whereunder B agrees to employ A for two years

IV. A written contract, signed by both parties, whereunder A cosigns her son's debt to B.

V. A written contract signed only by A, whereunder B agrees to marry A's daughter and A agrees to pay B $500,000

A. I and II

B. III, IV, and V

C. I, II, III, and IV

D. I, II, III, IV, and V

ANALYSIS.   All of these contracts are within the Statute of Frauds, meaning that all are of a type to which the Statute of Frauds applies. Some are written and signed by A, and those are the ones that B can enforce.

Option I describes a contract for the sale of an interest in land. The contract falls within the Statute of Frauds. B, who wants to sue A for breach, cannot show a writing signed by A. B can't enforce the contract (and neither, for that matter, can A).

Option II tells of a contract that falls within the Statute of Frauds' one-year provision. It is set forth in a writing signed by B but not by A — "the party to be charged." Hence B can't enforce it against A. (Yet, because B signed, A would be able to enforce it against B.)

Option III describes a contract between A and B that falls, also, within the Statute of Frauds' one-year provision. The contract is recorded in writing and signed by A. B *can* enforce the contract against A (but because B did not sign, A would *not* be able to enforce it against B.)

In Option IV, we read of a contract that falls within the Statute of Frauds' suretyship provision. It is recorded in a writing, signed by A and B. Consequently, it's enforceable by B against A (and would be enforceable by A against B).

Option V describes a contract made in consideration of marriage. It's recorded in a writing signed only by A. The contract is enforceable by B against A (but would not be enforceable by A against B).

Party B can enforce contracts III, IV, and V, but not contracts I or II. **B** is right.

QUESTION 4. On December 1, 2011, Sabrina and Barry form an oral contract under which Barry is to (a) decorate Sabrina's retail store for Christmas Day, 2012 and then, *after* Christmas, (b) take the decorations down. Sabrina is to pay Barry $15,000 on or before December 1, 2012. Twelve months later, on December 1, 2012 Sabrina comes to Barry with her $15,000 check. Barry refuses to accept it and tells Sabrina that he will not perform; he won't decorate her store for Christmas. Sabrina sues

Barry for breach. Barry moves to dismiss the suit, citing the fact that he signed no contractual writing. Should the court grant his motion?

A. Yes, because the agreement exacts no consideration from Sabrina
B. Yes, because the Statute of Frauds renders the contract unenforceable
C. No, because the agreement reflects a bargain in which both parties suffer a legal detriment
D. No, because Sabrina, if she wished, might have paid Barry before December 1, 2012

ANALYSIS.   The parties form their contract on December 1, 2011. It's possible, of course, for Barry to decorate Sabrina's store for Christmas of 2012 in late November 2012, which time will fall within one year of December 1, 2011. Yet Barry is to take down the decorations *after* Christmas. As a matter of logic, it is *not* possible that December 25, 2012, should fall within one year of December 1, 2011.

Sabrina is to pay Barry on or *before* December 1, 2012, meaning she might pay him one hour, one day, one week, or one month after the parties form their contract. She *can* complete her performance within one year of December 1, 2011. Yet, in order that a contract not fall within the Statute of Frauds it must be possible that *both* parties complete performance within the one-year period. Barry can't do that. Since the contract is within the Statute of Frauds, and the parties have created no writing at all, neither can enforce it against the other.

Choices **A** and **C** refer to lack of consideration, but each party did provide consideration to the other: Sabrina promised to pay, and Barry promised to decorate. **A** and **C** are wrong. **D** is wrong too. Although one contracting party might possibly perform within the one-year period, the contract is, nonetheless, within the Statute of Frauds if the other cannot.

B tells us that Sabrina can't enforce the contract because the Statute of Frauds renders it unenforceable. That's exactly correct. **B** is right.

B.   The Meanings of "Writing" and "Sign"

Ironically, the law disdains its own rule. Surrounding the Statute of Frauds is another judge-made doctrine to this effect: *Because the Statute of Frauds may deprive a contracting party of a contract genuinely formed, it is to be very narrowly construed so to allow the parties to enforce contracts they truly have made.* With that premise, the law is stunningly malleable in the meanings it gives to the words "writing" and "sign."

In order that two parties create "a writing," they need not put black ink to business-grade paper stock. They might make marks and scratches on tissues, paper towels, or candy wrappers, and thus create a "writing." If A and B form an oral contract, and A then sends B a signed napkin, on which she describes the contract, A has signed "a writing." B may enforce the contract against her. If A responds, with a signed dust rag, on which she, too, describes the contract, then she, too, has signed "a writing." B can enforce the contract against her. Taken together, napkin and rag make "a writing," signed by A and B.

Now shall we address the word "signature." With respect to the Statute of Frauds, a signature is any mark, stamp, or symbol intended as an authentication. One's initials, one's first name only, or last name only set forth in type or in handwriting, cursive, print, or scribble constitutes her "signature," as does one's fingerprint. As characterized by Restatement (Second) of Contracts §134 and cmt. A, a signature

> . . . may be any symbol made or adopted with an intention, actual or apparent, to authenticate the writing as that of the signer.
>
> a. *Types of symbol.* The traditional form of signature is of course the name of the signer, handwritten in ink. But initials, thumbprint or an arbitrary code sign may also be used; and the signature may be written in pencil, typed, printed, made with a rubber stamp, or impressed into the paper. Signed copies may be made with carbon paper or by photographic process.

C. Part Performance: Removing a Contract from the Statute of Frauds

Without a writing, two parties might form a contract falling within the Statute of Frauds, and then begin to perform. Under some circumstances, their performance or partial performance "removes the contract from the Statute of Frauds," meaning that one party (or both) can enforce it even though it is *not* set forth in a signed writing.

1. Part Performance and the Land Sale Contract

With respect to an unwritten (or unsigned) contract for the sale of land, most courts hold that certain forms of part performance allow the buyer to enforce the contract against the seller (although part performance does not, normally, allow the *seller* to enforce it against the *buyer*). If the buyer has paid the full purchase price, many (but not all) courts allow him to enforce the contract even in the absence of a writing signed by the seller. In such a case, the buyer is not normally entitled to recover monetary damages. Rather, he is entitled to the equitable remedy of specific performance, described in Chapter 30, section B.[5] Similarly, if, with Seller's permission, Buyer occupies the premises

---

5.   The emerging view, however, is that payment of the purchase price does not entitle the buyer to specific performance, because he can recover the relevant monies by way of restitution. Restatement § 129, and Chapter 28, section B.

and makes improvements,[6] then, too, most courts allow him to enforce the contract without a writing signed by Seller.[7]

Illustration: Benita and Sheldon.   On January 1, without a writing, Benita and Sheldon contract for the sale of Sheldon's vacant land. The contract calls for a closing date of March 1. On February 1, not yet owning the land, Benita asks Sheldon's permission to begin her occupancy. Sheldon is agreeable, whereupon Benita enters the land and begins to build a small home. On February 25, Sheldon tells Benita that he no longer wishes to part with the land and that he will not proceed with the sale.

The February 1 contract falls within the Statute of Frauds. Ordinarily, neither party would have power to enforce it without a writing signed by the other. However, when Benita enters on the premises and begins to make improvements, the contract undergoes such "part performance," as — *maybe, depending on the state and the court* — removes it from the Statute of Frauds. In that case, Benita can enforce the oral contract against Sheldon.

2. Performance and the One-Year Provision

If, without a writing, two parties form a contract that they cannot fulfill within one year, and one of them *fully* performs, then, most courts will declare that both parties may enforce the contract.[8] From Question 4 above, consider Barry and Sabrina. Their Christmas decoration contract falls within the Statute of Frauds. Suppose now that before Barry renounces the agreement, Sabrina pays him the full $15,000 contract price. In most states, Sabrina's full performance would render the contract fully enforceable by both its parties. Similarly, if Barry had decorated the store and, after Christmas, disassembled the decorations, his full performance would render the contract enforceable by both its parties.

3. Part Performance and the Sale of Goods

Regarding contracts for the sale of goods, the modern-day Statute of Frauds inheres in UCC §2-201(1), adopted in every state. It provides that a contract for the sale of goods at a price of $500 or more requires a writing signed by the party "against whom enforcement is sought." UCC §2-201(3)(a) renders the signed writing *un*necessary if (i) the contract calls for specially

---

6.   One makes "improvements" to realty by clearing it, building on it, or otherwise altering it in some way that enhances its utility over the long term. One improves realty when she makes "a permanent addition to or betterment of real property . . . designed to make the property more useful or valuable." Finn v. McNeil, 23 Mass. App. Ct. 367, 502 N.E.2d 557, 562 (App. Ct. 1987) (citations omitted).

7.   The conceptual and historical bases of that rule are subject to debate. Some authorities, including the Restatement assert that such an exception to the Statute of Frauds rule inheres, really, in the fact of the buyer's detrimental reliance, and that the Buyer should be entitled to specific performance only if he has been substantially prejudiced through his occupancy and the making of improvements. Restatement § 129.

8.   Restatement §130.

manufactured goods that (ii) are not suitable for sale to other of the seller's customers and (iii) the seller has begun, in some substantial way, to produce or acquire them (or the means necessary to produce them). Stripped to its essence §2-201(3)(a) means that the contract is enforceable if the seller has relied on it to his detriment, with (a) "reliance" meaning that she has begun, to a substantial degree, to make or procure the goods, and (b) "detriment" meaning that the goods at issue are not, in ordinary course, salable to others (because they are somehow "unique," or customized to the buyer). Further, UCC §2-201(3)(c) removes a contract from the Statute of Frauds to the extent that (i) the seller has received and accepted the buyer's payment, or (ii) the buyer has received and accepted the goods. In either such case to *that* extent, each party may enforce the contract against the other.

Suppose that on May 1, without a writing, Buyer and Seller agree that for $10,000 Seller will manufacture and sell to Buyer, a strange, weird, Bizarre looking, uniquely designed, custom-made bedspring. On May 15, Seller forms a contract with Vendor for the purchase of various parts he needs to create this oddly conceived article. The contract calls for the sale of goods at a price greater than $500. When first formed, therefore, it falls within the Statute of Frauds. The law then "removes it from" the Statute because (1) Seller is to specially manufacture the goods (the goods are to be custom-made), (2) he cannot, in ordinary course, sell them to other customers (because they are of so strange a nature), and (3) he has begun, in a substantial way, to procure necessary parts. The contract is, now, enforceable even though neither party signed any writing.

As to part performance of a suretyship contract or a contract made in consideration of marriage, there is such difference among the states as to prevent us from stating any general rule.

QUESTION 5. Without a writing, Kevin as seller, and Taylor, as buyer, contract for the purchase and sale of Kevin's farm. Thereafter, Kevin declines to proceed with the sale, and Taylor sues for specific performance. Which of the following additional facts, if proven, would most likely allow Taylor to sustain his action against Kevin?

A. Before Kevin announced his intention not to proceed, Taylor, with Kevin's permission, moved onto the farm and built a new barn.

B. Eight persons saw and heard the parties form their contract, and each is willing to so testify.

C. After the parties formed their contract, Taylor prepared and signed a writing that accurately described the agreement.

D. Before the parties formed their contract, each, by signed writing, declared to the other his tentative interest in concluding an agreement for the sale of the farm.

ANALYSIS. Without a writing, these parties formed a contract for the sale of land. It falls within the Statute of Frauds. Ordinarily, then, neither would be entitled to enforce it against the other. However, where two parties contract for the sale of an interest in land, part performance often removes the contract from the Statute, so to allow the buyer to enforce it against the seller (but not (usually) the seller to enforce it against the buyer). The two circumstances most likely to remove the contract from the Statute are that (1) the buyer fully pays the purchase price, and (2) the buyer occupies the land and makes improvements to it.

B refers to witnesses who saw and heard the parties form their contract. No such circumstance will remove it from the Statute of Frauds. Neither, certainly, would a writing have any such effect if signed only by Taylor, the *plaintiff*. Hence, **B** and **C** are wrong. **D** reports that before forming their contract, the parties wrote, signed, and exchanged invitations to deal. To that we say, "so what?" No such fact removes any contract from the Statute of Frauds.

According to **A**, Taylor, the buyer, moved onto the premises and made improvements to it. That means he has given such part performance as (in most states) is sufficient to remove the contract from the Statute of Frauds. **A** is right.

D. The Closer

QUESTION 6. Bernard Bailey and Sahar Scott are longtime friends and business associates. For several months, Bernard has spoken to Sahar about the possibility of purchasing a parcel of land that she owns. As Bernard and Sahar sit together one evening at a Chamber of Commerce meeting, Bernard takes hold of a wet cocktail napkin. On it he writes, in crayon, "About your land, 28 Pate Street, Addington, MT 78420 (Volume 909 land books, page 187), I'll buy for $940,000—let's close by the end of the week. Deal?" Bernard passes the napkin to Sahar. Sahar reads the message and takes from her pocket a piece of crumpled notepaper, personalized with her full name printed at its top. On the paper, with an eyebrow pencil, she circles her name, and writes, "Okay." Sahar passes her message to Bernard. On the following day, Bernard calls Sahar by telephone. "Let's set a date for closing, so I can pay you the $940,000 purchase price and you can hand me a deed to the Pate Street property." Sahar responds that she has changed her mind: "I'm not going to sell."

Can Bernard sustain an action against Sahar for breach of a contract to sell the land?

A. Probably not, because Bernard did not sign his name on the cocktail napkin

B. Probably not, because neither the napkin nor the notepaper represents a "writing"

C. Probably, because Sahar "signed" her notepaper

D. Probably, because the contract falls outside the Statute of Frauds

ANALYSIS. Of this, there's no doubt: Bernard offers to buy Sahar's land and Sahar accepts; these two form a contract. The contract provides for the sale of an interest in land, meaning that it's within the Statute of Frauds. Neither party can *enforce* the contract unless it is recorded in a "writing" "signed" by the other (the party to be charged). In all states, the words "writing" and "signed" are (*very*) liberally construed.

Here, the cocktail napkin and the notepaper together constitute a writing. Sahar's name printed at the top of the notepaper qualifies as her "signature." That she drew a circle around it makes that all the more certain. The parties did, therefore, record their contract in a "writing," "signed" by Sahar. That means the answer is "yes"; Bernard can enforce the contract against Sahar.

A and **B** say "no"; so they're wrong. As for **A**, it's true that Bernard has not signed the writing, but it's also irrelevant. When a contract falls within the statute of frauds one party can enforce it against the other whether he himself has or has not signed a writing. It is necessary only that his *defendant* have signed one. As for **B**, two or more separate papers addressing the same subject qualify as "a writing." **B** is wrong. **D** correctly answers "yes," but its reasoning is all wrong. This contract does fall within the Statute of Frauds. It's enforceable because it conforms to the relevant requirements; it is recorded in a writing (the napkin and notepaper together), signed by the party to be charged (via Sahar's name, printed and circled).

C tells us that Bernard can enforce this contract because Sahar "signed" the writing, which is true because her name appears on the notepaper. Her name there printed and circled (probably) qualifies as her "signature." Without it, Bernard would be unable to enforce the contract, and so **C** is right.

✦ Silver & Hochberg's Picks

1.	**D**
2.	**B**
3.	**B**
4.	**B**
5.	**A**
6.	**C**

16

Incapacity to Form a Contract

A. Rescission, Status Quo Ante, and Unjust Enrichment
B. When Minors Form Contracts
C. When Mentally Impaired Adults Form Contracts
D. When Incompetent Persons Contract for Necessaries
E. The Closers
✧ Silver & Hochberg's Picks

A. Rescission, Status Quo Ante, and Unjust Enrichment

Under some circumstances, two parties may form a contract that a court, or they themselves later "rescind," meaning the contract undergoes "rescission"; it is "undone." Rescission (an enormous topic in itself) is appropriate when a contract is premised on a "mistake" (Chapter 22, section B), "duress" (Chapter 20, section A), "undue influence" (Chapter 20, section B); "illegality" (Chapter 17); or fraud.[1] Further, as is the subject of this chapter, a contract may undergo rescission when one of its parties lacks "mental capacity."

For right now, let's know this: When a contract undergoes rescission, it "disappears" retroactively, to the time at which it was formed. The law goes back in time and "unforms" it. The contract goes away; it's erased; it vanishes. In the law's eyes, it ceases to exist and *never did exist.*

Daphne and Assureco. Daphne contacts Assureco, an insurance company, and states her wish to buy disability insurance, (thereby making an invitation

---

1. One commits fraud, a common law tort, when (1) she knowingly makes a materially false statement to another, (2) intending that other believe her, and (3) the other party does believe it and (4) for that reason, suffers harm. Hanson v. Ford Motor Co., 278 F.2d 586, 591 (8th Cir. 1960)

to deal). Assureco sends her its application form, and asks that she complete it (thereby *responding* with an invitation to deal). The application form describes Assureco's disability insurance policy and the annual premium (price) that Daphne will have to pay for it. It requires that Daphne disclose information concerning her health. Asked whether she has ever been diagnosed with a heart condition, Daphne writes "no," even though she *has* had a heart condition and knows it; Daphne deliberately answers untruthfully.

On October 1, Daphne submits her application, which constitutes her offer to buy the insurance. On October 15, Assureco "approves" it, meaning it accepts the offer. The parties form a contract requiring (1) that Daphne pay an annual premium of $6,000, and (2) that Assureco pay Daphne $50,000 yearly, for the remainder of her life *if* she should become disabled. Because Daphne made a materially false statement concerning her health, the contract, unbeknownst to Assureco, is founded on a fraud.

For one year, Daphne pays her annual premium of $6,000. Then, her preexisting heart condition does, in fact, disable her. She claims her benefit from Assureco. Assureco investigates and learns the truth — that Daphne falsely withheld information about her heart condition. On that basis, it refuses to pay.

Daphne sues Assureco for breach. Citing Daphne's fraud, Assureco counterclaims for *rescission* of the contract. The court orders the contract rescinded and requires, also, that Assureco return to Daphne the $6,000 she paid it.

Why Does the Court Do *That*?   To say that a contract undergoes rescission is to say that it disappears, retroactively, to the time at which it was formed. By (a fiction of) law, the contract never existed. It is extinguished *nunc pro tunc.*[2] If, under the contract, (before the contract vanishes), either party receives from the other, any money, property, or service, the law demands that she return it.[3] That's because one enjoys an "unjust enrichment"[4] if she retains property pursuant to a contract which, by law, *never existed.* For that reason, rescission of a contract ordinarily requires that each of its parties restore the other to "status quo ante" — to the financial position she occupied before the contract was formed. To sound like lawyers all the more, we invoke the word "restitution,"[5] and recite this rule:

> When a contract undergoes rescission, then to avoid unjust enrichment to either of its parties, each must make to the other such restitution as restores her to status quo ante — to the financial position she occupied before the contract was formed.

In *Black on Rescission and Cancellation* §1, we read:

---

2.   The Latin phrase *nunc pro tunc* means literally "now for then," or "retroactively."
3.   This precept and the notion of rescission, generally, arose first in *equity* and has since been adopted by the law. See: Appendix, section E.
4.   Chapter 28, section B.
5.   Chapter 28, section B.

To rescind a contract is . . . to abrogate and undo it from the beginning; . . . [to] restore the parties to the relative positions which they would have occupied if no such contract had ever been made. Rescission necessarily involves a repudiation of the contract and a refusal of the moving party to be further bound by it. But this by itself would constitute no more than a breach of the contract or a refusal of performance, while the idea of rescission involves the additional and distinguishing element of a restoration of the status quo [ante]. . . .

And Restatement of Restitution §65 provides:

The right of a person to [rescission] and restitution . . . is dependent upon his return . . . to the other party anything which he received as part of the transaction.

All that we have just discussed explains why Assureco must return to Daphne the $6,000 she paid it. Assureco must restore her to status quo ante—to the financial position she occupied before the parties formed their contract, so to ensure that it enjoys no unjust enrichment.

QUESTION 1. Nanette owns a 90-foot sailing yacht but knows nothing of the sea. She wants a licensed captain to take charge of the vessel, and she seeks to hire one. Carp represents himself as a licensed captain with decades of experience at sea. On May 1, the parties form a contract under which Nanette is to (a) pay Carp $200,000 per year, and (b) allow him to live aboard the vessel rent free. In exchange, Carp is to pilot the vessel whenever Nanette wants to use it, usually inviting business guests to accompany her.

When the parties form their contract, Nannette pays Carp his first year's salary of $200,000. Carp immediately takes up residence aboard the yacht and over the course of May, June, and July pilots it 30 times, for a total of 300 hours, as Nanette takes her business guests on luxurious cruises. Carp performs well, and Nanette is pleased with him.

On August 1, however, Nanette learns that Carp has no captain's license and little experience. She petitions the court and moves to rescind the contract. If the court rescinds the contract, it should give such judgment also, as will assure that:

I. the parties complete their performances for the remainder of the year.

II. Carp returns to Nanette $200,000.

III. Carp pays Nanette for the value he derived by using the vessel as a residence.

IV. Nanette pays Carp for the fair market value of his services as captain for 300 hours.

A. I and II
B. I and III
C. II, III, and IV
D. Neither I, II, III, nor IV

ANALYSIS.   When a court rescinds a contract, it renders the contract inoperative from the outset. The contract is "undone." And, to the extent possible, the law requires that each party restore the other to the position he occupied before the contract arose—to status quo ante—so that neither enjoys an unjust enrichment.

In performing under this contract, Nanette (a) paid Carp $200,000, and (b) allowed him to live rent free aboard her yacht. Carp served competently as a captain for 300 hours. In order that the parties be restored to status quo ante, Carp must (a) return to Nanette, the $200,000 she paid him, and (b) pay Nanette the fair market value[6] of his tenancy aboard the yacht. In turn, Nanette must pay Carp a fair market value for 300 hours of his professional service. Hence, **C** is right.

B.   When Minors Form Contracts

In most (if not all) of the 50 states, one reaches adulthood on her eighteenth birthday. Before that she is a "minor," also called an "infant." By common law, a minor/infant lacks the mental *capacity* to form a contract. That is (generally) so whether she be a 2-year-old toddler or a 17-year-old college freshman studying molecular biophysics.

Illustration: Kelly and Marcie I.   Kelly, an adult, owns a retail business, "Bicycles Are Best." On September 1, 17-year-old Marcie visits the store and declares her wish to buy a bike. Kelly helps her select a bike, tells her that its price is $289, informs her that it will be ready in two days, and takes from her a $50 deposit. Later that day, Marcie regrets what she has done. She does not care about the bike, and wants back her $50 deposit. She tells the story to her mother, who then telephones Kelly: "My daughter Marcie is a minor. She wants to extricate herself from her contract with you, and demands return of her $50 deposit."

---

6.   Fair market value is a matter of fact. Where, by law, one party owes another the fair market value of some good or service and the parties themselves cannot agree on what *is* the fair market value, then, as with any other contested fact, the answer must come from a court (and, in the case of a jury trial— from a jury).

With that, the contract dies, and Kelly must return the deposit. That's because *a contract between a minor and an adult is "voidable" at the minor's option*, which means the minor is empowered to rescind it, whereupon she renders it void—dead, erased, nunc pro tunc.

In this context, by tradition, most lawyers don't use the word "rescind," although they'd certainly be right to do so. Rather, you'll hear and read that a minor's contract with an adult is voidable and, therefore, that the minor has the power to "void" or "disaffirm" it. But do remember that when a minor is said to "disaffirm" or "void" a contract, she elects, really, to *rescind* it.

As already noted, when a contract undergoes rescission its parties must, ordinarily, restore each other to status quo ante. However, when one party is a minor, and the other an adult, the law does not impose that obligation, fully, on the minor, as is explained further on. But an adult, who, pursuant to the contract, receives money or property *from* the minor must return it to her (or pay her its value).

Consequently, Kelly must return to Marcie the $50 deposit, and we now know this much: *A contract formed between a minor and adult is voidable at the minor's option, which means that the minor may, if she chooses, rescind ("disaffirm," "void") it. If she does so, then, by law, (1) the contract is extinguished, nunc pro tunc, and (2) the adult must return or make payment for any value she has received from the minor.*

Illustration: Kelly and Marcie II.   Suppose now that Marcie does not rescind the contract. On September 3, she returns to Kelly's store, pays the $239 still due, and takes the bike. Then, after keeping and riding it for one month, she regrets the purchase and wants her money back. Marcie (or an adult on her behalf) tells Kelly that she elects to disaffirm the contract, and to have back the full $289 purchase price.

Even after Marcie pays the purchase price, takes the bicycle, and uses it, she retains the right to rescind (void, disaffirm) the contract. If she elects to do so, the contract vanishes, retroactively, and Kelly must make restitution to Marcie for what would otherwise be $289 in unjust enrichment. Marcie, in turn, must return the bicycle (or pay Kelly such fair market value as it has when she disaffirms the contract).

Now, let's ask: What if, as certainly will be so, the bike has suffered such wear and tear as drops its value below the $289 that Marcie paid for it? Let's answer: A minor who disaffirms her contract need not return the adult to *full status quo ante*. She must return property she has acquired under the contract or pay such market value as it has at the time she disaffirms. She need not, however, pay for any decline in the property's value. Marcie, therefore, must return the bicycle to Kelly or pay Kelly its value *at the time of disaffirmation*. She need not worry about wear, tear, or depreciation. If Marcie no longer has the bike because it has been lost or stolen, then she need pay Kelly nothing at all, but Kelly must, still, return the full purchase price.[7]

Illustration: Kelly and Marcie III.   Let's take one more look at Kelly and Marcie with yet another alteration in the facts: Marcie pays the purchase price and takes the bike. One year later, she turns eighteen, and on the very *next* day, she wants her money back. Kelly must return the money, because: *If a minor forms a contract with an adult, her right to disaffirm it endures until she reaches majority (adulthood), and for a reasonable time thereafter.* In this regard, one day certainly falls within a reasonable time. Kelly must return to Marcie the $289 she paid her, and, if Marcie still has the bike, she need only return it to Kelly, whatever its condition, or pay her the amount of its *present* market value, however low that might be.

Once a minor achieves majority, she has the power to *affirm* her contract. If, for a reasonable time, thereafter, she makes no attempt to disaffirm it, then, by law, she affirms it. If, during the six months after she turns eighteen, Marcie makes no attempt to disaffirm her contract with Kelly—she affirms it. The contract is no longer voidable. If Marcie then asks to have her money back, Kelly need not (and certainly *will* not) return it.

Three More Illustrations.

Facts: Phillip is 12 years old. Kacy is an adult. By contract, Phillip promises Kacy his computer, and Kacy promises Phillip her stereo music system. Phillip's computer is worth $200. Kacy's music system is worth $50. The parties make the trade. Three years later when he is 15, Phillip disaffirms the contract. At that time, the computer in Kacy's possession has a value of $40. The music system in Phillip's possession is broken, obsolete, and worthless.

The Result: Kacy must return the computer to Phillip, together with an additional $160 to account for its loss of value (or she may keep the computer and pay Phillip the full $200 of value the computer had at the time of the trade). Phillip need only return to Kacy the worthless music system (if she wants it). He need not pay her any money at all.

The Rule: When a minor disaffirms his contract, the adult must afford the minor restitution for all value he receives under the contract, but the minor need not make such full restitution to the adult. The minor need only return such property as is actually in his possession (or pay whatever value it has *at that time*).

Rule Applied to This Case: When Phillip disaffirms the contract, he has no more than the broken, outmoded music system. He need only return the worthless thing to Kacy (if she wants it). On the other hand, Phillip parted with a $200 computer now worth only $40. Kacy must make the lad whole—all the way. She may return the computer together with $160, or keep it and pay him $200.

---

7.   Although a bicycle is a good, the common law governs the matter before us. UCC Article 2 does not. Article 2 is silent on the subject of incapacity. Hence the common law applies, even for transactions that involve the sale of goods.

Facts: Pablo is an adult. Patience is a 14-year-old girl. The two form a contract under which Patience is to paint two portraits of Pablo, with Pablo to pay her a total of $200 when she completes them. The actual fair market value of Patience's service is $1,000—$500 per portrait. Patience paints one portrait and then disaffirms the contract.

Result: Pablo must pay Patience $500.

Rule: When a minor disaffirms her contract with an adult, the minor must return any property she actually holds under the contract and she need do nothing more. Yet the adult must afford the minor full restitution for all value he receives from her. As to property, he must restore to the minor the full value with which the minor has parted under the contract. As to services the minor provides him, the adult must pay not the agreed contract price, but the true fair market value of the service, whether that's greater than, less than, or equal to the contract price.

Rule Applied to This Case: Patience took no property from Pablo; she owes him nothing. Patience furnished Pablo with $500 in service. Pablo must pay her that amount.

Facts: Lester is an adult and Negev a 17-year-old who owns an automobile.[8] The two form a contract under which Lester will repair Negev's vehicle, for which Negev will pay him $400 when the work is done. Lester completes the repair, and Negev promptly disaffirms the contract.

Result: Negev need pay Lester nothing.

Rule: When a minor disaffirms a contract, he must return to the adult any property he retains under the contract, but he need not pay the value of any service with which the adult has provided him.

Rule Applied to This Case: Negev acquired no property from Lester. He did derive a service, but for that he need not pay.

Let's now state a rule:

> *If a minor forms a contract with an adult, then*
>   *(1) (a) the minor may disaffirm (void, rescind) the contract at any time until he reaches adulthood and for a reasonable time thereafter.*[9]
>   *(b) the minor may, if he wishes, affirm the contract when he reaches adulthood, but he cannot do so while still a minor; neither can he do so if he has already disaffirmed it.*

---

8.   That one may lack capacity to form a contract does not mean he lacks the capacity to own property. Indeed, all persons, including minors, have capacity to own property. If one lacks the capacity to *manage* his property, then a parent or guardian is empowered to do it for him. Even in those cases, however, the minor or other incompetent party continues to own the property.

9.   The cases decided on this point seem always to involve a minor who formed a contract shortly before attaining adulthood. The common law leaves unsettled a case in which, for example, a 9-year-old forms a contract and wishes to affirm it on turning 18, nine years later.

(2) If the minor exercises his right to disaffirm the contract while still a minor or as an adult, then

(a) the adult party must (i) return (make restitution for) the value of any money or property he has received from the minor, and (ii) make payment (restitution) also for the value of any services with which the minor has provided him, and thereby return him to status quo ante.

(b) the minor must return (make restitution for) the value of any property he has acquired from the adult, the value to be assessed at the time of disaffirmation, not at the time the adult parted with it.

QUESTION 2. Peter, age 18, is a skilled auto body worker. Paul, age 17, is skilled in piano repair. Peter and Paul agree that Peter will paint Paul's car and Paul will repair Peter's piano. Peter then paints Paul's car, but Paul does not repair Peter's piano. Peter sues Paul for breach, whereupon Paul disaffirms the contract.

The legal result will be that:

I. Paul must pay Peter the fair market value of the paint job that Peter provided Paul.
II. Peter must pay Paul the fair market value of the piano repair he failed to provide Paul.

A. I
B. II
C. I and II
D. Neither I nor II

ANALYSIS.   Peter, an adult, forms a contract with Paul, a minor. Peter performs under the contract (although, because Paul is a minor, he is not obliged to do so — *while* Paul *remains* a minor). Paul disaffirms the contract and thus puts it to an end. Paul did not perform, so Peter received nothing from him. Consequently, Peter need make no restitution to Paul. Paul retains the value of his painted car, but that represents a *service*. Because Paul is a minor, he need make no restitution for it. Fair or unfair, right or wrong, Paul has a newly painted car, and he need pay nothing for it. **D** is right.

C.   When Mentally Impaired Adults Form Contracts

Criminal and common law alike have had difficulty defining such mental incompetence as frees an adult from responsibility for what he says and does.

In order truly to understand the law surrounding that question, one must devote considerable study—and then, still, he'll finish by throwing up his hands. Nonetheless, with respect to contracts, we'll teach you the standard lyrics to the standard tune, warning you, however, that the rules are far easier to state than apply. The Restatement (Second) of Contracts purports to express modern law on the subject, and for that purpose, it is perhaps as good (and as bad) as any other summary authority.

Restatement (Second) §15(1) divides mentally incapacitated adults into two groups: those who, because of mental illness or defect, (1) do not understand "the nature or consequences" of their agreements, or (2) do understand their agreements, but as to the relevant subject matter demonstrate an inability to *behave* reasonably:

> A person incurs only voidable contractual duties by entering into a transaction if by reason of mental illness or defect
>
> (a) he is unable to understand in a reasonable manner the nature and consequences of the transaction [and that applies whether or not the other party to the transaction knows or should know of the illness or defect], or
>
> (b) he is unable to act in a reasonable manner in relation to the transaction and the other party has reason to know of his condition.

To category 1 belongs the profoundly impaired or intellectually challenged adult who speaks assent to a proposal or signs his name to paper not knowing what it means or what consequences will follow. Category 1 includes, also, those with judgment severely impaired by alcohol, drugs, or the like. To category 2 belongs, for example, a compulsive buyer or hoarder with an uncontrollable irrational urge to buy, possess, and accumulate things for which she has no use.

When such an incapacitated adult forms a contract, he has the option to rescind (disaffirm, void) it as does a minor. When before doing so, however, he receives from the competent party any money, property, or service, the Restatement treats him less generously than it does a minor. The incapacitated adult who disaffirms his contract (on his own or through a guardian) must generally make restitution in full for *all* money, property, or service he has received from the competent party. The competent party must, of course, make corresponding restitution for any value *he* has received.

Three Illustrations

Facts: A is a competent adult who sells clothing retail. Unbeknownst to A, B is so seriously impaired as not to understand the nature or consequences of his actions. A and B form a contract for the sale of a $500 suit of clothes. B pays the $500, and A hands him the suit. For three weeks, B wears the suit, tearing it and staining it to "kingdom come." B's guardian learns of the events. She contacts A and announces B's wish to rescind the contract.

Result: The contract is rescinded. A must return B's $500. B must pay A such value as the suit had *when A parted with it.*

Rule: *If*—a competent person forms a contract with an adult who does not understand the nature or consequences of her actions,— *then*—whether the competent person does or does not have reason to know of the disability, the incompetent one may, at her option (through a guardian, generally), rescind (disaffirm/void) the contract. If she does so, each party must (a) return any money or property received from the other, valued as of the time he first acquired it, and (b) pay the other the fair market value of services, if any, he has provided.

Rule Applied to This Case: A forms a contract with B, an adult who does not understand the nature or consequences of his actions. B disaffirms the contract. A retains B's $500 and must return it. B must return to A the tattered suit, and pay the difference between its present value (zero it seems) and such fair market value as it had *when A parted with it.* (Paradoxically, the final result is that A keeps B's $500, and B gets nothing back from A. Yet, B does not "walk away" empty handed. He has had the use of the suit. Indeed he has used it for so long and in such a fashion as to keep and consume for himself all of its value.)

Facts: A is an automobile dealer. B is an adult who understands the nature and consequences of his actions. B is, however, a compulsive purchaser of cars, although A has no reason to know that. Propelled by his compulsion, B contracts with A for the purchase of an automobile, for which A charges a perfectly fair price. B takes the car and drives it for one month. Thereafter, he attempts to disaffirm the contract.

Result: The contract is not rescinded.

Rule: *If*—Party A forms a contract with an adult Party B who understands the nature of his actions but who, with respect to the contract, is unable to behave reasonably, Party A having no reason to know of Party B's impairment,— *then*—Party B has no right to rescind the contract.

Rule Applied to This Case: A had no reason to know of B's compulsion. B has no power to rescind.

Facts: A is an automobile dealer. B is an adult who understands the nature and consequences of his actions. However, B is a compulsive, uncontrolled, purchaser of cars. B arrives at A's dealership with his brother C. C tells A of B's disability. Nonetheless, A contracts with B for the sale of a car at a fair price. B takes the car and drives it for one month. Thereafter, B attempts to disaffirm the contract.

Result: The contract is rescinded. A must return B's purchase price, and B must return the car, together with payment for any decrease in its value.

Rule: *If*—a Party A forms a contract with an adult Party B who understands his actions but is unable to behave reasonably in the transaction, and A has reason to know of B's impairment,— *then*—Party B may disaffirm the contract. If he does so, each party must (a) return to the other any money or property he has acquired under the contract, valued as of the time he first acquired it, and (b) pay the other the fair market value of services, if any, the other has provided.

Rule Applied to This Case: A knows of B's disability, meaning B has power to disaffirm the contract. A retains B's purchase price and so must return it. B retains the vehicle and must (a) return it together with such money as accounts for its depreciation in B's hands, or (b) pay such fair market value as it had *when A parted with it.*

D.   When Incompetent Persons Contract for Necessaries

When an incompetent person, child or adult, (a) forms a contract by which she secures "necessaries"—goods or services reasonably related to her survival, and (b) then elects to rescind it, she must pay the fair market value (not the contract price) of all goods *and* services provided her. Necessaries include food, clothing, shelter, medical care, and other such staples. Suppose an 8-year-old child, hungry and alone, enters a retail store. He asks for food and clothing, promising to pay at some later time. Thereafter, the child (or someone on his behalf) might pay the agreed price and be done with it. He might, on the other hand, take the goods, consume them, and then elect to rescind the contract. If he does that, he must pay the seller not the contract price to which he agreed (since the contract no longer exists), but whatever the court names as the *fair market value* of the goods given him (which might or might not differ from the contract price).

E.   The Closers

QUESTIONS 3 & 4. Larry buys two $100 tickets for the state lottery. He approaches Lucy, a stranger, and offers to sell her one of the tickets for $100. Lucy accepts because she is an unrestrained, uncontrolled, compulsive gambler. The parties consummate the sale. Larry then approaches Victor, also a stranger. Victor, a chronic alcoholic, is too impaired to appreciate the significance of his surroundings, his speech, or his behavior. To Victor, too, Larry offers a lottery ticket for $100. Victor accepts, pays Larry, and takes the ticket.

Later in the day, Lucy contacts Larry and proclaims her wish to disaffirm the contract through which she purchased the ticket. "I want my $100 back," she says. Victor, on sobering up, does not remember purchasing the ticket. But he sees on his floor a receipt indicating that he bought it from Larry for $100. From the receipt Victor acquires Larry's contact information. He contacts Larry, expresses his wish to "undo" the contract, and demands the return of his $100.

Before any of the parties take further action, the state conducts its lottery. The ticket in Lucy's possession wins $20 million, and the ticket in Victor's possession wins $10 million. Before Lucy or Victor can redeem their tickets for the prize money, Larry contacts both, asserting his readiness to refund $100 to each and his demand that both tickets be returned to him.

QUESTION 3. Is Larry entitled to have back the ticket he sold to Lucy?

A. Yes, because a mental disturbance caused Lucy to purchase the ticket
B. Yes, because Lucy cannot retract her decision to disaffirm the contract
C. No, because Lucy understood the significance of her earlier transaction with Larry
D. No, because it is Lucy's option to affirm, disaffirm, or reaffirm her contract with Larry

QUESTION 4.   Is Larry entitled to have back the ticket he sold to Victor?

A. Yes, because Victor had no memory of his interaction with Larry
B. Yes, because Victor had no understanding of his interaction with Larry
C. No, because Victor's intoxication resulted from his own decision to drink
D. No, because Larry had no reason to know of Victor's condition as a chronic alcoholic

ANALYSIS.   This story turns things upside down. The parties who attempted to disaffirm now want their contracts back. The competent adult is delighted at the disaffirmation, eager to restore the status quo ante.

As to Question 3, when Lucy bought the ticket, she knew what she was doing; she appreciated the nature and consequence of her action. Neurosis prevented her from behaving *reasonably*, but that would warrant disaffirmation only if Larry had reason to know it. He didn't, because Lucy was a stranger. Lucy's attempted disaffirmation failed (which is good news for her). She keeps the lottery ticket and Larry keeps the $100. The answer is "no," meaning that **A** and **B** are wrong.

A implies a false statement of law. There's no general rule that allows one to disaffirm a contract simply because a mental disturbance causes her to form it. Even if, as here, the disturbance prevents the party from behaving reasonably as to the relevant matter, she may disaffirm only if the other party has reason to know of her difficulty. **A** is wrong. **B** operates on a false premise, to wit, that Lucy *had* a right to disaffirm the contract (stating, then, that she had no right to reaffirm it). She had no right to *dis*affirm it. Hence, **B** is wrong, leaving us with **C** and **D**, one of which is right (we hope).

D makes a false statement. Larry had no reason to know of Lucy's compulsiveness, meaning Lucy had no right to disaffirm. **D** is for the dumper. **C** correctly reports that Lucy understood her transaction with Larry, and *that's critical.* If she hadn't known what she was doing, the disaffirmation *would* operate. The ticket would go back to Larry, and the $100 to Lucy. The answer would be "yes" instead of "no." Hence, *because* Lucy knew what she was doing, Larry doesn't recover the ticket. **C** is right.

And what of Question 4? Victor was so intoxicated as *not* to understand what he was doing when he dealt with Larry. As soon as he announced his wish to "undo" the contract, he disaffirmed it and had no right, then, to *re*affirm it. Victor and Larry must restore each other to status quo ante. Larry gets the ticket and Victor the $100. **C** and **D** reach the opposite conclusion, so they're wrong. Furthermore, **C** implies a false statement of law. That a party causes his own incapacity does not deprive him of the right to disaffirm a contract; there's no such rule. **D** too implies a false doctrine. If two parties form a contract, one who does not understand the nature of his actions is empowered to disaffirm it regardless of what the other did or did not know.

We're left with **A** and **B**. According to **A**, Victor is entitled to disaffirm the contract because he can't *remember* forming it. There's no such law. A competent person might well form a contract and then forget that he has done so. His poor memory affords him no right to disaffirm. According to **B**, Victor may disaffirm because, in forming the contract, he had no idea what he was doing. That's the law, and that's why **B** is right.

Should a case like this arise, however, it would likely produce protracted litigation. The "rules" in this area are full of give and play. No good lawyer dealing with this case would rely on standard statements of the so-called rules as predictors of the outcome. The truth is, we have little idea of how a state supreme court would really decide this case. **A** may be "right," but that doesn't mean it's *real.*

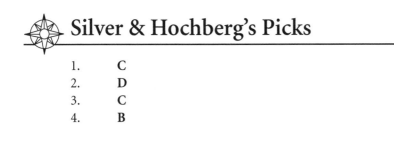 ## Silver & Hochberg's Picks

1. C
2. D
3. C
4. B

17

Illegal Contracts

A. "Illegal" Contracts: The Basics

The law surrounding so-called "illegal contracts" is mired in misleading and poorly conceived statements with the Restatement helping to move things from bad to worse. By the time Lord Chief Justice Mansfield took his seat on the King's Bench in 1754, the law had settled on the general rule that an "illegal contract" was unenforceable, Holman v. Johnson, 1 Crown 341 (K.B. 1775). Yet, as one author correctly writes, "courts have been consistently inconsistent" in applying that rule. 40 Virginia Law Review 1954 Note, 1067.

When used in this context, the word "illegal" does not refer to law as we usually understand that word. It doesn't refer, necessarily, to a violation of statute, regulation, or common law. Rather, "illegality" refers to violation of "public policy."

By modern common law, a contract is "illegal" if, to some meaningful degree, it conflicts with "public policy." "Public policy" as used here refers to that which promotes (in the judiciary's mind) cultural notions of "good," morals, of values central to a free and ordered society, and to those provisions of constitution, statute, administrative regulation ("positive law")[1] directed to serious matters of public health, safety, and welfare.

---

1. "Positive law" is that derived from some positive act of the government. It refers to law derived from constitution, statute, administrative regulation, or common law.

Thus characterized, "public policy" remains, still, poorly defined.[2] Nonetheless, we can illustrate its meaning with a few simple stories.

Illustration: Valdez and Ian.   Valdez, married to Wanda, is involved also with a paramour whom he plans to meet on Monday night. Not wanting Wanda to know about that, Valdez and Ian agree that (1) Valdez will pay Ian $50, and (2) if Wanda, should ask about Valdez's whereabouts on Monday night, Ian will say. "On Monday night. Valdez was, with me playing cards."

The agreement calls for Ian to practice deceit on Valdez's wife regarding a concern central to marriage which, in turn, constitutes a cherished social institution. Further, the agreement helps Valdez pursue marital infidelity which, too, contravenes "good" morals. Hence, the agreement calls for behavior that violates public policy. Most judges would brand it an illegal contract.

An Illegal Contract Is Void (Not Voidable, but Void)   Suppose that on Monday afternoon Valdez pays Ian the $50 and on Monday night he visits his paramour. On Tuesday Valdez's wife asks Ian "Do you know where Valdez was last night?" Ian decides to tell her the truth. "Not with me," he says, " I think he was with a girlfriend." Ian thus breaches his contract with Valdez. If Valdez brings an action against him for breach, the court will likely award him nothing, because the contract was "illegal" wherefore Valdez cannot enforce it.

Imagine now that the contract calls for Valdez to make payment not on Monday, but on Tuesday. On Monday night, Valdez visits his paramour. Ian receives no call from Wanda on Tuesday, but he does ask Valdez for the $50. Valdez refuses to pay. If Ian brings an action against Valdez, the court will award him nothing because the contract is illegal, wherefore it is void. Neither party can enforce it — not Ian, not Valdez, "not nobody."

Another Illustration: Bilea and Dale.   Dale wants to visit his mother. Bilea has a car, but is not licensed to carry passengers for hire. Nonetheless, in exchange for $25, Bilea agrees to drive Dale to his mother's home. The contract calls upon Bilea, literally, to violate the law, but it doesn't contravene "good" morality or any value important to a free and ordered society. Hence, it doesn't violate public policy, and few judges would call it an illegal contract. If either party breaches, the law will entitle the other to enforce it.

---

2.   *See* Horner v. Graves, 7 Bing. 735, 743 (1831) ("Whatever is injurious to the interests of the public [violates] . . . public policy."); Richardson v. Mellish, 2 Bing. 229, 252 (1824) (Burroughs, J.) ("Public policy . . . is an unruly horse and . . . you never know where it will carry you. It may lead you from the sound law."); 3 Samuel Williston, *The Law of Contracts* §1630 (1920) ("[P]ublic policy is a variable thing. It must fluctuate with the circumstances of the time.").

B.   Recovery in Relation to Illegal Contracts; Recovery for Unjust Enrichment

If a plaintiff sues defendant, alleging breach of an illegal contract, his recovery depends primarily on whether *his participation* in the contract violates public policy. One who asserts the breach of an illegal contract does not recover if he offends public policy through either

(1) *his* performance under the contract or

(2) *his wish* to induce the other party's performance.

The principle . . . is . . . *ex dolo malo non oritur actio*, meaning, said Lord Mansfield in 1775, that "no court will lend its aid to a man who founds his cause of action upon an immoral or an illegal act." Holman v. Johnson, 1 Cowp 341 (1775).

On the other hand one who is aggrieved by another's breach of an illegal contract might recover if his participation in the contract does not offend public policy in either of the ways described above. In other words, with respect to an illegal contract between A and B

(1) both parties might be "bad guys," in which case the law gives neither a remedy for an alleged "breach," or

(b) Party A might be a "bad guy" and B not, in which case the law gives no remedy to A, but might give one to B.

Illustration: Both Parties' Participation Offends Public Policy; No Recovery to Either One   For $50,000 X hires Y to kill Z. In forming their agreement, both parties offend public policy (big time): X by *wanting* Y to kill Z, and Y by promising to kill him. If either X or Y asserts a "breach" by the other, neither will recover.

Suppose the agreement requires that X pay Y his $50,000 fee in advance. X does so. Y then fails to do the "job." X sues Y. A court will award X nothing, because as to this illegal contract X is a "bad guy;" he sought the commission of a murder and thus offended public policy.

Suppose, on the other hand, the contract calls for X to pay Y *after* Y does "the job." Y does kill Z, but X refuses to pay him. Y sues X. The court will award Y nothing, because as to this illegal contract Y, too, is a "bad guy." He promised to commit a killing, and that too violates public policy.

Illustration: Only One Party's Participation Offends Public Policy; Recovery by the Other   For ten years, Fenn has worked full time for Esta. Needing additional income, he asks Esta for extra work — for "overtime" hours. Esta offers him ten additional hours per week, but says she won't pay the "time and a half" overtime wage required by law. Rather, she'll pay Fenn only his ordinary hourly pay. Fenn accepts.

These parties have formed a contract that conflicts with a significant policy of public wellbeing: a worker should receive a greater rate of compensation for overtime work. The contact is (probably) "illegal." As to this illegal contract Esta attempts to exploit her employee—to "get away" with receiving overtime service without paying overtime wage. Her participation in the contract offends public policy. Fenn, on the other hand, doesn't want to "get away" with anything. He is, simply, willing to work for a wager lower than the one to which he is lawfully entitled. His participation does not offend public policy. As to this illegal contract, Esta is a "bad guy;" Fenn is not.

Suppose, now, that (1) the agreement calls for Esta to pay Fenn in advance, (2) Esta does pay Fenn in advance, (3) Fenn fails to perform his extra ten hours of work, and (4) Esta sues him for breach. A court will likely dismiss her suit. She formed an illegal contract in which her participation offends public policy.

Suppose, now, that (1) the contract calls for Esta to pay Fenn *after* he completes the overtime work, (2) Fenn performs the overtime work, (3) Esta (for whatever reason) refuses to pay him anything—not even the ordinary wage, and (4) Fenn sues Esta.

A court will likely afford Fenn a recovery, *but the recovery will not be for breach of contract.*

Recovery?—But Not for Breach of Contract?—Why Not?   An illegal contract is void (not void*able*, but void). In the law's eyes, it doesn't exist, and no one can recover for breach of a contract that doesn't exist. For that reason, Fenn will recover from Esta, *not* under contract law, but for "unjust enrichment" (a phrase that arose not in law, but in equity; see Appendix, section E) and, more specifically, in "quasi-contract" (all discussed elaborately at Chapter 28, Part B). Fenn provided service to Esta with the reasonable expectation that he would be compensated—in this case because he and Esta had so agreed. Fenn's work "conferred" a "benefit" on Esta, and yet Fenn received nothing back. In the law's eyes, Esta is unjustly enriched at Fenn's expense. Fenn is entitled to a recovery for Esta's "unjust enrichment"

Let's ask: what *does* Fenn recover? Let's answer: Fenn recovers the "fair market value" of the "benefit" he has "conferred" on Esta, whether the benefit be money, property, labor, or service (see Chapter 28, section B). In a suit by Fenn against Esta, the court will admit evidence on the question of fair market value. It might then decide that the fair market value corresponds to the statutory overtime pay rate. It might, on the other hand, decide that the fair market value is the "going rate" in the community for the work Fenn performed. In any case, the court is to identify fair market value as a matter *apart from the contract price* because, once again, the contract between Esta and Fenn is void—nonexistent. One can't recover for breach of contract if he has not formed one.

Illustration: No Unjust Enrichment and No Recovery to Fenn.   Let's alter the story of Esta and Fenn. After they form their overtime contract, Esta quickly announces her intention to dishonor it. She instructs Fenn not to work, and actually prevents him from doing so. Fenn sues her. If this contract were not illegal, *contract law* would afford Fenn an action for Esta's breach; he'd be able to recover the pay promised him under the contract, regardless of the fact that he performed no work.[3] But the contract *is* illegal and any recovery to which Fenn might be entitled requires that he confer some benefit on Esta, so to make for unjust enrichment. However, Esta prevented Fenn from performing. Therefore, Fenn provided Esta with no money, effort, or service. He conferred on Esta no benefit; Esta enjoyed no unjust enrichment. Fenn recovers—zilch (see Chapter 28, section B).

Summary: The Law of Illegal Contracts   *(1) If and only if two parties form a contract whose terms offend public policy— whether or not they contravene statute, regulation, or common law— their contract is "illegal," wherefore it is void and hence, unenforceable by either party.*

(2) If either party performs under the contract, and his participation does not offend public policy, then to the extent he has parted with his own money, property, labor or service, he is entitled to recovery for unjust enrichment equal to whatever the court identifies as the fair market value of the benefit he thus confers on the other.

QUESTIONS 1 & 2. Tollins operates a construction business. Santos approaches him and asks for employment. "Can you operate a back hoe?" asks Tollins. Santos says yes, and Tollins continues: "My one remaining back hoe failed the legal safety inspection, but if you're willing to take your chances, you're hired—$30 per hour, 40 hours per week, Monday to Friday, 9 A.M. to 5 P.M. You'll be paid every two weeks, on Friday at 5 P.M., 20 weeks of work guaranteed if you'll guarantee me that you'll remain for 20 weeks." Santos agrees: "It's a deal." Assume that because Tollins authorizes Santos to operate an instrument that is, by law, unsafe, his participation in the agreement violates public policy. Assume that Santos' participation does not.

QUESTION 1. Santos performs his work for two weeks, and the back hoe functions well. When he requests his pay of $2,400 ($30/hour × 80 hours), Tollins refuses to pay, asserting that he is short of funds. He further advises Santos that he must "let him go" for that same reason. Alleging Tollins's failure to honor his agreement, Santos sues Tollins. The Court should rule that:

 I. the parties' contract is enforceable against Tollins.
 II. Santos will recover $2,400 in pay because that is the amount on which the parties agreed.

---

3. She would recover damages, however, only to the extent that she exercises a duty to "mitigate" (see Chapter 26, section A).

A. I
B. II
C. I and II
D. Neither I nor II

ANALYSIS.   Set your brain upon the law. These parties formed a contract under which Santos was to operate heavy machinery that had failed to pass a legally required safety inspection. The contract is illegal. That means it's void and, theoretically, nonexistent. Hence, neither party can sustain an action or derive recovery for breach of contract. Option I is false.

Tollins is a "bad guy"; Santos is not. Because Tollins dishonored his promise, Santos worked for no pay. Tollins has been enriched at Santos's expense. Santos is entitled to recover not for breach of contract but for unjust enrichment. According to option II, Santos recovers $2,400 because such is the amount Tollins promised him. Wrong. The Court will afford Santos a recovery based not on the terms of the illegal contract, but for the unjust enrichment enjoyed by Santos. It will hear evidence as to the *fair market value* of Santos' services, and quantify the award accordingly. Both options I and II are false. **D** is right.

QUESTION 2. Assume now that Santos works for ten weeks, and Tollins pays him $2,400 every other Friday, as agreed. On Friday of the twelfth week, Santos asks Tollins, "Can you pay me today for these past two weeks eleven and twelve, and pay me, also, in advance, for the next two weeks—thirteen and fourteen? I'm very short of cash." Tollins responds, "You've been working for ten weeks, performing wonderfully and handling that back hoe without difficulty. So my answer is yes." Tollins pays Santos $2,400 for weeks ten and eleven, and an additional $2,400 for work to be performed during weeks twelve and thirteen. On that Friday, Santos truly intends to do his work during weeks twelve and thirteen, but on Monday of week twelve, he changes his mind. He fails to appear for work. Neither does he appear on Tuesday—nor ever again. Tollins sues Santos for dishonoring his obligations (a) to work for 20 weeks, and (b) to earn the $2,400 paid him in advance. In relation to this suit,

 I. Tollins will be able to enforce the contract against Santos.
 II. Tollins will recover the $2,400 he paid Santos for the two weeks' work Santos did not perform.
 A. I
 B. II
 C. I and II
 D. Neither I nor II

ANALYSIS.   No one can enforce an illegal contract. Option I is false, so **A** and **C** are wrong. As to this illegal contract, Tollins is a "bad guy;" he attempted to "get away" with the use of a back hoe which, by law, was unsafe. Hence, even though he paid $2,400 for which he got back nothing, the court will award him — zip. Again, **D** is right.

QUESTIONS 3 & 4. Rory owns a suburban home where zoning regulations forbid him to build a yard fence higher than five feet without first obtaining permission (a "variance") from the local zoning board. He wishes to build a six-foot yard fence and offers to pay Ben $1,000 for doing so. Ben asks Rory whether he has obtained the necessary zoning variance, and Rory answers, truthfully, "no." Nonetheless, Ben accepts the offer and builds the fence. Thereafter, Rory refuses to pay.

QUESTION 3. Is the contract illegal?

A. Probably, because it conflicts with a lawfully enacted governmental regulation
B. Probably, because it conflicts with traditional notions of good morals
C. Probably, because both parties knew of the zoning ordinance when they formed their contract
D. Probably not, because it does not conflict seriously with public policy

---

ANALYSIS.   A contract is not illegal simply because it contravenes some legislative statute or administrative regulation. **A** is wrong. A contract is illegal only if it conflicts significantly with public policy. Public policy, in turn, refers to moral values that are conventionally "good" ones and, in general, values consistent with notions of a stable, free, ordered society as a court understands them. The zoning ordinance at issue here bespeaks no such concerns, and certainly it does not conflict with traditional notions of good moral values as stated in **B**. Neither is it relevant, as stated in **C**, that the parties knew of the zoning ordinance. **A**, **B**, and **C** are plainly wrong. **D** is right.

QUESTION 4. To what recovery is Ben entitled?

A. None
B. The fair market value of his services
C. The amount promised him under the contract
D. His usual and customary rate for performing substantially similar work

---

ANALYSIS.   Because the contract does not offend public policy, it's not illegal. It's enforceable. Ben has an action for breach of contract. He is entitled to recover the amount promised him under the contract, whether that's more or less than the fair market value of his services, and whether it is more or less than his customary rate of pay (which, in any case, is irrelevant even to unjust enrichment). **A**, **B**, and **D** are wrong. **C** is right.

C.   Illegal Contracts: Traditional Vocabulary

We have recited rules that refer to a party whose "participation" in a contract does or does not violate public policy. Those rules are, of course, correct. Although the courts follow them, they don't state them as we do. Rather, the rules as courts state them are a confused mixture of vestigial remains, each having left its fossil as the law of illegal contracts evolved. None of them truly expresses the basis on which courts reach their results. So remember the rules as we've taught them to you, but know that the courts (and your teachers) are likely to state them in different terms. Let's explain.

1.   Malum in Se *vs.* Malum Prohibitum

The Latin phrase *malum in se* means "wrong in itself." Murder, robbery, arson, and blackmail represent violations of law that are, to all legal minds, *malum in se*. *Malum prohibitum* means "wrong only because the law prohibits it." Suppose a 17-year-old girl looks older than her age. She swears to a new male acquaintance, aged 18, that she too is 18 and presents convincing (falsified) documentary evidence to that effect. This unfortunate chap believes her and, with her consent, has sex with her. This fellow, innocent and well meaning, has committed statutory rape, but his offense is, to most legal minds, *malum prohibitum*, not *malum in se*.

Once upon a time, a line of common law authority named a contract illegal only if it called for one or both parties to commit a tort or statutory violation that was *malum in se*. If the contract called for behavior that was merely *malum prohibitum*, it was *not* illegal. For instance, if X agreed to pay Y to kidnap Z, the parties formed an illegal contract because kidnapping is *malum in se*. But if X hired Y to build a six-foot fence on his property, both parties knowing that X had not acquired the necessary zoning variance, the contract was not illegal because the zoning ordinance created only a *malum prohibitum*.

This line of authority is now largely replaced by the rule we've described: A contract is illegal if it calls for a performance that violates public policy. Yet the Latin phrases appear in the older cases, and they might, even today, step on stage for cameo appearances because some court, here or there, just can't part with them.

2.   *Comparative Fault and Pari Delicto*

It's also been said, and still is said sometimes, that if two parties form a contract but one of them is at greater "fault," then the one at lesser fault will be entitled to recover for unjust enrichment, but the other will not. On the other hand, if the parties are in *pari delicto*, meaning at equal fault, neither is entitled to recover at all. In such a case, the court "leaves the parties where it finds them."

3. Illustrations

Consider the contract to kill described above. X's participation violates public policy, as does Y's. If X pays Y his $50,000 fee, Y fails to do the job, and X sues, a court will not award X anything at all. Suppose, on the other hand, that Y performs first; he commits the killing. If X then refuses to pay and Y sues, a court will award him nothing. In reaching these decisions, a court would likely state that the contract is illegal and the parties are in *pari delicto*, wherefore the court will award nothing to either.

Consider, now, the Santos/Tollins case at Questions 1 and 2. If, as in Question 1, Santos sues Tollins for failure to pay, the court will acknowledge the contract's illegality, but nonetheless award Santos the fair market value of his services because, as to this illegal contract, Santos's "fault" was less than Tollins's. If, as in Question 2, Tollins sues Santos for failure to honor his obligations, the court will likely rule, once again, that Tollins's "fault" is greater than Santos's and for that reason award Tollins nothing.

4. So, in Summary . . .

If a court rules that neither party to an illegal contract is entitled to an award for breach because the parties are in *pari delicto*, it means that both parties' participation in the contract offends public policy. Consequently, neither is entitled to recover if the other should dishonor the agreement.

If, as to a given illegal contract, a court rules that plaintiff is entitled to a recovery for unjust enrichment because his fault is less than that of the defendant, it means that defendant's participation violates public policy, but plaintiff's does not.

D. The Closers

Lafayette operates a fruit stand, and Habel is his customer. When Habel asks to purchase a peach, Lafayette explains that he has but one peach, 10 days old. "It looks all right and it's probably good," Lafayette says, "but the state law against distribution of potentially poisonous foods prevents me from selling you any fruit that is more than 3 days old, unless it is refrigerated, which this peach is not. And, who knows—maybe it's *not* safe." Habel responds "I'll take my chances," and the parties contract for the sale of the peach, at a price of $1.

QUESTION 5. Immediately after forming the contract, before either party has performed, Lafayette decides not to sell Habel the peach and refuses to do so. To what recovery (in (*very*) small claims court) is Habel entitled?

A. None
B. The fair market value of the peach
C. $1
D. The customary charge in the community for a peach

ANALYSIS. A food safety regulation certainly reflects public policy. The contract is illegal, wherefore it is void and unenforceable. Habel has no action for *breach of contract*. Further, he has not performed under the contract. He has parted with no value in money, property, labor, or service, meaning that Lafayette has enjoyed no unjust enrichment. He is entitled to no recovery at all. He recovers nothing—nada, rien, nusquam, zilch—which means **A** is right.

QUESTION 6. Assume that Lafayette hands the peach to Habel and that Habel then refuses to pay for it. To what recovery is Lafayette entitled?

A. None
B. The fair market value of the peach
C. $1
D. The customary charge in the community for a peach

ANALYSIS.   The contract is illegal, wherefore it is void and hence unenforceable. Lafayette has no action for breach of contract. Moreover, Lafayette is the seller of the forbidden fruit, wherefore *his* participation in the contract violates public policy. The law will not aid a willful wrongdoer; *ex dolo malo non oritur actio.* Notwithstanding that he has parted with the peach and that Habel (might) enjoy it, the law will award Lafayette nothing. **A** is right.

QUESTION 7. Assume that Habel pays Lafayette $1. Lafayette then refuses to hand him the peach and refuses, also, to return the dollar. Habel brings an action against Lafayette. *If* a court allows Habel to recover, it will award him:

A. the fair market value of the time devoted to forming the contract with Habel.
B. the fair market value of the peach.
C. $1.
D. the customary charge in the community for a peach.

ANALYSIS.   The contract is illegal, wherefore it is void and hence unenforceable. Habel has no action for breach of contract. Arguably, Habel's participation in the contract violates public policy since he has knowingly purchased and intends to ingest food that is, legally, substandard. If the court should so conclude, then Habel will recover nothing. With its first few words, "If a court . . . ," the question hypothesizes that Habel does recover and you're asked to identify the appropriate form of recovery.

Because the court cannot enforce the contract, it will afford recovery for unjust enrichment. Habel will be entitled to have the fair market value of any benefit he has conferred on Lafayette in money, property, labor, or service. In this case, Habel's payment of the $1 purchase price confers on Lafayette a benefit of that same amount (since the fair market value of a dollar is always a dollar). **C** is right.

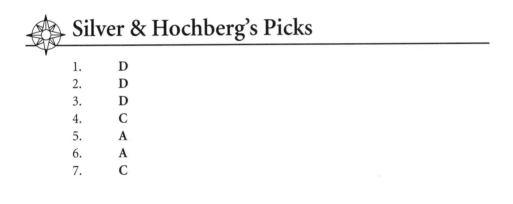 ## Silver & Hochberg's Picks

1.	**D**
2.	**D**
3.	**D**
4.	**C**
5.	**A**
6.	**A**
7.	**C**

18

How We Interpret Contracts

A. You've Already Mastered Most of This Topic

From Chapter 2 you know that: (1) a contract arises by offer and acceptance, (2) the terms of the offer have such meaning as would be given them by a reasonable offeree under all prevailing circumstances, and (3) an offeree accepts only if he assents to all of the offeror's terms without addition or exception.[1] That means (4) the terms of any true acceptance are identical to those of the offer, wherefore (5) the terms of the resulting contract are the same as those of the offer which are the same as those of the acceptance, wherefore (6) a contract includes such terms and has such meaning as conform to the parties' reasonable understandings and expectations.[2]

Suppose Darlene, a Canadian citizen visiting Idaho wants to buy a car. On an Internet site called "Ibuy," Chester advertises a car for sale, setting forth his address and telephone number in Boise, Idaho. Darlene responds to the advertisement with an email that bears her signature: "I have seen the vehicle you advertised on "Ibuy." I'll take it for $7,000. I'll send you a check today. Are we agreed?" Chester responds, "Yes."

Darlene sends Chester a check drawn on her Canadian bank, for seven thousand *Canadian* dollars. Chester receives it and telephones Darlene: "When

---

1. Except with respect to UCC §2-207, under which an offeree might accept an offer without a mirror image assent (Chapter 11, section B).
2. Remember that when two parties form a contract, the offer and the acceptance always have the same meaning. If they do not, then the parties don't form a contract. That includes the very rare case, like *Peerless*, in which each of two parties gives a different meaning to the same word or phrase, both of them reasonable under the prevailing circumstances (see Chapter 3, section C). That is true even in respect of UCC §2-207(1) (see Chapter 11, sections B-E).

we agreed on $7,000, I meant 7,000 *U.S.* dollars, not Canadian dollars. The check you've sent is worth only $6,650 in U.S. dollars." Darlene responds, "I'm from Canada, so I thought in terms of Canadian dollars. I'm only willing to buy for $7,000 *Canadian* dollars — $6,650 U.S. dollars."

These Parties Are In Dispute As to the Meaning of "Dollar." Within a contract, a word's meaning, we know, is that which reasonable persons would give it under the circumstances that surround them when they form the contract. The advertisement referred to an Idaho address, and Idaho is in the U.S. When Darlene offered to buy the car, Chester was justified in believing that she meant to pay seven thousand American dollars. When Chester accepted, Darlene *should* have understood that he assented to a price of seven thousand American dollars. Regardless of what Darlene herself truly thought or intended, these parties contracted for a price of seven thousand dollars, U.S. currency.

We have just interpreted a disputed contractual term. In this contract, "dollar" means "U.S. dollar." We did so according to this rule: contractual terms have such meaning as reasonable persons would give them under the relevant circumstances.

In its own tortured way, the Restatement (Second) of Contracts §20(2)(b) states the same rule.

> Where the parties have attached different meanings to a promise or agreement or a term thereof, it is interpreted in accordance with the meaning attached by one of them [and not the other] if at the time the agreement was made ... that party had no reason to know of any different meaning attached by the other, and the other had reason to know the meaning attached by the first party.

Let's take hold of Restatement §20(2) and "plug in," the facts pertaining to Chester and Darlene:

> Where the parties have attached different meanings to a promise or agreement or a term thereof [as happened here with Chester, Darlene, and the word "dollar"], it [the word "dollar"] is interpreted in accordance with the meaning attached by one of them [Chester, in this case] if [as happened in this case] at the time the agreement was made . . . that party [Chester] had no reason to know of any different meaning attached by the other [Darlene], and the other [Darlene] had reason to know the meaning attached by the first party [Chester].

When Darlene said "dollar," Chester thought she meant "U.S. dollar." In Restatement terms, he had "no reason" to think otherwise (meaning his understanding was reasonable under the circumstances). When Charles accepted the offer, Darlene "had reason to know" that in his mind, "dollar" meant "U.S. dollar" (meaning that she should reasonably have understood him to mean "U.S. dollar.") Hence, the Restatement dictates that in this contract, "dollar" means "U.S. dollar," Its tortuous sentence comes to mean only this: A contract has such meaning as would be given it by reasonable persons under the relevant circumstances.

B. "Usage of Trade," "Course of Dealing," and "Course of Performance"

The law never tires of fashioning words and phrases that add nothing to its good, basic principles. Here, now, we explore three of them.

1. "Usage of Trade"

The phrase "usage of trade" refers to usages and interpretations common among persons belonging to a particular trade, industry, or commercial community. As Restatement (Second) §222(1) provides:

> A usage of trade is a usage having such regularity of observance in a place, vocation, or trade as to justify an expectation that it will be observed with respect to a particular agreement.

Within most industries, for example, "working day" means 8 hours. "Full time" means 40 hours per week, 50 weeks per year. In the retail sales industry, the phrase "bird dog" means one who sends prospective buyers to some particular seller. In the real estate industry, a "FISBO" is one who attempts to sell his home without an agent's help. Among medical interns and residents, "boxcars" means death. Among gamblers, "house" means casino. Among bartenders and their patrons, "rocks" means ice cubes. All such expressions represent usage of trade.

2. "Course of Dealing"

"Course of dealing" refers to two parties who have, in the past, formed contracts with each other. It represents the meanings and interpretations that *they* explicitly or implicitly adopt in the contracts they form, so much so as to create a private code between themselves, which might differ from the prevailing usage of trade. Restatement (Second) §223(1) provides:

> A course of dealing is a sequence of previous conduct between the parties to an agreement which is fairly to be regarded as establishing a common basis of understanding for interpreting their expressions and other conduct.

Suppose that by usage of trade within the widget industry, "single" means 1 widget, "double" means 2 widgets, and "triple" means 3 widgets. Now suppose that Party B frequently buys widgets from Party S, and suppose that over time these parties have developed a little code of their own, different from the prevailing usage of trade. When B wants 100 widgets, she orders "a single," and S sends her 100 widgets. When B wants 200 widgets, she orders "a double," whereupon S sends her 200 widgets. When she wants 300 widgets, she orders "a triple," whereupon S sends her 300 widgets. This private code, developed between these two parties, represents their "course of dealing," and it happens to differ from the prevailing usage of trade.

3. "Course of Performance"

The phrase "course of performance" applies only to a contract that calls for *multiple occasions of performance*. Suppose B has two warehouses, warehouse 1 and warehouse 2, separated by 20 miles. B and S have a history in which B has repeatedly bought widgets from S under contracts that call for delivery to "B's warehouse." S has always delivered to B's warehouse 2, and B has never objected. According to the parties' course of dealing, therefore, delivery to "B's warehouse" means delivery to warehouse 2.

Now suppose B and S form another contract for the sale of widgets. Unlike their previous contracts, this one calls for multiple occasions of performance; it requires that S deliver to "B's warehouse" 450 widgets on January 2, and 450 widgets on the first day of every month from February through December, thus creating 12 occasions for performance. B is to pay $45,000 for each such lot of 450 widgets, three days after S makes delivery.

On January 1, S delivers 450 widgets to warehouse 1, as he had never done in the past. Without objection, B's agent accepts them and, without objection, B pays the $45,000 purchase price on January 5. The same occurs in February, March, April, May, June, and July. On the first day of each such month, S delivers 450 widgets to warehouse 1. Without objection, B's agent accepts them and, without objection, B timely pays the appropriate purchase price. These parties have established a "course of performance," meaning an interpretation developed by their behavior as they perform *this very contract*—whereby "B's warehouse" means warehouse 1. Their course of performance thus differs from their course of dealing, by which "B's warehouse" means warehouse 2.

As Restatement (Second) §202(4) provides:

> Where an agreement involves repeated occasions for performance by either party with knowledge of the nature of the performance and opportunity for objection to it by the other, any course of performance accepted or acquiesced in without objection is given great weight in the interpretation of the agreement.

4. A Hierarchy

In the law's eyes, a reasonable person, in interpreting a contractual term, would or should be keenly aware of any usage of trade, course of dealing, and/or course of performance relevant to the circumstances. Consequently, all such concepts are highly relevant to contractual interpretation. Furthermore, (UCC) §2-208(2) establishes a hierarchy among them. Where course of performance and/or course of dealing and/or usage of trade *conflict*, course of performance ranks first; it trumps course of dealing. Course of dealing ranks second; it trumps usage of trade. Usage of trade ranks third.

QUESTIONS 1 & 2. Within the woodget industry, "two hits" means 2,000 woodgets. Between 1990 and 2011, Bana and Soo have formed many contracts for the purchase and sale of woodgets. With respect to their contracts, they have developed a private language by which "two hits" means only *200* woodgets. On January 2, 2012, Bana and Soo form a contract under which Soo is to deliver to Bana "two hits" of woodgets on the fifth day of every month, January through December. Bana is to pay $10 for each woodget that Soo delivers. For the months January through June, Soo delivers only *20* units, and for each such month, Bana accepts and pays for them without objection.

QUESTION 1. With respect to this most recent contract:

I. by usage of trade, "two hits" means 2,000 woodgets.
II. by course of dealing, "two hits" means 200 woodgets.
III. by course of performance, "two hits" means 20 woodgets.

A. I
B. I and II
C. II and III
D. I, II, and III

ANALYSIS. You're asked only to know the meaning of the three phrases "usage of trade," "course of dealing," and "course of performance." The parties to this contract are two persons in the business of buying and selling woodgets. In that industry, "two hits," means 2,000 woodgets, and such, therefore, is the usage of trade. Option I is true, so **C** is wrong. We're told also that as to their previous contracts, *these two parties* have established a "code" whereunder "two hits" means 200 widgets. Hence, option II is true. If option III is true, then **D** is right. If it's false, **B** is right.

It's true. In performing *this very contract*, which calls for multiple deliveries of "two hits," Soo has repeatedly delivered only 20 units, and Bana has repeatedly accepted them without objection. Consequently, for this contract, "two hits" by course of performance means 20 woodgets. Option III is true, and **D** is right.

QUESTION 2. July 5 arrives. Soo delivers to Bana 20 woodgets. Bana protests: "You should be providing me with 2,000 units. That's what 'two hits' means in our industry. And certainly you should be providing me with no less than 200 units because that's what you've always provided in the past when our contract called for 'two hits.' I won't accept this shipment, you're in breach." Is Bana correct in alleging that Soo has breached with respect to the July 5 delivery?

A. Yes, because the July 5 delivery does not conform to usage of trade
B. Yes, because the July 5 delivery does not conform to the parties' course of dealing
C. No, because the July 5 delivery conformed to the contract, as properly interpreted
D. No, because Soo cannot be charged with knowing a usage of trade once she and Bana have established a course of dealing

ANALYSIS.   When a conflict arises as to the three phrases we've discussed, the law provides this ranking: course of performance ranks first, course of dealing ranks second, and usage of trade ranks third. In this case, as already noted, the parties established a course of performance (which, once again, is possible only for a contract that calls for multiple occasions *of* performance). According to their course of performance "two hits" means 20 units. That meaning trumps both their course of dealing in which "two hits" means 200 units, and usage of trade by which "two hits" means 2,000 units.

Soo delivered 20 units and, pursuant to course of performance for *this* contract, that's what "two hits" means; Bana is wrong. The answer, therefore is "no," which means that **A** and **B** are wrong. **A** implies a false statement of law. It's true that the July 5 delivery contravenes usage of trade, but that doesn't matter. Course of performance overrides usage of trade. **B** too implies a false statement of law. It's true that the July 5 delivery contravenes the parties' course of dealing, but that too is irrelevant. Course of performance trumps usage of trade *and* course of dealing.

We're left with **C** and **D**, both of which correctly answer "no." **D** is double talk at best and, more likely, false. Soo is in the woodget business, and the law *does* charge her with knowledge of the relevant usage of trade. That she does or does not know the usage of trade, however, is irrelevant to this question. These parties established a course of dealing, and that's the standard by which the law, in this case, construes "two hits." Hence, Soo delivered the appropriate quantity; she performed according to the contract, as properly interpreted. **C** is right.

But **C** doesn't mention course of performance. Why not? Because the question writer wants to see you choose the right answer without relying on some word or phrase to which you give "magical" meaning. He could have written:

- C. No, because pursuant to the course of performance that these parties established, the July 5 delivery conformed to the contract
- C. No, because on earlier occasions of delivery, Soo delivered 20 units without objection from Bana, meaning the parties established a course of performance under which "two hits" meant 20 units
- C. No, because pursuant to the course of dealing, the parties established in performing this very contract, "two hits" means 20 units, and course of performance supersedes both usage of trade and course of dealing

The writer offered no such choices because a multiple-choice question tests your ability to reason and your ability to read for meaning. Our knowledge together with our *reasoning—reasoning—reasoning*—tells us that for this contract on July 5, "two hits" means 20 units. Soo delivered 20 units, and so she performed according to the contract. We need not see the phrase "course of performance" to know that **C** is right.

C. Interpretation of Writings

Recall and/or review the discussion of signed writings in Chapter 2, section C. As explained there, most contracting parties record serious business agreements in writing. That is, they form a written, signed contract. If a dispute later arises, proper interpretation requires that we probe the history of the final written contract.

1. Draft Contracts

Before signing their final writing, contracting parties often exchange unsigned drafts, each draft usually representing an invitation to deal. When one party signs a writing, then generally he is the offeror because his signature manifests his definite willingness to enter the bargain the writing describes. If and when the other signs that same writing, she, as offeree, accepts by manifesting her assent to the bargain that the offeree proposes.

Suppose Wendy is a writer and Pablo a publisher. After discussing the possibility of Pablo's serving as publisher for Wendy's latest novel, Pablo sends Wendy a draft contract outlining all details that are customary to a contract between author and publisher—author name, book title, book length, advances, royalties, copyrights, licenses, derivative works and what not.

Draft 1 is Pablo's invitation to deal. (If he'd signed it, it would be his offer, but he didn't, so it's a mere invitation to deal.)

Wendy makes changes to the draft and sends it back to Pablo, unsigned. Draft 2 is Wendy's invitation to deal. Pablo makes changes to Draft 2, signs the resulting Draft 3, and sends it back to Wendy. Because Pablo signed Draft 3, it's his *offer*. If Wendy were to sign, she'd accept and the parties would form a contract according to the writing's terms. But suppose Wendy doesn't sign. Instead, she makes changes, thus creating Draft 4. She signs *that* and sends it back to Pablo. Draft 4 is Wendy's *counteroffer*. Pablo receives it, reads it, and signs. Now, finally, the parties have a contract whose terms are those of Wendy's counteroffer and Pablo's acceptance (which, of course, "mirrors" the offer (Chapter 7, section B)). When two parties form a contract through this common process of changing and exchanging drafts, they don't usually retain the unsigned ones. Rather, each keeps a copy of the final, signed document and both forget all about the unsigned drafts. If the signatures are dated, then, ordinarily, the first party to sign is offeror and the second is offeree. If both parties sign on the same date (or leave their signatures undated), the document does not indicate who is offeror and who is offeree. And generally, when two parties form a written contract, lawyers do not think in terms of offeror and offeree. They think in terms of a *contract* by which both parties are bound, the terms of which appear in the writing. If (years later, perhaps) the parties find themselves in dispute as to the meaning of some term, then their lawyers will certainly introduce (conflicting) evidence of what reasonable parties would have understood under the relevant circumstances. They'll adduce evidence concerning usage of trade, course of dealing and course of performance if any such thing is relevant, but they will not ordinarily trouble to identify the offeror and offeree.

2. *Printed and Handwritten Terms*

Suppose on November 1, 2012, Buyer and Seller are about to sign a contractual writing, thus evidencing their mutual assent to its terms. The document represents Seller's preprinted form, several pages long. Paragraph 19 appears thus:

> **19.** Buyer shall pay Seller the full purchase price named above one year from the date hereof with interest of 7 percent.

At the last minute, before either party signs, Buyer states that he needs only one month — until December 1, 2012 — in which to pay the purchase price, and that he wants to pay no interest. Seller agrees. By handwriting, with a pen, in the margin of the page, Seller writes, "Full purchase price to be paid on December 1, 2012, no interest." He does not, however, delete the original text. Both parties sign.

Let's ask: In the event of a conflict, which term governs — the one in print or the one in handwriting? Let's answer: If a preprinted or typewritten (computer-written) term conflicts with a handwritten term, the handwritten term ordinarily controls. That's because the handwriting presumably reflects that on which the parties separately and specifically agreed subsequent to the creation of the printed/typed text. Restatement (Second) §202(d) states it thus:

> [S]eparately negotiated or added terms are given greater weight than standardized terms or other terms not separately negotiated.

3. *Writings Are Construed Against the Drafter*

Often, two parties adopt or sign a contractual writing that one of them has prepared. That is always the case, for example, when two parties form a written contract pursuant to a preprinted form that one of them supplies. If after forming their contract, they should come to dispute the meaning of some term, it is said, that "the writing will be construed against the drafter."

Restatement (Second) §206 provides:

> In choosing among the reasonable meanings of a promise or agreement or a term thereof, that meaning is generally preferred which operates against the party who supplies the words or from whom a writing otherwise proceeds.

The fact that one party prepared the document is itself a *circumstance* under which the parties form their contract. The law's assumption is that the drafter chooses her words carefully and in writing the document resolves every ambiguity in her own favor. Both parties should assume, therefore, that any remaining ambiguity is to be resolved in favor of the *other* party. Some courts view the rule, simply, as one of fundamental fairness: "The rule of resolving ambiguities against the drafter "does not serve as a mere tie breaker; it rests upon fundamental considerations of policy." Goddard v. S. Bay Union High Sch. Dist., 79 Cal. App. 3d 98, 104 (1978).

QUESTION 3. On January 1, 2006, JKLM Radio Inc. and Kelly Kant form a written contract under which Kant, for five years, is to serve JKLM as a radio weather forecaster. The written contract is set forth on a preprinted form provided by JKLM, with some entries made by handwriting. Paragraphs 2 and 29 provide:

> **2. Term of Employment:** The parties agree that Employee will serve for *five* period(s) of *one* year.

Paragraph 29, with the handwritten word "Period" squished in between "Term" and "of" in its heading, provides that JKLM would have the right, at its option, to rehire Kant:

> **29. Additional Term *Period* of Employment:** Employer will have the option to rehire Employee at the same annual salary and under the same contractual terms as those provided herein.

Following paragraph 29, there appear the parties' signatures and, underneath both, the date of January 1, 2006.

In December 2011, when the five-year contract period is nearly expired, JKLM advises Kant that it wishes to rehire him for an additional five years. Kant refuses, stating that JKLM has the right to rehire him only for one additional year. JKLM sues Kant for breach of contract, citing Kant's unwillingness to be hired for an additional five-year period.

JKLM argues that the word "Term" in the heading of paragraph 2 refers to five years, as provided in the substance of paragraph 2 itself. The heading to paragraph 29, says JKLM, should be read with the printed word "Term" and without the handwritten word "Period." Therefore, paragraph 29, JKLM argues, means that at the end of the five-year period, it is entitled to rehire Kant for an additional "term"—an additional five years.

Kant agrees that his initial term of employment was five years, but that according to paragraph 2, the five-year term comprised five separate *periods* of one year each. Each employment *period*, he says, was one year. The heading to paragraph 29, he argues, should be read with the word "Period," not the word "Term." Read that way, Kant reasons, it gives JKLM a right to hire him for one additional year only.

In paragraph 29, the fact that the word "Period" is handwritten and the word "Term" preprinted argues for

A. JKLM, because a printed term generally carries greater weight than does a handwritten term
B. JKLM, because the printed term likely represents usage of trade
C. Kant, because a handwritten term generally carries greater weight than a printed term
D. Kant, because the addition of the handwritten term shows that the parties had a course of dealing

ANALYSIS.   It's important to Kant's position that the heading to paragraph 29 be read with the word "Period" and without the word "Term." Important to JKLM's position is that the heading be read the other way 'round. By common law, a handwritten term carries greater weight than does a conflicting printed (or typewritten) term. Consequently, the fact that "Period" is handwritten favors Kant and works against JKLM.

A is opposite to the truth; a handwritten term carries more weight than a printed term. **B** incorrectly invokes the phrase "usage of trade." Usage of trade refers to the usages, "codes," and private languages that obtain within a given industry. The fact that JKLM, in its form, chose to use a particular word does not render that word a part of its "usage of trade." **A** and **B** are wrong.

D improperly cites the phrase "course of dealing," which refers to meanings that two parties implicitly adopt by virtue of their patterns of behavior in performing their contracts. The fact that Kant and JKLM agreed, during their negotiations, to handwrite the word "Period" just above the printed word "Term" is wholly irrelevant to the phrase "course of dealing." With **A**, **B**, and **D** so terribly wrong, **C** had better be right—and it *is*. It tells us, simply, that a handwritten term carries greater weight than does a printed term, for which reason the handwritten word argues for Kant. **C** is exactly right.

D.   The Closer

QUESTION 4. GlassCo sells window glass to window manufacturers, and PaneCo is a window manufacturer. Both parties are located in the city of Alton, where, among buyers and sellers of window glass, the phrase "my place" refers to one's factory headquarters. PaneCo has its factory head-quarters on Main Street and its executive offices on High Street.

On October 1, PaneCo contacts GlassCo by signed writing and orders 100 panes of glass, to be delivered to "my place." GlassCo responds by signed writing with an acceptance. Thereafter, GlassCo's truck driver, Anne, delivers the 100 panes to PaneCo's executive offices on High Street, but PaneCo makes no objection. It pays the purchase price and moves the panes in its own trucks to its factory on Main Street. On November 1, the parties form another contract for the purchase and sale of glass panes delivered to "my place," and again Anne delivers to PaneCo's executive offices without objection from PaneCo.

Six months later, on May 1, GlassCo and PaneCo form a new contract for the purchase and sale of 400 glass panes to be delivered to "my place," in four installments of 100 units each on June 1, July 1, August 1, and September 1. On June 1 and July 1, GlassCo's driver on duty is not Anne, but Derek. In both months, June and July, Derek delivers the window panes to PaneCo's factory headquarters. PaneCo accepts the delivery without objection. On August 1, Anne is once again on duty. As before, she brings the window panes to PaneCo's executive offices, but this time PaneCo refuses the delivery and proclaims that GlassCo is obliged to deliver to the factory headquarters, not the executive offices.

Citing PaneCo's refusal to accept and pay for the window panes, GlassCo brings an action against PaneCo for breach. The litigation raises only the issue of whether GlassCo had tendered delivery to the appropri-ate location, GlassCo asserting that it had and PaneCo asserting that it had not. PaneCo would best support its position by observing that the appropriate place for delivery, in this case, is governed by

A. usage of trade.
B. course of performance.
C. course of dealing.
D. the parties' intentions.

ANALYSIS. These parties formed a contract for the sale of goods, meaning that UCC Article 2 governs. In interpreting a contract, UCC Article 2 provides that course of performance trumps course of dealing, which trumps usage of trade. In this case, usage of trade would require that GlassCo deliver to PaneCo's factory. However, the parties had a prior course of dealing reflected in their contracts of October 1 and November 1. For those contracts, GlassCo delivered to PaneCo's executive offices and PaneCo did not object. As between these two parties, therefore, *usage of trade* calls for delivery to the factory but *course of dealing* calls for delivery to the executive offices.

Then, under the May 1 contract, which called for multiple performances, the parties, established a course of *performance*. For the first two installments tied to that contract, GlassCo delivered to PaneCo's factory and PaneCo did not object. Between these parties, as of July 1, usage of trade dictated delivery to the factory, course of dealing called for delivery to the executive offices, and course of *performance* called for delivery to the factory. Course of performance trumps course of dealing, which trumps usage of trade. PaneCo should cite that law and point out that in this case course of performance requires delivery to the factory, not to the executive offices. Consequently, **B** is right.

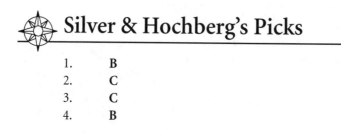 # Silver & Hochberg's Picks

1.	**B**
2.	**C**
3.	**C**
4.	**B**

19

The Parol Evidence Rule

A. The Parol Evidence Rule: Few Things Are Darker Than This[1]

The so-called "parol evidence rule" is a tangled mass of misunderstanding. Everywhere the "rule" rears its misshapen head, it spawns debate, dissent, discord, dysfunction, demoralization, disaffection, depression, dejection, and disgust — not to mention thousands of judicial decisions devoid of sense, coherence, and consistency. No two authorities seem ever to agree on the rule's purpose, meaning, operation, or application. Referring to the parol evidence rule, Professor Thayer wrote, in 1898 that:

> Few things are darker than this, or fuller of subtle difficulties[.] The chief reason is that most of the questions brought under this head are out of place;

---

1. James B. Thayer, A Preliminary Treatise on the Law of Evidence 390 (1898).

there is a grouping together of a mass of incongruous matter, and then it is looked at in a wrong focus. James B. Thayer, *A Preliminary Treatise on the Law of Evidence* 390 (1898)

Writing of the puzzlement that surrounds the parol evidence rule, Professor John Henry Wigmore wrote in 1904:

[T]he so-called parol evidence rule is attended with confusion and an obscurity which make it the most discouraging subject in the whole field of evidence. [T]he present condition of the subject is beyond endurance; unless improved, it threatens . . . irrational and incurable chaos. 4 Wigmore, A *Treatise on the Stem of Evidence in Trials at Common Law* 3368 (1904)

In 1952, Professor Arthur Corbin wrote:

The cases that consider and purport to apply the so-called "parol evidence rule" are so variable and inconsistent as to be the despair of the teacher, the lawyer, and the judge.

Corbin on Contracts (1 volume edition) 534 (1952).
And, in 1992 a Missouri Court wrote that, with respect to the parol evidence rule,

we, in Missouri, no different than the courts in most other jurisdictions, have used a variety of principles, chosen randomly with no consistency . . . The principles of one source . . . are not necessarily consistent with the principles of another[.] Thus, the random selection of principles from more than one source to resolve parol evidence issues has made the parol evidence rule a deceptive maze rather than a workable rule. John C. Byers, Inc. v. J.B.C. Investments, 834 S.W.2d 806 (Mo. App. 1992)

All of these authorities are absolutely right. On its surface the parol evidence rule is a morass of confusion, inconsistency, and misunderstanding. *Beneath* its surface it is — that same morass of confusion, inconsistency, and misunderstanding. Yet you must know about the parol evidence rule. You must know, at least, what it's said to be and immerse yourself temporarily in the abject muddle that comprises its core. You must see for yourself what it is, what it is not, and — maybe — that it is nothing at all.

Notwithstanding the diverse misunderstanding that surrounds the parol evidence rule, virtually all modern authorities (and teachers) agree that despite its name, it is a substantive rule of contract law, not a rule of evidence. So — when you speak of the parol evidence rule, begin, always, by saying "Despite its name, it's not a rule of evidence, but a substantive rule of contract law." That starts you moving in what all will agree is the right direction. From there, the terrain is replete with pits, potholes, and perils. But heed our teaching, and, to the extent possible, you'll master the parol evidence rule free of the confusion that surrounds it (maybe).

> **QUESTION 1.** The parol evidence rule is:
>
> **I.** a rule of evidence.
> **II.** a substantive rule of contract law.
> **III.** clear and well understood throughout the states and enjoys consistent and coherent interpretation and understanding.
> **A.** II
> **B.** I and II
> **C.** II and III
> **D.** I, II, III, and IV

ANALYSIS.   About the parol evidence rule you know this much:

(1) All authorities agree that it is a mass of confusion and inconsistency. That eliminates Item III, which eliminates options **C** and **D**. Item II makes a true statement, meaning that the answer is **A** or **B**, depending on whether Item I is true or false. Despite its name, the parol evidence rule is not a rule of evidence but a rule of contract law. I is false, II is true, so **A** is right.

B.   The Kind of Problem That the Rule Addresses

Suppose that in the presence of ten witnesses, two parties, on October 8, reach an oral agreement:

> **Abe:** I'll pay you $300 to set up my new computer and make it operate, together with all of its peripherals.
> **Betsy:** I'll do it for $400; I'll finish by Friday, three days from now; and I'll warranty my work for a year.
> **Abe:** It's a deal; let's put it in writing.

Betsy then creates this writing:

> In consideration of $400 to be paid to her by Abe Abrams, Betsy Best will set up Abe's newly purchased computer so that it operates properly, together with its peripherals, all such work to be completed by October 11 of this year.
>
> *This is our full and final agreement.*

Before signing, with ten witnesses still present and listening, the parties continue to talk:

> **Betsy:** So, shall we sign?
> **Abe:** The writing doesn't mention your one-year warranty.

Betsy: Don't worry. I'll shout it, now, before all ten of these folks: "I warrant that my work is good for one year."

Abe: Okay—so the warranty is absolutely a part of our agreement, right?

Betsy: Right.

The parties then sign the document. Betsy sets up the computer exactly as promised, and Abe pays her $400. One month later, the system goes down. Abe telephones Betsy asking that she honor her warranty and examine the system. Betsy responds:

Betsy: Our written contract provides for no warranty.

Abe: That's right, but you assured me that your work carried a one-year warranty.

Betsy: I worked hard enough for $400. I won't do any more.

Abe: Ten witnesses heard you make your one-year warranty a part of our agreement.

Betsy: We also have a signed, written contract in which we mention no such warranty, so I say you have no case.

Abe brings an action against Betsy alleging that she has failed to honor her warranty. Betsy's lawyer takes this position: Whether Betsy did or did not orally make the one-year warranty is irrelevant. After forming their oral contract, the parties created and adopted, with their signatures, a writing—and that writing mentions no warranty. By failing to include in the writing, the warranty term on which they orally agreed, they failed, legally, to include it in their contract. Even if Betsy did, orally, make the one-year warranty, the writing supersedes it.

Abe's lawyer takes this position: The parties' contract includes all terms on which they actually agreed. The writing is *evidence* of the terms on which they agreed, but it does not have the final say on that point. The true contract between these parties includes not only the terms of the writing but also another term—the one-year warranty. And if, as we are certain, our evidence is adequate to prove that Betsy promised the one-year warranty, then that promise is part of the contract.

We can't yet tell you who wins. We can only tell you that such is the kind of dispute to which the parol evidence rule is addressed. In more abstract terms, we can say that the parol evidence rule governs this question: *If* (1) as to some subject (such as the installation of a computer system), two parties first form an oral contract[2] and (2) then create a writing that purports to recite the contract's terms, but (3) fail to include in the writing some terms on which they did genuinely agree, *then* (a) is the contract, by law, limited to that which is

---

2. To make matters worse, the parol evidence rule as now commonly stated is relevant not only to an oral contract later reduced to writing, but also to a *written* agreement followed by a *later* writing on the same subject matter. See section H below.

in the writing, or (b) does it include also the terms on which the parties truly, provably agreed but failed to include in their writing?

Abe and Betsy's oral contract included Betsy's one-year warranty. Their writing failed to mention it. In Abe's and Betsy's case, therefore, the parol evidence rule will decide this question: Are Abe's contractual rights limited to the writing, in which case he has no one-year warranty, or do they include also the warranty on which the parties agreed but failed to record in their writing?

QUESTION 2. The parol evidence rule:

I. concerns the definition of signatures as to those contracts that are unenforceable unless set forth in writing.
II. concerns the enforceability of terms upon which two parties orally agree but then fail to include in a writing that purports to represent their contract.
III. is a substantive rule of evidence that concerns the relative probative values of signed and unsigned writings.

A. II only
B. I and II only
C. III only
D. II and III only

ANALYSIS.   About the parol evidence rule you now know *this* much:

(1) All authorities agree that it is a mass of confusion and inconsistency.

(2) Despite its name it is not a rule of evidence, but a substantive rule of contract law. That eliminates Item III. Further, the rule is in no way concerned with the difference in probative value between signed and unsigned writings, so Item III is false for that reason too.

(3) It concerns, generally, this question: When two parties form an oral contract and then purport to reduce it to writing, is their contract then limited to the terms *of* the writing or does it include, also, terms on which they orally agreed but failed to set forth in writing? That squares very nicely with Item II. That means the answer is either A or B, depending on whether Statement I is true or false.

And Statement I is — False.

Don't confuse the parol evidence rule with the Statute of Frauds. They're unrelated. The Statute of Frauds (Chapter 15) identifies those contracts that are unenforceable unless recorded in a writing "signed by the party to be charged." Because that doctrine turns, in part, on the word "signed," it concerns also the definition (for its own purposes) of "sign"/"signature." The parol evidence rule, although it does *relate* to writings, does not provide that any particular kind of contract must be in writing or that, if it is, it must be signed. Items I and III make false statements. Item II makes a true one, so **A** is right.

C. Before We *State* the Parol Evidence Rule, We Introduce the Word "Integration"

Before stating the parol evidence rule we introduce you to the terms "integration," "partial integration," and "total integration." Fundamentally the verb *integrate* means to take many and join them as one. In the realm of contract law the word refers to two parties who (1) form a contract orally or, perhaps, by creating several writings, all of which, together, embody their agreement, and (2) then finally settle on *one writing* (as is common) that they "intend" and "adopt"[3] as a *final* expression of their *contract.* An integration brings the parties' prior discussions, drafts, tentative agreements, oral promises, and understandings together in a single final writing that *appears* to recite what the parties finally understand as the terms of their agreement.

Integrations come in two flavors, "partial" and "total." Partial integration means a contractual writing that the parties "intend" as a final expression of their agreement regarding the terms it does recite, but not as a complete expression of *everything* on which they in fact agreed. "Total integration" means a contractual writing that the parties "intend" to be both (a) *final* as to all of the terms it recites and (b) *complete*, meaning they "intend" the writing to represent a full, final, exhaustive, and exclusive recitation of any and every term on which they agreed, so that nothing, but *nothing* else is a part of their contract. Finally, if the parties create a writing that they intend not to be final, even, as to those terms stated *in* the writing, then they create no integration at all.

> **QUESTIONS 3 & 4.** Shayna and Chris agree orally that Chris will act as supervisor and manager of Shayna's commercial ice skating rink, Monday through Friday from 9 A.M. to 5 P.M. Shayna is to pay Chris an annual salary of $150,000, in 12 monthly installments of $12,500 each, on the first day of each month. While negotiating, the parties exchange a number of notes and conduct a number of conversations. Ultimately they agree, orally and by handshake, to the terms described above, and to an additional 50 terms as well. Thereafter, in cursive, they sign their first names only to this short writing, labeled "Employment Contract":
>
> > The undersigned Shayna Signorelli ("Employer") and Chris Matus ("Employee") hereby agree, finally and unconditionally, that Employee will serve as Employer's general manager, on an ordinary full-time basis and that he will be paid for his service an amount satisfactory to him. Employee acknowledges that the skating rink operates from 8 A.M. to 10 P.M. seven days per week.

---

3. Although the conventional manner of "adopting" (assenting to) the terms of a writing is by signature, the parol evidence rule does not limit itself, per se, to signed writings It is possible for two parties to record their contract in writing and then, without signing it, manifest their mutual assent to its terms.

QUESTION 3. If a judge concludes that the writing is a partial integration and not a total integration, her reason will most likely be that

A. the writing names itself an "Employment Contract" and therefor must represent, in part, terms on which the parties have finally reached agreement.
B. the writing is dated and signed by both parties, each setting forth his or her cursive signature.
C. the writing specifies the number of days per week and hours during which the skating rink operates.
D. the parties intended the writing as a final statement as to some of what each party would do for the other, but they did not intend it fully to state all on which they had agreed.

ANALYSIS. The question tests only the superficial definition of "partial integration" as we describe it above. A partial integration (whatever its significance, to be discussed at section G below) refers to two parties who first form an oral contract and then reduce it to a writing, which in a judge's opinion, they "intended" as a final expression of those terms that do appear in the writing, but not as a complete expression of all terms on which they agreed. **D** very plainly and simply restates that definition, and that's why **D** is right.

QUESTION 4. If the judge were to conclude that the writing constitutes no integration at all, he would most likely do so because

A. the writing fails adequately to specify any commitment from either party to the other.
B. the parties did not intend the writing to be final even as to the terms it states.
C. each of the parties signed with a first name, but not a last name.
D. it does not refer to itself as an integration of the parties' agreement.

ANALYSIS. This question requires that you know the definition of "integration." An integration is a document that the parties "intend" as a final expression of their agreement as to the terms it sets forth. If in a judge's opinion the parties did not intend the writing to be final as to anything, then the writing is no integration at all. **B** restates that simple rule, and that's why **B** is right.

The "guts" of the parol evidence rule, and the confusion in which it bathes, lie in the meaning (or meaninglessness) of "partial" and "total" "integration." We address that unhappy subject in sections D, E, and F below. But, now, with what little we've told you about that topic let's, at least (and at last), *state* the parol evidence rule. Until we get to section H, we're going to omit two of the rule's words, and mark them with two blank lines.

D.   The Parol Evidence Rule — *Stated* (with Two Words Omitted)

(1) If contracting parties first form an oral _____ _____ contract and then create a writing that they adopt as a *partial* integration of their agreement, then —

(a) no term on which the parties orally agree, *prior* to or contemporaneous with their adoption of the writing, is enforceable if that term *contradicts* the terms of the writing, but

(b) any such terms as are *consistent* with the writing and, therefore, do no more than add to it, *are* enforceable.

(2) If contracting parties first form an oral _____ _____ contract and then create a writing that they adopt as a *total* integration of their agreement, then no term on which the parties agree, *prior* to or contemporaneous with their adoption of the writing, is enforceable whether it is or is not consistent with the writing; *the terms of the writing are the terms of the contract.*

Leaving aside, still, how we determine that a writing is an integration and, if it is, that it is a total or partial integration, let's illustrate the rule's operation when a court has already made that determination (however it does so).

Illustration 1: When the Court Has Determined That a Writing Is a *Partial* Integration.   Bart owns a white house that needs painting. He plans to be away on vacation for the month of October. On September 28, 2012, three days before his departure, in the presence of five witnesses (Al, Bob, Carol, Dave, and Ethel), Bart orally forms a contract with Andy under which (1) Andy, during the month of October, will paint Bart's house; and (2) Bart will pay Andy $2,000 in advance. They agree that Andy will paint the house in the color "robin's egg blue," shown as color #375, in the Bartholomew Mohr Paint catalog. The parties then sign this writing:

> The undersigned parties, Andy Anderson ("Andy") and Bart Bennett ("Bart"), agree that Andy will repaint Bart's house at 223 Amiel Avenue, Carson City, Nevada 15459. Andy will begin work on this next Monday, October 3, 2012, and will finish no later than October 31, 2012. In exchange, Bart will pay Andy $2,000, immediately upon the mutual execution of this writing. The parties acknowledge that Bart will be away from his home during the relevant four-week period.

Just after the parties sign, Bart pays Andy the $2,000. On October 1, he departs on vacation. Andy timely paints the house — *white*. Bart, on returning home, complains to Andy that he didn't use the robin's egg blue. Andy points out that the signed contract doesn't specify color. Bart counters, "Well, the writing doesn't mention color, but I know and you know that we agreed on the color robin's egg blue. Al, Bob, Carol, Dave, and Ethel know that too." Bart brings an action against Andy for breach of contract. At trial, Bart's lawyer calls Al as his first witness:

Bart's lawyer: Did you hear Plaintiff and Defendant make any kind of agreement on September 28, 2012?

Al: Yes, I did.

Bart's lawyer: On what subject did they agree?

Al: They agreed that while Bart was away, Andy would paint his house.

Bart's lawyer: Did you hear them agree on anything concerning the color of paint to be used?

Al: Ye . . .

Andy's lawyer: Objection, Your Honor.

Court (to Al): Don't answer yet, please.

Court (to Andy's lawyer): What's your objection?

Andy's lawyer: The parol evidence rule forbids plaintiff to introduce this testimony. The parties executed a writing, a copy of which has been admitted as Defendant's Exhibit 1, which Your Honor has before you. As Your Honor can see, the writing describes the parties' September 28 agreement as to the painting of plaintiff's house.

Court (interrupting): Remove the jury from the courtroom.

(Jury is removed.)

Court (to Andy's lawyer): Continue, please, Counselor.

Andy's lawyer: Thank you, Your Honor. As I was saying, and as you can see, these parties reduced their agreement to a writing, and that writing makes no mention of color — none. Furthermore, it shows itself to be final and complete. It is a total integration of their agreement. Pursuant to the parol evidence rule, any oral agreement these parties made prior to adopting the writing is ineffective and unenforceable. Consequently, the jury should not hear any of plaintiff's evidence intended to show that the parties agreed, orally, on any particular color. Hence the Court should not permit his attorney to ask any witness whether or on what the parties agreed orally. The terms of the writing are the terms of the contract.

Court (to Bart's lawyer): What is your response, Counselor?

Bart's lawyer: We expect this witness to explain that the parties agreed before adopting their writing that Defendant should paint Plaintiff's house in a particular color — other than the color in which he actually painted it. And it is our position, Your Honor, that the parties' writing is by no means a total integration of the parties' agreement. It is only a partial integration, which the parties did intend as a final expression of the terms it states, but not as a *complete* expression of all terms on which they agreed. Because the writing is a partial integration of the parties' agreement, Plaintiff has the right to prove, if he can, that before adopting the writing the parties agreed, orally, on a term that is consistent *with* the writing. Since the writing says nothing about color, an agreement as to color is consistent with the writing; it does not contradict or conflict with any of the writing's terms; it merely adds to them. Consequently, the Court should admit Plaintiff's evidence intended to show that the parties did, orally, agree on a color other than the one in which Defendant painted it.

Court: To resolve this dispute, I must apply the parol evidence rule. If the parties intended this writing as a total integration of their agreement, then the terms of the writing are the terms of the contract. I can admit no evidence as to any terms on which the parties orally agreed before they adopted the writing. On the other hand, if these parties intended the writing as a partial integration of their agreement, then I may admit evidence of terms on which the parties agreed orally before they adopted the writing, so long as those terms have the effect of adding to the writing's terms without contradicting them.

I have examined the writing and I find that the parties intended it to be final as to the terms it states, but that they did not intend it as a complete expression of all terms on which they agreed. I find, therefore, that the writing constitutes only a *partial* integration of their agreement. The writing makes no mention of color. Consequently, if these parties did reach an agreement, orally, as to color, that agreement would not conflict with or contradict the writing's terms. Rather it would add to them. Consequently, I rule that Plaintiff may present witnesses who will testify that the parties orally agreed as to the color in which Defendant should paint Plaintiff's house. If the jury finds that the parties did indeed make such an oral agreement, then it is part of the parties' contract. Let the jury return.

(Jury returns.)

Court: The court reporter will read back the last question and the witness will answer.

Reporter: Did you hear them agree on anything concerning the color of paint to be used?

Al: Yes, they agreed on the color.

Bart's lawyer: Do you remember on what color they agreed?

Al: Oh, yes, Bart was insistent on it and Andy absolutely agreed—the house was to be painted in a Bartholomew Mohr paint called robin's egg blue. They said that and then they shook hands, again, and then they signed a piece of paper.

Illustration 2: Partial Integration With a Change in the Story. Suppose now that after reaching their oral agreement, including their understanding as to the color robin's egg blue, Bart and Andy date and sign *this* writing, which (for whatever reason) expressly refers to the color white:

The undersigned parties, Andy Anderson ("Andy") and Bart Bennett ("Bart"), agree that Andy will repaint Bart's house at 223 Amiel Avenue, Carson City, Nevada 15459. Andy will paint the house white. He will work on this next Monday, October 3, 2012, and will finish no later than October 31, 2012. In exchange, Bart will pay Andy $2,000, immediately upon the mutual execution of this writing. The parties acknowledge that Bart will be away from his home during the relevant four-week period.

Imagine, again, that the parties go to trial and that Bart wants to present his evidence—five witnesses plus his own testimony to prove that notwithstanding the writing, the parties definitely agreed on the color robin's egg blue. And imagine too that the court rules this writing a *partial* integration.

A prior oral agreement that Andy should paint the house blue and not white would certainly contradict the writing. "Blue" is not consistent with "white." Hence, under the parol evidence rule, such a prior agreement—even if the parties really did reach it—is ineffective; it's not a part of their contract. Consequently, the court does not allow Bart even a chance to prove that the parties agreed on such a term. For even if they did, it's not a part of the contract. The court rules Al's testimony inadmissible; the jury is not to hear this irrelevancy.

Illustration 3: When the Court Has Determined That the Writing Is a *Total* Integration.   Suppose now that in front of five witnesses, Deborah and Elena agree orally that while Deborah is away on vacation, Elena will paint her house Nevada white. The parties agree also that Elena will sand and finish the wood on Deborah's front door. They shake hands and shortly thereafter, Elena presents Deborah with this writing, labeled "Contract":

WHEREAS Elena Pagonis ("Elena") warrants that she has all professional skills, knowledge, and expertise germane and necessary to the performances hereinafter assigned and allocated to her; and

WHEREAS Deborah Durbin ("Deborah") wishes, for a price, to avail herself of such skill, knowledge, and expertise,

NOW, THEN, the parties do agree that Elena will repaint Deborah's house at 447 Chance Avenue, Reno, Nevada 15388, pursuant to the following terms and conditions:

(1) Elena will paint the house using Bartholomew Mohr paint color #287, "Nevada white."

(2) If Elena is unable, through no fault of her own, to obtain the kind and color of paint hereinbefore described, then she shall, pursuant to professional judgment, use a paint of substantially similar color and quality, such professional judgment to conform to standards of the relevant profession.

(3) Elena will supply her own equipment, including but not limited to ladders, paint brushes, rollers, pans, rags, tapes, covers, and shields.

(4) Elena will purchase the paint as necessary and all other chemical products including, but not limited to thinners and brush cleaners, and for these expenses Deborah will reimburse her on completion of her performance as hereinbefore and hereinafter described and specified.

(5) As between themselves, Elena is serving not as Deborah's employee, but as an independent contractor, wherefore Deborah's duties and liabilities to Elena or to third persons are governed by that relationship except to the extent that applicable law provides otherwise meaning, *inter alia,* that as to any attempt by any third person or persons, to hold Deborah liable for any alleged damage arising as a result of or in direct relation to Elena's acts or omissions as pertinent hereto, Elena will indemnify Deborah and hold her harmless.

(6) Elena will begin work on or after this next Monday, October 3, 2012, and will finish no later than Monday, October 31, 2012.

(7) The parties acknowledge that Deborah will be away from her home during the relevant four-week period.

(8) In exchange for all that Elena does as hereinbefore prescribed and described, Deborah will pay Elena $2,000, immediately upon the mutual execution of this writing.

(9) Should Elena fail to complete the work/performance as hereinbefore agreed, prescribed, and described then, except to the extent that any such failure shall be due to the fault of Deborah, Elena will repay to Deborah $100 for each day of delay.

(10) The contract represented hereby shall, should the occasion arise, be construed and enforced according to the laws of Nevada.

TO THE FOREGOING terms and conditions the parties do commit themselves and, therefore, to this writing they do set their signatures on the date(s) of:

_____   _____

September 28, 2012   September 28, 2012

After Deborah examines the writing, she says to Elena, "The writing doesn't state that you'll sand and finish the wood on the front door." "Oh, I see you're right," replies Elena. "Well, I'm certainly going to do that. We've agreed to it, and of course I'll do it." Deborah is reassured, and both parties sign the writing.

Deborah returns from vacation to find a freshly painted Nevada white house and an untouched front door. Deborah contacts Elena to complain that she did not sand and finish the wood on the front door. Elena denies that she had any obligation to do so because, she says, "the written contract makes no mention of it." A lawsuit follows, and there arises once again the question of whether Deborah's lawyer may attempt to prove, with the testimony of five witnesses and that of Deborah as well, that Elena promised to sand and finish the wood, even though the writing features no term to that effect.

> **Deborah's lawyer:** Your Honor, we seek to prove that these parties orally agreed to a term that is perfectly consistent with the writing, for nothing in the writing contradicts a term by which Defendant is obliged, in addition to painting the house, to sand and finish the wood on its front door.
>
> **Elena's lawyer:** That may be true, Your Honor, but we believe that the writing is a total integration. Consequently any term to which the parties orally agreed but failed to include in the writing is not a part of

their contract, whether it does or does not contradict the terms of the writing. The terms of the writing *are* the terms of the contract.

Court: Defendant's lawyer correctly states the parol evidence rule, and plaintiff's lawyer has no quarrel with him on that point. The rule provides that if two parties first form an oral contract and then reduce it to a writing that they intend to be final as to the terms it states and, furthermore, a complete expression of all terms on which they agreed, then they have created a total integration of their agreement. In that situation, no term to which the parties agreed, orally, before adopting the writing is a part of their contract, unless the parties include it *in* the writing.

Having examined this elaborate writing, replete with terms that address a variety of contingencies and possibilities, I conclude that these parties intended it as a final expression of all terms it states and, furthermore, a complete expression of all terms on which they agreed. They intended that it be a final and complete expression of their agreement. The writing is, therefore, a total integration. Consequently, no term on which these parties agreed belongs to their contract unless it appears in the writing. This writing makes no mention of sanding or refinishing of any wood, wherefore no such term is part of this contract, even if the parties really did agree to it. The jury is to hear no evidence that the parties made any such agreement, meaning that Plaintiff may present no such evidence.

This judge concluded that these parties reduced their oral agreement to a total integration. Consequently, the terms of the writing *are* the terms of the contract. Elena's oral promise to sand and finish the wood is unenforceable, no matter how many witnesses stand ready to testify that Elena truly made that promise, no matter that the term is consistent with the writing or no matter than Elena herself might stand ready to acknowledge, on the witness stand, her promise to sand and finish the wood. A total integration wipes out any term to which the parties orally agreed and then failed to include in the writing.

E.   The Major Confusion: Deciding That a Writing Is an Integration, Total or Partial

In the first house painting case, the judge ruled Bart and Andy's writing a partial integration. Yet he did not explain how he reached his ruling, except to say, "I have examined the writing." In the second case, he gave no reason as to why he ruled Deborah and Elena's writing a total integration, except to say, "Having examined this elaborate writing, replete with terms that address a variety of contingencies and possibilities, I conclude that these parties intended it as a final expression of all terms it states and, furthermore, a complete expression of all terms on which they agreed." Like many others who have applied the parol evidence rule, the judge took his ruling from the "gut"—for there is, in the law, no trace, even, of a settled, workable rule as to how a court should determine that two parties did or did not "intend" their contractual writing as an integration or, if they did, that they intended it as a partial or total one.

What Authorities *Say* on the Subject. It's commonly *said* that on this matter the law features two opposing views. Before describing them, we advise you that probably no jurisdiction ever has adopted either one. Rather, the way in which courts make the determinations just described usually falls on a line that extends between the two—or, just as frequently perhaps, on a line that begins and ends nowhere, having nothing to do with either such view. Moreover, the "view" that any court purports to take in explaining a decision on this point usually lacks any logical connection to the ruling it ultimately issues.

1. The "Four Corners" or "Williston" View

Professor Samuel Williston (1861-1963) is rightly regarded as one of America's two greatest expositors of contract law. With respect to the parol evidence rule, lawyers, judges and teachers often speak of a "Williston view," which, as they commonly characterize it, certainly was not Professor Williston's view. According to this so-called Williston view (also called the "four corners" view), a judge determines whether a given writing constitutes no integration or a partial or total integration by examining the writing itself and nothing more. That is, a judge confines herself to the "four corners of the document." She is first to ask herself this question: does the writing show finality as to any term at all? If her answer is "no," then the writing is not an integration at all. The parol evidence rule does not apply, wherefore the terms of the parties' contract are those to which they manifested their mutual assent (through offer and acceptance), by whatever mode they did so, including, of course, spoken word. If her answer is yes" — the writing does show finality as to at least one of its terms — then it is an integration, either partial or total. In that case, the judge asks herself this second question: is the writing "complete on its face?" Does it show finality as to all that is necessary to a contract for the kind of performances it describes? If her answer is "no," then the writing is a partial integration. If her answer is "yes," the writing is a total integration.

According to the Williston view, therefore, the whole of the determination is made by examination of the writing itself; the court hears no extrinsic evidence (evidence outside the writing) as to whether and to what extent the parties "intended" the writing as an integration.

Illustrating the Williston View I. Think again of Elena, Deborah, the house painting, and the front door. Imagine this time that the parties date and sign this writing:

> The undersigned parties agree that Elena will perform service as to the house, as agreed, Elena to begin and finish as agreed. In exchange, Deborah will give consideration as agreed.

The words of this writing are insufficient to show agreement as to *anything.* In terms of the Williston view, it shows finality as to nothing. Consequently, it is not an integration at all, and the parol evidence rule does not apply. Should these parties fall into dispute and litigation, the Williston view will require that the court permit either one to introduce evidence of any kind to show that the parties did or did not form a contract and what, if any, were its terms.

Illustrating the Williston View II.   Imagine now that Deborah and Elena, having had their same conversation, date and sign *this* writing:

> The undersigned parties, Elena Pagonis ("Elena") and Deborah Durbin ("Deborah"), agree that Elena will paint Deborah's house at 447 Chance Avenue, Reno, Nevada 15388, color as agreed. Elena will begin work on this next Monday, October 3, 2012, and will finish no later than Monday, October 31, 2012. In exchange, Deborah will pay Elena immediately upon the mutual execution of this writing. The parties acknowledge that Deborah will be away from her home during the relevant four-week period.

This writing shows finality as to some matters, but not as to others. The phrase "color as agreed" makes plain that the writing is not final as to color. The writing's failure to specify Elena's fee means that it's not final as to that matter either. Yet the writing shows finality as to the fact that Elena *will* paint Deborah's house and the dates on which she will start and finish her work. Hence it shows some finality and, according to the Williston view, it's a partial integration. Either party may introduce evidence of an oral agreement as to any term, earlier adopted, that does *not contradict* the writing.

Illustrating the Williston View III.   Let's now look at the long writing Elena and Deborah adopted when first we met them. Before going further, reread their written contract from Illustration 3.

Under the Williston view, this writing is, certainly, "complete on its face," meaning that one who examines it objectively sees in it all terms that a house painting contract ought to have (and more). Reading this writing, two reasonable parties would have no question about what each is to do. Hence, under the Williston view, the writing is a total integration, and its terms *are* the terms of the contract. Neither party may seek to prove that the contract includes anything more or anything different.

Consider, for example, Item 6: "Elena will begin work on or after this next Monday, October 3, 2012, and will finish no later than Monday, October 31, 2012." Suppose Elena truthfully asserts that just prior to signing the writing, before 1,000 witnesses, the parties agreed that she would have until November 30 if the average low temperature for the days October 1 through October 31 fell below 40° F. Suppose further that Deborah is prepared to admit to that agreement.

Nonetheless, that term is not part of the parties' contract. Why not? Because it's not in the writing, and when the writing is a total integration, the writing is the contract — period.

2. The "Corbin" View

We said that Williston was one of America's two greatest expositors of contract law. Professor Arthur Corbin (1874-1967) was the other. According to the so-called Corbin view of the parol evidence rule, a court cannot decide that two parties "intended" a writing as an integration, partial or total, without examining all facts and circumstances in place when they adopted it, including the facts of whether, before adopting it, they had made any other agreements on the same subject. As is so throughout contract law, "intent," according to this view, should refer to what each party led the other reasonably to understand. Stated otherwise, the Corbin view considers that no writing can prove itself to be anything at all but ink on paper. In a disputed case, the writing is one item of admissible evidence as to what the parties, under all circumstances, should have understood to be the terms of their agreement. Admissible also, however, is any and all evidence, including the parties' conversations, statements, and agreements, as to what significance the writing should have.[4] The Corbin view thus *eliminates* the parol evidence rule. Should a court adopt the Corbin view of the parol evidence rule, it would, in fact, abolish the rule, and that is what Professor Corbin truly believed should happen.[5]

Consider the second house painting case in which the parties orally agreed that Andy should paint Bart's house blue, after which the parties signed a writing that specified the color white. In determining that the parties' writing was an integration, partial or total, Professor Corbin would admit evidence of all circumstances surrounding the parties when they adopted it, *including any statements they made to each other*. For this purpose — the purpose of establishing the parties' "intent" as to the writing — Corbin would have the court admit evidence of Andy's promise to paint the house blue. On that basis, it would decide that the parties did not *intend* the writing even as a partial integration of their agreement, since the writing was at odds with that on which they had truly agreed.

Consider, now the third house painting case, in which Deborah complains that Elena failed to refinish her front door. If the court had followed the Corbin view, then before finally characterizing the writing, it would have admitted evidence of all circumstances surrounding the parties when they adopted it, *including Elena's promise to sand and refinish the front door*. Since that testimony (if believed) shows that the parties omitted a term on which they had agreed, the court would rule the writing not to be a total integration. The

---

4. We have just purported to summarize, in a few sentences, Professor Corbin's views on the parol evidence rule. Know, please, that he himself wrote hundreds of pages in order to do so. *See generally* 3 *Corbin on Contracts* §§573-596 (2d ed. 1960).

5. As Professor Corbin wrote: "It would be better if no such rule ever had been stated[.]" Arthur L. Corbin, *The Parol Evidence Rule*, 53 Yale L.J. 603, 631-632 (1944).

Corbin view thus renders it impossible for any "parol evidence rule" to exclude evidence of agreements that parties make prior to adoption of a writing.

The Corbin View Predominates Today, or So They Say . . . It is said that modern law leans toward the Corbin view — toward admitting "extrinsic evidence" (evidence outside the writing). The Restatement (Second) of Contracts illustrates the point. It devotes ten sections to the parol evidence rule (§§209 through 218), each accompanied by comments and illustrations. Not one of its illustrations draws a conclusion that a given writing is or is not an integration, partial or complete. And although its writers obviously *purport* to recognize the parol evidence rule, the net effect of their rules, comments, and illustrations, if scrupulously studied, is probably to abolish it. Certainly — *certainly* — the Restatement abolishes the existence of a total integration, although once again the writers do not acknowledge that truth.

Restatement (Second) §213 first states the parol evidence rule in conventional terms:

> (1) A binding [partially] integrated agreement discharges prior agreements to the extent that it is inconsistent with them.
> (2) A binding completely integrated agreement discharges prior agreements to the extent that they are within its scope. . . .

Subsection 2 means, then, that a total integration ("binding completely integrated agreement") supersedes ("discharges") any prior agreement on the same subject matter ("within its scope").

Comment b then provides:

> To apply this rule, the court must make preliminary determinations that there is an integrated agreement and that it is inconsistent with the term in question. Those determinations are made in accordance with all relevant evidence, and require interpretation both of the integrated agreement and of the prior agreement. The existence of the prior agreement may be a circumstance that sheds light on the meaning of the integrated agreement, but the integrated agreement must be given a meaning to which its language is reasonably susceptible when read in the light of all the circumstances.

Restatement (Second) Contracts §214 provides:

> Agreements and negotiations prior to or contemporaneous with the adoption of a writing are admissible in evidence to establish
>
> > (a) that the writing is or is not an integrated agreement;
> > (b) that the integrated agreement, if any, is completely or partially integrated. . . .

Comment a reads thus:

> *Integrated agreement and completely integrated agreement*: Whether a writing has been adopted as an integrated agreement and, if so, whether the agreement is completely or partially integrated are questions determined by the

court preliminary to determination of a question of interpretation or to application of the parol evidence rule. . . . Writings do not prove themselves; ordinarily, if there is dispute, there must be testimony that there was a signature or other manifestation of assent. The- preliminary determination is made in accordance with all relevant evidence, including the circumstances in which the writing was made or adopted. It may require preliminary interpretation of the writing; the court must then consider the evidence which is relevant to the question of interpretation.

Restatement (Second) §210 provides:

(1) A completely integrated agreement is an integrated agreement adopted by the parties as a complete and exclusive statement of the terms of the agreement.
(2) A partially integrated agreement is an integrated agreement other than a completely integrated agreement.

Comment b then reads thus:

That a writing was or was not adopted as a completely integrated agreement may be proved by any relevant evidence. A document in the form of a written contract, signed by both parties and apparently complete on its face, may be decisive of the issue in the absence of credible contrary evidence. But a writing cannot of itself prove its own completeness, and wide latitude must be allowed for inquiry into circumstances bearing on the intention of the parties.

Taken together, the Restatement's material on the parol evidence rule is shot through with ambiguity, evasion, and inconsistency. The restatement writers leave the parol evidence rule just as they found it: a morass of circular statements that lead—nowhere. And notwithstanding the elaborate pretense to an exacting scholarly analysis, these ten sections of the restatement—if they do anything at all—abolish the parol evidence rule altogether.

F. The Merger Clause

Within a contractual writing, a "merger clause" is a provision, whatever its words, that characterizes the writing itself *as* a total integration. Each of the following three provisions constitutes a merger clause (whether or not it is *entitled* "merger clause"):

Merger. This writing represents the entirety of the parties' agreement, and it supersedes any and all prior agreements the parties may have reached on this same subject matter.
Entire Agreement. The parties hereby agree that this writing represents a merger of all to which they may have agreed or considered on this subject matter, and that it therefore represents a full and final integration of their agreement.
Total Integration. This document fully, finally, and totally integrates the parties' understandings and agreement as to its subject matter, wherefore no prior agreements or understandings on such subject matter is or are operative.

1. The Effect of Merger Clauses According to the Williston View

According to the Williston view, a writing that is not "obviously incomplete" *and* sets forth a merger clause is a total integration. Those who thus describe the "Williston view" give no definition of "obviously incomplete." Let's suppose that the phrase means a writing that "shows finality as to nothing"—the same writing that constitutes no integration at all. We might then come to this conclusion: According to the Williston view, a contractual writing that is otherwise a partial integration becomes a total integration if it features a merger clause. With that in mind, let's add a merger clause to the signed writing we earlier called a partial integration under the Williston view:

> **Agreement:** The undersigned parties, Elena Pagonis ("Elena") and Deborah Durbin ("Deborah"), agree that Elena will paint Deborah's house at 447 Chance Avenue, Reno, Nevada 15388, color as agreed. Elena will begin work on this next Monday, October 3, 2012, and will finish no later than Monday, October 31, 2012. In exchange, Deborah will pay Elena, as agreed, immediately upon the mutual execution of this writing. The parties acknowledge that Deborah will be away from her home during the relevant one-month period.
>
> **Merger/Entire Agreement:** The parties agree that this writing represents a full, final, and total integration of their agreement on this subject matter and that no prior terms or agreements bearing on the same are relevant hereto or binding on either of them.

Maybe the Williston view means to say that this writing, otherwise a partial integration, is, with its merger clause, a *total* integration. But—if it's a total integration, meaning that the writing *is* the contract, it leaves us with these two questions: (1) How shall a court identify the color in which Elena is to paint the house? (2) How shall it determine what fee Deborah is to pay her? The answer to both questions is, plainly: It can't. Hence, with respect to the so-called Williston view (not Professor Williston's view), the significance of a merger clause remains a mystery.

2. The Effect of Merger Clauses According to the Corbin View and the Restatement

The Corbin view gives merger clauses no significance at all. Under the Corbin view, no writing, however long and elaborate, can, on its own, "decide" that it is a complete expression of the parties' agreement. That view carries a good deal of logical appeal. All will agree that a signed paper, blank in all respects except for a merger clause, cannot constitute a "complete and final expression" of anyone's agreement about anything.

Likewise, the Restatement gives merger clauses no significance at all. We know that because it makes not even a mention of merger clause.

G.   The Parol Evidence Rule in Real Legal Life

In real life, as noted at the beginning of this chapter, there is no agreement on how a court should determine whether a given writing is an integration and, if it is, whether the parties "intended" it as a partial or total integration. Courts write of the Williston and Corbin views, but none adheres to either with any consistency. No *court could* possibly do so. For the Corbin view amounts to a negation of the rule. The so-called Williston view (which was *not* Williston's view) is devoid of logic and wholly unworkable. In parol evidence cases today, some courts, on some days, make their judgments on this critical question by looking exclusively to the writings themselves. Others claim to look only to the writings, but then in fact consider exogenous circumstances as well. There is, still, no true parol evidence rule on which the jurisdictions agree. As Professor Farnsworth writes, "Surprisingly little light is shed on the problem by the hundreds of decisions resolving the issue of whether an agreement is completely integrated. Opinions often fail to set out the text of the writing in full, and each case turns on its own peculiar facts." E. Allan Farnsworth, *Contracts* 435 (3d ed. 1999). And, as discussed above, the Restatement writers purport to recognize and state the parol evidence rule, but unwittingly abolish it.

As for the merger clause, a court that finds a writing to be a total integration will cite to a merger clause, if there be one, as additional support for its conclusion. But that same court, it appears, would call that same writing a total integration without the merger clause. Substantially every contractual writing formally drafted by an attorney does feature a merger clause. And in practical terms, if a court is faced with two credible arguments as to whether a writing is a partial or total integration, the merger clause will usually cinch the case for the party who argues that it is a total one.

Illustration: Effect of a Merger Clause.   Let's create another dated and signed writing for Elena and Deborah:

> The undersigned parties, Elena Pagonis ("Elena") and Deborah Durbin ("Deborah"), agree that
>
> (1) Elena will repaint Deborah's house at 447 Chance Avenue, Reno, Nevada 15388. Elena will begin work on this next Monday, October 3, 2012, and will finish no later than Monday, October 31, 2012.
>
> (2) The front door is to be refinished, also as agreed.
>
> (3) In exchange, Deborah will pay Elena $2,000 immediately upon the mutual execution of this writing. The parties acknowledge that Deborah will be away from her home during the relevant four-week period.
>
> (4) This writing constitutes the full and final expression of the parties' agreement as to this subject matter.

For a court inclined toward the Williston/four corners rule (as most courts claim to be), items 1, 2, and 3 leave room for debate as to whether the writing is (a) complete on its face and, therefore, a total integration, or (b) final only as to some matters and, therefore, a partial integration.

Item 1 does not expressly mention color. On that basis one might argue that it is complete as to the facts that Deborah must paint the house, but incomplete as to color. On the other hand, the writing provides that Deborah will *re*paint the house, which one might take to mean "paint in the same color as now shows itself on the house."

Consider item 2: "The front door is to be refinished, also as agreed." That provision, one might argue, renders the writing incomplete as to what Elena must do with the front door. One might, on the other hand, argue that the provision means only that the front door is to be repainted along with the rest of the house.

Faced with two plausible arguments as to the writing's status—partial or total integration—the judge must, of course, make a decision. To the extent that the judge limits his examination to the "four corners of the document," the merger clause adds weight to a finding that the writing is complete on its face. Where, in the court's mind, the question of total versus partial integration is arguable, the merger clause gives it a reason to decide that it is a total integration.

QUESTIONS 5 & 6. Aiden planned to produce a film called *The Whole Nine Days*. He wanted Madison to serve as director. The two conducted highly detailed discussions about

- the duties each would perform,
- the way in which each would perform, and
- that which would occur in the case of a great many contingencies and conditions.

Among the hundreds of terms on which they orally agreed, were these:

(1) Aiden would produce the film and Madison would serve as director.

(2) Madison would take custody of all moneys the film earned each year, and distribute them once on July 31 and again on December 31.

(3) Profits would be divided equally except for the first year, when they would be divided 60 percent to Aiden, 40 percent to Madison.

Finally, after weeks of discussions and after reaching, orally and by handshake, all of the agreements mentioned above, the parties conversed thus:

Madison: We've agreed on hundreds of details. Shall we put the whole thing in writing?

Aiden: Yes, eventually we should, but that will require lawyers and lots of time. Why don't we put in writing, for now, a general statement of our agreement and, specifically, our agreement as to division of profits? Once we've done that, we'll get going on the project and, as we do, we'll have our lawyers hammer out a writing in full.

Madison: Okay, let's do that.

The parties then created, dated, and signed this writing, enitled "Memorandum of Agreement":

> This writing concerns the creation of a film to be entitled *The Whole Nine Days* for which Aiden Anderson will be Producer and Madison Maise director. The parties will divide — 50 percent to each of them, always — any profits that the film earns, Madison Maise to receive, hold, and take custody of all moneys derived from the film until such time as they are so divided.

Notwithstanding their stated plans, the parties never did create another writing. They made the film, and, in 2012, it began to deliver profits. Madison took custody of all moneys and deposited them in a bank account. On December 28, 2012, he advised Aiden that he would in three days, divide the monies, 50 percent to each of them. Aiden spoke up: "If you'll remember, just prior to signing the writing we agreed that we would divide the first year's profits 60 percent to me and 40 percent to you, because the whole film was my idea." Madison replied, "I remember that, but our writing provides for a 50/50 split and says nothing about the 60/40 division for the first year." Madison distributed the profits 50/50. Aiden now sues Madison, demanding an additional 10 percent.

At trial, Aiden offers to testify to the conversation that he and Madison held just before signing the agreement. Further, he is prepared to produce three witnesses, all of whom are also prepared to testify that Madison and Aiden did indeed agree that they would divide the first year profits 60 percent to Aiden and 40 percent to Madison. Madison objects to all such testimony on the basis that the parties' writing clearly called for a 50 percent distribution of earnings to each party.

QUESTION 5. If the court adopts the Restatement's view of the parol evidence rule, it will most likely

A. exclude the evidence Aiden offers, because in the case of a partial integration, the terms of the writing are the terms of the contract.
B. exclude the evidence Aiden offers, because it would contradict the terms of the writing.
C. admit the evidence Aiden offers, because in the case of a partial integration, Aiden is allowed to testify to the prior oral agreement.
D. admit the evidence Aiden offers to determine the parties' intentions as to the significance of the writing.

ANALYSIS. Restatement (Second) §214 provides that "[a]greements and negotiations prior to or contemporaneous with the adoption of a writing are admissible in evidence to establish (a) that the writing is or is not an integrated agreement; (b) that the integrated agreement, if any, is completely or partially integrated." Consequently, this court will admit evidence of the parties' oral agreement for that purpose.

A and **C** are wrong because they expressly presuppose a decision as to the very question the court must answer — whether the writing is a partial or total integration. Further, **A** makes the false statement that the terms of a partial integration are the terms of the contract. The Restatement purports to subscribe to the conventional view that terms of a *total* integration are the terms of the contract: "a binding completely integrated agreement [total integration] discharges [supersedes] prior agreements to the extent they are within its scope [on the same subject matter]." **C** incorrectly states the rule. In the case of a partial integration, a court will not hear evidence of a prior agreement that contradicts the writing. **B** too jumps the gun because it implicitly presupposes that the writing is a total integration and that, once again, reflects the very question the court must answer.

D conforms to the Restatement's provisions on the parol evidence rule. It tells us that the court will admit the evidence of the prior agreement to answer the question of whether the writing is a total or partial integration. (Once having done so, the court will then, it seems, be forced to conclude that the writing is at most a partial integration since it omits a consistent additional terms on which the parties did actually agree.) For that reason, **D** is right (maybe).

QUESTION 6. If the court adopts the Williston view of the parol evidence rule, it will most likely

A. exclude the evidence Aiden offers, because in the case of a partial integration, the terms of the writing are the terms of the contract.
B. exclude the evidence Aiden offers, because it would contradict the terms of the writing.
C. admit the evidence Aiden offers, because in the case of a partial integration, Aiden is allowed to testify to the prior oral agreement.
D. admit the evidence Aiden offers to determine the parties' intentions as to the significance of the writing.

ANALYSIS. The Williston view provides that in ruling a contractual writing to be a partial or total integration (or no integration at all), a court is to restrict itself to the "four corners of the document." Consequently, this court will not, for this purpose, admit evidence of the prior agreement. **D**, this time, is wrong. The court must conclude that this writing is final as to some of its terms, so it must conclude that the writing is either a partial or total integration. And, in either case, it will then exclude the evidence Aiden offers, because the prior oral agreement does, indeed, contradict the terms of the writing. A division of 60/40 for one year is inconsistent with what the writing provides—a division of 50/50 "always." **B** reflects that reasoning, so **B** is right.

H. "Confusion Now Hath Made His Masterpiece":[6] The Two Missing Words

Throughout this chapter we have dealt with the parol evidence rule in terms of two parties who first form an *oral* agreement and then, as to the same subject matter, create and adopt a writing. Cases that call forth the parol evidence rule do usually involve that situation. (The word "parol" means "by the mouth" or "by the spoken word.")

Nonetheless, all authorities (purport to) agree that the parol evidence rule applies to prior *written* agreements as well as it does to prior oral agreements. Hence, a full statement of the rule requires that we account for that notion:

> **The Parol Evidence Rule *In Full***
>
> (1) If contracting parties first form a contract and then reduce it to a writing that the parties intend as a partial integration of their agreement, then the writing cannot be contradicted by evidence of any prior agreement, written or oral, or any contemporaneous oral agreement, but it may be supplemented by evidence of consistent additional terms on which the parties earlier agreed.
>
> (2) If the parties intend the writing as a total integration of their agreement, then the writing cannot be varied by evidence of a prior agreement, written or oral, or any contemporaneous oral agreement.

In terms of its application to written agreements, the rule probably means no more than what is otherwise true: A later agreement supersedes an earlier one. Furthermore, despite the rule's broad statement, purportedly excluding evidence of prior written agreements, it cannot be true and *is* not true (except pursuant to UCC §2-209; see Chapter 14, section B) that a later written agreement supersedes an earlier one if the later one fails to exact consideration from both its parties. If,

> (1) by writing, A and B agree that A will perform a service for B in exchange for $1,000, and then
>
> (2) by subsequent writing agree that the fee will be $800, the subsequent writing cannot supersede the earlier one, for it represents a modification in which A gives no consideration.

---

6. William Shakespeare, *Macbeth*, act 2, sc. 3.

Recognizing those truths, the notion that the parol evidence rule applies not only to prior and contemporaneous oral agreements but also to prior *written* agreements is of very dubious significance.

I.   Important Qualifications

1. Collateral Agreements

Suppose Buyer and Seller (1) first agree orally on the sale of a violin for $1,500; (2) then, at the same meeting, agree on the sale of a dog located 100 miles away for $200; and (3) then reduce to writing, finally and completely, their agreement as to the violin but not the one concerning the dog. All authorities agree that even in the face of a total integration, a prior agreement (oral or written) that is truly separate from the one to which the writing applies is enforceable as an oral contract that stands in its own right, apart from the one reduced to writing.

Restatement (Second) §212(2) sets forth that same precept:

> A binding completely integrated agreement discharges prior agreements to the extent that they are within its scope.

That sentence means "A total integration supersedes prior agreements to the extent that they address the same substance and subject matter." Hence the law recognizes, notwithstanding the parol evidence rule, that two parties might at the same meeting form two separate contracts and then reduce to writing only one of them. The second, it is then said, is "collateral" to—meaning *separate from*—the first. The parol evidence rule does not affect the collateral agreement; that agreement stands independent of the other. That it fails to appear in the writing is insignificant.

In order that an agreement qualify, in this regard, as collateral it must, of course, show a separate consideration and, in the court's opinion, bear on a separate subject matter. Any court would agree that Buyer and Seller above formed two *separate* agreements because the matter of dog and violin are so plainly distinct. The agreement concerning the dog is collateral to that which concerns the violin. It stands on its own as an enforceable oral contract.

> **QUESTION 7.** Isaac and Renee agree orally that Isaac will build a garage on Renee's land in exchange for $40,000. Renee then adds, "Would you be willing also to construct a cement walkway leading from my house to the driveway?" Isaac replies, "Yes. That will cost you an additional $5,000." Renee agrees. The parties then create and sign a writing that describes their agreement as to the building of a garage. It is long, elaborate, and exhaustively detailed, complete with a merger clause. It

provides that Renee will pay Isaac a total of $40,000 and makes no mention of a walkway.

Isaac builds the garage, whereupon Renee pays him $40,000. She then asks him to begin work on the walkway. He refuses. Renee brings suit, and the court determines that the writing is a total integration. If the court nonetheless hears evidence of the agreement relating to the walkway, it will most likely be because

I. in its opinion, the building of a walkway and garage represent different and distinct undertakings.
II. the parties agreed that the building of the walkway would occasion additional payment.

A. I
B. II
C. I and II
D. Neither I nor II

ANALYSIS. With respect to the parol evidence rule, an agreement qualifies as collateral if it shows, in the court's mind, a separate consideration and a separate subject matter. Unlike the matter of violin and dog, this story creates a close case. When the parties agreed on the building of the walkway, they also agreed that Renee would pay Isaac $5,000 beyond the $40,000 she was to pay for the garage. Nonetheless, one court might rule that the parties, having agreed on the garage and the $40,000, *added a provision to their then existing oral contract*: that for an additional $5,000, Isaac would build a walkway. Because that term does not appear in the writing, such a court would rule that the parol evidence rule renders it unenforceable.

Another court might rule otherwise, concluding that these parties (1) first formed a $40,000 contract for the building of a garage, (2) then formed a separate $5,000 contract for the construction of a walkway, and (3) then reduced the first one to writing, leaving the second as an oral agreement, fully enforceable, standing on its own. If a court were to reach that conclusion, it would necessarily conclude that the $5,000 represents a consideration separate from the $40,000 and that garage and walkway reflect separate substance and subject matter. Both I and II apply, and for that reason **C** is right.

Some refer to this collateral agreement doctrine as an "exception" to the parol evidence rule, but that notion is misconceived. The parol evidence rule purports only to affect *a* contract that two parties first form and then reduce to a final written expression. It does not purport to address any *set of contracts* formed by two parties at or near the same time.

2. *Interpretation, Fraud, Duress, Mistake*

Although the parol evidence rule may forbid two contracting parties to enforce agreements and terms omitted from their writing, it does not stop them from introducing evidence of prior discussions to establish the meaning of words and phrases that appear *in* the writing. Hence, if a partial or total integration features the term "blue," or "market price," or "unit," either party may introduce evidence of conversations and negotiations to show that the parties should reasonably have understood "blue" to mean navy blue or "market price" to mean opening price on the London market, or "unit" to mean bushel. To those ends, any evidence including usage of trade and course of dealing are admissible. Further, parol evidence is admissible always to show fraud, duress, or mistake. None of these realities constitutes a true exception to the parol evidence rule.

3. *Conditions Precedent*

Suppose Jermaine and Ty, after protracted negotiations, create a 90-page writing, exhaustively detailed, complete with merger clause, under which Jermaine, as owner of 24 patents, is to license all of them to Ty for $40 million. The parties are poised to sign the writing, but before they do, Ty says, "Can we agree that this contract will not be effective unless my lawyer approves it?" Jermaine says, "yes." The parties then sign. Notwithstanding the parol evidence rule, *that* oral agreement is effective. Jermaine is obliged to seek his lawyer's approval. But if she disapproves of the arrangement, the contract does not operate. This stands as a true exception to the parol evidence rule, for it allows the parties to enforce a term not included in their writing—that each party's duty to perform is subject to the condition precedent that Ty's lawyer should approve their arrangement.

J.   The Closers

QUESTIONS 9 & 10. Eston is producing a fashion show at a local arts chamber on May 10. He asks Falil to serve as announcer. Falil expresses interest, and before several witnesses, the parties talk and negotiate. Eston begins: "Well, it will require two rehearsals of about four hours each. Then the show itself will last for about two hours. I thought perhaps I'd pay you—for the two rehearsals and the show—$2,000 total." Falil replies, "That's fine; I'll do it. I'd like to be paid $1,000 after the first rehearsal and $1,000 at the completion of the show. Also, if I should put more than 20 hours into all of these efforts, I'd like to be paid an additional $50 for each such hour." Eston says, "It's a deal."

The parties then agree on every other detail they can think of, including rehearsal dates and times, Falil's wardrobe, and music to accompany the show. After the parties agree on all details, Falil says, "Shall we put all of this in writing?" "I don't think we need to, do we?" answers Eston. "I guess not," Falil says, "but I would like to put in writing some general statement to the effect that I will serve as announcer and how much I will be paid." On March 12, the parties create and sign this writing, which they label "Contract":

> Eston Eaves and Falil Ford acknowledge, between them, an agreement under which (1) Eston Eaves will produce a fashion show at the Hazelton Arts Chamber on May 10 of this year and (2) Falil Ford will serve as announcer for a total compensation of $2,000, no less and no more.

QUESTION 8. On April 9, Eston calls for the first rehearsal, and Falil properly performs his part. At the rehearsal's end, Falil asks Eston for his first $1,000 payment. Eston refuses to pay, asserting that "according to our contract of March 12, I need pay you only $2,000, which I will pay after the show itself is complete." Falil counters, "Don't you remember that before signing that short writing we agreed that you would pay me $1,000 after the first rehearsal and $1,000 after completion of the show itself?" "Yes," says Eston, "but we didn't put it in the contract, so as far as I'm concerned I need not do it. But I'll ask my lawyer her opinion." Eston consults with his attorney, who advises him, "You are probably obliged to pay in installments as you agreed, even though the writing recites no such obligation." The attorney's reasons most likely include which of the following?

I. The March 12 writing was a partial integration.
II. There were several witnesses to the parties' conversations of March 12.
III. Payment in two installments would not contradict the March 12 writing.

A. I
B. II
C. I and III
D. I, II, and III

ANALYSIS. These parties formed, orally, a detailed contract and then created a writing. They failed to include in their writing Eston's promise to pay Falil in two installments. If that term is a part of the contract, notwithstanding its absence from the writing, then it must be so that (1) the writing is a partial integration, and (2) the term adds to the writing without contradicting it. Consequently, if Eston's lawyer understands the parol evidence rule and concludes that the prior oral agreement is binding—that Eston is obliged to pay in installments—she must have reached those two conclusions. Options I and

III make statements identical to those conclusions, meaning that the answer is **C** or **D**, depending on whether option II is true or false.

Option II is false. The parol evidence rule provides that the law will or will not enforce a contractual term (a) on which two parties agree, but (b) fail to include in a contractual writing they create and adopt after forming their oral contract. If in a given situation the rule provides that such a term is enforceable, then of course the party who wishes to enforce it must prove that the parties did, indeed, agree on it, and the law allows him to present his evidence (his parol evidence) on that point. The parol evidence rule does not require that he present any particular kind or quantity of evidence. Rather, once permitted to offer proof as to the oral agreement, he must, as with any attempt to prove a fact, introduce that which convinces the jury by a preponderance of the evidence that the parties did in fact make the agreement.

Certainly if (a) Party X asserts that she and Party Y agreed on a contractual term that they failed to include in their writing, and if (b) circumstances are such that under the parol evidence rule the oral agreement is enforceable (if proven, of course), then Party Y's *own admission* that he and Party X did, indeed, make the agreement will be sufficient to prove that fact. Consequently, in deciding that under the parol evidence rule Eston's agreement, *to which Eston himself admits*, is enforceable, Eston's lawyer need not conclude that "there were several witnesses to the parties' conversations of March 12."

Again, the parol evidence rule is not a rule of evidence; it is a substantive rule of contract law providing that oral agreements followed by written "integrations" are or not enforceable. As to *how* and by what quantity of evidence the oral agreement, if enforceable, is to be proven, the parol evidence rule has nothing to say. (That, indeed, is a question of evidence law.) Since option II therefore is false, and options I and III are true, **C** is right.

QUESTION 9. The parties conduct the fashion show on May 10 as planned. By the time it's over, Falil has devoted 26 hours to the whole effort. He reminds Eston of their oral agreement under which Eston would pay him, in addition to the $2,000, another $50 for each hour he worked beyond 20 hours. Falil claims that he is owed a total of $2,300. Eston acknowledges the oral agreement, but nonetheless refuses to pay the additional $300, noting that "our actual contract provides for total payment of $2,000, no less and no more." If the parties' writing is a *partial* integration of their agreement, is Eston obliged to pay the additional $300 as orally agreed?

A. Yes, because the writing is not a total integration
B. Yes, because Eston acknowledges that component of the oral agreement
C. No, because the writing expressly voids all prior oral agreements
D. No, because that component of the oral agreement is inconsistent with the writing

ANALYSIS.   Orally, these parties formed a contract providing that Eston should pay Falil $2,000 plus $50 per hour to the extent that he worked beyond 20 hours. They then created a writing that, we are told to assume, was a partial integration of their agreement. Consequently, any term on which the parties orally agreed before adopting the writing (a) *is* admissible if it adds to the writing's terms, without contradicting them, but (b) is inadmissible if it conflicts with the writing's terms.

The writing expressly provides that Falil's "total compensation" will be $2,000, "no more and no less." The prior oral agreement that allows for the possibility of payment greater than $2,000 is *inconsistent* with the writing; the writing refers to $2,000 and "no more," whereas the oral agreement provides for $2,000 plus the possibility of more. The oral agreement thus contradicts the writing and so does not become a part of the contract.

A answers "yes," so it's wrong. That the writing is only a partial integration does not render the oral agreement enforceable. If the prior oral agreement were consistent with the partial integration, then it would become part of the contract. But this oral agreement *contradicts* the writing because of the words "total" and "no more." As for **B**, Eston's acknowledgment of the oral agreement is irrelevant. If the term on which the parties orally agreed contradicts the partial integration, as it does, it is not a part of the contract, acknowledgment or not. **C** correctly answers "no," but it makes a peculiar statement. The writing does *not* provide, in so many words, that "prior oral agreements are void," meaning it does not expressly void the prior agreements (and, furthermore, the parol evidence rule does not (insofar as we yet know) provide that any such written statement voids all prior agreements if the writing is, indeed, a partial integration. **C** is wrong.

D correctly answers "no" and properly states as its reason that the oral agreement contradicts the writing. That's why **D** is right.

✦ Silver & Hochberg's Picks

1.	**A**
2.	**A**
3.	**D**
4.	**B**
5.	**D**
6.	**B**
7.	**C**
8.	**C**
9.	**D**

20

Duress, Undue Influence, and Unconscionability

A. The Doctrine of Duress
B. The Doctrine of Undue Influence
C. The Doctrine of Unconscionability
D. The Closer
✤ Silver & Hochberg's Picks

A.   The Doctrine of Duress

Suppose X makes an offer to Y and asks, "Do you accept?" Y responds, "No, definitely not." X then repeats her offer, this time with a knife at Y's throat, saying, "How about now — *now* do you accept?" Rapidly and readily, Y says, "yes."

The doctrine of duress provides: *If parties A and B form a contract and B, by unlawful threat, has coerced A's assent, then at A's option, the contract is voidable.*[1] Restatement (Second) of Contracts §175(1) provides similarly:

> If a party's manifestation of assent is induced by an improper threat by the other party that leaves the victim no reasonable alternative, the contract is voidable by the victim.

In the knife case, therefore, this long-standing rule provides that X and Y form a contract, but the contract is voidable by Y.

1.   When Is a Threat "Improper"?

A threat is improper when one has no "legal right" to make it. Generally, that means that a party threatens to commit criminal or tortious conduct. Each of the following constitutes an improper threat:

---

1.   Regarding the meaning of a "voidable" contract, see Chapter 16, section B.

- "Sign this settlement document or I'll sue you, even though I have no good claim against you, and I'll allege the right to garnish your wages pretrial." That constitutes a threat to commit the tort of vexatious litigation.
- "I offer to buy your car for $100. Accept or I'll destroy it." That constitutes a threat to commit a crime, generically called vandalism, and the tort of trespass to property.

Suppose Buyer and Seller legitimately contract for the purchase and sale of a service and thereafter Seller says:

- "I won't perform the contract unless you agree to pay more than the contract price on which we have already agreed." Seller has threatened the unlawful behavior of contractual breach.[2]

One who threatens to exercise a right or discretion to which he is otherwise entitled, not for its legitimate purpose but for personal gain, also makes an improper threat. In most instances, that too is a crime or tort. Suppose S was once convicted of embezzlement. She has served her sentence and now lives as a good and productive citizen in a community of persons who do not know of her conviction. B proposes to buy S's home for $200,000. S says she is not willing to sell it for that price. Nonetheless, B prepares and signs a writing whose terms require that S sell her home to him for $200,000. He presents the writing to S, saying, "Sign or I'll tell the entire community of your criminal past." He has made an improper threat (and has, in most states, committed the crime generically called blackmail).

QUESTION 1. Thaddeus, Vore's employee, steals $10,000 from Vore's safe. Vore knows nothing of the theft, but Banya, unbeknownst to Thaddeus, witnesses it and shortly thereafter creates, dates, and signs this writing titled "Agreement":

October 12, 2012; 8:00 a.m.

Banya Banes, "Payee," hereby agrees not to report to Vore Volee or to any other person or authority the activities and conduct she witnessed on the part of Thaddeus Thames on the evening of October 11, 2012, between the hours of 6 P.M. and 7 P.M., in exchange for which the said Thaddeus Thames agrees to pay her $5,000 within 24 hours of the above-noted date and time.

---

2. Of course, any resulting "modification" would be unenforceable for lack of consideration, another showing that courts invoke the duress doctrine when they should rest on other fundamental rules of contract. Modification of a contract, like formation itself, requires consideration from both contracting parties (except as to contracts for the sale of goods; see Chapter 14, section B).

> Banya approaches Thaddeus, presents him with the writing, and says, "Sign or I'll report you to Vore and to the police. You know very well what I'm talking about." Thaddeus reads the writing and signs it. The parties
>
> A. formed no contract, because Banya did not make her offer in good faith.
> B. formed no contract because Thaddeus manifested no assent to Banya's offer.
> C. formed no contract because Banya made only a gratuitous promise.
> D. formed a contract voidable at Thaddeus's option.

ANALYSIS. The doctrine of duress provides that when an offeree accepts an offer in response to an offeror's improper threat, the parties form a contract that is voidable at the offeree's (victim's) option.

One generally has a right to report another's misconduct to whomever she pleases (unless she is bound, for example, by a professional confidence), but one commits a legal wrong (blackmail or extortion, depending on the state) when he offers not to exercise that right and to "keep quiet," demanding value in exchange for his silence. The misuse or abuse of such a right constitutes an improper threat, which in turn means the resulting agreement between black-mailer and victim is voidable for duress.

Banya has misused her right, precisely as described above (and, therefore, likely committed blackmail). Prevailing legal thought provides that the parties formed a contract voidable by Thaddeus, the victim, for duress. **A** is wrong for stating that the parties did not form a contract. Prevailing thought decrees that they did. Further, as to the failure of good faith, Banya, in making her offer, likely committed the crime of blackmail, but that does not mean, exactly, that she made her *offer* in bad faith. She made it honestly in the sense that (as far as we know) she intended to keep her promise of silence. Furthermore, one who proposes a bargain in bad faith — intending at the outset not to honor her own part of it — does not fail, for that reason, to make an offer. She likely commits a fraud, but her proposition stands nonetheless as an offer.

Regarding **B**, most authorities, including Restatement (Second) §175, would hold that Thaddeus did manifest assent by signing the paper and that he did thereby form a contract.[3] The contract is voidable at Thaddeus's option, but it is a contract nonetheless. **C** states, once again, that the parties formed no contract and according to prevailing thought, that's wrong. Further, it's wrong to

---

3. Logic (but not "black letter law") dictates that an "assent" elicited by duress is not an acceptance. An offeree accepts, after all, when he says or does that which would lead the offeror reasonably to believe that he assents — truly, by free will — to all terms of the offer (Chapter 2 section D). When, under unlawful threat, an offeree purports to "accept" an "offer," an offeror cannot reasonably believe that he has truly assented to the "offeror's" proposed bargain. Logic dictates that an "assent" produced by duress is no acceptance at all and, in logic, such parties should fail to form a contract. That the law does recognize a contract — a voidable contract — probably reflects its wish to punish the wrongdoer by "sticking" him with the "agreement" he forcibly obtained, should the offeree wish to enforce it.

characterize Banya's commitment as a gratuitous promise. One makes a gratuitous promise when she makes it in exchange for nothing. A gratuitous promise is unenforceable because the promisee gives no consideration, meaning the parties form no contract (Chapter 12). That is not this case. In exchange for her promise, Banya took back Thaddeus's promise to pay her $5,000. **A**, **B**, and **C** are wrong, so **D** had better be right. And it is. According to prevailing legal thought, these parties formed a contract, Thaddeus doing so under duress. The contract is therefore voidable at his option. **D** is right.

2. What If the Threat Comes from a Third Person?

Restatement (Second) §175(2) provides:

> If a party's manifestation of assent is induced by one who is not a party to the transaction, the contract is voidable by the victim unless the other party to the transaction in good faith and without reason to know of the duress either gives value or relies materially on the transaction.

Suppose at

Time 1, A presents B with an improper threat and says, "If C makes you an offer, you'd better accept it."

Time 2, A comes to B with an offer, and B proclaims his assent.

Let's ask: Is the resulting contract voidable? Let's answer: It depends. If when B proclaimed his acceptance, A knew or had reason to know what C had done, then the contract is voidable at B's option. But if A did *not* know and had no reason to know what C had done, and furthermore A has relied to his detriment on the contract, then the contract is not voidable. B must honor his contract with C. (B's remedy for the wrong is to sue C for her wrongful conduct in making the threat.)

QUESTION 2. Vincent, a married man, owns Blackacre. Fern makes a signed written offer to buy it for $1 million, and Vincent rejects the offer, both parties acting honestly in all respects. Diana is Fern's daughter. She badly wishes that her mother should own Blackacre. Without Fern's knowledge, Diana approaches Vincent and says, "If my mother makes another offer for Blackacre, you'll accept it. If you don't, I'll tell your wife about the affair we had." Fern again presents Vincent with her written offer to buy Blackacre for $1 million. Because of Diana's threat, Vincent accepts and signs the writing. Is the resulting contract voidable at Vincent's option?

A. Yes, because Vincent's assent followed from Diana's improper threat
B. Yes, if Fern had a basis on which to know the substance of Diana's conversation with Vincent
C. Yes, if Fern knew of Diana's affair with Vincent
D. No, if after forming the contract Fern acted in reasonable reliance on it, to her detriment

ANALYSIS.   If A and B form a contract, B having assented to its terms because a third party, C, subjected him to an improper threat, then (1) if A knew or had reason to know of C's threat, the contract is voidable at B's option. (2) If A did not know of C's threat and A has relied to his detriment on the contract, then the contract is not voidable; B must honor it. In this case, Fern is Party A, Vincent is Party B, and Diana is Party C. It takes only the single showing that Fern knew or should have known what Diana did to render the contract voidable. It takes *two* showings to render the contract fully enforceable: (1) that Fern did not know or have reason to know what Diana had done, and (2) that Fern reasonably relied on the contract to her detriment.

The story tells us nothing as to whether Fern did or did not know of Diana's threat to Vincent. Consequently, a correct answer choice, be it "yes" or "no," must provide us with facts on that subject. **A** fails to do that; reading **A** we still do not know the state of Fern's knowledge regarding Diana's threat to Vincent, and so we cannot say its "yes" answer is correct. **A** is wrong. **C** fails in the same way. It posits that Fern knew of the affair, but says nothing as to what Fern knew of *Diana's threat*. Without that information, we still cannot answer "yes" or "no." That leaves **B** and **D**.

D posits that Fern reasonably relied on the contract. That alone is not sufficient to render the contract enforceable. In order that **D** should be correct, it would have to posit also that Fern neither knew nor had reason to know of Diana's threat to Vincent. But **D** is silent on that point, and so we cannot answer the question "yes" or "no." **D** is wrong.

B posits that Fern "had a basis" on which to know "the substance of Diana's conversation with Vincent." Those words mean that Fern had reason to know of Diana's threat. That additional information allows us to conclude that **B** is right.

B.   The Doctrine of Undue Influence

The rule of undue influence arose in equity (see Appendix, section E), but the common law has now adopted it. It provides, generally: *If (1) the relationship between parties A and B affords A a position of "dominance" over B or justifies B in relying on A's judgment, and (2) exploiting such dominance or trust for his own interest, A induces B to enter a contract, then the contract is voidable at B's option.*

Illustration 1: Exploitation of Trust.   Yul inherits from his grandfather a 100 percent interest in his grandfather's business. He leaves day-to-day operation of the business to Mary, who has served as the grandfather's business manager for decades. At some point, Mary decides that she wishes to purchase for herself, for her own purposes, certain real property owned by the business, a transaction to which Yul would have to agree. Knowing that the property is worth $50 million and believing that it will soon appreciate dramatically, Mary "advises" Yul to sell the property to her for $10 million. Trusting Mary, Yul forms a contract to sell Mary the property.

Most courts would rule that Yul and Mary have such a relationship as justifies Yul in relying on Mary's judgment. Most would further rule that Mary induced Yul to enter the contract for her own purposes and thus abused Yul's trust. Consequently, it would rule the contract voidable at Yul's option on the ground of undue influence.

Illustration 2: Abuse of Dominant Position.   Wendy cares for Genna, a sick, weak woman of 98. Genna depends on Wendy for her care, day-to-day, hour-to-hour, and minute-to-minute. Her physician visits her at her home, which she has not left for seven years. Wendy decides that she wishes to purchase all of Genna's stock in ABC Corporation for $10 per share when, as Wendy knows, each share is indisputably worth $90. Wendy prepares and presents to Genna a writing that calls for Genna to sell her the shares for $10 each. Genna reads it and says, "I don't think I can do this without advice from an attorney or accountant." "Sign now," Wendy says, "or I'll cease to take care of you; I'll resign." Genna signs.

Most courts would rule that (1) Wendy's position in Genna's life was one of dominance, and that (2) she used her position to induce Genna's acceptance and, therefore, that (3) the contract is voidable at Genna's option because it was the product of undue influence.

Let's ask: Why is that not a case of duress? Most authorities would likely answer that Wendy's threat is not an "improper" one, as that term operates in the duress doctrine. By resigning her position, Wendy would not be committing a tort or crime. Neither would she thereby exercise, for an illegitimate purpose, some discretion that is hers (although that is debatable). On the other hand, the existing contract under which Wendy cares for Genna (probably not in writing) likely includes, implicitly, Wendy's promise not to leave her post without such notice as will allow Genna to secure a replacement. Consequently, if Genna reasonably understands Wendy's statements as a threat to leave her side immediately, without giving her opportunity to find a new caregiver, then, probably, Wendy *has* made an improper threat and the contract is voidable on both the grounds of duress *and* undue influence.[4]

C.   The Doctrine of Unconscionability

Through 1950 or so, contract law did not concern itself with the fairness of contractual terms. The common law nowhere provided that a contract was

---

4.   It might be that all cases of undue influence are, also, cases of fraud and, where the defendant is a fiduciary—a breach *of* his fiduciary duty.

enforceable only if its terms were fair or unenforceable if they were not.[5] The common law bound two parties to their agreement whether its terms were consummately fair or so inexpressively one-sided as to offend the conscience of right-thinking persons. "A deal was a deal," and "a contract was a contract."

In 1962, the Uniform Law Commission promulgated the Uniform Commercial Code, which all states have now adopted in one version or another. UCC §2-302 invested contract law, for the first time, with a rule that takes account of *fairness*: "If the court . . . finds [a] contract . . . to have been unconscionable at the time it was made the court may refuse to enforce [it]." Section 2-302, of course, is statutory and so does not represent the common law. Further, U.C.C. Article 2 applies only to contracts that concern the sale of goods, and to no others.

But between 1962 and the present, the doctrine of unconscionability as thus created by the UCC wiggled its way into the common law.[6] It now applies, in all states, to contracts for the sale of goods, pursuant to UCC §2-302, and to all other contracts as well, by modern common law. Restatement (Second) §208, promulgated in 1972, provides that:

> If a contract or term thereof is unconscionable at the time the contract is made, a court may refuse to enforce the contract, or may enforce the remainder of the contract without the unconscionable term, or may so limit the application of any unconscionable term as to avoid any unconscionable result.

Hence, contract law does, today, concern itself with the fairness of contractual terms. For contracts involving the sale of goods, UCC §2-302 provides that a court may refuse to enforce a contract or contractual term if it is unconscionable. As for other contracts, the common law now embodies an analogous provision, as reflected today in the Restatement.

1. How and By Whom Is it Decided That a Contract Is Unconscionable?

Under UCC Article 2 and by common law, the question of unconscionability is one of law, not fact, which is a fanciful way of stating that even in a jury trial, it belongs to the judge, not the jury. If, as to a suit for breach of contract, one party asserts that the agreement (or one of its terms) is unconscionable, the judge holds a hearing, without a jury, to decide whether the contract is unconscionable.

---

5. Courts of equity, however, have for centuries taken account of a contract's fairness or unfairness when deciding to enforce it. We discuss that matter later in this chapter and, more elaborately still, in the Appendix's section E.

6. For example, in 1965, borrowing from UCC §2-302, the U.S. Court of Appeals for the D.C. Circuit first announced that the D.C. common law would thenceforth render a contract unenforceable where "the element of unconscionability is present at the time a contract is made." Williams v. Walker-Thomas Furniture Co., 350 F.2d 445, 449 (D.C. Cir. 1965).

The courts are not unanimous in their conception of an unconscionable contract. Yet they do reflect some meaningful commonality as to the applicable criteria. The best general statement we (or anyone) can make on the matter is "soft" and uncertain of shape. Nonetheless it's meaningful:

If, in evaluating a contract, a court finds (a) unfairness in the bargaining process ("procedural unconscionability") and, in light of that unfairness, (b) "oppression" of one party ("substantive unconscionability"), then it will find the contract unconscionable. Let's take these words apart and see what they mean.

Unfairness in the Bargaining Process: *Procedural* Unfairness.   Modern decisions indicate that the *bargaining process* (meaning the combined processes of invitation to deal, offer, and acceptance) that ultimately spawns a contract between two parties A and B is itself unfair to Party B when the court finds, singly or in combination, to some critical degree, that

1. Party B lacked a meaningful opportunity to understand the contract's terms (leading to "unfair surprise"), and/or
2. Party A subjected B to some form of "pressure," and/or
3. Party A presented the terms to B as a take-it-or-leave-it proposition so that B had no opportunity to negotiate (in which case the contract is termed a "contract of adhesion"), and/or
4. Party A knew that B was subject to some infirmity or weakness.

As to a given bargaining process between two parties, a court "weighs" the total "quantity" of the four factors. If it sees some critical "quantity" of *total* unfairness, whether only one or all four factors be present, then it will find the resulting contract infected by an unfair bargaining process.

Let's Explain Further.   Think of the four factors just mentioned. By crude metaphor, imagine that each has "weight"—that each is measurable in pounds. Suppose, further, that a given judge believes that 10 pounds of these factors, in any combination, create an unfair bargaining process ("procedural unfairness"). Imagine, now, that, as to a given contract between Parties A and B, the judge finds to the extent of

• 2 pounds, that A lacked meaningful opportunity to understand the contract's terms;
• 5 pounds, that B exerted pressure on A;
• 3 pounds, that A proposed the terms to B as a take-it-or-leave-it proposition;
• 1 pound, that A knew B was suffering from some degree of dementia.

In sum, the process carries, in this judge's mind, 11 pounds of unfairness, which amount exceeds her 10-pound threshold, wherefore she finds that the parties formed their contract pursuant to an unfair bargaining process.

Oppression: *Substantive* Unconscionability. Generally, the authorities agree on (varied iterations) of this statement: *A contract or its terms are oppressive, meaning substantively unconscionable, if the court finds that, under the circumstances that surround formation, the terms are so harsh or one-sided as to shock the conscience of the court.*

The decisions indicate that the phrase "circumstances that surround formation" refers to the bargaining process, which we just considered. In other words, procedural unfairness (unfairness in the bargaining process) and substantive unfairness (oppressiveness of terms) do not reflect separate inquiries. Rather, the nation's courts deem a given term substantively fair or unfair depending on the nature of the bargaining process, that being, perhaps, the only relevant "circumstance" that surrounds the parties when they form their contract.

If a court deems a bargaining process perfectly fair, then never, it seems, will it find the contract's terms substantively unfair. If the court deems the bargaining process unfair, then the term at issue may be unfair, depending on how the court evaluates it in light *of* the unfairness that infected the bargaining process. As to one bargaining process, a given term might be perfectly fair. As to another, that same term might be unfair.

Illustration 1: A Term That, In Light of the Bargaining Process Is — *Fair*
Pam is a savvy, sophisticated lady who operates an investment bank. She contacts ConCorp to secure from it certain consulting services. After brief discussion, ConCorp presents Pam with its standard written form contract prepared by its lawyers, with its blank spaces completed so that they (1) name Pam as the "Client," (2) describe the services ConCorp will deliver, and (3) set forth ConCorp's fee of $500,000.

At ConCorp's offices, holding the writing already signed by ConCorp, Pam says to ConCorp's representative, "Before I read this document, are you negotiable on any of these terms?" "Perhaps," is the answer. "Why don't you and your lawyer read the document and get back to us with any changes you propose." Pam reads the document together with her attorney. The two of them note that the writing sets forth this clause titled "Arbitration Option"[7]:

> If either party hereto should assert that the other has breached this contract, then, at ConCorp's option — if and only if ConCorp so decrees — the parties will not, in that regard, resort to judicial litigation, but will instead submit the cause to arbitration pursuant to the rules and regulations of the American Arbitration Association. In this respect, Client shall have no reciprocal option; the decision that any allegation of breach should be resolved by judicial litigation or by arbitration shall rest solely with ConCorp, wherefore Client renounces his/her right to make any choice or decision in that regard

---

7. In nearly any legal dispute, two parties may waive their right to litigate in court and instead choose arbitration. In all states, and under federal law where relevant, such parties are bound by the arbitrators' decision. Except in very limited circumstances, arbitration decisions are unappealable.

and renounces, also, therefore, what would otherwise be his/her right to have the relevant dispute adjudicated by a court of competent jurisdiction.

After she and her attorney study the writing in full, Pam tells ConCorp's representative that she wants to eliminate or amend the arbitration clause. In response, ConCorp consults with its attorney and considers Pam's proposal carefully, but ultimately decides that it is not willing to eliminate or modify the arbitration provision. When she receives this news, Pam says, "Well, I've already thought about it and, although I'd prefer to eliminate or modify the arbitration clause, I do need your service and I am, reluctantly, agreeable to signing the document as it is." She then signs on the dotted line.

After three months, Pam asserts that ConCorp's performance is defective. The parties fail to settle the dispute between themselves, and Pam announces her intention to bring suit for breach of contract. ConCorp informs Pam that the dispute will be resolved by arbitration, and not by a court. Pam protests: "My attorney regards the arbitration clause as unconscionable; it's entirely one-sided. It allows you the option to compel arbitration, but gives me no such right. It requires that I waive my right to sue in court, if you so decree, but it exacts no such waiver from you." The parties then find themselves in court before a judge, who must decide whether the arbitration clause is unconscionable and hence whether it is enforceable.

Without question, any judge would rule this arbitration clause enforceable. She would hold a hearing and hear evidence, first, on the bargaining process, evaluating it according to the four factors previously described. No doubt, she would observe the following:

1. Pam had full opportunity to understand the arbitration provision, that she consulted with her own attorney as to its significance, that she did in fact understand it, wherefore it subjected her to no "unfair surprise."
2. ConCorp did not in any way subject Pam to pressure.
3. Although ConCorp was ultimately unwilling to remove or modify the arbitration provision, it did seriously *entertain* Pam's proposal and so did not present its terms to Pam as a take-it-or-leave-it proposition, meaning that ConCorp did not victimize Pam with a "contract of adhesion."
4. ConCorp had no reason to suspect any weakness or infirmity on Pam's part (and, indeed, Pam had none).

Then, having thus evaluated the bargaining process, a judge would examine the arbitration clause and conclude that it is not, under these circumstances, oppressive. Upon those findings, in turn, the court would certainly decide that the arbitration clause is not unconscionable and that ConCorp has every right to enforce it.

Illustration 2: Under Other Circumstances, the Same Arbitration Clause Is— *Unfair* Suppose Jackson visits a hospital emergency room in severe pain, with dizziness, nausea, and partial paralysis of his right arm. Before treating him, hospital personnel present him with a document entitled "Contract for Emergency Room Treatment," demanding that he sign. Frightened and in pain, he does so immediately. Unbeknownst to him, the document includes this provision labeled "Arbitration Option":

> If in connection with or as alleged result of treatment given to Patient, Patient should allege or contend that Hospital or any of its personnel has committed professional negligence or medical malpractice and if the parties are unable, themselves, to resolve the resulting dispute, then, at Hospital's option, and only at Hospital's option, Patient shall submit his cause to binding arbitration pursuant to the rules and regulations of the United States Arbitration Organization, and Patient shall bring his action in court only if Hospital does not decree that he/she shall submit it to arbitration. Patient expressly understands and agrees that he/she has no corresponding right and that should Hospital have cause to bring action against Patient for, without limitation, payment, then it shall, in that case too, have the sole, exclusive option to choose between litigation and arbitration, wherefore, in either such instance, Patient waives what would otherwise be his/her right to pursue judicial litigation.

Emergency room personnel do not treat Jackson for 30 hours, insisting that he has no serious condition and that he "can wait." In fact, Jackson is suffering from a meningeal infection, which curable with timely diagnosis and treatment. But for lack *of* timely diagnosis and treatment, Jackson is permanently rendered blind and deaf by the infection.

Jackson alleges medical malpractice by the hospital and its employees. Jackson wishes to sue in court. The hospital insists that the matter be submitted to arbitration. The parties find themselves in court before a judge, who must decide whether the arbitration provision is unconscionable and therefore whether it is enforceable.

We borrow the foregoing facts, by and large, from *Weidman v. Tomaselli*,[8] where the court made the following observations as to the four factors relevant to unfair bargaining:

1. The patient had no meaningful opportunity to know of the arbitration provision.
2. The urgency of the patient's situation subjected him to "pressure."
3. The hospital had presented the contractual document to the patient as a take-it-or-leave-it proposition, wherefore it gave rise to a "contract of adhesion."
4. The patient's condition was itself an infirmity or a weakness, and the hospital had plain and obvious reason to know that.

Then, evaluating the arbitration provision, the court observed that the purported waiver of the fundamental right to bring a civil action in a court of

---

8. 365 N.Y.S.2d 681 (City Ct.), *aff'd,* 386 N.Y.S.2d 276 (App. Div. 1975).

law is not enforceable under such circumstances; this arbitration clause was unconscionable.

As to what renders a contract or term unconscionable, we now have sufficient basis to articulate something akin to a rule. *As between two parties, A and B, a contract or contractual term is unconscionable as to Party A if, in the court's determination, the relevant bargaining process was, in sum total, unfair because to some critical degree:*

1. Party A lacked a meaningful opportunity to understand the contract (or the relevant term), thus producing "unfair surprise," and/or
2. B (or the relevant circumstance) subjected A to "pressure";
3. Party B presented the terms to A on a take-it-or-leave-it basis, so that A had no opportunity to negotiate (in which case the contract is termed a contract of "adhesion"); and/or
4. B knew that A was subject to some infirmity or weakness;

and if, in light of the unfairness in the bargaining process, the contract or terms at issue are harsh, oppressive, or so one-sided as to shock the conscience of the court.

Let's understand that the very same term appearing in two different contracts might be enforceable in one and unconscionable in the other if, in one case, the court deems the bargaining process fair and in the other it does not. In order that a court deem a contract or term substantively unconscionable it must first ask itself if the contract at issue suffers from procedural unconscionability. If its answer is yes, then and only then can it ask itself if the contract or term is substantively unconscionable (and, probably, it will answer yes to that question too).

QUESTIONS 3 & 4. Augusta is a wealthy and sophisticated businesswoman. Brigid is a poor widow, unable to read or write. With eight young children in her care, Brigid barely keeps her family fed and clothed by working her very small farm and laboring separately late into every night as a seamstress. Correctly believing that Brigid urgently needs money, Augusta approaches her with what she calls an "offer of kindness": "I am prepared to give you $100 right now, which you need never repay, in exchange only for such consideration as is provided in this document, which I have already signed. If you sign right now, I will immediately pay you the $100."

The document provides that Augusta will pay Brigid $100 on the execution of the writing, and, in consideration of that payment, Brigid will, three years later (a) convey to Augusta all of her property, real and personal, regardless of its market value (except for one set of clothes for

Brigid and each of her children); and (b) work ten hours per week as Augusta's personal seamstress for five years, without compensation. As consideration for all of that, Augusta promises only $100.

Brigid signs the document, whereupon Augusta immediately pays her $100. Three years later, Augusta demands that Brigid honor the terms of their contract; when Brigid learns what the contract provides, she refuses to honor its terms. Augusta brings suit against Brigid in a court of law, seeking monetary damage equal to the market value of Brigid's property, real and personal, plus the amount necessary to engage a seamstress ten hours weekly for five years. Brigid secures a lawyer who agrees to represent her pro bono[9] and who asserts that the court should not award damages. Brigid's lawyer offers to present evidence showing that the bargaining process was extremely unfair and the terms shockingly one-sided.

QUESTION 3. Assume all foregoing events occurred in 1880. The court rejects the defendant's contentions and ultimately issues a judgment against her for the monetary damages Augusta requests. Its reasons might include these:

I. Under the common law of 1880, the fairness of a contract's terms was not relevant to their enforceability.
II. A reasonable person would regard the contract as fair to both its parties.
III. One hundred dollars is adequate consideration for all of Brigid's promises.

A. I
B. I and II
C. I and III
D. I, II, and III

ANALYSIS. Before 1950 or so, the common law took no account of a contract's fairness. If two parties formed a contract by (what passed for) mutual assent (usually embodied, of course, in offer and acceptance), then they were bound by its terms no matter how unjust. If two parties formed a contract and one of them breached it, the common law offered its usual remedy of monetary compensation ("damages") without accounting at all for the contract's fairness.

Option II is false because no reasonable person would deem this contract fair to Brigid, and, more to the point, the 1880 common law did not "care"

---

9. The Latin phrase "pro bono" means, literally, "for the good" or "for the good of it." When, on occasion lawyers work without pay, for charitable purposes, they need some fancy Latin phrase to mark the occasion, wherefore, they don't use the simple phrase "without charge" or "just to be nice." Instead, they say, "I'm doing the work pro bono" (as though the Latin somehow elevates their undertaking above that of all others who work charitably).

whether contractual terms were fair. As to contract law, the matter of fairness was irrelevant. Because option II is false, **B** and **D** are wrong, leaving us with **A** and **C**. Both **A** and **C** include I, but **C** includes III as well. Option I, therefore, *must* be true, and it is: It's true for the same reason that option II is false. Pursuant to the common law of 1880, fairness was irrelevant to a contract's enforceability. If option III is true, then **C** is right. If statement III is false, **A** is right.

Option III is true. As discussed in Chapter 12, section C, courts do not ordinarily inquire into the adequacy of consideration; the common law features no general requirement that consideration by one party be equal, in objective value, to that given by the other. Option I is true, II is false, and III is true. **C** is right.

QUESTION 4. Now assume all foregoing events occurred in 2012. The court accepts the defendant's contentions and dismisses Augusta's suit. Its reasons might include these:

   I. Modern common law allows a court to refuse enforcement of what it deems to be an unconscionable contract.
   II. Brigid had no meaningful way to understand the writing at the time she signed it.
   III. Monetary compensation is a legal remedy.
   A. I
   B. I and II
   C. II and III
   D. I, II, and III

ANALYSIS.   As its principal remedy, the *law* (as opposed to equity) offers monetary compensation ("damages"), and a suit for breach of contract is a suit *in law* (Appendix, section E). Statement III is correct. **A** and **B** omit option III, so they're wrong. That leaves **C** and **D,** which means that option II *must* be correct, and it is; one of the factors that creates an unfair bargaining process is unfair surprise, meaning that one of the parties had no meaningful opportunity to know of the contract's terms (the first factor on our list of four factors). Brigid was unable to read, and Augusta gave her no description of the writing's terms, meaning that when Augusta demanded that Brigid convey all of her property to her and serve her as seamstress, Brigid suffered an unfair surprise. **C** and **D** differ in that **D** includes option I and **C** does not. If option I is true, **D** is right. If option I is false, **C** is right. And—option I is true. By modern common law, a court may refuse to enforce—to award damages for—breach of a contract it deems unconscionable (as reflected in Restatement (Second) §208). Options I, II, and III are true, and **D** is right.

QUESTIONS 5 & 6. As Bella emerges from TarMart Store, Sidney approaches and offers her membership in "Consumer's Club." He explains that Consumer's Club members are entitled to enormous discounts on an equally enormous number of goods. Bella, wearing a large hearing aid, responds, "I don't understand." Sidney says, "Take from your bag one item that you just purchased in TarMart." Bella pulls out a package of 12 Snow-White soap bars, marked $10.95. Sidney then opens the Consumer's Club catalog to show the same package of 12 Snow-White soap bars priced at $6.95.

As Sidney reaches into Bella's grocery bag for another item, Bella says, "I don't think I'm interested." Sidney responds, "But you should be—it's good for you and your family. Think of all the money you'll save that you can put toward other of your family's needs!" Bella asks, "What'd you say?" Sidney repeats his pitch and again opens his catalog. "I'm not sure I understand how the club works," Bella says, "and I really have to go." "Well, just sign right here at the bottom of this page," answers Sidney, "and you can go with the happy knowledge that you belong to Consumer Club." Bella, worn down and running late, says, "All right, where do I sign?" Sidney points, Bella signs after glancing at the document's tiny print, Sidney hurriedly gives Bella a copy of the writing, and departs.

Unbeknownst to Bella, the writing's terms provide that:

- Consumer Club's catalog prices are subject to change without notice.
- Members must pay a $200 membership fee within 30 days of signing and suffer a $25 penalty for every month or partial month for which such payment is late.
- Members who order less than $1,000 worth of merchandise from the catalog per year must pay a $1,000 "failure to purchase" charge.
- Members must pay an annual renewal fee, which is subject to change without notice.
- Members not wishing to renew must contact Consumer's Club by signed writing six months before their memberships end. (The paper from Sidney, however, provides no address or other contact information for Consumer's Club.)
- Consumer's Club does not send bills or requests for fee or penalty payments, but requires members to keep track of all required fees and send them as outlined in the signed writing.

Four years after Bella signs the document, Consumer's Club contacts her and demands payment of $2,000 in membership fees, $3,250 in penalties, and $4,000 in annual "failure to purchase charges," for a total of $9,250. Bella refuses to pay, Consumer's Club brings suit, and Bella's attorney asserts that the contract is unenforceable for the reason that its terms are unconscionable.

QUESTION 5. In deciding the question of unconscionability, the court should consider evidence tending to show that

  I. Bella's hearing aid was visible to Sidney.
  II. The document's writing was printed in very small type.
  III. Sidney had once been convicted of criminal mischief.
  IV. The terms gave very little to Bella and took much from her.
  A. I
  B. II and III
  C. I, II, and IV
  D. I, II, III, and IV

ANALYSIS. Any court using the modern rule of unconscionability stated earlier in the chapter would have to find compelling evidence of an unfair bargaining process. First, the writing was set forth in very small type, depriving Bella of a meaningful opportunity to read it and hence to understand it, thus subjecting her to unfair surprise. Option II, therefore, describes evidence relevant to the matter of unfair bargaining process/procedural unconscionability. The correct answer should include II, meaning that **B** is wrong.

Sidney subjected Bella to high-pressure sales talk, even after Bella made clear that she was not interested. Bella also made plain to Sidney that her hearing was impaired, meaning that Sidney had reason to know of that infirmity, wherefore option I makes a true statement. The correct answer must include options I and II; **A** and **B** are wrong.

As for substantive unconscionability, Consumer Club designed its writing on the philosophy of get-the-most-give-the-least, and surely its terms are so abjectly one-sided as to shock the conscience of any (sane) judge. They are in the nature of what we colloquially call a "scam" (even if they don't quite rise to the level of fraud). Option IV, therefore, describes evidence relevant to substantive unconscionability, and the correct answer must include it. The answer is **C** or **D**, both of which include I, II, and IV. They differ in that **D** includes option III and C doesn't. If option III is true, the answer is **D**. If option III is false, it's **C**. And—option III is false. As to this contract, Sidney's criminal record or other facets of his background are not relevant to unconscionability, procedural or substantive. Options I, II, and IV make true statements; III does not. Hence, **C** is right.

QUESTION 6. Beyond the facts already described, Bella's assertion of unconscionability would be most strengthened if she were able to show that she asked Sidney if she could have time to read the document where-upon Sidney responded,

A. "No, but if you choose not to sign today we might contact you again if you'll provide me with your contact information."
B. "Certainly you may take home a copy of the writing and read it. But if you wish to join Consumer's Club, we'll require that you sign this document as it is; we won't change it in any way."
C. "Yes, but our offices have not yet approved any proposed changes to this writing."
D. "Yes, but be aware that our fees and charges might increase between now and the time, if ever, that you sign."

ANALYSIS. None of the four choices concerns the contractual terms themselves. Rather, each adds a fact to the bargaining process, and we should search for that which touches most closely one of the four factors that create unfair bargaining/procedural unconscionability. In **D**, Sidney tells Bella about one of the writing's terms, to wit, that prices, fees, and charges are subject to change. Arguably, Sidney thus exerts pressure by implicitly encouraging Bella to sign then and there. Certainly the response does not reflect *intense* pressure, wherefore **D** *could* be right.

Perhaps, however, one of the other choices is better. In **C**, Sidney warns Bella that his offices have not yet approved changes to the writing. On the one hand, that raises the specter of an adhesion contract (where terms are presented as a take-it-or-leave-it proposition), but on the other, it suggests that the offices might have *considered* proposed changes to the document's terms and would *consider* any that Bella proposes. **C** is not outright wrong; neither is it strikingly correct. In **A** Sidney does nothing objectionable, but in **B** he expressly informs Bella that the terms are nonnegotiable—that to join the club, she'll have to sign the document as is. With that, certainly, Sidney presents the document as a take-it-or-leave it proposition, meaning that he proposed a contract of adhesion. Among the choices, therefore, **B** touches most closely one of the four factors that create unfair bargaining and so, **B** is right.

3. Unequal Bargaining Power

Two parties are said to have unequal bargaining power if one of them is, in some way, "holding all of the cards." If, in the desert, A is dying of thirst and B has an abundance of water for sale, A and B are said to be unequal in their bargaining power. A urgently needs what B has, but from A, B *needs* little or nothing. Consequently, B might demand from A $1 million for a glass of water.

More realistic situations of unequal bargaining power are those in which many buyers need or wish to secure some very scarce goods or service and one (or a few) sellers have the commodity available. In such situations, the sellers (it is said) have the superior bargaining power. They are in a position to demand a very high price for their goods. Similarly, a buyer could have the superior bargaining power. Imagine that a poor but brilliant chap named Inventor patents a process that will allow BigRichCorp, the world's only widget manufacturer, to create widgets at one-tenth its present costs and thus increase its profits by billions of dollars. Because BigRichCorp has no competitors, Inventor's process would be useful *only* to BigRichCorp. But BigRichCorp can get along without Inventor's patented process, certainly much better than Inventor can get along without some kind of payment from BigRichCorp. These two parties, therefore, have unequal bargaining power. Inventor needs badly what BigRichCorp has to give (money), but BigRichCorp doesn't so badly need (or need at all) Inventor's device.

Does Unequal Bargaining Power Render a Bargaining Process Unfair?   Both the Restatement (Second) §208 cmt. b and UCC §2-302 cmt. 1 answer "no." The Restatement, however, states that as to any allegation of unconscionability, the fact of unequal bargaining power should heighten the court's suspicion that one of the four relevant factors operates. Furthermore, courts frequently do cite unequal bargaining power, without consistency or explanation, as a factor that bears on procedural unconscionability. Consequently, we should consider that on some days in some courts for some cases, the factors that tend to create an unfair bargaining process are not four in number, but five—the fifth being unequal bargaining power.

4. Unconscionability in the Equity Courts

To the law, unconscionability is something relatively new, but in equity courts it's centuries old. As described in the Appendix, section E, our Anglo-American legal system once sharply separated courts of law from courts of equity. Today, in America, to a very significant degree, equity and law remain conceptually distinct, but in most (but not all) states, and in the federal system, the same *courthouses* serve both the jurisdictions of law and equity, and the law court's judges double as the equity court's chancellors when a petitioner invokes the court's equitable jurisdiction.

And What Does It Mean to "Invoke the Court's Equitable Jurisdiction?"   For a more elaborate answer to that question, please see the Appendix, section E. Reduced to very simple terms, we may say this: whether one brings his suit "at law," or "in equity," depends on whether he seeks (1) monetary damages, in which case he has brought an action at law, or

(2) a court order/injunction, in which case he has brought an action at equity. He who brings a suit at equity is termed not a plaintiff but a "petitioner," and his opponent is not a defendant, but a "respondent." The imposing figure seated at the bench, clad in a black robe, removes her hat, labeled "judge" (figuratively speaking) and dons the one labeled "chancellor in equity."

When one petitions an equity court, the chancellor first asks herself whether, in her opinion, the petitioner has suffered an "injustice" for which the "law offers no adequate remedy." If she answers "no," then the petitioner is not eligible for equitable relief (an order/injunction), and the chancellor dismisses his case. If she answers "yes," then, generally, she will issue the order the petitioner requests or, in any event, such order/injunction as, in her opinion, is necessary to correct the injustice.

Suppose, for example, by signed writing, Seller contracts to sell Buyer a Rembrandt original for $900,000. Buyer tenders the purchase price but Seller then refuses to convey the painting; he breaches the contract. Buyer wants the painting—*that* painting. Seller owns it and, obviously, Buyer cannot buy it elsewhere. Consequently, Buyer believes that monetary damage will not compensate him for Seller's breach. It is not clear, even, that Buyer has suffered *any* monetary damage; he does not have the painting but he does still have his $900,000. He wants that for which he bargained—the painting itself.

Hence, he brings not an action for breach of contract in a law court but, instead, a petition in equity demanding "specific performance" of the contract—which means a court order requiring that seller convey the painting for the agreed price. Quite likely, the Chancellor (that same robed figure who functions as a judge in "cases at law,") will issue the order for specific performance; Seller will be required to convey the painting or face imprisonment for contempt of court.

Equity's "Clean Hands" Rule   As instruments of "justice," the equity courts are to view every contest before them with an eye toward doing "justice" overall. Over the centuries, to serve that objective, they created a variety of defenses that respondents might assert against petitioners. If a petitioner seeks equitable relief but respondent shows that the petitioner himself, in connection with the very matter at issue, has behaved so badly as not to deserve the "justice" he seeks, then the chancellor is to dismiss his case upon the ground that he has not come to equity with "clean hands."

Let's illustrate, by adding a fact to the Rembrandt case just described. Buyer's first name is "Thief." He badly wants the Rembrandt painting and is willing to pay $1 million to have it. Hoping he might not have to pay at all, he attempts, first, to steal the painting. Seller catches him in the act, and demands an explanation. Buyer, answers, "Well, uh, I really like the painting; I was just looking at it with the plan of making you an offer to buy it." Seller responds, "Oh, really? So what's your offer?" Buyer replies, "$900,000." Seller accepts the offer and the parties create a perfectly structured writing that calls for Buyer to buy and Seller to sell, for $900,000, the Rembrandt original painting. Both parties sign and thus form a contract.

Buyer then tenders the purchase price and Seller, deciding he does not wish to sell, refuses the money and declines to convey the painting. Buyer brings an action at equity, requesting an order of specific performance—an order to Seller that he accept the purchase price and convey the painting, or face imprisonment for contempt of court.

Hearing Buyer/Petitioner's evidence of the events, the Chancellor concludes that he has "suffered an injustice for which the law offers no adequate remedy"—that no amount of monetary damage is assessable and that none will make Buyer whole. On that basis she is prepared to issue an order of specific performance—to order that Seller accept the purchase price and convey the painting to Buyer. However, Respondent/Seller demonstrates to the Chancellor's satisfaction that before contracting to buy the painting, Buyer attempted to steal it. On that basis, the Chancellor decrees, "This Petitioner, the buyer, has come to the equity court with unclean hands and so I will not issue the order of specific performance to which he would otherwise be entitled."

Clean Hands and Unconscionability   We wrote, earlier, that the doctrine of unconscionability is new to the *law* over these last sixty years or so, and that's true. It is not, however, new to courts of *equity*. If as to an alleged contractual breach one seeks a court order of specific performance then he is seeking an equitable remedy and is, therefore, "in" an equity court, subject to the defenses that equity has devised, including that of "clean hands." We noted above that a Buyer's attempted theft of a good that he later contracts to purchase means he comes to equity without clean hands. A petitioner's hands are similarly unclean if he seeks specific performance of a contract as to which he himself has subjected the respondent to a grossly unfair bargaining process, together with grossly one-sided terms. That means, really, that in the equity courts, a doctrine equivalent to that of unconscionability has operated for centuries.

In *Campbell Soup v. Wentz*, 172 F.2d 80 (3d Cir. 1948) Campbell Soup, Inc. had contracted with a grower/seller for the purchase of carrots. The grower/seller refused to honor the contract and Campbell's Soup sought specific performance (meaning it invoked the court's "equitable jurisdiction," alleging that the kind of carrot at issue was virtually unobtainable except from this particular grower, and that the law's remedy of monetary damages offered no relief adequate to make it whole).

The court agreed that monetary damages would not do justice and that specific performance would be an appropriate remedy were it not for the fact that the contract was too hard a bargain and too one-sided an agreement to entitle Campbell's Soup, Inc. to relief in a court of equity, "which is a court of conscience."

So, now we know: if, before 1952 (or so) a plaintiff brought an action *at law* for breach of contract, meaning that he sought the law's remedy of monetary damages for breach of contract, he was entitled to recover regardless of the fairness or unfairness of the relevant bargaining process or contractual terms. Today, the law embodies a doctrine of unconscionability; a law court may deny recovery to a plaintiff who sues at law for breach of contract if, in the judge's opinion, the bargaining process and terms are so unfair as to render the contract unconscionable.

If, *two hundred years ago*, a petitioner alleged a breach of contract and brought action in an *equity* court for specific performance, unconscionability of the contract (bargaining process and/or terms) would render him ineligible for relief pursuant to the "clean hands" rule, and that continues to be so, today. To law, unconscionability is relatively new. To equity, it's centuries old.

D. The Closer

> **QUESTION 7.** Do yourself a favor, please, and *read the Appendix, section E,* as you should already have done. (It will serve you well throughout the rest of your law school years and legal career.) Then read this next story. It's similar to that of Augusta and Brigid (Questions 3 and 4 above). This one, however, occurs in Texas in 1880 and involves a court of equity.
>
> Belle is a poor widow, unable to read or write. Caring for nine young children (two of them invalids), she barely keeps her family fed and clothed by working her very small farm and laboring separately late into every night as a seamstress. As a seamstress, Belle is uniquely talented. Cruella is a wealthy and sophisticated businesswoman. An engineer has advised her that oil is likely located beneath Belle's small farm. Correctly believing that Belle urgently needs money (always), Cruella approaches her with an "offer of love."
>
> **Cruella:** I am prepared to give you, now, $10, and you need never repay me. You need only sign this document, which states that I have given you $10. I'm very serious about wanting to help you, dear, so I've already signed. Look, here's a $10 bill. Sign right now and I'll give it to you.
>
> **Belle:** Well, Miss Cruella, I don't know my letters; I can't read words. Does the paper say anything else? Does it say only that you've given me $10? Is there more?
>
> **Cruella:** Just a little bit. It states that years from now—years from now, dear, you'll do a few small things for me—some sewing, for example. Really, dear, it's nothing much.
>
> **Belle:** That's very kind of you. I do know how to write my name, so I'll sign.
>
> The document provides that Cruella will pay Belle $10 on the execution of the writing and, in consideration of that payment, Belle will, three years later, convey to Cruella all of her property, real and personal, regardless of its market value (except for one set of clothing for Belle and each of her children), and work 30 hours per week as Cruella's personal

seamstress for five years, without compensation. It expressly provides that the $10 is consideration for all of Belle's property and for her five years' work as a seamstress, and that Belle is satisfied with such consideration. Belle signs, and Cruella promptly pays her $10.

Three years later, Cruella demands that Belle convey to Cruella all of her property, real and personal, with the exceptions provided in the writing. She further demands that Belle begin working as Cruella's personal seamstress 30 hours per week. By this time, Belle has heard rumors about oil beneath her farmland. Hearing Cruella's demands, she refuses to comply. Cruella engages a lawyer and sues Belle. She asserts that there is uniqueness in Belle's properties and in her skills as a seamstress. Money, she says, can't buy what Belle owes her "under our contract." She wants not a monetary judgment but a court order that Belle do as the contract requires.

On that basis, Cruella goes to an equity court and petitions for a court order directing that Belle convey all of her property to Cruella and serve Cruella as a seamstress 30 hours weekly for five years. Cruella's lawyer convinces the equity court that Belle's properties and services are unique, but the chancellor nonetheless declines to issue the order Cruella seeks. His reasons might include

I. that under the common law of 1880, the fairness of a contract's terms was not relevant to their enforceability.
II. that the agreement between Belle and Cruella was so unfair as to offend the "King's conscience."
III. that equity courts do not aid those who come to it with unclean hands.

A. I
B. I and II
C. II and III
D. I, II, and III

ANALYSIS. Equity courts are "courts of justice," with jurisdiction limited to situations in which, as the chancellor sees them, a petitioner has suffered an injustice for which the law (meaning common law or statute) offers no adequate remedy. Consequently where, in the chancellor's opinion, the petitioner has a legitimate grievance (has "suffered an injustice" such as would "offend the King's conscience") that monetary damages cannot correct, the court of equity will ordinarily issue a remedy (in the form of an injunction or court order).

Yet, precisely because its mission *is* to "do justice," the equity court will not enforce what it deems to be an unfair contract, for to do so would be to participate in an injustice. Stated in terms of a celebrated equitable maxim, "One who seeks equitable relief must come to court with clean hands,"[10] meaning that if, as to the very matter at issue, a petitioner has himself behaved badly (in the chancellor's opinion), then the equity court will not entertain his complaint of injustice. Consequently, an equity court will not aid a petitioner who first draws another into a wretchedly one-sided contract and then complains that the other has breached.

In this case, Cruella drew Belle into an abusive agreement knowing, moreover, that Belle could not read the contractual document. Further, Cruella told Belle that she would not have to repay the $10. Arguably, such was "technical," "legal" truth, but her statement was grossly misleading, since it implied, perhaps, that the money was Cruella's gift. Hence, with respect to this contract, Cruella behaved badly — very, very badly, and such is a reason that an equity court would likely deny her a remedy — even if, by *law*, Belle is in breach.

Option I is true but wholly irrelevant. In 1880, the common law took no account of fairness. Yet, this proceeding is not at law but at equity. The chancellor does not look to law for his decisions — she looks to precepts of what she sees as justice. **A** and **D** include option 1, so they're wrong. That leaves us with **B** and **C**. Both include option II, which must therefore be correct. And it is; the agreement is, arguably, so one-sided and oppressive as to "offend the King's conscience." If option III is true, **C** is correct. If option III is false, **B** is correct. And — option III is true. It cites an equitable maxim directly relevant to this controversy. Having lured Belle into so heinously abusive an agreement, Cruella comes to court without clean hands, and that is a reason for which equity would deny her relief. Option I is false, and options II and III are true. Hence, **C** is right.

✶ Silver & Hochberg's Picks

1. **D**
2. **B**
3. **C**
4. **D**
5. **C**
6. **B**
7. **C**

---

10. There's another equitable maxim of similar meaning: "One who seeks equity must do equity."

21

Condition and Contingency

A. Conditional and Unconditional Duties: Conditions Precedent, Conditions Subsequent, and Conditions Concurrent

Nearly every American law student stumbles when she reads the phrases "condition precedent," "condition subsequent," and "condition concurrent." That shan't happen to *you* because we'll make their meaning crystal clear—right here, right now.

1. Difference Between Conditional and Unconditional Contractual Duties

Contract 1. A and B agree that (1) A will drive B to Boston on March 1 and that (2) B will pay A $100 on March 2. A's duty is to drive B to Boston on March 1, period—no ifs, ands, or buts. A's obligation is *unconditional.*

Contract 2. Now suppose this: Highway 100 leads to Boston. It's been closed for a while but is due to reopen soon. C and D agree that (1) C will drive D to Boston on March 1 *if* Highway 100 reopens by that date, and (2) D will pay C $100 for C's service. C's duty is to drive D to Boston on March 1 *only if*

Highway 100 reopens by that date. C's duty is *conditional*, in this case, on the reopening of Highway 100.

QUESTION 1. By signed writing, Daniel and Melissa reach an agreement with these terms:

The undersigned parties Daniel Thorne ("Daniel") and Melissa Wright ("Melissa") understand and acknowledge:

A. That Daniel is currently negotiating actively and in good faith toward the formation of a contract with Harmony Hall under which Daniel will, if the negotiations succeed, deliver and be paid for a singing performance at that facility on the evening of August 18, 2012; and

B. That Melissa is an able and experienced piano accompanist.

Now, therefore, the parties agree:

Item 1: Melissa will and does now commit herself to remain available to provide Daniel with piano accompaniment during and throughout the concert described above.

Item 2: In exchange for the commitment just described, Daniel will pay Melissa the sum of $400 on the execution of this agreement.

Item 3: Should the aforementioned negotiations succeed, Melissa will provide the accompaniment, and Daniel will pay Melissa an additional $600 at the conclusion of the concert.

Item 4: The nature, type, and condition of the piano itself will lie within the discretion of Harmony Hall, and in that regard Melissa will raise no dispute.

Having formed the contract,

A. Melissa has undertaken a duty conditional on Daniel's successful completion of his performance at Harmony Hall.

B. Melissa has undertaken a duty conditional on the formation of a contract between Daniel and Harmony Hall.

C. Daniel has undertaken a duty conditional on the good faith of Harmony Hall's negotiations with him.

D. Daniel has undertaken a duty conditional on Harmony Hall's ability to furnish a piano satisfactory to Melissa.

ANALYSIS. As her part of this contract, Melissa assumes two duties: (1) Item 1 requires that she be *available* on August 18 to accompany Daniel, with no ifs, ands, or buts. She "will and does now commit herself to remain available." That duty is unconditional. (2) Item 3 requires that she actually provide the accompaniment "should the aforementioned negotiations succeed," meaning the negotiations between Daniel and Harmony Hall, as described in the contract's first sentence. *If* Daniel and Harmony Hall do form a contract, meaning that Daniel will in fact perform, Melissa must provide the accompaniment. Otherwise, she need not. So Melissa's duty actually to furnish the accompaniment is conditional.

Daniel also assumes two duties: (1) Item 2, with no ifs, ands, or buts, requires that he pay Melissa $400 as soon as the parties execute the writing. (That's Melissa's payment for remaining, so to speak, "on call.") Daniel's duty to pay $400 is unconditional. (2) Item 3 requires that he pay Melissa an additional $600 "should the aforementioned negotiations succeed." That obligation arises only if Daniel and Harmony Hall form a contract (the same condition that applies to Melissa's duty to provide accompaniment). So Daniel's duty to pay $600 is unconditional.

A correctly states that Melissa assumes a conditional duty, but it misrepresents the condition; it tells us that Melissa has a duty conditional on Daniel's successful completion of his performance. With the word "successful," the question writer has set you a trap. Don't fall in. Melissa's duty to provide accompaniment arises "should the *negotiations* succeed," meaning that Daniel and Harmony Hall form a contract. The success or failure of the performance itself is irrelevant to Melissa's obligations. **A** is wrong.

C correctly states that Daniel assumes a conditional duty, but Daniel's duty is not conditional on Harmony Hall's "good faith." The agreement does invoke the words "good faith," but they form no part of the condition to which one of Daniel's duties is subject. Daniel's obligation to pay Melissa the additional $600 is conditional on the success of his negotiations with Harmony Hall—on his formation of a contract with Harmony Hall. Hence, **C** is wrong.

D invokes the word "satisfactory" and thus attracts students who, when reading contract item 4, fix on the words "condition" and "satisfaction" without reading the whole of that provision. Item 4 means that Melissa will not assert dissatisfaction with the piano Harmony Hall provides. Nothing in item 4 creates a conditional obligation, and **D** is wrong.

That leaves **B**, which correctly tells us that Melissa's duty to accompany Daniel is subject to the condition that Daniel and Harmony Hall succeed in their negotiations—that they form a contract. Hence, **B** is right.

See here, as elsewhere, that the three incorrect choices draw on words that appear in the story, a common trapping technique. The one correct choice doesn't do that. Rather, it takes a phrase set forth in the contract ("should the negotiations succeed") and requires that you understand it as a reference to the formation of a contract between Daniel and Harmony Hall.

2. Conditions Precedent and Subsequent

Knowing now the difference between conditional and unconditional duties, we must distinguish a condition "precedent" from a condition "subsequent."

Examine these two promises:

Promise 1: I will go to the fair if tomorrow's weather is good.
Promise 2: I will go to the fair unless tomorrow's weather is bad.

Promises 1 and 2 seem to create the same result. In good weather I go to the fair; in bad weather I don't. Yet there is a subtle difference between them.

Promise 1: The Condition Precedent.   Promise 1 is subject to an "if"; I am obliged to go to the fair *if* tomorrow's weather is good. At the time I make the promise, my duty is not fully mature. Rather, it's a seedling that might or might not take root. If, when tomorrow arrives, the weather is good, my duty blossoms, ripens, and comes to life. If the weather is bad, it does not. With that in mind, we say that under promise 1, my duty is subject to a "condition precedent." Something stands "in front" of it. Some event or circumstance must occur before my duty comes fully to life. A condition precedent is marked by the words "if," "only if," "but only if," or some phrase of like meaning.

Think again about my duty to go to the fair under promise 1. We've said that it's subject to a condition precedent. The condition precedent is that tomorrow's weather be good. We might express that same thought like this: "Good weather tomorrow is a condition precedent to my duty to attend the fair."

Promise 2: The Condition Subsequent.   Look at promise 2: There's no "if" about it. My duty is *not* subject to a condition precedent. It's full born as soon as I make my promise. Yet the duty might "die" before I'm ever called on to perform it. I have promised to go to the fair tomorrow without an "if," but I will be *relieved of that duty* if tomorrow's weather is bad. With bad weather, my duty disappears. Put otherwise, my duty arises as soon as I make the promise, but bad weather will *discharge* it.

When a promise is so worded as to create a current duty that is subject to discharge by some subsequent event or circumstance, we say the duty is subject to a "condition subsequent." Something is standing "in back" of it. The duty exists as soon as the relevant promise is made, but on the occurrence of some condition, it will disappear. A condition subsequent is marked by the words "unless," "but not if," or words of similar meaning.

Regarding promise 2, we might say, "My duty to attend the fair is subject to a condition subsequent, that tomorrow's weather be bad," or "Bad weather tomorrow is a condition subsequent to my duty of attendance at the fair."

QUESTION 2. By signed writing, Chantalle and Bob form a contract of purchase and sale:

1. PURCHASE AND SALE
Except in the event that she shall not be able to acquire the product named below, Chantalle will sell, supply, and deliver to Bob 13 tons of Genetech Solvent, Formula 2, at a price of $20,000 per

ton, delivery and payment to be made as described in paragraph 2 below.

2. DELIVERY AND PAYMENT

Delivery is to be made on August 15 of this calendar year by Chantalle to Bob at Bob's warehouse facility, and the purchase price described above is to be paid by Bob, conditional on and subsequent to actual delivery.

3. RIGHT OF FIRST REFUSAL AS TO SUBSEQUENT PURCHASES

If Chantalle does supply and deliver the product as provided in paragraphs 1 and 2 above, then Bob agrees that he will for all subsequent months in the present calendar year provide Chantalle a right of first refusal to sell to and provide Bob with all Genetech Solvent that Bob may require during that period.

Pursuant to the contract between Chantalle and Bob,

A. Chantalle's acquisition from Bob of a right of first refusal is a condition subsequent to Chantalle's duty to deliver Genetech Solvent to Bob.

B. Payment by Bob to Chantalle of the purchase price is a condition precedent to Chantalle's duty to acquire the Genetech Solvent.

C. Delivery by Chantalle of Genetech Solvent to Bob's warehouse facility is a condition subsequent to Bob's duty to pay.

D. Unavailability of Genetech Solvent is a condition subsequent to Chantalle's duty to supply Bob with that product.

ANALYSIS. Examine the duties each party assumes. Determine which are conditional, on what conditions they depend, and whether each condition constitutes, in substance, an "if" (condition precedent) or an "unless" (condition subsequent).

Chantalle's duties arise in paragraphs 1 and 2. Chantalle promises to supply and deliver Genetech Solvent, and there's no "if" about it. Chantalle's duty, however, is subject to an "unless," even though that word doesn't appear. Look at paragraph 1's first five words: "except in the event that." They mean "unless." The contract provides that Chantalle must supply Genetech Solvent to Bob—unless she is unable to acquire it. Chantalle's duty is subject to a condition subsequent. The "except" clause creates a condition subsequent, even though it appears physically on the page *before* the promise to "sell, supply, and deliver."

Bob's duties flow from paragraphs 2 and 3. At paragraph 2, Bob agrees to pay the purchase price—subject to an "if." Bob is required to pay "conditional on and subsequent to" actual delivery. We may restate Bob's promise thus: "If Chantalle delivers, then, after she does, Bob will pay." Bob's duty to pay is subject to a condition precedent, and that's true even though the word "subsequent" appears in the sentence (placed there, of course, to mislead you). Bob's duty arises—comes to life—only if and after Chantalle delivers.

At paragraph 3 Bob affords Chantalle a right of first refusal as seller of all Genetech Solvent Bob might buy during the year. That duty, too, carries an "if." Bob will give the right of first refusal only "if Chantalle does supply and deliver the substance as provided in" paragraphs 1 and 2. Bob's duty is subject to a condition precedent. It matures—ripens—only if Chantalle delivers.

We've identified three conditional duties:

1. Chantalle's inability to acquire the product is a condition subsequent to her duty to deliver;
2. Chantalle's actual delivery is a condition precedent to Bob's duty of payment; and
3. Chantalle's actual delivery is a condition precedent to Bob's duty to afford her a right of first refusal.

A states that Chantalle's acquisition of the right of first refusal is a condition subsequent and, specifically, that it is a condition subsequent to her duty of delivery. That's false. Chantalle's acquisition of a right of first refusal is not, itself, a condition at all. It's a duty that Bob owes her, and so **A** is wrong. According to **B**, Bob's payment of the purchase price is a condition precedent to Chantalle's duty to acquire the Genetech Solvent. That, too, is false. Payment by Bob to Chantalle is no condition at all. It's a duty that Bob owes Chantalle, and it's *subject* to a condition precedent—Chantalle's actual delivery. **B** is wrong.

C tells us that Chantalle's delivery is a condition subsequent to Bob's duty to pay. It's true that Chantalle's delivery is a condition to something. But it is a condition precedent to (a) Bob's duty to pay, and (b) Bob's duty to afford Chantalle a right of first refusal. **C** is wrong.

D tells us that Chantalle's duty to deliver is subject to a condition subsequent. That's true. Chantalle is obliged to deliver unless she is unable to acquire the product. Consequently, unavailability of product is a condition subsequent to Chantalle's duty to supply Bob with Genetech Solvent. That's what **D** says and that's why **D** is right.

3. *Significance of Conditions Precedent and Subsequent: Burden of Proof*

Suppose Arthur and Beth contemplate a written contract for the washing of windows. They consider these two alternative drafts:

Draft 1: Arthur will wash Beth's windows on Monday if the weather is fair, and Beth will pay Arthur $100 for the job.

Draft 2: Arthur will wash Beth's windows on Monday unless the weather is foul, and Beth will pay Arthur $100 for the job.

Under draft 1, Arthur's duty to wash is subject to a condition prece-dent—that Monday's weather be fair. Under draft 2, Arthur's duty to wash is subject to a condition subsequent—that Monday's weather be foul. Draft 1 is better for Arthur; draft 2 is better for Beth. Suppose the parties adopt draft 1, and Arthur fails to wash the windows.

Under draft 1, Beth must plead and prove that (1) the parties actually formed the contract, (2) on Monday, *the weather was fair,* and (3) Arthur did not wash the windows. Those *three* propositions are essential to Beth's prima facie case.

Now suppose the parties adopt draft 2, and suppose again that Arthur fails to wash the windows. Beth sues. Under draft 2, Arthur's duty to wash arises without any condition precedent. True enough—it will be discharged if the weather is foul, but unless *Arthur* can show that the weather was foul, his failure to wash is a breach. That means, under draft 2, Beth need only plead and prove (1) that the parties formed the contract, and (2) that Arthur did not perform. Those *two* propositions make out Beth's prima facie case. If Arthur wishes to show that the weather was foul, *he'll* have to put on a defense and prove it.

Stated otherwise, if a duty is subject to a condition precedent, the burden of proving that the condition occurred is on the party asserting the breach. If a duty is subject to a condition subsequent, the burden of proving that the condition occurred is on the party who denies the breach.

Continue thinking about draft 1, draft 2, and Beth v. Arthur. Suppose the evidence shows that on Monday the weather was somewhat cloudy, a bit cold (45°), wet, and a little drizzly. Some jurors might think such weather "fair." Others might think it "foul." If Beth sues Arthur under draft 1, the court will instruct the jury that "if, on the evidence, you are in doubt about the status of the weather as fair or foul, then you must find that Beth has failed to meet her burden and return a verdict for Arthur." On the other hand, if Beth sues Arthur under draft 2, the court will instruct the jury that "if, on the evidence, you are in doubt about the status of the weather as fair or foul, then you must find that Arthur has failed to meet his burden of defense and return a verdict for Beth."

Alternatively, imagine this: (1) evidence shows that the contract was formed, (2) evidence shows that Arthur failed to wash the windows, but (3) no evidence is admitted on the status of the weather. Under draft 1, Beth loses and Arthur wins. That's because Beth failed to show occurrence of the condition that would make Arthur's duty come alive. Having failed to show a duty, Beth cannot show a breach. Under draft 2, Beth wins and Arthur loses. That's because Beth has shown that Arthur had a duty and Arthur has failed to show that his duty was discharged.

QUESTION 3. By signed writing, StarCo and PumpCo form an underwriting contract:

StarCo Inc., a licensed underwriter, and PumpCo, a corporation engaged in the business of manufacturing peristaltic pumps, mutually wishing to undertake a public offering of PumpCo shares, do agree:

Item 1: StarCo will and hereby does firmly commit itself to selling, on PumpCo's behalf, through public offering, 2 million shares of PumpCo common stock, pursuant to applicable law and regulation, unless PumpCo shall fail diligently, appropriately, and timely to file such registration statements as, for this purpose, are required by applicable state and federal law.

Item 2: StarCo warrants and promises that in selling the PumpCo shares as described in paragraph 1, it will receive from buyers thereof a price no lower than $2 per share.

Item 3: PumpCo agrees that it will pay to StarCo 5 percent of the monies received from buyers of the offered shares subsequent to the receipt of such monies from PumpCo by StarCo, such payment to be made if, in fact, StarCo does, as described in paragraphs 1 and 2, sell the said shares for no less than $2 each.

StarCo fails to sell any of the PumpCo shares, and PumpCo brings an action against StarCo for breach of contract. PumpCo's complaint alleges (1) the formation of the contract described above, and (2) StarCo's failure to sell any of the PumpCo shares. PumpCo's complaint does not, however, allege that PumpCo itself had diligently, appropriately, and timely filed such registration statements as were required by applicable law. Because PumpCo fails to make that allegation, StarCo moves to dismiss the complaint. Should the court grant StarCo's motion to dismiss?

A. No, because if PumpCo did not file the registration statements, StarCo must plead and prove that fact in its own defense

B. No, because the contract nowhere includes PumpCo's promise that it will file the registration statements

C. Yes, because the filing by PumpCo of the registration statements is a condition precedent to StarCo's duty to sell the shares

D. Yes, because PumpCo's complaint does not specifically allege that StarCo failed to use reasonable commercial efforts in trying to sell the PumpCo shares

ANALYSIS.   If StarCo's duty is subject to a condition precedent, then plaintiff PumpCo must plead (and prove) that the condition occurred. If, on the other hand, StarCo's duty is unconditional or subject to some condition subsequent, PumpCo need only plead and prove that the parties formed their contract and that StarCo failed to perform.

StarCo's duty to sell the shares arises from paragraph 1: "StarCo will and hereby does firmly commit itself to selling" the shares. But that duty is subject to an "unless"; "StarCo will and hereby does firmly commit itself to selling the shares *unless* PumpCo shall fail diligently, appropriately, and timely to file" the registration statements. That means StarCo's duty is subject to a condition subsequent. As a plaintiff alleging StarCo's breach, PumpCo need not plead or prove that it *did* file the statements. Rather, StarCo must show, if it can, that PumpCo did *not* do so. For that reason, PumpCo's complaint makes out a prima facie case and is not subject to dismissal. The right answer, then, should state in substance "no," PumpCo's complaint should not be dismissed because it is not PumpCo's burden to show that it filed the registration statements, but rather StarCo's burden to show that PumpCo did not.

C and **D** say "yes," the complaint should be dismissed. For that reason, they're wrong. Further, **C** continues in error by reporting that StarCo's duty to sell is subject to a condition precedent; it is in fact subject to a condition subsequent. As for **D**, "reasonable commercial efforts" have nothing—but *nothing*—to do with this contract or controversy. Under the contract, StarCo's duty is to sell the shares. That it does or does not use reasonable commercial efforts in doing so is irrelevant. **B** correctly answers "no," PumpCo's complaint should not be dismissed. Its reasoning, however, is wrong. It's true that PumpCo does not promise to file the registration statements, but that is not the reason StarCo's motion should be dismissed. **B** is wrong.

A correctly answers "no," PumpCo's complaint should not be dismissed because StarCo, if it wishes to avoid the contract, must plead and prove that PumpCo failed to file the statements. That's exactly right. StarCo bears the burden of showing, if it can, that its duty was discharged by the occurrence of that condition subsequent. Hence, **A** is right.

4. *Conditions Concurrent*

Often two parties agree on a transaction but do not specify who will perform first. Suppose Buyer and Seller contract for the purchase and sale of Blackacre. As is common for real estate sales contracts, this one is silent on the matter of who goes first. Does the Buyer first pay the selling price, or does the Seller first deliver the deed? When a contract fails, expressly or impliedly, to provide that one of the parties will perform before the other, then the law provides that neither need perform until the other first *tenders* his performance.

A party tenders his performance when he shows that he's ready, willing, and able to perform. Suppose in our example that, at the closing, both Buyer and Seller sit and stare at each other, each waiting for the other to make the first move. As long as they sit like this doing nothing, neither has tendered his performance, and so neither is in breach. Now suppose Seller says, "Here's the deed [he holds it up]. As soon as you hand over the check, I'll hand you this deed." When Seller does that, he tenders his performance. As soon as Seller tenders his performance, Buyer must actually *perform*; he must hand over the check. Then, when Buyer pays, Seller must hand over the deed.

The law, at some point, invented the phrase "condition concurrent" and hitched it to the situation just described. When two parties form a contract that does not (expressly or impliedly) provide who should perform first, we say, that each performance is a condition concurrent to the other.[1] We mean, simply, that (1) neither party need perform until the other first tenders performance; (2) if one party does tender her performance, then—and only then—the other must actually perform.

QUESTION 4. On May 1, Desi and Yan form a signed written contract requiring that Desi conduct a marketing study and prepare a report on the product that Yan manufactures and distributes; in exchange, Yan will pay Desi $25,000. The contract provides: "The parties will meet on November 1, 2012, at Yan's offices, at which time they will make the exchange of payment for marketing report—marketing report for payment." On November 1, Desi arrives at Yan's office with the complete marketing report in his briefcase. Yan has a cashier's check for $25,000, made payable to Desi, in his desk drawer. Yan asks for the marketing report. Desi states that he will not remove the report from his briefcase until Yan pays him. Yan states that he will not pay until Desi gives him the report. Is Desi in breach for failing to hand Yan the marketing report?

A. Yes, because by refusing to deliver the report, Desi failed to honor his contractual promise

B. Yes, because Yan had no duty to make payment until Desi first tendered the marketing report

C. No, because Desi had no assurance that Yan genuinely intended to pay him

D. No, because absent Yan's tender of payment, Desi was under no duty to perform

---

ANALYSIS.   Desi and Yan formed a contract that did not provide for the order in which they'd perform, meaning that each performance was a condition concurrent to the other. Neither party here was willing to tender performance, and since neither party tendered performance, neither was in breach.

A says "yes," Desi was in breach, so it's wrong. As for the reasoning, it's true that Desi has made a contractual promise to deliver the report, but he need not honor the promise unless and until Yan tenders payment. As for **B**, it's true that Yan had no duty to pay until Desi tendered the report, but that means only

---

1. The phrase "condition concurrent" ought never have been conceived. In truth, when we say that two promises are condition concurrent to each other, we're really describing a particular form of condition precedent—that is, the tender of performance by each party is a condition *precedent* to the other's promise/duty to perform. All that we henceforth teach about conditions precedent applies to conditions concurrent.

that Yan is *not* in breach. It doesn't mean that Desi *is* in breach. **C** is tempting because one might think of Yan's tender as an assurance that Yan does in fact have the check and intends to pay. If none of the choices was better than this, **C** would be correct.

But **D** is better than **C**. **D** states the relevant rule of law. Neither party is obliged to perform until the other first tenders performance. As for whether Desi breached the contract, the answer is "no"—precisely because, absent Yan's tender, Desi need not perform. So **D** is right.

B. Conditions "Intended to Benefit" One or Both Parties

1. One Party

It is said that most conditions precedent or subsequent are "intended to ben-efit" one of the contracting parties. A court determines whether a condition is intended to benefit a particular party by interpreting the contract according to the ordinary rules of interpretation (see Chapter 18). If the condition prec-edent or subsequent applies expressly to one party and not the other, then it is intended to benefit that party.

To illustrate, let's return to a contract we've seen before: C and D agree that (1) C will drive D to Boston on March 1 if Highway 100 reopens by that date, and (2) D will pay C $100 for C's service. C promises to transport D subject to a condition *precedent*—that Highway 100 reopen by March 1. The condition affords C a (legal) protection. If it fails to occur, C is off the hook, and D doesn't get his ride. The condition is intended to benefit C, not D.

The same would apply if the highway's reopening were a condition *subse-quent* to C's duty:

C will drive D to Boston on March 1 unless Highway 100 fails to reopen by that date.

With *that* formulation, C is, *ab initio*, under a duty to furnish the trans-portation on March 1, but the law releases him if Highway 100 does not reopen (for which the burden of proof rests on him). Again, the condition is intended to benefit C, not D.

QUESTIONS 5 & 6. On June 1, 2012, JelCorp and NetCorp form a con-tract that bears these terms:

Item 1: JelCorp hereby promises to buy from NetCorp, for the price of $450,000, its Hubdie machine, delivery to be made by NetCorp to JelCorp at JelCorp's main processing center on September 9, 2012, except that JelCorp need not make the purchase if, before August

1, 2012, the U.S Congress repeals the presently effective accelerated depreciation statute applicable to the purchase of a Hubdie
machine.

Item 2: NetCorp promises, in accordance with item 1 above, to deliver
the Hubdie machine to JelCorp.

On July 1, 2012, the U.S. Congress repeals the accelerated depreciation statute applicable to the purchase of a Hubdie machine.

QUESTION 5. JelCorp contacts NetCorp: "As you may know, Congress
has repealed the accelerated depreciation statute. Nonetheless, we wish
to proceed under our contract with you and purchase the machine."
NetCorp responds, "We no longer wish to sell it to you at the $450,000
price. And since Congress has repealed the law to which our contract
refers, we need not sell it to you." If NetCorp refuses to deliver the Hubdie
machine, will it breach its contract with JelCorp?

A. Yes, because the condition has no intended beneficiary
B. Yes, because JelCorp did not insist on the condition
C. No, because the contract is subject to a condition precedent that
   Congress not repeal the accelerated depreciation statute
D. No, because repeal of the accelerated depreciation statute is a
   condition subsequent to JelCorp's promise

ANALYSIS.   The contract subjects JelCorp's promise to a condition subsequent. JelCorp promises to purchase and pay for the Hubdie machine (whatever *that* is), but then by using the words "except that" gives itself an out. It
need not purchase if Congress repeals the accelerated depreciation statute pertaining to a Hubdie purchase.

To understand why the provision concerning the depreciation statute creates a condition subsequent, not a condition precedent, remember what you
learned in section A.2 above: A condition precedent is marked by the words "if,"
"only if," "but only if," or some phrase of like meaning. A condition subsequent
is marked by the words "unless," "but not if," or words of similar meaning.
JelCorp states its promise to purchase and pay for the Hubdie machine with
the words "except that," which function as the word "unless." That phrase creates a condition subsequent; it describes an event that will discharge JelCorp's
duty.

The condition subsequent to JelCorp's promise seems, on its face, to carry
an intended benefit for JelCorp and not for NetCorp. JelCorp wants to purchase the machine only if, apparently, certain advantageous tax laws will apply
to it. Hence, this condition is intended to benefit JelCorp.

*Only the party for whose benefit a condition is intended has the power to
insist on its fulfillment or occurrence.* NetCorp, therefore, has no such power,

and the answer to Question 5 is, first of all, "yes," NetCorp will be in breach. The reason is that NetCorp is not the condition's intended beneficiary, wherefore it has no power to insist on the condition, wherefore in the face of JelCorp's willingness to purchase, its failure to deliver the machine is a breach. **A** correctly answers "yes," but thereafter makes no sense. All conditions are intended to benefit one (or occasionally both) parties. This one is intended to benefit JelCorp. **C** incorrectly answers "no"; it's wrong for that reason alone. Furthermore, it mischaracterizes the condition with the word "precedent," whereas the relevant provision is a condition subsequent. **D** correctly characterizes the condition with the word "subsequent," but it incorrectly answers "no."

That leaves **B**, which does not, however, jump out as the correct answer. It does not mention the critical point, to wit, that this condition benefits JelCorp and only the condition's beneficiary has the power to insist on it. Yet **B** makes a correct statement in every way. It answers "yes," and then words the reason in a way that's exactly correct (even though the question writer has not used the wording you'd *like* to see). It is true that because JelCorp did not insist on the condition, NetCorp must deliver the machine or find itself in breach. If JelCorp *had* insisted on the condition, NetCorp would not be in breach for failing to deliver the machine. Implicit (and sort of hidden) in **B** is the reality that only JelCorp has the power to insist on the condition and, therefore, the power not to insist on it. **B** is right.

QUESTION 6. JelCorp contacts NetCorp: "As you may know, Congress has repealed the accelerated depreciation statute. We are not willing to purchase. Please do not deliver." NetCorp responds, "We don't insist on the condition that concerns the depreciation statute. We're ready to proceed and expect you to purchase." If JelCorp refuses to pay for the machine, does it breach its contract with NetCorp?

A. Yes, because the provision concerning the depreciation statute is a condition precedent to NetCorp's promise

B. Yes, because the provision concerning the depreciation statute is a condition precedent to JelCorp's promise

C. No, because the contract is subject to the condition that Congress not repeal the accelerated depreciation statute

D. No, because repeal of the accelerated depreciation statute is a condition subsequent to JelCorp's promise

---

ANALYSIS. JelCorp's promise to purchase is subject to a condition subsequent; its duty to purchase is discharged if and when Congress repeals the statute. Congress did repeal the statute and thus released JelCorp from what was otherwise its obligation to purchase. The answer, therefore, is "no," JelCorp is not in breach. The reason is that its obligation to purchase was subject to a condition subsequent that did occur.

A incorrectly answers "yes." It mischaracterizes the condition with the word "precedent" and ties the condition to NetCorp's promise, whereas it belongs to JelCorp's promise. **A** couldn't be more wrong. **B** incorrectly answers "yes," and it too mischaracterizes the condition with the word "precedent." **C** correctly answers "no" but ties the condition to "the contract" and that's not quite right. Properly characterized, a condition attaches to one or the other of the parties' promise(s) or, perhaps, to both. But it's poor form to characterize a condition as a provision attached to the whole of a contract. Even if the terms expressly provide that "this contract is subject to the condition that . . . ," still the condition belongs, truly, to one or both of the parties' promise(s), not to "the contract." In this case, the condition is plainly and expressly tied to JelCorp's promise, so that even one whose form is poor would know better than to state, in this case, that the condition applies to "the contract." **C** is bad.

D correctly answers "no," JelCorp will not be in breach, and it correctly states the reason, to wit, that its promise is subject to a condition subsequent, which *we* know has occurred, and thus relieved JelCorp of its obligation to purchase, so **D** is right.

2. One or Both Parties

Some conditions precedent or subsequent are intended to benefit both parties. But beware. Even when a condition applies to *both parties' promises*, it may be intended to benefit only one of them. Or then again, it may be just as it seems: intended to benefit both.

Let's use our driving-to-Boston example to illustrate. D, still trying to get to Boston, converses with C:

> **D:** Do you think you might be able to drive me to Boston on March 1?
> **C:** Yes, for $100 or so, but Highway 100 is closed.
> **D:** So what? There are other routes to Boston.
> **C:** Well, I won't do it unless I can travel Highway 100.
> **D:** Well, all right, I suppose I'll agree to that.

C and D then create this writing: C and D agree that (1) if Highway 100 reopens by March 1, then, for a price of $100, to be paid on arrival in Boston, C will drive D to Boston; and (2) D will pay C $100 for C's service.

The writing begins by stating a condition—that Highway 100 reopen by March 1. It then recites the two parties' promises, so that superficially the condition appears to attach itself to both sides of the contract. Read literally (and hence, superficially) the terms provide that if the Highway does not reopen by March 1, neither party need perform. Yet the parties' antecedent conversation makes plain that D is indifferent to the travel route. It is C to whom

Route 100 is important. Mindful of "intention" under contract law—reading the words to mean as, under all prevailing circumstances, reasonable persons would understand them, the condition is intended to benefit C.

Sometimes, in the nature of things, conditions reveal an intention to benefit one party absent the showing of any surrounding circumstance. Consider these contractual terms:

> If, by May 1, the zoning board approves Buyer's plan to build a hotel on Blackacre, now owned by Seller, then on June 1, for a purchase price of $12 million, Seller and Buyer will undertake and proceed with the purchase and sale of Blackacre.

The writing first states a condition—that the zoning board should approve Buyer's plan to build a hotel on Blackacre. It then recites the two parties' promises, so that on its face the condition appears to attach itself to both parties' promises. Read literally (and hence superficially), the terms provide that if the zoning board does not issue its approval, then neither party need perform.

Read with a mind toward "intention," meaning that which reasonable persons would understand all of the words to mean, we can conclude, without more, that Seller cares only to sell the property and receive her money; she doesn't care about the zoning board or the hotel. Buyer wants the Board's approval; he doesn't want Blackacre unless he can build the hotel on it. Hence, on the basis of the contractual words alone, without insight into any additional surrounding circumstances, a court will likely conclude that the condition is intended to benefit Buyer. (If Seller insists that the condition was intended to benefit him as well, then certainly he can present evidence of such surrounding circumstances as would tend to substantiate his claim.)

3. Only the Party Intended to Benefit May Insist on the Condition

Consider again C's and D's Boston travel contract. Suppose on February 15, C contacts D:

C: I don't think Highway 100 will be open by March 1. I've decided, however, that I'm willing to take old Route 4. So I'll drive you to Boston on March 1. Count on it.

D: I too have rethought the matter. If we can't go on Route 100, I don't want to go.

C: I'm coming to pick you up on the morning of the first; I expect you to be ready. And if you refuse to travel, I expect to be paid nonetheless.

C appears at D's home on the morning of March 1, ready to drive D to Boston via old Route 4. (C thus tenders his performance.) D refuses to travel and states, "The condition attached to our contract has not occurred; Highway 100 is not open. I don't have to travel or pay."

But party D is wrong. Because the condition is intended to benefit party C, D has no right or power to insist on it. If C wants to perform notwithstanding the nonoccurrence of a condition intended for his benefit, then he has every right to do so and to insist on D's performance as well. D has nothing to say about it. Stated otherwise, the party for whom the condition's benefit is intended has the power to insist on the condition or to "waive" it, as she chooses.

C.   Excuse of a Condition: Obstruction, Waiver, Estoppel

The law may "excuse" a condition (precedent or subsequent) for reasons of obstruction, waiver, or estoppel.

1. *Condition Excused by Obstruction*

If a condition that benefits Party A will occur or not depending on some conduct of Party A, and B prevents A from fulfilling the condition, then it's excused. Suppose A and B agree that (1) A will mow the lawn using B's lawnmower, and (2) B will pay A $50, on the condition that A refill the lawnmower's gas tank after using it to mow the lawn. If B will not give access to the lawnmower when A returns to refill its gas tank, B's "obstruction" excuses the condition precedent to B's performance. B must pay A, notwithstanding that the condition is unfulfilled—that A did not refill the gas tank.

2. *Condition Excused by Waiver*

Far more common and more involved than excuse by obstruction is the condition excused by "waiver." A contracting party for whom a condition's benefit is intended waives the condition (precedent or subsequent) when he expresses his willingness to perform notwithstanding the condition's nonfulfillment. C in the Boston example waived the condition concerning Highway 100, and D had nothing to say about it; *he* was obliged to perform. That raises another question: If one waives or promises to waive a condition, is he bound by that promise?

Suppose again that on February 15, C contacts D. This time, however, the conversation runs thus:

> **C:** I don't think Highway 100 will open by March 1. I've decided, however, that I'm willing to take old Route 4. So I'll drive you to Boston on the first. Count on it.
> **D:** That's great.
> **C:** I'll see you on March 1.

On February 18, C contacts D again:

> **C:** I've changed my mind again. I don't want to travel on any route other than Route 100. So we're back to our original agreement. If Highway 100 opens by March 1, we go. If not, we don't.

D: Oh, no. You promised just three days ago that you would perform regardless of Highway 100. You waived the Highway 100 condition.

C: Well, now, I'm "unwaiving" it.

D: You can't do that; you'll be in breach.

Is D right? Must C keep his promise of waiver? In Chapter 14, section B, you learned that to modify an existing contract, each party must provide the other with consideration—just as each must do in forming the contract to begin with. By waiving—promising not to insist on—the Highway 100 condition, C gives up a contractual right and receives nothing back for it. If the law requires that he keep the promise—if it holds him to the waiver—then, in effect, it binds him to a contractual modification for which he receives no consideration. Yet the law might hold him to the waiver, and the relevant rule draws on the notion of "detrimental reliance" (as does the doctrine of promissory estoppel addressed in Chapter 14, section F). The rule provides: *If a contracting party waives a condition intended for her benefit, then (1) she may effectively retract the waiver before the other party has reasonably, foreseeably, and detrimentally relied on it, but (2) she is bound by the waiver once the other party has reasonably, foreseeably, and detrimentally relied on it.*

Let's apply the rule to the Boston travel case in its most recent incarnation: (1) C waived the condition on February 15, and (2) attempted to retract his waiver on the 18th, three days later. Suppose, first, that on February 16, D, in reliance on C's waiver (a) confirmed his business appointment for that day; (b) purchased nonrefundable airline tickets for $600, with which his wife and children could fly to Boston on March 3 when his business would conclude; and (c) for that same purpose, reserved hotel rooms for the week March 3 to March 10. C's attempt to retract his waiver would be ineffective; the law would bind him to it. If, on the other hand, D had not altered his position in any way in reliance on the waiver, then C would be free to retract it.

Waiver Is Nonretractable Only If the Condition Is Immaterial to the Contract's Essence.   Reread the zoning board contract in section B.2 above. Now suppose that, on April 29, Seller contacts Buyer: "I have some information indicating that the zoning board is not going to approve your proposal by May 1. So that I may make plans, tell me, please: Are you willing to buy the property even if the board does not give its approval by the first?" The Buyer replies, "Yes, I'll buy anyway." Buyer has purported to waive the condition precedent tied to his performance. A court would likely rule, however, that this particular condition goes to the essence of Buyer's purpose in forming the contract. Both parties understood (or should have understood)—*when they formed the contract*—that Buyer wished to own Blackacre to build a hotel on it. With the condition thus touching on Buyer's principal contractual purpose, the waiver is retractable, and that is so even if Seller relies on it to his detriment, reasonably and foreseeably.

If the zoning board fails to approve Buyer's proposal by May 1 and then on June 1 Seller wishes to proceed with the purchase and sale, Buyer may still, if he wishes, insist on the condition, whether or not Seller has relied to his detriment on Buyer's wavier.

The Rule in Fuller Form.   Let's expand the rule of waiver:

If a contracting party waives a condition that is (a) intended for her benefit, and (b) *ancillary* to her principal contractual purpose, then
      (1) she may effectively retract the waiver before the other party has reasonably, foreseeably, and detrimentally relied on it, but
      (2) she is bound by the waiver once the other party has reasonably, foreseeably, and detrimentally relied on it.

Restatement (Second) of Contracts §84 provides:

[A contractual] promise to perform all or part of a conditional duty . . . in spite of the non-occurrence of the condition [meaning the promisor waives the condition tied to his promise] is binding . . . unless . . . occurrence of the condition was a material part of the agreed exchange [or, more precisely, it pertains to promisor's principal purpose in forming the contract]. The promisor can make his duty again subject to the condition [meaning he can retract his waiver] by notifying the promisee . . . of his intention to do so if . . . [retraction of the waiver] is not unjust because of a material change of position by the promise . . . [meaning the promisee has not relied on the waiver reasonably, foreseeably, and to his detriment].

QUESTIONS 7 & 8. FanCo and FireCo form a contract that includes these terms:

Paragraph 12: FanCo hereby promises and agrees that it will monitor the activities of FireCo's 400 franchisees throughout the United States and Europe and Asia, and report to FireCo once every three months in writing, according to details and specifications described in paragraphs 3 to 11 above, but FanCo will have no such obligation as to any nation if there should come to exist a state of war between any such nation and any nation anywhere.

Paragraph 13: FireCo will pay FanCo once every three months $4 million, representing $1 million per franchise, except that it will not pay as to any franchise that FanCo fails to monitor in any three-month period for the reasons referenced in Paragraph 12 above.

QUESTION 7. If FireCo announces a waiver of the condition set forth in Paragraph 13, beginning with the words "except that," and FanCo reasonably and foreseeably relies on the waiver to its detriment, will FireCo be empowered, thereafter, to retract its waiver?

A. Yes, because as to this contract FireCo's principal purpose is to receive FanCo's reports
B. Yes, because FanCo has the power to insist or not on a condition intended for its benefit
C. No, because reasonable, foreseeable reliance always renders a waiver nonretractable
D. No, because such retraction would subject FireCo to an unfair practice

ANALYSIS. Regardless of the promisee's reliance, a promisor cannot—even if she wants to—make a nonretractable waiver as to a condition that goes to the essence of her contractual purpose. As for this contract, FanCo's principal purpose is to receive payment. FireCo's principal purpose is to receive *reports*. Paragraph 13 subjects FanCo's promise to pay $1 million for each report to the condition that it *actually receive the report*. That condition goes to the heart of FireCo's purpose in forming this contract. If FanCo announces its waiver of that condition, it *can*, thereafter, retract the waiver and reinstate the condition no matter how or to what degree FireCo relies on it. The answer, therefore, is "yes"—FanCo is empowered to retract its waiver. The reason is that the condition goes to the essence of FanCo's contractual purpose.

D incorrectly answers "no," so it's wrong. As a reason, it offers up some happy-sounding "fluff" concerning "an unfair practice." **C**, too, incorrectly answers "no," and it's wrong. It makes the false statement that detrimental reliance always renders a waiver nonretractable; wrong again. Detrimental reliance is necessary to but not sufficient for nonretractability. Stated otherwise, retractability requires, always, detrimental reliance. But a waiver does not, in every case, become nonretractable simply because the promisee has detrimentally relied on it. Retractability requires, also, that the condition at issue be ancillary or immaterial to the promisor's principal contractual purpose.

B correctly answers "yes," but it reports an irrelevancy. It's true that FanCo (and any contracting party) has the power to insist or not on a condition intended for its benefit. But this condition is intended to benefit FireCo, not FanCo. **B**'s observation is wholly irrelevant to the question. **A** correctly answers "yes" and correctly states the applicable reason: FireCo's principal contractual purpose is to receive FanCo's reports. Consequently it cannot waive the condition—that it receive the reports. Hence **A** is right.

QUESTION 8. If FanCo announces a waiver of the condition set forth in Paragraph 12, beginning with the words "but FanCo will have no such obligation," and FireCo reasonably and foreseeably relies on the waiver to its detriment, will FanCo be empowered, thereafter, to retract its waiver?

A. Yes, because as to this contract FireCo's principal purpose is to receive FanCo's reports

> **B.** No, because FireCo has the power to insist or not on a condition intended for its benefit
> **C.** No, because reasonable, foreseeable reliance renders this waiver nonretractable
> **D.** No, because such retraction would subject FanCo to an unfair practice

ANALYSIS. This condition (subsequent) relieves FanCo of its duty to monitor any franchisee if the nation in which it sits goes to war. Quite obviously (any court would likely rule), FanCo wants freedom from the obligation to travel to or enter into nations at war. The condition expressly attaches itself to FanCo's promise and plainly is intended for FanCo's benefit. Yet, it does not pertain to FanCo's principal contractual purpose. Surely any court would rule that, although FanCo might well regard the condition as terribly important, FanCo did not form this contract to prevent war among nations. It did so to sell its service — to receive payment. Hence this condition, unlike the one that appears in Paragraph 13, is ancillary to its beneficiary's principal contracting purpose.

Based on the rule of waiver given in the section above titled "The Rule in Fuller Form," if FireCo relies (somehow) reasonably, foreseeably, and to its detriment, can FanCo thereafter retract its waiver? The answer is "no" — FanCo cannot retract its waiver. The reason is twofold: (1) the condition is ancillary to its beneficiary's principal contracting purpose, and (2) the promisee (FireCo) has relied on the waiver.

A incorrectly answers "yes," so it's wrong. For a reason it states an irrelevant truth — that FireCo's principal purpose is to receive FanCo's reports. For this question it matters not where lies FireCo's principal purpose. **B** is just as bad. It offers another "yes," wrong in itself, and another irrelevant truth — that FireCo has the power to insist or not on a condition intended for its benefit. FireCo does have such power (within limits), but this condition is not intended for *its* benefit; it benefits FanCo. As it did in Question 8, **D** refers us to the "fluffy" concept of unfairness — which does not, with precision, explain the answer.

C is right all the way 'round, and it differs by one word from the **C** that appears with Question 8. The difference lies in "this waiver" versus "a waiver." *This* waiver is ancillary to FanCo's primary contractual purpose. And so it is that FireCo's reliance on *this* waiver renders it nonretractable. **C** is right.

3. The Doctrine of Estoppel Touches on the Nonretractable Waiver

We've said that one party may not retract his waiver because the other has relied on it. To that statement, we should add the word "estoppel," like this:

*If as to a contract between Parties A and B, A waives a condition and B rea-
sonably, foreseeably, and detrimentally relies on the waiver, then, by reason of
estoppel, A may not retract his waiver.* Let's explore the word "estoppel."

Suppose (1) Shayna has a baby. By judicial proceeding, she alleges that
Marvin is the biological father and asks that the court issue a support award
against him. (2) Marvin responds by admitting his fatherhood and by demanding also shared custody of the child. (3) Shayna, wanting to keep sole custody,
responds by alleging now that Marvin is *not* the father.

The court rules:

> This mother, Shayna, first took the position that Marvin was the baby's father
> and on that basis sought a support award. Faced now with a custody claim,
> she reverses course, contending that Marvin is *not* the father and so has no
> custodial rights. We hold that she cannot want it one way and then another.
> That is, we invoke the doctrine of estoppel and rule that Shayna, having first
> claimed that Marvin was the child's father, will not now be heard to say he
> is not. She is *estopped* now to assert that Marvin is not the father, and so
> whether he is or is not, we shan't entertain her claim that he is not.

Now imagine that Francis and Ethel, each driving her own car, collide. A few
days later Fran receives a letter from Ethel's lawyer:

> We represent Ethel Elanda, with whom you were recently involved in an
> automobile accident. Having thoroughly investigated the matter, we con-
> clude that you were at fault. We have also thoroughly investigated all aspects
> and details of the damage to our client's vehicle and we have determined that
> it amounts, monetarily, to $2,700. Please write a check to our offices in the
> amount of $2,700 in order that our client may be properly reimbursed.

Francis refuses, and the attorneys send another letter asserting, again, that they
have thoroughly investigated the accident and the damage in all aspects and
details. Again, they demand payment in the amount of $2,700, which, they
assert, represents the damage done to their client's automobile. Again, Francis
refuses to pay. Ethel's attorney brings suit in the amount, not of $2,700, but
$11,100, asserting now that he stands ready to prove in court that the collision
damaged Ethel's vehicle to that degree.

Citing the doctrine of estoppel, Francis's lawyer contends that whatever
the true damages to Francis's vehicle, she (by her lawyers) may not now claim
or be allowed to prove, even if she can, that they exceed $2,700. Even if the
vehicle really is damaged to the extent of $11,100, he argues, Ethel and her
attorneys are estopped to ask for any more than $2,700 (and, of course, that
they'll have to prove damages even of that amount). Ethel's attorney addresses
the court:

> Your Honor, Plaintiff's attorneys, having repeatedly demanded that Defendant
> pay $2,700 upon their claim that they had "*thoroughly investigated* all aspects
> and details" of the accident and damages cannot now be heard to say that
> the damage is three times what their "thorough investigation of all aspects

and details" first revealed, upon which they demanded that Defendant pay $2,700. Even if the vehicle truly was damaged to the extent of $11,100, as Plaintiff and her attorneys claim, they should be estopped now even to make that claim and estopped, likewise, to present any evidence that would support it. They demanded that Defendant pay $2,700 in accordance with their "thorough investigation." Under the doctrine of estoppel, they should not and cannot now be heard to say that the damages were greater than that.

The court might well agree and rule that (and her attorneys) are estopped to claim $11,100 after first purporting to have conducted a thorough investigation as to every aspect and detail of the damage and, on that basis, made a demand for $2,700.

The Doctrine of Estoppel Stated   The doctrine of estoppel provides generally:

> A first party will not be heard to assert against a second what would otherwise be a proper position if, as to the matter at issue,
>   (a) the first has induced the second to believe she would not take such a position, wherefore the other, on that belief, has reasonably, foreseeably, and detrimentally relied; or
>   (b) the position she first asserts so contravenes some statement or stance she has earlier taken as to create incongruity that amounts to injustice.

Part (a) of the foregoing definition applies to the Boston travel case in which D relied on C's waiver by committing to the purchase of airline tickets and hotel accommodations. C is estopped to retract his waiver; that's clear. Part (b) applies to Shayna, who first demands a support award, claiming that Marvin fathered her child and then, faced with a custody dispute, flip-flops and claims he did not. (A fair-minded person wants to say to Shayna: "Having claimed that Marvin was the father to obtain a support award, you're in no position now to claim — and you will not be heard to say — that he is *not* the father. And when fair-mindedness invites a statement such as that, the doctrine of estoppel becomes relevant.)

Part (b) above applies, likewise, to Francis, Ethel, and the attorneys who first demand $2,700 upon their purported "thorough investigation," but then, when Ethel refuses to pay, bring an action for $11,100. (The fair-minded person wants to say: You claimed to have made a "thorough investigation of all aspects and details" relating to the damage and were ready to take $2,700 from Defendant without her having a day in court. You're in no position now to claim, in court, that the damages are higher — you won't be heard to say so.)

There's Much More to Estoppel Than We've Described   In all (conceptual) directions, estoppel reaches far beyond what we've discussed, and it embodies a variety of types and categories including "estoppel in pais," "estoppel by deed," "collateral estoppel," "estoppel by acquiescence," and "promissory estoppel" (discussed in Chapter 14, section F). Estoppel is not—not at all—limited in application to the law of contracts. All that we've said about estoppel is *correct*, but it's not *complete*. We have only touched on the subject in order to explain why, when a waiver of condition is nonretractable, the words "estoppel" and "estopped" rear their heads. Now you know why they do.

D. An Implied Condition Precedent: Substantial Performance, Total Breach, and Partial Breach

The common law provides that an "express" condition—one that the parties explicitly state or write—calls for *full and literal fulfillment*. When C promises to drive D to Boston *if Highway 100 reopens*, his duty arises only if Highway 100 does fully reopen (whatever the court decides "reopen" means). If it's a five-lane highway and only four lanes reopen, then it has not fully reopened; the condition does not occur, and C has no duty to transport D to Boston (unless the court decides, as is unlikely, that "reopen" includes the opening of only four lanes).

Now Suppose Corp X and Corp Y agree that: (1) Corp X will ship 36 tons of the chemical substance known as Trentoran to Corp Y, if Corp X can secure, for a total of $10,000 or less, a 24-hour rental of 18 trucks, each with a payload capacity of no less than 2 tons; and (2) Corp Y promises to pay $20 million for the Trentoran.

Corp X's promise to deliver the Trentoran is subject to the express condition precedent that it be able to secure for a total of $10,000 or less a 24-hour rental of 18 trucks, each with a payload capacity of no less than 2 tons. If Corp X can secure only 12 trucks, each with a payload capacity of 3 tons, its duty to deliver the Trentoran does not arise. In substance and in essence, perhaps, the condition is fulfilled because 12 trucks with a payload capacity of 3 tons will facilitate the transport of $(12 \times 3) = (18 \times 2) = 36$ tons of Trentoran. Nonetheless, this express condition has not enjoyed complete, absolute, literal fulfillment. Consequently, Corp X is not obliged to deliver the Trentoran.

1. Conditions Implied by Law Call Only for Substantial Fulfillment

The law will, at times, impose its own condition upon a party's performance in order, 'tis said, to "do justice." An implied condition calls not for complete and literal fulfillment, but only for "substantial" fulfillment. The only implied/constructive condition of general consequence is described below, and it spawns the doctrine of "substantial performance."

Suppose Jack and Jill agree that (1) on Monday Jack will paint the kitchen, and (2) on Tuesday Jill will pay Jack $500. The terms don't seem on their face to provide for any conditions—precedent *or* subsequent.

But the law implies one: the doctrine of substantial performance. As to the contract just described, the law subjects Jill's duty to this condition *precedent*: that Jack shall *substantially perform* the painting of the kitchen. The *law* reads the contract thus: (1) on Monday Jack must paint the kitchen, and (2) *if Jack substantially performs on Monday*, then on Tuesday Jill must pay Jack $500. The law adds the italicized text as a condition precedent to Jane's duty: *Where a contract provides that Party 1 is to perform first in time and Party 2 is to perform second in time, the law implies as a condition precedent to Party 2's duty that Party 1 shall timely deliver a substantial performance.*

Think about the kitchen painting contract and imagine that on Tuesday Jill refuses to pay. If Jack sues for breach he'll have to prove that (1) the parties formed the contract, (2) on Monday he substantially performed the painting service, and (3) on Tuesday Jill failed to pay. Stated otherwise, if on Monday Jack fails to give substantial performance, then Jane's duty to pay does not arise—at all.

And What's "Substantial Performance?"   One furnishes substantial performance when she—pretty much, by and large—performs her obligations, even if she doesn't *fully* and *completely* perform them to perfection in every detail. One substantially performs if, as to her obligations, she leaves undone only a portion that is slight, small, relatively unimportant, immaterial. It helps, perhaps, to think numerically:

- Performance to the extent of 50 percent, 60 percent, 70 percent, 80 percent, or 85 percent certainly is *not* substantial performance.
- Performance of 99 percent *is* substantial performance.
- Performance to the extent of 90 percent, 92 percent, or 95 percent creates a "gray area"; it might or might not be substantial performance.

Understand, however, that not every performance or breach is readily quantifiable in true numeric terms. Suppose Party A is to deliver a music lesson and Party B alleges that A failed substantially to perform because the lesson was, to a substantial degree, unprofessional. One cannot measure "professionalism" in numbers. Hence in many (maybe most) cases, the numerical guide set forth above is valuable in figurative terms only.

Suppose Xavier and Thalia form a contract by which they agree that

Item 1: Xavier will clean Thalia's fireplace on Wednesday and then clean any areas of the nearby floor that become unclean as a result, so to restore the surrounding area to its original condition, completing all work by 5:00 P.M. sharp—no delays or extensions.

Item 2: Thalia is to pay Xavier $100 on Wednesday at 5:00 P.M.

Xavier works on the fireplace all day Wednesday. At 5:00 P.M., he finishes cleaning the fireplace, but he has created an ugly mess on the floor that will take, say, another 30 minutes to clean. He says to Thalia, "Well, I have left only to clean the floor. I'll stay and do that now, or I'll come back tomorrow and do it then—whatever you prefer." She replies, "I don't want either. You had until 5:00 and you haven't finished. I don't want you to stay on now and I don't want you back. I'm not going to pay you—not anything."

Thalia is within her rights. The contract calls for Xavier to perform first in time. Thalia is to perform second. By implication of law, therefore, contract item 2 reads thus: "*If Xavier substantially completes the cleaning of the fireplace (and the surrounding floor) by Wednesday at 5:00, then* Thalia is to pay Xavier $100 on Wednesday at 5:00." The italicized words represent the condition precedent imposed by implication of law. With the fireplace clean and surrounding floor markedly unclean, Xavier has (probably) not given a substantial performance. It's hard to assess the breach numerically, of course, but the percentage numbers presented above are useful as figurative guides. Left with a soot-covered floor, Thalia can't consider Xavier's work and conclude that it's done to near perfection. Xavier's failure to clean the floor by 5:00 P.M. is, probably, a failure to furnish substantial performance, meaning Thalia's obligation is subject to an unfulfilled condition precedent, wherefore she need not pay.

What if Xavier does clean the floor, but leaves one tiny speck of soot? If Xavier does, by 5:00 P.M. clean the floor, leaving however, one small speck of soot, then he does, certainly, furnish substantial performance—a performance that is almost entirely complete even though not complete "to the letter" in every single detail. In that case, (1) Xavier *is* in breach (ever so slightly), but (2) Thalia is nonetheless obliged to pay Xavier *in full*, and (3) Thalia has an action against Xavier for this teensy breach (if she cares to pursue it), but she must pay *in full* or she herself will be in breach.

QUESTIONS 9 & 10. TCorp binds books, booklets, and magazines. UCorp publishes a magazine called *RoofTop*. In May 2012, UCorp has 1 million copies of its August issue printed. The copies, however, are not bound. UCorp contracts with TCorp to take possession of the 1 million copies, bind them, and return them to UCorp by July 25. Relevant portions of the parties' written contract appear below.

The undersigned parties TCorp and UCorp do agree on May 6, 2012, that: [Paragraphs 1-120 not shown]

Paragraph 121: TCorp will bind 1 million copies of UCorp's magazine *RoofTop* according to the specifications set forth in paragraphs 10-120 hereof, and deliver the said 1 million bound copies to UCorp in 10,000 bound packages of 100 copies, each on or before July 25, 2012.

> **Paragraph 122:** On or before July 27, 2012, UCorp will pay TCorp a $300,000 fee.
>
> **QUESTION 9.** On July 25, TCorp tenders delivery to UCorp of 800,000 copies of the bound magazine in 8,000 packages of 100 copies each. TCorp apologizes for not having finished the job and promises to deliver the remaining 200,000 magazines within 10 days, on or before August 4. UCorp refuses to accept the 800,000 magazines because they are deficient in quantity. On July 27, TCorp demands payment from UCorp of $240,000, or 80 percent of the total fee. UCorp refuses to accept the magazines and refuses to pay. Is UCorp in breach of contract?
>
> **A.** Yes, because TCorp promised to complete its work within a reasonable time after the initial due date
> **B.** Yes, because TCorp furnished 80 percent of its performance and is entitled to 80 percent of the payment provided in the contract
> **C.** No, because TCorp gave UCorp no reliable basis on which to believe it would complete the work on or before August 4
> **D.** No, because a condition precedent to UCorp's duty of payment has not occurred

ANALYSIS.   If two parties form a contract under which Party 1 is to perform first in time and Party 2 second in time, substantial performance by Party 1 is a condition precedent to Party 2's duty to perform. Consequently, if Party 1 fails to give substantial performance, Party 2 need not perform—at all.

TCorp and UCorp formed a contract under which TCorp was to perform first in time (on or before July 25) and UCorp was to perform second in time (on or before July 27). By implication of law, UCorp's duty to pay on or before July 27 was subject to the condition precedent that TCorp should, on July 25, furnish substantial performance. By law, paragraph 122 of their contract means that *if TCorp furnishes substantial performance on or before July 25, then* on or before July 27, UCorp will pay TCorp a $300,000 fee. The italicized words represent the condition precedent implied by law. On July 25, TCorp furnished performance of only 80 percent, which does not amount to substantial performance. The relevant condition precedent, therefore, did not occur, and UCorp need not pay. For that reason, the answer is "no"—UCorp is not in breach of contract.

A answers "yes," so it's wrong. Further it misstates the law, implying that one who fails to furnish substantial performance is entitled to performance if he promises to complete performance within a reasonable time. There is no such rule. **B** also answers "yes," and it too is wrong. It too misstates the law. If Party 1 performs to the extent of 80 percent, she is not entitled to 80 percent of Party 2's performance. Rather, she is entitled to nothing.

C correctly answers "no," but its reasoning is wrong. It implies that if Party 1 fails to furnish substantial performance but promises to complete performance within a reasonable time and gives Party 2 a reliable basis on which to believe that representation, then Party 2 is obliged to perform. Again, there is no such rule.

D correctly answers "no." UCorp is not in breach of contract because there failed to occur a condition precedent to UCorp's duty. That's correct. UCorp's duty to pay is subject to the condition precedent that TCorp substantially perform. TCorp failed to do that, meaning that UCorp need not pay, meaning in turn that by refusing to pay it commits no breach. Hence, **D** is right.

QUESTION 10. Assume for this question that on July 25 TCorp tenders delivery to UCorp of 10,000 packages of magazines and advises UCorp: "The total number of magazines in the packages is 1 million, as agreed, and all but two packages contain exactly 100 magazines, as agreed. One package contains only 99 magazines and another contains 101." UCorp refuses to accept the magazines, and on July 27, it refuses to pay. Is UCorp in breach of contract?

A. Yes, because the condition precedent to UCorp's duty was satisfied
B. Yes, because TCorp honestly disclosed its breach
C. No, because TCorp failed to furnish substantial performance
D. No, because TCorp did not deliver a perfect service, as provided by the contract

---

ANALYSIS. If two parties form a contract under which Party 1 is to perform first in time and Party 2 is to perform second, then the law implies, as a condition precedent to Party 2's duty, that Party 1 will *substantially* perform, not that Party 1 will perfectly perform "to the letter." If Party 1 provides a nearly perfect performance, incomplete or flawed only in some immaterial way, then he is in breach, but has nonetheless given substantial performance, and Party 2 must perform.

These parties formed a contract requiring that TCorp perform first in time and UCorp second. TCorp timely delivered 1 million bound magazines as required, but deviated ever so slightly from its obligation. Its failure constitutes a breach, but a breach so small as to mean that it did still furnish substantial performance. Consequently, TCorp satisfied the condition precedent provided by law, and UCorp is obliged to pay (and is entitled, of course, to the magazines that it refused to accept). The answer then is "yes"—UCorp is in breach, and the reason is that TCorp furnished substantial performance, thus fulfilling the condition precedent to UCorp's duty to pay.

C and **D** say "no," so they're wrong. **D** implies that UCorp would be obliged to pay only if TCorp delivered a perfect service. That is not the rule. UCorp's failure to deliver a perfect service constitutes a breach on its part. UCorp is entitled to recover any damages it sustains as a result, but it may not, for that reason, withhold its own performance. It must pay in full. **C** incorrectly concludes that TCorp failed to furnish substantial performance. Certainly TCorp did furnish substantial performance. **B** correctly answers "yes," but its reasoning is wrong. It implies that one who honestly discloses his breach is entitled to a return performance for that reason. There is no such rule. **B** is wrong.

A is correct. It says "yes," UCorp is in breach, and correctly states the reason. By furnishing substantial performance, TCorp fully satisfied the condition precedent to UCorp's duty to pay. That's why **A** is right.

2. *Material (Total) Breach; Immaterial (Partial) Breach*

If a contracting party furnishes substantial performance but does not give "letter perfect" performance in every detail, then she has committed an "immaterial" breach, also called a "partial" breach. An immaterial breach is one so slight as not to negate a substantial performance. If as to a contract between Parties X and Y, we say "X committed an immaterial breach," we're saying that Party X (1) did furnish substantial performance, and (2) did also commit a (very small) breach entitling Party Y to damages (whatever they are).

If a party commits a breach sufficiently large as to fail to furnish substantial performance, then he commits a "material" breach, also called a "total" breach. One who performs to the extent of 10 percent, 30 percent, 50 percent, 70 percent, 80 percent, or 85 percent commits a material breach and, concomitantly, fails to furnish substantial performance.

In Question 9 above, TCorp delivered only 80 percent of the bound magazines it had promised. Consequently, TCorp committed a material breach and failed to give substantial performance. That means UCorp had no obligation to pay TCorp anything and had an action against TCorp for damages sustained by its breach. In Question 10 above, TCorp delivered an incomplete, but very *nearly* complete performance and so, TCorp committed an immaterial breach and furnished substantial performance. Consequently, UCorp was obliged to make full payment and nonetheless had an action against TCorp for the damages (if any) it suffered because of the partial breach.

3. *Seller's Substantial Performance Is Not Enough to Trigger Buyer's Duty*

Under UCC §2-206 (and older law on which it draws), the seller of goods must make a "perfect tender" to trigger what would otherwise be the buyer's duty to accept the goods and pay the price. Suppose Buyer and Seller form a contract that calls for Seller to deliver 100 widgets, each wrapped in light blue paper, Seller to deliver the goods to Buyer's facility on July 11, Buyer to pay the purchase price on July 12. On July 11, Seller delivers 100 widgets, all of them in perfect condition, wrapped in *dark* blue paper. Even if all concede that the color of the wrapping paper is a trivial matter, still, Buyer may reject the goods, refuse to pay the price, and sue for Seller's breach. (If a buyer first pays all or part of the purchase price, she is entitled to have it back and can sue for her damages. See Chapter 26, section C.)

E.   The Contractual Term That Is Both a Condition and a Promise

Consider two contract terms: In term 1, A promises to do X on Monday, in exchange for term 2, in which B promises to do Y on Tuesday. We've just learned that term 1 has significance in two separate respects: (1) It represents A's promise; if she dishonors it, she commits a breach; and, separately, (2) its substantial performance represents a condition precedent to B's promise; if A fails substantially to perform (commits a material breach), then B need not perform—at all.

Now consider these contractual terms: In term 1, Buyer, on Wednesday, August 19, will pay Seller $4 million, such payment to be made by certified check. In term 2, Seller, in consideration of such promise, will, on Thursday, August 20, convey Blackacre to Buyer.

Term 1 sets forth (1) B's promise to (a) pay (b) by certified check, and (2) two conditions precedent to Seller's promise, one implied/constructive and one express: (i) that Buyer pay, and (ii) that Buyer pay by certified check. Suppose on August 18, Buyer asks Seller whether she will accept a cashier's check rather than a certified check. When Seller replies, "Yes, I will," she has just waived the condition that Buyer pay by certified check. In reliance on the waiver, Buyer buys a cashier's check, but on the morning of August 19, Seller contacts Buyer to say that she's changed her mind; she wants a certified check after all. Buyer explains, "But it's too late for me to get one today." Seller's attempt to retract her waiver is ineffective because Buyer has relied on it to his detriment (reasonably and foreseeably). Seller can no longer demand a certified check as a condition of conveying Blackacre. When Buyer arrives at Seller's office and tenders the cashier's check, Seller must deliver the deed to Blackacre.

But, as odd as it seems, Buyer is in breach. One can waive a condition precedent (or subsequent) to his promise, but he cannot, without consideration, modify the contract. Consequently (and most paradoxically, it seems) (1) although payment by certified check is, after the waiver, no longer a condition to Seller's duty to perform, (2) Buyer's failure to pay by certified check is a breach (immaterial to Seller's principal purpose, of course, or Seller's waiver would not be effective). Seller has an action against Buyer for whatever damages (probably none) she suffered from the substitution of a cashier's check for a certified check. It's a fine point, paradoxical, a little crazy—but it's law and belongs to the basic contracts course.

F.   The Closers

QUESTION 11. PayCo, a payroll accounting firm, forms a contract with SoluCo, a computer programmer:

> (1) SoluCo will create for PayCo, and PayCo will purchase from SoluCo, together with all applicable rights of ownership and copyright, four computer programs to be designed and to function according to the specifications set forth in Appendix A attached to this writing.
> (2) The price to be paid by PayCo will be $360,000 in total, on final completion and delivery of all of the four programs to be produced by SoluCo. The first program, as described in Appendix A, shall be due and delivered on January 15, 2012, the second on February 15, 2012, the third on March 15, 2012, and the fourth on April 15, 2012.

SoluCo timely delivers the first three programs, properly designed and properly functioning. On April 15, 2012, SoluCo notifies PayCo that the fourth program will be delivered one month late, on or about May 15. SoluCo demands that in the interim, PayCo pay it the amount of $270,000 for the three programs already delivered, noting that $270,000 represents three-quarters of $360,000. PayCo refuses to make any payment. Which of the following is true?

I. By failing to deliver the fourth program on time, SoluCo committed a partial breach.
II. By delivering three of the four programs SoluCo provided PayCo with substantial performance.
III. By refusing to pay SoluCo any money at all, PayCo committed a total breach.

A. I
B. II and III
C. I, II, and III
D. Neither I nor II nor III

ANALYSIS.   By failing timely to deliver a full 25 percent of the programs for which the contract called, SoluCo committed not a trivial partial breach, but a serious, material (total) breach. Consequently, option I is false. To say that a contracting party commits a material breach is to say that he fails to give substantial performance. That means option II is false as well. SoluCo, who was to perform first in time, did not provide PayCo with substantial performance, meaning it did not fulfill a condition precedent to PayCo's duty to pay. Hence

PayCo had no obligation to pay SoluCo *anything*, and by refusing to do so it committed no breach. Option III, therefore, is false. And so, **D** is right.

QUESTION 12. On March 1, MetalCorp and GreenCorp agree on the following contractual terms by signed writing:

Paragraph 1: GreenCorp will overhaul the landscaping on the 100 acres surrounding MetalCorp's corporate offices according to the specifications set forth in paragraphs 3-20 of this written agreement, GreenCorp to begin work on or about March 1 and to complete its work on or before March 22.

Paragraph 2: MetalCorp will pay GreenCorp (a) $100,000 when GreenCorp begins work; (b) an additional $100,000 when GreenCorp completes such portion of the work as is specified in paragraph 12 of this agreement, the parties agreeing that such work constitutes approximately one-half the total work GreenCorp is to perform; and (c) $100,000 when GreenCorp completes the work—for total payment from MetalCorp to GreenCorp of $300,000.

[Paragraphs 4-11 concern other matters]

Paragraph 12: On the 50 acre portion of the property called Colleague Quadrangle, rectangular in shape, GreenCorp will plant, along each of the four sides, so many trees as fully cover each such side with no spaces visible between trees.

[Paragraphs 13-20 concern other matters]

On March 1, GreenCorp begins work and MetalCorp pays it $100,000. On March 12, GreenCorp completes the work (approximately one-half the total work) described in paragraph 12, and MetalCorp pays it an additional $100,000. On March 22, GreenCorp announces that it has completed the work, and on March 23 requests that MetalCorp pay the final $100,000 installment. MetalCorp truthfully informs GreenCorp that "on the Colleague Quadrangle, which represents only 50 acres of our 100 acres, you planted 300 trees. Having done that, you left, on one of the Quadrangle's four sides, a two-foot space between two of the trees. To conform your performance of paragraph 12 of our contract, you should have planted one additional tree." For that reason, MetalCorp refuses to pay GreenCorp any portion of the final $100,000 installment and, further, refuses to allow GreenCorp to plant the one additional tree. MetalCorp brings an action against GreenCorp for breach. Which of the following facts, if found, is most favorable to MetalCorp?

A. With respect to landscaping and plantings, MetalCorp has always paid serious attention to its Colleague Quadrangle.

B. The Colleague Quadrangle is the only portion of MetalCorp's property used by employees and visitors, and the space between the two trees is sorely noticeable.

> **C.** GreenCorp failed to plant the 300th tree in the Quadrangle because it had run short of trees.
> **D.** Each tree carries a cost of about $40.

ANALYSIS.   To be innocent of breach, MetalCorp must show it had no duty to make the final $100,000 payment. If, by March 22, GreenCorp failed to furnish substantial performance, meaning it committed a material breach, then MetalCorp would have no such duty because, once again, GreenCorp's substantial performance is a condition precedent to MetalCorp's obligation to pay. The correct answer is that which reflects a finding that GreenCorp, by failing to plant the one missing tree, committed a material breach and, therefore, failed to give substantial performance.

D reports that the cost of a single tree is about $40. If that fact is relevant at all, it works not in MetalCorp's interest, but against it; $40 is a miniscule portion of $100,000. **D** therefore is wrong. **C** too is wrong; it states an irrelevancy. GreenCorp's reasons for failing to plant the missing tree are unrelated to the question at issue: Does the missing tree represent a material breach? **A** has some vague overtone of relevance. It suggests that the quadrangle is important to MetalCorp, but that does not allow us to call GreenCorp's omission a material breach (unless **B** is worse).

B is better, and best among the four. It reports two facts: (1) that the quadrangle is the only portion of MetalCorp's property occupied by employees and visitors, and (2) the absence of the missing tree is significant to its appearance. Those two facts together would make for an argument that GreenCorp's failure to plant this single tree represents a material breach. Hence, **B** is right (more right, anyway, than **A**, **C**, or **D**).

✴ Silver & Hochberg's Picks

1.	**B**
2.	**D**
3.	**A**
4.	**D**
5.	**B**
6.	**D**
7.	**A**
8.	**C**
9.	**D**
10.	**A**
11.	**D**
12.	**B**

22

Interpretation as to Allocation of Risk: Mistake, Frustration, and Impracticability

A.   Interpretation as to Allocation of Risk

L ife is full of risk, and contracts are a part of life. Suppose XYZ stock is traded publicly over the New York Stock Exchange. Divestor owns 10,000 shares of XYZ stock and believes its value will soon decline—he thinks the stock will "go down." Meanwhile, Investor has a tip that XYZ stock's value soon will rise—she thinks the stock will "go up."

Investor pays $1 million for 100 of Divestor's shares of XYZ stock, the transaction mediated by a stock broker in the ordinary way so that neither party knows the other's identity. Each party knowingly assumes a risk. If the stock goes down, Investor loses and Divestor wins (because he did not suffer a loss; he got out in time to avoid it). Investor wishes she could go back in time, undo the purchase and have her money back. If the stock goes up, Investor wins and Divestor loses (because he did not enjoy the gain; he got out too soon to reap it). Divestor wishes he could go back in time and have the stock back.

In either case, we know and they know that they can't do that. By law, the gains and losses lie where they fall; the law saddles each party with the outcome of the risk he assumed.

The law that does that is the law by which we interpret contracts. In Chapter 18, section A, we learned that the terms of any contract have such meaning as would be given the offer, as accepted, by a reasonable offeree and offeror under all prevailing circumstances. When two parties contract for the purchase and sale of publicly traded stock, each, as a reasonable person, should know (and usually does know) that her contract implicitly includes this term:

> To the buyer there is allocated the risk that the stock's value will decrease, and to seller there is allocated the risk that the stock's value will increase. Consequently, neither party on the ground of disappointment as to any such outcome shall have the right to rescind (undo) the agreement hereby recorded or the purchase and sale that follow herefrom.

As to the unknown matter of future increase or decrease of the stock's value, the contract *allocates risk* to each party, and that is so because this contract, like all contracts, carries such terms as reasonable persons under the circumstances would understand it to carry.

Illustration: Blueacre *Might* Be Hiding Oil.   Suppose Seller owns Blueacre, which is unsuitable for farming, building, or anything else, except that many think oil might lie beneath it. Seller announces that the land is for sale for $20 million. Buyer contacts Seller and the two converse.

Buyer: So — many think that oil lies beneath your land. What do *you* think?

Seller: I don't know any more than anyone else knows. If I *knew* that oil lay beneath the land, I would keep it, drill, and make billions. But I *don't* know and I don't want to invest any money trying to find out. If oil lies beneath Blueacre, someone else will make the billions. If it does not, someone will lose $20 million, my selling price.

Buyer: Yes, yes, of course. That's right.

Buyer decides to buy. The parties form a signed, written contract and proceed to closing. Buyer pays the purchase price, Seller conveys the land, and Buyer becomes owner. Buyer spends $1 million exploring the land for oil and finds none — not a drop.

Buyer wants his money back. But plainly, the contract does not entitle him to that. As to what should transpire if Blueacre does or does not yield oil, this contract resembles a contract for the sale of publicly held stock. Again, from Chapter 18, section A, the terms of any contract have such meaning as would be given the offer and acceptance by a reasonable offeree and offeror under all prevailing circumstances. The circumstances under which Buyer and Seller formed this contract included, notably, their conversation in which each led the other reasonably to understand that each was taking his chances as to the matter of oil. Seller assumed the risk that he would receive a mere $20 million for property that might harbor billions in oil. Buyer assumed the risk that he would pay $20 million for useless land. Properly interpreted, the contract allocated risks to each of its parties, as just described. The contract does not entitle Buyer to a return of his money should the land prove useless. Neither would it entitle Seller to reverse the transaction if the property produced oil.

Furthermore, if the parties had not expressly conversed about the oil prospects still, as reasonable persons, they would or should know that their agreement implicitly and unquestionably provided that (1) if the land held oil, Seller would not be entitled to take it back; and (2) if the land held none, Buyer would not be entitled to return of his money. Say, if you wish, that such is simple common sense. In so saying, you mean that reasonable persons would so understand their agreement.

Illustration: This Contract for the Sale of Woodacre Is Different.   Now suppose Seller owns Woodacre, which when she purchased it was rich with timber, holding a stand of 140,000 trees. Buyer wants the land for its timber. On May 18, the parties converse.

> **Buyer:** Am I right to understand that Woodacre has a stand of approximately 140,000 trees?
> **Seller:** Yes, that's right.
> **Buyer:** Well, I don't care about the land itself, but I want the timber, which I think to be worth about $12 million. I'll purchase the property for that amount.
> **Seller:** I'll sell for $14 million.
> **Buyer:** It's a deal.

On May 20, the parties create and sign the appropriate writing. The contract provides that the closing should occur on July 1. Unbeknownst to the parties, all of Woodacre's trees had been destroyed by fire on May 1, 19 days before they formed their contract. Buyer discovers that fact on June 1 and informs Seller that she will not honor the contract.

> **Buyer:** I've just learned that at the time we formed our contract, the trees were no longer standing on Woodacre; they had burned on May 1.
> **Seller:** Well, *I* didn't know that.
> **Buyer:** I realize that you didn't know that, and I'm not accusing you of any deceit. Still, we both honestly understood that I was to buy and you were to sell property on which there stood some 140,000 trees. In fact, even as we formed our contract, there were no trees on the property.
> **Seller:** Well, what do you want *me* to do about it?
> **Buyer:** I want out. I want back my $2 million deposit, and, of course, I don't want to buy the land.
> **Seller:** Well, we have a contract for the sale of Woodacre, and I expect you to buy it.

Buyer refuses to buy the property, and Seller sues. Buyer counterclaims for the return of her $2 million deposit. In the conversation Buyer and

Seller conducted just before forming their contract, they spoke of the trees as though their presence on Woodacre was a fact, not a possibility. Further, Buyer's statements should have led Seller to understand that Buyer wanted the land only for its trees and that absent the trees, she would not buy it. Thus interpreted, the contract does not allocate to either party any risk as to the presence or absence of the trees. Rather, its terms assume that the trees do sit on Woodacre. The parties have manifested no recognition of such a risk and hence, no intention to allocate it to either of them.

When that is so — when, as to some fact(s) relevant to their contract, the contracting parties *assume* its truth, meaning they do not allocate to either of them the possibility of its falsehood — the law invokes its so-called doctrines of mutual mistake, frustration of purpose, or impracticability — all identical in concept, but different as to details that, in the law's eyes, make a difference as to which doctrine applies. Let's discuss each such doctrine, one at a time.

B.   Mutual Mistake

The doctrine of mutual mistake provides: *A contract between two parties A and B is voidable by A if (1) when forming their contract, the parties manifest their mutual belief, to the point of absolute fact, that some set of circumstances is in place; and (2) when forming the contract B should, under the circumstances, understand that but for that belief A would be unwilling to enter the contract (except, perhaps, on materially different terms); and (3) that belief is mistaken — then the contract is voidable at Party A's option.*

Let's apply that rule to the Woodacre case. Before forming their contract, the parties conversed, each making clear to the other her understanding — not as a chance or possibility, but as an absolute *fact* — that Woodacre held a large stand of trees. Each manifested her belief in that circumstance, and, further, Seller should have understood that Buyer would not have agreed to the purchase had she known Woodacre held no trees. They then learned that *at the time they formed their contract,* Woodacre had no trees. Consequently, Buyer may void the contract. And if she does, the court will afford her the remedy of rescission, meaning it will "undo" the contract, that to be coupled with the remedy of restitution, meaning it will require Seller to refund Buyer's $2 million deposit.[1]

The Restatement (Second) of Contracts §§152 and 153 (which we have here combined into one sentence) states the rule of mutual mistake:

> A mistake is a belief that is not in accord with the facts[,and] [w]here a mistake of both parties at the time a contract was made as to a basic

---

1.   Regarding the law of restitution, see Chapter 29, sections B and C.

assumption on which the contract was made has a material effect on the agreed exchange of performances, the contract is voidable by the adversely affected party. . . .

The phrase "basic assumption on which the contract was made" refers to what we describe in element 1 of the rule, to wit, that each party manifests to the other — to the degree of absolute fact — a belief that some circumstance is in place. The phrase "has a material effect on the agreed exchange of performances" means that one of the parties should know that the other, if he knew the truth, would not form the contract (except, perhaps, on significantly different terms).

QUESTION 1. Walker owns a cow that she can not breed. A veterinarian thoroughly examines the animal and advises Walker that the cow is infertile. Walker then offers the cow for sale at a price of $1,000, whereas a fertile cow of the same type, variety, and age would command a price of $15,000. On April 1, Sharewood expresses interest in purchasing the cow and asks Walker why her price is so low. Walker explains that the cow is infertile. Manifesting his understanding that the cow is indeed infertile and that such is the reason for the low price, Sharewood accepts the offer and thus agrees to purchase the cow. The parties create and sign a writing by which they agree to the purchase and sale of the cow for $1,000. The contract provides that Sharewood will pay the purchase price and that Walker will deliver the cow on May 1.

On April 15, Walker, still possessing the cow, thinks it might be pregnant. Surprised at what she thinks to be so, she calls her veterinarian again. The veterinarian examines the cow and advises Walker that his earlier diagnosis of infertility had been wrong, that the cow is pregnant, and that it had been pregnant for some two months. On May 1, Sharewood tenders the $1,000 purchase price. Walker explains that the cow is fertile and, indeed, pregnant. She refuses the payment, and declines to convey the cow.

Sharewood sues Walker for breach. Referring to the cow's fertility and citing mutual mistake, Walker attempts to void the contract. Which of the following facts is legally relevant to Walker's claim of mutual mistake?

A. Walker had a reasonable basis on which to believe the cow was infertile.

B. The parties formed their contract before they were to complete the sale itself.

C. Each party led the other to understand that he or she took the cow's infertility for a fact.

D. Sharewood believed the cow was infertile only because Walker had so represented it.

ANALYSIS.   Apply the rule to the facts. Walker can avoid this contract on the ground of mutual mistake if she proves that (1) when the parties formed the contract, each manifested a belief *to the point of fact* that the cow was infertile; and (2) under the circumstances, each should have understood that Walker, had she known the cow to be fertile, would not have agreed to sell it for so little as $1,000; and (3) that the cow was in fact fertile at the time the parties formed the contract.

Referring to the Restatement's formulation, Walker can void the contract if she shows that (1) both parties believed the cow to be infertile, which belief was not in accord with the facts (meaning it was false); (2) their mistaken belief in the cow's infertility was a "basic assumption" on which they formed their contract, meaning each manifested such a belief to the point of fact; and (3) the mistake had a material effect on the agreed exchange of performance (meaning that Sharewood should have known that Walker, if she knew the truth, would not have formed the contract).

All such elements apply to this case, but among the four answer choices, only one is mentioned. The veterinarian advised Sharewood that the cow was infertile, and **A** correctly reports, therefore, that Walker had good reason to adopt that belief. That fact, however, is irrelevant to mutual mistake. The doctrine requires that each party manifest to the other his belief in some fact, which belief they later learn to be false, but it matters not how or why either party comes to manifest that belief or whether does so for good or bad reason. **A** is wrong. **D** is wrong for the same reason; *how or why* Sharewood came to manifest his mistaken belief is irrelevant. **B**, too, cites an irrelevancy. That time does or does not intervene between the dates on which two parties form a contract and on which they actually perform plays no role in the doctrine of mutual mistake.

That leaves **C**, which is correct. **C** recites an element critical to the mutual mistake doctrine, to wit, that each of these parties manifested his or her belief to the point of absolute *fact* that the cow was infertile. Referring to the Restatement's formulation, these parties manifested a belief that was not in accord with the facts, and that belief served as a basic assumption on which they formed their contract. Hence, **C** is right.

QUESTION 2. Nancy's great uncle dies, leaving his home and its contents to Nancy. She decides to sell the home and commissions Oliver to empty it for that purpose.

> **Nancy:** I'll pay you $20 per hour if you'll empty the house.
> **Oliver:** I normally charge $35 per hour.
> **Nancy:** What if we agree that you can keep anything you find in the house?
> **Oliver:** Well, what's *in* the house?
> **Nancy:** As far as I know—junk. But who knows? Sometimes old junk is valuable.

> **Oliver:** You're right. Who knows?
> **Nancy:** Do we have a deal—$20 per hour and you keep the junk?
> **Oliver:** Yes.
>
> Oliver empties the house. Buried among items in its attic he seizes on a cluster of 1910 stock certificates, which upon his research and consultation reveal a value of $20 million. Nancy learns of the find and insists on having the certificates herself. She engages a lawyer who, on the ground of mutual mistake, brings an action seeking rescission and a return to Nancy of the stock certificates. Oliver contends that mutual mistake does not apply. Which of the following most *weakens* Nancy's position?
>
> **A.** If Nancy had not promised Oliver the contents of the home, she would fail to provide consideration adequate to create a contract.
> **B.** In accepting Nancy's offer, Oliver assented to its terms as he understood them.
> **C.** In using the word "junk," the parties manifested their belief that the home likely contained nothing of great value.
> **D.** In using the phrase "who knows?" the parties mutually manifested their intention to allocate between them, as a risk, that the home did or did not contain items of great value.

ANALYSIS. In order that the mutual mistake doctrine apply to this case, Nancy would have to show that (1) before forming their contract, the parties led each other to understand that each believed—not as speculation, but to the point of fact—that the home contained nothing of significant value; (2) she led Oliver to understand that she would not have entered the contract absent that belief; and (3) the mutual belief was mistaken—that the home did, in fact, contain one or more items of significant value.

Easily she can show item (3); the home did contain stocks worth $20 million. It is not clear that she can establish elements (1) and (2), and the right answer is that which negates a showing of either such element.

A is false and irrelevant. Nancy provides consideration to Oliver by promising him both $20 per hour and the home's contents. Further whether one does or does not provide consideration goes not to the matter of mutual mistake, but to the question of whether they form a contract at all. **B** states a falsehood. When one accepts an offer, he does not do so according to his own understanding of its terms, but rather according to the meaning that a reasonable person would give its terms under all prevailing circumstances. **C** argues *for* Nancy's position. If the parties mutually manifested a belief that the home contained only "junk," then the stock certificates shows they *were* mistaken.

We're left with **D**, and it's correct. It posits that the parties mutually manifested their understanding that the presence or absence of valuable articles within the home amounted to a risk, each side of which rested on one of the parties. To finish the argument that **D** starts, we would say that the contract, properly interpreted, allocated (a) to Nancy the risk that the home harbored items of significant value and (b) to Oliver the risk that it did not. If as to some circumstance in place at the time they form their contract, two parties manifest their uncertainty and allocate the relevant risk between them, then they have made no "mistake," and the mutual mistake doctrine does not apply. That's why **D** is right.

QUESTIONS 3 & 4. AuctionCorp conducts an auction in which it attempts to sell memorabilia. The auction is "with reserve," meaning that AuctionCorp is not obliged to sell any item unless the highest bid is, in its judgment, *sufficiently* high, in which case it will sell to the highest bidder. At the auction site, AuctionCorp posts a sign that reads: "All sales are final."

Auctioneer: We have here lots 15 and 16, each representing one hat. I put up first lot #15 — a hat that belonged to Vice President Spiro Agnew. Do I hear $5,000? . . . $500? . . . $50? . . . $5? . . . $1? . . . 50 cents? . . . 1 cent?

Bidder 1: Yes, 1 cent; it's good for cleaning oil spills in my garage.

Auctioneer: Sold for 1 cent.

Auctioneer: I show you now lot #16 — a hat that belonged to President Abraham Lincoln. Do I hear . . .

Bidder 1: $50,000

Bidder 2: $500,000

Bidder 1: $5 million

Bidder 2: $50 million

Auctioneer: Do I hear $55 million? Going once, twice — sold for $50 million.

Bidder 1 paid 1 cent and took the hat labeled lot 15. Bidder 2 paid $50 million and took the hat labeled lot 16. Three days later, all discover that the auctioneer had accidentally mislabeled the hats. The lot 15 hat had belonged to Lincoln and the Lot 16 hat to Agnew;

QUESTION 3. On the ground of mutual mistake, AuctionCorp brings an action against Bidder 1 seeking rescission of the contract and return of the Lincoln hat. Which of the following facts should AuctionCorp prove and cite as a basis for its claim?

A. That the contract, properly interpreted, allocated to Bidder 1 the risk that the hat might in fact have belonged to Abraham Lincoln

B. That AuctionCorp and Bidder 1, to the point of certainty, manifested their belief that the lot 15 hat had belonged to Vice President Agnew

C. That the auctioneer put up first the hat he thought had belonged to Vice President Agnew and second the one he thought had belonged to President Lincoln

D. That the difference in value of the two hats is attributable not to any inherent quality of each, but to their divergent histories

---

QUESTION 4. On the ground of mutual mistake, Bidder 2 brings an action seeking rescission of his contract with AuctionCorp and a return of his $50 million. He should probably

A. win, because all components of the mutual mistake doctrine are operative and in place.

B. win, because the Agnew hat does not carry a fair market value substantially equal to the $50 million that Bidder 2 paid for it.

C. lose, because AuctionCorp posted the sign reading "All sales are final."

D. lose, because AuctionCorp acted in good faith throughout.

ANALYSIS. The situation bears all elements tied to the mutual mistake doctrine, which therefore renders voidable both of AuctionCorp's contracts — that with Bidder 1 and that with Bidder 2. In both cases, Auctioneer and the bidder should reasonably have understood each other to take not as a chance but as a fact that the hat was what Auctioneer said it was. In Restatement terms, both parties, contrary to the truth, believed lot 15 to be the Agnew hat, with that mistaken belief constituting a "basic assumption" on which they formed their contract. Bidder 1, as a reasonable person, should have known (and certainly did know) that Auctioneer would not have let the hat go for 1 cent if he'd known it belonged to Lincoln and not Agnew. In Restatement terms, the mistaken belief had a material effect on the agreed exchange of performances.

As for the second contract, Auctioneer should have known (and certainly did know) that Bidder 2 would not have paid $50 million for Spiro Agnew's hat. Hence, both contracts answer to the doctrine of mutual mistake. Each is voidable by the injured party, the first by Auctioneer and the second by Bidder 2.

The right answer to Question 3 is that which, as to this dispute, reflects at least one of the doctrine's elements: (1) that each party manifested to the other his understanding — the point of absolute fact — that the lot 15 hat had belonged to Agnew and not Lincoln; (2) that the hat had belonged to Lincoln, not Agnew; (3) that Bidder 1 should have understood that Auctioneer would not have accepted a 1 cent bid for Lincoln's hat.

A does the opposite. It states that the contract did allocate risk. **C** refers to an utter irrelevancy. It is insignificant to the doctrine of mutual mistake in which order the auctioneer put up the two hats. **D** correctly states that the two hats carry different values because they have different histories. But the mistake doctrine takes no account of why two items might have different values. **B** states, in substance, that each party manifested his belief to the point of fact that the lot 15 hat belonged to Lincoln. That reflects the first criterion tied to the mutual mistake rule, and so **B** is right.

In Question 4, **B**, **C**, and **D** make correct statements—all of them irrelevant. No doubt the fair market value of the Agnew hat is far less than $50 million. Indeed, the auction is potent evidence that the hat is worth exactly 1 cent. But that does not go to the elements of mutual mistake. Further, it is true that AuctionCorp posted an "All sales are final" sign. Nothing in the law allows any such sign to supersede the doctrine of mutual mistake or to supercede any other law pertaining to contracts. Finally, that AuctionCorp acted honestly is, similarly, irrelevant. The mutual mistake doctrine does not concern the matter of honesty or dishonesty.

A correctly states that Bidder 2 should win because all elements of the mutual mistake doctrine apply to his contract. Hence, **A** is right.

C. Frustration of Purpose

Suppose it's July 3 and Party A wants to see tomorrow's July 4th parade from a high building that overlooks Main Street. B owns such a building. A explains to B that he wants to see the July 4th parade from a spot high in B's building, and the two agree that B will allow A to occupy a room on the 25th floor of her Main Street building "in order that A be able to view tomorrow's July 4th parade in exchange for $500 to be paid by A to B at the conclusion of the parade."

Early on the morning of July 4th, the city cancels the parade due to a terrorist incident. With no parade to see, A has no use for the room. He wants "out" of the contract. The mutual mistake doctrine affords no relief to B for the reason that the parties did not manifest belief in some fact or circumstance *in place at the time they formed their contract*. The case thus differs from the timber and pregnant cow cases. In the timber case, the parties manifested their belief—to the point of absolute fact—that there stood on Seller's realty, *at the time they formed the contract*, 140,000 trees, when in fact the trees were, at that time, no longer there. In the cow case, the parties manifested their belief—to the point of absolute fact—that the cow, *when they formed their contract*, was infertile, when in fact it was at that time "with calf."

Here, the surprise relates not to a circumstance relevant to the time at which the parties contract, *but to a future event*, the July 4th parade that, contrary to their certain belief—contrary to their basic assumption—did not occur. Upon that (conceptually unimportant) distinction, the law distinguishes between mutual mistake and "frustration of purpose." It provides: *With respect to a contract between Parties A and B, A is discharged from any performance not yet given if (1) when forming their contract, the parties manifest their*

*mutual belief, to the point of absolute fact, that some event will or will not occur;
(2) when forming the contract B should, under the circumstances, understand
that the occurrence or nonoccurrence of the event is critical to A's principal purpose in forming the contract; and (3) contrary to their belief, and through no fault
of A, the event at issue does or does not occur.*

Restatement (Second) §265 states the doctrine thus:

> Where, after a contract is made, a party's principal purpose is substantially
> frustrated without his fault by the occurrence of an event the non-occur-
> rence of which was a basic assumption on which the contract was made, his
> remaining duties to render performance are discharged[.]

The parade case answers to the rule. A and B mutually manifested a belief—to
the point of absolute fact—that the July 4th parade would occur—not that it
might occur—not that it *probably* would occur, but that it *would* occur. On the
basis of A's statements, B should have understood that the parade represented
A's principal purpose in arranging for the room. Finally, contrary to the parties' belief, the parade did not occur.

Where frustration of purpose applies, it does not render a contract voidable, but rather creates the equivalent of a condition subsequent (Chapter 21,
section A) and so discharges the aggrieved party from any remaining obligation to perform. In our July 4th case, A has not yet paid B, and the frustration
of his purpose discharges him from his duty to do so.

D.   Impracticability

Think again of the July 4th case. Parties A and B form a contract under which
B will allow A to occupy a room in her building on Main Street. Imagine now
that the terrorist incident occurs, and that this time it destroys B's building. The city, however, does not cancel the July 4th parade; the parade goes
on. With the building destroyed, B cannot possibly perform her part of the
bargain; she can't allow A to occupy the room because the room and building
are gone.

The case differs from our first July 4 case in this way: In the first case,
the supervening (after-occurring) event rendered valueless to A that which
B was to provide him; cancellation of the parade "frustrated" A's "purpose"
in forming the contract. In this second case, neither party's purpose is frustrated. Rather, the supervening event—destruction of the building—renders
it impossible for B to perform.

Therein lies the difference between the doctrines of frustrated purpose
and impracticability (the latter formerly called the doctrine of "impossibility").
If two parties premise their contract on a mutual assumption that some event
will (or will not) occur, and contrary to their manifest belief the event does not
(or does) occur, then we invoke (1) the doctrine of frustration of purpose, if

the supervening event denies one of the parties the value or benefit he justifiably anticipated; but (2) the doctrine of impracticability, if the supervening event renders one of the party's performance far more costly, burdensome, or difficult than he justifiably anticipated. It may, indeed, render his performance *impossible*, which constitutes the infinite extreme of cost, burden, or difficulty.

The doctrine of impracticability provides: *As to a contract between A and B, B is discharged from the duty of further performance if (1) when forming their contract, the parties manifest their mutual belief, to the point of absolute fact, that some event will or will not occur; (2) when forming the contract, A should, under the circumstances, understand that the occurrence or nonoccurrence of the event will render it unreasonably difficult or impossible for B to continue her performance; and (3) contrary to their belief, and through no fault of B, the event at issue does or does not occur.*

The difference between the frustration and impracticability rules lies in a few words of element (2) that describe *the effect* of the supervening event. The same difference is evident in the relevant Restatement sections. Compare Restatement (Second) §265 (frustration) with Restatement (Second) §261 (impracticability). Finally, remember the difference between these two doctrines and the doctrine of mutual mistake. Mutual mistake operates when the parties adopt their contract upon a manifest (mistaken) basic assumption that some fact or circumstance is *in place at the time they form their contract.* As for its effect, the mistake might in any way materially affect one party's difficulty or cost of performance, value with which he parts, or value that he justifiably expects to receive.

QUESTIONS 5-7. ShowCo, located in Pottsfield, produces shows for theater owners. StageCo, located in Cincotti, owns and operates a theater. On July 1, 2012, ShowCo and StageCo form a contract including these terms:

> Whereas StageCo plans to sell seats in its theater for $100 each on such dates and for such performances as are described below, and whereas Morton Green is a world-renowned baritone revered, moreover, for his portrayal of the part of Kaha in the opera hereinafter mentioned, the parties do agree that:
>
> 1. ShowCo will produce, at StageCo's facility, on the dates October 1 to October 15, 2012, inclusive, the comic opera *Makado*, for which ShowCo will hire, furnish, and pay the entire cast and orchestra, the leading baritone role of Kaha to be played by the celebrity Morton Green; and
>
> 2. StageCo will, on November 1, pay ShowCo $500,000 for such service.

> **QUESTION 5.** Which of the following facts, if proven, would most likely render the contract voidable by ShowCo on the theory of mutual mistake?
>
> **A.** On July 1, Morton Green was dead.
> **B.** On August 1, Morton Green died.
> **C.** On July 1, just before forming their contract, the parties mutually acknowledged their understanding that *Makado* might not be appealing to a Cincotti audience.
> **D.** On August 1, through no fault of StageCo, the Daily-Carta opera company obtained a court order against StageCo forbidding it to present *Makado* to a paying audience.

ANALYSIS. Mutual mistake operates only if, *at the time they form their contract,* the parties mutually manifest, to the point of fact/basic assumption, a mistaken belief as to a circumstance existing at the time they form their contract. The doctrine, of course, requires more than that, but that, first, it demands. **B** and **D** describe supervening events—events that arise in August—*after* the parties form their contract, so both are wrong. **C** too refers to a matter of the future—whether an audience will or will not wish to see the opera. Furthermore, **C** describes as an allocated risk, the possibility that Cincotti audiences will or will not wish to see *Makado.* **A** reports that Morton Green is dead *on July 1,* and thus hypothesizes a fact in existence *at the time the parties form their contract.* Among these choices, therefore, only **A** cites a fact essential to ShowCo's claim of mutual mistake.

> **QUESTION 6.** Which of the following facts, if proven, would most likely discharge ShowCo's duty to perform on the theory of impracticability?
>
> **A.** On July 1, Morton Green was dead.
> **B.** On August 1, Morton Green died.
> **C.** On July 1, just before forming their contract, the parties mutually acknowledged their understanding that *Makado* might not be appealing to a Cincotti audience.
> **D.** On August 1, through no fault of StageCo, the Daily-Carta opera company obtained a court order against StageCo forbidding it to present *Makado* to a paying audience.

ANALYSIS. Like frustration of purpose, impracticability requires a supervening event—an event that occurs *after* the parties form their contract that, of course, they assumed would not occur. (As already noted, both doctrines apply also when the parties assume that some event will *not* occur and, contrary to their assumption, it does.) Impracticability applies when that event renders it far more difficult, costly, or burdensome—or indeed, impossible—for one of the parties to perform. The right answer is that which refers to an event that (a) according to their manifestations at the time they formed their contract, the parties believed would certainly not occur and (b) makes it unreasonably difficult or impossible for one of them to perform.

A hypothesizes a fact *in place at the time the parties contract.* For that reason, it's wrong. **C**, once again, describes not a "basic assumption," but uncertainty — an allocated risk, wherefore it invokes none of the doctrines discussed in this chapter. **D** does hypothesize an event that occurs after the parties form their contract, but its effect is to deprive *StageCo* of the value it anticipated receiving; if StageCo can't produce Makado, then it is subject to frustration of purpose. Yet, we are looking for a fact that subjects *ShowCo* to the doctrine of *impracticability.*

B describes an event that occurs after the parties form their contract whose effect is to render it impossible (and, a fortiori, impractical) for ShowCo to perform. With Morton Green dead, ShowCo cannot secure him for the *Makado* cast. Hence, **B** is right.

QUESTION 7. Which of the following facts, if proven, would most likely discharge StageCo's duty to perform on the theory of frustration of purpose?

A. On July 1, Morton Green was dead.

B. On August 1, Morton Green died.

C. On July 1, just before forming their contract, the parties mutually acknowledged their understanding that *Makado* might not be appealing to a Cincotti audience.

D. On August 1, through no fault of StageCo, the Daily-Carta opera company obtained a court order against StageCo forbidding it to present *Makado* to a paying audience.

ANALYSIS.   Like impracticability, frustration of purpose applies when there occurs some supervening event that the parties manifestly believed, to the point of basic assumption/absolute fact — would not occur. (And, as earlier noted, it applies too when as a basic assumption the parties believe an event *will* occur, but it does *not.*) Its effect must be to frustrate for Party 1 that which Party 2 knows or should know to be the Party 1's essential purpose in forming the contract.

Here StageCo formed the contract in order that it be able to present *Makado* to a paying audience. The right answer, therefore, must describe an event that occurs after the parties contract, whose effect is to prevent StageCo from presenting the opera. **A** describes a fact or circumstance in place at the time the parties contract, and for that reason it's wrong. **B** describes an event that renders ShowCo's performance impossible (and so it's the correct answer to Question 10 above). **C**, once again, describes a circumstance or an event as to which the parties manifest uncertainty, which, therefore, cannot answer the criterion of "basic assumption." **D** describes an event that occurs after the parties form their contract, whose effect is to prevent StageCo from presenting the opera, thus frustrating StageCo's essential contractual purpose. Hence, **D** is right.

E.   Unilateral Mistake

The courts have little common understanding of what they mean by the phrase "unilateral mistake." Judges most often invoke the phrase when two parties purport to contract but give materially different meanings to some critical word or phrase both of them reasonable. Such are the cases we described in Chapter 3, section C, to which some courts also apply the phrase "meeting of the minds" and others as just noted, the phrase "unilateral mistake." Let's put out of our discussion, therefore, those many, many cases in which courts *write* the words "unilateral mistake" when (whether they know it or not) they *mean* that two parties fail to form a contract because they give different, reasonable meanings to some word or words on which they purport to agree.[2]

There Remain Two Kinds of Unilateral Mistake; Here They Come

Case 1.   On May 25, DemCo a political organization, asks BusCo, a busing company, whether it can transport 200 DemCo members round-trip from Los Angeles to Washington, D.C., some ten months later, with departure from Los Angeles on March 1, arrival back in Los Angeles on March 15. In response, BusCo contacts LeaseCo to discuss leasing eight buses for the first two weeks of March, and LeaseCo assures BusCo that the buses will be available. BusCo then contacts DemCo offering to transport the 200 DemCo members to Washington, D.C., on the dates specified by DemCo, for a total fee of $40,000. DemCo accepts the offer, and the parties reduce their contract to a signed writing which provides that DemCo is to pay BusCo $40,000 and BusCo is to furnish the round-trip transportation from Los Angeles to Washington, D.C., on the specified dates.

In February, BusCo contacts LeaseCo to secure the necessary buses and discovers that, on May 30 of the prior year, LeaseCo had ceased to do business. BusCo wants "out" of its contract with DemCo, stating that its belief in LeaseCo's existence was its own "unilateral mistake." Now—before we probe the relevant law, let's read the next case.

---

2.   *See, e.g.,* Beatty v. Depue, 103 N.W.2d 187 (S.D. 1960); *cf.* Fleischer v. McGehee, 163 S.W. 169 (Ark. 1914); Goodrich v. Lathrop, 29 P. 329 (Cal. 1892); Perlmutter v. Bacas, 149 A.2d 23 (Md. 1959); Winkelman v. Erwin, 165 N.E. 205 (Ill. 1929); Stong v. Lane, 68 N.W. 765 (Minn. 1896).

Case 2.   Suppose Contractor and Developer form a contract under which Contractor is to construct a building on Developer's land. To fulfill her obligations, Contractor must secure the services of subcontractors—electricians, masons, heating specialists, ventilation specialists, and many others—with whom she will form contracts for the purchase of their services.

Contractor asks five electricians to bid on the electrical components of the project. (When one asks for bids, be he a contractor or an auctioneer, he makes an invitation to deal (Chapter 4, section A). A bid, itself, is an offer.) From four of the electricians, Contractor receives these bids (1) $920,000, (2) $890,000, (3) $1,110,000, and (4) $990,000. The fifth bidder, ElCo, intends to bid $975,000, but in writing the bid, one of its clerks mistakenly writes "$97,500." On receiving ElCo's bid, Contractor immediately writes to ElCo, "We accept your offer." When ElCo discovers its error, it wishes not to perform the work for so little. The $97,500 figure, it says, was its own "unilateral mistake."

These Two Cases Represent Two Very Different Forms of Mistake   In case 1, BusCo formed its June 1 contract upon its own belief, to the point of basic assumption, that LeaseCo was in business and ready to supply buses. In fact, LeaseCo like the Woodacre trees, had "burned;" it no longer existed. BusCo made the same sort of mistake as underlies the doctrine of *mutual* mistake, but BusCo alone made the mistake. DemCo did not. Hence the law applies to BusCo the phrase "unilateral mistake."

In case 2, ElCo did not form its contract with Contractor upon any basic assumption or belief as to a nonexistent fact. Rather, it made a clerical error in transcribing the bid it meant to make. This sort of error, too, the law treats as a unilateral mistake, although in its nature it differs markedly from the mistake at issue in the BusCo case.

The Law Affords Cases 1 and 2 Two Different Treatments   As to case 1—the contracting party who commits the first form of error—the law seldom, if ever, allows him to void the contract. That's because a reasonable contracting party normally understands (even if subconsciously) that his contract allocates to him the risk that he enters it due to some misinformation or misapprehension. One's own misinformation is one's own problem. If BusCo promises to transport passengers falsely (though faultlessly), believing that LeaseCo will make buses available to BusCo, then BusCo's personnel, as reasonable persons, should understand that LeaseCo's disappearance is their problem—that the contract allocates that risk to *them*. (Likewise, as reasonable persons, the DemCo folks should understand that if they fail to secure a sufficient number of passengers to pay BusCo's $40,000 fee, that is their problem; the contract allocates that risk to DemCo.)[3]

---

3. Yet the Restatement writers, recklessly and without cited authority, describe the law otherwise. According to Restatement (Second) §152, one who makes the sort of unilateral mistake just

As to the contracting party who commits the second form of unilateral mistake—a simple careless error—the law works a discharge if the other party should, as a reasonable person, perceive the error.[4] In the ElCo case above, Contractor received four bids all falling within the "ballpark" of $1 million. She should have known that ElCo did not really mean to offer its service for $97,500 but rather that it had misplaced a comma and then omitted a zero. Certainly a court would rule that the contract is voidable by ElCo. Stated otherwise, ElCo made a careless clerical error, and Contractor should have known that.

So What Do We Know About Unilateral Mistake?   We know that when courts write "unilateral mistake," they refer to these three very different kinds of mishap:

1. That in which two parties give materially different interpretations to the words on which they purport to agree, both of them reasonable. In those cases, "unilateral mistake" is improperly used. The parties fail to form a contract because they have not achieved offer and acceptance or, objectively, a "meeting of the minds." They are addressing, really, a "Peerless" kind of case, incorrectly invoking the phrase "unilateral mistake." (Chapter 3, section C).
2. That in which two parties form a contract with one of them (but not the other) believing to the point of certainty or "basic assumption" that some fact or circumstance is then in place when in fact it is not. Probably, that sort of mistake never renders a contract voidable.[5]
3. That in which one contracting party commits an ordinary careless error in expression—a "slip" of the pen or tongue. That sort of unilateral mistake renders a contract voidable if the other party knows or should know of the error (which certainly includes any situation in which he himself has caused the error).

---

described may void the contract if (a) the contract does not allocate the risk of the mistake to him, and (b) by enforcing the contract (awarding damages for breach), the court would subject him to unconscionability. The Restatement writers offer not a whit of authority to support their thinking. Not one of the judicial opinions cited in §152 invokes any words similar to "allocation of risk" or "unconscionability." And although the cited cases do refer to "unilateral mistake," all describe, as discussed above, offerors and offerees who give two different interpretations to the terms of their agreement, *both of them reasonable*. Those cases do not properly belong, even, to the subject of unilateral mistake.

4. However, in this context the Restatement, again, recklessly and without cited authority, again invokes the word "unconscionable." Restatement (Second) §152 provides in full: "Where a mistake of one party at the time a contract was made as to a basic assumption on which he made the contract has a material effect on the agreed exchange of performances that is adverse to him, the contract is voidable by him if he does not bear the risk of the mistake . . . and (a) the effect of the mistake is such that enforcement of the contract would be unconscionable, or (b) the other party had reason to know of the mistake or his fault caused the mistake.

5. Yet, the Restatement, without authority or relevant illustration, states that it does so where enforcement would be "unconscionable."

QUESTION 8. C-Corp, a construction company building a high-rise office building, invites bids from eight plumbing companies in relation to the plumbing for which the project calls. Seven plumbing companies respond with bids that range from $15 million to $16 million. The eighth company, PlumbCo, bids $15.6 million. But in calculating that bid, it omits, by simple oversight, to account for a $150,000 expense it would have to bear in completing the project. If it had not made the error, therefore, its bid would have been $15,600,000 plus $150,000 = $15,750,000 = $15.75 million, instead of $15.6 million.

C-Corp receives Plumbco's $15.6 million bid and immediately accepts it. It does so even though other of the bids it receives are lower, because C-Corp's president has faith in PlumbCo. After C-Corp issues its acceptance, PlumbCo discover its $150,000 error and seeks to void the contract. In all likelihood, PlumbCo

A. can void the contract because C-Corp received seven additional bids, any one of which it can accept or could have accepted.

B. can void the contract because C-Corp had good reason to believe that PlumbCo had made the error in addition.

C. cannot void the contract because such would subject C-Corp to a possible loss of profit.

D. cannot void the contract because, under the circumstances, C-Corp had no reason to believe that PlumbCo had made the error in addition.

ANALYSIS. All authorities agree that if one enters a contract whose terms reflect a clerical error, he may void the contract if the other party, as a reasonable person, *should have known of the error.* In this situation, C-Corp received seven bids, all of them within the range of $15 million to $16 million. PlumbCo's bid fell squarely within that range, notwithstanding its error. Consequently, C-Corp had no reason to believe that PlumbCo, due to its own error, submitted a bid of $15.6 million instead of $15.75 million. For *that* reason, PlumbCo's mistake does not afford it the right to void the contract.

A and **B** report that PlumbCo can void the contract, and for that reason, they're wrong. In addition, **A** makes a statement of abject irrelevancy; that C-Corp had other offers available to it plays no role in the doctrine of unilateral mistake. **B** makes the false statement that C-Corp had reason to know of PlumbCo's error. **C** correctly states that PlumbCo cannot void the contract, but its reason is no reason at all: the phrase "loss of profit" has no place in the realm of unilateral mistake. **D** is right in all respects. It tells us that PlumbCo must abide by its contract notwithstanding the error because C-Corp had no reason to think it was "snapping up" an offer that arose through error. Hence, **D** is right.

QUESTION 9. On September 20, EmCo, owner of a property known as the Wrightworth Estate, by signed writing, offers to sell it to ZeCo for $50 million. The Wrightworth Estate has no house on it, but in the same vicinity is a property also owned by EmCo known as the Wentworth Estate, which includes an enormous mansion. Misreading EmCo's offer, ZeCo thinks that it pertains to the Wentworth Estate, and, wanting property only with a mansion, ZeCo accepts EmCo's offer, also by signed writing. When ZeCo learns that it has confused "Wentworth" with "Wrightworth," it seeks to void the contract. If the court does not permit ZeCo to void the contract, it might state among its reasons that

I. the contract implicitly allocated to ZeCo the risk that it had misunderstood EmCo's offer.
II. the contract falls within the Statute of Frauds.
A. I
B. II
C. Both I and II
D. Neither I nor II

ANALYSIS. The law seldom, if ever, allows a contracting party to void a contract because she (and not the other) enters it through some mistaken belief or assumption. The reason is that a reasonable person normally understands (even if she does not think in these words) that her agreement allocates to her the risk that she, alone, through no fault of the other party, is misinformed or otherwise acting under a misapprehension. EmCo's error is its own. The contract implicitly allocates to EmCo the risk that it is misinformed or otherwise operating under a misapprehension.

Option II states an irrelevancy. The contract does fall within the Statute of Frauds because it provides for the sale of realty (Chapter 15, section A). That, however, has no bearing on *mistake*. Option I states the relevant truth, and so **A** is right.

F.   The Closers

QUESTION 10 & 11. ArmCo is in the business of selling weapons to governments. On September 1, the nation of Qarat is at war with Bohrein and, as was widely publicized, the parties are conducting peace negotiations even as they fight. Also on September 1, by signed writing, ArmCo as buyer contracts with WeapCo as seller for the purchase of 100 tanks at $200 million, delivery to be made 11 months later on August 1. ArmCo forms the contract in order that it be able to supply Qarat and its enemy with additional tanks if and as the two nations sought to purchase them. ArmCo pays WeapCo $20 million on September 1 and promises to pay the remaining balance on August 15.

On July 1, the warring nations reach a peace accord and the war ends. Consequently, ArmCo is unable to sell the tanks and wants not to pay WeapCo any remaining purchase price.

QUESTION 10. Whether or not Armco is entitled to a discharge from its obligations, in seeking to obtain one it would be best advised to cite the doctrine of

A. frustration of purpose, because at the time the parties formed their contract, the peace accord represented a future event.
B. frustration of purpose, because at the time the parties formed their contract, each party knew that it was in no position to know for how long the war would continue.
C. mutual mistake, because when they formed their contract, the parties were mistaken about the likely duration of the war.
D. mutual mistake, because when they formed their contract, the peace negotiations were in progress.

ANALYSIS. Mutual mistake and frustration of purpose differ most significantly in that (1) mutual mistake requires that the contracting parties be mutually mistaken as to a fact or circumstance *in existence at the time they form their contract*, whereas (2) frustration of purpose requires that they be mistaken as to the occurrence or nonoccurrence of some *future* event (that one party should know will frustrate the other's essential purpose). Both, of course, require that their mistaken belief constitute a "basic assumption" on which they form the contract.

In this case, ArmCo cannot conceivably establish a mutual mistake as to a fact or circumstance in existence at the time they formed their contract. Both parties knew (or certainly should have known) that Qatar was at war and that peace talks were in progress. If ArmCo is entitled to withhold payment, it would have to resort to frustration of purpose and show that both parties manifested their belief, to the degree of fact — but they took as a basic assumption — that the war would continue for at least 11 months — that the warring parties would reach no peace accord during that period.

C and **D** state that ArmCo should look to the doctrine of mutual mistake, so both are wrong for that reason. Further, **C**, while referring to mutual mistake, cites also a future circumstance, to wit, the likely duration of war. Again, mutual mistake requires that the parties be mistaken as to a fact or circumstance existing at the time they form their contract. **D** refers to a fact in place at the time the parties formed their contract, but that fact is one of which each party had reason to know. Furthermore, that fact suggests the possibility of peace, not the continuation of war.

B reports that neither party could predict the prospects for war or peace. That suggests that they could not as reasonable persons assume that war would continue, and so **B** is wrong. **A** correctly refers to frustration of purpose and properly cites to the peace accord as a future event. That's why **A** is right.

QUESTION 11. If ArmCo claims discharge by frustration of purpose, which of the following facts, if proven by WeapCo, would weaken ArmCo's claim?

A. As they formed their contract, the parties manifested their mutual belief that the war was certain to endure for more than 11 months.

B. As they formed their contract, the parties mutually acknowledged that the war might not endure for 11 months.

C. After forming their contract, the parties manifested their mutual belief that the war was certain to endure for more than 11 months.

D. After forming their contract, the parties mutually acknowledged that the war might not endure for 11 months.

ANALYSIS. WeapCo would weaken ArmCo's claim of frustrated purpose if its proof negates one or more elements of the relevant rule. **A** affirmatively states one of the doctrine's elements, to wit, that the parties took as a fact—assumed—that the war would not end within the period September 1 to August 1. If WeapCo were to prove *that*, it would *strengthen* ArmCo's claim. **C** and **D** refer to the parties' state of mind after forming their contract, and that certainly is irrelevant. Both the mutual mistake and frustration doctrines (as well as the impracticability doctrine) require that the contracting parties manifest erroneous beliefs at the time they form their contract. With mutual mistake, the erroneous belief must relate to a fact in existence at that very time. With mutual frustration, it must pertain to an event that will or will not occur in the future. Hence, **C** and **D** are wrong.

Now consider **B**. It hypothesizes that WeapCo proves this fact: As these parties formed their contract, they manifested their mutual belief that by August 1 the war might or might not end. If that was their manifest belief, then certainly the war's continuation was not a basic assumption on which they contracted. Rather it was a matter of uncertainty, with ArmCo, as buyer, assuming the risk that the war might end by the date. Hence, the frustration doctrine would offer it no relief, and for that reason **B** is right.

✵ Silver & Hochberg's Picks

1.	**C**
2.	**D**
3.	**B**
4.	**A**
5.	**A**
6.	**B**
7.	**D**
8.	**D**
9.	**A**
10.	**A**
11.	**B**

23

Warranty

A. What's a Warranty?

A warranty is one's contractual promise that the commodity he purveys will be of some specific quality concerning its function, utility, or durability (among other matters). All authorities divide warranties into two categories: "express" and "implied." An express warranty is one that the seller creates by his own word or behavior. An implied warranty is a warranty that the law creates on its own.

B. Warranties as to Service

1. Nonprofessional Sellers of Service: Express Warranties

When a nonprofessional sells a service, the law implies no warranties. If, however, the seller makes an express warranty, she is bound by it as she is by any term of her contract. Suppose Bard sees on his car a scratch, which he mentions to his next-door neighbor Lola. Lola says, "I'd be happy to remove the scratch and refinish the affected area." Bard queries, "Do you know how to do that work?" She replies, "Yes. I warrant that after I complete my work, you will be unable to identify the affected area of the car." Bard asks to know "how much," Lola says "$200," and he replies, "It's a deal." The parties thus form a contract under which Lola, for $200, will remove the scratch and refinish the affected area. Further, the contract includes Lola's express warranty that after she completes her work, Bard will be unable to identify the scratched area.

In order to communicate her express warranty, Lola need not use the words "I warrant." She could simply say, "After I complete my work, you will be unable to identify the affected area of the car." Or she might show Bard other high-quality fender repairs she has done when he asks "Do you know how to do that work?" In that case, Bard, as a reasonable person, will conclude that in promising to repair his car, Lola promises also that her work will conform to the sample she showed him. Lola might (1) use the words "I warrant," or (2) expressly describe the quality of the work she will do, or (3) show Bard a sample of her work as a means of telling him how her work will appear. In every such case, she makes an express warranty.

Express Warranty: A Rule   *One expressly warrants the service she sells if in forming her contract with buyer by written or spoken word, description, display, depiction, sample, or simulation she leads the buyer reasonably to believe in some fact pertaining to its nature, quality, or durability.*[1]

2. *Professional Sellers of Service: Implied Warranties*

Depending on the jurisdiction and the industry, a seller who holds himself out as a professional provider of a service warrants that he will perform in a "good and workmanlike" manner. That phrase, in turn, refers to a performance that would ordinarily be given by one who has the knowledge, training, and/or experience necessary for the successful practice of the seller's same trade or occupation. Where such an implied warranty applies, it means the service provider must perform his work as would the ordinary reasonable person *in his same profession.* The warranty does not pertain directly to outcome. The fact that a mechanic agrees to "repair the leaking gas tank" does not imply a warranty that when he completes the job, the gas tank will not leak. Rather, it implies a warranty (if any) that he will think, judge, decide, and perform as would the provider of fair and average ability. If, in doing so, he fails to stop the leak, he has not breached any implied warranty. It is said that such a warranty applies by common law to construction workers, and by statute, in some states, to other providers as well.

QUESTION 1. VentCo installs and repairs heating, air conditioning, and ventilation equipment. BuildCo is a builder. Both are located in a jurisdiction that imposes an implied warranty on all providers of building construction services. In connection with its construction of a residential

---

1. That rule, of course, is but a corollary to a set of more basic ones that we presented at the very beginning of Chapter 18, section A.

apartment building, BuildCo, by signed writing, forms a contract with VentCo under which VentCo, for $700,000, is to "perform all services relating to the installation, placement, connection, and adjustment of all vents and related conductors appurtenant to the heating, air conditioning, and ventilation systems in the said building." Although the written agreement comprises 35 pages, it nowhere expressly describes the quality of the work or service VentCo is to perform. When VentCo announces completion of its work, BuildCo inspects it and finds it unsatisfactory. BuildCo brings an action alleging that VentCo is in breach of warranty.

At trial, BuildCo calls as witnesses various VentCo personnel, who describe in detail the way in which they think about their work, make their judgments, and perform their installations. Separately, BuildCo introduces evidence of the way in which the heating, ventilation, and air conditioning systems, as installed, do and do not function. Thereafter, BuildCo calls as a witness a professional expert in the field of heating, ventilation, and air conditioning systems. That witness will most directly support BuildCo's claim if he testifies that

A. in his opinion, VentCo's work product would not suit the ordinary and reasonable needs of the residents who occupy BuildCo's building.

B. he himself would have performed the work differently from the way in which VentCo performed it.

C. in his opinion, VentCo did not reach its professional decisions with the same care as would a professional in the same field with the ordinary degree of skill.

D. having examined the building's heating, air conditioning, and ventilation systems after VentCo installed them, he would not hire VentCo to do the sort of work for which BuildCo hired it.

ANALYSIS. Under the contract, VentCo made no express warranty as to the quality of its work. Consequently, any breach by VentCo of a warranty must relate to an implied warranty—a warranty that the law imposes on it. The only warranty that the law imposes on providers of a service (and it does not impose one on all of them; some states impose it only as to construction work) is that of "good and workmanlike" performance, which relates not to the outcome of one's work but to the way in which one performs it (which, of course, does *affect* the outcome). Most relevant to BuildCo's claim in breach of warranty is evidence not of the way in which the various systems function, but the way in which VentCo actually performed its work.

A relates not to the way in which VentCo performed its work but to the way in which the systems will or will not meet the needs of reasonable persons. It's wrong. **B** relates not to whether VentCo performed as would an average professional in its field, but to how the expert witness himself would have chosen to do the work. It too is wrong. **D** is also off the mark. It tells us only that the expert witness thinks VentCo's work product inadequate to the standards by which *he* would hire a professional in the same field.

C is best; it affords the fact finder a basis on which to conclude that VentCo performed its work in a manner not equal to the standard that prevails among average persons in its field. That denotes a breach of VentCo's warranty to perform its service in a "good and workmanlike manner," and that's why **C** is right.

C. Express Warranties Relating to Goods

UCC Article 2 governs warranties related to goods. UCC §2-313 provides:

(1) Express warranties by the seller are created as follows:

(a) Any affirmation of fact or promise made by the seller to the buyer which relates to the goods and becomes part of the basis of the bargain creates an express warranty that the goods shall conform to the affirmation or promise.

(b) Any description of the goods which is made as part of the basis of the bargain creates an express warranty that the goods shall conform to the description.

(c) Any sample or model which is made part of the basis of the bargain creates an express warranty that the whole of the goods shall conform to the sample or model.

(2) It is not necessary to the creation of an express warranty that the seller use formal words such as "warrant" or "guarantee" or that he have a specific intention to make a warranty, but an affirmation merely of the value of the goods or a statement purporting to be merely the seller's opinion or commendation of the goods does not create a warranty.

The definition is much like the common law definition we present in section B above, relating to service, and it carries the same meaning.

QUESTION 2. Channah visits TronCo to purchase a set of wall-mountable shelves on which to place her stereo equipment. The salesperson shows her a set of shelves mounted in its showroom and says, "How about this?" Channah asks to know the price, receives an answer of "$195," and then says, "I'll take it." The salesperson retrieves a large box from the back room. Channah pays $195 and receives a receipt that reads "$195 received for X23 Wall Unit." At home, Channah opens the box and finds shelves that resemble the ones shown her at TronCo's, except that they are white instead of black. Is TronCo in breach of an express warranty?

A. Yes, because the receipt expressly identifies the product for which Channah paid

> **B.** Yes, because of the color difference between the product TronCo supplied to Channah and the one it showed her
> **C.** No, because TronCo made no expression or communication as to the color of the shelves it supplied Channah
> **D.** No, because Channah asked no questions and made no statements about color or preference as to color

ANALYSIS. Reread UCC §2-313(1)(c) above. The TronCo salesperson showed Channah the model attached to the walls of the showroom, and by his doing so, TronCo made an express warranty that the good supplied to Channah would conform to the model, which, because of its color, it did not. The answer therefore, is "yes," and the reason is that the contract included TronCo's *express* warranty that the shelves sold to Channah would be the same color as those she was shown.

C and D answer "no," so they're wrong for that reason alone. Further, C makes a (legally) false statement. By showing Channah its model, TronCo did make an expression as to the color of the shelves it would provide her. D implies that Channah's failure to mention color denies her an express warranty, and that's false. That TronCo showed her the model, making it a "basis of their bargain," creates the express warranty. A correctly reports that the receipt (in some way) identifies the product sold, but that creates no warranty.

B correctly answers "yes" and correctly states the reason: The color of the shelves Channah took home was different from those shown to her. The shelves did not conform to the sample or model presented to her. Hence, B is right.

D.   Implied Warranties Relating to Goods

For the sale of goods, UCC Article 2 creates two implied warranties: (1) the warranty of "merchantability," which applies to virtually all contracts for the sale of goods; and (2) the warranty of "fitness for a particular purpose," which applies to *some* contracts for the sale of goods.

1. Merchantability

UCC § 2-314 provides generally that a merchant who sells a good (to a merchant or non-merchant) implicitly warrants it to be "merchantable," which means it must be of such quality (a) as ordinarily characterizes that same product when sold, generally, throughout the relevant industry, and (b) as renders it that suitable to the purpose for which reasonable persons use it. In stating that principle, the Code writers describe merchantable goods as those that are of such quality as "pass without objection in the trade," are of "fair and average quality," and are "fit for the ordinary purposes for which they are used."

2. *"Fitness for Particular Purpose"*

With the Code's implied warranty of merchantability, a seller promises that his goods are fit for their *ordinary* purpose—that a sponge will absorb water, a grass seed will grow grass, and a pair of scissors will cut paper. Labeled by the Code as an implied warranty, it reflects, really, the broader rule that a contract includes such terms and has such meaning as will afford its parties their reasonable expectations. The implied warranty of fitness for a *particular* purpose represents that same rule.

Suppose Buyer contacts Seller, a professional dealer in widgets and widget covers: "I need a 2011 widget cover that will fit over a 1911 widget. Do you have any such thing?" Seller shows Buyer a widget cover and says, "Certainly we do. Here it is. It's $9.99." Buyer buys it. A reasonable person in Buyer's position would take Seller's statement to mean, "For $9.99, I will sell you this widget cover, and I promise it will fit over a 1911 widget."

Contemplating such situations as that one, the Code creates the implied warranty of fitness for a particular purpose, for which the relevant rule is this: *If a commercial seller of any good knows (or should know) (1) of some specific purpose for which the buyer wishes to secure the goods, and (2) that the buyer is looking to the seller's expertise in order that the good should serve that purpose, then the seller warrants that his good will do so. If he wishes not to make the warranty, then he must refrain from selling the good.* UCC §2-315 states it thus:

> Where the seller at the time of contracting has reason to know any particular purpose for which the goods are required and that the buyer is relying on the seller's skill or judgment to select or furnish suitable goods, there is . . . an implied warranty that the goods shall be fit for such purpose.

Can a Seller Somehow Disclaim the Implied Warranties?   Yes, the Code allows a seller to "exclude" both the implied warranties of merchantability and fitness for particular purpose, but only if she does so according to the dictates of UCC §2-316. That section provides that the seller may exclude the warranty of merchantability (a) orally or (b) by conspicuous writing and that, in either case, she must use the word "merchantability" or words that in "common understanding" indicate the absence of implied warranties. By way of example, the Code cites to the phrases "as is" and "with all faults." A long string of big arcane words supplied by a lawyer will not disclaim the warranty. (And do remember that the seller who relies on an oral statement sets herself up for a potentially difficult task as to proof.)

A seller may exclude the warranty of fitness for a particular purpose *only by* "conspicuous" writing. In the writing, the phrases "as is," "with all faults," and "no implied warranties" are sufficient to work the exclusion. An attempt to exclude the fitness warranty by spoken word is ineffective, as are any words that a reasonable person of ordinary ability cannot understand.

E.   The Closer

QUESTION 3. On November 1, SurfCo contacts PlexCo.

SurfCo: We plan to manufacture a new line of vacuum-formed sandwich-riding surfboards and so wish to purchase polyurethane foam.

PlexCo: We have 120 different polyurethane foam preparations. Can you be more specific about the sort you'd like to have?

SurfCo: No, we can't. We know only what we wish to do with it.

PlexCo: Well, we can offer you our #99 polyurethane foam at $100 per commercial unit, delivered to your facility on November 20.

SurfCo: We'll take 100 units.

The parties then create a signed writing identifying SurfCo and PlexCo by name and address. It otherwise provides only this: "PlexCo will, on November 20, 2012, deliver 100 commercial units of its #99 polyurethane foam to SurfCo's facility, with SurfCo to pay $100 per unit for a total price of $10,000." If the #99 polyurethane foam is not suitable for the manufacture of vacuum-formed sandwich-riding surfboards, then, under UCC Article 2, PlexCo is in breach of

A. an express warranty of merchantability.
B. an express warranty of fitness for particular purpose.
C. an implied warranty of merchantability.
D. an implied warranty of fitness for particular purpose.

ANALYSIS. PlexCo made no express warranty. Yet the law, under UCC §2-314, warrants that the product will be "merchantable"—that it will serve its ordinary purpose and be of such fair and average quality as is ordinarily provided by sellers who provide the same or analogous product. The case presents no evidence that PlexCo's product fails in those respects.

But—SurfCo informed PlexCo that it needed the polyurethane foam for construction of a vacuum-formed sandwich-riding surfboard, and that it did not know what sort of foam would serve that purpose. PlexCo therefore knew (or should have known) "the particular purpose for which the goods [were] required and that the buyer [was] relying on [its] skill or judgment to select or furnish suitable goods." Consequently, PlexCo made a warranty of fitness for a particular purpose. By law, it promised that the polyurethane preparation #99 would be suitable for the manufacture of vacuum-formed sandwich-riding surfboards. If the product is not fit for that purpose, PlexCo is in breach of that warranty. Hence, **D** is right.

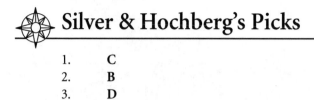

Silver & Hochberg's Picks

1.   **C**
2.   **B**
3.   **D**

Third-Party Beneficiaries, Assignment, and Delegation

A. Third-Party Beneficiaries

1. Intended and Incidental Beneficiaries

A "third-party beneficiary" to a contract formed between two others may sustain an action for breach if he is an "intended beneficiary," but not if he is an "incidental beneficiary." An intended beneficiary is one whom the contracting parties understand (or should understand) is *meant* to benefit from the contract. An incidental beneficiary is one whom the parties have no reason to understand that any benefit is intended.

Let's illustrate. B is a pianist and C her next-door neighbor. C frequently hears B play and enjoys her music, until one day he begins to notice that B's piano is falling out of tune. B too knows that her piano is losing its tune and forms a contract with A, a piano tuner, under which A will tune B's piano and B will pay him $150. C is not a party to the contract. A breaches; he fails to tune B's piano. Consequently, when B plays, C continues to hear piano music that is not in tune. For that reason, C sues A for breach. The court dismisses his suit.

Now suppose F owns a piano and E is her friend. As a gift to her friend, E wishes to have F's piano tuned. E forms a contract with D under which D will tune F's piano and E will pay D $150 for that service. F is not party to the contract. D breaches; he fails to tune F's piano. F sues D. The court does *not* dismiss her suit.

In the first piano case, the contracting parties A and B have no reason to believe that either intends A's service to benefit C. Neither, in forming the contract, has reason to believe the other is thinking of C. Consequently, C is an *incidental* beneficiary and has no power to sustain an action for A's breach. In the second piano case, E intends to benefit her friend F and, as a reasonable person, D should know that. Consequently, F is an *intended* beneficiary, and the law entitles her to sustain an action against F for breach.

Restatement (Second) of Contracts §§302, 304, and 315 provide:

> **§302.** The beneficiary of a promise is an intended beneficiary if recognition of a right to performance in the beneficiary is appropriate to effectuate the intention of the parties and . . . the circumstances indicate that the promisee intends to give the beneficiary the benefit of the promised performance. . . . An incidental beneficiary is a beneficiary who is not an intended beneficiary.
>
> **§304.** A promise in a contract creates a duty in the promisor to any intended beneficiary to perform the promise, and the intended beneficiary may enforce the duty.
>
> **§315.** An incidental beneficiary acquires by virtue of the promise no right against the promisor or the promisee.

Again, let's note that behind the veil of doctrines and definitions tied to the status of third-party beneficiaries, the rule truly at work is this one: *A contract includes such terms and has such meaning as conform to the parties' reasonable understandings and expectations.* When, in the first case, A and B form their contract, neither has reason to understand that C has any interest in A's performance. But when, in the second case, D and E form their contract, each should understand that F has an interest in D's performance. That is the principle that underlies the rules of third-party beneficiaries.

QUESTION 1. Jeffrey's employer is sending him on a six-month overseas business trip. Not wanting to disrupt his 12-year-old son Kyle's school year, Jeffrey forms a contract with Kandy under which Kandy promises to live in Jeffrey's house as a full-time caregiver to Kyle, in exchange for which Jeffrey promises to pay Kandy $35,000 for the full six-month period. If Kandy fails properly to care for Kyle, can Kyle (through his guardian ad litem) sustain an action against her?

A. Yes, because Jeffrey and Kyle have a direct familial relationship
B. Yes, because contract law affords Kyle that right

C. No, because Kyle is not a party to the contract between Jeffrey and Kandy

D. No, because Jeffrey was not within the jurisdiction at the time of the breach

ANALYSIS.   In relation to a contract between parties A and B of which C is not a part, C is an intended third-party beneficiary if the contracting parties, as reasonable persons, should understand that one (or both) of the promised performances is meant for the benefit of C. The story here makes plain that both these parties, as reasonable persons, should have such an understanding as to Kyle. Consequently, the answer is "yes," for the reason that Kyle is an intended third-party beneficiary.

C and **D** answer "no," and they're wrong for that reason. C offers a blatantly false statement, implying that no third party ever acquires a right to bring an action for breach. **D** raises a matter of irrelevancy. Whether a party to the contract is or is not within the relevant jurisdiction at the time of breach has no effect whatever on the beneficiary's rights (nor on his own, for that matter; when he returns to the jurisdiction, Jeffrey, too, may sustain an action against Kandy).

A accurately reports that Jeffrey and Kyle are family, but that has no bearing on Kyle's status as an intended beneficiary. **A** too is wrong. **B** correctly answers "yes" and correctly states its reason: Because Kyle is an intended beneficiary, contract law does afford him the right to sustain this action. Hence, **B** is right.

2. Creditor Beneficiaries and Donee Beneficiaries

When first the law described its rules of third-party beneficiaries, it distinguished beneficiaries not with the words "intended" and "incidental" but with the designations "creditor" and "donee." It was said that a third-party *creditor* beneficiary could sustain an action for breach but that a third-party *donee* beneficiary could not.

Suppose A borrows $10,000 from C and so owes C a debt of that amount; C is A's creditor. Thereafter, A and B agree that A will perform some service for B, in exchange for which B will pay A's $10,000 debt to C. In that circumstance, the law recognized (and in most quarters still does recognize) C as a "creditor beneficiary" of the contract between A and B, meaning that the third-party benefit he stands to derive arises because A actually owed C a debt and formed a contract in which B was obliged to pay it.

Now, suppose G and H form a contract under which G will rebuild H's transmission and H will relandscape G's yard. Party I is G's next-door neighbor and stands to benefit from the beauty added to G's yard. Neither G nor H owes I any obligation; the benefit of beauty that I stands to derive through the contract between G and H amounts, in older legal terms, to a mere "donation." Consequently, it used to be said that as to the contract between G and H, I was a mere "donee" beneficiary.

And what relevance do these older terms have today? As already noted, modern common law distinguishes between an *intended* and an *incidental* beneficiary. Any creditor beneficiary is also an intended beneficiary; "creditor beneficiary" represents a subset of "intended beneficiary." Hence, it remains so today that the law allows every creditor beneficiary to sustain an action for breach against a contracting party who, by breaching her contract, deprives the creditor beneficiary of his benefit. And although the significance of "creditor beneficiary" is eclipsed now by that of "intended beneficiary," modern courts still invoke the phrase; it's not yet dead.

A donee beneficiary might be an intended beneficiary and might be an incidental beneficiary. In the first piano case above, C was a donee beneficiary and also an incidental beneficiary. In the second piano case, F was a donee beneficiary but also an intended beneficiary. The phrase "donee beneficiary," therefore, is no longer significant to the law of contracts except for historical purposes.

QUESTION 2. StopCo owns a restaurant at the corner of Highway 21 and Highway 22. FuelCo, a gasoline dealer, and BuildCo, a builder, form a contract under which FuelCo is to pay BuildCo $300,000 and BuildCo is to build a gasoline station near the corner of Highway 21 and Highway 22. BuildCo fails to build the gas station and thus breaches its contract with FuelCo. StopCo is disappointed because it expected that the new gasoline station would bring additional business to its restaurant. Does the law afford StopCo the right to sustain an action against BuildCo for its breach?

A. Yes, because StopCo reasonably expected and understood that it would benefit from the presence of the new gasoline station
B. Yes, because FuelCo might reasonably expect to benefit from the location of StopCo's restaurant
C. No, because StopCo's expectation was insignificant to BuildCo's and FuelCo's contractual purpose
D. No, because StopCo had chosen its location before BuildCo and FuelCo formed their contract

---

ANALYSIS. StopCo stood to benefit from this contract in the same way as did the pianist's next-door neighbor in our first piano case above. Two parties, FuelCo and BuildCo, contracted with no manifestation of an intention to benefit StopCo; neither had reason to understand that the other was concerned with any gain StopCo might reap from the contract. (And that is true even though FuelCo might have selected the site because of StopCo's presence there. That FuelCo might have sought a benefit from StopCo's presence is not to say that FuelCo formed its contract to benefit StopCo.) StopCo is a mere incidental beneficiary, and for that reason the answer is "no."

A and **B** answer "yes," and they're wrong for that reason alone. **A** is tempting to some because it correctly states that StopCo's expectation was a reasonable one. Reasonable understandings and expectations are significant insofar as they apply to the *contracting parties*. If either FuelCo or BuildCo reasonably expected or understood that the other wished to benefit StopCo, then such by law would be *their* intention, and they would thus constitute StopCo as an intended beneficiary. But no such reasonable understanding or expectation obtained between the two contracting parties. As for **B**, FuelCo's expectation that it might benefit from StopCo's presence does not constitute StopCo as an intended beneficiary.

D correctly answers "no," but its reasoning is all wrong. Let's ask: If StopCo had selected its own site after BuildCo and FuelCo formed their contract, would it then become an intended beneficiary? Let's answer: No, it would not. **D** is wrong. **C** correctly answers "no," but some students fail to see its correctness because it does not feature the phrase "incidental beneficiary." Nonetheless, it accurately reports the reason that StopCo is an incidental beneficiary; StopCo's well-being played no role in FuelCo's and BuildCo's contractual purpose. **C** is right.

B.   Assignment

Recall again the broad precept that arises from all we discussed in Chapter 2 (see also Chapter 19, section A): *A contract includes such terms and has such meaning as conform to the reasonable expectations of its parties.* Keep this rule in mind and read about X and Y.

X and Y form a contract under which Y will weed X's garden on Monday and X will pay Y $100 on Friday. Thinking in terms of contract *rights*, see that the contract affords X the right to a weeded garden and Y the right to $100 (subject to the implied condition precedent that he substantially perform his obligation on Monday, as discussed in Chapter 21, section C). On Monday, Y weeds the garden, meaning that on Friday X must pay him $100. On Wednesday, Y approaches Z and says, "X owes me $100, to be paid on Friday. I give to you my right to have X pay that money. Now she owes the $100 to you, not to me." Y then contacts X and instructs her to pay the $100 directly to Z.

X has no good reason to object. As the law sees things, a reasonable person in X's position should expect to have her garden stripped of weeds and to pay $100 for the service. That she should be asked to pay the $100 to Z instead of Y does not compromise her reasonable expectations in the law's eyes. In a sense, where the contract provides that "X will pay Y $100," the law reads it to *mean* "X will pay $100 to Y or to any other person as Y directs."

When a first party manifests his intention presently to transfer his existing contractual right to a second party, he is said to "assign" it. The law then names the first party "assignor" and the second "assignee." In our weeded garden case, Y is the assignor and Z the assignee. X has a place in all of this, so she too acquires a title. It's her obligation to pay the $100, so the law names her the "obligor."

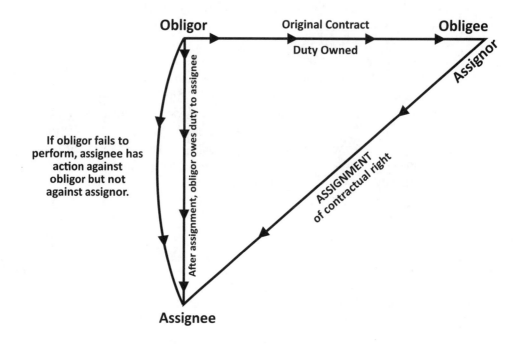

Assignment is a conveyance of property. When one conveys his property, he parts with the substantive privileges tied to his ownership and likewise loses the standing to enforce them. The grantor of real property loses his right to occupy and, of course, his right to sue another for trespass.

A contract right *is property*. More specifically, it is intangible personal property (and, more specifically still, a "chose in action"). By assigning a contract right, one conveys his property. All that was his belongs to his assignee. He loses his right to have the obligor perform in his favor and concomitantly loses the right to bring an action against her if she does not. And what the assignor loses, the assignee acquires. The obligor must perform in the assignee's favor, and if she fails, the assignee has an action against her for breach.

All of that creates this common law rule: *Ordinarily, a contracting party may assign his contractual rights, and if he does so, with notice to the obligor, then*

(1) the obligor must perform for the assignee; (2) if the obligor fails to perform, the assignee has an action against her for breach, but the assignor does not.

As Restatement (Second) §317 provides:

> An assignment of a right is a manifestation of the assignor's intention to transfer it, by virtue of which the assignor's right to performance by the obligor is extinguished . . . and the assignee acquires a right to such performance.

C.   Delegation

Consider again the original contract between X and Y. Imagine this time that Y does not assign his rights. Instead he decides that he doesn't want to weed the garden. He forms a contract with Z under which Y will pay Z $75 and Z will weed X's garden; Z will do X's job for him (and Z will make a "profit" of $25). With that arrangement, Y "delegates" his contractual duty to Z. Y is the "delegator" (also called the "delegor" and the "delegating obligor"), and Z is the "delegate" (also called the "delegee"). Because X is the party who is owed the performance, we name him the "obligee."

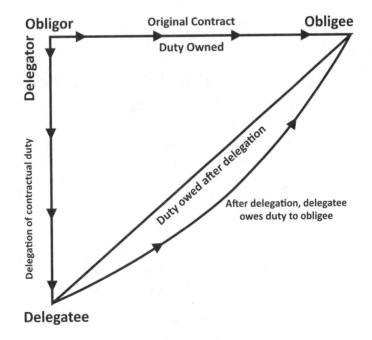

In effect, where the original contract provides that "Y must weed X's garden," the law reads it to *mean* "Y must see to it that someone weeds X's garden." The law gives X no right to object if Z and not Y arrives at X's garden on Monday ready to remove its weeds. So long as Z does then perform, X has her reasonable expectations fulfilled. That Y himself doesn't do the work gives her no cause to complain.

Consequently, the common law provides generally that *(1) each party to a contract is entitled to receive the performance promised by the other, but neither has, generally, a right to have that other party himself provide it, wherefore(2) if one contracting party delegates his duty and the delegatee does in fact perform, the delegator is not in breach.*

What if the delegatee does not perform—who's in breach then? Think again of X, Y, Z, and the weeds. Under the original contract as the law reads it, Y promises to see that X's garden is stripped of weeds. He may have Z do the weeding, but if Z fails to perform, then Y has broken his promise and he—Y—is in breach. Hence, the law provides: *If a delegatee fails to perform the contractual duty at issue, the delegator is in breach and the obligee has an action against him.* Restatement (Second) §318 provides: "[D]elegation of performance [does not discharge] any duty or liability of the [delegator]."

All of these rules apply to contracts for the sale of goods as they do to all others. UCC §2-210(1) and (2) specifically addresses assignment and delegation, and its provisions are the same in substance as those of the common law.

D. Assignment and Delegation Together: Assignment of a Contract

Ordinarily one assigns his contractual rights not as a gift but in exchange for something. And that "something" is in most cases the assignee's promise to perform the assignor's contractual duties. In other words, assignment and delegation usually occur together. In this regard, the law recognizes the phrase "assignment of a contract," which means an assignment of rights together with a delegation of duties. As UCC §2-210 (5) provides:

> An assignment of "the contract" or of "all my rights under the contract" or an assignment in similar terms is an assignment of rights and unless the language or the circumstances . . . indicate the contrary, it is a delegation of performance of the duties of the assignor and its acceptance by the assignee constitutes a promise by him to perform those duties.

Let's think again of X, Y, Z, and the weeds. X and Y first form a contract under which Y must, on Monday, weed X's garden and X must, on Friday, pay

Y $100. Suppose now that Y "assigns his contract" to Z. That means that Y and Z form a contract of their own under which Y assigns to Z his right to receive $100 from X, and Z promises to weed X's garden. Y, therefore, has assigned his rights *and* delegated his duties, meaning that Y has assigned *the contract* to Z. The delegation has also a separate effect: It renders X an intended third-party beneficiary of the contract between X and Z.

So—who is liable to whom for what? Once Y assigns his contract to Z, there stand two separate contracts: (1) the contract between X and Y, and (2) the contract between Y and Z.

Under contract 1, Y must see that someone strips the weeds from X's garden. That's a duty he owes to X. X must pay $100 as Y directs. That's a duty she owes to Y. Under contract 2, Y must instruct X to make payment to Z, and because of contract 1, X then owes that duty to Z, not X. Z must weed X's garden. That's a contractual duty he owes to Y. X stands as an intended third-party beneficiary.

If Z fails to weed the garden, then Y is in breach of his contract with X, Z is in breach of his contract with Y, and X has failed to derive his intended third-party benefit. Consequently, X has an action against Y, Y has an action against Z, and X has an action against Z (as intended third-party beneficiary). If, on the other hand, X fails to pay Z, Z has an action against X, but Y does not have an action against X.

Assignment & Delegation
"Assignment of a Contract"

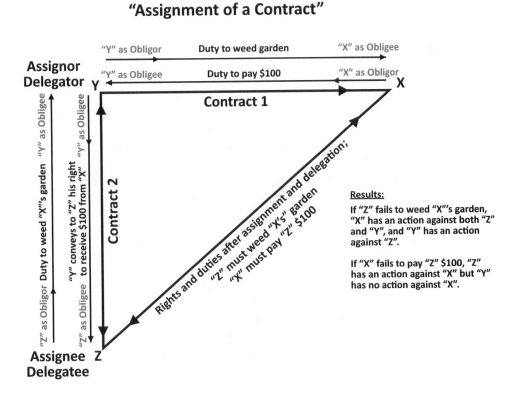

After assigning his contract to Z, X owes nothing to Y, but Y is obliged, still, to see that X's garden is weeded. He need not weed it himself, and he has arranged for Z to do so. But still Y remains liable to X; if Z fails to weed the garden, X has an action against him.

Y can free himself of that obligation only all three partices agree to a "novation," which means that X and Y mutually release each other from their original contract and, simultaneously, Z and X form a contract in which Z promises to weed X's garden and X promises to pay Z $100. Y is then "out of it" and contractual relations run only between X and Z. Again, the law calls that new arrangement a "novation."

The law, it is said, favors the free transferability ("alienability") of property. If two parties form a contract whose terms are silent on the subject of assignment, then each is ordinarily free to assign her rights. A party is forbidden to assign her rights only if the contract so provides, explicitly. If two parties form a contract whose terms are silent on the subject of delegation, then each is ordinarily free to delegate her duties. Even in the absence of an express contractual provision that prohibits delegation, there remains one circumstance under which an obligor is, nonetheless, forbidden to delegate her duties: that in which the would-be delegator owes the obligee a "personal service," as discussed below.

E.   Delegation and the Personal Service Contract

Reasonable persons (as the law sees them) do not ordinarily fuss over who it is that weeds their gardens, sweeps their floors, paints their cars, or shovels their snow. When competently performed, those services do not differ with the person who performs them. To the reasonable person, a shoveled driveway is a shoveled driveway regardless of who it is that wields the shovel.

Yet reasonable persons consider that the work products of a graphic artist, musician, poet, or cook do differ depending on the person doing the work, and one who contracts with another for receipt of such services reasonably expects (and the other should understand) that the same service nominally performed by some third person will not fulfill the promise made her. With regard to this so-called rule, be mindful again (and always) that *contracts include such terms and have such meaning as conform to the parties' reasonable understandings and expectations.* With that, read about Elan and Fay.

Elan, a renowned painter of portraits, forms a contract with Fay under which Elan promises to paint Fay's portrait and Fay promises to pay Elan $100,000. Jetta, Elan's daughter, timely arrives at the appointed location and truthfully advises Fay that Elan has delegated to her his duty to paint Fay's portrait, wherefore she stands ready, willing, and able to paint Fay's portrait.

Of that situation the courts used to say this: "Although a contracting party may generally delegate his duties to another, in the case of a personal service contract, that rule does not apply. One who contracts to deliver a personal service must deliver it himself." The phrase "personal service contract" was mischosen since, by ordinary usage, one who collects the garbage, cleans the furnace, or repairs the roof does personally deliver a service. The decisions make plain that when haplessly writing of "personal service contracts" courts meant and mean to designate those contracts for which the services of a particular person on one side of a contract are critical to the reasonable expectations of the party on the other. More fundamentally, the courts mean to recognize (although they may not know it) that when one party says "I promise to paint your portrait," the other reasonably understands him to *mean* "I—*myself*—promise to paint your portrait," wherefore by law that *is* what he means; that is what he "intends" to promise, and that is the promise he makes. The law does not allow him to delegate.

Let us then state the law of delegation more fully: *Except as to a contractual duty for which a reasonable person would deem it significant that actual performance be given personally by the obligor (often called a "personal service" contract), a contracting party may effectively delegate his duty to another and when he does so: (1) the obligee has no cause to complain, so long as the delegatee does in fact perform; but (2) if the delegatee fails to perform, the delegator is in breach and the obligee has an action against him and also against the delegatee.*

Restatement (Second) §318 makes its statement on the topic rather badly:

> An obligor can properly delegate the performance of his duty to another . . . [but] a promise requires performance by a particular person . . . [if] the obligee has a substantial interest in having that person perform . . . the acts promised.

That section's comment c then runs 'round in circles as well, citing to the old phrase "personal service," meanwhile offering no attempt to define the Restatement's own words, "substantial interest," and failing to relate the relevant principle to that of reasonable expectations, from which, certainly, it arises:

> Delegation of performance is a normal and permissible incident of many types of contract. . . . The principal exceptions relate to contracts for personal services and to contracts for the exercise of personal skill or discretion.

With its illustrations 1 and 5, §318 does properly report that when A owes money to B, he may effectively delegate to C his duty to pay, but that when A contracts with B to sing, he may not effectively delegate that duty to C, another singer.

QUESTIONS 3 & 4. TeleCo provides television conferencing services, and StockCo is a nationwide stockbroker. TeleCo and StockCo, by signed writing, form a contract under which TeleCo will service, for three years, all of StockCo's needs for teleconferencing among its various offices, with StockCo to pay for that service in installments every three months, beginning three months after formation of the contract. The contract features no provision that concerns assignment or delegation.

QUESTION 3. Before the first three-month period expires and hence before StockCo makes its first payment, TeleCo assigns to ElectriCo its right to receive the first payment from StockCo. TeleCo notifies StockCo of the assignment, and StockCo acknowledges the notice. When its first payment is due, StockCo contacts TeleCo and asks for permission to pay one month late. TeleCo gives permission and so notifies ElectriCo, but ElectriCo objects to the one-month extension. It contacts StockCo and demands immediate payment. In light of the extension that TeleCo has given StockCo, is ElectriCo entitled to immediate payment?

A. Yes, because as to that payment TeleCo and StockCo have no contractual relationship

B. Yes, because StockCo sent no notice to ElectriCo of the extension given it by TeleCo

C. No, because as assignor of a contract right, TeleCo maintains its power under the original contract to modify StockCo's duties

D. No, because ElectriCo's position is subordinate to TeleCo's and ElectriCo is bound by any waiver TeleCo might make in respect of StockCo's obligations

ANALYSIS. When one assigns a contract right, he conveys property to his assignee and so relinquishes all rights and privileges associated with ownership. Before making the assignment, TeleCo was entitled to the first payment and upon StockCo's failure to make it, had the right to an action for the breach or, alternatively, the right to forgive it. With the assignment, TeleCo lost all such privileges and passed them to ElectriCo. Consequently, TeleCo had no power to extend StockCo's payment deadline by one month or one moment. That right belonged to ElectriCo, and ElectriCo wants immediate payment. For *that* reason, the answer is "yes."

C and **D** say "no"; they're wrong. Both make statements contrary to the law. As to the right it assigned, TeleCo maintains no power to modify StockCo's duty; neither is ElectriCo's position "subordinate" to StockCo's. **B** correctly answers "yes," but then cites an irrelevancy. An assignor has no power to alter a contractual right it has assigned to another. That is so whether the obligor (StockCo) does or does not notify the assignee that the assignor has attempted to do what he cannot do. **B** is wrong.

A answers "yes" and correctly states the reason. As to the first payment StockCo owed, TeleCo relinquished its contractual relationship and so lost its power to deal with StockCo as to StockCo's obligation. **A** is right.

QUESTION 4. MeetCo too provides teleconferencing services and is known to have a status, capacity, and reputation equal to TeleCo's. For this question, assume that TeleCo does not assign any right to ElectriCo. Instead, before beginning its performance, TeleCo signs a writing on which it writes "Contract with StockCo is hereby assigned to MeetCo." TeleCo staples to that writing a copy of its written contract with StockCo and delivers the two stapled writings to MeetCo. MeetCo takes the papers and gives back to TeleCo a signed writing on which it writes "Assignment of StockCo's contract with TeleCo is accepted." TeleCo and MeetCo then notify StockCo of these events.

Thereafter, MeetCo visits StockCo's facility and announces its readiness to provide teleconferencing service. StockCo refuses to accept the service on the ground that its contract is with TeleCo. It then contacts TeleCo, insisting that TeleCo is in breach of contract. Which of the following facts most strongly suggests that StockCo is wrong?

A. TeleCo and MeetCo made their arrangement in writing.
B. The contract provides for the sale of a service, not for the sale of goods.
C. MeetCo is capable of offering service equivalent to TeleCo's.
D. TeleCo not only delegated its duties but also assigned its rights.

ANALYSIS. TeleCo has "assigned its contract" to MeetCo, meaning that it has, to MeetCo, assigned its rights and delegated its duties. Critical to this question is the delegation. When one party to a contract delegates her duty to some third party, the original obligee (StockCo in this case) has no cause to complain unless the original contract, as fairly interpreted, provides that the obligee is entitled to service from the party with whom she actually contracted. That is so only if the contract expressly forbids one or both parties to delegate performance or if the service at issue, in the mind of a reasonable person, will differ depending on the party who actually furnishes it (wherefore there arises the unhappy phrase "personal service contract").

We are told that this contract featured no provision relating to assignment or delegation. Hence, TeleCo is permitted to delegate (and assign). We *are* told that MeetCo's abilities are equal to TeleCo's. For both reasons, TeleCo's assignment is effective, and so long as MeetCo performs (or tenders performance in the face of StockCo's refusal to accept it) MeetCo commits no breach.

A, **B**, and **D** cite truths—all of them wholly irrelevant. StockCo would be obliged to accept performance from MeetCo if TeleCo and MeetCo had made their arrangement without a writing. It would be so obliged, too, if the contract were for the sale of goods and if the delegation had not been accompanied by TeleCo's assignment of rights.

C is correct because it cites a matter of significance. If MeetCo were not capable of offering service equivalent to TeleCo's, StockCo would not be obliged to accept MeetCo as provider of the service and TeleCo would be in breach. Hence, C is right.

F.   The Closer

QUESTION 5. FlyCo, an airline, forms a contract with ServeCo, a packaged food sales company, under which ServeCo will supply FlyCo with packaged meals suitable for delivery to passengers during flight. The contract is specific as to quantities, time periods, and the nature of the packaged meals. FlyCo pays ServeCo its full fee under the contract and awaits ServeCo's performance. ServeCo then meets with MealCo, which is in the business of preparing packaged meals. ServeCo explains to MealCo its contractual obligations to FlyCo and that FlyCo had fully paid for the services it was to perform. Thereupon, ServeCo and MealCo form a contract under which ServeCo will pay MealCo and MealCo would actually prepare and package the meals to be delivered to FlyCo. MealCo fails properly to perform and, as a result, ServeCo is unable to deliver meals to FlyCo as required by its contract. FlyCo brings an action naming both ServeCo and MealCo as defendants. MealCo moves to dismiss the action as to itself. In reaching its decision, a court might logically observe that FlyCo's status is that of

  I. creditor beneficiary
  II. donee beneficiary
  III. intended beneficiary
  IV. incidental beneficiary

  A. I
  B. I and II
  C. I and III
  D. I, III, and IV

ANALYSIS.   When ServeCo approached MealCo, it owed FlyCo a contractual duty, and FlyCo fully explained its nature to MealCo. Hence, MealCo had reason to know that ServeCo wished to secure MealCo's services to fulfill those obligations. Consequently, in older legal parlance, FlyCo might well be called a "creditor" beneficiary, and courts do still invoke that phrase. In more modern terms, FlyCo is an intended beneficiary (as is every creditor beneficiary), and for that reason the law affords it the right to sustain an action against MealCo for its breach. A creditor beneficiary cannot be a donee beneficiary, and an intended beneficiary cannot be an incidental beneficiary (although a donee beneficiary might well be an intended beneficiary).

A court might today invoke both the phrases "creditor" and "intended" beneficiary (even though the latter alone is significant to this purpose). Consequently, options I and III make true statements. II and IV do not, wherefore **C** is right.

Silver & Hochberg's Picks

1.	B
2.	C
3.	A
4.	C
5.	C

25

Breach, Remedies, and Damages, Part I

A. What's a Contract?

Many define "contract" like this: A contract is a promise or set of promises that, when breached, entitles the aggrieved party, by law, *to a remedy*.[1] So crucial is the concept of remedy to the law of contracts that many teachers (and some casebooks) begin the contracts course with that subject. If your teacher is in that group, then begin *this* book right here. Most likely, your teacher's unit on remedies will take you through Chapter 30. He or she will likely turn then to either offer and acceptance (Chapters 1-11) or consideration (Chapters 12-14).

If your teacher begins with remedies, he or she may well begin with the substance set forth in section E, "Calculating the Damages: Expectation Interest and Benefit of the Bargain." Even so, we urge you first to read section B (it's short). Okay? Let's get started.

---

1.   That's a better crafted version of the Restatement's definition.

According to Restatement (Second) of Contracts §1: " A contract is a promise or a set of promises for the breach of which the law gives a remedy. . . ."

If you are beginning this book with Chapter 25, you will not yet know what is meant by the "Restatement." See Appendix, section C.

B.   Three Little Words: "Breach," "Remedies," and "Damages"

If a contracting party fails to honor one or more of her contractual promises, she commits a breach of contract (unless she has some viable defense[2]). Breach of contract constitutes a *cause of action*, meaning that if a plaintiff alleges facts that describe a defendant's contractual breach (see Appendix, section A), the law entitles him to sustain an *action* (lawsuit) through which to prove his allegations and, if he succeeds in doing so, a *remedy*.

"Remedy" refers to some process or device by which the law attempts to right a legal wrong. The law's customary remedy for breach of contract is an award of "monetary damages" (sometimes called, simply, "damages"), meaning a monetary recovery that, in the law's eyes, corresponds to the harm or loss caused the plaintiff by the defendant's breach. So we say that for breach of contract, the usual remedy is damages.

Now STOP! Before going further in this chapter, read (or reread) Chapter 21, section D, which thoroughly discusses material (total) breach and immaterial (partial) breach. Don't come back, please, until you've finished doing that.

Welcome back. Now, please answer Questions 1 and 2.

QUESTIONS 1 & 2. On January 1, Jack and Jill form a contract under which Jack is to build a house on Jill's land, the work to be complete by July 31. When the house is built, Jill will pay Jack $400,000. On July 31, Jack announces his completion, but unknowingly fails properly to nail one last nail into one last shingle on one corner of the newly built roof. Believing he has done his job, Jack gathers his equipment and leaves. On the morning of August 1, Jill inspects the house and sees a loose shingle. She so advises Jack, who responds, "Well, I've taken all my equipment away, and I have other commitments to fulfill. I can't come back right away to place one nail in one shingle. I'm sorry. I will be able to return, however, in about ten weeks."

QUESTION 1. Is Jill obliged to pay Jack the $400,000, as provided by their contract?

A.   Yes, because if two parties A and B form a contract and A breaches, B has an action against A, but B must nonetheless perform *her* contractual duties

---

2. Defenses include the Statute of Frauds (Chapter 15); incapacity (Chapter 16); illegality (Chapter 17); duress, undue influence, and unconscionability (Chapter 20); mistake, frustration of purpose, and impracticability (Chapter 22). You have studied or will study all such topics earlier or later in your course.

> **B.** Yes, because Jack committed a partial breach, which does not deny his efforts the status of substantial performance
> **C.** No, because as to two contracting parties A and B, if A is to perform first and B second, any breach by A allows B to withhold her performance
> **D.** No, because Jill gave Jack notice as to his breach and he declined to make prompt correction and cure

ANALYSIS. This question tests the law described in Chapter 21, section D: *If Parties 1 and 2 form a contract and Party 1 commits a partial breach, then Party 2 must nonetheless continue in her performance. If she doesn't do so, then she too is in breach*—total breach.

Jack gave substantial performance; he *almost* fully completed his work. The missing nail *is* a breach, but it's an immaterial breach called, also, a partial breach. Hence, Jill may not withhold her performance. By law, she must pay Jack the full $400,000 she owes him. She can then sustain an action against him for the damages, if any, caused her by the missing nail, but she cannot withhold her own performance—not even a little bit.[3] So the answer to this question is "yes," which shoves **C** and D out the window. Let's look at them as we say goodbye. **D** implies a false statement of law, to wit, this one: Where Party B notifies Party A that he has committed a breach—even a "teensy" one—then if Party A fails promptly to correct ("cure") it, Party B may withhold her performance. There is no such rule! And that illustrates an important test-taking strategy: As always, read a multiple-choice option *for its meaning* and not for the appearance of familiar words. Once you've done so, if you find that it states or implies a rule you've never heard of—eliminate it. The chances are that if, on an exam, after studying, you're faced with a rule of which you never have heard—it doesn't exist.

By omitting the word "material" or "total" before "breach," **C** states that *any* breach by Party A allows Party B to withhold performance. That's false, so **C** is wrong. **A** is wrong for the same reason. Omitting the words "partial" or "immaterial" before "breach," **A** says that Jill would have to perform even if Jack had left the building without any roof at all. Both **A** and **C** fail to distinguish between partial and total breach.

And what of **B**? It says, "yes," Jill must pay Jack the full $400,000. Why? Because Jack committed only a partial breach. That alone would be enough to make a correct answer. Yet **B** goes on. To commit only a partial breach, it explains, is to give substantial performance. And we know that if Party A gives

---

3. In reality, Jill, if honest, would pay Jack all but the amount necessary to place the last shingle. Imagine that she pays Jack $399,900, reserving $100 to hire someone to place the last shingle. She would then be in breach. In theory, Jack would have an action against Jill for the $100, but Jill would have a counterclaim against him for the $100 damage occasioned by his breach. Jack (unless crazy) would accept the $399,900 and the parties would not—certainly not—find themselves in court.

substantial performance, then Party B must perform—fully. There's no doubt about it: **B** is right.

> **QUESTION 2.** Now assume that on July 31, the house is complete, except that it does not yet have a roof; it has no roof at all. Is Jill obliged to pay Jack the $400,000, as provided by their contract?
>
> **A.** Yes, because if two parties A and B form a contract and A commits a significant breach, B has an action against A, but B must nonetheless perform her contractual duties
>
> **B.** Yes, because Jack completed most of his work, and in the case of this partial breach the law does not excuse Jill from honoring her contractual obligations
>
> **C.** No, because as to two contracting parties A and B, if A is to perform first and B second, a total breach by A deprives B of substantial performance
>
> **D.** No, because Jill gave Jack notice as to a material breach, and he declined to make prompt correction

---

ANALYSIS. This time Jack committed a total breach. A house without a roof certainly bespeaks a material breach, which entitles Jill to withhold her performance entirely, cancel the contract, and sue Jack for monetary damages. Plainly, then, the answer to this question is "no," Jill is not obliged to pay Jack anything at all. That means we show **A** and **B** to the door. **A** refers to a "significant breach" and thus refers to a material breach—a failure of substantial performance. Where a first party commits a material breach, the second is *not* obliged to perform, because the first party's substantial performance is a condition precedent to the second party's duty to perform. So—**A** is wrong. It answers "yes," when the answer is "no," and makes a false statement of law.

B too is a loser. The "yes" makes it wrong, of course, as does the double-talk that follows. We're told that Jack completed most of his work. That's true; he did. Then we're told that he has committed only a partial breach. That's false; he committed a total breach. Even though Jack completed most (more than 50%) of his work, he did not give substantial performance. He committed not a partial breach, but a total breach. The absence of a roof denotes, certainly, a material breach, even though it represents less than one-half the task of building a house. So as for **B**, we confidently say this: it's wrong.

D properly answers "no" but then implies a false statement of law, invoking the word "material" to trap the unwary. There is no such rule as given in **D**. If Party A commits a material breach, then B need not perform. Party A can't revive B's duty to perform by curing the material breach. (If she wishes, however, Jill certainly can allow Jack to cure the breach and then pay him. Sensible people in Jack and Jill's position behave that way when they can. Lawsuits aren't fun, except for the lawyers.)

C, alas is correct. It correctly says, "no," Jill is not obliged to pay Jack any money at all, and it correctly states the relevant law: When a first party commits a material breach, the second need not perform. **C** is right.

C.   Anticipatory Repudiation as Total Breach

Suppose that on February 1, Cook and Darworth form a contract under which Cook is to perform on March 1 and Darworth is to perform on March 2. On February 15, Cook tells Darworth: "I regret forming this contract and I won't perform." Cook thus commits an "anticipatory repudiation" (or "anticipatory breach"). Darworth may treat the anticipatory repudiation, immediately, as a total breach. Without waiting until March 1 when Cook's performance is actually due, Darworth may inform Cook that the contract is terminated, and/or contract with some other party to furnish Cook's performance, and/or bring an action for breach. (But as discussed in section E below, Darworth must mitigate his damage or risk losing some of his recovery.)

Restatement (Second) of Contracts §253 provides:

> Where an obligor repudiates a duty before [his performance is due,] his repudiation alone gives rise to a claim for damages for total breach, [and the repudiation] discharges the other party's remaining duties to render performance.

Darworth, on the other hand, may sit still and wait until March 1, hoping perhaps that Cook will have a change of heart, retract his repudiation, and perform. If, however, before Cook retracts his repudiation, Darworth advises Cook that he is terminating the contract, and/or contracts with some other party to substitute for Cook, and/or brings suit against Cook, and/or otherwise alters his position in response to or reliance on Cook's repudiation, then Cook loses his power to retract. He remains in breach, and Darworth may sue for damages.

As Restatement (Second) §253 provides:

> [A] repudiation . . . is nullified by a retraction of the [repudiation] if notification of the retraction comes to the attention of the injured party before he materially changes his position in reliance on the repudiation or indicates to the other party that he considers the repudiation to be final.

So let's write a rule:

> *If with respect to a contract one party manifests her intention not to furnish substantial performance when it comes due, she commits an anticipatory repudiation, whereupon*
>
> *(1) the aggrieved party may consider that the repudiating party has committed a total breach and, in response, without waiting until performance is due, advise the repudiating party that the contract is at an end, and take any and all*

other actions that she would be entitled to take had that party failed to furnish substantial performance on the very day it was due, including the initiation of a lawsuit for total breach, and if the aggrieved party does initiate suit or take any other action in reliance on the repudiation, the contract is at an end and the repudiating party loses his right to reaffirm it; or

(2) the aggrieved party, if she chooses, may do nothing in response, in which case, if the repudiating party retracts her repudiation before the day on which her performance is due, she thereby reaffirms the contract, the aggrieved party loses her right to respond to the breach, and both parties are once again obliged to perform as agreed.

D. Calculating the Damages: Expectation Interest and Benefit of the Bargain

Fairfax is an orchestra leader and Gaelle a planner of corporate events. On April 1, the two form a contract under which Fairfax, before June 6 and at his own expense, will engage 25 musicians, thereby assembling an orchestra; and then, on June 6, conduct the orchestra at a corporate event to be arranged by Gaelle. In exchange, Gaelle will pay Fairfax, on April 5, a total, final fee of $40,000.

On April 2, Fairfax spends $25 for a list of orchestral musicians available for performance on June 6. Then, on April 6, Fairfax contacts Gaelle: "Your $40,000 payment was due yesterday, April 5, but I haven't received it." Gaelle responds, "I won't be paying because I have decided that I don't want to proceed with our contract. I'm out." Gaelle thus commits an anticipatory repudiation. When Fairfax announces that he'll take Gaelle to court for breach, she asks, "Have you made any commitments or payments to anyone because of our contract?" Fairfax replies that he has spent $25 for the musician's list. Gaelle then says that she'll reimburse Fairfax the $25. Not satisfied, Fairfax promises to sue, but Gaelle counters, "Go ahead, but you'll only recover $25."

Gaelle Is Wrong; Fairfax is entitled to Much More Than the $25 He Spent "Out of Pocket" Long-standing common law provides that recovery for a plaintiff who suffers breach of contract is not measured by the amount he loses out of pocket. Rather, *for breach of contract, the plaintiff is normally entitled to recover such amount as will move him from the position he occupies at the time of breach to the position he would have enjoyed had the contract been fully performed by both its parties.* Restatement (Second) §347 cmt. a tells us:

> Contract damages are . . . intended to give [plaintiff] . . . a sum of money that will, to the extent possible, put him in as good a position as he would have been in had the contract been performed.

Suppose Fairfax does sue Gaelle. At trial, evidence makes plain that if both parties had fully performed under the contract, Fairfax would have paid

- $25 for the available musicians list (which he has in fact paid),
- $1,000 for a rehearsal hall, and
- $20,000 in fees to the musicians.

To calculate the appropriate recovery, we establish a number line on which the zero mark represents plaintiff's monetary position just before forming the contract:

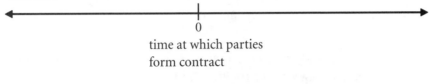

0
time at which parties
form contract

Second, we ignore what *actually* occurred after the parties formed their contract and instead look at what plaintiff *would* have received and what plaintiff *would* have paid out if both parties had fully and properly performed:

- Fairfax would have received: $40,000
- Fairfax would have paid: $25 + 1,000 + 20,000

Had both parties fully performed, Fairfax would have enjoyed a *net gain* of $18,975. The result represents the position plaintiff would have occupied had both parties fully and properly performed under the contract:

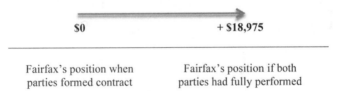

$0	+ $18,975
Fairfax's position when parties formed contract	Fairfax's position if both parties had fully performed

Third, we identify the position that plaintiff does occupy in light of the breach. Fairfax has received nothing from Gaelle and has spent $25 on the available musicians list:

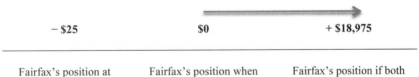

− $25	$0	+ $18,975
Fairfax's position at time of breach	Fairfax's position when parties formed contract	Fairfax's position if both parties had fully performed

The law awards plaintiff the amount of money that will move him from the position (1) that he actually occupies at the time of breach, to (2) the position he would have occupied if both parties had fulfilled their contract. When Gaelle breaches, Fairfax is "down" $25 from the time the parties formed their contract. If both parties had fully performed, Fairfax would have been "up"

$18,975. We call that amount the "benefit of the bargain" or the plaintiff's "expectation interest." Fairfax justly "expected" that the contract would afford him an $18,975 gain. Stated otherwise, Fairfax stood to enjoy an $18,975 "benefit" of his "bargain." Consequently, the law will award him monetary damages of ($25 + 18,975) = $19,000. That amount affords Fairfax his expectation interest—the benefit of his bargain.

We state the general rule like this: *For breach of contract, the plaintiff is normally entitled to recover such amount as will move him from the position he occupies at the time of breach to the position he would have enjoyed had the contract been fully performed by both its parties, and thus affords him his expectation interest, also called the benefit of his bargain.*

QUESTIONS 3 & 4. On July 1 Sintara and Tanya form a contract under which Sintara is to cut 100 trees on Tanya's property, Sintara to begin work on August 1 and complete it by August 15. Tanya is to pay Sintara a total of $6,000 in three installments: $2,000 immediately upon formation of the contract, an additional $2,000 on August 1 when Sintara arrives to begin work, and $2,000 when Sintara completes her work.

On July 1 Tanya pays Sintara $2,000 as agreed. On August 1 Sintara arrives, demonstrating that she is ready, willing, and able to begin work. Tanya announces that she will not pay the second or third installments of $2,000 because she is "bowing out" of the contract; she anticipatorily repudiates, thus committing a total breach.

QUESTION 3. Sintara brings an action against Tanya. At trial it is proven that to perform, Sintara would have spent $500 in equipment rental, which in light of the breach, she will not in fact have to pay. Sintara is entitled to a total recovery of

A. $6,500 – $2,000 = $4,500
B. $6,000 – $500 = $5,500
C. $5,500 – $1,500 = $4,000
D. $5,500 – $2,000 = $3,500

ANALYSIS.   For breach of contract, a plaintiff ordinarily is entitled to recover damages in such amount as will fulfill her expectation interest or, stated otherwise, as will afford her the economic position she would have enjoyed if both parties had properly performed. If both these parties had fully performed under their contract, Tanya would have received $6,000 and paid $500, for a net expectation interest of $5,500. That amount represents the benefit of Sintara's bargain—Sintara's expectation interest. Tanya did pay Sintara $2,000, so that at the time of the breach, Sintara is up by $2,000. To move her from the position of $2,000 to $5,500, the law must award her (from Tanya's pocket) $3,500. Hence, **D** is right.

> **QUESTION 4.** Assume now that when Tanya breached, Sintara had already paid the $500 for equipment rental. In that case, the law should afford Sintara recovery of
>
> A. $6,500 − $2,000 = $4,500
> B. $6,000 − $500 = $5,500
> C. $5,500 − $1,500 = $4,000
> D. $5,500 − $2,000 = $3,500

ANALYSIS. The change to the story does not affect Sintara's expectation interest; it does not alter the gain she would have derived if both parties had fully performed. That remains at $5,500. The fact that Sintara paid the $500 for equipment rental alters the position she in fact occupies. It is not + $2,000 but rather ($2,000 − $500) = + $1,500. Consequently, the recovery necessary to fulfill her expectation interest is $5,500 − $1,500 = $4,000. **C** is right.

E.   The Closers

> On September 1, Team and Legs form a contract under which Legs will play basketball for Team during the months January to April of the following year, and Team will pay Legs a salary of $1 million monthly, on the thirtieth day of each such month. On September 15, Legs announces to Team that he will not, under any condition, play for Team, and that he will not report to work in January.
>
> **QUESTION 5.** Team takes no action in response. On January 1, Legs reports for play as required by his contract, announcing that he has changed his mind and that he will honor it after all. Team Owner advises Legs that he is not welcome to play, that he will not be paid a salary—that he is "fired." Which party has an action against which party?
>
> A. Team has an action against Legs for total breach, arising from the anticipatory repudiation Legs made on September 15.
> B. Legs has an action against Team arising from Team Owner's declaration, on January 1, that Legs was "fired."
> C. Each party has an action against the other because each has manifested an intention not to honor the relevant contractual obligations.
> D. Neither party has an action against the other because each has behaved improperly as to the other.

ANALYSIS.   If one party to a contract commits an anticipatory repudiation, the other (the aggrieved party) may consider that he has committed a total breach. Without waiting for the day on which performance is due, he may announce that the contract is terminated, contract with a substitute and initiate suit against the repudiating party for total breach. If, however, the aggrieved party does nothing at all in reliance on the contract, then at any time up to the moment that performance is due the repudiating party may retract his repudiation and reaffirm the contract.

Legs committed an anticipatory repudiation on September 15, but Team took no action in reliance on it. It did not hire another player to take Legs's place. Neither did it initiate suit nor advise Legs that it was terminating the contract. When Legs reported for duty on January 1, he reaffirmed his contract. When Team Owner then "fired" him, Team committed an anticipatory breach by announcing (implicitly) that it would not pay his salary when due. Because Legs reaffirmed the contract, Team has no action against him. Because Team then committed its own anticipatory breach, Legs has an action against Team. For those reasons, **B** is right.

QUESTION 6. Assume that in response to Legs's September 15 announcement, Team, on December 31, hires another player to replace Legs. On the next day, January 1, Legs reports for play as required by his contract. Team Owner advises Legs that he is not welcome to play, that he will not be paid a salary—that he is "fired." Which party has an action against which party?

A. Team has an action against Legs for total breach.
B. Legs has an action against Team for total breach.
C. Each party has an action against the other for total breach.
D. Neither party has an action against the other for breach.

ANALYSIS.   In this case, Team took action in reliance on the repudiation before Legs attempted to retract it. Team, therefore, has an action against Legs for total breach. **A** is right.

QUESTION 7. Assume now that in response to Legs's September 15 announcement Team brings an action against Legs for breach. On receiving notice of that action, Legs promises that he will indeed perform under the contract. May Team proceed with its action?

I. Yes, because the initiation of suit constitutes reliance on Legs's repudiation
II. Yes, because one who commits an anticipatory repudiation loses his right to reaffirm the contract if the aggrieved party brings suit against him

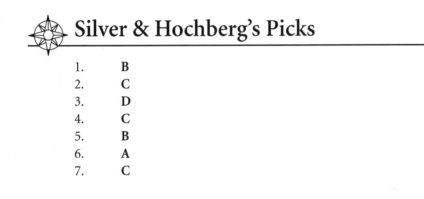

A. I
B. II
C. I and II
D. Neither I nor II

ANALYSIS. When a party commits an anticipatory breach, the other party's initiation of a lawsuit is, by law, a form of reliance on the breach. If and when the other party begins his suit, the repudiating party can no longer retract the repudiation. The situation is thus akin to that of Question 2 above, in which Team hired a replacement for Legs. It acted on the repudiation in that case and in this one. Options I and II make true statements, and **C** is right.

✦ Silver & Hochberg's Picks

1.	**B**
2.	**C**
3.	**D**
4.	**C**
5.	**B**
6.	**A**
7.	**C**

Breach, Remedies, and Damages, Part II

A. Plaintiff Does Not Recover for Damage She Could Reasonably Have Avoided: *Mitigation of Damages*

1. *Mitigation of Damages: The Rule*

Suppose that on May 1 Marnoff and Namly form a contract for the sale of Marnoff's home to Namly for $550,000. Their contract provides for an August 1 closing.[1] On May 15, real estate values in the area begin to turn downward, and Namly believes he will save money if he waits longer to buy a home. On May 20, he tells Marnoff, "I no longer wish to buy the home. I'm not going forward with our contract." Two days later, Orshan offers to buy Marnoff's home for $490,000, but Marnoff refuses. By August 1, the home's value declines to $350,000.

Marnoff sues Namly for breach of contract His lawyer argues, "Had both parties fully performed this contract, my client, Mr. Marnoff Marnoff would have received $550,000 for his property. The real estate now, however, is worth

---

1. The contract for sale of the realty and the sale itself are not the same. The contract obliges each party to appear at a "closing" and perform his part of the sale. At the closing, the seller transfers title and the buyer pays the purchase price (less the down payment amount).

only $350,000, meaning that my client is entitled to damages of ($550,000 − $350,000) = $200,000. That amount will move him from the position he now occupies to the position he would have occupied had the parties performed.

Namly's lawyer responds, "Two days after my client withdrew from the contract, another buyer stood ready to buy the property for $490,000. Had Marnoff sold for that amount, he would have had, in his pocket ($490,000 − $350,000) = $140,000 of the $200,000 for which he now asks. From my client, he would need only ($200,000 − $140,000) = $60,000 to fulfill his expectation interest, and that is all he should recover. The remaining $140,000 of his "damage" represents his own fault— his own failure to sell his property for $490,000 and thus spare himself $140,000 of the $200,000 lost to him.

Namly's lawyer is right. The common law has long provided that a party who suffers a breach of contract has an obligation to "mitigate,"—lessen— her damages. One who suffers a breach cannot sit idly by and let her damages run upward if some reasonable means of mitigating them is available. The consequences of a party's not mitigating damages are that he will be denied recovery for damages he could have avoided by reasonably and diligently mitigating. Plaintiff will be entitled to $60,000 in damages; he himself caused the $190,000 loss by failing to mitigate when he had the opportunity.

Knowing, now, about the plaintiff's obligation to mitigate her damages, we must amend the rule we stated in Chapter 25, section E—the rule by which we ordinarily calculate a plaintiff's damages for breach of contract: *For breach of contract, the plaintiff is normally entitled to recover such amount as will move her from the position he would have enjoyed had he taken reasonable action to mitigate his damage, if any such action was available to her, to the position she would have enjoyed had the contract been fully performed by both its parties.*

2. What Constitutes a "Reasonable" Effort to Mitigate?

One who suffers a breach of contract must make such efforts to mitigate her damage as do not expose her to unreasonable risk, cost, burden, or humiliation. Restatement (Second) of Contracts §350 provides that "damages are not recoverable for loss that the injured party could have avoided without undue risk, burden or humiliation."

Suppose Ladner owns realty that's covered in poison ivy. She forms a contract with Karson under which Karson will remove the poison ivy and Ladner will pay her, on completion, $20,000. Before she begins her work, Karson announces that she will not perform. Ladner immediately seeks to find a qualified substitute, and he finds only one person willing to perform the job. Her price is six times Karson's: 120,000. Ladner hesitates to commit to so high a payment in hopes of going to court and recovering the difference of ($120,000 − $20,000) = $100,000. Probably, he need not do so, for that would expose him to unreasonable risk or unreasonable cost.

If, on the other hand, Ladner had found a qualified substitute willing to do the work for $23,000, then he would be obliged to hire her. Assuming the substitute properly performed, Ladner would then have an action against Karson for $3,000.

3. Mitigation When an Employer Breaches an Employment Contract

For an employee who suffers breach of contract by her employer, the rule on mitigation is fundamentally the same. However, the law offers more refined a statement of what is reasonable in that circumstance: *When an employer, in breach of contract, terminates an employee, the employee must use reasonable efforts to mitigate her damages by seeking alternative employment of a similar nature, in a similar location, and of similar status. If she finds but fails to accept such alternate employment, her recovery is limited to the difference between the financial position she would have occupied had she accepted it and the position she would have occupied had both parties fulfilled their contract.* The phrase "similar status" reflects Restatement §350's word "humiliation."

Let's Illustrate   Multinational Corporation X hires Raelle as its new president under a ten-year contract at a salary of $10 million per year. For one year, the corporation honors its contract, but then fires Raelle and thus breaches. On those facts alone, Raelle's expectation interest would be ($100 million − $10 million) = $90 million = Raelle's position had the parties fully performed minus Raelle's position at breach.

Now add these facts: Upon firing Raelle from the presidency, the corporation offers her a full-time job making photocopies at $15/hour, 40 hours per week, 50 weeks per year, for the nine additional years during which she was to have been president. By accepting this alternative employment, she would reduce her damages by $270,000 — from $90 million to $89,730,000. Raelle refuses the copy job, announcing that it would be "humiliating to move from corporate president to corporate photocopier."

Maybe Raelle is a snob. But the law, too, is a snob. Recall our rule's requirement that any alternative employment be similar in location, nature, and status. Because the photocopying position is not similar in nature or "status," Raelle may refuse the job without reducing her damage award. The law entitles her to the full $90 million difference between the $100 million Corporation X should have paid her, and the $10 million it did pay her.

Now suppose that for the remaining nine years of her original contract, Corporation Y offers Raelle the position of executive vice president at an annual salary of $7 million. She refuses the job, thereby refusing alternative employment whose nature and status *are* similar to that of her job with Corporation X. Her recovery from Corporation X will be such amount as moves her from the position she would have occupied had she accepted the alternative employment to the position she would have occupied had Corporation X honored its contract: [**$100** million *minus* (**$10** million, the amount Corporation X paid her for one year) *minus* (**$63** million, the amount offered her by Corporation Y)]

= **$27** million. That's the amount Raelle would truly have lost had she accepted the vice-presidential position with Corporation Y. In fact, she has lost $90 million, but of that $90 million, $63 million represents her own fault—her failure to mitigate damages. Hence she recovers only the difference: $27 million.

QUESTION 1. Bowman and Chance form a contract under which Bowman is to serve as Chance's public relations consultant for one year at an office 5 miles from Bowman's home, and Chance is to pay Bowman $45,000 per month for the duration of that year.

All's well for September, October, and November. Bowman does his job, and Chance pays him. On December 1, Chance announces that he no longer needs a consultant, fires Bowman, and refuses further to pay him. With nine months remaining under the contract, Bowman searches diligently for alternative work. He finds one and only one job, as a parking lot attendant 40 miles from his home at $8 per hour, 40 hours per week, for all nine months. From that job, over nine months, he would earn $12,480. If Bowman rejects the parking lot job and sues Chance for damages, he is likely to collect

A. nothing, because he failed to mitigate his damages.
B. the amount he would collect from the parking lot employer over nine months.
C. his regular salary from Chance, for so much time as a reasonable person in his position would need to find alternative employment.
D. his full expectation interest because he had no reasonable opportunity to mitigate.

ANALYSIS. An employee discharged in breach of contract must make reasonable efforts to seek and accept alternative employment of a similar nature, in a similar location, and of a similar status (meaning without humiliation, as states the Restatement). Bowman's diligent search for alternative employment resulted in only one job offering—as a parking lot attendant, which differed in nature from his job with Chance. Further, it was located 35 miles farther from his home than was his job with Chance, and it offended the law's snobbery because it was not of similar status. This alternative employment fails all three of the pertinent tests, and the law will not reduce Bowman's recovery for failing to accept it. That means he is entitled to recover the difference between the financial position he would have occupied had both parties fulfilled their contract minus the financial position he occupies in view of the breach.

A gives Bowman nothing "because he failed to mitigate." Failure to mitigate does not reduce one's damages to zero unless mitigation would have done the same. Suppose, for example, a new employer offered Bowman nine months' work as an executive consultant for $45,000 monthly, 5 miles from his home. By accepting that job, he'd reduce his damages to zero. The law would award him zero, whether he accepted it or not. The parking lot job, however, offers him only about $1,375 per month. Arithmetically, it would not reduce his damages to zero, even if it passed all three tests named above.

According to **B**, Bowman is entitled to the amount he would have earned from the parking lot job, $12,480. That is not the recovery Bowman would derive even if the parking lot job passed the three tests. Rather it is the amount the law would *subtract* from his expectation interest in assessing his recovery.

C tells us of law that does not exist: that an employee discharged in breach of contract is entitled to receive his regular salary for so much time as a reasonable person would need to find alternative employment. To one who does not know the law, that's an appealing statement. It features the word "reasonable," and (in a way) it seems reasonable. But there's no such law; **C** is wrong. Remember, if you have studied appropriately, and a multiple-choice option states or implies a rule you've never heard of, then it is almost certainly wrong. Don't let an appealing set of words shake your confidence.

D states that Bowman had no reasonable opportunity to mitigate, and that's true. He diligently searched for alternative employment but could find none that passed the three pertinent tests of nature, location, and status. Hence, he is entitled to his full expectation interest, which is $405,000. **D** is right.

B. Contracts for the Sale of Goods: Buyer's Mitigation When the Seller Breaches

1. Wholesaler vs. Distributor, Episode I

Suppose that on January 1, Wholesaler and Distributor form a signed, written contract under which Distributor will deliver 100,000 widgets to Wholesaler on February 1, and Wholesaler will pay Distributor $100,000 on delivery. Furthermore, Wholesaler has a customer who will buy the widgets from *her* for $150,000. On February 3, Distributor contacts Wholesaler and repudiates the contract. Wholesaler finds 100,000 widgets elsewhere, for $120,000 — $20,000 more than she was to pay Distributor. She buys the widgets, pays the $120,000, and, as planned, sells them to her customer for $150,000.

When a seller of good breaches his contract by failing to deliver the goods at issue, and buyer secures substitute goods, we say that she "covers," meaning she mitigates her damages by elsewhere purchasing the relevant goods. When Distributor breached, Wholesaler responsibly mitigated by securing widgets elsewhere; she covered. She is entitled to recover the difference between [− ($100,000) she would have paid to Distributor + ($150,000, she would have collected from her customer)] = **$50,000**, and [− ($120,000 she paid to her substitute seller + ($150,000, she collected from her customer)] = **$30,000**; $50,000 − $30,000 = **$20,000**. That amount will move her from the monetary position she now occupies to the position she would have occupied had both parties fully honored the contract.

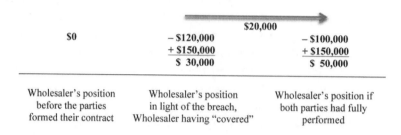

$0		$20,000	
	– $120,000		– $100,000
	+ $150,000		+ $150,000
	$ 30,000		$ 50,000

Wholesaler's position before the parties formed their contract	Wholesaler's position in light of the breach, Wholesaler having "covered"	Wholesaler's position if both parties had fully performed

2. Wholesaler vs. Distributor, Episode II

Suppose now that on learning of Distributor's breach, Wholesaler immediately finds cover (substitute goods) for $100,000, the same price she was to pay under the contract. She purchases the goods and sells them to her customer for $150,000 as planned. She has no damage; she walks away with the same $50,000 profit she would have had had both parties fully performed.

3. Wholesaler vs. Distributor, Episode III

This time, suppose that on learning of Distributor's breach, Wholesaler diligently searches for cover but cannot find any. As a result, she loses her $150,000 sale. In that case, she would recover $50,000. So she occupies, once again, the financial position she would have occupied had both parties fully performed.

The three Wholesaler and Distributor episodes teach us that: if a buyer of goods is able to find cover, her recovery is equal to the cover price minus the contract price. In episode I, the cover price minus the contract price was $20,000, and that's what Wholesaler recovered. In episode II, the cover price minus the contract price was $0, and that's what Wholesaler recovered; she was unharmed by the breach. In episode III, Wholesaler tried to cover but could not do so; her damages were equal to the full $50,000 gain that she would have enjoyed had Distributor properly performed.

C. Contracts for the Sale of Goods: Seller's Mitigation When the Buyer Breaches

1. Supplier vs. Retailer, Episode I

Supplier deals in widgets and has in her warehouse ten million type A widgets for which she paid 50¢ each, each identical to every other. She also has in her warehouse one million type B widgets, which are out of production. The one million type B units were made in 1956 for which, *in* 1956 Supplier also paid 50¢ each. Few if any businesses have any use for the Type B product.

Nonetheless, on March 1, Retailer contacts Supplier and wants to know, if by chance, Supplier has in stock any of the "old Type B widgets from the 1950s." Supplier tells Retailer that she has one million units purchased decades earlier. Later that same day, March 1, by signed writing Supplier and Retailer form a contract under which Supplier will deliver to Retailer the 1 million old Type B widgets on March 10. Retailer will pay, on delivery, $1.00 for each unit, for a total purchase price of $1 million.

Since Supplier has paid 50¢ per widget, she properly anticipates a profit of [($1.00 − 50¢) x ($1 million) = $500,000. On March 8, Supplier packs the widgets and prepares them for delivery to Retailer. On March 9, Retailer contacts Supplier and repudiates, "I've changed my mind. I don't want the widgets. Don't send them." Hence, Retailer breaches; he commits an anticipatory repudiation (Chapter 25, section D).

Coincidentally, on that same day, March 9, a party named Lastuser contacts Supplier. He asks, "Do you happen to have any of the old Type B widgets from the 1950s. I need about 1 million of them." Supplier responds, "Yes, I do. I was just about to sell them to a customer who backed out of our contract. So they're available to you at the same price I quoted him; $1.00 per widget, delivered to you, $1 million total, payable on delivery." Lastuser accepts, and the parties reduce their agreement to a signed writing.

Supplier takes the 1 million Type B widgets he had planned to send Retailer and sends them to Lastuser, whereupon Lastuser pays the $1 million purchase price. Having resold to Lastuser for $1 million the 1 million Type B widgets that Retailer should have purchased, Supplier achieves the monetary position in which she would have stood had Retailer honored his contract. Supplier has the same $500,000 profit she would have derived from the sale to Retailer. If she wishes, now, to sue Retailer for breach, she will recover nothing (except perhaps "nominal damages" of $1 or so).[2] The breach caused her no harm; she's whole.

2. *Supplier vs. Retailer, Episode II*

Remembering that Supplier has *10* million Type *A* widgets, having paid 50¢ for each one, let's change the story. Retailer and Enduser, complete strangers, happen to contact Supplier at the same time. Each contracts to purchase 1 million type A widgets for $1 million, so that on each sale, Supplier stands to earn a $500,000 profit. Enduser honors his contract, he buys the widgets and pays the $500,000 price. Retailer repudiates; he breaches, and refuses to purchase the widgets. The 1 million widgets that Retailer should have purchased remain in Supplier's warehouse.

---

2. Breach of contract is, theoretically, actionable without a showing of damages. If a plaintiff who suffers no harm from defendant's breach of contract wishes nonetheless to bring suit, she is entitled to "nominal damages," usually in the amount of $1 or $10.

It is absolutely plain (we hope) that the sale to Enduser does not compensate Supplier for Retailer's breach. Supplier had formed two contracts, each unrelated to the other and, since Retailer dishonored her contract, Supplier lost one of her expected $500,000 profits. In order to fulfill her expectation interest, therefore, the law affords her a recovery from Retailer of $500,000. And that simple little story prepares us for —

3. Supplier vs. Retailer, Episode III

Remembering, still, that Supplier has 10 million Type A widgets, let's change the story yet again. On March 1, Supplier and Retailer form a signed written contract under which Supplier will deliver to Retailer 1 million type A widgets on March 10. Retailer will pay Supplier, on delivery, $1 per unit, for a total of $1 million. As before, Supplier has paid 50¢ per unit and anticipates a profit of $500,000. On March 9, Retailer repudiates; he refuses to purchase the widgets. On that same day, it just so happens that Finaluser contacts Supplier: "I need 1 million type A widgets. Have you got them?" Supplier replies, "Yes, I have ten million of them; nine million in my warehouse, and, on my truck, 1 million units that I was preparing for delivery to another buyer who breached his agreement to buy them. I was about to return them to my warehouse, but I'll deliver them to you tomorrow, March 10, for $1.00 per unit, $1 million total, on delivery." Finaluser agrees, the parties record their agreement in a signed writing, and both parties fully perform.

Retailer has delivered to Finaluser the very same 1 million widgets she had prepared for Retailer, and she has collected from Finaluser the same $1 million price that Retailer was to have paid. Let's ask: does Supplier occupy the same position she would have occupied if Retailer had honored his agreement? Let's answer: No, she doesn't, and she has an action against Retailer for $500,000.

That's Because This Episode III Is Really the Same as Episode II

In episode II, Supplier had 10 million Type A widgets. She formed two separate contracts with two separate buyers, each for the sale of 1 million units, each contract wholly unrelated to the other. Wholeseller fulfilled his contract, wherefore Supplier, of course, had no action against him. Retailer breached his contract. Supplier was left with a single profit of $500,000, and nine million unsold units in her warehouse, whereas, if Retailer had honored the contract, she would have had two $500,000 profits and eight million units remaining in her warehouse. Hence, Supplier was entitled to recover from Retailer the full $500,000 profit she lost because of his breach. That we saw very clearly.

Here, in episode III, in all meaningful respects, the story is the same. Supplier has 10 million Type A widgets. She forms two separate contracts with two separate buyers, Retailer and Finaluser, each for the sale of 1 million units, each contract wholly unrelated to the other. Finaluser performs properly, and Supplier, plainly, has no action against him. Retailer breaches his contract. Supplier is left with a single profit of $500,000, and nine million unsold units in her warehouse, whereas, if Retailer had honored the contract, she would have had two $500,000 profits and eight million units remaining in her warehouse. Supplier is entitled to recover from Retailer the full $500,000 profit she lost because of the breach.

Between episodes II and III, there are two differences, both legally meaningless: (1) In episode II, Wholeseller and Retailer happened to approach Supplier simultaneously, and formed their separate contracts at the same time. In episode III, Finaluser approaches Supplier and forms his contract with her after Retailer has already breached; (2) When Finaluser contacts Supplier, Supplier, Supplier is about to take from her truck the 1 million units she has prepared for Retailer, and return them to the warehouse. If Retailer had not committed his March 9 anticipatory repudiation then, when, on March 9, Finaluser contracted to buy 1 million units, Supplier would have gone to her warehouse, removed another 1 million units, and tossed them on the truck. On March 10, she would have made two separate deliveries—one to Retailer and one to Finaluser. From each she would have collected two separate, unrelated amounts of $1 million and, thus derived two $500,000 profits, each unrelated to the other. By selling to Finaluser the same 1 million units that just happen to be, still, on her truck, Supplier in no way reimburses or compensates herself for the $500,000 profit lost through Retailer's breach. Rather, she saves herself a trip to the warehouse; that's all.

The Unfortunate Phrase "Lost Volume Seller"

Here, in episode III, we say that Supplier is a "lost volume seller," meaning that by selling to Finaluser the goods she intended to sell Retailer, Supplier does not make herself whole. She derives one profit whereas she ought to have had two; the volume of her sales on March 10 was one instead of two. She lost a sale; she "lost volume."

Let's state a rule: *If as to a contract for the sale of goods, a buyer breaches and the seller sells the relevant goods to some other party, then (1) if, absent the buyer's breach, the seller would nonetheless have made the second sale, she is a "lost volume seller" and is entitled to recover the profit lost through the buyer's breach; but if, absent the buyer's breach, the seller would not have made the second sale, then the buyer's breach has caused seller no loss of profit and she is not entitled to recover from buyer the profit she anticipated deriving from the contract.*

QUESTION 2. Saul operates an automobile dealership that sells the popular Jip Mangler-X. When Saul runs low on inventory, he orders more vehicles from the manufacturer at $18,000 each. On August 1, by signed writing, Saul contracts to sell one Jip Mangler-X to Berringer for $25,000. Berringer agrees to take delivery and pay the purchase price on August 15. When August 15 arrives, Berringer tells Saul that he won't purchase

the vehicle; he commits an anticipatory repudiation — a total breach.[3]
One hour later, Bennington walks in to Saul's showroom wanting to purchase a Jip Mangler-X. For $25,000, Saul sells Bennington the vehicle he
had planned to sell Berringer. Saul then brings an action against Berringer
seeking damages for his lost profit, $7,000. Should Saul recover that
amount?

I. Yes, because he is a lost volume seller
II. Yes, because he would have sold a Jip Mangler-X to Bennington even
if Berringer had honored his contract
III. Yes, because the sale to Bennington does not cause Saul to recoup the
profit he would have earned on the sale to Berringer
IV. No, because the resale to Bennington affords Saul the economic
position he would have occupied had Berringer honored his contract
A. I
B. I and II
C. I, II, and III
D. IV

ANALYSIS.   Ask yourself: Would seller have made the sale to Bennington if
Berringer hadn't breached? The answer is "yes." Bennington's wish to purchase
the Jip Mangler-X had nothing to do with Berringer's ultimate refusal to buy
one. If Berringer had honored his contract, Saul would have sold Bennington
not the very same vehicle he had prepared for Berringer, but an identical vehicle at the same price, for the same $7,000 profit. The two contracts are unre-
lated; Berringer's breach caused Saul a loss of $7,000. Hence, Saul is entitled to
recover the profit lost through Berringer's breach.

Option IV, therefore is false, meaning **D** is wrong. Options I, II, and III are
different formulations of the same thought, and they're all correct. Berringer
is a lost volume seller; he had sufficient inventory to supply both Berringer
and Bennington with vehicles. Option II correctly makes the simple, critical
statement that Saul would have sold a vehicle to Bennington even if Berringer
hadn't breached. Option III properly states that the sale to Bennington did
not compensate Saul for the profit he lost through Berringer's breach. Had
Berringer bought the vehicle, Saul would have had two $7,000 profits. Hence,
C is right.

---

3. Chapter 21, section D.

D.   The UCC on Expectation Interest, Mitigation, and the Lost Volume Seller

In section A, B, and C above, we taught you the *common law* concerning expectation interest, mitigation, and the lost volume seller. Where two parties form a contract for the sale of goods, their damages are, today, governed not by the common law but by the Uniform Commercial Code, Article 2 (except where Article 2 is silent, in which case, the common law does govern). With respect to expectation interest, mitigation and the lost volume seller, its rules are fundamentally the same as the common law's, although one who quickly examines the relevant provisions would not immediately see that truth.

The U.C.C. embodies nine "articles," the first of which is Article 1.[4] The provisions of Article 1 apply, generally, to all other of the code's nine articles if and as the context requires. UCC §1-305 provides

> [All of the] remedies provided by the Uniform Commercial Code must be liberally administered to the end that the aggrieved party may be put in as good a position as if the other party had fully performed.

1.   Buyer's Remedies as Described in UCC, Article 2

When the seller repudiates or otherwise fails timely to deliver conforming goods, then, as the UCC puts it, the buyer may "cover" (see section B above). If she does so, UCC Article 2 entitles her to recover, generally,[5]

- any contract price already paid the seller, *plus*
- the quantity [(cover price) *minus* (contract price)], *plus*
- "incidental damages," *plus*
- "consequential damages," *minus*
- expenses saved as a result of the breach.

"Incidental damages" refers to ancillary expenses the buyer incurs because of the breach. If, for example, he spends $500 searching for cover, he has incidental damage of $500. If seller delivers defective goods and buyer spends $1,000 storing them for seller or returning them to seller, buyer has $1,000 in incidental damage.

"Consequential damage" refers to damages that are indirectly or remotely caused by the breach. The classic example is that of the middleman buyer who contracts to buy goods, with another contract already in place, by which he

---

4.   Regarding the history, purpose, and structure of the UCC (Uniform Commercial Code), see Appendix, section D.

5.   UCC §2-713.

plans to resell them to his own customer for a profit. If the seller fails to deliver the goods and, as a result, the buyer cannot resell to his own customer, the buyer's lost profit constitutes consequential damage,[6] and such lost profit is the most common form of consequential damage. (If buyer's customer sues buyer for breach, the resulting costs to buyer also constitute consequential damage caused to buyer by seller.) Article 2 does not include as consequential damage any expense or injury that a buyer who does not attempt to cover could have avoided by doing so. U.C.C. § 2-715(a)(2) provides that consequential damage does not include any loss that "could reasonably be prevented by cover or otherwise."

All of This Comes to the Same as the Common Law Rules Taught at Sections A, B, and C Above

Suppose Buyer sues a breaching Seller, and at trial the evidence indisputably shows that:

- On May 1, Buyer and Seller formed a contract under which Seller was to deliver 100,000 widgets on July 1.
- Buyer was to pay $20,000 on May 1 as a down payment and an additional $80,000 on delivery, for a total purchase price of $100,000.
- Buyer was to pay a delivery charge of $500.
- Buyer, as "middleman," had a customer ready to purchase the widgets from him for $150,000.
- On May 1, Buyer made the $20,000 down payment.
- On May 15, Seller contacted Buyer and repudiated; she committed a total breach.
- Buyer spent $700 searching for "cover." He found substitute goods and bought them for $112,000 under a contract that occasioned no delivery charge.
- Buyer sold the goods to his own customer for $150,000 as originally planned.
- In connection with the purchase of cover, Buyer had to pay no delivery charge, and because Seller never delivered her goods to Buyer, Buyer never paid the $500 delivery charge required by the original contract between Buyer and Seller.

Let's Calculate Buyer's Damages, First Under the Common Law, and Then Under UCC Article 2

Under the common law, in order that Buyer occupy the monetary position he would have held absent Seller's breach, he needs $32,200:

---

6. U.C.C. §2-715 cmt. 6, Kunstsoffwerk Alfred Huber v. R.J. Dick Inc., 621 F.2d 563 (3d Cir. 1980).

$32,200
Buyer's recovery

Buyer has paid no money, owns no goods	$ 20,000 (down payment) − $ 700 (search for cover) − $112,000 (cost of cover) + $150,000 (resale)	− $100,000 − $ 500 + $150,000
$0	+ $ 17,300	+ $ 49,500

Buyer's position at the time parties form contract	Buyer's position in light of Seller's breach, cover, and sale to customer	Buyer's position if both parties had honored their contract

Under UCC Article 2, Buyer is entitled to:

(1) his down payment:	$20,000
(2) [(cover price) − (contract price)]:	$12,000
(3) incidental damage (search for cover):	$ 700
(4) consequential damage (No consequential damage because Buyer was able to sell to his own customer at the anticipated $150,000 price.):	$ 0
LESS	
(5) expenses saved because of the breach	$ 500 (delivery charge not paid)
	$32,200

Now, suppose Buyer finds the substitute goods but doesn't buy them. Let's calculate his recovery. Buyer's actual position would then be -$20,700, and he would need $70,200 to attain his position of expectation:

$70,200

−$20,000 (down payment) − $ 700 (search for cover)	−$ 20,000 (down payment) −$ 700 (searching for cover) −$112,000 (cost of cover) +$150,000 (resale)	−$100,000 −$ 500 (delivery) $150,000 (resale)
−$20,700	+$ 17,300	+$ 49,500

But failure to purchase the substitute goods is a failure to mitigate. The common law affords Buyer only the $32,200 that will move him from the position he would have occupied if he had mitigated, to his position of expectation. That amount will afford him not the +$49,500 position but the +$49,500 position *minus* the $32,000 in damage he caused himself by failing to mitigate:

- $20,000	- $ 20,000	- $100,000
- $ 700	- $ 700	- $ 500
	- $112,000	+$150,000
	+$150,000	
-$20,700	**$17,300**	**$49,500**

$$\xrightarrow{\hspace{2cm}} \qquad \xrightarrow{\hspace{2cm}}$$

$38,000	$32,200
Damage Buyer caused herself by failing to cover	*Buyer's actual recovery*

Buyer's position having failed to cover	Buyer's position if she had covered	Buyer's position if both parties had fully performed

Under UCC Article 2, Buyer would recover:
(1) his down payment: −$20,000
(2) incidental damages (search for cover):   −$ 700
(3) [(cover price − contract price)]:   −$12,000
(4) consequential damages (lost profit on resale): $ 0
(Consequential damage under UCC §2-715(2)(a),
does not include any loss that a buyer
could have avoided "by cover or otherwise.")

                                                    LESS
(4) delivery charge not paid: $ 500
                                                    _____

                                                         $32,200

3. So Article 2 Does a Good Job with Damages?

No, it doesn't; it does a bad job—a *very* bad job. In many situations, one must mash and manipulate its words to reach the right result—the one dictated by UCC §1-305, to wit, the same as that of the common law: such amount as will afford buyer the position he would have occupied had both parties fully performed their contract.

For example, Article 2 does not account for the buyer who diligently attempts to cover but cannot do so. Suppose that on spending his $700 attempting to find cover, Buyer is unable to find any equivalent goods. Hence, he buys none and is unable to resell to his customer, thus losing his justly anticipated $50,000 profit. The common law and UCC §1-305 dictate that he recover $70,200:

$$\xrightarrow{\hspace{8cm}}$$

	$70,200	
has paid no money owns no goods	-$20,000 (down payment) -$ 700 (searching for cover)	-$100,000 -$ 500 (delivery) +$150,000 (resale)
$0	-$20,700	+$49,500
Buyer's position at time parties, formed contract	Buyer's position having attempted to mitigate but unable to do so	Buyer's position if both parties had fully performed the contract

Yet UCC §2-713(a) provides that for a buyer who does not cover, the measure of damages is "the difference between the market price at the time [delivery is due] and the contract price together with any incidental or consequential damages. . . ." As we already know, §2-715(2)a *excludes* from consequential damage only such loss as buyer could have avoided "by cover or otherwise." If a buyer *tries* to cover but cannot do so, his consequential damage is not avoidable by cover and so, the Code (by clear implication) provides that the Buyer will recover his full consequential damage including, of course, lost profit on resale. If we take § 2-715(2)(a) seriously, we find that it entitles Buyer to:

(1) the down payment:	**$20,000**
(2) [(market price) − (contract price)]:	**$12,000**
(3) incidental damages (search for cover):	**$ 700**
(4) consequential damages (lost profit on resale because this loss could not have been avoided by cover):	**$50,000**
LESS	
(5) delivery charge not paid:	**$ 500**
	$82,200

That amount gives him $12,000 more than his loss, loss, which fact arises only through the Code writers' bungling ineptitude. By awarding Buyer the [$112,000 − $100,000] when in fact he did not make the $112,000 purchase, and then awarding him also the whole of his lost $50,000 profit, the writers give Buyer $12,000 too much. They would save themselves from this one of their (many egregious) errors by adding to §2-713 this text: *If the buyer diligently attempts to cover but cannot do so, then he does not recover the quantity [(cover price) − (contract price)], but his consequential damages are not restricted.*

4. UCC Treatment of the Lost Volume Seller

The Code writers address the lost volume seller with a consummate poverty of articulation and understanding; their mastery of the issue is too meager, it seems, to facilitate a meaningful explication and resolution. To begin, UCC §2-706(1) provides:

> [T]he seller may resell the goods concerned . . . [and] the seller may recover the difference between the contract price and the resale price together with any incidental or consequential damages. . . .

That rule is worthless. For as we know, a seller may resell the goods intended for the breaching buyer at the same price the breaching party was to pay, in which case [(resale price) − (contract price)] = 0. Yet, if that second sale would have occurred regardless of buyer's breach, the seller is a lost volume seller and entitled to the profit lost on the contract that buyer breached.

Don't the Code Writers Account for That?

They do so only in the most pitiful of ways. UCC §2-208(2) provides:

> If the measure of damages provided . . . in Section 2-706 is inadequate to put the seller in as good a position as performance would have done, the measure of damages is the profit . . . that the seller would have made from full performance by the buyer, together with any incidental or consequential damages. . . .

Official Comment 4 then explains:

> Subsection 2 is used in the cases of . . . lost-volume sellers. This remedy is an alternative to the remedy under . . . Section 2-706, and it is available when the damages based upon resale of the goods . . . do not achieve the goal of full compensation for harm caused by the buyer's breach.

5. What Can We Conclude About Article 2?

About Article 2's rules regarding expectation interest, mitigation, and lost volume sellers, we can conclude that:

- The writers intended to mirror the common law's rules, and UCC §1-305 proves that point.
- The writers were not equal to that task, and their provisions on these points offer a web of misconception and mistake.
- When calculating damages under Article 2, one should first calculate them under the common law and then make the result "fit" Article 2 (which in some cases the Code drafters make impossible through their pervasive inability to address legal concepts of any complexity).

E.   The Closers

> **QUESTION 3.** On June 1, Attly and Bartley form a contract under which Attly is to design a dam on or before August 1, and Bartley is to pay her $250,000 when she completes the design.
>
> Attly begins work and, during the month of June, spends $10,000 in work-related expenses. On July 1, Bartley advises Attly that he no longer needs the dam design and will not pay her, thereby committing a total breach. Nonetheless, Attly completes the design, spending an additional $20,000. Attly then sues Bartley for breach, claiming damages of $250,000. She asserts that
>
> - if Bartley had not breached, she would have received $250,000 and paid $30,000 for a net gain of $220,000;
> - in light of Bartley's breach, she has spent $30,000 and received nothing; and
> - to fulfill her expectation interest, she is entitled to $250,000 ($220,000 − [−$30,000]).
>
> Attly should recover:
>
> A. $250,000
> B. $230,000
> C. $220,000
> D. $210,000

ANALYSIS.   When Attly learned of Bartley's breach, she had spent $10,000. Because she knew that Bartley intended not to pay, mitigation required that she not spend additional sums. By spending yet another $20,000, she "ran up" her damages. Had Attly properly mitigated, her position, in face of the breach, would have been negative $10,000 instead of negative $30,000. She herself caused $20,000 of her loss. Hence she is entitled to ($250,000) − (−$20,000) = $230,000. **B** is right.

> **QUESTION 4.** Brothers Martin and Nate decide to purchase a photocopier for their home. Martin visits Phil, who operates a retail electronics store that carries photocopies. He contracts for the purchase of a Repro Model 13 photocopier for $1,200. Phil has in stock 50 of these same machines, and he paid $700 for each one. Further, he is free to order from the manufacturer, for $700 each, as many additional ones as he might want.

Martin and Phil agree that Martin will return on the following day to make payment and take delivery of the machine. Phil immediately sets aside a machine for Martin. One hour later, however, Martin returns to say that he will not purchase the machine. Phil moves the photocopier back to his storage room. When Nate learns what Martin has done, he goes to Phil's store, tells Phil that he wants to buy a Repro Model 13. Phil tells him that the price is $1,200, and Phil agrees to buy. Phil brings out a second machine from his storage room, whereupon Nate pays him $1,200 and takes the machine.

Is Phil entitled to recover from Martin a $500 profit ($1,200 − $700) lost to him because of Martin's breach?

A. Yes, because he is a lost volume seller
B. Yes, because he had sufficient inventory to supply *both* Martin and Nate
C. No, because he did not sell to Nate the very same unit he had planned to sell Martin
D. No, because if Martin had purchased a machine, Nate would not have done so

ANALYSIS. Ask the key question: Would Phil have made the sale to Nate if Martin hadn't breached? The answer is "no." Between the two brothers, there never were to have been two sales. Nate bought the photocopier only because Martin did not. If Martin had bought the photocopier, Nate would not have done so. Consequently, by selling the photocopier to Nate, Phil recouped the profit he lost through Martin's breach.

As for **A**, Martin's breach didn't cause Phil to lose a sale; Phil is not a lost volume seller. **A** is wrong. **B** correctly states that Phil had sufficient inventory to supply both Martin and Nate, but that's irrelevant to this circumstance. The facts are such that he did not stand to make two sales, so the answer "yes" makes **B** wrong. **C** cites a fact that's true but irrelevant. The whole question of whether a seller resells to some other customer the very same goods that a breaching buyer failed to buy is irrelevant to the lost volume issue. The question is only whether the second sale is separate from, independent of, and unrelated to the first. In this case, it's not. **D** correctly says "no" and offers the right reasoning. Between the brothers, there was never to have been more than *one* sale. Hence, **D** is right.

QUESTION 5. Quenn owns a yacht (which is a good; see Appendix, section D). She engages Broker 1 to sell it. Under her contract with Broker 1, Broker 1 is entitled to receive 6 percent of the sale price if he finds a buyer who forms a contract with Quenn to purchase the yacht at any price above $700,000. Broker 1 is entitled to his commission as soon as such a contract arises. The fact that either party might then breach the contract does not affect his entitlement to the 6 percent fee.

On March 1, Broker 1 finds a buyer, Remsen, willing to pay $1 million for Quenn's yacht. On March 5, by signed writing, Quenn and Remsen contract for the sale of the yacht at a price of $1 million, the actual payment and transfer of title to occur on April 1. Also on March 5, Quenn pays Broker 1 his $60,000 fee.

On March 10, Remsen contacts Quenn and repudiates the contract, thus committing a total breach. On March 15, Quenn engages a new broker, Broker 2, to whom she contracts to pay the same 6 percent commission should he find a buyer who actually contracts to purchase the yacht at a price above $700,000. She also advertises the yacht on her own and spends $1,000 doing so. On April 1, Broker 2 introduces Quenn to Leonards, who stands ready to buy the yacht for $750,000. On April 5, Quenn and Leonards form a contract calling for the purchase and sale of the yacht at that price. Also on April 5, Quenn pays Broker 2 his $45,000 fee. Leonards does purchase the yacht for $750,000 as agreed.

Quenn brings an action against Remsen. Itemized according to the UCC, to what recovery, if any, is Quenn entitled?

A. $45,000
B. $250,000
C. $296,000
D. $300,000

ANALYSIS. Forget about the UCC and solve the problem, first, by common law. Quenn is entitled to occupy the financial position she would have occupied had both parties fully performed minus the financial position she occupies (or would have occupied) having made a reasonable attempt to mitigate. Quenn did make a reasonable attempt to mitigate and succeeded. She is entitled to damages of $296,000:

Owns Boat	$296,000 →	
	− $ 60,000 to Broker 1	+$1,000,000
	− $ 45,000 to Broker 2	− $ 60,000 to Broker 1
	− $ 1,000 advertising	
	+$750,000 on sale	
$0	+$644,000	+$940,000
Quenn's position before forming contract with Broker 1	Quenn's position in face of breach	Quenn's position Remsen and Quenn had fully honored their contract

Now, force UCC Article 2 to yield that same result:

(1) purchase price paid:	$ 0
(2) [(contract price) − (resale price)]	$250,000
(3) incidental damages	
(a) advertising:	$ 1,000
(b) commission, Broker 2:	$ 45,000
	———————
	$296,000

C is right.

Silver & Hochberg's Picks

1. **D**
2. **C**
3. **B**
4. **D**
5. **C**

27

Breach, Remedies, and Damages, Part III

A. Expectation Interest and Foreseeability of Damage: *Hadley v. Baxendale*

Suppose it's 1854. Hadley operates a mill whose shaft breaks, leaving the mill inoperable. For each day the mill is idle, Hadley loses money. He hurriedly contacts the shaft's manufacturer, who instructs Hadley to send the broken shaft itself as a model for a new one. Hadley and Baxendale form a contract under which Baxendale will deliver the shaft to the manufacturer in one day's time and Hadley will pay for the service. At the time these parties form that contract, Baxendale has no reason to know that Hadley's mill will remain inoperative until fitted with a new shaft. Alas, Baxendale delivers the broken shaft to the manufacturer in one week instead of in one day, as the contract requires. Consequently, the mill is idle for that additional week and causes Hadley to lose £200 in revenue. Hadley sues Baxendale, claiming damage of £200.

Faced with (something close to) this story, an English court ruled that because the defendant had no reason to know that plaintiff's mill would remain inoperative without the new shaft, plaintiff's damages did not include the revenue lost because of defendant's lateness:

> Now we think the proper rule . . . is this: Where two parties have made a
> contract which one of them has broken, the damages which the other party

ought to receive . . . should be such as may fairly and reasonably be considered either arising naturally, i.e., according to the usual course of things . . . or such as may reasonably be supposed to have been in the contemplation of both parties, at the time they made the contract, as the probable result of the breach of it. . . . Now, in the present case . . . we find that the only circumstances here communicated by the plaintiffs to the defendants at the time the contract was made, were, that the article to be carried was the broken shaft of a mill, and that the plaintiffs were the millers of that mill. . . . [And] in the great multitude of cases of millers sending off broken shafts to third persons by a carrier under ordinary circumstances . . . [the mill itself continues to operate].

Hadley v. Baxendale, 156 Eng. Rep. 145, 151 (1854).

With that, we amend the rule earlier stated in earlier chapters, and we come to this: *For breach of contract, the law's ordinary remedy is monetary damages in an amount that allows plaintiff to enjoy "the benefit of his bargain," meaning the amount necessary to fulfill the plaintiff's "expectation interest," but such benefit and expectation do not account for any fact, circumstance, or event that the defendant had no reason to foresee.*

In this regard, Restatement (Second) of Contracts §351(1) provides: "Damages are not recoverable for loss that the party in breach did not have reason to foresee as a probable result of the breach when the contract was made."

QUESTION 1. Harriet plans to attend a business meeting 2,000 miles from her home. She purchases a nonrefundable airline ticket for $1,000 and makes a cancelable hotel reservation for $1,000. Harriet then forms a contract with Indo, a cab driver, under which Harriet will pay Indo $55. Indo will pick up Harriet on Wednesday at 6:00 A.M. and transport her to the airport. Indo neither knows nor has reason to know why or to where Harriet is traveling.

On Wednesday morning, Indo, running twenty minutes late, reaches Harriet's home at 6:20 A.M. As a result, Harriet reaches the airport at 7:20 A.M. She pays Indo $55 and dashes from cab to boarding gate. Nonetheless she misses her plane by 2 minutes and, for that reason, misses her business meeting, thus losing a business opportunity that would have paid her $5 million. After canceling her lodging reservation without penalty, Harriet decides to sue Indo. Harriet calculates her expectation interest as she sees it. If both parties had fully performed, she would have spent $1,000 for airline tickets, $1,000 for lodging, and $55 for Indo, for a total of $2,055. She would have received $5 million. Her position would have been positive **$4,997,945**. In fact, Harriet spent $1,000 on airfare, even though she did not travel. She paid Indo $55, and she did not, of course, enjoy the $5 million. Her position, therefore, is *negative* $1,055. On this basis, Harriet sues Indo, alleging damages of $4,999,000.

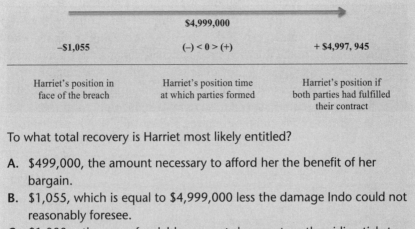

To what total recovery is Harriet most likely entitled?

A. $499,000, the amount necessary to afford her the benefit of her bargain.
B. $1,055, which is equal to $4,999,000 less the damage Indo could not reasonably foresee.
C. $1,000—the nonrefundable amount she spent on the airline ticket.
D. $0 because Indo did, in fact, substantially perform his obligations.

ANALYSIS.   For breach of contract, a plaintiff does not recover for any loss not reasonably foreseeable to defendant at the time the parties formed their contract. Indo had no reason to foresee that a 20 minute lateness on his part would occasion damage of so staggering an amount as $4,997,945. Consequently, in calculating Harriet's recovery, the law does not include the $4,997,945 profit lost to her. On the other hand, a reasonable person in Indo's position should foresee that the lateness could cost his passenger the price of an airline ticket, and that an airline ticket cost as much as $1,000 (or more). That amount belongs to Harriet's recovery.

D reports that Indo substantially performed. That's not true. With respect to travel to an airport, minutes count, and a 20-minute delay is material. Further, even if Indo had substantially performed but committed some partial breach, Harriet would be entitled at least to have back the amount of her damage, however small (Chapter 21, section D). She would be entitled to have back, at least, the $55 she paid Indo. C gives Harriet the nonrefundable amount she paid for the airline ticket, but it omits to award her the $55 paid to Indo. A awards Harriet her full expectation interest and thus includes the damages that Indo could not reasonably have foreseen. It too is wrong. B awards Harriet that same amount *minus* the amount of damage Indo could not reasonably foresee: $4,999,000 − $4,997,945 = $1,055. For that reason, B is right.

B.   Expectation Interest When Cost of Performance Exceeds Value of Performance

Suppose Olan and Portia form a contract under which Portia is to build a house for Olan and Olan is to pay her $400,000 when she completes the work.

The contract provides that for purposes of all internal plumbing, Portia is to use Rodding copper piping. Portia completes the house with perfect conformity to the contract except that she uses Conan copper piping, whose quality is the same as the Rodding product. Olan obtains three good faith estimates for the cost of replacing the Conan piping with the Rodding; all three estimates report a cost of $50,000. Olan sues Portia claiming damages of $50,000, which amount, he asserts, he will need to replace the piping and thus afford himself the position he would have enjoyed had Portia properly performed.

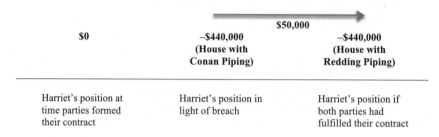

Portia admits the accuracy of Olan's estimates, but her own evidence demonstrates that (a) with the Conan piping in place the home's value is $500,000 and (b) with the piping replaced by the Rodding product its value would likewise be $500,000. Hence, the cost of correcting Portia's performance would be $50,000 whereas the corrected performance would add to the home a value of $0. Portia thus argues that Olan does in fact occupy the position he would have occupied if she had used the Rodding product. Her breach, she says, has caused Olan no recoverable damage.

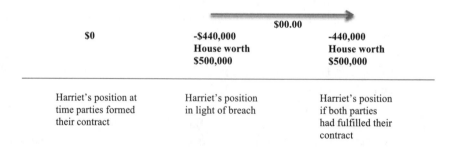

That leaves us with this critical question: When the *cost* of correcting or completing a defendant's faulty performance exceeds the market *value* of the corrected performance, does fulfillment of the plaintiff's expectation interest require recovery of the cost ($50,000 in this case) or only the value ($0 in this case)?

The pat answer to that question turns on the phrase "economic waste," and many law students learn to recite "when, as to a building or construction contract, the cost of performance exceeds the value of performance and correcting performance would wreak economic waste, then the plaintiff recovers not the cost but the value." The phrase "economic waste" derives from the *first* Restatement of Contracts §348:

> (a) For defective or unfinished construction [plaintiff] can get judgment for either
>
>   (i) the reasonable cost of construction and completion in accordance with the contract, if this is possible and does not involve unreasonable economic waste; or
>
>   (ii) the difference between the value that the product contracted for would have had and the value of the performance that has been received by the plaintiff, if construction and completion in accordance with the contract would involve unreasonable economic waste.

Comment b then provides:

> The purpose of money damages is to put the injured party in as good a position as that in which full performance would have put him; but this does not mean that he is to be put in the same specific physical position. . . . There are numerous cases . . . in which the value of [a] finished product is much less than the cost of producing it after the breach has occurred. . . . The law does not require damages to be measured by a method requiring such economic waste. If no such waste is involved, the cost of remedying the defect is the amount awarded as compensation for failure to render the promised performance.

The Restatement nowhere defines its own phrase "economic waste." Neither does that phrase go far to explain the judicial decisions on this point. A number of courts have purported to state that a plaintiff should recover cost of performance, even where it exceeds the value of performance if the defendant's breach is willful—if he breaches "on purpose" (meaning that the defendant did not in good faith attempt to honor his contract). Yet if defendant's breach is not deliberate then, say some courts, recovery is limited to the monetary value of correcting performance where the cost of performance would be more.

> Where the contractor's performance has been incomplete or defective, the usual measure of damages is the reasonable cost of replacement or completion. . . . That rule does not apply if the contractor performs in good faith but defects nevertheless exist and remedying them could entail economic waist. Then, diminution in value becomes the proper measure of damages.

City Sch. Dist. of the City of Elmira v. McLane Constr. Co., 85 A.D.2d 749, 750 (N.Y. App. Div. 1981).

But the distinction between willfulness and good faith breach doesn't hold up. The cases don't support it. In one celebrated case, plaintiff and defendant formed a contract under which defendant paid plaintiff for the right to remove valuable sand and gravel from plaintiff's land. Defendant was obliged not only to pay money to plaintiff, but also to restore the land to a certain condition after it completed the removal. Defendant paid plaintiff as required, removed the sand and gravel, but then failed to restore the land. The cost of the restoration would have exceeded $60,000. Yet, *if* restored, the land would have a market value only $12,000 higher than it had when loaded up with defendant's mess. Noting that the breach was willful, the court ruled that plaintiff was entitled to have the *cost* of performance.[1]

In an equally renowned decision, the result was opposite. Defendant strip miner formed a contract with plaintiff landowner under which defendant would pay plaintiff for a lease of plaintiff's land and have the right to mine it. The contract further required that when defendant concluded its mining activity, it was to restore the land. Defendant paid plaintiff as required and mined the land. When finished, however, defendant did not restore the land. The court found that restoration would cost $29,000 but would increase the land's value by only $300. On that basis, citing the Restatement's phrase "economic waste," the court limited damages to $300.[2] In that case too, the breach was willful. The two cases are not reconcilable (as certainly can happen, especially between two separate jurisdictions). Simply and plainly, *there is no reliable rule* whereunder willfulness or innocence of the breach dictates the recovery when cost of correcting improper performance exceeds its monetary value.

Restatement (first) § 346, Illustration 2 tells us this:

> A contract to erect a dwelling for B for $70,000, according to plans and specifications, one of which is the use of "Alpha" pipe for all plumbing. After completion, B learns that A has used "Beta" pipe, an equally good brand. To replace the "Beta" pipe with the "Alpha" would now require tearing down the walls and would cost almost as much as a new house. The value of the house as built is not less than the value of the house as promised. B can get judgment for only nominal damages.

Illustration 4 then tells us *this*:

> A contract to construct a monumental fountain in B's yard for $5,000, but abandons the work after the foundation has been laid and $2,800 has been paid by B. The contemplated fountain is so ugly that it would decrease the number of possible buyers of the place. The cost of completing the fountain would be $4,000. [B's contract required that he pay $5,000 for the fountain and he has thus far paid only $2,800. He is entitled to $4,000, the costs of completing performance, less the additional $1,200 he would have had to pay ($5,000 − $2,800) as the remainder of the $5,000 contract price.] He can get judgment for $1,800, the cost of completion . . . [.] less the part of price unpaid.

The Restatement writers don't explain—not anywhere, not anyhow—why in Illustration 2, plaintiff recovers only the value of performance whereas in Illustration 4 he recovers the cost.

So, let's take the Restatement rule and set it aside. Let's state a better rule—the *real* rule—the rule that explains the decisions. To do so, we return

---

1. Groves v. John Wunder Co., 286 N.W. 235 (Minn. 1939).
2. Peevyhouse v. Garland Coal & Mining, 382 P.2d 109 (Okla. 1962).

to the basic doctrine of contractual interpretation. With it, we'll resolve this issue by giving more precise a meaning to the phrase "the position plaintiff would be in if defendant had not breached."

All reported cases in which the *cost* of performance differs substantially from the market *value* of performance bear on contracts for building, construction, or other activities that touch on realty. Where correcting the flawed performance would occasion the physical destruction or substantial disassembly of a physical structure, then, citing the phrase "economic waste," courts are quite likely to limit recovery to the value of performance.

Time Out.   For those students whose courses have not yet dealt with contract formation/offer and acceptance/mutual assent, we urge you to stop here and read Chapter 2, sections A, B, D; Chapter 3, section A; Chapter 7, section A; and Chapter 18, section A. Skip the multiple-choice questions for now; just read the text. It will go very quickly (we promise) and give you a leg up in understanding the material in the next part of this chapter. When your course addresses these three topics, then you'll read those chapters in full and address the multiple-choice questions. Please. Okay?

Time In.   In earlier chapters, you learned that

- a contract arises by offer and acceptance (with each party providing consideration to the other);
- the terms of the offer have such meaning as would be given them by a reasonable offeree under all prevailing circumstances;
- an offeree accepts only if he assents to all of the offeror's terms without addition or exception; *wherefore*
- the terms of any true acceptance are identical to those of the offer; *wherefore*
- the terms of the resulting contract are the same as those of the offer, which are the same as those of the acceptance; *wherefore*
- a contract includes such terms and has such meaning as conform to the parties' reasonable understandings and reasonable expectations.

Consider the Difference Between These Two Contracts.   Here's the first:

> **Party A:** I'd like you to rip up all of the grass and flowers on my residential property. I'll pay you $3,000 for the service.
>
> **Party B:** Why do you want me to do that?
>
> **Party A:** Well, I'm somewhat eccentric. I prefer my yard to be absolutely devoid of greenery.

Party B: But that will diminish the market value of your property.
Party A: I know it will, but I don't care. That's the way I want it.
Party B: Okay, if that's what you want—it's a deal.

Here's the second:

Party C: I'd like you to build a house on my land according to the specifications shown in these architectural diagrams. I'll pay $350,000.
Party D: What are your plans for the house after it's built?
Party C: I think it will be worth about $550,000 and I'm going to sell it.
Party D: I agree that it will be worth about that amount. You should make a handsome profit. In any case, I agree. I'll build the house for $350,000.

Now let's compare the two contracts. Any reasonable person in B's position should understand that A is not interested in raising his property's value but in stripping it of greenery even if he thus impairs its value. B, as a reasonable person, should understand that the "position" in which A seeks to be placed is that of a person who owns residential realty devoid of greenery. Both A and B should understand that when these parties make their contract, B makes this promise: "I will strip your property of all grass, plants, and flowers, and if I fail to do that I will owe you the cost of completing that job, regardless of what that means to the value of your property." If B breaches, A's expectation interest should be measured not according to the monetary value of his property, but according to the cost of correcting B's performance.[3]

With regard to contract 2, a reasonable person in D's position should understand that C is interested not in obtaining some particular result touching on his own peculiar taste, but rather in erecting a structure that he anticipates will be worth more than it costs him to build it. When the parties form their contract, D, as a reasonable person, should understand that the position C seeks is to own a house with a value greater than the cost of erecting it. That does not mean that D guarantees any such result. It means only that if D fails properly to build, C's expectation interest should be measured as the difference between the value the house would have had if properly constructed and the value it has as D improperly constructed it.

No real case in a real court has ever involved conversations that so explicitly define a contractual purpose as those that created contracts 1 and 2 above. Nonetheless, in all real cases in which cost of correcting performance exceeds the value of correction, it is the court's job to determine what, under the circumstances, the parties should reasonably have understood as their objectives in forming a contract. On *that* basis and no other, the court should identify plaintiff's expectation interest according to either monetary value or cost of completing/correcting performance. And, whether, consciously, they know it or not, that is what the courts generally do

---

3. *See* Chamberlain v. Parker, 45 N.Y. 569, 572 (1871) (an owner is "entitled to recover the value of the work and labor that the defendant was to perform, although the thing to be produced had no marketable value").

So What Rule Can We Write About Cost of Performance vs. Value of Performance? This one:

If (1) two parties P and D form a contract under which D is to perform a service for P, and (2) D breaches, creating a situation in which the cost of completing or correcting D's performance exceeds the market value to be obtained by doing so, then the measure of recovery depends on the circumstances surrounding the parties — including their own communications — when they formed their contract and what they should have led D to understand regarding P's objective.

    (a) Where such circumstances have led D reasonably to understand that P's purpose was to derive increased monetary value, then P's recovery is the value of corrected performance.

    (b) Where such circumstances should have led D reasonably to understand that P's purpose was not pecuniary but something else — related, perhaps, to sentiment, emotion, personal taste — then P's recovery is the actual cost of correcting performance, even though that exceeds the monetary value of correction.

QUESTION 2. Kinelman is an auto body servicer. Leder owns an old car that once belonged to her grandmother. Leder approaches Kinelman and, as she displays her car, the parties speak:

Leder: How much would you charge to restore this car's body to showroom condition, repainting it in its original color, mint green?

Kinelman: Far more than the car would be worth after I completed the work.

Leder: Well, it was my grandmother's car, and I love it. So, what would you charge?

Kinelman: $18,000, in advance.

Leder: Yes, let's do it.

Kinelman: Okay.

Leder pays Kinelman $18,000, and Kinelman begins work. In three weeks, he notifies Leder that the vehicle is ready. When Leder arrives at Kinelman's shop, she sees that the color is sky blue, not mint green.

Leder: It's beautiful, but it's the wrong color. I'd like you to repaint it mint green, the color we agreed on.

Kinelman: [Kinelman checks his notes.] You're right. I'm sorry, I painted it the wrong color. But, as you say, it's beautiful, isn't it?

Leder: Yes, but I want it to be mint green, the color it was when my grandmother first bought it.

Kinelman: I can't do that. I would have to remove this brand new paint, re-sand, prepare the whole surface of the car, and then apply four coats of mint green. That would take several days of my time.

> **Leder:** I insist.
> **Kinelman:** I'm sorry. I won't do it.
>
> Leder brings an action against Kinelman. At trial, undisputed evidence shows that the cost of having a well-qualified auto body expert repaint the vehicle mint green would be $5,000, and the change in color would make no difference to the car's market value. Is it likely that the court will award Leder a judgment of $5,000?
>
> A. Yes, because the circumstances surrounding formation of their contract indicated that Leder bargained for the position of one who owned a mint green car
>
> B. Yes, because a judgment of a lesser amount would reward Kinelman for his breach and unjustly enrich him at Leder's expense
>
> C. No, because changing the vehicle's color from sky blue to mint green would constitute economic waste
>
> D. No, because when Party A contracts with Party B for the purchase of a service and Party B fails properly to perform it, Party A is entitled to receive only the monetary value of which the breach deprives her

ANALYSIS. Whether cost or value of performance measures the plaintiff's expectation interest depends on the expectations the parties had — or, as reasonable persons, *should* have had — when they formed the contract. In this case, Leder made plain that her wishes arose from sentiment, not from a quest for monetary gain. Consequently, Leder's expectation interest is to be measured according to the vehicle's appearance, not its market value. In this case, then, plaintiff is entitled not to the difference in market value tied to the two different colors, but to the cost of correcting performance.

C and **D** say "no," so they're wrong. **D** makes the incorrect statement that a plaintiff is never entitled to receive the cost of completing performance. **C** invokes the tired phrase "economic waste" (which, unfortunately, your contracts teacher too will invoke) and hence misses the point. Some will say that one commits economic waste when she buys a thing or service whose monetary value is less than its price. More sophisticated economics, however, recognizes that value is an individual matter. The mint green is worth more to Leder than to the ordinary person. The restoration of the vehicle, obviously, is worth $18,000 to Leder, even though it has no such value to others. Although commonly used in this context, "economic waste" is an unavailing phrase; it gets us nowhere.

B correctly says "yes," but its reasoning is wrong. To award Leder less than $5,000 would not "reward" Kinelman for his breach. Kinelman worked diligently on the vehicle. He took no shortcuts and cut no corners. He simply made an honest mistake as to color. **A** reports the $5,000 figure and reasons correctly. Under the circumstances, Kinelman should have known that Leder was unconcerned with market value — that she expected the car to be mint green. Hence, **A** is right.

C.   Expectation Damages Require "Reasonable Certainty"

Imagine that Starr is a theatrical celebrity. After discussions, Starr and *Watch* magazine form a contract under which Starr will pose for a photograph and permit *Watch* to publish it on its January cover. *Watch* promises that it will in fact print the photograph on its January cover. The exchange calls for neither party to pay any money to the other.

As the contract requires, Starr poses and *Watch* snaps the photo. *Watch* then decides to publish the picture of some other celebrity on its January cover, thus committing total breach of its contract with Starr. Starr brings an action alleging that the published photo would have benefited her career and enhanced her earnings. At trial, she calls two witnesses, both experts in theatrical publicity. Asked what financial benefit Starr would have derived from the published picture, Witness 1 testifies: "Who knows? It might have brought her millions. It might have brought her nothing. That kind of thing is impossible to predict." Answering the same question, Starr's Witness 2 says, "There's no way to tell—maybe a lot, maybe a little, maybe nothing."

When Starr rests her case, *Watch* moves to dismiss on the ground that Starr has shown no damage. The court rules:

> Whether the action be breach of contract or any other, a plaintiff cannot recover damages that would require a jury to guess or speculate as to their amount. Rather, a plaintiff must present such evidence as, in the court's opinion, will allow the jury to quantify her damages with *reasonable certainty*. This plaintiff has failed to satisfy that requirement. She has presented two witnesses, neither of whom offers any meaningful answer as to whether this bargain would have afforded the plaintiff any benefit at all. Consequently, this Court lacks an evidentiary basis on which to submit this case to the jury on the question of Plaintiff's expectation interest. Plaintiff is entitled only to nominal recovery. Judgment is for the plaintiff in the amount of $1.

The Relevant Rule.   *With respect to breach of contract, a plaintiff cannot recover for expectation interest unless she shows with reasonable certainty an amount that, under the contract if properly performed, she stood to benefit.*[4] *If she can make no such showing, then she has, by law, no expectation interest.*

And that raises this question: If plaintiff has no expectation interest, does she recover anything? The answer is "yes," as described in Chapter 28. So, answer the closer and move on to the next chapter.

---

4.   The doctrine as to reasonable certainty and proof of the plaintiff's anticipated gain is another redundancy of law. It is but an application of a general (and obvious) rule: The jury will not be allowed to make a finding of fact on any matter unless, in the court's opinion, the trial has produced evidence sufficient for a reasonable person to make such a finding.

D.   The Closer

QUESTION 3. Parties P and D form a contract. D performs improperly, thereby committing breach. The nature of the breach and surrounding circumstances are such that the cost of actually correcting D's performance will exceed the monetary value P will derive from correction. In which of the following cases is a court most likely to award P the cost of correcting performance, notwithstanding that it exceeds the monetary value of the correction?

A. Where, at the time D made the error in his performance, there was no difference between the cost of performing correctly and cost of performing incorrectly

B. Where no reasonable person would consider significant the difference between the way in which D did perform and the way in which he should have performed

C. Where because of circumstances surrounding the parties at the time they formed their contract, D should have known that P's objective was not pecuniary in nature, but sentimental

D. Where D deliberately and knowingly performed contrary to the contract because it was economically advantageous for him to do so, and he believed in good faith that P would be unconcerned with the difference between the performance as given and the performance as called for by the contract

---

ANALYSIS.   On the question of recovery when cost of correcting an improper performance exceeds the monetary value of correcting it, the cases — and most especially the Restatement — do not offer a meaningful rule. The common thread among the cases (in their results more than in their espoused reasoning) strongly suggests that the rule truly, silently at work is this one: When two parties contract for the purchase and sale of a service, and the seller should, as a reasonable person, realize that the buyer is not concerned with monetary gain but with something else, then the law will award the buyer not the value of corrected performance, but the cost of corrected performance.

A has a nice ring so long as you don't read it for meaning. It suggests a rule that does not exist: If, at the time of breach, the cost to the performer of doing things the right way was the same as the cost of doing them the wrong way, then the law is more likely to award plaintiff the cost of correcting performance, even though it exceeds the value of correction. What can we say? It's nonsense. **A** is wrong (*way* wrong). **B** is truly appealing, but only if you don't comprehend the difference between one's *reasonable expectations* and the usual expectations of a *reasonable person*. They're different. **B** is wrong because it refers, generally, to what reasonable persons would think significant and fails to refer to P's reasonable expectations given the circumstances surrounding contract formation.

D sings a song about willfulness of breach, meanwhile throwing in a verse about good faith. It, too, implies a rule that doesn't exist. Whereas some courts do, at times, state that willfulness is significant in this regard, none refers to the good faith belief that P would be unconcerned with the breach. Further, most cases do not support the significance of willfulness as making the difference between recovery for cost versus value of correcting improper performance.

C tells us what the New York court stated in 1871:

> [One] may do what he will with his own, . . . and if he chooses to erect a monument to his caprice or folly on his premises, and employs and pays another to do it, it does not lie with a defendant who has been so employed and paid for building it, to say that his own performance would not be beneficial to the plaintiff.

Chamberlain v. Parker, 45 N.Y. 569, 572 (1871).

We could add to the court's words this clarification:

> If the party hired to erect the monument fails to do what *he knows or should know is wanted*, it is not for him to say that correcting his flawed performance would be worth less on the market than the correction itself. It is for him to do as he promised or to pay the cost of having it done.

This meaning is consonant with the whole science of interpreting offers and contracts, and with all that attends the meaning of "manifest intention" (Chapter 3, section A) **C** is right.

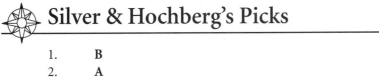 **Silver & Hochberg's Picks**

1.   **B**
2.   **A**
3.   **C**

28

Breach, Remedies, and Damages, Part IV

A. Reliance Interest

"Reliance interest" refers to money or property—but not time or effort—with which plaintiff parts in reliance on a contract that defendant has breached. For illustration, let's add a few facts to the Starr and *Watch* magazine story from Chapter 27, section C. Please reread that now before continuing.

Now assume that after *Watch* contacts Starr but before the parties form their contract, Starr spends $2,000 in consultant fees attempting to determine whether the photograph will promote her celebrity. Starr decides that the photograph will promote her celebrity and so she accepts *Watch*'s offer. After thus forming the contract, Starr spends $3,000 on clothing and grooming to style her appearance for the photograph.

Thereafter, *Watch* breaches, as in Chapter 27. As before, Starr can't establish her expectation interest with any certainty. But she can show that she spent money *in reliance* on the contract. *Because* of the contract—in preparation for her performance *under* the contract—Starr spent $3,000. *With reference to the time before she formed the contract*, she's "in the red" by $3,000. That amount, therefore, represents her reliance interest. One's reliance interest is such an amount of money as restores the plaintiff not to the position she would have occupied had both parties fully performed, but to *the position she occupied before the parties formed their contract.* In order that the law restore Starr to the position she occupied *before forming the contract*—to make her whole—it must award her $3,000. And because Starr cannot show her expectation interest, that is what the law will (usually) do.

What About the $2,000 Consulting Fee?

Starr secured consulting services *before* forming the contract. She did so to determine whether she wished to accept *Watch*'s offer. Amounts that are spent investigating and studying a prospective contract before it is formed do not belong to a party's reliance interest.

With that, let's amend our rule: *For breach of contract, the law's ordinary remedy is monetary damages in an amount that allows plaintiff to enjoy "the benefit of her bargain" meaning the amount necessary to fulfill the plaintiff's "expectation interest." If that amount cannot be quantified with reasonable certainty, then the law awards the plaintiff such amount as corresponds to her reliance interest, meaning the value of money or property (but not of time, effort, or labor) with which she parted in reliance on the contract.*

QUESTION 1. Orson secures a patent on her new invention. Penn knows of the invention and believes he can, over ten years, earn $500 million manufacturing and marketing it. Consequently, Penn wishes to buy Orson's patent. The parties become serious about contracting for the sale of the patent from Orson to Penn. Each engages an attorney, and Penn pays $10,000 for his attorney's services. He also spends $12,000 consulting with technical experts as to what would be involved in manufacturing and marketing the device. Thereafter, the parties form a contract under which Penn is to pay Orson $1 million immediately; Orson is to convey the patent to Penn one year hence; and Penn, as he sells the device to buyers, is to pay Orson a royalty of 5 percent on each sale.

Penn makes the $1 million payment as required and, over the next year, begins to prepare for manufacture. Spending 100 hours of his time, he secures a factory and equipment, all at a cost of $3 million. On January 2, 2012, Orson refuses to convey the patent, and Penn sues Orson for breach.

At trial, Penn produces two expert witnesses who testify about how much profit Penn would have earned manufacturing and marketing Orson's invention. One witness testifies, "It's very hard to know—maybe a billion dollars, maybe nothing." The other testifies, "These things are highly speculative. It's impossible to say." After Penn and Orson present all of their evidence, the court rules, as a matter of law, that Penn has not shown with reasonable certainty how much money he stood truly to derive if Orson had honored the contract. Penn is entitled to recover

A. nothing.
B. $22,000, the amount spent on a lawyer and consultants.

> **C.** $4 million, the amount spent after forming the contract.
> **D.** $4 million plus the fair market value of his time and effort.

ANALYSIS. Start with the rule. Then recognize that just before forming this contract, Penn *had already spent* the $22,000 on a lawyer and consultants. That's "on him." He doesn't recover it, and **B** is wrong. *After* forming the contract, Penn spent $4 million and invested 100 hours of his time and effort, relying on the contract. Reliance interest does not include the value of time, effort, or labor that plaintiff puts forth in reliance on the contract, so **D** is wrong. Penn does recover the $4 million in money he spent in reliance on the contract. Hence, **A** is wrong and **C** is right.

1. Reliance Is a Subset of Expectation

Look again at the final number line tied to the *Fairfax v. Gaelle* case from Chapter 25, section E:

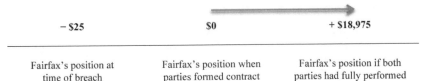

$-\$25$	\$0	$+\$18,975$
Fairfax's position at time of breach	Fairfax's position when parties formed contract	Fairfax's position if both parties had fully performed

The $25 represents the amount Fairfax spent on the available musicians list, in reliance on the contract. The $18,975 represents the overall *net gain* he would have enjoyed had both parties fulfilled their obligations ($40,000 [Gaelle's payment] minus $21,025 [Fairfax's expenses]). Fairfax's total recovery, therefore, is equal to the $25 he actually paid in reliance on the contract plus the $18,795 gain he would have derived absent Gaelle's breach.

Hence, *expectation interest = reliance interest + expected net gain.* Further, one (who keeps good records) can usually show the degree to which she made expenditures in reliance on a contract. She will (or should) have little difficulty in showing that portion of her expectation interest. The reasonable certainty rule usually raises its head in relation to the plaintiff's inability to show what gain, if any, defendant's performance would have afforded her. Hence, when the authorities (and teachers) say that "one recovers his expectation interest only if he can prove it with reasonable certainty," they're usually referring to the plaintiff who cannot show the portion of her supposed expectation interest that represents her expected gain. That was so of the Starr/*Watch* magazine illustration and also of *Penn v. Orson* in Question 1. The same principle expresses itself in the case law.[1]

---

1. *See, e.g.,* Sperry & Hutchinson Co. v. O'Neill-Adams Co., 185 F. 231, 239 (2d Cir. 1911) ("Plaintiff . . . made a claim for lost profits, but [failed to] marshal any evidence that would support a finding of exact figures").

QUESTION 2. On November 1, Beller and Gall form a contract under which Beller, by February 1, is to design audio speakers for Gall's audio speaker business, and Gall is to pay Beller $400,000 when she completes the work. Relying on Beller timely to complete the design, Gall launches an advertising campaign relating to the new, forthcoming speaker and, in so doing, spends $1 million. Beller, however, never even begins the work and thus breaches the contract. Consequently, Gall withholds payment of the $400,000 and brings suit, alleging that sales of the new speaker, over the next many decades, would have afforded him approximately $100 million in profit. Consequently, he demands damages in the amount of $99,600,000 ($100 million less the $400,000 he would have paid Beller on full performance).

At trial, Gall calls witnesses who, to his disappointment, testify that the profit one might derive from a new audio speaker is wholly unpredictable. Several add that a new speaker could just as easily fail to capture any market share at all, causing enormous losses for manufacturers such as Gall. When Gall finishes with his prima facia case, the court rules that he has failed to present any meaningful evidence as to the gain he would have derived through marketing of the new speakers. The court also rules that Gall has presented indisputable evidence that he spent $1 million on his advertising campaign. It issues a judgment against Beller for that amount. In doing so, the court has fulfilled

I. that portion of Gall's expectation interest as to which Gall presented adequate evidence.
II. Gall's reliance interest.
A. I
B. II
C. I and II
D. Neither I nor II

ANALYSIS. A plaintiff's expectation interest represents the sum of two parts: (1) amounts she expends in reliance on the contract (reliance interest) and (2) (provable) gain she would have derived absent defendant's breach.

In this case, Gall could not prove the second component of his expectation interest; he could not show what gain he would have derived from Beller's performance. In awarding Gall $1 million, the court fulfilled his reliance interest or, stated otherwise, fulfilled that portion of his expectation interest that he proved. Both I and II are accurate, so **C** is right.

B.   Restitution Interest; Unjust Enrichment and Quasi-Contract

1. Builder v. Developer

Suppose Developer owns vacant land with a market value of $2 million. Builder and Developer form a contract under which Builder will build an office building on Developer's land. Developer will pay all expenses that Builder incurs during the process. When Builder completes the building, Developer will pay her the (relatively small) sum of $100,000. Developer will then attempt to rent the building and for the next 50 years pay Builder 5 percent of the rents. For those next 50 years, Developer will not sell the building without Builder's consent.

Builder builds the building, spending a total of 400 hours doing so. As she builds, she incurs expenses of $7 million, all of which Developer promptly pays. When Builder completes the building, Developer pays her $100,000 as the contract requires. Then, in flagrant breach, Developer sells the building for $15.1 million to a buyer who has no knowledge of Developer's contract with Builder. Hence, Builder stands to receive no portion of any rent the building might produce.

Developer is plainly in breach of contract and Builder sues him. At trial, Builder produces witnesses who, to her disappointment, testify that the amount of rent Builder might have received under his contract over the next 50 years is a matter of pure speculation. Further, Builder can show no reliance interest; in reliance on the contract, she has parted with neither money nor property. (She has parted only with her time and effort.) Hence, Builder cannot show that Developer's breach has caused her any loss.

Does Builder Recover Anything?

Yes, The equity courts long ago recognized an action for "unjust enrichment," and it is now recognized, too, at law.[2] The relevant rule is that: *If Party B is unjustly enriched at the expense of Party A, then Party A is entitled to such remedy as will correct the injustice.* The phrase "unjust enrichment" in its fullest sense embodies a large body of lawsuits bearing on a great many scenarios—most of them *not* involving contracts. Suppose, for example, A visits her friend B at B's home. During the visit, B asks A to change a $100 bill into five $20 bills. A does so, and B, in turn, lays a $100 bill on her coffee table for A. When A departs B's home, she inadvertently leaves the $100 bill on B's coffee table. When A asks to have the $100 bill back, B refuses and insists on keeping it.

---

2. Regarding the equity courts and the difference between law and equity, see Appendix, section E.

Let's ask: what action does A have against B? B hasn't stolen the money; she hasn't taken it wrongfully in any way. A *left* it at her home. Hence, A has no suit in the long-standing legal action of conversion. A did not borrow the money, meaning that she owes B no debt or contractual obligation.

Among all of the actions long recognized at law, none offers A recovery of the $100 that, in justice, should be hers, except that: A has an action against B for "unjust enrichment." In the law's eyes, B has been unjustly enriched at A's expense. A did not give the $100 to B, and B in no sense earned it. Consequently, A is entitled to a $100 judgment against B.

Let's Shore Up Our Vocabulary

Unjust Enrichment is a *cause of action* in which plaintiff alleges that defendant has been unjustly enriched at her expense.

Restitution is the *remedy*, whatever its form by which the court rectifies the unjust enrichment. Restitution is always and only the remedy for the action of Unjust Enrichment.

Contract Implied in Law, also called Quasi-contract is one *kind* of action for unjust enrichment. It's a *subset* of unjust enrichment; it's an action for unjust enrichment in which plaintiff seeks restitution in the form of a money judgment. *For all unjust enrichment actions discussed in this book, plaintiff will seek restitution in the form of a monetary judgment. Stated otherwise, in this book, all actions in unjust enrichment are, more specifically, actions in quasi-contract, also called actions for breach of contract implied in law.*

We have touched on unjust enrichment in several earlier chapters. In Chapter 16, section A, we discuss contracts between minors and adults. (If your class has not yet covered this topic, please read, now, Chapter 16, section A but skip over the multiple-choice questions.) All that we learned about voidability and status quo ante as related to contracts between minors and adults has its historical roots in unjust enrichment.

Similarly in cases where a defendant successfully asserts the defense of mutual mistake, unilateral mistake, impracticability, or frustration of purpose (Chapter 22), either party might be left with some degree of unjust enrichment, and the law requires that each make appropriate restitution so that all comes out right. The same applies to discharge for duress and undue influence (Chapter 20).[3]

The doctrines of unjust enrichment and restitution do not, per se, belong to *contract* law. They arise in hosts of cases having naught to do with a contract. In a few situations, however, they apply to contractual disputes that, by tradition, belong not to contract law but to a basic contracts *course.* Of those situations, we now will teach you. -

---

3.   *See* Restatement (Second) of Contracts §376.

So Let's Get Back to Builder and His Recovery

Builder is entitled to recover for the unjust enrichment Developer has enjoyed at her expense. Stated otherwise, Builder is entitled to fulfillment of her "restitution interest." *If two parties P and D form a contract, D materially breaches, and P can show neither an expectation nor a reliance interest, then if P can show that because of her performance under the contract D has been "enriched," the amount of the enrichment represents P's restitution interest, and she is entitled to recover it.* The measure of her recovery—the unjust enrichment that D enjoys—goes by the nickname "benefit conferred," meaning the amount of monetary benefit that P, through her performance under the contract, has conferred on D, the breaching party.

Builder can show neither expectation nor reliance interest, but she *can* show that because of her performance under the contract, Developer derived a benefit of $6 million ($15.1 million, less the $7 million Developer paid in expenses, less the $2 million value of Developer's land when vacant, less the $100,000 that Developer paid Builder). To the extent of $6 million, Developer has been unjustly enriched at Builder's expense—at the expense of Builder's time and effort. Stated otherwise, Builder, through her performance under the contract, "conferred" on Developer a "benefit" of $6 million. To that amount Builder is entitled—to fulfill *not* her expectation or reliance interests but her restitution interest, which means her interest in having back from defendant any amount by which defendant has been unjustly enriched at her expense.

2. *Recovery for Breach vs. Restitution for Unjust Enrichment: Recovery "On" and "Off" of the Contract*

By issuing to plaintiff a recovery for expectation damages, the law attempts to afford her the position she would have occupied absent defendant's breach. It tries to create a *substitute* for the defendant's performance. Consequently, in awarding full expectation damages, the law recognizes the contract and, by considering available admissible evidence, takes account of (1) what each party did and did not do, (2) the consequences that followed from what they did and did not do, (3) what each party ought to have done, and (4) the consequences that would have followed had they done as they ought to have done. When the law awards a recovery for full expectation damages, it thus *enforces the contract.*

The same is so of a reliance award. A plaintiff's reliance interest, we know, represents the position she occupied *before forming her contract* with defendant. It is, also, a component of her expectation interest. She recovers for that component alone—her reliance interest—when she cannot establish (with such reasonable certainty as a given court demands) the amount of the second component—her expected net gain. Hence, in making an award in reliance, the law, once again, recognizes the contract and, by considering available admissible evidence, takes account of (1) what each party did and did not do, (2) the consequences that followed from what they did and did not do, (3) what each party ought to have done, and (4) the consequences that would have followed had they done as they ought to have done. When the evidence does not make a showing of the gain that plaintiff would have enjoyed, the numerical finding at number (4) is equal to *the position plaintiff occupied just before the parties formed their contract.* In issuing plaintiff an award that affords her that position, the law, as far as the evidence will allow, once again *enforces the contract.*

Hence, recovery for full expectation or reliance alone represents the law's *enforcement* of the breached contract. And, for short, it is often said that full expectation and reliance represent recoveries "on" the contract; recovery "on" the contract means a recovery that enforces the contract, providing the plaintiff with money designed to substitute for defendant's failed performance.

And so what? Here's the "so what:" As already noted, restitution for unjust enrichment (and, more specifically, quasi-contract/contract implied in law) is not a remedy for breach of contract. Rather, it reflects the long-standing doctrine of unjust enrichment. Hence, traditional thinking provides that in affording plaintiff a recovery in restitution the law does *not enforce* the contract. Rather, it cancels (or some say "rescinds") the contract—makes it go away—so that (by fiction of law) it never existed. Having done that, the court then seeks to take from defendant and give back to plaintiff any benefit defendant derived through plaintiff's performance under the contract (less any benefit that plaintiff might retain from defendant's performance under the contract). According to this traditional thought, restitution does not constitute recovery "on" the contract. It's recovery "off" of the contract. When a plaintiff seeks restitution, she elects, in theory, to cancel the contract and have back from the defendant anything of value that she conferred on him in attempting to perform. Because restitution carries with it an implicit cancellation of the contract, some speak of the remedy as "rescission with restitution for benefit conferred,"[4] which has the same meaning as "recovery off of the contract."

QUESTION 3. When defendant commits a breach and, according to traditional thought, plaintiff recovers "off" of the contract,

I. the contract terminates retroactively to the time at which it was formed.
II. defendant must pay plaintiff for such benefit as she has enjoyed through plaintiff's performance.
III. plaintiff is entitled to fulfillment of his expectation interest.
A. I
B. II

---

4. A relatively few modern authorities reject the historical distinction between recovery "on" and "off" of the contract. They regard a restitution award as one form of recovery for breach. But we'll stick with the traditional thinking because it still prevails.

C. I and II
D. II and III

ANALYSIS. Recovery "off" of the contract refers to restitution for benefit conferred or, as some call it, recovery off of the contract. As the traditional thinking goes, a court that awards a restitution rescinds the contract. Hence, option I makes a true statement. That means the answer is **A** or **C**, depending on whether option II makes a true statement. And it does. The restitution that characterizes this remedy refers to the plaintiff's right to have back the benefit he has conferred on defendant. Option III, as expected, makes a false statement. Plaintiff's expectation interest is relevant to recovery *on* the contract — to monetary damages designed not to rescind it, but rather to *enforce* it (and the same is so of recovery in reliance). Hence, **C** is right.

Let's Summarize What We Know So Far

When two parties form a contract, and one of them breaches, the other, as plaintiff, is entitled either to:

(1) monetary damages in such amount as fulfills
   (a) Her "expectation interest," which represents the benefit of her bargain — the position she would have occupied had the contract been fully performed (subject to her obligation to mitigate damages); or if she cannot show her expectation interest with reasonable certainty,
   (b) her reliance interest, which represents the position she occupied before the contract was formed (and is, also, a *component* of her expectation interest),

OR

(2) an award of such money as fulfills her restitution interest, meaning the amount by which, through her performance, she has unjustly enriched the defendant, also called the "benefit conferred" by her on the defendant through her performance.[5]

Once again, according to traditional thought, still prevalent in most quarters, expectation and reliance damages represent recovery "on" the contract, and restitution recovery represents recovery "off" of the contract.

3. Who Decides That Plaintiff Recovers for Expectation, Reliance, or Restitution?

From the mouths of judges, authors, and teachers, three statements frequently emerge:

1. The plaintiff in a breach of contract action may "elect his remedy;" he may seek to recover for his expectation, reliance, or restitution interests as

---

5. Regarding this summary, see Restatement (second) Contracts § 344.

he chooses, but he can recover *for only one* such interest — whichever he selects.

2. Ordinarily, the plaintiff will choose to recover for his expectation interest as that will usually yield him the largest recovery.

3. If, however, he cannot show his expectation interest with reasonable certainty, then he will choose between the greater of his reliance interest (if he has one) and his restitution interest (if he has one).

These three statements are true, but they carry a number of ifs, ands, and buts. Here's one now:

4. Restitution Is Available Only When Defendant Commits Total Breach

Because a suit in restitution involves a rescission of the contract, it's available only when defendant commits a *total breach* (see Chapter 21, section C; Chapter 25, section C). For partial breach, plaintiff may sue for expectation damages (or, if she can't show her expected gain, then her reliance damages). She cannot in that case, however, sue in restitution. If, on the other hand, defendant commits a total breach, then plaintiff may sue to fulfill her expectation or reliance interests. And, in that case she may elect, instead, to sue in restitution. As Restatement (Second) of Contracts §373 cmt. a explains: "[The] alternative of [restitution] . . . is available only if the breach gives rise to a claim for damages for total breach and not merely to a claim for damages for partial breach."

C.   The Measure of Restitution; Benefit Conferred, Quantum Meruit, and Quantum Valebant

1. Reliance and Restitution Compared

Remember that plaintiff's reliance damages include any expenditure that plaintiff makes in (reasonable) reliance on the contract,

- whether or not she confers any benefit on defendant,
- whether she pays it to defendant or to any other person, and
- whether she spends it in preparing to perform under the contract or in actually performing her contractual obligations.

As Restatement (Second) §349 provides: "As an alternative to [damages for expectation interest,] . . . the injured party has a right to damages based on his reliance interest, including expenditures made in preparation for performance or in performance." The reliance interest is limited to expenditures of money (or property). It does not include the value of any time, effort, labor, or service that plaintiff expends or delivers in performing the contract or in preparing to perform.

Plaintiff's restitution interest includes any money paid *to* defendant and includes, by curious fiction of law, any time, labor, effort, or service that plaintiff devotes *actually to performing his contractual obligations, whether or not defendant actually receives or retains any of plaintiff's work product.* Suppose, for example, that D hires P, an architect, to design a building. D makes it halfway through the work and P anticipatorily repudiates the contract (Chapter 25, section D). *Even though P has not taken or retained any portion of the design,* the law considers that he received a "benefit" equal to the value of D's time, labor, and effort.

Restitution interest does not, however, include any time, effort, or labor that plaintiff devotes to *preparation* for performance. In that regard, think again of P, the architect. Imagine that before he begins work on the design, he spends time and effort cleaning and organizing his office. Because that time and effort represents preparation for performance, it does not belong to P's restitution interest. Stated otherwise, in the law's eyes, time and effort that plaintiff devotes to *preparing* for performance does not confer a benefit on defendant.[6]

Hence, reliance and restitution have in common this single element: money (or property) that plaintiff conveys *to* defendant in performing his obligations under the contract (Figure 28-1, area 2). Such a payment forms part of plaintiff's reliance interest and also part of his restitution interest. Time, effort, labor, or service that plaintiff devotes to actual performance of his contractual obligations belong to his restitution interest but not to his reliance interest (Figure 28-1, area 3). *Money* that plaintiff pays to prepare for performance belongs to his reliance interest but not to his restitution interest (Figure 28-1, area 1).

2. Learn These Latin Phrases: "Quantum Meruit" and "Quantum Valebant"

The Latin phrase "quantum meruit" means, literally, "amount deserved." In contract law, it refers to that component of a plaintiff's restitution interest inherent in the value of time, labor, effort, or service that he devotes to performing his contractual obligations. On the other hand, "quantum valebant" means, literally, "amount of worth" or "amount of value." In contract law, it refers to that component of a plaintiff's restitution interest inherent in the money or property she conveys to defendant in performing her contractual obligations. Hence, if we want to "talk the talk," we say that with respect to

---

6. *See* Restatement (Second) of Contracts §371 & cmt. a.

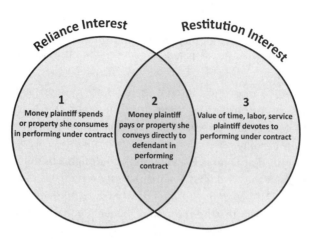

Figure 28-1.   Reliance vs. Restitution Interests

breach of contract, a plaintiff's restitution interest includes quantum meruit and quantum valebant.

Hence, between restitution and reliance interests is an area of potential overlap. Money paid or property conveyed by plaintiff directly to defendant belongs to both plaintiff's reliance interest and plaintiff's restitution interest (Figure 28-2, area 2). When this money or property belongs to restitution interest, we call it quantum valebant. Some lawyers, judges, and teachers are unaware of the phrase "quantum valebant" and think that "quantum meruit" is wholly synonymous with "benefit conferred." Be ready to encounter that common but erroneous usage of the phrase.

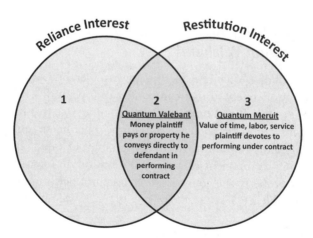

Figure 28-2.   Quantum Meruit vs. Quantum Valebant

3. *The Measure of Quantum Meruit; Valuing Plaintiff's Time, Effort, and Labor*

When, in performing a contract, plaintiff pays money to the defendant, it's easy to assess its monetary value: $1 is worth $1 and $1,000 is worth $1,000. But if instead or in addition plaintiff devotes time, effort, labor, or service in performing the contract, there arise two measures by which, logically, we might quantify the benefit (quantum meruit) his efforts confer on the defendant.

Suppose Scape and Ohn form a contract under which Scape is to cut down all of the trees on Ohn's land, and Ohn is to pay Scape $25,000 when Scape completes the job. Scape completes half of the job, whereupon Ohn advises Scape that he has changed his mind, that he does not want any more trees cut, that he will not pay Scape anything, and that Scape is to leave the land immediately. Scape leaves, and Ohn, of course, is in material breach of his contract.

Scape elects to recover his restitution interest. He has paid no money and conveyed no property to Ohn. Hence, his restitution interest has no component of quantum valebant. Scape, however, has spent time and effort cutting down trees, and that invests his restitution interest with quantum meruit. At trial, Scape proves these two additional facts: (1) to hire a person with Scape's credentials to cut down half the trees on Ohn's land, Ohn would have to pay $18,000; and (2) the value of Ohn's land with half its trees removed has been increased by $90,000.

Do we identify the benefit conferred through Scape's labor (quantum meruit) as $18,000 or $90,000? Stated more abstractly: Does quantum meruit equal the market value of plaintiff's services or the net increase in financial value that defendant derives? Restitution for services rendered in performance of a contract is usually measured by the fair market value of the services performed, not by the actual financial gain that the defendant enjoys. It is said that in most instances the fair market value measure will afford the greater recovery. But whether it offers the greater or lesser recovery, it is, usually, the preferred measure.

In some jurisdictions, if a court that believes the defendant has behaved with particular impropriety by, say, willfully breaching with some element of malice, it might well decide to award the plaintiff the larger of the two recoveries. And if the larger recovery happens to be the defendant's true financial gain, then the court makes its award accordingly. But, once again, that's only a "maybe." The state of the law on this point is sufficiently uncertain and the results sufficiently variable across the jurisdictions as to leave us only with a disappointingly vague rule on the measure of quantum meruit.

Here's our rule: *When defendant breaches and plaintiff seeks recovery in restitution for services she has delivered under the contract, she usually will recover what evidence shows to be the fair market value of her services. But in the relatively uncommon case where fairness seems so to demand, a court might decide deliberately to award her the greater of the two amounts. If the greater amount corresponds to the defendant's true financial gain, then that's what she'll recover.*

The Restatement (Second) §371 (not, in this case, reflecting any distinct majority of jurisdictions) states it thus:

> If a sum of money is awarded to protect a party's restitution interest, it may *as justice requires* be measured by either
>   (a) the reasonable value to the other party of what he received in terms of what it would have cost him to obtain it from a person in the claimant's position, or
>   (b) the extent to which the other party's property has been increased in value or his other interests advanced.

We *underscore* the phrase "as justice requires" to demonstrate that the Restatement writers can find in the judicial decisions no principle or precept more specific than that. And although the writers go on, as usual, to comment on their own writing, their comments (also as usual) offer little clarification (or sophistication of thought). They essentially come to this: It's up to the court to choose whether fair market value or actual financial gain better serves justice. To Scape in his restitution suit against Ohn, the court would almost certainly refuse to award $90,000; under the operative circumstances, almost any judge would consider $90,000 excessive and unjust. It would award Scape $18,000, the fair market value of his service.

In the case of Builder v. Developer, described earlier, we said that Builder would recover $6 million, and that's probably right. Developer behaved very badly. His breach was willful. Probably, a court would choose to fashion Builder's award according to the larger of the two available measures, which in this case was the true financial gain that defendant derived.

QUESTIONS 4 & 5. Harris and Danforth form a contract under which Danforth is to make a market study for Harris, Harris is to pay Danforth $50,000 immediately on formation of the contract, and Harris is to pay Danforth another $250,000 when Danforth completes the study and delivers his report. Harris pays Danforth the $50,000, but Danforth never begins the study and thus breaches the contract. Harris sues Danforth for breach but cannot show what profit or benefit, if any, he would have enjoyed had Danforth completed the study and delivered his report.

QUESTION 4. If Harris elects to recover for his *reliance* interest, and not his restitution interest, the court should award him

A. $50,000, because that is the amount of benefit he conferred on Danforth.
B. $50,000, because he spent that amount in reliance on the contract.
C. nothing, because he cannot show that he would have enjoyed any benefit if Danforth had fully performed.
D. nominal damages, because he can show no damage, but Danforth is nonetheless in breach.

ANALYSIS. Any money (or property) with which the plaintiff parts in reliance on the contract—whether or not conveyed to the defendant—belongs to his reliance interest. In this case, Harris paid $50,000 in reliance on the contract. Hence, that's his reliance interest. To the extent plaintiff makes that payment (or conveys property) *to* defendant, it belongs not only to his reliance interest, but also to his restitution interest. In this case, Harris paid the $50,000 *to* Danforth (and not, for example, to some other party to prepare for performance). Hence, that same $50,000 belongs not only to his reliance interest, but also to his restitution interest. In this case, therefore, reliance and restitution interests wholly overlap; they are equal. Harris elects to recover his reliance interest, meaning the $50,000, characterized, however, not as a benefit conferred on Danforth, but as the amount he spent in reliance on the contract. The right answer will report an amount of $50,000, and describe it as the amount of money Harris spent in reliance on the contract, and not as the benefit that Harris conferrred on Danforth (although that, too, is equal to the same $50,000).

C and **D** are wrong because they fail to recognize that Harris is, indeed, entitled to a recovery, to wit, of $50,000. **A** correctly states that Harris will recover $50,000, but its reasoning is wrong. Harris, we're told, elects to recover in reliance, but **A** recites reasons that pertain to restitution. It's wrong. **B**, on the other hand, correctly cites a $50,000 recovery and properly relates it to reliance. So, **B** is right.

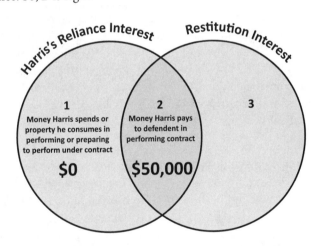

QUESTION 5. If Harris elects to recover his *restitution* interest the court should award him

A. $50,000, because that is the amount of benefit he conferred on Danforth.
B. $50,000, because he spent that amount in reliance on the contract.
C. nothing, because he cannot show that he would have enjoyed any benefit if Danforth had fully performed.
D. nominal damages, because he can show no damage, but Danforth nonetheless is in breach.

ANALYSIS.   Harris's restitution interest happens to be the same as his reliance interest because he spent exactly $50,000 in reliance on the contract, paying all of it *to* defendant, thus conferring on defendant that same $50,000 benefit. Since Harris, for this question, elects to recover in restitution, both **A** and **B** correctly recite the $50,000 figure, but only A correctly cites the reasoning. **A** is right.

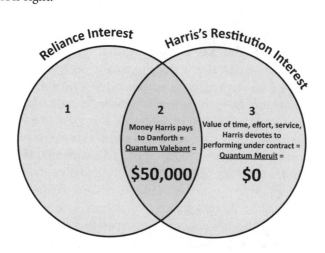

QUESTION 6. Writer has studied the novel *No News Is Bad News*. He believes it lends itself to adaptation as a good motion picture. Writer contacts Angelante, who wrote the novel. Writer and Angelante form an option contract (Chapter 6, section B) under which Writer pays Angelante $10,000 immediately, and Angelante agrees that Writer will be entitled, for two years, to purchase from her, for $1 million, all such rights as are necessary to adapt her novel to a screenplay. Writer then approaches Goldwine, president of Goldwine Studios:

Writer: I have acquired a two-year option on the right to make a movie from the novel *No News Is Bad News*. I have paid $10,000 for the option and have the right to buy the right, in full, for $1 million. I have also brought you an elaborate proposal, complete with 30 pages of dialogue. If, after reading the proposal, you want the screenplay, I'll write it.

Goldwine: And you'll want what in exchange?

Writer: Assuming that you want me to write the screenplay and that my screenplay conforms to the quality of the proposal, then you will (1) pay Angelante the $1 million for the rights to create the film, (2) produce the film, and (3) pay me 20 percent of the net profits it produces.

After Goldwine reads the proposal, he tells Writer, "I'm inclined to move forward." The parties' lawyers create a lengthy contractual writing that provides for a great many details the parties did not discuss. The writing also includes the terms that Writer proposed to Goldwine during their first conversation.

Writer begins diligently to work on the screenplay and timely completes it. He submits it to Goldwine, who rejects it without reading it because he no longer is interested in the project. Writer brings against Goldwine an action for breach of contract. At trial, all witnesses for both parties testify that

- the quality of Writer's screenplay is superb and at least as good as that embodied in the proposal he gave to Goldwine at their first meeting;
- the amount of net profit that the motion picture might have produced is wholly speculative, not subject, even to an estimate; and
- the cost of hiring a writer to produce a screenplay as good as this one would be $250,000.

The court decides that there are no relevant matters on which any reasonable juror could disagree and so, without jury participation, it issues a judgment in Writer's favor. The court should issue a judgment for

A. nominal damages, because the evidence shows no right of recovery "on" or "off" of the contract.
B. $10,000, the amount Writer paid Angelante, which represents his reliance interest.
C. $250,000, because that amount represents quantum meruit.
D. $1 million, because that amount represents Writer's expectation interest.

ANALYSIS. Writer fulfilled his contractual obligations. Had Goldwine done the same, Writer would have received 20 percent of net profit that the film produced. The court found as a matter of law that such amount was purely speculative and could not be quantified. Consequently, Writer has no expectation interest. Writer paid $10,000 to Angelante, but she did not do so in reliance on her contract with Goldwine; she paid Angelante *before* forming her contract with Goldwine. Having neither expectation nor reliance interest, we must ask whether Writer has a restitution interest. The answer is "yes," she does. Writer devoted time and effort to writing the screenplay. By law, that qualifies as a benefit conferred on Goldwine and, more specifically, quantum meruit. Consequently, Writer is entitled to recover the fair market value of her services, which according to undisputed evidence is $250,000.

A, B, and **D** name the wrong numbers, so all are wrong. Further, **A** makes a false statement. The evidence shows that Writer is entitled to no recovery "on" the contract (meaning he can show no expectation or reliance interest), but he is entitled to a recovery "off" of the contract to fulfill his restitution interest. **B** incorrectly identifies $10,000 as Writer's "reliance interest," which it is not. Again, Writer spent that money *before* forming his contract with Goldwine and so did not spend it in reliance on that contract. **D** falsely characterizes $1 million as Writer's expectation interest. If Goldwine had honored the contract, he would have paid $1 million not to Writer, but to Angelante.

That leaves us with **C**. It tells us, correctly, that Writer is entitled to $250,000 because that amount is equal to quantum meruit—the value of the time, labor, and effort he devoted to performing his contractual duties. **C** is right.

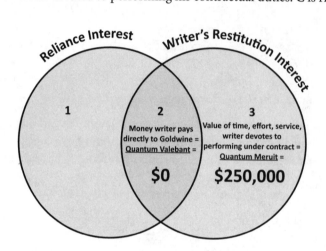

4. Sometimes Reliance Interest Exceeds Restitution Interest

In our second Starr and *Watch* magazine case above, Starr conveys to *Watch* no value and devotes no time or effort to performing under the contract. Her restitution interest is zero. Yet she had paid $3,000 in preparing to perform, meaning her reliance interest equals that amount, which she recovered.

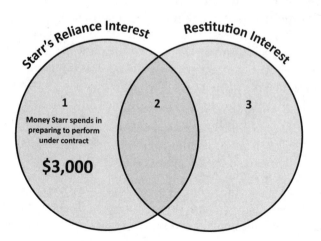

In Question 1 above, Penn paid $1 million to Orson when the two parties first formed their contract. That amount belonged to Penn's reliance *and* restitution interests. Further, Penn spent 100 hours of his time and $3 million in securing a factory and equipment, as he prepared to perform under the contract. That $3 million expenditure belonged to Penn's reliance interest, but not to his restitution interest. Hence, Penn's restitution interest was $1 million and his reliance interest was $1 million plus $3 million = $4 million. Reliance exceeded restitution, and so Penn elected to recover not in restitution but in reliance.

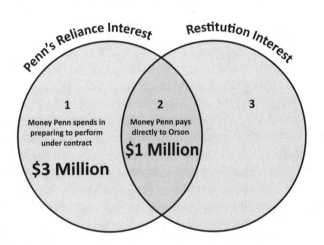

QUESTION 7. Lawrence and Meadows form a contract under which Lawrence is to market Meadows's patented device for five years, and Meadows is to pay Lawrence a royalty of 8 percent on each unit of product sold.

After the parties form their contract, Lawrence begins to prepare for performance. He hires marketing consultants, contracting to pay them nonrefundable fees of $100,000, and commits to advertisements for a nonrefundable cost of $50,000. After Lawrence makes those $150,000 in expenditures, Meadows commits a total breach. Lawrence cannot show, with any reasonable certainty, how many units he would have sold over the five-year period, and therefore cannot show what his royalties might have been. By way of remedy and recovery, Lawrence is most likely entitled to

A. nothing, because he conferred no benefit on Meadows.
B. nothing, because he can show no expectation interest.
C. $150,000, as fulfillment of his reliance interest.
D. $150,000, as fulfillment of his restitution interest.

ANALYSIS.   Lawrence cannot show where he would have stood financially had both parties honored the contract and so has no (provable) expectation interest. Neither does he have any restitution interest; he paid no money to Meadows and performed no service for her. Yet, Lawrence spent or committed to spending $100,000 plus $50,000 = $150,000. That amount represents his reliance interest, and he is entitled to recover it.

A and **B** correctly tell us that Lawrence has neither an expectation nor a restitution interest (having conferred no benefit on Meadows). Yet, by ignoring his reliance interest, they incorrectly report that he recovers nothing; **A** and **B** are wrong. **D** names the right number, but incorrectly attributes it to Lawrence's restitution interest. Lawrence's restitution interest is zero. **C** correctly identifies Lawrence's $150,000 reliance interest and tells us that he recovers that amount. **C** is right.

QUESTIONS 8 & 9. On March 1, 2012, Landers and Cleft form a contract under which Cleft is to study Landers's missiles and devise for them a satellite-directed guidance system, his work to be complete in one year, by February 28, 2013. In exchange, Landers is to pay Cleft a royalty on missile sales, equal to 2 percent of net receipts. For that purpose, Cleft situates himself at Landers's office facilities and, for six months, studies Landers's missiles and their design. At the end of that six-month period, Landers advises Cleft that he has decided not to develop guidance systems for his missiles, that Cleft should leave Landers's premises, and that "the deal is off." Landers thus commits a total breach of his contract. During the six-month period, Cleft spent no money relating to the contract. Neither could he gather any meaningful evidence as to how much money in royalties he would have collected had he finished the project.

QUESTION 8. By way of recovery and remedy, Cleft is most likely entitled to

A. nothing, because he can show neither a reliance interest nor an expectation interest.
B. nominal damages, because he can show no actual damage.
C. restitution recovery equal to the fair market value of the time and effort he devoted to the project during the six-month period.
D. recovery in reliance equal to the fair market value of the time and effort he devoted to the project during the six-month period.

ANALYSIS.   Cleft can offer no evidence that would quantify with reasonable certainty the royalties he stood to earn had both parties fulfilled their contractual duties. Hence, he has no expectation interest. Cleft spent no moneys in preparing for or performing the contract. Hence, he has no reliance interest.

Cleft, however, did perform services, work, labor in performing the contract. And although his efforts likely leave Landers with no financial gain, Cleft did, by (fiction of) law, confer a benefit on Landers equal to the fair market value of his services.

A correctly states that Cleft has neither expectation nor reliance interest, but it incorrectly states that he's entitled to no recovery. **B** is wrong because it too denies that Cleft is entitled to a meaningful recovery. **D** correctly states that Cleft should recover the fair market value of his services, but incorrectly attributes that recovery to his reliance interest. That leaves **C**, which correctly tells us that Cleft should recover the fair market value of his services and properly attributes the recovery to his restitution interest. Hence, **C** is right.

QUESTION 9. By way of recovery and remedy, Cleft is most likely entitled to

A. money for quantum meruit.
B. money for quantum valebant.
C. money for both quantum meruit and quantum valebant.
D. money for neither quantum meruit nor quantum valebant.

ANALYSIS.   From Question 8, we know that Cleft has neither an expectation nor a reliance interest. Neither did he pay money or convey property directly to Landers, meaning Cleft recovers no quantum valebant. Cleft did devote time, effort, and labor to performing under the contract. Consequently, he has a restitution interest arising from quantum meruit. **A** is right.

D.   Reliance, Restitution, and the Losing Contract

On April 1, Tripp and Unis form a contract under which Tripp will rewire Unis's house by May 1, and Unis will pay Trip $50,000 when the work is complete. Before forming the contract, Tripp calculates that in performing the work, he will incur $40,000 in expenses, meaning he'll earn a gain of $50,000 minus $40,000, or $10,000. To his surprise, however, his expenses come to $60,000. Tripp honors his contract, pays out $60,000 in expenses, and finishes the work on May 1. When he receives $50,000 from Unis, Tripp sustains a *loss* of $10,000. Tripp, therefore, has formed and performed a "losing contract," a—contract in which he suffers a loss.

1. *The Losing Contract and Reliance Damages*

When a defendant breaches and plaintiff cannot show what gain, if any, his contract would have brought him, and elects to sue for reliance damages, the law makes an assumption, right or wrong, that the plaintiff has not entered a losing contract. If Unis had committed an anticipatory breach on April 20 and Tripp had spent $53,000 up to that point in performing the contract, Tripp would recover only $50,000. The law will not award such reliance damages as would reflect, on the plaintiff's part, a losing contract. Stated otherwise, when issuing a judgment in reliance, the law will not require the defendant to pay more than she was obliged to pay under the contract. If the law were to allow Tripp to recover the full $53,000 he spent in reliance, while the total amount owed him was only $50,000, it would not be enforcing the contract; it would be, in a sense, punishing Unis for her breach—demanding that she do more than the contract required of her.

With That, Let's Write a Rule   *With respect to breach of contract, a plaintiff who elects to recover his reliance damages cannot recover more than the amount of money (or other value) that defendant owed him under the contract; that is, a defendant will not be held to pay more than she would have had to pay under the contract.*

2. *For Restitution, the Rule Is Different*

Remember that restitution constitutes a remedy "off" of the contract; the remedy does not enforce the contract. Rather, it represents a cancellation or rescission of the contract, retroactively, and a restoration to the plaintiff of the benefit conferred on defendant through plaintiff's performance under the contract, before the law "threw it out."

For that theoretical reason, a recovery in restitution isn't limited to the amount of money (or other value) that the contract requires defendant to pay plaintiff. When the court issues a restitution award, it might require that the defendant pay *more* (*much* more) than the contract requires of her. Reciprocally, the plaintiff might recover more than her entitlement under the contract.

Suppose Muir and Boomer form a contract under which Boomer is to build a dam during the ten-month period from April to January. During that period, as Boomer needs and requests, Muir is to furnish him with critical supplies and equipment so that Boomer *can* build the dam, and Muir is to pay Boomer, in ten $2,000 monthly installments, on May 1 to February 1, a total of $20,000.

Boomer starts building on April 1, and for April, May, and June works diligently to fulfill his obligations. During that period, Muir fails to make a single $2,000 payment, but Boomer keeps working through July. Then, in August, September, and October, Muir fails repeatedly to provide Boomer with the supplies and equipment he needs to do his job. For that reason, on November 1,

Boomer stops working. Citing Muir's material breach/total breach, he declares the contract terminated (Chapter 21, section D). Then he brings an action for unjust enrichment and hence, as remedy, seeks restitution (for an action in unjust enrichment imports, *always*, the remedy of restitution).

To the jury's satisfaction, Boomer proves that the fair market value of the services he delivered over seven months was $258,000, even though total payment due him under the contract was only $20,000. Now, then, Boomer's action in unjust enrichment, is a suit "off" of the contract. The court awards him $258,000 because (a) in an action for restitution, the contract, by law, disappears; it plays no role in measuring or limiting the recovery, and (b) plaintiff's recovery is equal to the fair market value of his performance (plus any money actually paid to defendant).

So, even though the *contract* entitled Boomer to only $20,000, Boomer's suit in unjust enrichment affords him a judgment in the amount of $258,000.

That Can Really Happen?   It *did* happen in 1933, with the case of *Boomer v. Muir*:

> To hold that . . . [the contract price] may limit recovery where the contract is afterwards rescinded through the defendant's fault seems to us to involve a confusion of thought. A rescinded contract ceases to exist for all purposes. How then can it be looked to for one purpose, the purpose of fixing the amount of recovery? "A contract is extinguished by its rescission." . . . "Generally speaking, the effect of rescission is to extinguish the contract. The contract is annihilated so effectually that in contemplation of law it has never had any existence. . . ." "When the [plaintiffs] rescinded the contract, they put it out of [defendant's] power to enforce it, . . . but [plaintiff] may . . . claim pay [for the fair market value of his services] just as though [the contract] had never existed."[7]

Hence, that which would have been paid him under a contract does not limit a plaintiff's recovery if he sues in unjust enrichment and hence for the remedy of restitution, measured by quantum meruit. The law lets the fact finder (ordinarily a jury) award the plaintiff so much as (on the admissible evidence) it (reasonably) finds to be the value of plaintiff's time, effort, and labor, ignoring the payment to which the contract entitled him since, in the case of rescission and suit for unjust enrichment, the contract is erased.

Hence, Plaintiff Might Recover Large Amounts Even When He Gets Himself into a Losing Contract.   Let's revisit Tripp's losing contract with Unis, and make a change to the facts. This time, Tripp unhappily discovers that he has *already* spent $60,000 on April 15, halfway through his work. Nonetheless, as an honorable chap, he continues in his obligation, continues spending, and continues rewiring. On April 20, by which time Tripp has spent $63,000

---

7.   24 P.2d 570, 577 (Cal. Dist. Ct. App. 1933) (citations omitted).

performing his work, Unis advises him that she does not want the work done and that he should leave her house.

Tripp engages a lawyer who, after investigating for several days, tells Tripp of her opinion that Unis has committed a total breach and that Tripp has badly undersold his service. The lawyer tells Tripp that the value of the labor and service he had provided before Unis breached is approximately $225,000.

On Tripp's behalf, the lawyer brings suit against Unis, electing the remedy of restitution for benefit conferred. At trial, the lawyer presents evidence tending to show that the market value of Tripp's performance falls somewhere between $200,000 and $300,000. The jury returns a verdict for $210,000, and the court enters judgment on the verdict. Hence, depending on the market value of the service he gives (or money he pays) *to* the defendant in performing the contract before defendant breaches, a plaintiff who makes a losing contract and then sues a breaching defendant in unjust enrichment might fare better than the contract itself allowed.

F.   The Closers

TCorp binds books, booklets, and magazines. UCorp publishes a magazine called *RoofTop*. In May 2012, UCorp has 1 million copies of its August issue printed but not bound. On June 1, UCorp contracts with TCorp to take possession of the 1 million copies, bind them, and return them to UCorp. UCorp is to pay TCorp $30,000 on June 15, an additional $10,000 on June 30, and another $10,000 on July 15, for total payment of $50,000. TCorp is to deliver the bound magazines to UCorp on July 30.

QUESTION 10. TCorp begins work on the project, pays $12,000 for various expenses, and binds 500,000 magazines. On June 15, UCorp fails to make any part of the $30,000 it owes and announces, further, that it will not proceed with the contract. TCorp is able to prove that if it had finished the project, it would have spent $16,000 more in expenses and, on receiving $50,000 from UCorp, would have derived a gain of $50,000 minus ($12,000 + $16,000) = $22,000. With respect to UCorp's breach, TCorp may bring an action

   I. "on" the contract.
  II. "off" of the contract.
  A. I, but not II
  B. II, but not I
  C. I or II, at TCorp's option
  D. Neither I nor II

ANALYSIS. When a defendant commits a total breach, the plaintiff may choose to sue (a) "on" the contract, meaning she recovers for her expectation interest or (or, if she cannot show her expected gain, then) her reliance interest, or (b) "off" of the contract, meaning she may rescind the contract and recover for any benefit she has conferred on defendant through her own performance under the contract. Benefit conferred means money (or property) conveyed *to* the defendant, or the market value of time, effort, and labor that plaintiff devotes to performance. By fiction of law, such time, effort, and labor "confer" a "benefit" on defendant whether or not defendant actually takes or retains any of plaintiff's work product.

In this case, UCorp fails to pay any part of the $30,000 it owes on June 15, which $30,000 amounts to 60 percent of all moneys it is to pay under the contract. On April 15, UCorp announces that it will not proceed with the contract and so commits an anticipatory repudiation and material breach. TCorp's reliance interest is $12,000 the amount of money it had spent performing the contract when UCorp breached. Its expectation interest is of ($12,000 + $22,000) = $34,000, the amount that will afford it the full benefit of its bargain. If TCorp elects to recover "on" the contract, it will, of course, choose its expectation interest over its reliance interest. TCorp's restitution interest is equal to the fair market value of the services it delivered in binding 500,000 of the magazines. What that amount might be, we don't know; it remains to be proven in court. It might be more than or less than $34,000. We do know, however, that among recoveries "on" or "off" of the contract, the choice is plaintiff's. Hence, **C** is right.

> **QUESTION 11.** Now assume that on June 15 UCorp pays only $29,000 of the $30,000 it owes and promises to make up the $1,000 difference by paying $11,000 instead of $10,000 on July 15. With respect to that breach, TCorp may bring an action
>
>   I. "on" the contract.
> II. "off" of the contract.
> **A.** I
> **B.** II
> **C.** I and II
> **D.** Neither I nor II

ANALYSIS. By paying 29/30 (96.67 percent) of the amount it owes on June 15, UCorp furnishes substantial (but not complete) performance. It commits only a partial breach, meaning that TCorp has no right to rescind the contract. Hence, TCorp cannot sue "off" of the contract in restitution. Rather, it must continue to perform. It may sue immediately for the breach, but its recovery is limited to its expectation interest as of June 15. It can recover such amount as will put it in the position it should have occupied *on June 15*. That amount is exactly $1,000, which would afford TCorp the position it was entitled to occupy on June 15. (TCorp cannot recover its June 15 reliance interest of $12,000 because that exceeds its June 15 expectation interest.) Because TCorp committed only a partial breach, UCorp can sue only for its expectation damages (calculated as of the time of partial breach) and thus has a suit only "on" the contract. Hence, **A** is right.

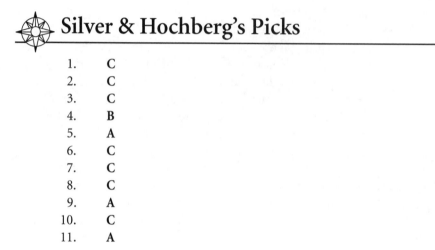

Silver & Hochberg's Picks

1.	C
2.	C
3.	C
4.	B
5.	A
6.	C
7.	C
8.	C
9.	A
10.	C
11.	A

29

Breach, Remedies, and Damages, Part V

A. Restitution Interest for the Plaintiff in Breach

Think of a Party A who forms a contract with Party B. Suppose Party A partly performs under the contract, thus "conferring" on B a "benefit," and then *himself* breaches (e.g., by failing to complete performance). On some occasions, Party A—the *breaching* party—secures a recovery not for breach of contract, of course, because B has not breached. Rather, he secures a recovery upon the theory of "restitution for unjust enrichment."

The rule is that *if Party P and D form a contract and Party P breaches but, nonetheless, has genuinely conferred a benefit on Party D, then Party P—the breaching party—is entitled to recover from Party D, restitution for unjust enrichment.*

Let's Illustrate: Panwith and Randolph. Panwith and Randolph form a contract under which Panwith will build for Randolph three cottages on Randolph's land, and Randolph will pay him $165,000 upon completion. Panwith begins his work and finishes two of the cottages, paying $20,000 in expenses. He never begins work on the third and thus commits a material breach of contract.

Randolph, certainly, has an action against Panwith for breach of contract, but he has no expectation interest, no reliance interest, and no restitution interest. He'll recover only nominal damages. Why's that exactly? Let's assess Randolph's expectation interest. Had both parties fully performed, Randolph would have acquired three cottages and paid $165,000. He'd be out $165,000 and up three cottages (which, of course, would have market values).

Let's now assess, by number line, Randolph's economic position at the time the parties formed their contract. We'll refer to the $165,000 that Randolph has not yet paid Panwith as $165,000 in Randolph's "bank."

$0

(Randolph is ahead of his expectation position)

no cottages and + $165,000 in bank	+ two cottages and + $165,000 still in bank	+ three cottages and $0 in bank
Randolph's position, at time parties form their contract	Randolph's position at time of breach	Randolph's position if both parties had fully performed

When Panwith breaches, Randolph has paid him nothing; Randolph still has his $165,000 in the bank. Meanwhile, he has acquired two cottages on his land. He has suffered no damage (unless he can show that it will cost him more than $165,000 to have another person build the third cottage). Rather, he has enjoyed a genuine benefit; he has acquired two cottages on his land and paid nothing for them. Hence, his expectation interest is $0; indeed, he is now in a better position that he would have been had both parties fully performed. Randolph has spent no money in reliance on the contract and, certainly, he has conferred no benefit on Panwith (not even as the law fictitiously uses that phrase). Consequently, Randolph has no expectation interest, no reliance interest, and no restitution interest. For Panwith's breach, Randolph is entitled only to nominal damages.

Panwith, of course, has no action for breach of contract because Randolph committed no breach. The contract required that Randolph pay Panwith $165,000 after all three cottages were completed, and Panwith never built the third one. Nonetheless, Panwith, the breaching party, has conferred a benefit on Randolph — not a fictitious one, but a genuine one. He has built two cottages on Randolph's land, and Randolph has acquired them "for free." In this situation, equity found (and the law now finds) that Randolph has enjoyed a windfall; he has been "unjustly enriched." For that reason, the law affords Panwith a cause of action and recovery — not in breach of contract, but in restitution for unjust enrichment.

How much does Panwith recover? Here's a pretty reliable rule: *When one breaches a contract and the breaching party sues in restitution for unjust enrichment, he is entitled to receive the amount by which the other party has been unjustly enriched at his expense. In most such cases, the breaching plaintiff will recover the lesser of what he has given up in money (or other property) in performing the contract or the degree by which defendant's position exceeds the position she would have enjoyed had both parties fulfilled the contract.*

Let's Show You How Simply It Really Works: Panwith and Randolph (continued).   Suppose that when Panwith breaches, Randolph engages another party to build the third cottage and pays her $40,000. Randolph then sues Panwith. At trial, evidence shows that

- just before Panwith and Randolph formed their contract, Randolph's land was worth $300,000.
- when Panwith breached, the two cottages he had built increased the value of Randolph's land by $140,000 so that its value was $440,000.
- Randolph paid $40,000 to another builder for construction of the third cottage.
- with the third cottage completed, Randolph's realty increased its value by another $70,000, for a total increase of $210,000, and total value of $510,000.
- Panwith spent $20,000 of his own money in expenses related to his work and *would have* had to spend an additional $10,000 in building the third cottage.

Now we can calculate the amount by which Randolph was unjustly enriched at Panwith's expense. If both parties had fully performed the contract, Randolph's position would be:

⟵――――――――――――――

$55,000
(Randolph is "ahead' of his expectation position
by $55,000)

land worth $300,000 and $165,000 "in bank"	land worth $510,000 and $125,000 "in bank"	land worth $510,000 and $0 "in bank"
Randolph's position, at time parties form their contract	Randolph's position in face of breach	Randolph's position if both parties had fully performed

In light of the breach, Randolph has his three cottages, which have raised the value of his land to $510,000. He has spent only $40,000, so that of his original $165,000 in the bank he has $125,000 remaining. His monetary position, therefore, is $510,000 + $125,000 = $635,000. If both parties had properly performed, Randolph would have had land worth $510,000 and spent all of the $165,000 in the bank, so that his monetary position would have been $510,000. The difference between his actual position in light of the breach and his expectation position is, therefore, $635,000 − $510,000 = $125,000. He is *better off* by $125,000 than he would have been if both parties had fully performed.

Panwith, meanwhile, spent $20,000 performing under the contract. As a breaching party suing in restitution for unjust enrichment, he recovers the lesser of $125,000 and $20,000.

But Doesn't Randolph Still Reap a Huge Windfall?

No, he doesn't. It's true that when all is said and done, and Randolph has paid Panwith his $20,000 award, he'll have $105,000 ($135,000 − $20,000) more than he would have had under the contract. That's his good fortune, but in the law's eyes, it's not unjust enrichment enjoyed at Panwith's expense. That's easy to see if we parse the transaction and account for the $105,000.

Panwith was to build each cottage for $55,000 ($165,000 ÷ 3). He would have spent $10,000 in building each one, so that his profit per cottage, had he honored his contract, would have been $45,000 ($55,000 − $10,000). For the two cottages he did build, therefore, Panwith's profit would have been $90,000 had he not breached. Panwith failed to build the third cottage and Randolph found a substitute whose fee was $40,000 instead of $55,000, meaning that because of Panwith's breach, Randolph saved $15,000 on the third cottage. Randolph's $105,000 gain in good fortune is the sum of the $90,000 in profit that Panwith would have earned had he honored the contract, and the $15,000 savings that Randolph saved on building the third cottage.

From Randolph's original enrichment of $135,000, the $20,000 restitution award gives back to Panwith only so much as Panwith actually spent. It denies him any part of his anticipated profit. The law sees no injustice in depriving a breaching plaintiff of the profit he would have earned by honoring his contract and, instead, leaving that profit with the nonbreaching defendant. In the law's eyes, that affords the defendant some good fortune, but not a windfall. The $15,000 that Randolph saved by engaging the substitute certainly should not, "in justice," go to Panwith, the breaching plaintiff. Randolph found someone to perform Panwith's work for $15,000 less than Panwith would have charged. That too is Randolph's good fortune, but it's not a windfall; it represents no unjust enrichment to Randolph at Panwith's expense.

QUESTIONS 1 & 2. On October 1, Seretan contracts to sell a parcel of commercially zoned real estate to Boshen for $2 million. At the time the parties form their contract, Boshen makes to Seretan a $400,000 down payment. The contract provides for a closing on December 1, at which time Seretan will transfer title and Boshen will pay the remaining $1.6 million in purchase price. On November 15, Boshen advises Seretan that she will not purchase the property. Seretan immediately advertises the land for sale.

QUESTION 1. After advertising the land for one month, Seretan finds a buyer. The value of the land apparently has increased: The buyer offers $3 million for the land, and Seretan sells it for that amount. Thereafter, noting that Seretan has lost nothing from Boshen's breach, Boshen asks Seretan to return her $400,000 down payment. Seretan refuses, and Boshen brings against her an action in restitution for unjust enrichment. The court is most likely to award Boshen

A. nothing, because Seretan is not in breach of contract.
B. $1 million, because that is the amount of Seretan's windfall.
C. $400,000, because that is the amount by which Seretan has been unjustly enriched at Boshen's expense.
D. $1.4 million, the sum of Seretan's unearned down payment and his $1 million windfall.

ANALYSIS.   Start with the rule. Then reason thus: if both of these parties had honored their obligations, Boshen would have paid $2 million and acquired the realty. Seretan would have received $2 million and parted with the realty. In light of her breach, Boshen has paid $400,000 and has nothing to show for it. Seretan, meanwhile, has parted with his realty and received $3.4 million. Relative to where he would have stood under the contract, Seretan is ahead by $1.4 million ($3.4 million − $2 million).

	$1.4 million gain (Seretan is "ahead" of his expectation position by $1.4 million)	
$0.00 **owns realty**	**+ $3.4 million** **no longer** **owns realty**	**+ $2 million** **no longer** **owns realty**
Seretan's position before parties form their	Seretan's position in light of Boshen's breach	Seretan's position if both parties had fully performed

Boshen has spent $400,000, and the lesser of $400,000 and $1.4 million is, of course, $400,000. That's what Boshen recovers because that's the degree to which Seretan has been unjustly enriched at Boshen's expense.

Seretan is left with $3 million, which means he emerges still with a gain of $1 million. That $1 million does not represent an unjust enrichment at Boshen's expense. As with Randolph and Panwith, it represents the profit Boshen would have earned had she honored her contract.

	$1 million	
$0.00 **owns no realty**	**$0.00** **owns no realty**	**− $2,000,000** *owns* **realty worth** **$3 million**
$0.00	**$0.00**	**+ $1 million**
Boshen's position before parties formed contract	Boshen's position in light of her breach and recovery of $400,000 down payment	Boshen's position if both parties had fully performed

If Boshen had honored her contract, she would have paid $2 million and acquired realty worth $3 million (since that's the price for which Seretan was able to sell it). As a breaching plaintiff, she doesn't get that $1 million gain. Seretan keeps it; it's good fortune, but it's not unjust enrichment. Once again, in the law's eyes there's nothing unjust about depriving a breaching plaintiff of the profit she ought to have earned and leaving that profit, instead, in the hands of the nonbreaching defendant. Boshen recovers $400,000. **C** is right.[1]

QUESTION 2. Assume now that one month after Boshen repudiates, Seretan finds a buyer who offers not $3 million, but $1.85 million; Seretan sells the realty for that amount. Thereafter, Boshen asks Seretan to return her $400,000 down payment. Seretan refuses, and Boshen brings against her an action in restitution for unjust enrichment. The court is most likely to award Boshen

A. $400,000, because that amount represents Seretan's unjust enrichment at Boshen's expense.
B. $250,000, the amount of Seretan's windfall.
C. $250,000, the amount by which Seretan has damaged Boshen.
D. nothing, because Seretan is not in breach of contract.

ANALYSIS.   Once again, reread the rule. Then reason thus: had both parties fully performed the contract, Seretan would have parted with his realty and received $2 million. In light of what actually has happened, Seretan has parted with his realty and received $1.85 million + $400,000 = $2.25 million.

His actual monetary position exceeds his expectation position by $2.25 million - $2 million = $250,000.

Boshen has paid $400,000 performing under the contract. Seretan's actual position exceeds his expectation position by $250,000. The second number is lower than the first, and Boshen recovers $250,000. That leaves Seretan with no particular good fortune, but it does leave him as well off as he'd have been if Boshen had not breached. Meanwhile, it restores to Boshen $250,000 in windfall that Seretan would otherwise enjoy.

D correctly states that Seretan is not in breach, but it ignores all that we've just discussed, to wit, that a breaching party is sometimes entitled to recover in restitution for unjust enrichment. **A**, too, is wrong. As explained above, Seretan has been unjustly enriched at Boshen's expense by $250,000, not by $400,000. If we were to award Boshen $400,000, we would leave Seretan with a $150,000 loss; he'd have $1.85 million instead of the $2 million to which he was entitled under the

---

1.   As discussed in the next chapter's first section, a contract for the sale of real estate often provides explicitly that if the buyer breaches, the seller may keep her down payment.

contract. We'd be giving Boshen more than the unjust enrichment at issue. **B** and **C** both report the correct award of $250,000. **C**, however, describes it as damage done by Seretan to Boshen, and that's inaccurate. Seretan has done nothing wrong. Rather, Seretan unjustly retains money at Boshen's expense; he retains what the law calls a windfall, precisely as **B** describes it. Hence, **B** is right.

B.   Restitution Interest for the Nonofficious Volunteer

Neff and Olson are next-door neighbors. Neff leaves his home to travel on business. He owns a dog that he intended to board in a kennel. Yet, in his hurry, he wholly forgets to do so and unwittingly leaves the dog in his backyard tied to a leash. Olson sees the dog tied up in Neff's backyard and takes it into his own home, feeding and caring for it for the four weeks Neff is away. Further, during that period the dog becomes ill and needs veterinary attention. Olson sees to that as well. All in all, in caring for the dog and securing the needed veterinary attention, Neff spends $500 during the four week period.

When Neff returns, Olson alerts him to the matter of the dog and Neff expresses his thanks. Olson then presents Neff with a $700 bill, itemizing $100 for food, $400 for veterinary bills, and $200 for Olson's time, effort, and attention. Neff refuses to pay. Let's ask: is Olson entitled to any recovery?

Let's answer: yes. Olson is entitled to recover in quasi-contract (contract implied in law). These parties formed no true contract. Olson, as a good neighbor, took it on himself to care for the dog Neff had unwittingly neglected. In any court's opinion, no doubt, he acted reasonably in caring for the dog did not behave officiously (meaning that he was not a meddlesome busybody pushing himself into a situation where he did not belong), and reasonably expects some compensation. Consequently, the court will award him restitution for the unjust enrichment enjoyed by Neff at Olson's expense. The amount of the award will be, once again, the benefit conferred on Neff by Olson, which in turn includes all moneys Olson spent in caring for the dog and the reasonable value of his time and effort.

Olson's recovery represents monetary restitution for unjust enrichment in an amount equal to benefit conferred, which in turn includes quantum meruit, the fair market value of Olson's time and effort, plus quantum valebant, the actual money or property that Olson spent and by which Neff benefited. In this particular kind of restitution/unjust enrichment case—that of the nonofficious volunteer—courts (and teachers) are *particularly* likely to invoke the phrases "quasi-contract" and "breach of contract implied in law." They may invoke them too with respect to the plaintiff who has breached (see section A above). But you are far less likely to hear or read those words in cases in where a defendant has breached and the plaintiff elects to recover his restitution interest. Although "quasi-contract" and "contract implied in law" do properly apply to those cases, by habit, lawyers seem to prefer in those cases, the designations "restitution," "unjust enrichment, "benefit conferred," "quantum meruit," and, of course, recovery "off" of the contract.

Now let's state the rule: *If (1) Party A sees that Party B is in need, and Party B is unable or unavailable to meet the need by forming a contract, and (2) Party A acts to meet Party B's need, reasonably, nonofficiously, with the reasonable expectation of compensation, then the parties form a quasi-contract ("contract implied in law") under which Party B must pay Party A reasonable compensation. He must compensate A fully for his disbursements (if reasonable) and, for the fair market value of his time and effort.*

QUESTION 3. Johnson is away on business. Kohr, his neighbor, inspects Johnson's yard and thinks the garden should have in it more perennial plants. On his own initiative, making necessary expenses, he plants a large number of perennials in Johnson's garden. When Johnson returns from travel, Kohr presents him with a bill for his disbursements and his labor, at $15 per hour. In response, Johnson says, "get lost." Kohr is not entitled to recovery in quasi-contract because

A. Johnson was enriched in no way by Kohr's activities.
B. Kohr's behavior was meddlesome.
C. the parties did not, in truth, form a contract.
D. the rate of $15 per hour is excessive for the kind of work that Kohr performed.

ANALYSIS.   A party recovers as a volunteer only if he behaves *nonofficiously*. But Kohr behaved officiously; no one asked him to meddle with Johnson's garden. He had no reason to think that Johnson, if present, would want him to, and no reason to expect compensation for what he did.

A makes a false statement (in the law's eyes anyway). Johnson did benefit from Kohr's activities; Kohr spent money and put forth effort enhancing Johnson's garden. **C**'s statement is true but irrelevant. You're asked to determine why the law would likely deny Kohr a recovery in quasi-contract. The absence of a true contract offers no answer, for the whole point of quasi-contract for a nonofficious volunteer is that the relevant parties do not, truly, form a contract. **D** makes a statement that might or might not be true; it's a matter for the jury to decide. But we cannot say, on our own, that the rate of $15 an hour for landscaping work is per se unreasonable. Hence, **D** too is wrong. **B** correctly observes that Kohr butted in where he had no business; he was meddlesome, meaning he acted officiously. Kohr had no reason to think Johnson would want him to redesign his garden, and no reason to expect Johnson to pay for it. Hence, **B** is right.

C.   The Closer

QUESTION 4. Harrison falls out of a train and is badly injured. Bystanders take an unconscious Harrison to a hospital where a surgeon operates on him for hours. Harrison survives for a time, but dies many weeks later never regaining consciousness. Thereafter, the doctors and hospital who attended to Harrison demand that his estate pay for their services. The estate refuses to pay, stating that Harrison formed no contract with the doctors or hospital and was not enriched in any way, justly or unjustly.

The hospital and doctors bring an action against Harrison's estate, and the court issues a money judgment to the plaintiffs in an amount (set by the jury) equal to the fair market value of the services delivered. The state's appellate court affirms the decision. In writing its opinion, is the appellate court likely to invoke the words "contract implied in law" or "quasi-contract?"

A. Yes, because the plaintiffs were volunteers, acting nonofficiously
B. Yes, because for all suits in unjust enrichment, lawyers and courts are in the habit of invoking those phrases
C. No, because those designations are customarily reserved for cases that do not involve a nonofficious volunteer
D. No, because those phrases have no relationship to unjust enrichment, restitution, or benefit conferred

---

ANALYSIS.   Don't let your contracts class confuse you on this point: For every action in unjust enrichment (no matter what the scenario), the remedy is restitution. When (as in every case we discuss in this chapter) the court awards restitution *in the form of a money judgment* (as opposed, say, to impressing a constructive trust or giving an order that property be returned), the suit for unjust enrichment belongs to a subcategory called "breach of contract implied in law" or "quasi-contract." By habit and custom, however, lawyers, judges, and teachers usually reserve those two designations for the unjust enrichment cases that involve no contract at all but rather a volunteer who, in the court's opinion, acts unofficiously to deliver service to a party who cannot form a contract, with the reasonable expectation of receiving compensation.

This is such a case. Harrison was unconscious; he was unable to form a contract. As volunteers (not butting in where they don't belong), physicians and hospital tried to save his life. They failed in that effort, but they are nonetheless entitled to fair compensation for their services. It is perfectly correct to characterize their suit as an action in unjust enrichment seeking restitution for benefit conferred. More commonly, in this kind of case, we say that their suit is in quasi-contract or that their suit is for breach of a contract implied in law. The measure of the damage, however, remains as the monetary amount called benefit conferred/quantum meruit. For these reasons, **A** is right.[2]

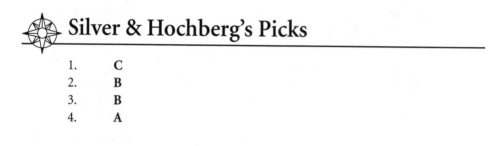

Silver & Hochberg's Picks

1.	C
2.	B
3.	B
4.	A

---

2.   This closer is inspired by *Cotnam v. Wisdom*, 104 S.W. 164 (Ark. 1907).

30

Breach, Remedies, and Damages, Part VI

A. Liquidated Damages
B. Specific Performance
C. The Closer
✧ Silver & Hochberg's Picks

A. Liquidated Damages

1. What Are Liquidated Damages?

"Liquidate" has several meanings, one of which is "to reduce or transform to money or cash." One who owns corporate stock might decide to liquidate her investment by selling it, thus converting its value to money. Where one party owes another 5 percent of the value of copyright X, the parties might decide to liquidate the amount of the debt by subjecting the copyright to appraisal, taking 5 percent of the result and thus assigning to the debt a cash figure. When two parties form a contract, the law sometimes allows them to create and enforce a "liquidated damage provision."

Suppose Meere is a renowned expert in investment, finance, and insurance, so much so that she is commonly understood to have no equal in all of the United States. Greeney contacts Meere, and the parties discuss forming a contract under which Meere will review all of Greeney's investments and insurance policies, thereafter reporting, in writing, her opinion as to what changes she recommends. Meere will submit to Greeney an itemization of time spent on the project, whereupon within ten days of receiving such itemization, Greeney will pay Meere at the rate of $800 per hour for her work.

Before forming the contract, it occurs to Greeney (or his lawyer) that if Meere fails substantially to perform that he will withhold payment. Beyond that, he thinks, he will sustain a loss—a loss of the uniquely expert services for which he has contracted. Not knowing how he might demonstrate the monetary amount of that loss, he suggests that the parties add to their contract this provision:

> **Liquidated Damages.** If Meere should fail substantially to fulfill her obligations under this contract, then (a) Greeney may withhold all payment that he would otherwise owe her, and (b) Meere will pay Greeney damages of $100,000.

That's a liquidated damage provision, meaning a contractual term by which the parties agree on the amount of damage one (or each) shall pay the other in the case of breach. Meere agrees to it, and the parties form their contract by signed writing. So, let's ask: if Meere commits a material breach, will a court award Greeney $100,000?

Let's answer: Maybe; here's the rule: *If contracting Parties A and B agree to a liquidated damage provision, the law will enforce it if it finds that (1) at the time the parties formed their contract, reasonable persons in their positions would agree that the actual damages caused by the contemplated breach are difficult to predict in monetary terms; and (2) from the perspective of reasonable persons, at the time they form their contract, the liquidated damages on which they agree represents a reasonable attempt to compensate the prospective plaintiff for the breach, meaning they are neither excessive nor punitive.*

If, for example, Meere and Greeney had agreed to a figure of $10 million, their liquidated damage provision would violate criterion (2). Ten million dollars would not, to persons in their positions, represent a reasonable attempt to compensate Greeney in the event of Meere's breach. Indeed, an award of that amount would be punitive.

Suppose, now, that Meere were willing to agree to the liquidated damage provision only if it provided for liquidated damage in his favor as well, so that they agree ultimately, on this:

> **Liquidated Damages.** (a) If Meere should fail substantially to fulfill her obligations under this contract, then (i) Greeney may withhold all payment that he would otherwise owe her, and (ii) Meere will pay Greeney damages of $100,000; and (b) if Greeney should fail timely to make to Meere the $800 hourly fee, Greeney will pay Meere in damages the sum of $2,500 per hour of service performed by Meere.

Imagine that Meere submits her report to Greeney, on time, in perfect form. She also provides Greeney with a detailed itemization of time she devoted to the work, showing that she spent in total 100 hours, meaning that Greeney owes her $(100 \times \$800) = \$80,000$. Greeney informs Meere that he will not be able to raise that amount of money for three weeks. In three weeks, he raises it, but Meere then refuses to accept the $80,000. She demands, under the liquidated damage provision, payment of $2,500 times 10, or $250,000.

Meere won't get $250,000 because no court will enforce the liquidated damage provision's part (b). That part of the clause fails to answer criterion (1) of the rule stated above—that actual damages be difficult to predict in monetary terms. Reasonable persons under the circumstances in which Meere and Greeney formed their contract would conclude quite the opposite, that damages to Meere for Greeney's failure timely to pay Meere $800 per hour are readily foreseeable: $800 per hour is—after all—$800 per hour. Greeney's failure to pay the $800 when due would cause Meere damages of exactly $800 for each such hour (plus some interest, depending on the degree of the lateness).

QUESTION 1. On April 1, Shuva and Bimra contract, by signed writing, that Shuva (Seller) will convey his real property to Bimra (Buyer), in exchange for which Bimra will pay a purchase price of $800,000, 10 percent of which ($80,000) she will pay immediately, on April 1, and the remainder, $720,000, at a closing that is to occur on or about June 1. The contract also includes this provision:

> **Deposit/Down Payment as Liquidated Damage.** The parties agree that if Buyer should fail at closing to purchase the property, then Seller may keep, as liquidated damage, the 10 percent ($80,000) down payment Buyer is to make on the formation of this contract, and that such shall be the only damage to which Seller shall, in such case, be entitled.

On May 20, Bimra advises Shuva that she will not purchase the realty, thus committing an anticipatory repudiation. She says simply that she has found another property that she prefers and that she intends to buy it. Consequently, she asks Shuva to return her $80,000 deposit. Shuva refuses, claiming that under their contract he is entitled to keep the $80,000 as liquidated damages. Shuva sues Bimra for unjust enrichment, claiming restitution in the amount of $80,000. The court enforces the liquidated damage clause and denies Bimra's claim for a return of the money.

The court should not have made that decision, unless it found that

I. under these circumstances, $80,000 is not excessive or punitive.
II. when these two parties formed their contract, the actual amount of damage sustained by Shuva on Bimra's breach would be difficult for reasonable persons in their positions to foresee.
III. Bimra's breach was knowing and willful.
IV. Bimra not only breached her contract with Shuva, but also decided to buy other realty from another seller.

A. I
B. I and II
C. I, II, and III
D. I, II, III, and IV

ANALYSIS. Recall from the rule given above that a liquidated damage clause is enforceable if it meets two criteria. In this case, since we're told the court enforces the liquidated damage provision against the breaching buyer, it should first have concluded that (1) as reasonable people, these two parties, at the time they formed their contract, believed it would be difficult to foresee the actual monetary damage that Shuva would suffer from Bimra's breach, and (2) Shuva's retention of the $80,000 deposit is a reasonable means of fixing damage at the outset; it is neither excessive, nor punitive. There is little (if anything) else that the court need find to enforce the liquidated damage provision.

Options I and II reflect those two criteria. Hence, they belong to the right answer. Option III correctly reports that Bimra's breach was knowing and willful, and option IV accurately tells us that Bimra decided to purchase other property elsewhere. But both those facts are irrelevant; if Bimra had breached because he was unable to raise the purchase price and if he had no intention of buying property elsewhere, the court would not alter its ruling. Options I and II reflect the two criteria that render a liquidated damage provision enforceable. **B** is right.[1]

3. More About Criterion 1: Actual Damages Difficult to Foresee

Focus, please, on criterion 1 above, as related to the enforceability of a liquidated damage clause: If when two parties, A and B form a contract, reasonable persons in their positions would think themselves able to predict within a meaningful range the damages likely to arise from Party A's breach, then as to the damages A is to pay under a liquidated damage clause, the clause is *unenforceable*. If B sues A for breach, B is entitled to the actual damages he proves, whether they be less or more than those prescribed by the liquidated damage clause; the liquidated damage clause is irrelevant. The same applies, of course, if the amount of damage A is likely to suffer from B's breach is reasonably foreseeable *when the parties form their contract*; if A sues B for breach, A recovers the actual damages he proves, irrespective of the liquidated damage clause.

If reasonable parties would deem foreseeable the damage to be suffered by A or B in the case of the other's breach, then a liquidated damage clause is wholly unenforceable as to both parties. Should either sue the other for breach his award will be equal to the actual damages proven—no more and no less. The court will take the liquidated damage clause and "throw it out."

---

1. Some jurisdictions hold that as to a contract for the sale of realty, a seller's prospective damages for buyer's breach are, as a matter of law, "difficult to foresee." In those states, a 10 percent, 15 percent, or perhaps 20 percent down payment is, by law, reasonable; it's neither excessive nor punitive. Even where the parties' contract does not provide that the down payment will serve as liquidated damage, these states hold that *unless the parties contract otherwise,* a 10 to 20 percent down payment implicitly represents a liquidated damage provision, with the down payment representing the liquidated damage.

QUESTION 2. Xanzi and Yorta form a contract that carries this liquidated damage clause:

> **Liquidated Damage.** If either of the parties hereto should commit a material breach hereof, then he shall pay the other liquidated damages of $5 million.

The nature of the contract and surrounding circumstances would cause reasonable persons, at the time they form the contract, to predict that Xanzi's material breach would probably cause Yorta damage in the amount of $100,000 to $150,000, and Yorta's material breach would probably damage Xanzi in the amount of $400,000 to $500,000.

Xanzi commits a material breach. Both the circumstances surrounding the parties at the time of breach and the effect of the breach on Yorta are not at all what a reasonable person would have predicted. Nonetheless, by mode and manner that no reasonable person would have predicted when these parties formed their contract, Yorta's damages are in fact $6 million—not so different from the liquidated damage of $5 million on which the parties agreed. Taking a traditional view of liquidated damage provisions, should the court award Yorta $5 million or $6 million?

A. $5 million, because as between the damage quantified in a liquidated damage clause and that which a plaintiff actually sustains, the court, upon a standard of reasonableness, will award the smaller of the two amounts.

B. $5 million, because Yorta explicitly agreed to accept that amount as compensation for Xanzi's breach, in exchange for a mirror-image provision regarding Yorta's potential breach, and under such a circumstance, the law holds him to his agreement.

C. $6 million, because it is reasonably close to the $5 million figure to which the parties manifested their mutual asset as reflected in their liquidated damage clause.

D. $6 million, because the $5 million figure did not reflect a reasonably foreseeable quantification of Yorta's damage at the time these parties finalized their contract.

ANALYSIS. Before assessing the choices, think of the law—the law—*the law*! As to any prospective defendant sued for breach of contract, a liquidated damage clause is unenforceable *if, at the time plaintiff and defendant form their contract,* the damage to be suffered by plaintiff on defendant's breach would be meaningfully foreseeable to reasonable persons in the positions of the two contracting parties. (It's unenforceable, too, if the amount of liquidated damage identified is unreasonable; excessive, punitive.)

Here, we're told that when these parties form their contract, reasonable persons would foresee that Xanzi's material breach would cause Yorta damages of $100,000 to $150,000. As for damages caused Xanzi by Yorta's breach, they would foresee an amount of $400,000 to $500,000. Hence, the degree of damages flowing from each party's prospective breach was reasonably foreseeable, so we take the liquidated damage provision and trash it. For that reason, Yorta recovers his actual damages (as proven, of course) — $6 million.

A awards plaintiff $5 million, so it's wrong for that reason alone. Then it states a nonexistent rule. It implies that when a liquidated damage clause names one figure and evidence identifies another, the court awards the smaller of the two figures. There's no such rule. The test writer invented it to throw you off balance. Once again, *when a multiple-choice option states or implies a rule you've never heard of, you must indulge a very strong presumption that it's wrong.* And don't be sucked in by the phrase "standard of reasonableness" simply because you're familiar with it. **A** states the wrong answer, justified by a rule that doesn't exist. Hence, **A** is wrong.

B too gives plaintiff $5 million, so it's wrong. It too implies a nonexistent rule: If two contracting parties agree to a liquidated damage provision that, upon each party's potential breach, entitles the other to the *same* damage award, then the clause is enforceable. That's nonsense; there's no such law. And don't let the words "mirror-image" seduce you, just because you've heard them before (which you have if you've already read Chapter 7). **B** is wrong.

C correctly awards plaintiff $6 million, but its reasoning is wrong. It too implies a nonexistent rule: that only if plaintiff's actual damage is reasonably close to the amount damage defendant is to pay under the liquidation clause, then the court is to award actual damages. According to **C**, then, if plaintiff's actual damages had been $15 million, the court would award him $5 million. It would not. Alas, **C** is wrong.

That leaves **D**, which must be right; and it is. It awards plaintiff $6 million — his actual damage — and its reasoning is right. When the parties formed their contract, **D** tells us, reasonable persons would (right or wrong) believe they could, by foresight, approximate the actual damages to be suffered by each party should the other commit a material breach. *That fact* renders the damage clause unenforceable, and plaintiff is entitled to recover his actual damages, whether they are close to or far from those provided in the liquidated damage provision. **D** is right.

QUESTION 3. On February 1, Winston, a screenwriter, and Antwon, a motion picture screenplay agent, form a contract requiring that Winston, by or before December 31, write a screenplay for the largely forgotten novel *Alone But Yet Alive*; Antwon then, for three years, will make diligent commercial efforts to market the screenplay to motion picture producers. If Antwon should be successful in that effort, which he cannot and does not guarantee, Winston will pay Antwon 15 percent of whatever moneys a motion picture production company pays Winston for the screenplay.

The parties and their lawyers conclude that if Winston should fail to write the manuscript, it would be nearly impossible to calculate what damages Antwon would suffer. Similarly, the parties conclude that if Antwon should fail to make diligent commercial efforts to market the screenplay, it will be nearly impossible to quantify and prove Winston's damages because, even if Antwon does exert serious effort in marketing the manuscript, neither party can now predict that any production company will purchase it, or what price, if any, it might pay. Consequently, the parties include in their contract this provision:

> **Liquidated Damages.** (a) If Winston should fail substantially in his obligation timely to create the aforementioned screenplay, he will pay Antwon 15 percent of $20 and (b) if, after Winston does timely create the manuscript, Antwon fails substantially in his obligation to use diligent professional efforts in attempting to market it to motion picture production companies as aforesaid, then Antwon will pay Winston $20 million.

Winston timely completes the screenplay, but Antwon never lifts a finger to market it.

During the next year, Sarahn, another screenwriter, writes a screenplay for *Alone But Yet Alive*, hoping to market it to production companies. Shortly after he finishes it, the original author of the novel *Alone But Yet Alive* is involved in a widely publicized scandal whose facts are similar to those of her novel. She and her novel gain enormous notoriety, and Sarahn, who has a good and diligent agent, sells his manuscript to a production company for $25 million—twice the highest price ever paid for a screenplay.

Thereafter, Winston seeks to recover from Antwon the liquidated damages to which, he says, the contract entitles him. He brings an action against Antwon demanding $20 million. The court finds as facts that

- at the time the parties formed their contract, no screenwriter had been paid more than $8 million for a screenplay; wherefore
- the amount of $25 million as provided in the parties' contract, viewed from their perspective when they formed it, was positively unreasonable, excessive, and punitive;
- as matters evolved, another screenwriter did sell his screenplay for $25 million, so that the liquidated damage provision, examined today, turns out not to have been excessively high.

The court then rules:

> According to a long-standing traditional view of liquidated dam-
> age clauses, this one is unenforceable. If plaintiff Winston wishes to
> recover from defendant Antwon, he will have to prove his damages.
> He will have to prove that Antwon, if properly discharging his con-
> tractual duties, would have sold Winston's manuscript and for how
> much. Plaintiff Winston's manuscript, let us remember, is the same
> as Miss Sarahn's.

The court's reason for ruling the liquidated damage clause unenforceable
is most likely that

A. at the time they formed their contract, the parties had no reason to
believe that either of them would commit a material breach.
B. the parties' liquidated damage provision did not treat equally a
breach by Winston on the one hand and Antwon on the other.
C. as to the amount of liquidated damage on which two parties
agree, reasonableness is to be judged by the court in light of all
circumstances that surround the breach.
D. as to the amount of liquidated damage on which two parties agree,
reasonableness is to be judged from what should be their perspective
at the time they form their contract.

ANALYSIS. According to traditional thought, the enforceability of a liquidated damage clause rides on two criteria, each to be applied from the perspective of reasonable persons in the parties' positions *at the time they form the
contract.* If the parties choose as liquidated damages a figure that is unreasonably high, as reasonable persons should visualize the prospective breach *at that
time,* then the provision is unenforceable. And that is true even if it turns out,
as no one would reasonably have predicted, that the figure was not too high.

In this case, the parties agreed on $20 million in liquidated damages for
Winston, even though at the time they formed their contract no screenwriter
had ever been paid any amount nearly so high. The fact that a screenwriter
did, through unpredictable events, later receive an amount even higher than
that does not affect the reasonableness of the parties' figure as of the time they
chose it. That's why this court, citing to a long-standing traditional view, ruled
the liquidated damage clause unenforceable.

As for **A:** The validity of a liquidated damage agreement does not require
that the parties anticipate a breach. That thought has nothing to do with the
subject, wherefore **A** is wrong. **B** too is wrong; the viability of a liquidated
damage clause does not depend on any sort of mutuality or equality. As we
already know, a contract might provide for liquidated damages respecting one
party's breach, but not the other's. **C** speaketh nonsense. The reasonableness of
a liquidated damage figure depends not on what a court thinks in light of all

circumstances surrounding a breach. It depends on what a court, on evidence, thinks reasonable parties should have thought at the time they formed their contract. **D** says exactly that, and that's why **D** is right.

4. The More Modern Trend

According to a more modern and emerging view, a court may assess the reasonableness of a liquidated damage figure by looking not only backward in time to what the parties should have thought when they formed their contract, but also to the present for reasonableness of amount *in light of what truly has occurred.*

Restatement (Second) of Contracts §356 appears to take that view:

> Damages for breach by either party may be liquidated in the agreement but only at an amount that is reasonable in the light of the anticipated or actual loss caused by the breach and the difficulties of proof of loss. A term fixing unreasonably large liquidated damages is unenforceable on grounds of public policy as a penalty.

The three words "or actual damage" seem to mean that a liquidated damage clause is enforceable if it approximates the actual damage a plaintiff suffers from defendant's breach. UCC §2-718(1) provides similarly:

> Damages for breach by either party may be liquidated in the agreement but only at an amount that is reasonable in the light of the anticipated or actual harm caused by the breach[.]

The words "or actual harm" mean the same as the Restatement's words "or actual damage."

That innovation in the law is of dubious significance. It would seem to be relevant only when the plaintiff is, in fact, able to show his actual damage and the liquidated damage clause provides for damages slightly higher than the actual ones.

QUESTION 4. Altering the facts given in Question 3, assume now that Sarahn sold her screenplay for $17 million. The court, at a bench trial, finds as fact that

- at the time the parties formed their contract, no screenwriter had been paid more than $8 million for a screenplay; wherefore
- the amount of $20 million as provided in the parties' contract, viewed from their perspective at the time they formed it, was positively unreasonable, excessive, and punitive; and
- if Antwon had fulfilled her contractual duty, she would have sold Winston's screenplay for $17 million, before Sarahn had a chance to sell hers.

If the court were to follow the newer, emerging trend on the matter of reasonableness of liquidated damages, it would most likely award Winston

A. nominal damages only.
B. $17 million, his actual damages, as proven.
C. $20 million, the liquidated damages provided by contract.
D. $37 million ($17 million + $20 million).

ANALYSIS. The words "or actual damage" that appear in Restatement § 356 bespeak some emerging trend (maybe) by which liquidated damages that are unreasonable in amount when the parties agree on them may nonetheless be awarded if, as matters turn out, they are not "out of whack" with the actual damages the plaintiff suffers (which means, of course, that he must prove those damages). Hence, if some court really does adopt this Restatement view, it would note that the plaintiff's actual damages of $17 million, as proven, are not so far from the $20 million figure provided in the contract, and it would, therefore award the amount provided by contract. Hence, **C** is right (*maybe*, and *maybe* the view is endorsed by Equitable Lumber Corp. v. IPA Land Dev. Corp., 381 N.Y.S.2d 459 (N.Y. 1976)).

B. Specific Performance

1. What Is Specific Performance?

A long-standing precept adopted by the equity courts provides that when the law's remedy of money damages is insufficient to rectify the injustice wrought by breach of contract, the injured party may petition the equity court for an order of "specific performance," meaning a court order to the other party that he *actually perform the contract* or, if he refuses, to face incarceration for contempt of court.

Suppose Bertha conducts a garage sale where Hattie finds an old 78 RPM recording of her great aunt Lottie playing the violin. Lottie, in her day (the 1910s), had been a well-known concert violinist. Hattie wants badly to buy the record. Bertha offers it for $5, and Hattie accepts. The parties thus form a contract for the sale of the record by Bertha to Hattie. Hattie roams among the other merchandise for a while and then approaches Bertha to pay for and take the record. Bertha says she has changed her mind and wants $100 for the record. Bertha, therefore, is in material breach of contract.

Hattie's lawyer tells her that in an ordinary suit for breach of contract, she'll be entitled to recover only the fair market value of the record, whatever that is — $5 or $100. Hattie tells him that no such amount of money will give her what she bargained for. The record she contracted to buy has a special meaning to her. Tearful, she tells her lawyer, that "nothing will do but to have the record itself." On Hattie's behalf, the lawyer brings an action against Bertha

(1) citing Bertha's breach of contract; (2) citing the particular significance of the very recording Hattie contracted to buy from her; and (3) asserting therefore that a monetary award equal to the value of the record will not put Hattie in the same position she would have occupied had the contract been performed. The lawyer then advises the court of his position: (4) that the case is one in which Bertha's breach subjects Hattie to an injustice "for which the law (through a judgment for monetary damages) offers no adequate remedy," and (5) that the court therefore should invoke its jurisdiction as a court of equity and order "specific performance" of the contract, meaning it should issue no judgment, but rather issue an order to Bertha that she convey the record itself when Hattie tenders her $5.

With that argument on these facts, Hattie's lawyer will likely succeed and the court will likely issue an order of specific performance, meaning an order that Bertha do as she contracted to do or find herself in contempt of court, which in turn subjects her to imprisonment (for ten days, perhaps, and then as long as she refuses still to comply). If, when Hattie tenders her $5, Bertha refuses to turn over the record, Hattie's lawyer will return to court asking that it find Hattie in contempt of court and send her to prison until she is willing to comply. The court should, ordinarily, do just that.

QUESTION 5. With respect to breach of contract, the remedy of specific performance

   I. inheres in a court order, which if disobeyed puts its recipient in contempt of court, for which she is subject to incarceration.
   II. is intended to afford the aggrieved party the position he would have occupied absent the breach.
   III. is no longer available in the United States.
   IV. is awarded only if the court concludes that a monetary award will not meaningfully afford plaintiff the position he would have occupied absent the breach.

   A. I
   B. III
   C. I, II, and III
   D. I, II, and IV

ANALYSIS. Specific performance is a remedy for breach of contract. It's a court order compelling the breaching party actually to perform. Option I is true. The remedy is intended to afford the aggrieved party the position she would have occupied absent the breach, meaning that option II is true as well. A court is to issue such an order when, in its opinion, monetary recovery (the *legal* remedy) will fail to achieve that end. Hence, option IV is true. Option

III reports that specific performance is not available in the United States, and that's false. It is available—from every state in the union. It is an "equitable remedy," meaning that it arose in the English equity courts. When issued in the United States today, the court invokes its jurisdiction as a court of equity. "Merger" does not alter that fact, wherefore option III is false. I, II, and IV are true. **D** is right.

2. Specific Performance as the Remedy in Real Estate Sales Contracts

Before proceeding, please read Appendix, section E. We'll wait for you right here.

Welcome back. Equity considers all real estate as unique (just as Great Aunt Lottie's record was unique to Hattie).[2] If seller and buyer agree on the sale of Blackacre for $500,000, and seller then wrongfully refuses to sell, then (1) equity acknowledges that the return of any purchase buyer paid in advance plus any difference between current market value and the contract price will afford buyer the *financial* position he would have occupied absent the breach, but (2) equity believes that such will not truly afford the buyer *the* position he would have occupied absent the breach.

The monetary award, equity believes, will not allow buyer to buy equivalent realty because no two parcels of realty are equivalent. In such a case, if buyer so chooses, the judge changes "hats" and becomes a chancellor. The court converts itself briefly from a law court to an equity court, whereupon the chancellor issues an order of specific performance. It *orders* seller to convey the property to buyer (subject, of course, to buyer's tender of the purchase price). Should the seller disobey, he'll be in contempt of court, for which the court (once again, acting as an equity court) might incarcerate him until he avows his willingness to obey the order.

QUESTION 6. On May 1, Sasha, owner of Redacre, forms a contract with Basha under which Basha is to make a $75,000 down payment on May 1; and, at a closing to occur on July 1, Sasha is to convey Redacre to Basha and Basha is to pay Sasha an additional $425,000 for a total purchase price of $500,000.

On May 31, Sasha correctly determines that during the previous two months Redacre has increased in value. She contacts Basha and advises her that she will return the $75,000 down payment and she will not,

---

2. Realty earned its special place in equity's heart because, in centuries past, English and American economies were largely agricultural. Land, more than any other asset, was the greatest show of wealth. Only one hundred fifty years ago, after all, to his daughter Scarlet, Gerald O'Hara imparted this wisdom: "Why land is the only thing worth working for, worth fighting for, worth dying for, for it's the only thing that lasts."

under any circumstances, convey the property. Basha receives from Sasha a $75,000 check, but she does not deposit it. Basha then brings an action against Sasha. Basha is probably entitled to

I. a remedy at law in the form of a judgment in an amount equal to $75,000 plus the difference between Redacre's present value and the $500,000 contract price.
II. a remedy at law in the form of specific performance.
III. an equitable remedy in the form of specific performance.
IV. an equitable remedy in the form of a court order requiring that Sasha convey Redacre to Basha.

A. I
B. III
C. I, III, and IV
D. II, III, and IV

ANALYSIS. Generally speaking, court orders such as those for specific performance are creatures of equity, not law. Option II characterizes specific performance as a legal remedy, so it's wrong. For a seller's breach of a contract to sell realty, equity is generally willing to grant the remedy of specific performance, as it believes that no parcel of realty is equal to any other. Consequently option III is true. Because specific performance is, in fact, a court order that a breaching party honor his contract by actually performing under its terms, option IV is true too. A buyer of realty may choose an ordinary legal remedy—a monetary judgment—if he prefers. Hence, I is true as well. I, III, and IV are true; II is not. So **C** is right.

C. The Closer

QUESTION 7. Adams is a theatrical celebrity. *Showstopper* magazine wants to publish her photo on the cover of its January 2013 issue. Adams and *Showstopper* contemplate a contract under which Adams will pose for a photograph and permit *Showstopper* to publish it on its January cover; *Showstopper* promises that it will in fact print the photograph on its January cover. Before making any agreement, the parties' lawyers speak:

Adams's Lawyer: There's something I don't love about this arrangement. If you folks breach, my client will be unable to show what damage she suffers—other than any money she spends in reliance on the contract. It will be difficult to know or show what gain, if any, she would have derived from the published picture.

Showstopper's Lawyer: I agree, that will be hard to show. And now that you mention it, if Adams should breach, it will be hard for *Showstopper* to show what gain it has lost.

Adams's Lawyer: True. I suggest that we include in the contract a liquidated damage provision for each of our clients.

Showstopper's Lawyer: Yes, I suppose we can do that. You know the drill, I'm sure: By law, we must choose an amount that is reasonable, not excessive or punitive.

Adams's Lawyer: Yes, I know. I, too, have read the Glannon Contract Guide.

Showstopper's Lawyer: Exactly. So we're talking about a big celebrity and a big magazine. I say that a $100,000 liquidated damage provision for each of us will be enforceable.

Adams's Lawyer: Agreed.

The lawyers prepare and the parties sign a document that includes these provisions:

1. Adams ("Celebrity") will pose for a photograph and permit *Showstopper* magazine to publish it on the cover of its January 2013 issue.
2. *Showstopper* magazine ("*Showstopper*") will in fact take the photograph and print it on the cover of its January 2013 issue.
3. **Liquidated Damages.** WHEREAS the parties hereto do agree that if either should commit a material breach, the damages to be suffered by the other, in the nature of this contract, will be difficult to quantify and prove, and do further agree that in light of that fact, a nonpunitive, nonexcessive amount of damage, reasonably calculated to compensate each party for a potential breach by the other, would be $100,000, wherefore the parties agree that (a) if Adams should fail substantially to fulfill her obligations hereunder by refusing to pose for the aforementioned photograph or by any other failure, then she will pay *Showstopper* damages in the amount of $100,000, and (b) if *Showstopper* should substantially fail to fulfill its obligations hereunder by failing to take and publish the aforementioned photograph, or by any other failure, then *Showstopper* will pay Adams damages in the amount of $100,000.

As the contract requires, Adams poses and *Showstopper* snaps the photo. *Showstopper* then decides, however, to publish the picture of some other celebrity on its January 2013 cover, and thus commits total breach of its contract with Adams. Pursuant to their contract, Adams seeks to recover from *Showstopper* $100,000 in liquidated damages.

At trial, Adams introduces the contract and its liquidated damage clause. Adams also introduces expert witnesses who testify that at the time the parties formed the contract there was no plausible basis on which to predict what damages *Showstopper*'s breach would cause Adams. *Showstopper* does not dispute that evidence but seeks to introduce evidence that Adams was offered the opportunity to have her photograph published by another prominent magazine but did not avail herself of that opportunity. Adams (through her lawyer) objects to the introduction of that evidence.

> **Adams's Lawyer:** Defendant *Showstopper* does not dispute that at the time these parties formed their contract, it was virtually impossible for reasonable people in their positions to predict what actual economic damage either would suffer from the other's breach. Consequently, they settled on a liquidated damage provision not for $100 million, or $10 million, or $1 million, but $100,000. Even if defendant can show now that plaintiff might have turned down an opportunity to have her photograph published in another magazine, such a showing is irrelevant. We object to the introduction of the evidence and, if defendant has no other evidence to present, we move for a directed verdict in our favor.

> **The Court:** I sustain the objection. Whatever the situation might truly be now, the validity of the liquidated damage clause depends on whether reasonable parties *at the time they formed their contract* would have believed that damages upon breach would be difficult to show, and that they agreed on liquidated damages that represented a reasonable attempt not to punish, but to compensate. Now, have you anything more to introduce?

> **Showstopper's Lawyer:** No, your honor, the defense rests.

> **The Court:** There is, then, nothing for a jury to consider. Plaintiff's motion for directed verdict is granted. Judgment for plaintiff in the amount of $100,000.

Which of the following changes to the foregoing story would most likely cause the court to deny Plaintiff's motion for a directed verdict?

A. The amount of liquidated damage on which the parties agreed was $1 billion.

B. The amount of liquidated damage on which the parties agreed was $25,000.

C. The liquidated damage provision provided for damage of $100,000 in the case of *Showstopper*'s breach, but did not set any amount of damage for Adams's breach.

D. The liquidated damage provision did not include the italicized text beginning with "whereas."

ANALYSIS.   Think of the law: In deciding to enforce a liquidated damage clause, a court wears the lens of reasonable persons at the time they form their contract. It will enforce the provision only if, thus taken back in time, it sees that the party who now wishes to recover on the clause would have thought when forming the contract: "If the other party breaches, the damages he causes me will be difficult to quantify and prove," and the amount of money chosen as liquidated damage is neither excessive nor punitive, but rather represents a reasonable attempt to compensate for true, actual damage.

The law does not require that a liquidated damage provision address a breach by both parties. It may address a breach by only one of them. For that reason, **C** is wrong. The law requires that the applicable criteria apply, but it certainly does not require that the parties, in their contract, state their belief that they apply. Hence, **D** is wrong as well. A liquidated damage provision cannot provide for excessive or punitive damages, but the parties do not invalidate their liquidated damage provision by choosing a figure that is *lower* than what they might justifiably have chosen. So **B** is wrong too. **A** refers to liquidated damages in the amount of $1 billion. That excessive amount would render the provision unenforceable. Hence, **A** is right.

That would leave Adams unable to collect through the liquidated damage provision. She would have to prove her actual damages. Should she be unable to do so, she would collect, of course, any moneys she had spent in reliance on the contract, but her expectation interest would be $0.

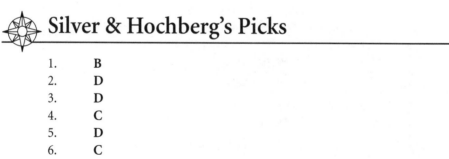

Silver & Hochberg's Picks

1.	B
2.	D
3.	D
4.	C
5.	D
6.	C
7.	A

31

Closing Closers

Here are some final questions to test your comprehension of the material covered in the preceding chapters. The answers are at the end, along with references to the chapter and section in which the tested material was covered.

Good luck!

QUESTION 1. Alicia says to Frank, "If you will offer me $100 to shovel the snow out of your driveway this morning, I promise that I will definitely accept. So, you need only make the offer and that will seal the deal." Frank replies, "I hereby offer you $100 to shovel the snow out of my driveway this morning." To his surprise, Alicia counters, "Well, I've changed my mind; I do not accept." If Frank insists that the parties have formed a contract, then his best argument is that

A. if at a first party's request a second party makes an offer, the first has no right then to reject it.

B. notwithstanding that Alicia purported to request an offer from Frank, Alicia herself made an offer that Frank accepted.

C. with their first two communications, Alicia and Frank formed an option contract.

D. one's promise to accept an offer needs no consideration to be binding.

QUESTION 2. George and Jacqueline are friends. On Monday, they meet by chance at a shopping mall. Jacqueline is accompanied by another of her friends whom George has never met. He has never heard of her and she has never heard of him. The friend's name happens also to be Jacqueline. When George encounters the two friends, he says, "Jacqueline, I've been meaning to call you, so I'm glad I've bumped into you. I need twelve illustrations for my next book and, of course, would like you to produce them. I'll need them by December 1, and I'll pay you $1,200. Will you do it?" George's friend Jacqueline does not immediately respond.

Rather, the other Jacqueline immediately responds, "Yes, I'll do it." A few seconds later, George's friend Jacqueline says, "No, he means me, and yes, I'll do it." Has George formed a contract with the other Jacqueline?

A. Yes, because when one makes an offer in the presence of two persons, only one has power to accept it

B. Yes, because, by law, the offer went to both women, and the other Jacqueline was first to manifest assent

C. No, because the other Jacqueline knew or should have known that George did not her know *name*.

D. No, because the other Jacqueline knew or should have known that George did not know *her*.

QUESTION 3. In each of the following cases, Party B proposes a modification to her preexisting contract with Party A. In which case does Party A's silence most likely amount to an acceptance of Party B's proposal?

A. On February 1, Parties A and B form a contract under which B is to empty A's basement on March 1, and A is to pay B $200 when the job is done. On February 15, B sends A an e-mail that reads, "As to our agreement that I empty your basement, I'd like to be paid $250 instead of the $200 on which we first agreed. I assume that you are agreeable." As of February 28, A makes no response.

B. On February 1, Parties A and B form a contract under which B is to empty A's basement on March 1, and A is to pay B $200 when the job is done. On February 15, B sends A an e-mail that reads, "As to our agreement that I empty your basement, I'd like to do the work on March 10 instead of March 1." As of February 28, A makes no response.

C. Party A is a professional seller of used carpenter's tools. Party B is a carpenter. On February 1, A makes to B this offer: "I will sell you the used lathe that you saw in my garage for $300, delivered on March 1 to your home, 46 Shepherd Drive." B promptly responds, "Yes, I accept, but I will not be home on March 1. Please deliver to my next-door neighbor, 48 Shepherd Drive, instead. I will alert her and she'll be there to accept delivery." As of February 28, A makes no response.

D. On February 1, A makes to B this offer: "I will sell you the used lathe that you saw in my garage, delivered to your home, 46 Shepherd Drive, on March 1, for $300." B promptly responds, "Yes, I accept, but I will pay only $200." As of February 28, A makes no response.

QUESTION 4. By signed writing, Randolph, an attorney, offers to sell his automobile to Endicott for $400. The writing is complete in all material respects and correctly identifies the vehicle's identification number. By signed writing, Endicott responds immediately, "I'd like to think it over for four or five days." Randolph responds with another signed writing: "That's fine." Two days later, Endicott observes someone other than Randolph driving and parking what appears to be Randolph's automobile. After the driver parks the car and emerges, Endicott asks her: "Is this your car?" She responds, "Yes, I bought it yesterday." With the driver's permission, Endicott examines the vehicle's identification number and correctly concludes that the automobile is the same one Randolph has offered to sell him. Later that same day, Endicott reaches Randolph by telephone and says, "I accept your offer to sell me your car." Randolph responds, "I'm sorry, it's sold." Which of the following facts most clearly indicates that Randolph is not in breach of contract?

A. When Endicott attempted to accept Randolph's offer, Randolph no longer owned the vehicle he had offered to sell Endicott.
B. Before attempting to accept Randolph's offer, Endicott learned that Randolph had sold the vehicle to another party.
C. By the time Endicott attempted to accept Randolph's offer, it had expired by passage of time.
D. Endicott, in making his offer, did not expressly provide that it would be irrevocable.

QUESTION 5. Sandoff and Barlow reach an agreement, recorded in a signed writing that embodies 25 paragraphs. Paragraphs 1 to 19 describe the parties' promises and set forth a variety of additional terms and conditions. Paragraph 20 provides:

> The parties agree and understand that notwithstanding any other agreements, commitments, or terms hereinbefore set forth, Barlow is free at any time, for good cause, before or after either party begins performance to cancel, renounce, dishonor, and withdraw from all promises, agreements, terms, and commitments by which he is, herein, otherwise bound.
>
> After the parties form their agreement, but before either begins to perform, Sandoff announces to Barlow that he will not honor their agreement. Sandoff claims the right to dishonor the agreement on the ground that Barlow made only an illusory promise, wherefore he and Barlow formed no contract. Which of the following phrases from paragraph 20 most weakens Sandoff's position?

A. "for good cause"
B. "before or after"
C. "purportedly bound"
D. "notwithstanding any other"

QUESTION 6. Chadwick walks through the center of Tarleton City and, for three hours, shouts repeatedly, on and on: "To any person who gives me an Indian head nickel, I will pay $500 right now." After three hours, Sheila and Charise emerge from their two homes, each holding an Indian head nickel. Sheila reaches Chadwick first. She tenders to him her nickel. Chadwick takes it and pays Sheila $500. Charise then reaches Chadwick. She tenders her nickel, but Chadwick rejects it, and refuses to pay her. The matter goes to court, Charise claiming that Chadwick had made an offer, that she had accepted, wherefore Chadwick owed her $500. Which of the following changes to the facts would most strengthen Charise's claim?

A. Instead of proposing to pay $500 for the nickel, Chadwick had proposed to pay only $200.
B. Instead of shouting "To *any* person . . . ," Chadwick had shouted, "To *every* person . . . "
C. Instead of dispatching his message by voice on the streets, Chadwick had dispatched it using written flyers left at all homes he passed.
D. Instead of shouting "anyone who *gives* me . . . ," Chadwick had shouted, "anyone who *in exchange gives* me."

QUESTION 7. Jones sends to Kirkwood an unsigned writing in which she states, "I am prepared to refurbish and rebuild your computer—the one we discussed—for $250, payable when I finish the work. Sign at the bottom of this writing and we have a deal (unless I am unable to secure the parts I need for the job)." At the bottom of the writing is a space designated for each of the parties' signatures. The space designated for Jones's signature is blank. On receiving the writing, Kirkwood signs in the space designated for his signature and sends the writing back to Jones. Two days later, Jones receives it. She telephones Kirkwood and says, "I've received back my writing, signed by you, but I have decided not to sign it. We don't have a deal." Has Jones committed an anticipatory repudiation?

A. Yes, because Jones's unsigned writing constituted his offer, which Kirkwood accepted by signing his name and returning the writing to Jones

B. Yes, because Jones made an offer for a unilateral contract and Kirkwood, by signing the writing, began his performance, thus forming with Jones an option contract

C. No, because Jones's unsigned writing constituted only an invitation to deal, meaning that Kirkwood, by signing and returning the document, made not an acceptance but an offer

D. No, because the parenthetical clause in Jones's letter meant that her proposal failed to exact consideration from her

---

QUESTIONS 8 & 9. Lampert, a professional musician, says to Norberg, a manufacturer of computer motherboards, "I'm interested in buying your land, Blueacre." Norberg responds, "Well, you can have it for $3 million. That's my offer." "I'd like you to promise that you'll hold that offer open for four months so that I may consider it," replies Lampert.

QUESTION 8. The conversation continues: "Absolutely," says Norberg. "The offer is good for four months. I won't take it back." Lampert answers, "Great. Let's put it in writing." The parties then sign a writing that fully sets forth their names and addresses. It describes Blueacre in full legal detail, and provides that:

> Norberg hereby offers to convey Blueacre to Lampert for $3 million, this offer not to be revoked or withdrawn for four months."

Is Norberg free, immediately, to advise Lampert that he will not sell him Blueacre and then sell it to some other buyer?

A. Yes, because the prescribed period of irrevocability exceeds three months

B. Yes, because the subject matter of the sale is not a computer motherboard

C. No, because the parties have effectively formed an option contract

D. No, because equity considers that all realty is unique and its owner cannot be compelled to part with it, even if he has contracted to do so

---

QUESTION 9. Now assume that the parties continue their conversation thus: "Okay," replies Norberg, "but you'll have to pay me $25,000 now for that privilege. Agree to that, and I won't take the offer back for four months." Lampert agrees, again saying, "Great. Let's put it in writing." The parties then sign a writing that fully sets forth their names and addresses. It describes Blueacre in full legal detail, and provides that:

In exchange for $25,000 to be paid by Lampert one month from the date hereof, Norberg hereby offers to convey Blueacre to Lampert for $3 million, this offer not to be revoked or withdrawn for four months.

Is Norberg free, immediately, to advise Lampert that he will not sell him Blueacre and then sell it to some other buyer?

A. Yes, because the prescribed period of irrevocability exceeds three months
B. Yes, because the subject matter of the sale is not a computer motherboard
C. No, because the parties have effectively formed an option contract
D. No, because equity considers that all realty is unique and its owner cannot be compelled to part with it, even if he has contracted to do so

---

QUESTIONS 10 & 11. On March 1, Janus and Kellman agree, orally, that Janus will replace all windows in Kellman's office building. Kellman is to buy and pay for the windows and all other supplies. Janus is then to install the windows. He is to begin work on April 15 and finish by June 30. Kellman is to pay Janus $1.5 million for the entire job, in three installments: $500,000 on April 15, $500,000 on April 30, and $500,000 when the work is complete on June 30.

Question 10. The parties also agree, as part of that same oral contract, that Janus will repaint all of the building's window sills. Having formed their contract orally, the parties create a writing that fully, exhaustively, and completely describes every detail concerning the way in which Janus is to replace the windows, the kind of windows and sealants he is to use, and the timing by which Kellman will pay him. The writing is silent as to the painting of any window sills, and its last paragraph provides:

This writing represents the whole of the parties' agreement on this subject matter, wherefore in this regard, no other term on which they might have agreed, by whatever mode, means, or medium, is binding on them.

On April 1, each party has his own copy of the writing, but neither has signed it. By telephone, they speak:

Janus: Well, I have my copy of the writing, and it's fine. Are we agreed—definitely—that this writing is our contract?
Kellman: Yes, we're agreed—definitely—that this writing is our contract.
Janus: Okay, then. Next time we meet we'll sign it. Right?
Kellman: Right.

> **Janus:** So I'll begin work on April 15, and on April 15 you'll pay me $500,000.
>
> **Kellman:** Yes, that's what our contract requires.
>
> **Janus:** Very good.

Is Janus obliged to paint the window sills?

A. Probably, because the window sills are separate from the windows
B. Probably not, because the contract would otherwise be unconscionable
C. Probably not, because the writing is most likely a total integration of their agreement
D. Probably not, because neither party signed the writing

QUESTION 11. Now assume that with their oral contract the parties agree also that Janus warrants that the windows, as installed by him, will remain free of leaks for ten years. That provision the parties do include in their writing, although as noted in Question 10, they do not include in the writing any term as to the repainting of the window sills. The parties then conduct the same conversation described in Question 10. As of April 15, after the parties have their conversation, have they formed an enforceable contract?

A. Yes, because the parties adopted the writing as a total integration
B. Yes, because the writing specifically includes the warranty term
C. No, because neither party signed the writing
D. No, because the writing is probably a total integration of their agreement

QUESTION 12. On July 1, Buyer calls Seller to say, "I may need some widgets on September 1 — 3,000 of them. If I decide that I do need them, will you be able specially to manufacture them for me?" Seller replies, "I'm not sure. Let me find out and get back to you." The next day, Seller sends Buyer this signed writing labeled "sales confirmation":

> Regarding our conversation of yesterday: Yes, I'll be able to specially manufacture the widgets — 3,000 of them for delivery to you on September 1.

Seller then begins work and tenders 3,000 widgets to Buyer on September 1. Buyer refuses to accept or pay for them. Is Buyer in breach of contract?

A. Yes, because Seller's July 2 writing removed the contract from the Statute of Frauds
B. Yes, because Seller's special manufacture of the goods removed the contract from the Statute of Frauds
C. No, because the parties did not agree on price
D. No, because the parties did not form a contract

QUESTION 13. After attending his cousin's wedding reception, Andrews, 50 years old, with $2,000 to his name—all of it sitting in his pocket as cash—is so wholly inebriated as not to understand his own actions or the results they might produce. Notwithstanding his state of intoxication, he appears to ordinary persons to be sober. In that condition, he enters the Black Bear Smoke Shoppe and there sees for sale a box of ten cigars with a $2,000 price tag, "all taxes included." Black Bear Smoke Shoppe had bought the box of cigars for $1,000. Andrews takes the box to the cashier, who is a stranger, and states that he wishes to purchase it. He then puts on the cashier's counter $2,000 pulled from his pocket. The cashier processes the purchase and hands Andrews the box of cigars. Andrews leaves the store and promptly chain-smokes all ten cigars. On the following day, Andrews returns to the store. He tenders back the cigar box empty of cigars, and asks to have back his $2,000. He is entitled to have back

A. nothing, because he smoked all of the cigars.
B. nothing, because his inebriation was not obvious to a reasonable person in the cashier's position.
C. $1,000, the difference between $2,000 paid by Andrews and $1,000 paid by Black Bear Smoke Shoppe to its supplier.
D. $2000, all of the money he paid for the cigars.

QUESTION 14. Bruce, 14 years old, enters ElectroniMart, a retail electronics store, and for $300 purchases a device called HiPod. Before the day is out, Bruce decides to sell the HiPod for $250, which he does, then spending the $250 on spray paint, all of which he uses to write graffiti on his high school's exterior walls. Bruce then demands from ElectroniMart a return of his $300, offering the store nothing back in exchange. Is ElectroniMart obliged to return the $300?

A. Yes, because it is in the business of selling electronic equipment at retail
B. Yes, because Bruce is empowered to disaffirm the contract and retains no value related to the HiPod

C. No, because Bruce's use of the spray paint probably violates public policy

D. No, because Bruce voluntarily disposed of the HiPod for money, and knowingly spent the proceeds on another commodity

---

QUESTION 15. Marjorie and Dalia are 19-year-old girls, both of them competent (but stupid). They decide to play their own version of the game called chicken, using trains instead of automobiles. Each girl is to take a turn standing on the local railroad tracks as a train approached her. She who allows the moving train to come closest to her before jumping off of the tracks wins the game. The loser is to pay the winner $1,000.

After agreeing by offer and acceptance to play the game according to those rules, Marjorie takes the first turn on the tracks. She allows the train to come within 30 feet of her body and jumps from the tracks. Dalia takes her turn and allows a train to come within 25 feet of her body. As winner, Dalia demands that Marjorie pay her $1,000. Is Marjorie obliged to pay?

A. Yes, because the parties are competent adults, generally free to form their contracts as they wish

B. Yes, because each party's conditional promise to pay $1,000 to the other makes for mutuality of consideration

C. No, because Dalia's participation in the contract violates public policy

D. No, because Marjorie's participation in the contract violates public policy

---

QUESTION 16. Sanford employs Bella by signed written contract to serve as a pharmacist for one year in Sanford's pharmacy. The agreed compensation is $9,400 per month, payable monthly with ordinary income and payroll taxes to be deducted, thus leaving a monthly take-home amount of about $6,100. At the end of that first month, Sanford pays Bella $6,100 (properly withholding and crediting the unpaid amounts) but says that he is dissatisfied with her work. He offers to pay her an additional $9,400 in full if she gives up her employment with him. Bella refuses. Nonetheless, Sanford sends Bella a $9,400 check with a signed note that reads: "I tender this check as per our earlier conversation regarding your employment with me." Bella deposits the check. On the following day, Bella reports for work at the pharmacy and says to Sanford, "I thank you for the additional check. I will consider it an advance on the salary due me at the end of this month." Sanford responds, "You no longer work here; by agreement, you have given up your employment." Bella brings suit against Sanford for breach of an employment contract. As a defense, Sanford asserts accord and satisfaction. Bella moves to dismiss the defense. Which of the following additional facts, if proven, would most strengthen Bella's position?

A. Sanford's check "bounced"; it did not clear his bank.
B. By depositing Sanford's check, Bella did not genuinely intend to accept Sanford's proposal that she give up her employment.
C. Bella's job performance, although not satisfactory to Sanford, was adequate under ordinary standards prevailing among pharmacists.
D. Bella was reasonably relying on the $9,400 monthly salary to meet commitments she had made before accepting employment with Sanford.

QUESTION 17. At the trial of a suit by plaintiff Seller against defendant Buyer for alleged breach of a contract for the purchase and sale of Lift Springs, undisputed evidence tended to show:

1. On many occasions during each of the years 2002 through 2007, Buyer ordered Torto Lift Springs from Seller, whereupon Seller, on each such occasion, delivered the goods together with a billing statement showing a "catalog list price" and "billing price" of $1,500 per unit. On each such occasion, Buyer paid the $1,500 per unit, and Seller accepted it as full payment.
2. During the years 2008 to 2012, Buyer made no purchases from Seller.
3. On January 1, 2013, Buyer issued to Seller a signed, written purchase order requesting "prompt shipment of 200 Torto Lift Springs; appropriately priced." On January 2, Seller confirmed the order in a signed writing that did not mention price, and then immediately shipped and delivered 200 such units together with a billing statement showing a "catalog list price" and "billing price" of $2,500 per unit. The total bill was $500,000 ($2,500 × 200).
4. On January 2, 2013, Seller's catalog list price for the Torto Lift Springs was, in fact, $2,500 per unit.
5. The average price actually billed by suppliers other than Seller for Torto Lift Springs within 100 miles of Buyer's facility during the preceding 12 months was $1,900 per unit, although the average *catalog* price for such other suppliers was $2,550.
6. When the goods arrived at Buyer's premises, Buyer examined the billing statement, whereupon she rejected the goods and refused to pay for them, advising Seller that the price was "too high."

In Seller's suit against buyer, which of the following phrases would least likely appear in the court's charge to the jury?

A. "course of dealing"
B. "prevailing market price"
C. "course of performance"
D. "reasonable price"

QUESTIONS 18-20. On June 1, Georgia Morales receives by mail from Universal Insurance Co. a document entitled "Offer of Life Insurance." Although Georgia has had no previous contact with the company, the "offer" correctly states her name and age. Under its title, the document reads:

> We are pleased to offer you a $2 million life insurance policy. Should you die within the next 20 years, Universal Insurance will pay $2 million to the beneficiary you name. If you wish to accept, complete the health questionnaire that appears on the next page and, in the indicated space, provide the name, address, and social security number of the person whom you wish to receive the benefit under your policy. Send the completed form back to us at the address shown above. Our approval and premium/cost will depend on our evaluation of your responses.

Georgia completes the health questionnaire, reporting the truth as she knows it. Asked if she has ever had any disease of the brain or blood vessels, she answers "no." As beneficiary, she names her daughter Angela Morales, providing Angela's name, address, and social security number. On June 2, Georgia mails the completed form back to Universal Insurance. On June 15, she receives from Universal a second mailing entitled "Insurance Approval." It states:

> Based on your responses to our health questionnaire, we are pleased to advise you that a $2 million insurance policy is available to you, for 20 years, at a cost of $300 per month. The initial beneficiary will be Angela Morales subject to change at any time, if and as you wish. You need only sign and send back to us the enclosed purchase form in the enclosed envelope, together with a check or money order in the amount of $300.00 for your first month's premium, payable to Universal Life Insurance Co.

The "purchase form" states only this: "I wish to purchase Universal life insurance, as described to me." Georgia signs the form and, together with her $300 check payable to Universal, packs it in the designated envelope. She deposits the envelope in the U.S. mails on June 16.

Although Georgia does not know it, and has no reason to know it, she has been born with a cerebral aneurysm. On June 17, the aneurysm ruptures and she instantly dies. On June 18, Universal receives the mailing she had dispatched on June 16. On that same day, Universal learns of Georgia's death and refrains from depositing her check. It writes to her daughter Angela:

> Your mother, Georgia Morales, applied with this office for a life insurance policy naming you as beneficiary. We learned today of her death, and we express our sympathies. We presently hold, undeposited, the check that she tendered to us as her first premium payment. Please provide us with the name and address of the party handling her estate, and we will return the check to him or her.

Angela visits an attorney who, on her behalf, brings an action against Universal, demanding judgment in the amount of $2 million. At trial, undisputed evidence establishes all of the facts described above. Universal argues that it owes nothing to Angela because it never formed a contract with Georgia and, even if it had, (a) it never formed a contract with Angela, and (b) it was freed from its obligations under any such contract on the ground of mutual mistake. As to mutual mistake, Universal observes that when it interacted with Georgia, (1) the cerebral aneurysm was in place, (2) neither Georgia nor Universal knew of it, (3) neither party was at fault for failing to know of it, and (4) Georgia's responses on the health questionnaire were basic assumptions on which the parties had dealt.

QUESTION 18. Did Georgia and Universal form a contract?

A. Yes, when Georgia dispatched her mailing of June 2
B. Yes, when Georgia dispatched her mailing of June 16
C. No, because Universal did not deposit Georgia's check
D. No, because $300 is inadequate to constitute consideration for a promise to pay $2 million

QUESTION 19. If Universal and Georgia did form a contract, is Universal entitled to avoid it on the basis of mutual mistake?

A. Yes, because from June 1 to June 16, both parties were justifiably ignorant of the cerebral aneurysm
B. Yes, because as between the two parties, Georgia was in the better position to discover that she had a cerebral aneurysm
C. No, because each party to the transaction deliberately undertook risk
D. No, because Universal did not insist that Georgia undergo a medical examination

> **QUESTION 20.** If Universal did form a contract with Georgia and is unable successfully to assert mutual mistake as a defense, does it owe $2 million to Angela?
>
> **A.** Yes, because both parties should have understood that Georgia wished Angela to benefit from the contract
> **B.** Yes, because Georgia, in effect, assigned her contractual rights to Angela
> **C.** No, because Angela is an incidental third-party beneficiary
> **D.** No, because Angela fails to constitute a creditor beneficiary

✦ Silver & Hochberg's Picks

Question 1.   From Chapter 2, section B, you know that one makes an offer when, to some other person, she proposes an arrangement in such a way as would lead the other reasonably to believe that a definite bargain is proposed to him, that he is invited to assent to it, and that if he does, he will finalize the bargain. You know also that one may make an offer without using the *word* "offer" (Chapter 2, section B). Here, Alicia purported to *solicit* an "offer" of specified terms and promised absolutely that she would accept it; she promised that Frank's "offer" would "seal the deal." Alicia thus *made* an offer (even though she purportedly invited Frank to make one). She invited Frank to assent by *purporting* to make an offer. When, in response, Frank purported to make the offer, he assented to the bargain that Alicia had proposed, and therefore issued an acceptance (even though he termed it an "offer"). That these parties turned upside down the *words* "offer" and "acceptance" matters not. Alicia made an offer and Frank accepted it. **B** is right.

Question 2.   In Chapter 2, section D, you learned that we identify an offeree according to reasonable beliefs: With respect to any offer, an offeree is any person who, under the circumstances, reasonably believes that the offeror has made his proposal to her and that she is invited to assent to it.

Under these circumstances, the other Jacqueline could not reasonably believe that George intended to make his proposal to her. She knew (or certainly should have known) that George did not know her and would not say, to *her*, "I've been meaning to call you, so I'm glad I've bumped into you." Hence, she should have known that George was not addressing her. **D** reflects that reasoning, and it's the right answer.

What's wrong with **C**? It tells us that the other Jacqueline was not the offeree because she should have known that George was unfamiliar with her *name*. That's not quite right, and here's how we prove it: Suppose that when the three parties met, George's friend Jacqueline had said, "George, I want you to meet my friend, whose name happens also to be Jacqueline." At that point, the other Jacqueline would have reason to think that George now knew her name. Yet, that would not change our answer from "no" to "yes." When George said, "I've been meaning to call you, so I'm glad I've bumped into you," this lady should know, still, that George was not addressing her, because even having learned her name, he did not know *her*. In concluding that this lady was not an offeree, our critical observation is not George's unfamiliarity with her *name*, but his unfamiliarity with *her*. Hence, **D** is right.

Question 3.   In Chapter 14, section B (and elsewhere), you learned that by common law if two parties first form a contract, they may effectively modify it only if, in doing so, each provides consideration to the other. But you also learned that UCC §2-209(1) departs significantly from that rule when the contract involves the sale of goods, by stating: "An agreement modifying a contract within this article needs no consideration to be binding." Further, UCC §2-207(1) and (2) govern "expressions of acceptance," contract modifications, and a merchant party's silence as assent (Chapter 11, sections B, C, and D).

In **A**, Party B proposes to modify an existing contract without providing that he will give consideration to A. Even if A had overtly purported to accept, the attempted modification would be ineffective. That alone means **A** is wrong. **B** and **D** are wrong for the same reason. In **C**, Party A makes an offer and Party B responds with an "expression of acceptance," thus (1) forming a contract on A's terms and, at the same time, (2) proposing to modify that very contract as to the place of delivery. Both parties are merchants, the proposed change is immaterial, Party A, in his offer, did not object to any change in terms, and finally, after receiving B's response, Party A remained silent for a full two weeks. Hence, Party B's proposed change as to place of delivery likely becomes part of the contract; A's silence acts as his acceptance. (And although the UCC allows two parties to modify an existing contract irrespective of consideration, this particular modification did exact consideration from both parties. B released A from the obligation to deliver to B's home, and A, in exchange, took on a new obligation: to deliver at the next-door neighbor's home.) **C** is right.

Question 4.   In Chapter 6, section D, you learned that an offeror may dictate the time at which his offer expires. If he doesn't do that, it expires at such time as is reasonable under the circumstances. On learning that Endicott wished to ponder the offer for several days, Randolph responded, "That's fine." Randolph thus restated his offer (implicitly) and provided that, for at least a week, it would not expire. Two days later, therefore, it had not expired by passage of time. **C** is wrong.

It's true that Randolph offered to sell a good, and that UCC Article 2 applies generally to the transaction. But Randolph is an attorney; for this transaction, he's not a merchant. Consequently, the Article 2 "firm offer" provision (Chapter 11, section A) does not apply to him as to this offer. Even if Randolph's signed, written offer had proclaimed itself irrevocable (with or without stating an associated time period), it would be revocable. Hence, **D** is wrong. **A** too is wrong, and here's why: Revocation is effective only when communicated to the offeree (Chapter 8, section A). If one offers to sell a good to one party and then sells it to another (or otherwise loses ownership), he does not, with that alone, communicate revocation to his original offeree. Yet, as you learned in Chapter 8, section C, effective revocation requires no *direct* communication from offeror to offeree. If an offeree learns not from the offeror but from some other source that the offeror cannot or will not stand by her offer, then the offer is effectively revoked. That's what happened here, and **B** properly attributes revocation to that fact. **B** is right.

Question 5. In Chapter 14, section D, you learned that if one purports to make a promise but then by some attached term reserves the right to dishonor it unconditionally, for any reason or no reason, then he makes an "illusory promise," or no promise at all. One party who, with respect to a purported contract, makes to the other only an illusory promise gives no consideration, and the two parties fail to form a contract.

Here, however, Barlow does not quite reserve for himself the right to dishonor his promise at his own unbridled whim. Rather, he reserves the right to do so for "good cause." Although the agreement may nowhere define that phrase, those two words do refer to some objective standard that sits apart from Barlow's own unfettered fancy. Hence, a court will take it on itself to decide how two reasonable parties should understand the phrase "good cause"—that it means, perhaps, grave illness, unforeseen weather conditions, family emergency, or the like. Of all phrases listed in answer choices **A** through **D**, only "good cause" arguably means that Barlow's promises (whatever they be) are genuine and not illusory ones. That's why **A** is right.

Question 6. In Chapter 5, section A, you learned that an ordinary advertisement is a mere invitation to deal, but an advertisement that is extraordinarily specific as to available quantity and/or the person(s) addressed is an offer.

The fact that Chadwick shouts his message personally on the streets tends to make the message more personal than would be a printed advertisement. Hence, **C** is wrong. Chadwick's message clearly contemplates an exchange and adding the *word* "exchange" would make no significant difference. Hence, **D** is wrong. The price that Chadwick proposed to pay is wholly irrelevant to the question of whether he made an offer and, if so, how many persons became offerees. Hence, **A** is wrong.

If Chadwick's message is an offer, then the words "every person" make relatively plain that he directs it at all persons who hear him. The words "any person" arguably mean that he contemplates paying for only one nickel. Pursuant to that argument (a decent one), all who heard Chadwick shouting his message should have understood him to mean that he would pay $500 only to the *first person* who tendered an Indian head nickel. Hence, **B** is right.

Question 7. In Chapter 5, section C, you learned that *ordinarily* a proposal or "draft contract" that bears a marked space for the proposor's signature is an offer if the proposor has signed, and an invitation to deal if she has not. But "ordinarily" doesn't mean "always." If she who sends the unsigned proposal makes abundantly clear that she intends it to constitute a definite proposal for a bargain that awaits only the recipient's assent, then the unsigned proposal *is* an offer. The recipient has power to accept it.

B and **D** are wrong. Jones did not demand that Kirkwood manifest his assent by actually making the $250 payment. Hence, she did not make an offer for a unilateral contract (Chapter 9, sections C and D). Jones's parenthetical remark did not create an illusory promise (Chapter 14, section D). Rather, it subjected her commitment to a condition subsequent (Chapter 21, section A).

If Jones had sent this same unsigned writing without its last sentence, then certainly the writing would have constituted only an invitation to deal. Upon signing the document and returning it to Jones, Kirkwood would then make an offer that Jones would be free to accept or not. And in that case, **C** would be right. By including in her message that last sentence, however, Jones made abundantly clear that she intended it to constitute a definite proposal for a bargain. For that reason, **A** is right.

Question 8.   Generally the common law provides that one who makes an offer may revoke at any time before the offeree accepts. That's so even when he promises not to do so (Chapter 6, section A). Yet, two parties may form an "option contract," which is a contract in and of itself, requiring offer, acceptance, and consideration from both its parties. More specifically, an option contract is a contract in which one party, for a consideration, agrees to hold an offer open and irrevocable for some stated period (Chapter 6, section B).

These parties have formed no such thing because Lampert gave no consideration for Norberg's promise to hold his offer open. **C** is wrong. As for **D**, it's true that equity regards all realty as unique (Appendix, section E). That means, only, that when one breaches his contract to sell realty, the buyer might obtain the remedy of specific performance, compelling the seller to convey the realty. Hence, **D** is wrong. UCC Article 2 provides that if a merchant who by signed writing makes an offer to buy or sell goods and proclaims it irrevocable, the offer *is* irrevocable for any time stated or, if none is stated, for a reasonable time, but in no case for more than three months. This transaction involves the sale not of goods but of realty. Hence, that rule does not apply in any respect. Whether Norberg had specified a time period of three seconds or three hundred years, he would be entitled, immediately, to revoke his offer. (Furthermore, where the Code's "firm offer" rule does apply, an offeror who proclaims his offer irrevocable for four months creates an offer that's irrevocable for *three* months (Chapter 11, section A)). **A** is wrong.

As to motherboards, Norberg is a merchant (Chapter 11, section A). If this signed written offer *had* pertained to a motherboard, then the Code's "firm offer" rule would apply, and the offer would be irrevocable for three months, not four. Reciprocally, we may say that because the transaction does *not* involve motherboards, Lampert is free immediately to revoke his offer. So, **B** is right.

Question 9.   Question 9 differs from Question 8 in that Norberg promised to *pay* Lampert for the option to accept his offer at any time during a four-month period. These parties thus formed an option contract, and for four months Norberg (the optionor) must remain ready, willing, and able to sell Blueacre to Lampert (the optionee). That's why he is not "free, immediately, to advise Lampert that he will not sell him Blueacre and then sell it to some other buyer." **A**, **B**, and **D** are wrong; **C** is right.

Question 10.   In order that a contractual writing should constitute an integration, the two contracting parties must "adopt" it as an expression of their agreement. Ordinarily they manifest the adoption by signing, but they need not do it that way. These two parties formed an agreement orally and then reduced it to a writing, which via their conversation, they plainly adopted as a final expression of their contract — even though they did not sign it (Chapter 19, section C, footnote 3). This writing is probably a total integration since it shows finality as to all matters ordinarily necessary to a contract for replacement of windows and, furthermore, features a merger clause (Chapter 19, sections F and G). Consequently, the parol evidence rule renders unenforceable the prior oral agreement as to the window sills. The exception concerning a "collateral agreement" (Chapter 19, section I) is inapplicable here because the oral agreement as to the window sills, we are told, was part of the same oral contract. Hence, **B** is right.

Question 11.   In Chapter 15, section A, you learned that the Statute of Frauds applies to all contracts that, in their nature, cannot be fully performed within one year. A contract wherein one warranties his work for ten years cannot complete his performance in one. Until the ten years pass, his performance is not complete. Hence, this contract falls within the Statute of Frauds, which requires that the contract be set forth in a writing, *signed* by any party against whom it is to be enforced. Neither party signed the writing, wherefore, after these parties form their contract and adopt the writing, it is unenforceable under the Statute of Frauds, precisely because they did not *sign* it. **C** is right.

Question 12.   The rule given in Chapter 11, section F, concerning UCC §2-207 and the written confirmation, has no bearing on this case. The parties' conversation reveals that they never formed a contract. Seller's "sales confirmation" was in fact an offer, nothing more, and Buyer never accepted it. Seller moved ahead as though he and Buyer had created a contract, but that was his mistake, and the result his problem. Furthermore, because the parties never formed a contract, any matter bearing on the Statute of Frauds or on "gap filling" are similarly irrelevant to the problem. Hence, **A**, **B**, and **C** are wrong. **D** is right.

Question 13.   Chapter 16, section C, teaches that when a competent adult forms a contract with an adult who is so mentally impaired as not to appreciate the nature or consequences of his actions, the contract is voidable at the option of the incompetent adult, *whether or not the impairment was objectively* *apparent.* If the impaired adult elects to rescind the contract, then each party must make the other whole—restore the other to status quo ante.

In order that these parties make each other whole, Black Bear Smoke Shoppe must return $2,000 box of cigars so that it may buy a new one from its supplier. In net terms, therefore, Black Bear Smoke Shoppe must pay Andrews $1,000. **C** is right.

Question 14.   By contract Bruce, a minor, bought a good from ElectroniMart. According to the rule given in Chapter 16, section B, Bruce may disaffirm the contract, whereby he rescinds it. That leaves ElectroniMart with unjust enrichment in the amount of $300. It must return that amount to Bruce. Having sold the HiPod, thereafter spending the proceeds of that sale, Bruce no longer retained any value that came to him via the contract. Hence, he need return nothing to ElectroniMart. Like it or not—**B** is right.

Question 15.   In Chapter 17, section A, you learned that an "illegal contract" is one that violates public policy, which almost certainly includes a monetary bet in which each party seriously risks her life. And when a party alleges breach of an illegal contract, her recovery depends primarily on whether *her participation* in the contract violates public policy. She does not recover if public policy is offended by her own performance under the contract or by her wish to induce the other party's performance (Chapter 17, section B).

Here, each party's participation violates public policy: Each party risks her life to win a $1,000 bet, and induces the other to do the same. (To the right of the word "because," Choices **A** and **B** make true statements. (As to Choice **B**, see Chapter 14, section A.) Each begins, however, with the word "yes," and that makes both **A** and **B** wrong.) Because it is Dalia who seeks to enforce the contract, *her* participation—*her* violation of public policy—denies her the right to recover. That's why **D** is wrong and **C** is right.

Question 16.   In Chapter 14, section C, you read about "accord and satisfaction" as a defense to an action for breach of contract. It often happens that (1) two parties form a contract, (2) one of them plausibly alleges that the other breached, (3) the other acknowledges (or, more often, denies) that she has breached, and (4) the parties agree to settle their dispute by revising their contract in some way that provides consideration to both. In that situation, the revised agreement is an "executory accord."

Very often, a first party proposes an accord to a second by tendering a check for some amount below an agreed contract price, offering it in final settlement of a dispute as to the second party's breach. By sending such a check, with notice or prior notice that it is offered in settlement as to a (plausible) allegation of breach, the sender offers to make an executory accord. If the recipient deposits the check, she accepts that offer and the parties form the accord. If, however, the sender's check then "bounces," the sender fails to satisfy the accord. In that case, the defense of accord and satisfaction is unavailable to him.

Here, Sanford said he was dissatisfied with Bella's work. If his dissatis-faction arose through some colorable belief that Bella was in breach of her contract, then his statements to her, his check, and his note made an offer of accord. Bella accepted by depositing the check, thus forming an executory accord. But if Sanford's check were then to bounce, Sanford would fail to give satisfaction (fail to honor his obligations under the accord). Bella would then be free to sue Sanford for breach of the accord or the original contract. In either case, Sanford would lose any possible defense of accord and satisfaction. That's why **A** is right.

Question 17. Since this case concerns the sale of goods, the relevant provi-sions are those of the UCC, Article 2 (which on this point are substantially identical to those of the common law). As explained in Chapter 18, section B, according to UCC §2-208(1), "course of dealing" refers to the meanings and interpretations that evolve between two particular parties over the contracts they form with one another over time. "Course of performance" applies only to a contract that calls for *multiple occasions of performance*. It refers to the meanings and interpretation on which the parties, by behavior and silence, appear to agree as they give performance of one particular contract.

This contract does not call for multiple occasions of performance and so the phrase "course of performance" has no relevance. For that reason, **C** is right.

Question 18. Look for an offer and acceptance. Universal named its first communication "offer" but proposed no bargain; it did not describe what Georgia was to pay in exchange for the $2 million insurance coverage. Rather, it indicated that cost/premium were not yet identified, and further stated that Universal had not yet "approved" the arrangement. As a reasonable person, Georgia could not believe that a definite bargain had been proposed to her, to be finalized only by her assent. Universal's first communication was a mere invitation to deal, meaning that Georgia's June 2 response was not an accep-tance. **A** is wrong.

Universal's June 15 communication proposed that Georgia pay $300 per month for 20 years, in exchange for Universal's promise to pay, if Georgia should die during that period, $2 million to Angela or any other beneficiary whom Georgia might someday name in her stead. Universal thus made an offer. Universal specified the manner by which Georgia might accept (although it did not use the *word* "accept"). She was to sign a paper and send a $300 check. Georgia manifested her assent exactly as Universal requested, and her acceptance was effective on June 16 when she dispatched it (Chapter 8, section A). That Universal did not deposit her check is irrelevant (in *this* case). **C** is wrong. As for **D**: If Georgia truly agreed to pay $300 per month in exchange for an absolute promise of $2 million, the arrangement might fail to exact consideration from Georgia (Chapter 12, section C). But that didn't happen. Universal promised to pay $2 million subject to the condition precedent that Georgia die (Chapter 21, section A). **D** is wrong, and **B** is right.

Question 19.   We interpret contracts according to each party's manifestation of intent—according to the understandings that each party should reasonably attribute to the other (Chapter 18, section A). In Chapter 22, sections A and B, you learned that mutual mistake applies only if two parties form a contract, each manifesting to the other a belief—to the point of fact or basic assumption—that some fact is or is not so. If, on the other hand, two parties form a contract that, properly interpreted, allocates to one or both the risk that some fact is or is not so, then as to that fact, each party takes his chances.

Insurance of any kind is, perhaps, the quintessential contract in which each party leads the other to understand that she knowingly, deliberately, takes on a risk. Any insurer that sells a homeowner's fire insurance policy should understand that the purchaser/insured intends to take the risk that her home will *not* burn and that, in the end, she will have paid insurance premiums without recovering a monetary benefit. The purchaser should reasonably understand that the insurance company takes on the risk that the future is unpredictable and that the home *will* burn. The same applies, of course, to life insurance. Georgia and Universal formed a contract in which each deliberately took a risk as to unknown circumstances, present and future. Georgia took the risk that she might live beyond 20 years and have nothing to show for the $72,000 she will have paid Universal. Universal took the risk that Georgia might die 10 years, 1 year, 1 week, or 1 minute after making her first premium payment. Universal has no defense in mutual mistake. **C** is right.

Question 20.   One assigns her contractual right by manifesting her intention presently to transfer her own existing right to another (Chapter 24, section B). As Universal's offer and hence the resulting contract provide: "The initial beneficiary will be Angela Morales subject to change at any time, if and as you wish." It is Georgia's right, if she should die within the 20-year period, to have Universal pay $2 million to Angela or to any other person she might later select. Georgia did not transfer *that* right to Angela. **B** is wrong.

One who stands as a third-party beneficiary to a contract formed between two others may sustain an action for breach as to a benefit of which she is deprived if she is an *intended* beneficiary, but *not* if she is a mere *incidental* beneficiary (Chapter 24, section A). Universal knew or should have known that Georgia intended her named beneficiary (Angela, at present) to benefit from this insurance contract. Accordingly, Georgia was reasonable in believing that Universal did know that. Consequently, as to this contract, Angela is an intended third-party beneficiary. **C** is wrong. It's true that Angela is not a creditor beneficiary (Chapter 24, section A), but that doesn't negate her status as *intended* beneficiary. **D** is wrong, and **A** is right.

Appendix: All About Law

A. What Is Law, and Who Makes It?

Law is our government's decree as to how we should behave. To the degree that our government is of, by, and for the people, law is our own collective code of right and wrong. For "unlawful" (wrongful) behavior, the government holds us "liable" (responsible). Depending on whether one's unlawful behavior constitutes a civil or criminal wrong, it imposes (a) civil liability or (b) criminal liability.

1. Civil Liability; Actionable Conduct," "Cause of Action"

Suppose Party P complains to her lawyer, "Party D's cat scratched me." Then she asks, "Can I sue?" In legal terms she means, really: *Has D committed the sort of unlawful behavior that makes him civilly liable for the harm he has caused me?* Stated in more lawyerly a form, she means: *Does D's behavior afford me a civil cause of action against him?* Stated in shorter a lawyerly form, she means: *Has D committed against me an actionable wrong?*

"Civil cause of action" and "actionable wrong" refer to behavior by one party for which the law affords another the right to sustain a civil action—a lawsuit—and, on proving both the truth of her allegations and the harm caused her—to recover compensation, usually in the form of money (as fully discussed in Chapters 25 through 30).

Most actionable wrongs are called "torts" (from the French noun of the same spelling, which means "wrong").[1] Your first year law school curriculum will likely include a course *called* Torts, in which you'll study a variety of actionable

---

1. That, in turn, derives from the Latin word "tortus" which means "twisted."

wrongs ("torts"), including assault, battery, conversion, trespass, defamation, nuisance, negligence and professional malpractice.

QUESTION 1. Danielle allows her dog to run free around her community. The dog makes its way into Peter's yard and scratches him. In letting her dog run free so that it scratches Peter, Danielle commits a tort against Peter. That means that

I. Peter has a cause of action against Danielle.
II. Peter has a basis on which to sustain a lawsuit against Danielle
III. If Peter proves his allegations and his damage, Danielle must compensate him.
IV. Danielle has committed against Peter an actionable wrong.
A. I
B. II
C. I, II, and III
D. I, II, III, and IV

ANALYSIS. To say that D commits a tort against P is to make all four of these statements, each roughly equivalent to every other. Hence, I, II, III, and IV make true statements. **D** is right.

2. *Criminal Liability*

One is *criminally liable* when she commits conduct that the government identifies as a crime. Generally, then, the phrase "criminal liability" means "subject to governmental punishment for the commission of a crime."[2]

For most crimes, the law recognizes corresponding torts (although the inverse is not true; most torts do not carry corresponding crimes). One who commits the crime of robbery or larceny also commits the tort of "conversion." For the robbery or larceny, the government prosecutes. For the conversion, the victim may sustain an action in conversion, demanding judgment in the amount of the stolen property's value. One who commits the crime of murder also commits the tort called "wrongful death." For the murder, the government prosecutes. For the wrongful death, the decedent's estate and survivors have an

---

2. To their most serious crimes, most jurisdictions give the name "felony," and to the (relatively) less serious ones the name "misdemeanor." "Felony" usually means a crime that is punishable by one year or more in prison, and "misdemeanor" a crime punishable by less than one year in prison (or by no imprisonment at all). Lesser offenses called "infractions" or "violations" are punishable by fine or community service, but strictly speaking, they do not qualify as "crimes."

actionable wrong for which they may recover moneys. In every state, a driver who operates a motor vehicle while intoxicated commits a crime. For that the government may prosecute and, if it prevails at trial, punish him. If by driving while intoxicated the driver injures someone, then that injured party has a civil cause of action against the driver for the tort of negligence. If by driving while intoxicated the driver *kills* another, he commits homicide for which the state may prosecute and, if it prevails, punish her. The deceased's survivors have against him the civil action of wrongful death.

QUESTION 2. Victoria's bicycle is worth $200. Daryl steals it, and for that behavior the state charges him with the crime of larceny. After trial, Daryl is convicted and sentenced to pay a fine of $3,000. Does Victoria receive that $3,000?

A. Yes, because she is the victim of Daryl's crime
B. Yes, because the purpose of the criminal law is to compensate victims of tortious conduct
C. No, because the bicycle's value was less than $3,000
D. No, but Victoria may sustain against Daryl a civil action to recover $200

ANALYSIS. Criminal law does not compensate victims of wrongful behavior. Rather, it visits punishment on those who commit crimes. Daryl pays his $3,000 fine to the state, and the state keeps it. Hence, **A** and **B** are wrong. **C** correctly says "no," but its reasoning is wrong. If the bicycle were worth 2 cents or $2 million, then, still, Daryl would pay his $3,000 fine to the state, and the state would keep it. **D** correctly states that separate from the criminal charge and conviction, Victoria has a civil cause of action against Daryl. As noted above, it's an action in conversion. Via that action, she will recover from Daryl the $200 value of the bicycle. **D** is right.

3. All Law, Civil and Criminal, State or Federal Comes From Government—From One of Its Three Branches—Legislative, Executive, or Judicial

Every person (other than a foreign diplomat) who is physically present within the United States is subject to the laws of the United States government ("federal law), and, separately to those of the state in which he is physically present at any given moment.[3] The civil and criminal law of the United States

---

3. One might be present in the United States, but not within one of the fifty states. The United States owns fourteen "territories," including, for example, American Samoa, Guam, Howard Island, Midway Islands, Northern Mariana Islands, Puerto Rico, the U.S. Virgin Islands, and Wake Islands. One who is located in a U.S. territory is subject to the laws of the United States and to the relevant territorial law.

government ("federal law") generally arises from the U.S. Congress through its enactment of "statutes" (which non-lawyers usually call "laws"). Congress derives its existence and its authority to make law from the U.S. Constitution's Article 1.[4] In addition to the statutes through which it creates substantive provisions of law, Congress has created fourteen executive "departments," from which there arise hundreds of administrative agencies (generally called "bureaus" or "offices"). Congress empowers the agencies to promulgate "regulations," and those too, constitute federal law. The agencies exist at Congress's pleasure, and Congress is empowered to abolish any or all of them at its will.

In any given state, law arises from both (1) statutes enacted by the *state* legislature, and (2) *common law* (described and discussed at section 4 below).[5] And every state legislature, like the federal government, has by statute created administrative agencies, empowering them to promulgate regulations. Those regulations constitute state law, just as federal regulations constitute federal law.

Ultimately, all statutes and common law are subject to "judicial interpretation," also called "judicial construction." When two parties dispute the meaning or applicability of a statute, courts step in to interpret it, and thus to resolve the dispute. Some disputes work their way up to the "court of last resort," meaning the highest court in the relevant jurisdiction, which most (but not all) jurisdictions call their "supreme court." Hence, each of the states California, Colorado, and North Carolina has its own supreme court. The federal government's highest court is, of course, the Supreme Court of the United States.

4. *Common Law: Courts Not Only Construe It, They Create It*

As to any question for which a state has enacted no constitutional provision, no statute and no administrative regulation, the relevant law comes from precepts, principles, and doctrines that the courts themselves have created over the last 1,000 years, beginning about 150 years after the Norman Conquest of 1066. Under the English king Henry II and his successors, there came to be a system under which judges (1) rode (by horse) about the land hearing and deciding disputes, (2) returned to the King's Court, (3) discussed their decisions, and (4) described in writing the controversies they decided and the decisions they made.

Over time there arose, among the king and his judges, an understanding that to the best of his ability, each judge should decide each controversy in a

---

4. The Constitution establishes the whole of the federal government, describing and *con*scribing its powers. It creates and defines the authority of a Congress, a president, and the federal courts.

5. Cities, towns, counties, villages, and other municipalities are created by the states in which they sit. Hence, municipal law (enacted by town councils or similar bodies) is, really, state law that is applicable only in some portion of the state.

manner consistent with the way in which some other judge had decided a similar one. Stated otherwise, the common law came to be a bundle of rules created by judicial decisions with every judge (supposedly) attempting to make "today's" decision on some given matter consistent with "yesterday's" decision that some other judge made as to a similar one. The very phrase "common law" refers to a system where the law is *common* to all persons and places — the same everywhere within the nation. Commonality, in turn, requires consistency. The demand that judicial decisions show consistency gave rise to the notion of "precedent" and the doctrine that courts were bound *by* precedent (which doctrine goes, also, by the Latin phrase *stare decisis*, meaning "to stand by the [earlier] decision").[6] Hence, in England it became a common law principle that every judge, deciding every controversy, should look to precedent and issue a decision consistent with it.

Within the 13 North American British colonies, courts bound themselves by the English common law, reaching their decisions by looking to English decisions as precedent. And when the 13 colonies became the United States of America, each state by its own constitution or by proclamation of its highest court "accepted" the existing common law of England as it then stood. Each state thus adopted, by and large, the rules and doctrines embodied within the English common law. In reaching their decisions, early American courts searched for precedent in decisions that emanated from both the colonial courts and the courts of England.

Then, as the American courts themselves decided more and more controversies, and as the United States took on ever more states, the state courts came ever more to cite back to their *own* precedents, seldom needing to cite to an English or colonial case. Read a Massachusetts appellate opinion from 1790 and you'll find citations to English precedent. Read a Massachusetts appellate opinion from 1990 and you won't. You'll find citations to Massachusetts precedent (which, of course, has its *origins* in the English common law).

Common Law Is *State* Law, Meaning There Are 50 Sets of Common Law. Although we refer to "*the* common law" as though it were a single discrete set of rules, there are really fifty sets of common law — one for each state. Because each state's judiciary *tends* to keep its common law consistent with that of every other state, the common law of any one state does not differ *much* from that of any other.[7] Kentucky's common law of contracts might differ a tad from Missouri's on one matter or another; New York's might differ

---

6. Expect your law school orientation program to bathe you in that phrase, and to invest it with some sort of silly mystique. Whatever the orientation folk tell you, remember that "stare decisis" refers only to the notion that law should, generally, remain constant and consistent; a court decision made "this" year, should be consistent with the one it made "last" year.

7. The one exception is Louisiana, which because of its French colonial history, does not even recognize anything called the common law. Like all other states, Louisiana is bound by federal law including, of course, the U.S. Constitution. Yet, in many respects its legal system differs from those of the other 49 states.

from California's. On some questions, it is often said that there are two views: a minority view and a majority view, meaning that as to some particular matter, in one whole group of states the common law provides for one rule and in another group it provides for another.

In every state, for example, the common law provides that contracts ordinarily arise upon offer and acceptance. Further, in every state, the common law provides that two parties form a contract only if each furnishes consideration to the other (as taught in Chapters 12 to 14). In all states, the common law provides that two parties may not modify an existing contract unless the modification exacts consideration from both. To that last rule, however, the common law in some states recognizes an exception: If D owes money to C, and D agrees to settle the debt by taking less money than he is owed, the common law in a minority of states provides that the agreement is enforceable, notwithstanding the absence of consideration from D to C. The common law of others (a majority) provides that it is not enforceable because D provides no consideration to C. (This whole topic is addressed at Chapter 14, section B.)

So here's the point: when, generally, a lawyer, judge, or teacher refers to "*the common law*" as though it's one uniform set of rules throughout the nation, she takes a liberty with legal language. She is referring, en masse, to that large body of common law rules as to which each state is by and large the same as every other. But the truth is that here in the United States, there are 50 bodies of common law, one for each state, each, as it happens, similar — but not identical — to every other.

And Is There *Federal* Common Law? No — not since 1938 when the U.S. Supreme Court decided *Erie Railroad v. Tompkins*, 304 U.S. 64 (1938). Certainly, you'll study that case in your first-year civil procedure class.[8]

The U.S. Constitution, Article III, §2(1) provides that "[t]he judicial Power [of the United States] shall extend to Controversies between — Citizens of different States[.]" In 1798, pursuant to that constitutional provision, Congress enacted this statute:

> The laws of the several States . . . shall be regarded as rules of decision in trials at common law, in the courts of the United States, in [controversies between citizens of different states].

28 U.S.C. §25 (found now, as revised, at 28 U.S.C. §1652).

In *Erie*, the Supreme Court construed the phrase "laws of the several States," ruling that it did not refer to any notion of "general [federal] common law" assembled by the federal courts from common law provisions of the various states. Rather, the court ruled that there was no such creature as "federal common law." In a suit between citizens of different states brought in federal

---

8. Which, in some law schools, lately goes by other names — because each new generation of law teachers thinks itself innovative when it gives new names to old things.

court, the Supreme Court ruled that the governing law would be such state law (common law or statute) as would apply if the plaintiff had brought the suit *in* state court:

> [T]he law to be applied in any case is the law of the state. And whether the law of the state shall be declared by its Legislature in a statute or by [state common law] is not a matter of federal concern. There is no federal general common law . . . [a]nd no clause in the Constitution purports to confer such a power upon the federal courts.

Id. at 78. According to Justice Holmes:

> The fallacy underlying the [notion of a federal common law] rests upon the assumption that there is "a transcendental body of law outside of any particular State but obligatory within it unless and until changed by statute," that federal courts have the power to use their judgment as to what the rules of common law are, and that, in the federal courts, "the parties are entitled to an independent judgment on matters of general law: 'but law in the sense in which courts speak of it today does not exist without some definite authority behind it. The common law so far as it is enforced in State, whether called common law or not, is not the common law generally but the law of that State existing by the authority of that State without regard to what it may have been in England or anywhere else. . . .'"

Id. at 79. So — there is no such creature as *federal* common law.

What Law *Does* Govern When Citizens from Different States Sue in Federal Court? In a suit between citizens of two different states, X and Y, a federal court must apply either the law of State X or the law of State Y[9] because there is no such thing *as* federal common law.

QUESTION 3. In State X, by common law decision of the state's highest appellate court, "an advertisement to the general public, however or wherever posted, if otherwise sufficiently definite to constitute an offer, does in fact amount to an offer and, if any person should attempt properly to accept it, a contract arises between that person and the person who issued the advertisement." However, in State Y, by common law decision of the state's highest appellate court, "an advertisement made by newspaper, radio, television, Internet, or other means does not constitute an offer unless it specifically names the party to whom the offer is made." In a great majority of states, an advertisement made to the general public does not ordinarily constitute an offer (Chapter 5, section A).

---

9. Which, according to the state's choice of law rules might refer the court, finally, to the law of a State Z, all such complexities covered, generally, in a law school course called Conflict (or Choice) of Law.

Esther is a State X citizen in the business of manufacturing paper products. On the Internet site u-buy, she sees this advertisement: "Offered for sale 1 Orson Paper Cup Manufacturing Machine Model #4587-A, 1998, used 10,000 hours, $50,000, pay by cashier's, teller's, or certified check. Any person who wishes to buy or to ask a question about this item should contact seller at Goods@ubuy.com." To that e-mail address, Esther writes, "I wish to buy the Orson Paper Cup Manufacturing Machine Model #4587-A, and I accept your offer. Please send instructions as to how I should make payment. I will retrieve the machine at my own expense wherever it is now located or at such other place as you may direct." Esther receives a response, signed by Frances, to this effect: "I posted the u-buy advertisement for the Orson machine. Thank you for your interest, but I have decided not to sell it."

Esther locates Frances and finds that she is a citizen of State Y. Esther brings suit against Frances for breach of contract, exercising her right to bring the suit in federal court. At trial, Esther cites the State X statute and her own State X citizenship. On those bases, she contends that the u-buy posting was an offer. Frances cites the State Y statute and her citizenship in State Y. On those bases, she contends that the u-buy posting was not an offer.

Which of the following, if put forth by the federal court, plausibly represents an appropriate decision?

I. The law of State X governs this controversy, wherefore the u-buy posting was an offer, meaning that these parties did not form a contract.

II. The law of State Y governs this controversy, wherefore the u-buy posting was not an offer, meaning that these parties did not form a contract.

III. Federal common law governs this controversy, wherefore the u-buy posting was not an offer, meaning that these parties did not form a contract.

A. I
B. II
C. I and II
D. I, II, and III

ANALYSIS. The U.S. Constitution affords the federal courts jurisdiction to hear suits between citizens of different states. In 1798, Congress provided that in such suits the federal court shall apply the "laws of the several States." For 150 years, the federal courts took that phrase to signify some mélange of state common law doctrine, which, as assembled by the federal courts, over time, came to be called federal common law or "general common law." But in 1938, the U.S. Supreme Court put an end to that. There was, it said, no such thing as federal common law. The phrase "laws of the several States" as used by Congress meant the common law (or statutory law) of the state whose law would govern a given controversy if it were, in fact, brought in state court.

In this case, the federal court will have to apply the common law of State X or State Y (making that decision according to another complicated body of doctrine called conflict of laws). Options I and II make plausible statements. But this much is sure: The federal court cannot apply to this controversy anything called federal common law because there is no such thing. Option III is clearly unacceptable. **C** is right.

Even Though There Is No Federal Common Law Federal Courts Do, With Their Decisions, "Make Law;" They *Have* To   The federal courts (by and large) decide cases involving federal law that *others* enact. U.S. Const. art. III. For example, the Constitution's first amendment provides that "Congress shall make no law . . . abridging the freedom of speech[.]" No court had any part in creating that rule. Congress wrote it (in 1798) and the states ratified it.

Now suppose, a century later, Congress enacts a statute forbidding any person to wear on his clothing a button with a message that criticizes the president, or to place on her car, in time of war, a "bumper sticker" that reads "Bring Our Troops Home." Suppose now that Citizen X does wear a button that reads "Impeach the President." The FBI arrests him for violating the statute just described. He contends that his button is a form of speech under the first amendment. The U.S. Justice Department contends that it's not.

As to what the first amendment does or does not mean by "speech," the federal courts *must* decide. That's their job. Many in our nation like to say "It's a court's job to interpret law, not to create it." The statement is meaningless. Such persons don't know that to do its job, a court must, in the very sense to which they object — "make law."

Thousands of times daily, two parties A and B (one of whom might be the federal or a state government), come to court disputing the meaning of some words within a federal statute, regulation, or the Constitution. A insists that the words in a given provision mean "this," and B insists they mean "that." The court's job is to *make a decision as to what the words do mean*. In doing so, it *must* pronounce that the *behavior* at issue is or is not lawful.

Love it or hate it, call it (through ignorance) "legislation from the bench," "judicial activism," or anything else. The federal courts must, when faced with a controversy, take hold of the statutes, regulations, or constitution that others have written, *interpret* them, and so decide that the behavior at issue is or is not lawful.

Consider the Controversial Topic of Abortion   In 1972, The Supreme Court of the United States decided (with some qualifications) that no state could prevent a pregnant woman from securing an abortion within the first two trimesters of pregnancy. Any state that did so, it ruled, behaved unlawfully. Plainly, the Constitution makes no such statement in "black and white." Rather the Supreme Court so construed/interpreted various of its provisions as to reach that decision. *Roe v. Wade*, 400 U.S. 113 (1973) (And there is scarcely a Supreme Court decision more controversial than that one.) In 1992, the Court, by *re*interpretation of the Constitution, modified that ruling, holding that a state may, to some degree, restrict a woman's right to procure an abortion during pregnancy's first two trimesters. In that case, it faced a Pennsylvania statute requiring that a pregnant woman (1) if married, notify her husband of her plan to secure an abortion and, married or not, (2) after advising her physician that she wished to abort her pregnancy, wait 24 hours before actually undergoing the procedure.

The Court ruled that requirement (1) was unconstitutional; Pennsylvania could not impose that restriction on a pregnant woman; its attempt to do so was unlawful under the U.S. Constitution. It ruled that requirement (2) *was* constitutional; the state's imposition of *that* requirement was lawful. *Planned Parenthood of Southeastern Pennsylvania v. Casey*, 505 U.S. 833 (1942).

But Here's The Point: That Decision Did Not Reflect Federal *Common Law*   When a federal court decides on the meaning of some word(s) within a federal statute, it announces *statutory law*; it tells the public what the statute *means*. When it decides on the meaning of some word(s) within the U.S. Constitution, it announces constitutional law, by advising the public on the meaning tied to some portion of the Constitution. In that way, we might say, casually, that Federal judges do "make law," but only by doing their job—by interpreting some statute, regulation, or the Constitution—for which the court did not ask and that it did not write. There is (since the *Erie* decision cited above), no federal *common law*.

What If a State Legislature Enacts a Statute That Conflicts with Its Own Common Law Rule?   Statutes supersede the common law. That's a principle of the common law itself. In Chapter 2, we teach that two parties may generally form a contract without a writing. If, however, some state should enact a statute that no agreement constitutes a contract unless set forth in writing, then such would be the law in that state. For once again, it's a principle of the common law itself that *statutory law supersedes common law*. Stated otherwise, common law governs in any given jurisdiction for only so long as its legislature fails to enact a statute that conflicts with it. Once it does so, the common law on that point ceases to operate.

B.   What Is Contract Law, and Who Makes It?

When we use the word "contract," we usually mean a "bilateral contract."[10]
A bilateral contract is *an exchange of promises each of which the law enforces
by providing, in the case of breach, a cause of action and compensatory remedy.*
(Compare "unilateral contracts," discussed in Chapter 9, sections C and D.)
Restatement (Second) of Contracts §1 defines "contract" as "a set of promises
for the breach of which the law gives a remedy, or the performance of which
the law in some way recognizes as a duty."

Throughout the 50 states, contract law is largely common law (see section
A4 above). You won't likely find in any state, a statute defining "offer," "acceptance," "rejection," or "revocation." Rather, the use, meaning, and significance
of all such terms arose, grew, and evolved, slowly, by judicial decision; they
belong to the common law.

So Where, in One Place, Is the Common Law of Contracts Written?   It isn't.
The common law lies in judicial decisions. In order truly to read the common
law of contracts for any given state, one must read, for that state, every judicial
opinion put forth by every judge or, at the very least, every decision put forth
by the state's highest court. All together those decisions, for any given state,
are — that state's common law of contracts.

In the 1800s and early 1900s, some scholars did very nearly that. They
include Oliver Wendell Holmes, Samuel Williston, Arthur Corbin, and others. Their scholarly works have gone far to "pull together" the common law
so that one may read (their interpretations and understandings of) the common law in organized fashion. Their multivolume treatises (now updated
and revised by others) constitute revered authority on the common law of
contracts. Judges frequently cite to them as they do, also, to the works of
Professors Farnsworth, Calamari, and Perillo, and to various articles written
(usually) by law professors who, too, have achieved expertise in the common
law of contracts (maybe).

---

10.   Historically, the word "contract" referred to three kinds of binding obligation: (1) The "formal contract" which, in turn referred to (a) the "covenant under seal" (section E below), (b) the "recognizance" (not discussed in this book or in any ordinary law school Contracts course), (c) the negotiable
instrument (the topic of a separate course usually *called* "negotiable instruments" or "payment systems"), and (2) the "simple contract" which is what we all mean, today, when we say "contract." If ever
you cross paths with the phrase "simple contract," know that it means "contract" as we all, today, use
that word and that the word "simple" distinguishes it from what once were called "formal contracts,"
as described above.

C.   Restatement of the Law of Contracts

1. *What Are Restatements of the Law?*

In Philadelphia, Pennsylvania, there sits an entity called the American Law Institute ("ALI"), founded in 1923. Among its self-assigned missions is to gather groups of (supposed) authorities on various subjects, and through their conjoined efforts, to "restate" the common law. Each of the ALI's Restatements appears as a set of "rules" partitioned into "sections" that resemble statutes and that, *according to the ALI*, accurately reflect the common law. (In some cases, clearly they do not, and in some others, the rules reflect the common law as ALI would *like* it to be.)

With the word "*re*statement," ALI acknowledges that the common law on any subject is *stated* in the thousands of judicial decisions, each made (supposedly) with an attempt at ongoing consistency. The ALI's work-product characterizes itself as a *re*statement of such common law; it represents the ALI's effort to take hold of the judicial decisions and to "restate" their common law principles in a cohesive, accessible form.

The ALI has now put forth a large number of restatements on a variety of common law subjects, including agency, property, torts, trusts and—contracts. The first Restatement of the Law of Contracts, published in 1932, represents the ALI's purported exposition of the common law of contracts as of 1932. The Restatement (Second) of the Law of Contracts, published in 1979, we are to believe, accounts for changes in the common law between 1932 and 1979, and so represents the ALI's purported exposition of the common law of contracts as of 1979 (and just as much, perhaps, its opinion as what the common law *should* be). Someday, no doubt, will follow Restatements (Third), (Fourth), and so on.

2. *So, At Any Given Time, The Most Current Restatement Is The Common Law of Contracts?*

No, No, No; don't ever say that. Whatever the Restatement of contracts might be, it's *not* law. It represents, at best, a private committee's joint opinion as to what is the common law of contracts, based on *its* reading of the cases, and *its* reading of the various scholars who have written on the subject (some of whom themselves participated in writing the first and second Restatements). Nonetheless, rightly or wrongly, state courts around the country regard the Restatement of Contracts with reverence. They refer to it, they *de*fer to it, and they cite to it almost as though it *were* law, which it is not.

Whether, on the one hand, the Restatement is a well-conceived work of useful scholarship or, on the other, a recitation of obvious unavailing generalities, devoid of intelligent analysis, that avoids always the difficult issues and resolves in trite terms the easy ones—lawyers, judges, and teachers regrettably regard it as an important authority. Some teachers base the whole of their Contracts course upon it. Nearly all refer to it regularly and require that their students (*you*) read many of its provisions. Hence, we cite to it very frequently in this book, for as to some matters you must know its contents.

QUESTION 4. The Restatement (Second) of the Law of Contracts is best described as

A. statutory law.
B. common law.
C. an opinion.
D. a precedent.

ANALYSIS. Restatements of the Law come forth from the American Law Institute, an arm of the American Bar Association. They are not statutes because the American Law Institute is not, certainly, a legislature. They are not common law because the common law inheres only in judicial decisions. They are not precedent because precedents, too, arise from judicial decisions. They represent the opinion of the American Law Institute as to what is or should be the common law of contracts. **C** is right.

3. *What We Mean When We Refer to the "Common Law of Contracts"*

When we say "common law of contracts," we mean that large body of contract law created over a millennium by the courts of England and the United States, each judge, theoretically, reaching her decisions with an effort to be consistent with her predecessors and by precedent—an effort to abide by precedent and also, at times, to "break new ground," so that the common law of contracts is said, always, to "grow" (as is so of the common law on any subject).

D. Statutory Contract Law: Uniform Commercial Code Article 2, and Miscellaneous State Statutes

In 1892 there occurred a first meeting of what is now called the National Conference of Commissioners on Uniform State Laws, headquartered today in Chicago, Illinois. Commonly called the "Uniform Law Commission" ("ULC"), this entity is not a government agency, but a private not-for-profit association.

Nonetheless, by ULC invitation, each of the 50 states (plus a few U.S. territories) names several "commissioners" to participate, on the state's behalf, in the ULC's self-appointed task.

1. *What* Is *the ULC's Self-Appointed Task?*

Because we are a nation of 50 states, each with its own power to make common law (via the judiciary) and statutory law (via the legislature), one state's laws sometimes conflict with another's. Where persons partake of interstate transactions, those conflicts raise questions as to the rights and duties of the participating parties. Suppose, for example, that by statute in State B, a check is valid only if dated at its top. Suppose that by statute in State A, a check is valid whether or not dated at its top. If a State A buyer sends to a State B seller a check that is undated at the top, there might well arise the question of whether the buyer has or has not sent a check that's valid. Under statutory law in the state from which the buyer sent it, the check is valid. In the state where the seller received it, it's not — and that's a problem.

Suppose a State A statute provides: "The retail seller of any electronic consumer product automatically, as a matter of law, warranties that the product will function properly for two years after the date of purchase." Suppose a State B statute provides: "The retail seller of any electronic consumer product automatically, as a matter of law, warranties that the product will function properly for three years after the date of purchase." If, by on-line, mail-order purchase, a State B buyer purchases a consumer electronic product from a State A retail seller, there arises the question of whether Seller warrants the product for two years or three years — and that's a problem too.

In order to avoid such conflicts, the ULC assigned itself the mission of drafting and proposing to each state legislature for enactment, various "uniform statutes" addressing areas of commercial law in which interstate conflicts often arise. The thinking ran thus: If every state were to adopt as statutes the laws that the ULC proposed, then as to the subject at issue, the law would be uniform throughout the states and thus unburden interstate transactions from potential conflicts among state law.

Among the several uniform acts that the ULC put forth in its earlier years was one called the Uniform Sales Act of 1906. It concerned those transactions in which two parties formed or negotiated toward a contract for the sale of *goods*. The Uniform Sales Act addressed no other sort of contract; it addressed only contracts *for the sale of goods* (presumably because the purchase and sale of goods often involved interstate transaction, particularly with the advent of railroads). The purchase and sale of service (at that time) was usually a local matter undertaken between persons closely located. (In 1906, American businesses did not engage employees in India to answer customer service telephone lines and instruct us on how to operate our computer equipment.)

About 30 states adopted the Uniform Sales Act, and in those states, therefore, the Act governed contracts for the sale of goods. All other contracts were governed still by the common law, and even contracts for the sale of goods were governed by the common law as to matters on which the Uniform Sales Act was silent. For example, the Act at various points invoked the terms "offer" and "acceptance," but nowhere defined them. Even in those states that adopted the Act, therefore, the definitions of those terms continued to be creatures of the common law (as did all other matters that the Act did not address).

In 1952, the ULC sent a call to all 48 states: repeal the Uniform Sales Act and certain other uniform acts related to commercial transactions. Adopt in its place our new Uniform Commercial Code (UCC). The UCC was (and is) a long statute (hundreds of pages long) partitioned into several "articles," each such article revising and replacing a pre-existing single uniform statute that the ULC had earlier put forth, each of which some (but not all) states had enacted. In 1952, UCC Article 2 dealt (and still deals today) with contracts for the sale of goods, the ULC intending that it replace the Uniform Sales Act. The states were slow to adopt the UCC, and so the ULC revised it in 1955. Even then many states declined to enact it, and so ULC revised it again in 1962, hoping all states would find it acceptable. In its 1962 version, the UCC's Article 2 still concerned contracts for the sale of goods (but no other contracts). And, during the 1960s, all states did adopt the UCC, including its Article 2 (some with minor alterations in language, and Louisiana with very significant alterations).

2. What's a "Good," Exactly?

All property is divisible, first, into "real property" and "personal property." Real property means land and all things firmly affixed to it such as a house, building, or flagpole. Personal property is all property other than real property. We may then divide personal property into two categories: "tangible" and "intangible." Tangible personal property means (by and large) any personal property that has a physical existence, such as a paper clip or the Hubble telescope; both are tangible personal property. Intangible personal property means personal property that has no physical existence. One's right to enforce a contract is intangible personal property. If one is injured by another's negligence, then his right to recover under negligence law is intangible personal property. A copyright, a trademark, and one's right to receive his income tax refund are all intangible personal property.

Article 2 (UCC §2-205) defines "good" generally as a "movable thing." With certain additions and exceptions set forth in that same section, "movable thing" means, really, tangible personal property. A wristwatch is a good. So is a jet, a nuclear bomb, a safety pin, a contact lens, a ball bearing, a marble, a loaf of bread, and an ocean liner. A patent, contract right, or right to take a gift left by a decedent through a will all qualify as personal property, but they have no physical existence. They all constitute intangible personal property, but they are not "goods," and UCC Article 2 does not govern contracts for the sale of any such property. Contracts for the sale of real property or intangible personal property are governed by the common law (or by some statute outside the UCC if the relevant jurisdiction has enacted one).

Since the ULC first put forth the UCC, it has revised Article 2 (and other of the code's articles) several times, so that over time it has issued Article 2 in various versions: a 1952 version, a 1955 version, a 1962 version (the one first adopted by substantially all states), and a 2003 version (which, as of today, no state has adopted).

Hence, UCC Article 2 as now enacted in all states (with some variation in text here and there) is, by and large, the 1962 version. For that reason when we, in this book, refer to UCC Article 2, we refer to the 1962 version, for that is the only version that is in fact law. Further, when we refer generally to "the code" or to the "UCC," we mean Article 2 of the UCC, 1962 version, for that is the one that specifically addresses contracts — *again, not all contracts, but only contracts for the sale of goods.*

QUESTION 5. When the Uniform Law Commission first completes the writing of any one of its uniform laws, its written work product at that moment constitutes

A. state common law.
B. state statutory law.
C. administrative regulatory law.
D. no law at all.

ANALYSIS. The Uniform Laws Commission is not a governmental entity, and it has no power to enact law. Pursuant to the mission it has declared for itself, it writes what, in its opinion, *would make* good uniform law throughout the states and then submits its work product to the state legislatures, suggesting that all enact it as statutory law. In some cases, the states do adopt the recommended law, and in some cases they don't. If one state adopts the law, then its provisions become law in that state. If two states adopt it, its provisions become law in that state too. If ultimately all states adopt it (as has happened with Article 2), then it becomes statutory law in all states. But — when the ULC first completes writing one of its "uniform laws" and before a first state adopts it, it is no law it all; it represents no more than ULC's *suggestion* to all states that they *enact* it as law. **D** is right.

3. The Code Comes with "Official Comments"

For all of the UCC's provisions, the writers have supplied their own "official comments." These purport to explain the origin, meaning, and application of the code provisions themselves. When the ULC encouraged all state legislatures to adopt the UCC, it did not proclaim that its official comments should be part of the law per se, and it is said in all states that the official comments do not enjoy the status of law. Indeed, where a state's statute books show the UCC as statutory law, they do not show the official comments; the comments are not a part of the law. The comments are, however, readily accessible, and courts do frequently read and refer to them when interpreting and applying the code's provisions. In that way, the official comments heavily influence the judiciary's understanding of the code and therefore certainly do inform the law. Without doubt, your contracts teacher, when asking that you read provisions of the code, will ask that you read, too, the relevant official comments.

4. *Other State Statutes Related to Contract Law*

Beyond UCC Article 2, the various states have enacted, to greater or lesser degrees, miscellaneous statutes that bear on contract law. In those states, *those* statutes form a part of the state's law of contracts. In Chapter 2, sections E and F, for example, we discuss acceptance by silence and dominion. We address the common law as well as the federal statute 39 U.S.C. §3009(b). Know this too: Some states have enacted their own statutes on the subject. New York General Obligations Law §5-332, for example, provides:

> No person, firm, partnership, association or corporation . . . shall . . . offer for sale . . . merchandise, where the offer includes the voluntary and unsolicited sending of such . . . merchandise not actually ordered[.] The receipt of any such . . . merchandise shall for all purposes be deemed an unconditional gift to the recipient, who may use or dispose of such . . . merchandise in any manner he sees fit without obligation on his part to the sender.

So — as to any topic or subtopic you study in your contracts course, there may well be, beyond the common law and beyond UCC Article 2, "this" or "that" miscellaneous statute in "this" or "that" state. In each state, all such statutes represent a part of *that* state's contract law.

5. *So Is the Common Law of Contracts Obsolete?*

No, certainly not. UCC Article 2 governs only *contracts for the sale of goods.* A contract for the sale of any service (including, notably, a contract for construction) is governed still by the common law (except where some miscellaneous state statute supersedes it). And even as to contracts for the sale of goods, where the code is silent, the common law governs.

QUESTION 6. In any given state, statutes that address contract law include

   I. UCC Article 2, as enacted by the state's legislature.
  II. the Restatement of the Law of Contracts, as enacted by the state's legislature.
 III. miscellaneous statutes, as enacted by the state's legislature.

A. I
B. I and II
C. II and III
D. I and III

ANALYSIS. In any given state, the law of contracts is largely a matter of common law. Statutes supersede the common law, and every state has enacted UCC Article 2, which governs contracts for the sale of goods. In every state, therefore, the code forms part of the statutory contract law. Option I is true. If the UCC and the common law conflict, the code governs. If as to some matter bearing on contract law, Article 2 is silent, the common law governs. In addition, every state has enacted, to greater or lesser degrees, its own statutes pertaining to contract law. Those form the remaining portion of state statutory law on the subject of contracts. Option III is true. As to any matter on which any such statute conflicts with the common law, the statute governs. The Restatement is *not* a statute. Neither is it common law. It is no law at all. It is, rather, the ALI's opinion as to the state of the common law (and in some cases, as to what the common law should be). When courts must decide contractual controversies governed by the common law, they do frequently look to the Restatement for guidance, but the Restatement isn't law. Options I and III are true, and II is false. **D** is right.

QUESTION 7. If two parties wish to form a contract concerning the construction by one of a home for the other, the law governing the formation, interpretation, enforceability, breach, and remedies pertaining to their contract and any alleged breach herein

A. UCC Article 2 only.
B. UCC Article 2 and any other pertinent state statute.
C. the common law only.
D. the common law and any other pertinent state statute.

ANALYSIS. The question describes a contract that does not concern the sale of goods, and for that reason UCC Article 2 is irrelevant. *Article 2 of the Code applies only to contracts for the sale of goods, and no others.* Let's say it again: *Article 2 of the Code applies only to contracts for the sale of goods, and no others*. **A** and **B** are wrong. If the state has enacted any statute that applies to the contract or controversy at issue, then that statute does certainly apply. As to matters for which there is no statute, the common law applies. **D** is right.

E.   Law vs. Equity

Throughout law school, a student reads and hears of "equity" contrasted with "law." She hears also that equity has "merged" with law, and she is led *wrongly* to conclude that the difference between them is today largely insignificant. Unless she takes a (good — *good*) course called remedies, equity, or equitable remedies, she will all too likely graduate law school with a wholly inadequate understanding of what is meant by "equity courts," "equitable jurisdiction," the "merger" of law and equity, and "equity vs. law." When, in her practice, the significance of equity vs. law steps up to jolt her with reality, she'll have to learn about it *then*, which is why, once again, every law student should take a (*good*) course that teaches equitable remedies.[11]

We can't, in this book, teach you fully (or anywhere *near* fully about the meaning of equity courts, equitable jurisdiction, or equity vs. law. A full apprehension of equity you shan't achieve by reading this chapter, nor as a first-year law student, nor in all your years at law school, nor perhaps in your lifetime on this planet. *But, as President Kennedy urged— let us make a beginning.*

Seat thyself in medieval England where the courts of law were, conceptually, like our courts of law today. As to the (*very many*) differences between the English law courts of that era and our own modern-day law courts, we'll do the serious, difficult, and responsible thing: *We'll forget about them and pretend there were and are no such differences.*

For our present purposes, that will work just fine. The English law courts developed and applied the common law and in so doing created forms of action, those giving rise today to what we call causes of action. If, however, some party felt he had suffered an injustice for which the law offered no cause of action and hence no adequate remedy, he had the right, under some circumstances (depending on who he was and what year it was) to petition the King for some form of relief. He thus became not a "plaintiff" in a lawsuit but a "petitioner" for the King's own justice. His adversary was not a "defendant" but a "respondent" who, the petitioner asserted, had caused him an *injustice for which the law offered no adequate remedy.*

The King (or his "right-hand man," the Lord Chancellor), 'twas said, would hear the matter and test it against "the King's conscience." If by such conscience he concluded that the petitioner had indeed suffered an injustice for which the law offered no action and hence no remedy, the King *ordered* the respondent to do "this, that, or the other" to give the petitioner his justice.

For example, in medieval England the law had not yet come to the point where it enforced contracts as we know that word. What we today call a contract (more properly, a "simple contract") was then a mere "private agreement,"

---

11. Alternatively, you might read all six volumes (with footnotes) of John Norton Pomeroy, *Equity Jurisprudence* (1881-1883) (originally three volumes, later expanded to six).

unenforceable at law. Hence, if two parties made an agreement, orally or by signed writing, the law wanted nothing to do with it. If one party breached, that gave the other absolutely no grounds on which to sue. Agreements, per se, were not enforceable; they had no status under the law; the law did not recognize them.

Let's Make That Very Clear.   *Ask yourself:* If on Monday, A and B agree that lavender is the prettiest of all colors, but on Tuesday B changes her mind and decides that wine-red is the prettiest of all colors, does A have a cause of action against B?

Answer yourself: No, of course not. As between two persons, sameness, difference, or change of opinion has no legal status. The law doesn't care about it. No person can sustain a suit against the other because the other holds an opinion different from his own, and that's obviously true even if at one time they held the same opinion.

Similarly, in medieval England if Parties A and B formed an agreement by handshake, or by signed writing, the law took no account of it. There was no name for what they had formed except a mere "private agreement." If Party A breached, Party B had no cause of action against him. Party B would perhaps learn not to make private agreements with A ever again, but the law offered him no cause of action and, therefore, no remedy or relief.

But the Law Did Furnish a Means to Enforce a Promise: Covenant Under Seal.   If, in 1660, (1) X made a promise to Y, setting it forth in writing; and (2) X applied to the writing—his *seal* ("seal" meaning one's own special stamp-like raised imprint, in those days, made of wax); and (3) X delivered the sealed instrument to the promisee, then his promise became a "covenant under seal," and the law enforced it.[12]

Hence, it became the common wisdom that a promise was enforceable when it was set forth in a writing that was "signed, sealed, and delivered" (which in today's parlance means "all done—complete").

An Illustration: Bullworth and Sterling.   Suppose it's November 1, 1621. Bullworth wants to buy Sterling's horse for £5. He wants to make the exchange of money for horse four months hence, on March 1, 1622. Sterling wants to sell the horse to Bullworth for that same price on that same day. The parties want to achieve what we, today, would call a contract for the sale of the horse. They can't do *that*, but here's what they *can* do. Bullworth writes his promise to pay Sterling, on March 1, 1662, the sum of £5. He provides the document with his seal and his signature. Sterling creates his own writing, promising delivery of the horse, on March 1, 1622, to Bullworth, providing the writing with

---

12. Although the promisor need not have *signed* the instrument to render his promise enforceable, he customarily did so.

his signature and seal. The parties then meet. Each delivers his writing to the other, so that each has, from the other, a written promise, signed, sealed, and delivered and, therefore, a covenant under seal. Each thus has from the other an enforceable promise. Should either of the parties breach his covenant, then, in order to enforce the promise in court, the other had to show and present the document to the judge.

And on that point, the law took itself quite seriously. Suppose Bullworth and Sterling prepare their signed, sealed, written promises as just described, Sterling covenanting to deliver a horse on March 1, 1662, and Bullworth covenanting to pay Sterling £5 on March 1, 1662. On November 3, 1661, they exchange writings so that each has from the other an enforceable promise, each promise to be performed on March 1, 1662. On December 15, Bullworth accidentally drops Sterling's covenant in the hearth. It burns to ash. No longer possessing the covenant, Bullworth cannot enforce Sterling's promise to deliver the horse. Yet Sterling still has Bullworth's covenant and Sterling must honor it; he must pay Sterling the £5.

You Mean Bullworth Had To Pay the Money But Had No Right to Receive the Horse?   Yes, that was so. But the law didn't then see the situation as we do; it did not consider that £5 was the price of a horse. Bullworth had to pay £5, not for a horse, but rather because (for whatever reason about which the court did not care) he promised to pay Sterling £5, in a writing signed, sealed, and delivered, wherefore the writing became a covenant under seal — enforceable — period. The *law enforced the covenant*, and cared not a whit about the reasons for which Bullworth created it. Bullworth had to pay not for a horse. He had to pay to make good on his covenant.

Bullworth, of course, knows that he made the covenant to Sterling in exchange for Sterling's covenant to deliver the horse, but the law took no account of "exchanges" or "bargains." Such things had no legal status. Their status at law was nada, nilch, zilch — just as today, for example, a difference of opinion between two persons has no legal status. Quite simply, if one was in possession of another's covenant, signed, sealed, and delivered to him, then he had a right to enforce it regardless of the whys and wherefores surrounding its creation.

Suppose Bullworth refused to pay the £5 unless Sterling should deliver the horse. Sterling would sue Bullworth for breach of covenant, and the court would award Sterling a judgment for £5.

That Takes Us on a Little Detour: "Judgment" vs. "Order."   When a court issues a *judgment* against some defendant, it does not *order* the defendant to pay the plaintiff. It is up to defendant to pay the judgment. If she doesn't, she is not in "contempt of court;" she suffers no punishment; the court isn't "mad at" her. Rather, the plaintiff must undertake a whole, new separate procedure to collect on his judgment. That procedure involves discovering and locating the defendant's assets and acquiring from the court something called (in many jurisdictions) a "writ of execution," which directs some judicial officer (a sheriff, constable, or someone else, depending on the jurisdiction) to seize the defendant's property, sell it at auction, deliver to plaintiff so much as the judgment requires, and return the excess, if any, to defendant. Or, if the defendant has money in the bank, the writ will direct the judicial officer to seize from the bank the amount of the judgment and pay it to plaintiff. Or, in an amount limited by statute in most jurisdictions, the writ will permit the judicial officer to garnish the defendant's wages, so that her employer withholds, say, 10 percent of her wages every pay period and pays them over to the court, which in turn pays the plaintiff.[13]

So Understand This. The enforceability of one's promise or covenant, signed, sealed, and delivered, did not arise because the parties had formed an agreement or exchange; the law knew and cared nothing for *agreement*s. It looked at each covenant individually. If the instrument was signed, sealed, and delivered, the law enforced it, and *that was that.*

So One *Could*, in Those Days, Make an Enforceable Naked Promise? Exactly right. There was, at that time, no such concept as "consideration." If, for whatever reason, Party 1 promised by covenant under seal to pay Party 2 on her eighteenth birthday £500, then he was bound to do so — so long as Party 2 could produce the instrument when she reached her eighteenth birthday. Without the paper, she had nothing.

QUESTION 8. The common law developed the legal creature called covenant under seal

A. after it had already invented the enforceable contract in which two parties exchanged promises.

B. because the doctrine of consideration was excessively complex and the law wished to create a device by which one could make an enforceable promise without receiving consideration in exchange.

C. as a means of allowing two parties to form what we today would call a contract.

D. before it recognized any such creature as an enforceable agreement.

---

13. The matter becomes more complicated when a state legislature (or the U.S. Congress) enacts a statute creating some cause of action specifically authorizing the court to issue, against a defendant, a court *order.* Since the relevant authority arises from the legislature and not from either the common law or equity per se, it is difficult to state confidently that such a court order is an equitable remedy. We are safer saying that such a court order is "*in the nature* of an equitable remedy." Hence, while all equitable remedies come in the form of court orders, we cannot say that all court orders constitute equitable remedies.

ANALYSIS.   Long before the law recognized that which we now call "contract," one could make an enforceable promise via the covenant under seal. At that time, the law knew nothing of and cared nothing for what it regarded as private agreements between private persons. It did not enforce agreements; it enforced *promises* that were signed, sealed, and delivered. In later centuries, the law came to recognize consideration as the substitute for a seal, although the history of that particular development is long and complex. This much, however, is simple and sure: The law recognized and enforced the covenant under seal long before it knew of what we today call a contract — an exchange of promises, each serving as consideration for the other.

A, B, and C all state or imply that the doctrine of consideration predated the covenant under seal. That makes all of them wrong. D makes the simple and correct statement that the law honored, recognized, and enforced the covenant under seal before it developed what we, today, call a contract. Hence, **D** is right.

End of Detour: Back to Bullworth, Sterling, and the Horse.   Because Sterling holds Bullworth's covenant under seal, the court issues against Bullworth a judgment for £5 in favor of Sterling. Having lost the covenant that Sterling gave him, Bullworth, in 1622, has no *legal* right to the horse for which (in *his* mind) he has paid.

So Bullworth Appeals to the "King's Conscience."   Bullworth petitions the King, asserting that he has suffered an injustice for which the law affords no action and hence no remedy. The King hears Bullworth's plea and hears too from Sterling, the respondent. The King decides that Bullworth is right — that he has suffered an injustice for which the law offers no action and hence no remedy. The King *order*s Sterling to convey the horse to Bullworth. His Highness does not issue a *judgment* at law, for he has no power to do so. He issues an order, and *that*, in 1622, he has power to do. A King's order is a thing quite different from a court's judgment. Should one disobey it, the King will order him imprisoned.

The King Sent His Conscience Around The Country: "Courts of Equity."
To oversimplify a little (or a lot), the King ultimately established what we might call "satellites" of his conscience by setting up equity courts around the realm and appointing "chancellors" to hear "petitions in equity." Hence, one who claimed to have suffered an injustice for which the law would give no remedy needed no longer to take himself to the King's Court and wait in line to see him (or his right-hand man, the Lord Chancellor). Rather, the petitioner might go to an equity court closer to his own location and present his grievance to the chancellor who sat there. Each chancellor, as "keeper of the King's conscience," was to ask himself, in each such case, whether the petitioner had indeed suffered an injustice for which the law offered no remedy. If he answered "yes," then he fashioned an order as, in his judgment, would correct

the injustice by requiring the respondent to do or to refrain from doing some certain thing. One who disobeyed the order was incarcerated for "contempt of His Majesty's court," that phrase later shortened to "contempt of court."

When the United States first established itself, the federal government and all 13 states, modeling themselves on the English system, had separate courts of law and equity (courts of equity being sometimes called courts of chancery). In 1938, the federal government "merged" its law and equity courts. The effect was not to abolish the separate *jurisdictions* of law and equity, but rather to house both jurisdictions in the same court buildings. A federal judge, figuratively speaking, had in his closet two hats, one labeled "judge at law" and the other "chancellor at equity." Depending on the nature of the matter before him, he put one or the other atop his head. When there came before the federal court the construction and application of either a federal statute, the U.S. Constitution, or the common law, the judge wore his "law hat;" the interpretation and application of common law and statutes are matters of *law*. When the federal court faced a petitioner who sought a court order to rectify an injustice for which the law offered no remedy, the federal judge donned his "equity hat."

It is said that in most states law and equity are similarly merged. Unfortunately, too many equate the "merger" with the abolition of equity as a separate jurisdiction, and they're much mistaken for doing so. Some states still do retain separate law and equity courts, and in virtually all states some courts of special purpose (the probate court, for instance) remains, still, a court of equity. In any event, you'll hear and read in your first year of law school (probably in civil procedure class) that law and equity are largely merged. Your teacher might (or might not) skate so quickly over the subject as to make you think there is no longer any distinction between equity and law. That (if it happens) does you a terrible disservice. Hence we say again: Take a course called remedies, equity, or equitable remedies. (And if you can't, then read *Examples & Explanations: Remedies*, by Richard L. Hasen (Aspen, 2d ed. 2010). It's a great *(great)* teach-yourself book on the subject.)

For Our Purposes, the Two Most Important Truths About Equity vs. Law Are These.   (1) When a court sits "at law" (as a court of law), an award of monetary damage is (just about) the only remedy it can offer. The law's principal remedy is monetary damages. (2)(a) When a court issues an *order* as opposed to a money judgment, it ordinarily invokes its jurisdiction as a court of equity, and (b) it does so only if, in its opinion, the petitioner before it has suffered an injustice for which a legal remedy (monetary award) is either unavailable or unavailing.

QUESTION 9. In general (with exceptions created by statute), when one seeks a court order as opposed to an award of monetary damages, she invokes a court's jurisdiction

A. at law and not at equity.
B. at equity and not at law.
C. both A and B.
D. neither A nor B.

ANALYSIS. Generally speaking, when a plaintiff wins an action at law, she receives the remedy of monetary damages, an award of money calculated (theoretically) to compensate her for the harm done her by the defendant (as elaborately discussed in Chapters 25 to 30). If she seeks a court order, then, generally, she must invoke the court's equitable jurisdiction — ask it to don its "equity hat." She must convince the judge that she has suffered an injustice for which the law affords no adequate remedy.

If she succeeds in that effort, the judge will issue an *order* that the defendant do (or refrain from doing) some particular thing that will, in the judge's mind, correct the injustice. As a general rule, monetary damages represents the remedy available "at law." A court order represents the remedy available "at equity." Hence, **B** is right.

QUESTION 10. Historically, equity courts and the equitable jurisdiction of today's courts have their roots in

A. common law court orders.
B. court orders authorized by statute.
C. an appeal to the "King's conscience."
D. an appeal to "the law's justice."

ANALYSIS. Equity is distinct from law (although the distinction is less visible today than it was 100 years ago). In theory (and in fact, still), the courts of equity are distinct from the courts of law, although the difference today represents not two different court houses or two different judges, but, usually, two different "hats" worn by the same judge sitting in one court house. Hence, equitable jurisdiction, yesteryear and now, is separate from legal jurisdiction and separate, therefore, from the common law. Consequently, **A** and **D**, which refer to "law," are wrong. The tasks of construing and applying statutes belong, also, to the law courts. **B** is wrong. The first equity court was the King's own court, where he entertained petitions from those who alleged that they had suffered an injustice for which the law offered no remedy. The King (or his delegate) then resolved the matter, according to his "conscience." **C** is right.

✦ Silver & Hochberg's Picks

1.	**D**
2.	**D**
3.	**C**
4.	**C**
5.	**D**
6.	**D**
7.	**D**
8.	**D**
9.	**B**
10.	**C**

Index